REFERENCE GUIDE TO SCIENCE FICTION, FANTASY, AND HORROR

Reference Sources in the Humanities Series
James Rettig, Series Editor

The Performing Arts: A Guide to the Reference Literature. By Linda Keir Simons

American Popular Culture: A Guide to the Reference Literature. By Frank W. Hoffman

Philosophy: A Guide to the Reference Literature. Second Edition. By Hans E. Bynagle

Journalism: A Guide to the Reference Literature. Second Edition. By Jo A. Cates

Children's Literature: A Guide to Information Sources. By Margaret W. Denman-West

Reference Works in British and American Literature. Second Edition. By James K. Bracken

Reference Guide to Mystery and Detective Fiction. By Richard Bleiler

Linguistics: A Guide to the Reference Literature. Second Edition. By Anna L. DeMiller

Reference Guide to Science Fiction, Fantasy, and Horror. Second Edition. By Michael Burgess and Lisa R. Bartle

REFERENCE GUIDE to SCIENCE FICTION, FANTASY, and HORROR

Second Edition

Michael Burgess
Lisa R. Bartle
California State University, San Bernardino

2002
LIBRARIES UNLIMITED
A Division of Greenwood Publishing Group, Inc.
Westport, Connecticut

LIBRARIES UNLIMITED
A Division of Greenwood Publishing Group, Inc.
88 Post Road West
Westport, CT 06881
1-800-225-5800
www.lu.com

Library of Congress Cataloging-in-Publication Data

Burgess, Michael.
  Reference guide to science fiction, fantasy, and horror / Michael Burgess, Lisa R.
Bartle.—2nd ed.
      p. cm. — (Reference sources in the humanities series)
  Includes bibliographical references and index.
    ISBN 1-56308-548-8 (alk. paper)
    1. Science fiction—Reference books—Bibliography.   2. Science fiction—History
and criticism—Bibliography.   3. Fantasy fiction—Reference books—
Bibliography.   4. Fantasy fiction—History and criticism—Bibliography.   5. Horror
tales—Reference books—Bibliography.   6. Horror tales—History and criticism—
Bibliography.   I. Bartle, Lisa R.   II. Title.   III. Series.
  Z5917.S36 B87 2003
  [PN3433.5]
  016.8093′876—dc21

                                                                                2002151707

DEDICATION OF LISA BARTLE

For Steve and Sydney,
With Many Thanks to Michael

DEDICATION OF MICHAEL BURGESS

In Memory of My Beloved Granddaughter,
Whitney Louise Rogers
(6 July 1986 – 9 November 2001)

CONTENTS

PREFACE TO REFERENCE SOURCES IN THE HUMANITIES SERIES

Every discipline continuously renews its reference literature to record new theories, revised theses, discoveries, deaths, and developments in the application of theory. New editions of standard works and new titles appear from time to time, while serials bibliographies index each year's outpouring of journal articles, monographs, and Festschriften. Furthermore, new media appear and new forms of reference tools develop to make optimal use of each new medium's strengths, opportunities, and features. This series, Reference Sources in the Humanities, takes as its purpose the identification, description, and organization of the reference literature of the humanities disciplines. This series, emphasizing the Anglo-American reference literature of recent decades, has been planned to meet the needs of undergraduates, graduate students, professors exploring adjunct disciplines, librarians building and using reference collections, and intellectually curious adults interested in a systematic, self-guided study of the humanities. It emphasizes print resources—vital both to current and retrospective understanding of the reference literature of each of the humanities—but it also includes the most recent electronic sources.

Like bibliographic guides to the literature of any discipline, guides in this series are intended to serve various users in different ways. Students being initiated into the ways of a discipline can use these guides to learn the structure of the discipline's secondary literature, to find sources that will enable them to find definitions of specialized terms, to identify significant historical figures, and to gain an overview of a topic. Specialists may use them to refresh their memories about once-familiar sources and to advise their students on approaches to problems. Librarians will use them to build and evaluate reference collections and to answer patron questions.

The Reference Sources in the Humanities Series is designed to serve all of these users and purposes. Each title in the series is organized principally by reference genre, including types specific to each discipline. As electronic reference works have evolved, they have blended the boundaries between and among genre. These have been placed in appropriate chapters, sometimes integrated with print resources, other times set apart because of their unique characteristics. This organization will facilitate their efficient use by reference librarians, a group trained to think in terms of reference genre (e.g., encyclopedias, dictionaries, indexes and abstracts, biographical directories, bibliographies) within subject categories, when they seek a particular type of reference work in one of the humanities disciplines. Because no discipline's reference literature can completely convey its most recent discoveries, each title also includes information on key journals, associations, and research centers—the sources from which much of any discipline's new knowledge emanates and the means by which that knowledge is disseminated. While each of these guides describes the reference literature of its discipline as that literature presently exists, each also contributes to that literature's renewal and growth.

—James Rettig, Series Editor

INTRODUCTION

Science fiction has, from its very beginnings as a literary genre in 1926, attracted an inordinate amount of fan interest, and these fans have, in turn, contributed a large number of indices, bibliographies, and other books about the field, far more than in the comparable genres of mystery and western fiction. Beginning in the late 1950s, fantastic literature also began receiving the serious attention of academic critics, who have added their own fair share of critical monographs and reference materials, leaving the genre with a vast amount of coverage for its size. This bibliography is one small attempt to provide the librarian, researcher, and fan with a path through the labyrinthine maze of amateur and professional reference materials in the related fields of science fiction, fantasy, and horror.

Included herein are annotations for all the major (and most minor) SF reference volumes. The books are grouped in sections by subject, then listed alphabetically by main entry. Each entry provides complete bibliographical data, a description of the book's organization, content, and purpose, and an evaluation of how well the author met his or her stated objective. We have tried in every instance to synthesize general critical reactions to the volumes covered, showing each book's weaknesses and strong points, with a balanced summation. We have rated or compared similar volumes when such comparison seems appropriate; and have also provided suggested core collection lists for librarians and scholars at several different interest levels. The indices at the end of this volume allow complete access to the individual monographs by author, title, and subject correlated to item number.

The world of SF criticism is a small one indeed, involving no more than a few hundred individuals, most of them having some near or distant acquaintanceship with each other. No evaluation has been inflated or deflated based on any personal knowledge of the author. Our sole purpose here has been to dissect these publications in such a way that their construction becomes obvious to all, and then to provide some clear idea of how well each has met its objectives, and how useful each may be to the librarian or scholar.

Readers may also wish to know something about the critical perspective that we bring to this book. We believe that reference volumes should normally include certain apparatus. Except for those works that already consist of nothing but an author- and/or title-arranged data base, all books should be indexed, and we will invariably mention the absence of same. We believe that bibliographies and literary guides should include paginations and other significant bibliographical data for both monographic and periodical works, and we will reduce my evaluation of any book lacking them. We expect reference books to be well and consistently organized, with data obviously and conspicuously arranged and displayed, so that even a casual user will be able to tell at a glance how the volume works and what it contains. The overuse of abbreviations is the sure sign of an amateur at work, and we will criticize those works that employ them too frequently. We will also point out obvious physical deficiences with the book, including faint printing, poor binding, and other substandard production values. We do not state or imply that there is only one way to organize data, for in fact there are as many ways to construct a reference volume as there are bibliographers and indexers; but if a work requires forty hours of classroom time before it can be used, then there are obvious construction problems present. We regard our function here as a guide to the uninitiated, pointing out the obvious and not so obvious, the good points and the bad of each of the works evaluated, with occasional pithy comments tossed in to enliven the tour. We have tried to apply these same standards throughout this work—even-handedly, fairly, consistently.

This second edition includes 150 new entries completely original to this version. In addition, many of the earlier entries have been reworked, sometimes extensively, either to cover newly published versions of the reference works in question, or to reflect the impact of amendations and/or additions elsewhere in the text. Perhaps half of the entries from the first edition of this guide have been revised or rewritten for this new rendition.

The primary sources for the books have been our own collection, which includes most of the items annotated; the J. Lloyd Eaton Collection of Science Fiction and Fantasy Literature at the Tomás Rivera Library, University of California, Riverside; and the John M. Pfau Library at California State University, San Bernardino.

Our special thanks to Dr. George Edgar Slusser, founding Curator of the Eaton Collection at UCR; Arthur E. Nelson, Library Director at CSUSB from 1963-88; Marty Bloomberg, Acting Library Director in 1988; Dr. William Aguilar, University Librarian from 1989-93; and Johnnie Ann Ralph, University Librarian from 1993, for their generous accommodation. A tip of the hat also to Robert E. Briney and Edward Wood for their pioneering work, *SF Bibliographies* (Chicago: Advent, 1972), which covers many early fan productions now impossible to locate. Thanks to Hal W. Hall of the Texas A&M University Libraries, who took the time to preview significant portions of the manuscript, and who also provided last-minute photocopies of hard-to-locate pamphlets and books; his input made this a better book than it would have been otherwise. Thanks also to Paul David Seldis, Mary A. Burgess, and Daryl F. Mallett, who helped proofread the original manuscript, and to Chickie Huizar and Lee Bayer at CSUSB, who obtained hard-to-locate monographs on interlibrary loan.

Kudos also to the publishers who generously sent review copies of their books, including The American Library Association, The Borgo Press, Carroll & Graf Publishers, Creatures at Large Press, Crossing Press, Drumm Books, Facts on File, Galactic Central Publications, The Gale Group, Garland Publishing Co., Greenwood Press, HarperCollins, Haworth Press, Hypatia Press, Kent State University Press, Locus Press, McFarland Publishing Co., Meckler Publishing, Niekas Publications, Oryx Press, Salem Press, Scarecrow Press, Charles Scribner's Sons, SFBRI, Soft Books, Starmont House, and the University of Iowa Press, among others.

Thanks to Dr. Fran J. Polek, who gave Michael Burgess the opportunity to work on his first bibliography during his senior year at Gonzaga University. Kudos to Neil Barron, Fred Lerner, Daryl F. Mallett, Ted Taylor, and Marsh Tymn, for their assistance in locating specific items; and to Buckley Barrett, Ned Brooks, Charlie Brown, Scott

Burgess, Bill Contento, Lloyd Currey, Jack Dann, Barry Levin, Doug Menville, Bill Nolan, Mark Owings, and Leslie Kay Swigart, who have, over the years, always been willing to "talk shop." Finally, our appreciation to our long-suffering editors at Libraries Unlimited, particularly to Jim Rettig, who conscientiously reviewed the first edition of this book, and to Barbara Ittner, who just as diligently parsed the second; both provided many valuable and useful suggestions for improving the text.

Additions and corrections are always welcome, and should be sent to the authors c/o the John M. Pfau Library, California State University, San Bernardino, 5500 University Parkway, San Bernardino, CA 92407.

—Michael Burgess and Lisa Bartle
28 April 2002

HOW TO USE THIS BOOK

To locate a specific work, please check the title or author index; the item number of the volume will locate it in the text. The monographs included herein are numbered consecutively from the number one throughout the entire volume. Index references correlate with the item numbers only. Specific books may also be found by broad type, arranged alphabetically by main entry. Similarly, author bibliographies are grouped together into one section, organized by the name of the writer being covered. The subject index at the end of this book will give the reader still another access point.

ABBREVIATIONS

Assoc. = Associate

Ed. = Editor or edition

Eds. = Editors

Exp. = Expanded

Pbk. = Paperback

Rev. = Revised

SF = Science Fiction

ENCYCLOPEDIAS AND DICTIONARIES

SCOPE NOTE: This chapter includes all those publications that call themselves encyclopedias of fantastic literature, plus dictionaries of critical or fan terminology. Character dictionaries are listed under the section of that name later in this book.

1. Ash, Brian, ed. **The Visual Encyclopedia of Science Fiction.** London & Sydney, Pan Books, 1977. 352 p. (pbk.). New York, Harmony Books, 1977. 352 p. index. LC 77-7036. ISBN 0-517-53174-7; ISBN 0-517-53175-5 (pbk.). London, Triune Books, 1978. 352 p. ISBN 0-85674-077-2.

A highly eclectic reference book masquerading as an encyclopedia, Ash's work jumps widely all over the literary landscape, although its organization is not quite as eccentric as might appear on the surface.

The first section of the book, "Program," is a sixty-page timeline of science fiction, listing prominent books, authors, stories, magazines, awards, and fan events, in year-by-year order, with numerous mini-illustrations scattered throughout. Ash's chronology is unique in the SF field for its detail and extensive development. Part Two, "Thematics," is a series of nineteen ten-page articles, each focusing on a particular SF theme, such as "Spacecraft and Star Drives," "Galactic Empires," "Cities and Cultures," or "Religion and Myths," all apparently penned by Ash himself. Each of these essays is prefaced with an original 500-word introduction by a famous SF author, one per chapter; Ash then provides a popular history of the subgenre or theme, giving background material and touching on many different stories and novels and authors involved with the particular theme.

Individual bibliographies (there is sometimes more than one in a particular chapter) focus on stories and novels employing the featured subject(s). The book is copiously illustrated throughout with magazine and paperback cover reproductions and drawings and photos of the authors, many in color. Also inserted into each chapter are such miscellanea as the timelines from the future histories developed by Poul Anderson and Robert A. Heinlein for their stories and novels in the section "Future and Alternative Histories."

Section Three, "Deep Probes," includes essays by three SF writers on "Interface," "Science Fiction as Literature," and "Recurrent Concepts." The fourth and last section, "Fandom and Media," focuses on fandom, SF art, SF cinema, SF magazines and comics, including lists of awards, a timeline of major SF films, and a brief checklist of SF anthologies (by editor). At the front of the book is a checklist of SF themes, keyed to page number. Detailed separate author/title and artist indexes complete the work.

The Visual Encyclopedia is a fascinating book to browse through, filled with eye-catching illustrations, hundreds of details, and marvelous mini-vignettes by many of the field's best-known writers. As a reference work, however, it lacks obvious organizational keys for the casual or serious reader, skipping from theme to theme without any clear pattern. Also, the mini-bibliographies, while organizing hundreds of stories and novels by subject, nonetheless miss a great many works that could (or should) have been included; and because they are fragmented into dozens of examples scattered throughout several hundred pages of material, the biblios are useless except as very general guides to further reading. Ash never pretends otherwise, stating in his introduction: "There is something [here] for everyone." Unfortunately, that's just the problem.

Now lamentably outdated.

2. Bunson, Matthew. **The Vampire Encyclopedia.** New York, Crown, 1993. x, 303 p. LC 92-42005. ISBN 0-517-88100-4 (pbk.). New York, Gramercy, 2000. x, 303 p. ISBN 0-517-16206-7.

This A-Z guide for fans attempts to include information on vampires "in film, literature, folklore, poetry, art, medicine, religion, and comedy," with approximately 2,000 entries on these topics, covering much of interest to the cape-enshrouded *littérateur,* all written in clear, informed, and humorous language. Entries range in size from a few sentences to two pages, averaging 200 words; perhaps half of the text deals with film and literary topics. The addition of twenty-eight black-and-white photographs of famous actors playing famous vampires adds little to the text.

The appendices provide brief bibliographies for further reading. Appendix One lists 50 fiction anthologies devoted to vampires. Appendix Two similarly notes 121 vampire novels. Appendix Three notes 89 secondary works for further study, but does not represent the complete list used in the research of the book. A typical appendix entry includes: author, title (in italics), year and place of publication, and publisher. A list of noteworthy vampire motion pictures is included between p. 92-97. A fourth Appendix lists major vampire fan societies and organizations, with addresses that are now wholly outdated.

While Bunson's work can be sipped and even occasionally enjoyed by the connoisseur of vampire literature, its bouquet travels less well than that of Melton's guide (see #10), since the *Encyclopedia* fails to indicate the sources of the specific data used in the text. The well-encaped vampirophile will soon find another blood bank to pillage.

3. Clute, John; Candida Frith-Macdonald and Tracie Lee, project editors. **Science Fiction: The Illustrated Encyclopedia.** London, New York, Dorling Kindersley, 1995. 312 p. LC 95-8083. ISBN 0-7894-0185-1.

Contents: "Chapter One: Future Visions"; "Chapter Two: Historical Context"; "Chapter Three: Influential Magazines"; "Chapter Four: Major Authors"; "Chapter Five: Classic Titles"; "Chapter Six: Graphic Works"; "Chapter Seven: Genre Film"; "Chapter Eight: International Television"; "Glossary"; "Index"; "Acknowledgments."

This pictorial A-Z guide to science fiction topics by a well-known critic is a beautiful coffee-table-style book filled with interesting and visually stimulating materials. However, while Clute acknowledges that he wrote the accompanying text, the illustrations and layout of the book derived from the expertise of the editorial team, in particular the art editors.

Each chapter looks at an aspect of science fiction, usually decade by decade, up to 1994, though it occasionally delves into the nineteenth century. The chapter "Future Visions" presents a hodgepodge of interesting images, and briefly explains their relationship with SF, the past, and the present, also examining "the hopes and fear of [the twentieth] century through the eyes of SF, of politicians, and of the news and current events of the day." The second section uses time charts to put "works of SF into historical context, comparing them with the backdrop against which they were created." Chapter Three, "Influential Magazines," profiles 32 SF periodicals, with each entry displaying a cover from one of the magazines, and including for each: title, years of publication, editor(s), and a historical description, averaging 50 words.

Chapter Four uses time charts to "list the major literary works of each era, themes and icons that were important to each generation, and the authors who made their debuts in each year. . . . Author profiles, with bibliographies, follow the charts." Each of the 110 author entries includes: photograph, birth and death dates, nationality, key works, signature facsimile, bibliography, and brief biography/commentary. Chapters Five and Six showcase graphic novels (covering illustrators as well as titles), providing details of first publication, publisher, title, and an image from the cover of a first or early edition.

Chapter Seven (film) and Eight (television) provide: title, nationality, director, writer, airtime, and a summary of each show. A star system (from 0-3, three stars being best) rates each media work. Films are arranged chronologically by release year, and TV programs by decade, with barebones information being provided for individual entries. The one-page glossary gives succinct definitions for well-known SF genre terms, and the index is easy to use (boldfaced page numbers indicate main entries), although the six-point typeface is difficult to discern for middle-aged eyes. The book is beautifully illustrated with color photographs and stills from books, films, magazines, comics, and graphic novels.

This volume is competing for the same dollars as Pringle's *The Ultimate Encyclopedia* (see #14). Both feature chapters on novels, film, television shows, and magazines, and include a who's who and glossary. Clute covers comics and illustrators, while Pringle focuses on characters. Pringle's guide appears more oriented towards U.S. authors, while Clute often has a more international perspective. Thus, both are good purchases for fans, but neither provides much in the way of reference value for library collections.

4. Clute, John, and John Grant, ed. **The Encyclopedia of Fantasy.** London, Orbit, 1997. xvi, 1049 p. ISBN 1-85723-368-9. New York, St. Martin's Press, 1997. xvi, 1049 p. LC 96-37472. ISBN 0-312-15897-1. New York, St. Martin's Press Griffin, 1999. xvi, 1079 p. LC 98-50905. ISBN 0-312-19869-8 (pbk.).

Contents: "Introduction"; "Contributors"; "Acknowledgements"; "Abbreviations and Symbols"; the *Encyclopedia* proper.

This companion volume to the 1993 edition of *The Encyclopedia of Science Fiction* (see #12) was created when the editorial team working on the latter project quickly recognized that the vast amount of speculative literature they were encountering required that fantasy, "a field of literature radically different from science fiction," be addressed as a separate project. There are, indeed, many similarities between the two books, most especially in format, and some entries have been cross-referenced to the first volume to acknowledge those authors who have produced work in both arenas.

The lengthy Introduction discusses the scope, background, and history of the project. As with *ESF,* the bulk of the volume consists of an A-Z listing of authors, titles, films and television, publishers, subjects, and other topics of interest. Many listings also contain helpful suggestions for further reading, as well as critical/historical works pertaining to the issue at hand. Numerous "See" and "See Also" references enable the user to navigate the text without difficulty.

The *Encyclopedia* concentrates on those fantasy authors and works that first appeared just before the beginning of the nineteenth century, and thence down through the modern era. Pre-nineteenth-century subjects, such as "Fairytale," "Folklore," and "Myths," as well as such "taproot texts" as works by John Milton and William Shakespeare, which provided some of the basic ideas and influences for modern fantasists, are touched upon as well. Supernatural fiction is covered in depth, although horror is treated more selectively, horror writers and films being chosen primarily for their fantasy content and for their influence on the field of fantasy, rather than for their horror content *per se*.

Coverage of the topics is as complete as the editorial team could make it through 1995, with less comprehensive discussion of items first appearing in 1996. However, the meat of the book, so to speak, lies in the numerous subject-oriented essays on fantastic literature scattered throughout the text, which themselves comprise an important philosophical history of the genre. Perhaps 3,000 entries are included, with over a million words of text.

An outstanding team of well-known editors and writers participated in the project. John Clute and contributing editor Roz Kaveney helped define the project, and the prolific Clute also wrote the bulk of the motif and author entries. John Grant and contributing editor David Langford were responsible for shaping the copy into a comprehensible text, as well as providing the many cross-references. In addition, Grant copyedited the text and wrote most of the Cinema entries. Contributing editors Mike Ashley and Ron Tiner penned a large number of essays, and consultant editors David G. Hartwell and Gary Westfahl provided overall editorial comment. At least thirty other worthy contributors, including such heavyweights as Brian Stableford and Franz Rottensteiner, were also involved in the project.

The 1999 reprint includes a supplement appended to the end of the volume, updating the book through 1998, and updated supplements are also available online.

As with the science fiction volume, this book would have greatly benefited from a comprehensive index to its myriad titles, authors, and subjects. But also like its companion, *The Encyclopedia of Fantasy* is an altogether thorough and well-conceived work, and should be considered an essential adjunct to any reference library of the field, and to all library collections.

5. Collins, Paul, ed.; Steven Paulsen and Sean McMullen, asst. eds. **The MUP Encyclopaedia of Australian Science Fiction & Fantasy.** Carlton South, Victoria, Australia, Melbourne University Press, 1998. xvi, 188 p. LC 99-530614. ISBN 0-522-84771-4; ISBN 0-522-84802-8 (pbk.).

This volume is an A-Z bio-bibliography of Australian science fiction and fantasy writers active from 1950-98, plus a handful of longer, topical essays on Australian SF comic books, horror works, radio, television, and fantasy. The approximately 1,500 entries include copious "See" references from author pseudonyms to the name under which the writer is best known. The *Encyclopaedia* covers SF and fantasy writers born in Australia and those settling there from other parts of the world.

A typical entry includes: author's name (boldfaced and inverted, with the surname in all caps), profile (100-500 words in length), and a chronological bibliography divided into two sections, covering the author's published books and short stories. References to the writer's monographs include: title (in italics), author's byline (if different from that used in the main entry), publisher, and year of publication only. Short stories citations include: title (in quotation marks), magazine abbreviation (in italics), and publication date.

A few pre-1950 authors and works "deemed particularly important" to the development of fantastic literature in Australia are also featured. Excluded from coverage are horror fictions (even when the author of the material has already been included for other reasons), picture books for children aged six or less, fanzine publications, and traditional tales by Aboriginal writers. Only writers with at least three short fiction pieces and/or one book publication are covered.

Without question, this guide will become the standard reference work to Australian SF writers and their works, which is not to say, however, that the *Encyclopaedia* is wholly without flaws. Hilary Bell, for example, is noted as having been born in the same year that her only fantasy book was published (a tad precocious, that!). As is often the case with compiled reference works, the content, tone, and length of the individual essays are very uneven. Though the stated intent of the book is to provide non-evaluative profiles of each writer, some entries are very critical, while others become almost frothy in their ecstatic insignificance. Personal biographical material on the authors can either be very detailed or utterly nonexistent, depending upon factors that are not always clearly indicated.

Most of the author entries are unsigned; according to the preface, the reader can assume that all such information was provided by the editors themselves. Many of the longer, more substantive subject entries, however, have been contributed by outside critics. Specific entries covering magazine and book editors can be succinct almost to the point of terseness, lacking any descriptive material and only listing the editor's tenure at a magazine, but on other occasions, the information on a particular author's editorial contributions will be buried deep within the text of his or her personal entry.

The seventeen major theme articles (averaging 1,000-4,000 words in length) are signed, but often provide no more than basic introductory guides to common science fiction topics, although from an Australian perspective. Bibliographical citations are skeletal for a volume with such high goals.

The short story references are often very difficult to read or follow, with a column or more of heavily-impacted text running together, entries being separated only a semicolon. Similarly, the descending chronological movement in each bibliography is often disrupted by the insertion of reprints after the first edition of each book or story; for major authors, discerning their specific publications can truly become a challenge, even to the aficionado. What was obviously done to save space has made this guide much less useful than it should have been. Many of these organizational difficulties could be improved by giving each major bibliographical citation its own line. The lack of a title index is keenly felt.

Still, the *Encyclopaedia* is the best single work available on Australian science fiction and fantasy, and is likely to remain so for many years to come. It establishes without question the increasing importance of "Down Under" writers to the advancement of modern fantastic literature. The volume is attractively typeset in double-column format, and is bound to library standards. Recommended for research libraries and large public library systems.

6. Davis, Richard, ed. **The Encyclopedia of Horror.** London, Octopus Books, 1981. 192 p. index. ISBN 0-7064-1507-8. Twickenham, England, Hamlyn, 1987. 192 p. index. ISBN 0-600-55359-0 (pbk.).

This companion volume to Holdstock's *Encyclopedia of Science Fiction* (see #9) is similar in organization and style to the earlier book.

Contents: "Foreword," by Peter Cushing; "Introduction," by Richard Davis; "Evil Monsters," by Tom Hutchinson; "The Frankenstein Saga," by Michel Parry; "The Devil's Army," by Richard Cavendish; "Vampires & Werewolves," by Basil Copper; "The Supernatural," by Michael Ashley; "The Undead," by Richard Davis; "Travelling Beyond," by Douglas Hill; and "The Catalogue," by Richard Davis and Denis Gifford.

As with Holdstock, this volume is actually a well-illustrated coffee-table history of weird and supernatural horror in literature and film. The quality and coverage of each subject vary widely from chapter to chapter, with more than half of the text consisting of black-and-white, tinted, or (occasionally) full-color reproductions of motion picture stills, drawings, and book and magazine covers. There are separate chronological lists of horror comic books and films at the end of the book; the film list also includes year of production, title, director, principal star(s), and distribution company (and country where produced); none of these items are anywhere near comprehensive. The index references all persons and titles mentioned in the text, with very scanty subject access.

Lightweight and wholly forgettable, and now wholly outdated.

7. Franson, Donald. **A Key to the Terminology of Science-Fiction Fandom.** Heiskell, TN, The National Fantasy Fan Federation, 1962. [17] p. (Fandbook, no. 1). (pbk.).

This brief mimeographed dictionary is designed to be used by the "neofan" ("new fan, usually only such for a few months") or the "faaan" ("fan who is interested more in fans and fandom than in stf" ["stf" = SF]), and includes, in addition to common fan terminology, acronyms and initialisms used by the major fan groups and conventions. The latter are now somewhat out-of-date, but many of the terms themselves remain in current use. An updated and expanded guide and study to the peculiar word usage of SF fandom is long overdue.

8. Gunn, James, ed. **The New Encyclopedia of Science Fiction.** New York, Viking, 1988. xix, 524 p. LC 87-40637. ISBN 0-670-81041-X.

With the prolonged delay in the preparation of a second edition of the Nicholls/Clute *Encyclopedia* (see #12), Gunn's book was eagerly awaited by the science fiction world; unfortunately, it generally received poor reviews, for reasons that become all too apparent upon close examination.

Like Nicholls's volume, Gunn's book is arranged alphabetically by main entry, including science fiction writers and artists, plus individual entries on major SF films and magazines. Basic entries range in length from 100-1,500 words (averaging 400-500); interspersed throughout the text are an additional 96 mini-essays (ranging from 1,000-2,000 words in size) on somewhat broader topics as "Alien Worlds," "Children's Science Fiction," "Cyberpunk," "Scientists and Science Fiction," and "Utopias and Dystopias."

A typical author entry includes: name under which the author is best known, middle name or real name (if the main entry is a pseudonym), years of birth and death, nationality, brief chronological evaluation of the writer's life and career (focusing on his or her works), plus selected "Other Works." The 250 film entries include: title, year of production, director, photographer, screenwriter, film musician, principal actors, running time, an indication whether the picture was made in color or black-and-white, plot summary, and significance. The general essays are usually chronological assessments of the particular topic, subgenre, or subject. The book is profusely illustrated throughout with author photographs, paperback and magazine cover illustrations, and movie and TV stills; there are also sixteen pages of color cover reproductions inserted into an unpaged signature at the center of the book.

Comparisons with Nicholls are inevitable. Although the original edition of *The Science Fiction Encyclopedia* is not significantly longer than Gunn's work, it actually contains almost twice the text, due to differences in layout and type size. Thus, while Gunn includes writers and films that have become prominent only in the 1980s (and that therefore are not mentioned in Nicholls), the latter actually has far more entries covering a much broader range of subjects and personages, including many peripheral figures of importance to the field.

Entries in Gunn are also usually shorter than their Nicholls counterparts, particularly for lesser-known writers. For example, the essays on Raymond Z. Gallun and Daniel F. Galouye, neither of them household names, average in Gunn 100 words each, with evaluations of two books by Galouye and one story by Gallun (plus a barebones listing of five additional titles); in Nicholls, Gallun's entry is 300 words and Galouye's 400, with many more works evaluated, plus "See" references to other entries in which both writers are mentioned and a further reference in the Galouye essay to an interesting attack on "new wave" SF that he contributed to an important reference work. (Not all of this is Gunn's fault; reportedly, the publisher drastically cut the projected length of the book long after essay assignments had been made, forcing many last-minute parings of both text and entries.)

Both works use outside contributors, most of them acknowledged experts in the field, but Gunn relies on more than 100 such critics, while Nicholls uses just 34; and even this figure is deceptive, because a large percentage of the entries in the latter were actually contributed by Nicholls and Clute, the editors, by John Brosnan (for films, often in collaboration with one of the principals), or by the two contributing editors, Malcolm Edwards and Brian Stableford. These five men account for 80-90% of the text in Nicholls, giving it overall a much stronger editorial focus. The lack of such guidance in Gunn's work becomes clearer when one examines typographical and textual errors, with which the book overflows in profusion, and the lack of "See" and "See Also" references (or index). One must also question some peculiar editorial standards for the inclusion and exclusion of specific personages and films: why, for example, if space was such an obvious problem, does the book provide so many entries on relatively worthless and unknown films while excluding such important figures as David G. Hartwell, a prominent book editor of the 1970s? *The New Encyclopedia* is better laid out, more attractive physically, and more current than its principal competitor, but in every other respect, Nicholls's work is by far the superior.

These differences have now been exarcerbated by the publication in 1993 of the Second Edition of *The Encyclopedia of Science Fiction* (see #12), which has corrected some of the problems of the 1978 version, and has updated entries through the mid-1990s (with the subsequent publication of a supplement).

Now largely outdated.

9. Holdstock, Robert, consultant ed. **Encyclopedia of Science Fiction.** London, Octopus Books, 1978. 219 p. ISBN 0-7064-0756-3.

A coffee-table picture book masquerading as an encyclopedia, this colorful British production includes 13 chapters contributed by such well-known (mostly British) critics and SF writers as Brian Stableford, Patrick Moore, Mike Ashley, Alan Frank, Harry Harrison, and Christopher Priest, on the following topics: "Locations" ("a modern perspective of science fiction"), "Marriage of Science & Fiction," "Major Themes," "Pulps & Magazines," "Screen Trips," "Machine as Hero," "Alien Encounter," "Art & Artists," "Fiction to Fact," "Outer Limits," "New Wave," and "Yesterday, Today & Tomorrow."

There is also a "Catalog" section, which includes brief essays on collecting SF, fandom, SF pseudonyms, major awards, a table of SF magazines (title, dates of publication, number of issues published, general subject evaluation [*e.g.,* "SF" = science fiction], including many foreign titles), a brief alphabetical table of major SF films (listing title, date, director, nationality), and a table listing the world science fiction conventions through the mid-1970s. None of these lists are in any way complete or comprehensive, and all are now very much outdated. A detailed author/title index completes the book.

The essays are popularly oriented and written, and tend to jump from title to title and writer to writer without any evident guiding plan for the book as a whole. However, the volume is well designed and illustrated, filled with full- and partial-page color illustrations reproduced from book and magazine covers and cover paintings, plus a few color stills from prominent motion pictures. Light, fun, pretty, Holdstock's book is also utterly worthless as a reference tool, and has now been superseded, even in its own format, by Clute (see #12). See also the companion volume on horror (see #6).

10. Melton, J. Gordon. **The Vampire Book: The Encyclopedia of the Undead.** Detroit, Gale Research, Visible Ink Press, 1994. xxxviii, 852 p. index. ISBN 0-8103-9553-3; 0-8103-2295-1 (pbk.). **The Vampire Book: The Encyclopedia of the Undead.** 2nd ed., rev. and expanded. Detroit, Visible Ink Press, 1999. xxxviii, 919 p. index. LC 99-161873. ISBN 1-57859-071-X (pbk.).

Contents: "Illustration Credits"; "A Brief Cultural History of the Vampire," by Martin C. Riccardo; "Preface: What Is a Vampire?" by Melton; "Introduction," by Melton; "Vampires: A Chronology"; A-Z listing of people, places, and things associated with vampires; "Appendices" (Resources, Vampire Filmography, Vampire Drama, Vampire Novels, Master Index).

Contents (Second Edition): "Foreword: A Brief Cultural History of the Vampire," by Martin V. Riccardo; "Preface: What Is a Vampire?" by Melton; "Introduction," by Melton; "Vampires: A Chronology"; "Photo and Illustration Credits"; [alphabetical list of entries].

The Vampire Book contains more than 375 descriptive entries arranged in a single alphabetic sequence. Some are very brief (100-300 words), and cover either definitions of terms associated with the vampire, or offer brief descriptions of places. The medium-length entries (500-1,000 words) include: accounts of such well-known fictional vampires as Count Yorga and Morbius; biographies of major figures associated with vampires, from actors who have played Dracula (*e.g.,* Bela Lugosi, Frank Langella, and John Carradine) to the major authors of vampire fiction (Bram Stoker and Anne Rice); and accounts of real-life vampire organizations (such as the Vampire Research Center and the Count Dracula Society).

Longer entries (up to 5,000 words) explore major topics associated with vampires (vampire bats and sexuality, for example), the appearance of the vampire in various cultures (like Romania or China), vampiric creatures and deities in different countries, and the life of the vampire in the media, from the stage to movies and comic books. There are over 100 black-and-white illustrations reproduced from movie and TV stills and photographs of the authors. Cross references are noted in bold type.

The foreword, "A Brief Cultural History of the Vampire," makes for fascinating and informative reading. The appendix offers a section of vampire resources, including addresses of vampire organizations, a brief, annotated vampire filmography, and a bibliography of vampire novels. Citations for further study follow almost every entry in the book.

The second edition contains 409 descriptive entries arranged in the same alphabetic sequence as the first. Most of the entries that appeared in the original volume have been reprinted unchanged, with a few exceptions, but the many new entries include pieces specifically oriented towards the contemporary audience (*e.g.*, "Internet, Vampires on" and "Angel"). The size and content of the entries are very similar to those in the earlier volume. The Second Edition also features a new, unnumbered, 15-page section of color illustrations, taken mostly from movie stills or posters. The Vampire Resources section has been expanded to include a list of vampiric websites and a brief bibliography of criticism on vampire literature. The index is highly useful for finding mentions of actors, writers, television programs, and movies.

The new edition completely supersedes the previous volume. Suitable for reference in all libraries.

11. Naha, Ed. **The Science Fictionary: An A-Z Guide to the World of SF Authors, Films, & TV Shows.** New York, Seaview Books, 1980. xii, 388 p. LC 80-5195. ISBN 0-87223-619-6. New York, Wideview Books, 1981. xii, 388 p. LC 80-16748. ISBN 0-87223-629-3 (pbk.).

The Science Fictionary focuses primarily on SF films and television programs, with only marginal attention given to science fiction authors and other topics. After brief introductions by Naha, the book is divided into four major sections: "Films," "Television," "Authors," and "Awards, Magazines, Themes."

The first chapter, by far the longest in the volume (237 pages), is an alphabetical guide to the major and minor motion pictures of the genre. Each entry includes title, nationality (if other than U.S.), date, black-and-white or color format, running time, plot summary, and lists of the production crew and cast (other than those mentioned in the annotation). The essays range in size from 20-400 words, averaging 50-100, and tend to be light and breezy, focusing on plot rather than content. The second chapter adds fifty pages of similarly arranged material on fantastic television programs. In both of these sections, "science fiction" is loosely defined to include fantasy and horror productions, as well as classic "sci-fi" videos.

The "Authors" section is a sixty-page "who's who" of the field, arranged alphabetically by surname, including writers mainly identified with a strict definition of the SF genre. A typical entry provides: name (including middle name), years of birth and death, brief biographical data (in some entries nonexistent), plus a chronological account of the author's career, including mentions of the writer's major works, with years of publication and (occasionally) one-sentence summations. The evaluations seem fair and "centrist," but provide little material that cannot be found in other, more complete reference sources.

The final chapter includes lists of the Hugo and Nebula award winners through 1978; the Oscars awarded to SF films; a description of other awards presented in the field (but no mention of winners); an alphabetical guide to the major SF magazines, with brief histories giving lists of editors, numbers of issues published, years published, and other data; and a wholly useless list of twelve major science fictional themes, with fifty-word descriptions. The book is illustrated throughout with small, black-and-white inset photographs and stills. The absence of a title index makes access more difficult than it should have been.

The motion picture and television data are remarkably complete and concise through the late 1970s, but the remaining sections appear to have been added almost as afterthoughts: the chapter on SF writers accounts for less than one-sixth of the entire text. Under such circumstances, one wonders why it was included at all.

Now wholly outdated, of course.

12. Nicholls, Peter, ed., John Clute, assoc. ed. **The Encyclopedia of Science Fiction: An Illustrated A to Z.** London, Granada, 1979. 672 p. LC 80-480051. ISBN 0-246-11020-1. London, Toronto, Panther Books, Granada, 1981. 672 p. ISBN 0-586-05380-8 (pbk.). As: **The Science Fiction Encyclopedia.** Garden City, NY, Doubleday & Co., 1979. 672 p. LC 77-15167. ISBN 0-385-13000-7. Clute, John, and Peter Nicholls, eds.; Brian Stableford, Contributing ed.; John Grant, Technical ed. **The Encyclopedia of Science Fiction.** 2nd ed. London, Orbit, 1993. 1370 p. ISBN 1-85723-124-4. New York, St. Martin's Press, 1993. xxxvi, 1370 p. LC 92-47048. ISBN 0-312-09618-6. New York, St. Martin's Griffin, 1995. xxxvi, 1386 p. LC 95-32883. ISBN 0-312-13486-X (pbk.).

Contents (Second Edition): "Introduction"; "Contents of This Book"; "Checklist of Contributors"; "Acknowledgements"; "Checklist of Themes"; "How to Use this Book"; "Checklist of Abbreviations"; A-Z listings.

An encyclopedic dictionary in one volume, Nicholls and Clute's work is arranged alphabetically by main entry, with individual entries on major and minor authors, general themes, motion pictures, publishers, series, television and radio programs, original anthologies, comics, science fiction and fantasy in various countries, terminology, awards, fanzines and fandom, and miscellanea. Contributions for the First Edition were solicited from thirty-four critics (including the editors), many of them British; the great majority (more than 90%) of the entries, however, were written by the two editors and three other critics, John Brosnan, Malcolm Edwards, and Brian Stableford.

The biographical entries, comprising the greater part of the text, typically include: person's name (in boldface), years of birth and death, a brief summary of his or her career (with minimal biographical material), and brief evaluations of the individual's principal works and/or contribution to the field, with dates of publication of the former, but no other publication data. Anyone who had written a book with fantastic content through the late 1970s is included, as are numerous writers prominent in the pulp era; also covered are the major foreign-language authors in the field, particularly those who have had at least one of their works translated into English; artists; film directors; major fans; and many other figures associated with the genre. The book is copiously illustrated with photographs, film stills, and reproductions of book and magazine covers. An acknowledgments page provides a brief bibliography of major sources.

The book includes an enormous amount of material on science fiction, virtually everything one would want to know in a quick-reference volume. Even comparatively minor writers receive generous 300- to 400-word entries evaluating their careers and major works, and always mentioning any secondary sources in book form. Although the book lacks an index, this deficiency is partially exculpated through numerous "See" and "See Also" references embedded at the end of almost every entry.

The 1993 edition represents more than a simple updating, being completely revised and almost wholly rewritten, and taking the editors many years to prepare. The new version has been expanded to include such '90s phenomena as games, shared worlds, technothrillers, and also includes such miscellaneous related topics as magic realism. The Second Edition contains over 4,300 entries and approximately 1,300,000 words of text, with some 2,000 cross-references.

Although listed on the title page as a contributing editor, Brian Stableford is acknowledged in the text as a "senior" editor for the project, which indicates that he was one of the three persons responsible not only for this newer version, but for the original volume as well. Editorial differences between Clute and Nicholls on the first edition were addressed, with Clute taking over responsibility for almost all of the author entries in the revised version. The three senior editors, Clute, Nicholls, and Stableford, contributed nearly 85% of the text, with the clear intention of providing more editorial control than is usual for such large, collaborative efforts. The result is a highly-focused, philosophically-uniform examination of SF throughout its history. In particular, the long, discursive essays scattered throughout the text, on such diverse topics as "Atlantis," "Definititions of SF," "Galactic Empires," "Genetic Engineering," "Heroic Fantasy," "Media Landscape," "Paranoia," "Religion," "Sociology," "Superheroes," and "Villains," to name but a few, themselves provide a significant addition to the critical literature of the genre.

The 1995 reprint includes a supplement at the end of the volume, and further updates are readily available online. A now-outdated CD-ROM version of the *Encyclopedia* was issued in the mid-1990s; this version enabled one readily to search every name and term included in the work.

The *Encyclopedia* has been criticized for its slightly pro-British slant, for its failure to include a comprehensive index (a lapse that is occasionally felt most keenly), and for disparities in the lengths of entries on certain authors. Despite these comparatively minor caveats, and the fact that the volume once again needs revising, Nicholls and Clute's book remains a thoroughly sound piece of work, outstanding in its conception and execution, the most comprehensive single-volume reference guide to science fiction and related fields, and certainly one of a handful of volumes that can truly be called "essential" to libraries and researchers everywhere.

Used in conjunction with the Clute's *Encyclopedia of Fantasy* (see #4), this updated encyclopedia is the last word in speculative source material, and as such, is a highly-recommended addition to the discriminating science fiction connoisseur's collection. It should also be part of any library worthy of the name.

13. Pringle, David, ed. **The Ultimate Encyclopedia of Fantasy: The Definitive Illustrated Guide.** London, Carlton Books; Sydney: Reader's Digest, 1998. 256 p. index. ISBN 1-858-68373-4; ISBN 0-864-49357-6. Woodstock, NY, Overlook Press, 1998. 256 p. index. LC 99-10503. ISBN 0-87951-937-1. Contributors: David Langford, Brian Stableford, Tim Dedopulos.

Contents: "Foreword," by Terry Pratchett; "Introduction"; "Types of Fantasy"; "Fantasy Cinema"; "Television Fantasy"; "Who's Who of Fantasy"; "A-Z of Fantasy Characters & Entities"; "Fantasy Games"; "Fantasy Worlds"; "Fantasy Magazines"; "Glossary"; "Index."

This beautiful volume, a companion to Pringle's *The Ultimate Encyclopedia of Science Fiction* (see #14), is filled with color illustrations and photographs. Pringle covers the highlights of the fantasy world across many different media. There is no standard entry.

The introductory essay describes the development of the genre from epic to fairy tale to the present. "Types of Fantasy" discusses nine subgenres, each mini-essay describing its history, development, and major authors and texts. The "Fantasy Cinema" and "Television Fantasy" chapters are more recognizably reference-oriented, being ordered chronologically by year, and thence by title, with notable fantasy productions for each year, including: title (all caps), country of origin, director, main cast, screenwriter, running time, and a 100-word evaluative summary/commentary.

"Who's Who of Fantasy" includes over 200 novelists, arranged alphabetically by surname, excluding older, classic writers of world literature (such as Aesop and Irving), all but a few children's writers, cartoonists, illustrators, comic-strip writers, and pulp-magazine writers of the first half of the century. Pringle also attempts "to include a number of very new people, whose first books have appeared just in the last two or three years." Entries in this section include: name, nationality, year of birth, and general description running from 30-500 words.

"A-Z of Fantasy Character & Entities" provides a "who's who" taken from novels, poems, plays, short stories, comic-strips, films, and television programs. The character "should have lived beyond the original source. That is to say, the majority of characters included here have been perpetuated by the original author from work to work, or have been perpetuated by other authors and by adaptations to different media, or have names which have entered the language for one reason or another." Entries include: character name, name of creator, source, date of first appearance, and a commentary averaging 200 words.

"Fantasy Games" contain mini-essays on role-playing games and their accompanying board games, books, live-action gaming, fantasy war gaming and figurines, computers in fantasy gaming, and trading card games. The section "Fantasy Worlds" comments on nine worlds found in epic series. "Fantasy Magazines" covers twelve major magazines "which have carried fantasy fiction over the past century." The glossary is a nearly pointless exercise of 118 terms that the average fan, and most non-fans, already know, such as "witches," "wizards," "quest," and "Oz." Each section of the book is color-coded for easier navigation through the text, and the index provides access to all authors mentioned.

This enjoyable coffee-table book is not really intended for reference, but oriented towards the fan who will read it from cover to cover. Future editions might expand further on this multi-media approach to the genre by including more information on comics and graphic novels by authors and illustrators such as Rumiko Takahashi and Wendy Pini, as well as providing a section on fantasy art and illustrators such as Boris Vallejo, Larry

Elmore, and Julie Bell. Also, the inclusion of some very new writers, rather than established authors in the genre, contradicts the generalist nature of the book, particularly since many of these are British figures relatively little known in the United States.

Still, there is no denying the sheer beauty of this book, and the very great pleasure that many readers will take in dipping through it. Recommended for public libraries.

14. Pringle, David, ed. **The Ultimate Encyclopedia of Science Fiction: The Definitive Illustrated Guide.** North Dighton, MA, JG Press, 1996. 304 p. index. ISBN 1-57215-212-5. Brookvale, NSW, Australia, The Book Company International, 1996. 304 p. index. ISBN 1-86309-255-2. Evanston, IL, Carlton, 1996. 304 p. index. ISBN 1-85868-188-X. Contributors: David Langford; Brian Stableford; Paul Di Filippo; John Grant; Chris Gilmore.

Contents: "Foreword," by David Pringle; "Introduction"; "Astounding Stories"; "They Came from Hollywood"; "TV 2000"; "The SF Files"; "Heroes and Villains"; "Propaganda"; "Glossary"; "Index."

A companion volume to *The Ultimate Encyclopedia of Fantasy* (see #13), Pringle's guide includes over 200 color illustrations and photographs, arranged in a coffee-table-style format. It covers the highlights of science fiction across many media, without trying to be comprehensive. There is no standard entry.

The introduction is a collection of brief essays, each covering the science fiction of a particular period of history. "Astounding Stories" is "a guide to the major plot templates which science fiction employs in its exploration of time and space and the ideas it has generated in the process." Included in these mini-essays are ten templates arranged in no discernible order, twenty-four alphabetical motifs, and fourteen alphabetical movements, trends, or buzzwords. Each entry defines the term, discusses its development, and lists the books and authors most significant to it.

"They Came from Hollywood," covers international films released from 1924-95, while "TV 2000" notes the highlights of television series and serials produced in the U.S. and U.K. between 1949-95. Both sections are arranged chronologically. Entries include: title, nation of origin, director, screenwriter, stars, duration, whether in black-and-white or color, and a summary and evaluative commentary running between 15-350 words.

"The SF Files," the book's "who's who" section, includes both authors and a few television and film producers and directors who are considered pioneers or groundbreakers of the genre. Entries are arranged alphabetically by surname, and include: name, nationality and profession, year of birth, and a general description of the figure and his or her genre-oriented work (30-500 words). "A-Z of Heroes & Villains" includes "the characters and entities of science-fiction literature and film, human and alien, robotic and trans-human." Alphabetical entries include: name, creator, source, date of first appearance, and a commentary on the character averaging 50 words.

"Propaganda" looks at the fifteen most influential science fiction magazines, with a brief history of each. The Glossary defines about sixty terms that fans reading the books should already know, such as bionics, hyperdrive, and zero gee.

This volume competes for the same dollars as Clute's *Science Fiction: The Illustrated Encyclopedia* (see #3). Both contain chapters on novels, film, television, magazines, a "who's who," and a glossary. However, Clute also covers comics and illustrators while Pringle focuses primarily on characters. Pringle's presentation is oriented more towards U.S. authors and productions, while Clute often displays a more international perspective.

Both books provide unique material that the other lacks, and thus neither can be preferred over the other. Academic libraries can skip both titles.

15. Rovin, Jeff. **The Fantasy Almanac.** New York, E. P. Dutton, 1979. 312 p. LC 79-11757. ISBN 0-525-47600-8 (pbk.).

Another misnomer, Rovin's book is *not* an almanac, nor does it deal strictly with fantasy, but comprises a dictionary of persons, events, places, and characters significant in the folklore, literature, comic books, television, films, and other media of the SF and fantasy genres. This poor man's version of *Brewer's Dictionary of Phrase and Fable* is arranged alphabetically by main entry. Each essay averages between 100-200 words and includes: topic name, classification key (*e.g.,* "FT" = Fairy Tale, "U" = Unexpected, etc.), description and background material (the bulk of the entry), and "See" references to related topics. The book also contains numerous black-and-white line drawings, a one-page "Key to Classifications," and a brief "Selected Bibliography." Some author entries are interfiled with the rest.

Rovin's annotations are straightforward, readable, and easy to digest, but he fails to cite any sources for his material (other than the general bibliography at the end of the book) and gives no indication anywhere in the volume of the criteria used in selecting the entries, or why certain authors and their creations were intermingled with figures from classic Greek and Roman mythologies, while other myths and authors remained untapped. The casual reader will thus find essays on Edgar Rice Burroughs, Ray Bradbury, Mr. Ed, Prince Ivan, Tribbles (cuddly critters from *Star Trek*), the Incredible Hulk, Batman, the *Galactica* (from the TV series, *Battlestar Galactica*), Fu Manchu, Brigadoon, and Aphrodite, to cite but a few, all jumbled together into one alphabetical sequence. Why? Random records do not a reference work make. Now wholly outdated.

16. Skal, David J. **V Is for Vampire: An A to Z Guide to Everything Undead.** New York, A Plume Book, 1996. xii, 288 p. LC 95-15522. ISBN 0-452-27173-8 (pbk.). London, Robson, 1996. xii, 288 p. ISBN 1-86105-055-0 (pbk.).

Contents: "Acknowledgments"; "Introduction"; an A-Z list of films, books, authors, actors, and other subjects relating to the vampire theme; "Appendix A: Cinema" (includes a checklist of vampire feature films in chronological order, followed by separate lists of Documentary Films; Fleeting Visitations [brief mentions of vampires or "vamps"], and Erotica, both Heterosexual and Homosexual); "Appendix B: Names of Vampires and Vampire-like Creatures" (an A-Z list of terms used for the undead, with country of origin indicated in parentheses); "Appendix C: Novels" (a very brief chronological checklist through 1995, giving title and author only, with no bibliographical information); "Bibliography."

This brief guide to vampire films, literature, and associated persons and terms attempts to provide a "one-stop, one-shop" introduction to the vampire theme in all genres, arranged in an A-Z format.

A typical film entry gives: title (bold type), category (*i.e.,* cinema), nationality, year of first release, and a plot summary-*cum*-commentary averaging 250 words. A typical book entry provides: title (bold type), category (*i.e.,* fiction), nationality, year of first publication, and plot summary averaging 300 words. In both instances, additional information (production company, director, and writer for films, author and publisher for books) may or may not be provided in the body of the entry. A few entries suffer from the interjection of author Skal into the proceedings, but the overall tone is light, airy, with fan-to-fan bantering commonplace.

All of the bulleted entries in the appendices appear in greater detail in the main section, thus forcing the reader to flip back and forth between the various lists to gain complete information on a particular topic. The book is sparsely (and muddily) illustrated with black-and-white stills and book covers.

An index would have been helpful in finding the obscure mentions buried in the entries; however, materials are cross-referenced throughout the volume in small caps. Academic libraries will much prefer Melton's more complete and more authoritative guide, *The Vampire Book: The Encyclopedia of the Undead* (see #10).

One fang on the vampire scale.

17. Sullivan, Jack, ed. **The Penguin Encyclopedia of Horror and the Supernatural.** New York, A Promised Land Production, Viking, 1986. xxviii, 482 p. LC 85-40558. ISBN 0-670-80902-0.

This first attempt at a true encyclopedia of horror film and literature includes contributions from sixty-four major and minor critics and fiction writers.

Contents: "Editor's Foreword" (by Sullivan); "How to Use This Book" (by Sullivan); "Contributors" (in alphabetical order, with brief bio squibs); [List of Major] "Essays"; Introduction: "The Art and Appeal of the Ghostly and Ghastly," by Jacques Barzun; the encyclopedia proper, with items arranged in alphabetical order by main entry; "Checklist of Film and Television Entries"; "Illustration Credits and Acknowledgments."

As with Gunn's *New Encyclopedia of Science Fiction* (see #8), Sullivan's book includes three different types of entries: critical biographies (of authors, artists, film makers, etc.), motion pictures critiques, and major theme essays.

Biographical entries range in size from one short paragraph to several pages and typically include: name (bold caps), middle names or real names (in parentheses), years of birth and death (where known), brief biographical data, an analysis of his or her writings or contributions to the horror genre, and a list of major "Works" (titles and years of first publication only); most essays focus on the person's contributions rather than on his or her life.

Film or television entries include: title, year(s) of production, basic credits (names of the director, script writer, major actors, etc.), running time, whether produced in color or black-and-white, a summary of the picture's or series's story line, and a brief critique; film entries typically average two to three paragraphs in size.

The fifty-four major essays cover such diverse topics as "Arkham House," "B Movies," "Ghosts," "Japanese Cinema," "Opera," "Sex," "Writers of Today," and vary from 1,000-8,000 words in length. Each entry is signed with the contributor's initials. Internal "See Also" references in the articles to related topics are indicated by putting the [sur]name or film or subject referenced in all caps; the volume also includes a few "See" references throughout the main alphabetical sequence to authors or topics covered elsewhere, but no overall index. The book is attractively designed and illustrated with black-and-white photographs, stills, and drawings taken from a wide variety of sources.

Sullivan's work displays many of the same problems as Gunn's *New Encyclopedia* (see #8), most of them apparently due to loose editorial control. For example, some entries in Sullivan record the middle or full names of their subjects, while others do not, for no apparent reason. R. Chetwynd-Hayes's first name is readily known, as are Agatha Christie's middle and married names; J. Sheridan Le Fanu's first name [Joseph] is given, but not his second middle name; Theodore Sturgeon is *not* a pseudonym of Edward Hamilton Waldo, but the legalized version of his stepfather's name, to cite but a few examples.

There is a greater difficulty, however, in the editorial selection of entries and subjects. Several of the major essays, particularly "Writers of Today," are used as "dump" entries to cover large numbers of comparatively minor writers; "See" references to these writers are then made in the main alphabetical sequence (*e.g.,* "McCAMMON, ROBERT R.: see WRITERS OF TODAY"). One may, of course, employ this approach, but it inevitably results in questions concerning the placement of certain writers (for example, are Clive Barker or Dean R. Koontz, each of whom has one paragraph in "Writers of Today," really lesser writers [by any definition] than R. Chetwynd-Hayes, who has a four-paragraph entry in the main sequence?). As employed by Sullivan, this particular format is both badly and inconsistently applied. Michael McDowell and James Herbert, for example, are listed in *both* sections, the former with overlapping, single-paragraph articles that essentially duplicate each other; other writers who are very little known have short, single-paragraph entries in the main text no greater in length or treatment than the "lesser" authors covered in "Writers of Today."

And the alphabetical "See" references do not really help the situation: the "Writers of Today" section is one of the longest in the book, exceeding 8,000 words; without an index, quick or easy access to the material in this essay is virtually impossible. Finally, there are great inconsistencies in coverage between, say, the authoritative articles on early supernatural writers contributed by Everett F. Bleiler (a well-known authority in the field) and the detailed coverage by Kim Newman of such minor films as *The Howling* and *I Walked with a Zombie,* which receive three paragraphs each. This lack of editorial balance permeates the text.

Sullivan's book is better proofread than Gunn and lacks the latter's obvious typographical and textual errors; but as a reference book, it must be placed somewhere between the Isles of Mediocrity and Lackadaisia, a far lesser work than it should have been.

18. Tuck, Donald H. **The Encyclopedia of Science Fiction and Fantasy Through 1968: A Bibliographic Survey of the Fields of Science Fiction, Fantasy, and Weird Fiction Through 1968.** Chicago, Advent:Publishers, 1974-82. xxviii, 920 p. in 3 v. index. LC 73-91828. ISBN 0-911682-20-1 (v. 1); ISBN 0-911682-22-8 (v. 2); ISBN 0-911682-26-0 (v. 3). Previously published in shorter and somewhat different form as: **A Handbook of Science Fiction and Fantasy.** Hobart, Tasmania, Australia, Tuck, 1954. 151 p. LC A55-3612 (pbk.). And as: **A Handbook of Science Fiction and Fantasy: A Collection of Material Acting As a Bibliographical Survey to the Fields of Science Fiction and Fantasy (Including Weird), Covering the Magazines, Books, Pocket Books, Personalities, Etc., of These**

Fields up Through December 1957. Hobart, Tasmania, Australia, Tuck, 1959. viii, 396 p. in 2 v. LC 60-40710 (pbk.).

Tuck's massive compilation had two previous self-published incarnations as oversized paperbound volumes, but since neither of these achieved much circulation and both were completely superseded by subsequent editions, they will be mentioned only in passing here.

Volumes 1-2 of the *Encyclopedia* are an A-Z listing of the major and minor writers in the field and their works, incorporating all known monographs (and their writers) published in fantastic literature from 1945-68, with selected works prior to that time.

A typical entry includes: writer's name (in bold caps), middle or real name(s), dates of birth and death (when known), a one- to three-paragraph biography (when data are available) and critical summary, an annotated bibliography of the author's major books in alphabetical order by title (including all monographs published in the field between 1945-68), giving (for each) title in boldface, type (*e.g.,* "C" = collection), publisher, place of publication, year, pagination, stock number, original price, and similar data for all known reprint editions through 1968, plus foreign translations (with foreign-language titles), contents (if a collection or anthology), original magazine publication data, and a one-sentence plot summary (for novels). Anthologies and nonfiction books on fantastic literature appear in their own alphabetical sections after the listing of the author's fictional monographs. A comprehensive title/author index completes the two-volume who's who set.

Volume 3 contains five sections, the first of which covers the SF magazines, with a complete A-Z listing of all professional periodicals in the field, including many peripheral publications; a typical entry provides title, nationality, type (*e.g.,* "weird"), number of issues published, dates, physical size, usual page count, usual price (with dates in effect), editor(s) (with time spans), publisher(s) (with time spans), frequency of issue (with time spans), major cover artists, a short critique and history, notable fiction published by the periodical (chronologically), a table of issues, dates, and volume numbers actually released (for long-running publications such as *Galaxy*), plus a summary of overseas editions by nationality.

The second section of Volume 3 is a guide to paperback publications in the genre through 1968, indexed firstly by author and title, giving publisher, stock number, year of publication, pagination, price, and type (*e.g.,* "J" = Juvenile); and secondly by publisher, giving publisher, place of publication, price codes, and a year-by-year summary of the publisher's paperback books (both trade and mass market) in order by stock number, author, and title; and thirdly by title and author. The third part of Volume 3 lists pseudonymous authors, first by pseudonym and real name, then reversed. The fourth chapter, "Series, Connected Stories, and Sequels," lists references to the appropriate entries in Volumes 1-2 for books and an actual list of stories (with magazine title and dates of issues) in order of publication for short periodical series; all series listed also include the author's name. The final section includes miscellanea such as television series, major SF films, awards listings and histories, comic books, and related topics.

Tuck includes such an incredible amount of raw data that it is difficult to see how any serious researcher could work in the genre without having access to these volumes. One obvious problem with the books is currency: although the final volume was not published until 1982, the cut-off date for all material except death dates was 1968, making the set now more than three decades out-of-date, and excluding much of importance in modern science fiction.

Tuck promises in his introduction to provide supplements at five- or six-year intervals, but none has appeared. Another difficulty with the set is a certain "fuzziness" in focus, since much of the data was derived secondhand from Tuck's correspondents; one wonders whether certain of the books and authors included really belong in an encyclopedia of fantastic literature, by whatever definition one is using (and that vision of imaginative fiction is never articulated by Tuck anywhere in these volumes, leaving us to wonder whether he did, on occasion, throw in the proverbial kitchen sink).

Yet, despite these minor carpings, most of the material *is* sound, well-organized, easy to use, and filled with prime research data; and there is no doubt whatever that these volumes are "must" purchases for academic institutions everywhere. Let us hope they are updated at regular intervals in the future.

19. Versins, Pierre. **Encyclopédie de l'Utopie, des Voyages Extraordinaires, et de la Science Fiction.** Lausanne, Switzerland, L'Age d'Homme, 1972. 997 p. LC 73-327497. [Rev. ed.] Lausanne, Switzerland, L'Age d'Homme, 1984. 1,037 p.

This French-language volume is the only foreign encyclopedia of science fiction and fantasy yet published, and, as might be expected, its coverage of European SF far surpasses that of any other one-volume source. Versins includes in one alphabetical sequence hundreds of biographies of major and minor figures in the field, as well as historical and critical articles on magazines, SF fandom, the history of SF, the subgenres, major fictional characters and some fictional places, countries, films, and other topics of interest. Personal surnames that are the subject of biographies are listed in all caps; real and imaginary places appear in boldface all caps; other topic heads run in small letters with initial capital letters only. The book is illustrated throughout with black-and-white cover reproductions, line drawings, and many old woodcuts, some of them full-page.

Versins covers a large number of writers, American and European, including many on whom very little information is available in the United States. The critiques range from 50-5,000 words in size, averaging 250, and typically include minimal biographical information (years of birth and death, plus one or two sentences of background data), with a focus on the writer's career, covering the author's major books (listed in boldface) in roughly chronological order. For minor writers, a list of additional titles is sometimes given without critical comment at the end of the entry.

The book is particularly strong in its coverage of seventeenth- through nineteenth-century fantastic literature, in its lists of major French science fiction publishing series, and in its critical evaluations of many writers whose works have never been translated into English. Versins shows no consistency, however, in his citations of English-language works, sometimes using the original titles, but often mentioning only the French translations of these titles without further reference. Since the original title is not always obvious, even to those fluent in French, he should, perhaps, have included the original appellation in parentheses when citing French translations. The numerous antique illustrations are quite simply marvelous. The 1984 edition updates and corrects the original but adds no significant amount of new information, and the author's recent death means that no other version of this book will likely ever be published.

This wide-ranging reference work should grace the shelves of every major American university library. See also Gunn (see #8) and Nicholls/Clute (see #12).

20. Wolfe, Gary K. **Critical Terms for Science Fiction and Fantasy: A Glossary and Guide to Scholarship.** New York, Westport, CT, Greenwood Press, 1986. xxxvi, 162 p. index. LC 86-3138. ISBN 0-313-22981-3.

This first true dictionary of fan and critical terms relating to fantastic literature is a carefully considered compilation and analysis of those words and phrases that have special meaning to the genre. Wolfe's lengthy introduction discusses the history of SF scholarship and the problems scholars have had in agreeing upon common definitions when discussing science fiction and fantasy literature. He then provides a comprehensive A-Z listing of the major terms used by fans and scholars, with copious "See" and "See Also" references. A bibliography and an index to the authors mentioned in the definitions complete the book.

Most entries quote from or cite other published sources from the list of 218 works provided in the "Works Consulted" section at the end of the book. The roughly 700 terms range in size from 15-2,000 words in length (the longest covers "science fiction" itself), averaging 100 words, and are balanced, authoritative, and readable, although oriented toward the scholarly rather than the popular reader. Indeed, Wolfe's book is as much a guide to the development of SF scholarship in the 1980s as it is a dictionary of science-fiction terminology, and as such it should be read and consulted by any student of fantastic literature. By defining these terms, he helps define the genre itself.

A most valuable and enlightening scholarly synthesis, one that should haunt the shelves of all academic libraries.

ATLASES AND GAZETTEERS

SCOPE NOTE: Included in this chapter are general atlases of fictional universes, map books of specific created worlds, and volumes that call themselves gazetteers of fantastic geography, general or specific. Character dictionaries are covered in the chapter of that name later in this book.

21. Falconer, Lee N. **A Gazeteer [*sic*] of the Hyborian World of Conan, Including Also the World of Kull, and an Ethnogeographical Dictionary of Principal Peoples of the Era, with Reference to the Starmont Map of the Hyborian World.** West Linn, OR, Starmont House, 1977. xiii, 119 p. LC 77-79065. ISBN 0-916732-19-3; ISBN 0-916732-01-0 (pbk.).

Falconer, a pseudonym of popular SF author Julian May, provides a brief introduction explaining the difficulties of elucidating the geography of Robert E. Howard's invented mythos, and details the history of previous attempts by fans to prepare maps of the Hyborian World (including her own separately published map for Starmont House).

The main section of the book (102 pages) is an A-Z guide to the people, places, and kingdoms mentioned in the entire Conan and Kull sagas (through 1977), including the non-Howard contributions to the series. A typical entry includes a description of the place in one or more paragraphs (as paraphrased from Howard's writings), with occasional paren-thetical remarks by May, plus an indication at the end of the entry of the story or stories in which the name appears (cited in italics). The appendices provide a chronological checklist of the Conan and Kull stories, including the non-Howard novels; "Notes on Various Peoples of the Hyborian Age," by Robert E. Howard; "Notes on Hyborian Heraldry and Cartogra-phy"; and "Source Maps of the Hyborian World," with reproductions of previous attempts to map Howard's intricate fictional world (the separately published map by May herself is not included here, however).

This type of work has the same value (primarily entertainment) to the reader and researcher as the numerous character dictionaries included elsewhere in this volume; May's contribution is readable, tastefully and attractively designed, and could certainly be useful to the scholar interested in Howard's literature, or in the development of series fiction by hands other than the original creator.

22. Fonstad, Karen Wynn. **The Atlas of Middle-earth.** Boston, Houghton Mifflin Co., 1981. xiv, 208 p. index. LC 80-22132. ISBN 0-395-28665-4. **The Atlas of Middle-earth.** Rev. ed. Boston, Houghton Mifflin Co., 1991. xi, p. 210 p. index. LC 91-25932. ISBN 0-395-53516-6 (pbk.).

This was the first of Fonstad's atlases, and it set the pattern for all the rest. A general introduction provides background material on J. R. R. Tolkien's Middle-earth, the created universe of *The Lord of the Rings* Trilogy, and includes a key to map symbols. Because Tolkien's fictional world covers a timespan of many thousands of years, encompassing wholesale changes in the historical geography of Middle-earth, Fonstad divides her coverage into several different periods corresponding with Tolkien's timeline of The First Age, The Second Age, and The Third Age.

Following these three sections are additional chapters providing regional maps of Tolkien's fictional geography, maps dealing specifically with the events chronicled in *The Hobbit* and *The Lord of the Rings,* and thematic maps (population, climate, languages, etc.). End matter includes an appendix listing major mountain chains, river systems, inland lakes and other bodies of water, and major political divisions; "Notes" providing the sources of quotations and other data included in the main text; "Selected References"; and an "Index of Place Names," giving name, map coordinates, and page number(s) (primary page number references are shown in italics, and site maps are underlined).

Each chapter of the atlas includes a general introduction giving background historical and geographical data, and is then subdivided into several sections (ranging from 5-31 in number), each corresponding to major events or characters or places in Tolkien's world. These subchapters typically include one to three pages of background textual material, accompanied by an illustrative map or maps occupying one-half to four pages. The descriptive material is taken directly from Tolkien's writings, including many quotations straight from the master's pen; all such citations are footnoted, with exact page references being given in the notes section at the end of the book. The maps themselves are carefully and exquisitely rendered (and attractively reproduced) in black and brown ink.

The 1991 revision stays true to the structure and content of the original. The table of contents is exactly the same, down to pagination, until the very end of the book, where the Index of Selected Place Names for the History of Middle-earth, the primary new addition, appears. A few of the maps have been redrawn, but most remain exactly the same, with no more than minor layout changes throughout.

A superbly researched and excellently drawn volume, Fonstad's book will be of equal interest both to the Tolkien fan and to the serious researcher, providing a very careful synthesis of the entire Tolkien corpus through *The Silmarillion.* Those already owning the first edition need not buy the revision.

See also the Strachey atlas, *Journeys of Frodo* (#29).

23. Fonstad, Karen Wynn. **The Atlas of Pern.** New York, A Del Rey Book, Ballantine Books, 1984. xvii, 169 p. index. LC 84-6511. ISBN 0-345-31432-8; ISBN 0-345-31434-4 (pbk.). London, Corgi Books, 1985. xvii, 169 p. index. ISBN 0-552-99148-1 (pbk.).

The second in this series of guides to major science fiction and fantasy worlds focuses on Anne McCaffrey's *Dragonriders of Pern* series. Following a general introduction to the geography of the world Pern as described in McCaffrey's series of books, Fonstad includes three different types of maps: detailed regional maps of those parts of Pern articulated by McCaffrey in her novels; a novel-by-novel chronology and geography, with each locale, "hold," and set of buildings mapped in great detail (again, based on descriptions from the series); and, finally, a set of thematic maps, including a depiction of Pern's eccentric orbital path, climates and ocean currents, land use and occupation, and population density. Each map is accompanied by descriptive text based around (and frequently quoting from) McCaffrey's original prose. Completing the book are notes referencing these descriptions to appropriate passages in the original novels by volume and page number; a selected bibliography; and an index of place names coordinated to page numbers of the maps in question, with latitude and longitude.

The maps are well drawn, clear, and distinctly reproduced in black and brown ink, with easy-to-follow keys and guides. Any fan of McCaffrey's series, or researcher into her fiction, will want this well-researched and executed atlas.

24. Fonstad, Karen Wynn. **The Atlas of the DRAGONLANCE™ World.** Lake Geneva, WI, and Cambridge, England, TSR, Inc., 1987. xx, 168 p. index. LC 86-51273. ISBN 0-88038-448-4 (pbk.).

The fourth of Fonstad's atlases pictures the proprietary universe of DRAGONLAN-CE™, a series of interactive games and separately published novels developed by the staff of TSR, Inc.

Contents: "Introduction" (including map key); "The South"; "The East"; "The West"; "The North"; "Paths and Battles"; "Thematic Maps" (*i.e.,* climate, population, etc.); "Footnotes"; "References"; "Index of Place Names."

Each chapter includes a general introduction, plus additional chapters on places of interest in those regions. A typical entry includes one to two pages of descriptive text, including numerous quotations from DRAGONLANCE™ games and literature, and one or more maps illustrating structures, cities, or locales. Quotations are cited in the "Footnotes" section at the end of the book. The maps are clearly reproduced in blue, black, and reddish-brown ink. The index correlates place names with page numbers and map coordinates; site map page references are underlined, primary locations being listed in italics.

The potential audience for this atlas is much more limited than with Fonstad's previous three books, due to the proprietary nature of this series; as usual, however, her research is impeccable and her draftsmanship clear, competent, and straightforward. Recommended.

25. Fonstad, Karen Wynn. **The Atlas of the Land.** New York, A Del Rey Book, Ballantine Books, 1985. xix, 201 p. index. LC 85-6203. ISBN 0-345-31431-X; ISBN 0-345-31433-6 (pbk.).

The third in Fonstad's map guides to science fiction and fantasy universes is arranged much like its companions. A general introduction describes the map keys and symbols and gives some background material on Stephen R. Donaldson's *Chronicles of Thomas Covenant the Unbeliever.* The book follows Thomas's journeys into the Land by dividing its geography into four roughly equal quarters, and then detailing the sites described in the two, three-volume sets of *Chronicles* (Covenant's several journeys to the Land are separated by thousands of years of relative time; however, the geography changes little over the eons).

Accompanying each map are descriptive paragraphs quoted or paraphrased directly from Donaldson's novels, with footnotes. End matter includes a detailed chronology of both series, a section referencing the notes to Donaldson's books, a selected bibliography, and an index of place names keyed to the page number of the specific map with coordinate numbers to find the locale.

The maps are attractively printed in black and brown ink, the drawings legibly produced, and the entire volume easy to read and follow, with clearly indicated guidelines. Fonstad's books have little general reference value, but this atlas will appeal to fans of Donaldson's work and to scholars interested in the development of his fiction.

26. Manguel, Alberto, and Gianni Guadalupi. **The Dictionary of Imaginary Places.** New York, Macmillan Publishing Co., 1980. 438 p. index. LC 80-11128. ISBN 0-02-579310-1. London, Granada, 1981. 438 p. index. ISBN 0-246-11560-2. **The Dictionary of Imaginary Places.** Expanded ed. San Diego, New York, A Harvest/HBJ Book, Harcourt Brace Jovanovich, 1987. 454 p. index. LC 86-26063. ISBN 0-15-626054-9 (pbk.). **The Dictionary of Imaginary Places.** Newly updated and expanded ed. New York, Harcourt Brace & Co., 2000. xvi, 755 p. index. LC 99-46994. ISBN 0-15-100541-9.

This *Baedecker* of imaginary geography includes in one A-Z sequence a selection of invented cities, countries, volcanoes, islands, deserts, and other places located in wholly fictitious geographical settings. Excluded are fictional depictions of Heaven or Hell, places with a future setting, or locales that are "disguises" for existing real-life places, such as Proust's Balbec or Hardy's Wessex.

A typical entry includes: place name (in bold caps), and a description and history (ranging in size from 50-3,000 words, averaging 200-400), with background data paraphrased from the text of the original works, which are cited by author, title, publisher, and date at the end of each annotation. A comprehensive author/title index completes the book; each author listing also includes (in all caps) a list of the geographical entries included in the *Dictionary,* referenced by book title.

The 1987 expanded edition inserts an eleven-page A-Z addendum of newly-discovered fictional locales after the main text, plus a two-page author/title index for the new entries after the main index, but is otherwise identical to the original (the text does not vary through the first 424 pages). The book is beautifully illustrated throughout with original maps and line drawings, some full-page, and is very attractively designed and printed.

The 2000 edition supersedes all previous versions of this guide. The more compact size of the new book lacks some of the charm of the larger, nineteenth-century gazetteer-style original, but happily, many of the illustrations therefrom have been retained. Manguel and Guadalupi have maintained the same standards for inclusion as before, continuing to exclude such places as Pooh's 100 Acre Wood and Richard Adams's *Watership Down.* The new edition has something less than 1,600 entries, including such significant new additions as Grand Fenwick (Wibberley), Neverwhere (Gaiman), Realm of the Jaguar Throne (Atwood), and Hogwarts (Rowling).

One major source cited by these European authors is Versins's *Encyclopédie de l'Utopie, des Voyages Extraordinaires, et de la Science Fiction* (see #19), the use of which results in a number of entries referencing older, rather obscure (at least to American readers) Continental works of imaginative literature, many of which have never been translated into English. And while all the standard fantasy classics are included (Tolkien is well represented here, as are the works of Edgar Rice Burroughs, Richard Adams, E. R. Eddison, Ursula K. Le Guin, and others), one might still have wished for a more catholic selection, or even for a more thorough coverage of the geographies actually mentioned.

Where, for example, is The Commonwealth of John Myers Myers's *Silverlock* or the land of Zimiamvia (there are ten geographical entries from E. R. Eddison's fantasy world, but not the place itself), or Hentzau from Anthony Hope's *The Prisoner of Zenda* and *Rupert of Hentzau* (only two entries are included for these books)? The text as presented is well written and illustrated, but one is struck by how much more could have legitimately been included (by the authors' own definitions) from modern fantasy literature, and by how many of the existing entries could have been omitted from an American edition without the reader or researcher ever missing them.

Still, this remains a fun book through which to browse, and should be acquired by all large library collections.

27. Post, J. B. **An Atlas of Fantasy.** Baltimore, The Mirage Press, 1973. xi, 283 p. LC 73-75640. ISBN 0-88358-108-6; ISBN 0-88358-011-X (pbk.). **An Atlas of Fantasy.** Rev. ed. New York, Ballantine Books, 1979. xiv, 210 p. index. LC 79-63506. ISBN 0-345-27399-0 (pbk.). London, Souvenir Press, 1979. xiv, 210 p. index. ISBN 0-285-62424-5 (pbk.).

Jeremiah Post, former Map Librarian at the Free Library of Philadelphia, compiled this volume as a labor of love, collecting over a hundred maps of imaginary and invented lands, dating from a map of Eden devised in the year 776, and continuing through the medieval Utopia to the modern fantasy worlds of Stephen R. Donaldson, Katherine Kurtz, and Anne McCaffrey. The original volume is 8.5" x 11" in size, the revised edition a more workable 11" x 8.5" (lying on its side), reducing the size of some maps in the latter by as much as a third (others, however, remain unchanged).

A typical entry in both books places the map on the right-hand page and a description of the place, author, artist, on the facing left-hand page. Some maps in the original edition were dropped or reshot from clearer copies in the Ballantine version, and a handful of newer maps were also added to the later book. The latter volume further contains a very useful index of artists not included in the first edition. It's worth noting that some of the maps represent authors and books not usually associated with fantasy or science fiction, particularly Raintree County, from Ross Lockridge's book of the same name, and Jefferson and Yoknapatawpha Counties, Mississippi, from the works of William Faulkner.

While Post makes no claim of having compiled a *complete* atlas of fantasy lands, this is an attractive, well-presented, and entertaining guide to some of the more interesting iconographies of fantastic literature. An expanded, updated edition covering some of the newer fantasy writers and their created worlds would be greatly appreciated.

28. Stableford, Brian, illustrated by Jeff White. **The Dictionary of Science Fiction Places.** New York, Wonderland Press, 1999. 384 p. index. LC 98-31937. ISBN 0-684-84958-5 (pbk.).

Contents: "Preface"; "Dictionary"; "Dedication and Acknowledgments"; "Works Cited"; "Entry List."

Stableford is a highly respected and prolific critic and science fiction author in his own right. His graceful, informative preface describes this fascinating volume as "a directory of imaginary places devised by writers of science fiction." He goes on to explain the purpose and scope of what he calls the "sciencefictional universe." He sees the primary bias of this fictional realm as the fact that science fiction writers are not particularly interested in portraying that part of the universe that is uninhabitable to humans. Thus, he has coined the term "Earth-clone" to describe the habitable, Earth-like worlds that proliferate the "sciencefictional" universe, and that provide the bulk of the entries he has explicated here. The admitted bias of the directory is that it "concentrates much of its attention on the least likely parts" of these Earth-type worlds, thus measuring "the ambition of the science fictional imagination far more accurately than it measures the genre's grasp of probability."

The author covers 625 entries from the created worlds of 293 authors, including material from 1893-1998. Entries are arranged alphabetically by place name. A typical entry includes: place name (bold caps), the body of the entry (averaging 275 words), and a reference to the novel or story from which the locale is derived. The overall tone is so completely matter-of-fact that it is sometimes difficult to distinguish between Stableford's own commentary and the material on which he is commenting. This can become confusing, as with the entry on Vulcan, where previous historical beliefs and Ross Rocklynne's use of the place become almost indistinguishable.

Stableford includes the name of the city or planet, the conditions and history of the site, and a summary of its fictional "history." The section at the end of each entry includes, in parentheses, the title of the work cited (italics for novels, quotation marks for short fiction), the author, the year of publication, known reprints, and similar entries cross-referenced with small caps. The Author Index correlates the writers with the list of works included (in italics or quotation marks), as well as the imaginary places drawn from those works (in small caps).

The Entry List indexes the main entries (small caps), noting the title of the work from which it was drawn (in italics or quotation marks), the author, and the year of original publication. The absence of a title index makes searching the title data almost impossible, unless one already knows the author's name. Jeff White's imaginative, black-and-white sketches of the places dress up the text. The editing is sometimes sloppy in both the indices and the text, with misplaced punctuation and incorrect fonts all-too-common occurrences.

Stableford's stated purpose in preparing this volume is to "fascinate and entertain," while reminding readers of the infinite possibilities and alternatives contained in both the imaginary universes he so vividly describes, and the mundane world in which we all must reside. He has succeeded handsomely in both goals. This is a lovely book, compelling the reader to return to it again and again, both for research and for serendipitous perusal. Highly recommended.

29. Strachey, Barbara. **Journeys of Frodo: An Atlas of J. R. R. Tolkien's** *The Lord of the Rings*. London, Boston, George Allen & Unwin, 1981. [110] p. ISBN 0-04-912016-6; ISBN 0-04-912011-5 (pbk.). New York, Ballantine Books, 1981. [110] p. LC 80-70523. ISBN 0-345-29723-7; ISBN 0-345-29633-8 (pbk.).

Journeys of Frodo provides a straightforward series of fifty-one maps in 7.5" x 9.5" format, the first of which gives an overview of Middle-earth based upon the maps originally drawn by J. R. R. Tolkien for his fantasy trilogy, the rest taking the reader on a step-by-step journey through various parts of the land, as Frodo and his companions make their epic journey from Hobbiton.

Each map is reproduced in black and red and faces a page of descriptive text by Strachey, who cites specific chapters from Tolkien's novels as authorities. Unlike the Fonstad volumes, which take a more systematic approach to the fantasy worlds they depict, this volume is less a reference work than a traveler's guide to Middle-earth, designed to be used with a reading of Tolkien's popular novels. However, it should be noted that Fonstad's *Atlas of Middle-earth* (see #22) is a much more detailed guide, and thus will prove more useful to the scholar and researcher.

CATALOGING GUIDES

SCOPE NOTE: This section includes cataloging schemes, introductions to cataloging practice, and guides to the assignment of literary numbers to science fiction, fantasy, and horror writers.

30. Burgess, Michael. **A Guide to Science Fiction & Fantasy in the Library of Congress Classification Scheme.** San Bernardino, CA, The Borgo Press, 1984. 86 p. index. (Borgo Reference Library, Vol. 8). LC 80-11418. ISBN 0-89370-807-0; ISBN 0-89370-907-7 (spiral-bound pbk.). **A Guide to Science Fiction and Fantasy in the Library of Congress Classification Scheme.** 2nd ed. San Bernardino, CA, The Borgo Press, 1988. 168 p. index. (Borgo Cataloging Guides, No. 1). LC 87-6308. ISBN 0-89370-827-5; ISBN 0-89370-927-1 (pbk.).

A university cataloger, Burgess prepared these guides for librarians using the Library of Congress classification scheme to catalog SF books and materials, for students seeking to know more about the way the LC classification arranges books, and for researchers examining the development of subject specialties in the SF genre. Some familiarity with cataloging theory and practice is presumed, particularly in the first edition.

Contents (first edition): "Subject Headings," "Author Main Entries and Literature Numbers," "Artist Main Entry and Artist Numbers," "Motion Picture Main Entries and Classification Numbers," "Subject Classification Numbers," "Index to Subject Classification Numbers." Bibliography numbers are included for those authors who have them. The second edition adds these additional chapters: "LC Literature Tables," "Television and Radio Program Main Entries and Classification Numbers," "Comic Strip Main Entries and Classification Numbers," "About the Author," in addition to expanding and revising those previously included.

In the first edition, Burgess tried to anticipate some of the changes wrought by the adoption of the second edition of the *Anglo-American Cataloging Rules* (AACR2), with mixed results. This version also failed to include sufficient "See" references from pseudonyms to the main entries established by the Library of Congress and was clearly designed for the technician, thus limiting its usefulness for the casual user.

The second edition was extensively revised to make it more accessible to non-professionals. In addition to doubling the size of the author base, with the inclusion of many more "See" and "See Also" references, Burgess also added extensive introductions to each section to better explain LC usage and practice, plus literature tables to demonstrate how author numbers are generated, and several new sections. He closely examined the changes in name forms resulting from LC's adoption of AACR2 in 1980, and returned all other main entries to the names used prior to AACR2, until and if new versions are actually generated by the Library of Congress.

The result was a current (in 1988), fairly accurate rendition of modern LC cataloging practice as it relates to fantastic literature in all its complexities and contradictions. Now out-of-date.

31. Cameron, Alistair. **Fantasy Classification System.** St. Vital, Canada, Canadian Science Fiction Association, 1952. 52 p. index. LC 53-33139 (pbk.).

Cameron uses a decimal-based cataloging scheme to classify fiction, particularly short stories, by theme. Following an introduction in which he defines fantasy literature and elucidates his cataloging theory, the author outlines his classification system, then expands upon it in much greater detail. Concluding sections cover "The Literary Information Profile," and profiles for "Single Stories," "Collections and Anthologies," and "Non-Fiction"; "Using the Classification Scheme"; "Examples of Classification"; "Index to Classification Numbers" (by subject and number); and "Some Remarks on Indexing."

The schematic is really an attempt to define and analyze fantastic literature in all its myriad forms in very great detail, and as such will certainly be of interest to those scholars interested in the theory of science fiction and fantasy. But it is clear from the examples he provides that Cameron's classification scheme fails in any practical demonstration, producing very long, cumbersome numbers that could never actually be used to organize a collection of monographs. Thus, as with Lerner (see #32), Cameron's system at best remains an interesting intellectual curiosity.

32. Lerner, Fred. **"The Cataloging and Classification of Science Fiction Collections,"** in *Science/Fiction Collections: Fantasy, Supernatural, & Weird Tales,* ed. by Hal W. Hall. New York, The Haworth Press, 1983, p. 151-170.

Although Hall's book is covered elsewhere in this book (see #131), Lerner's article has been extracted because it is the only known development of a classification scheme specifically designed for science fiction and fantasy literature and for the many nonfiction books published about these genres.

Lerner, a well-known academic librarian, first discusses existing classification schemes, particularly the Dewey Decimal and the Library of Congress systems (as well as Cameron's book [see #31]), and how they treat literature in general and SF in particular. His essay, though brief, is thorough and illuminating, clearly indicating the difficulties of housing an SF collection intermingled with other literatures. He then proceeds to extrapolate an LC-based classification scheme, the "PX" Class, "Fantastic Literature" (PX is currently unused by the Library of Congress), specifically to arrange a large science fiction and fantasy collection. His development is logical, elegant, and thorough, employing a typical LC literature arrangement, with applications and subsidiary tables designed to handle the peculiarities of the genre, plus plenty of room for expansion.

While it seems unlikely that any library will actually employ Lerner's scheme, the fact that it exists is testimony in itself to the field's growth, and to the serious interest many academics are now devoting to its study.

YEARBOOKS, ANNUALS, AND ALMANACS

SCOPE NOTE: This chapter includes literary annuals, yearbooks, and annual almanacs. Excluded are annual periodical indexes (listed in the "Periodical Indexes" section), and barebones annual bibliographies of the literature (these can be found in the "General Bibliographies" chapter). Descriptions are based on the latest years published.

33. Brown, Charles N., and William G. Contento, eds. **Science Fiction, Fantasy, & Horror: A Comprehensive Bibliography of Books and Short Fiction Published in the English Language, 1984-1991.** Oakland, CA, Locus Press, 1986-92. Annual. index. LC 88-645572. ISSN 0898-4077. (NOTE: The first *published* volume in the series was called **Science Fiction in Print: 1985**). **The Locus Index to Science Fiction (1984-2000); Combined with, Index to Science Fiction Anthologies and Collections.** Oakland, CA, Locus Press, 2001. CD-ROM. Updated annually, and produced on demand.

Charlie Brown, publisher and editor of *Locus,* the standard monthly news magazine of the SF field, teamed with William Contento, author of the standard guides to stories published in SF anthologies (see #145), to develop the first true literary annual of English-language fantastic literature. Initiating the series with the 1985 annual (published in 1986), Brown and Contento continued to add subsequent volumes at regular intervals through 1992, and also released a retrospective volume for 1984 (published in 1990).

The editors attempted to compile a complete descriptive (and partially annotated) book and periodical bibliography for each calendar year, plus additional features on topics of interest to the fan, professional, and researcher. Typical contents include (1988 annual) "Preface," by William G. Contento; "Author List: Books"; "Title List: Books"; "Author List: Stories"; "Title List: Stories"; "Contents List: Books [and] Magazines"; "Research Index," by Hal W. Hall, including "Subject List" and "Author List"; Appendices: "Book Summary," by Charles N. Brown; "Magazine Summary," by Charles N. Brown; "Cinema Summary," by Frank M. Robinson; "1988 Review," by Ed Bryant; "U.K. Year in S.F.," by Phil Stephensen-Payne; "Recommended Reading," by Charles N. Brown, Faren Miller, Tom Whitmore, Carolyn Cushman, Dan Chow, and Mark Kelly; "Awards," by Harlan McGhan; "Publisher Addresses"; and "Abbreviations."

Much of the bibliographical data for these volumes is taken from monthly listings in *Locus* magazine (with corrections and emendations), but many of the summaries (and secondary source bibliography) are original to the published books.

The primary "Books" section lists the volumes alphabetically by author or editor. A typical entry includes: author (all caps), series and title (boldface), publisher, ISBN number, month and year of date first seen (plus similar data for actual publication date, if different, in brackets), price, pagination, format (*e.g.*, "pb" = paperback), reprint/reissue information (with mention of publisher and year of first edition), book type (*e.g.*, anthology, novel, original anthology, etc.), brief annotation (usually one sentence), additional series information and/or data on related editions or books. Books are listed under the pseudonyms that appear on the title pages, but there are numerous "See Also" references from known pen names to others used by the same author.

Similarly, short stories published in magazines or books are listed alphabetically by author's name, with a typical entry including: name (all caps), title (regular type), format abbreviation (*e.g.*, "ss" = short story), source (*i.e.*, the earliest known publication of the piece if this appearance is not original, with title of original anthology or magazine in which it appeared, plus publication date), magazine abbreviation (*e.g.*, "F&SF" = *The Magazine of Fantasy & Science Fiction*) or book title (for collections and anthologies, in boldface), and date of publication. Anthology entries also include editor and publisher in addition to year of publication. The title indexes correlate titles and authors only.

The "Book Contents" section provides complete contents of story collections and anthologies, with editor (all caps), title (boldface type), bibliographical data, and a list of the stories as they appear in the book, including beginning page numbers for each item covered, and title and author.

The "Magazine Contents" chapter provides similar data for each magazine issue published throughout the year, arranged by periodical title (italics), then by volume and issue number and date, with editor's name, publisher, price, pagination, format (*e.g.*, "pb" = paperbound), and a complete contents listing, arranged by page number, with title and author.

Hall's research index (beginning with the 1988 book), a continuation of his *Science Fiction and Fantasy Reference/Research Index* (see #117), includes all known essays, indexes, bibliographies, and monographs published throughout the world relating to the study of fantastic literature. The first part of this section is arranged by subject, author, and title, with complete bibliographical data; the second part rearranges the same data by author. The appendices provide statistical tables, lists of awards, reading lists, and other material of interest.

The books are well designed and presented, attractively and legibly typeset in an 8.5" x 11" double-column format, and bound in sturdy library cloth editions. The 1988 edition includes 471 pages of closely packed data. While the bibliographies are not 100% complete, they include the vast majority of fictional publications actually released each year, missing only very peripheral or minor items; and the addition of Hall's secondary source lists in the newer annuals provides a valuable adjunct for researchers in the genre.

Sales for the volumes gradually declined in the early 1990s, and the series was discontinued with the 1991 annual. Subsequently, the bibliographical data and much of the other content of these volumes were put on-line by Locus Press (www.locusmag.com), and also released in annually-revised CD-ROMs under the title, *The Locus Index to Science Fiction*. With the reason for the bound books having been outdated by the advance of technology, the print volumes have now become mere peripheral adjuncts to the science-fiction library.

The CD-ROM version combines material taken from the printed volumes with the contents of Contento's *Index to Science Fiction Anthologies and Collections* (see #145). The CD enables the user to search the entire span of years from 1984 to date in one sequence, while the on-line database is broken into different spans of years. However, the CD is made up entirely of "html" pages, so that one significant feature found in the on-line product is absent. The "Search for Book or Story Title" link on the web-based version employs "cgi" protocol to search the database using boolean logic, while the CD-ROM is driven solely by alphabetical listings. Fortunately, the lists are (in most cases) as clear and simple to use as those duplicated on the Web product.

Some users may wonder, however, why they should pay good money for a CD product with somewhat less functionality, when the on-line databases are available to everyone for free.

34. Collins, Robert A., and Robert Latham, eds. **Science Fiction & Fantasy Book Review Annual, 1988-1989.** Westport, CT, London, Meckler, 1988-90, 2 volumes. **Science Fiction & Fantasy Book Review Annual, 1990-1991.** New York and London, Greenwood Press, 1991-94, 2 volumes. annual. index. LC 89-642022. ISSN 1040-192X.

When *Fantasy Review,* then the leading SF review magazine in the field, ceased publication in the summer of 1987, its editors, Collins and Latham, reincarnated its essence in this annual series of literary guides to the primary and secondary literature of science fiction and fantasy. The first of these books, published in 1988, covers the year 1987; the second volume (with 1988 reviews, but called 1989) did not appear until 1990; a third annual was published by Greenwood Press at the end of 1991, covering the year 1989 (but was called 1990); and the fourth and final volume was published in 1994, covering the year 1990 (but called 1991).

SF&FBRA is both similar and dissimilar to its ancestral periodical. The first edition includes the following introductory sections: "Author of the Year: Orson Scott Card," by Mark Van Name; "The Year in Fantasy," by Charles de Lint (with "Recommended Reading List"); "The Year in Horror Literature," by Michael Morrison (with "Recommended Reading List"); "The Year in Science Fiction," by Michael Levy (with "Recommended Reading List"); "The Year's Research & Criticism," by Neil Barron (with "Bibliography"); and "Award Winners in 1987."

These general survey essays summarize the literary highpoints of the year, covering both monographs and short fiction, as well as SF publishing, magazines, and the specialty press, with suggested readings lists of the best fiction of the year. Neil Barron's learned but dispiteous analysis of the major critical works published in 1987 includes some material not covered in the review section, plus a bibliographical checklist of the works (including author, title, publisher, pagination, price, and ISBN number); unfortunately, the number "9" was transcribed by the typesetting program as "6" throughout his bibliography in Volume One, making hash of the data.

The bulk of the 1988 volume, "Reviews of 1987 Books," is broken into three sections: "I. Fiction"; "II. Young Adult Fiction"; "III. Nonfiction." Each of these is arranged alphabetically by author, then by title. A typical entry includes: author (boldface), title (italics), publisher, place of publication, month and year of publication, pagination, price, ISBN number, and a contributed review.

The reviews themselves range in size from 100-1,000 words, averaging about 300. Reviewers include both well-known and unknown critics, academics, professionals, and fans, and the quality of the material varies widely, as might be expected. Generally, about half of a typical entry summarizes the plot or content of the book, with a paragraph or two of analysis and summary, including mention of related books or authors. Most are at least readable; the best provide flashes of literary insight into the author and his work.

The title index correlates title, author, and page number(s) for every book and film title mentioned in the volume (including those buried in the introductory essays, and those mentioned in passing in the bodies of each review), providing comprehensive access to the casual reader. The fourth volume in the series added a survey article reviewing children's science fiction and fantasy, but otherwise the format remained substantially the same for the life of the series.

In their general introductions to the books, the editors acknowledge some gaps in coverage, but the great majority of noteworthy SF titles published during the years 1987-90 are reviewed in the four, 500- to 900-page volumes. The books are attractively designed and typeset, well bound in a library cloth edition, and exceptionally easy to read and use (save for the glitches in Barron's article in the first volume, and for some faint pages that occur throughout the fourth volume).

Although *SF&FBRA* provided a comprehensive survey of the literature of science fiction during its brief run, the books never sold very well, and the series was discontinued after the fourth volume. This is a great shame, since no other comparable source for critical information currently exists in the field. However, as worthy as these volumes might have been when they were first published, they are now more than a decade out-of-date, and possess only historical value.

35. Lester, Colin, ed. **The International Science Fiction Yearbook 1979.** London, Pierrot Publishing; New York, Quick Fox, 1978. 394 p. ISSN 0143-1390. ISBN 0-905310-16-0 (pbk.).

The first volume in what was intended to be an annual series includes a large amount of rather dated material arranged very peculiarly.

Contents: "How to Use the Book"; 1. "Introduction"; 2. "The Year in Fantasy Fiction"; 3. "New Works, New Worlds: A Survey of SF in Latin America"; 4. "The State of the Art in Determining & Delimiting SF"; 5. "Obituaries"; 6. "Book Publishing"; 7. "Magazines"; 8. "Organizations"; 9. "Fanzines"; 10. "Agents"; 11. "Anthologies"; 12. "Criticism, Commentary, Bibliography"; 13. "Translators"; 14. "Libraries"; 15. "Book Clubs"; 16. "Booksellers"; 17. "Pseudonyms"; 18. "Conferences & Workshops"; 19. "Conventions"; 20. "Awards"; 21. "Artists"; 22. "Films"; 23. "TV"; 24. "Radio & Drama"; 25. "Music & Recordings"; 26. "APA's"; 27. "Miscellaneous Services"; 28. "Name-Interests" [summaries of critical and associational material available on six major names in the field—*e.g.*, Robert E. Howard]; 29. "Fringe Interests."

Lester compiled a huge amount of data for this book, derived both from direct-mail questionnaires and a network of correspondents worldwide; the coverage is international, although a great many of the listings perforce reflect English-language sources and publications. Many chapters include a descriptive introduction, then an alphabetical arrangement of the data. Much of the information is presented in abbreviated form, keyed to boldfaced numbers buried in each paragraph, with the description of the key located after the textual material at the beginning of each chapter.

The presentation is unnecessarily confusing and frequently difficult to elucidate, even for the experienced researcher: the text often seems to run together on the page, and one must constantly flip back and forth to decipher each entry. Also, the choice of a double-column format with no running page heads is particularly unfortunate in this type of publication, as is the utter absence of an index (which was not, however, the fault of the compiler; Lester prepared a comprehensive index that was rejected by the publisher). These major design flaws, plus the absence of any bibliographical details, and the fact that much of the material was originally oriented toward fans (and is now wholly out-of-date), render this work almost useless decades after the fact.

36. Stewart, Elke, and Alan Stewart, eds. **The SF Yearbook 1976.** London, BSFA Ltd., 1976. 57 p. (pbk.).

This very amateurish chapbook from the British Science Fiction Association summarizes happenings in the SF world (with particular attention to UK events) during the calendar year 1975.

Contents: "Foreword," by Kenneth Bulmer; "Introduction," by Alan Stewart; Articles: "Books in 1975," by Philip Stephensen-Payne; "Magazines in 1975," by David Ross; "Films in 1975," by Andrew Tidmarsh; "Television in 1975," by Graham Poole; "Fandom," by Elke Stewart; "Writing SF," by David Penny (essay); "Story of a Group," by Sonya Porter. Reference: "Awards of 1975"; "Publications"; "Booksellers"; "Publishers"; "Clubs and Groups"; "Past Conventions"; "Future Conventions."

This pamphlet was clearly intended for fans and contains very little of library interest, and much of that is now long outdated. The book is shot from photo-reduced (and often hard-to-read) typed copy and is saddle-stitched in plain (and very flimsy) paper covers. There is absolutely nothing here that can't be found elsewhere.

ANNUAL DIRECTORIES

SCOPE NOTE: Included herein are the annual membership directories of professional and fan societies. Descriptions are based on the latest years published.

37. Hopkins, Harry, and Mariane S. Hopkins, eds. **Fandom Directory.** Various cities [currently Springfield, VA], Fandata Publications, 1979-DATE. Annual. ISSN 8756-8349.

Published annually since 1979, the *Directory* was originally edited by Harry Hopkins, then jointly edited with his wife, Mariane, and then edited solely again by Harry, and then solely again by his wife.

Contents (of Number 18, 1998-1999): "How to Use Fandom Directory"; "Foreword"; "Status and Interest Codes"; "Geographic Distribution of Listings in this Edition"; "Contributing Artist Credits"; "*Fandom Directory* Online Edition"; "Fan Publications Index"; "Convention Index"; "Zine/Club/Con Annual Recertification Form"; "Fan Club Listing"; "Research Libraries of Interest to Fandom"; "Alphabetical Listing of Entries in This Edition"; "*Fandom Directory* Free Listing Form"; "Retail Stores Index"; "Artists' Gallery"; "Zip Code Listing of Entries in This Edition"; "Last Minute Additions and Updates"; "Classified Advertisements"; "*Fandom Directory* Back Issues"; "Index to Advertisers"; "*Fandom Directory* Advertising Rates"; "Customer Response Form."

With 20,000 listings, this is an enormous directory of anything (organizations, clubs, conventions, galleries, stores, libraries) and anyone (collectors, artists, editors, translators, writers) of interest in SF (and related fields) fandom.

Major sections include: current alphabetical list of SF fan magazines (fanzines), giving title, type of contents (*e.g.*, "*Star Trek* fiction and humor"), frequency, price, publisher, and address; conventions announced for the year by date, with dates, title, featured programming, sponsor, address, and telephone number; an alphabetical directory of fan clubs, with name, interests, frequency of meeting, publications, organization name or coordinator, and address; major research libraries arranged by state, then alphabetically by institution name, with a description of holdings, date of survey (*e.g.,* "6/96" = June, 1996), contact person or curator, address, and phone number; an index of retail stores selling materials of interest in SF, comics, and related fields arranged by state, then alphabetically by store name, with name, address, and phone number; an alphabetical index to all persons and organizations mentioned, including interested fans who have submitted data sheets on themselves, giving name (personal or institutional or society), state, and zip code (to find more information, one must look in the zip code directory); a zip code index arranged by state and then by zip code number, listing name, address, city, state, zip code, phone number (for about two-thirds of the addresses), and codes giving status (*e.g.*, "D" = Mail Order Retailer) and interests (*e.g.*, "FK" = filking).

Canadian listings follow the United States directory by province and postal code; fans living in other foreign countries are listed following the Canadian directory, in alphabetical order by country, then alphabetically by main entry. The directory also includes a portfolio of fan art selected from pieces submitted by budding artists in the field.

Some information that would aid the user's navigation through the text is difficult to find, and the volume as a whole can sometimes feel rather overwhelming to the novice, between the multitudinous data listings and the ample advertisements. The instructions on page 14 of the 1998-99 edition do provide answers to basic searching questions, and also point the user to the online version of the same product (at www.fandata.com).

The *Fandom Directory* is particularly useful as a very current guide to fan publications, conventions, and groups. Librarians and researchers may also find the retail store and library collection directories helpful for bibliographical control and interlibrary loan purposes. There is an enormous amount of worthwhile data buried within the pages of this annual guide, but it sometimes feels as if one needs a shovel to dig them out.

38. Horror Writers Association Membership Directory. Horror Writers Association, 1986-DATE. Annual.

HWA is a relatively new organization, having been founded in 1986 by Dean R. Koontz and others, but its annual directory of members is organized similarly to that of its rivals.

The first page of the directory lists the officers of the organization. Then the roughly 600 members are arranged alphabetically by surname. A typical entry includes: name, status (*e.g.*, "AC" = active), address, phone number(s), fax number, e-mail address, and agent. A second section lists agents alphabetically by business name, with an alphabetical list of the authors each represents. The third part of the directory is a geographical index to the authors, by state or country, and then alphabetically by surname.

With the expansion of the horror field into a separate paperback genre in the 1980s, HWA rapidly increased its membership and seems destined to grow even further. Access to the directory is restricted to members only, and membership qualifications are as stringent as they are for other writers' organizations, including SFWA.

39. International Association for the Fantastic in the Arts Membership Directory. Boca Raton, FL, International Association for the Fantastic in the Arts, 1986?-DATE. Annual.

This rival organization to the Science Fiction Research Association (see #40) was founded by well-known critic and bibliographer Marshall B. Tymn about 1985.

The first page of the directory lists the officers of the organization. Page 2 records the winners of the six different awards the Association has presented, arranged chronologically by presentation date. The main section is arranged alphabetically by surname, and lists the roughly 350 members, all of the scholars interested in the serious study of fantastic literature and the arts. A typical entry includes: name, academic affiliation, address, phone number, e-mail address, and a brief list of the individual's scholarly interests (in italics).

The final section of the directory records the constitution and bylaws of the organization. Copies of this annual volume are available for sale to the public. Since some academics only belong to one of the two organizations devoted to the study of science fiction, the directories of both associations are necessary to follow current research trends in SF and fantasy.

40. Science Fiction Research Association Annual Directory. Science Fiction Research Association, 1971?-DATE. Annual. index.

This directory of approximately 300 scholars interested in serious research into fantastic literature has been published annually by the association since about 1971.

The first page of the directory records a brief history (in three paragraphs) of SFRA, a list of past presidents of the organization, and current officers. The second page records a list of the annual conferences sponsored by the group, in descending, chronological order by year, with the specific dates and places where the meeting took place, and the conference direction.

The main section lists members alphabetically by surname, typically including: name (boldfaced), academic affiliation, address, phone number, e-mail address, plus a one- or two-sentence description of the member's interest in the genre (*e.g.*, "teaching SF at secondary level").

The Geographical Index rearranges the members by state or country, then alphabetically by surname. The Interest Index records the specialities mentioned by the scholars, with alphabetical listings of those associated with each subject. A fourth section reproduces the bylaws of the organization. The final section records the speeches of the Pilgrim, Clareson, Pioneer, and Graduate Student Paper Award winners for the previous year.

Copies of the directory are available for sale to the public. This is a very useful annual guide to the major scholars in the field and their current research interests. See also the directory of a rival organization, IAFA (see #39).

41. SFWA Membership Directory. Science Fiction and Fantasy Writers of America, Inc., 1965?-DATE. Annual.

This organization of professional science fiction writers has published an annual directory of its roughly 1,400 writers and institutional members since its inception.

The inside front cover records SFWA Contacts and Member Services. The main directory records members in alphabetical order by surname. A typical entry includes: name (boldfaced), status (*e.g.*, "A" = active member), address, phone number, fax number, e-mail address, and a three-letter code referring to the author's agent.

The second sections lists foreign members by country. Section three records U.S. members by state and zipcode. Section four gives the three-letter codes for literary agents, arranged in alphabetical order, including: agent, agency name, address, phone number, fax number, and a list of the authors affiliated with that agency, in alphabetical order by surname.

The fifth section provides a record of representatives of authors' estates. A sixth section records "alternate names" (*i.e.*, pseudonyms or real names) of members. The final section records the bylaws of the organization.

The directory is generally available to members only, but may be purchased by those with "a professional interest" in the field. Libraries may also join as institutional members. Most currently active American SF writers belong to SFWA (pronounced "Séfwa"), plus some fifty Canadian authors and sixty more from other countries.

STATISTICAL SOURCES

SCOPE NOTE: Included herein are books made up largely of tables, statistical charts, and comparative lists relating to the study of fantastic literature.

42. Ashley, Mike. **Illustrated Book of Science Fiction Lists.** London, Virgin Books, 1982. 190 p. ISBN 0-907080-45-6 (pbk.). As: **The Illustrated Book of Science Fiction Lists.** New York, Cornerstone Library, Simon & Schuster, 1983. 190 p. LC 83-235099. ISBN 0-346-12628-2 (pbk.).

Ashley, a well-known British bibliographer, divides his book into four sections: "A. What Is This Thing . . . ?," including fifty lists on the best or most noteworthy stories and novels in the genre, the best magazines, artists, and films, and novels about specific topics (*e.g.*, mutations, matter transmission, other dimensions, etc.); "B. Expert Opinion," forty-four lists generated by various experts in the field (SF writers, artists, and editors) on their favorite works in particular categories (for example, "Stephen R. Donaldson's 10 Favourite Fantasy Novels"); "C. The Recordholders," comprising thirty-four statistical lists on the most prolific, oldest, youngest, and most award-winning writers, the highest advances paid in the field for particular SF titles, and many other similar renditions; and "D. Oddities and Entities," with thirty-eight lists providing odd statistics or facts about SF writers (*e.g.*, "10 SF Writers Whose Careers Were Cut Short," "10 Pen Names That Hide the Identity of Two or More Authors," etc.).

Ashley's lists are authoritative, and he frequently provides annotations that enlighten the reader further about the author or his records, or that give further illuminations about the book or story or magazine in question. The very detailed contents pages help substitute for the lack of an index. Section C, "The Recordholders," includes a number of statistical tables unavailable in any other source, and could provide a valuable launching point for further sociological analyses of the genre and its writers. A second, updated edition is definitely past due.

43. Jakubowski, Maxim, and Malcolm Edwards. **The Complete Book of Science Fiction and Fantasy Lists.** London, Granada, 1983. 350 p. ISBN 0-586-05678-5 (pbk.). As: **The SF Book of Lists.** Expanded ed. New York, Berkley Books, 1983. 384 p. LC 83-237697. ISBN 0-425-06187-6 (pbk.).

Jakubowski and Edwards's book appeared almost simultaneously with Ashley's and covers much of the same material. The book is very loosely organized, without division, into specific subject lists covering the works, the awards, the authors, and the films of science fiction literature. The heart of the book is the ninety-page section called "The Years of Futures Past," which attempts to identify the major stories and novels of the field. This chapter is arranged chronologically, noting major award winners in the field, award nominees, stories selected for "Best of the Year" anthologies, and prevailing critical opinion for the very early periods, before any specific SF awards existed. This is a uniquely valuable guide to the literature of the genre.

The rest of the book is often interesting and fun to read, but is so loosely arranged that, without either an index or contents page, it cannot really be used as a reference tool. The American edition is identical to the British through page 350, adding thirty-four pages of further lists, except that the final list, on pages 382-384, repeats verbatim the list on pages 347-350, with which the British version ends.

Comparisons with Ashley (see #42) are inevitable, since the books were released within months of each other in the United States, and since they cover much of the same material (indeed, the premises, although not the contents, of many lists overlap wholly or in part). However, while Ashley's volume clearly works better as a reference tool and includes statistical material not found in Jakubowski/Edwards, the latter has its own unique and very detailed chronicle of the best SF from its beginnings to modern times, and incorporates many more tables in a much larger number of pages. Both books also include contributions by major SF authors and critics.

Thus, while each work has value in its own right, neither really displays any marked advantage over the other.

44. Pickard, Roy. **The Hamlyn Book of Horror and S.F. Movie Lists.** London, Hamlyn Paperbacks, 1983. 223 p., [16] p. of plates. ISBN 0-600-20778-1 (pbk.).

Pickard's volume focuses specifically on fantastic films and is arranged in alphabetical order by topic. Despite its superficial aura of superior organization, Pickard's book, like Jakubowski/Edwards's guide (see #43), is really a potpourri of popularly oriented associational items, sequels, directors' lists, and other miscellanea, as can be gleaned from a sampling of the chapter heads: "Awards," "Ray Bradbury," "Budgets," "Curses," "Peter Cushing," "Hammer Films: All of Them," "George Lucas," "The Most Popular Science-Fiction Films of the 1950s," "Priests," "*Star Trek,*" "Unusual Names," and "Last List," a chronological checklist of the major events in the development of science fiction, fantasy, and horror films.

The book includes sixteen pages of plates reproducing black-and-white stills from various pictures mentioned in the book (but uncorrelated to the text). The volume is fun and eminently readable, but very slight; the lack of an index makes it almost unusable as a reference work.

AWARDS LISTS

SCOPE NOTE: This chapter includes monographs consisting largely or entirely of lists of science fiction and fantasy awards. It should be noted that most general guides to the literature include some awards listings, although none are as complete as those covered below.

45. Franson, Donald, and Howard DeVore. **A History of the Hugo, Nebula, and International Fantasy Awards.** Dearborn Heights, MI, Misfit Press, 1985. 185 p. index. LC 71-25327 [for 1971 ed.] (pbk.). DeVore, Howard. **The Hugo, Nebula, and World Fantasy Awards.** [revised ed.]. Chicago, Advent:Publishers, 1998. 332 p. index. ISBN 0-911682-32-5 (pbk.).

At least nine editions of this book were issued between 1970-85, many of them not clearly labeled, but each slightly larger than the last; no attempt has been made to list the earlier versions here.

A basic guide to the three premier awards in the genre (plus an earlier precursor now no longer presented), DeVore's book in its 1998 edition includes short histories of the awards, and chronological listings of the nominees and winners, the latter being listed in boldface type. Each year of the award is broken into its component categories ("Best Novel," for example), arranged as per usual practice with the major fiction awards listed first, and the nonfiction and other categories second. The detailed index cross-references the appropriate page numbers with winners (authors, motion pictures, magazines, publishers), titles, and all other individuals and publications mentioned. The index is occasionally difficult to use for such prolific authors as Harlan Ellison, who has been nominated for (and received) dozens of awards. The book is nicely typeset and printed, a very great improvement over the sometimes amateurish production efforts of the earlier versions.

DeVore's latest incarnation covers the Hugo Awards through 1997, and the Nebula Awards and International Fantasy Awards through 1996. Reginald and Mallett's guide (see #47) includes many more awards (through 1992), but does not, however, list any nominees, thus making both books necessary purchases for the scholar, fan, or librarian.

46. Reed, Donald A., and Patrick Pattison. **Collector's Edition: Science Fiction Film Awards.** La Habra, CA, ESE California, 1981. 107 p. ISBN 0-912076-39-9; ISBN 0-912076-40-2 (pbk.).

The late Donald Reed founded The Count Dracula Society in 1962 to promote the study of horror films and literature, and a decade later created the Academy of Science Fiction, Fantasy and Horror Films to promote "the arts and sciences of science fiction, fantasy, and horror films." The first annual "Science Fiction Film Awards" were presented by the Academy later that year (1972).

This 8.5" x 11" volume lists the award winners from 1972-80 inclusive, being decorated with numerous film stills and pictures of the actors and actresses nominated for the awards, as well as photographs from the awards ceremonies. The text also provides career summaries for the winners and plot summaries and background data on the best films of the year. There is a complete chronological list of the winners at the end of the book, but no alphabetical index, making location of specific data unnecessarily difficult. A new, updated edition (with index) would be appreciated.

47. Reginald, R. **Science Fiction and Fantasy Awards, Including Complete Checklists of the Hugo Awards, Nebula Awards, Locus Awards, Jupiter Awards, Pilgrim Awards, International Fantasy Awards, Ditmar Awards, August Derleth Awards, World Fantasy Awards, Eaton Awards, Gandalf Awards, British Fantasy Awards, John W. Campbell Memorial Awards, Milford Awards, Prometheus Awards, and Selected Foreign Awards, with a Complete Index to Winners, a List of Officers of the Science Fiction Writers of America from the Beginning of That Organization, a Checklist of World Science Fiction Conventions and Their Guests of Honor, and Detailed Statistic Tables.** San Bernardino, CA, The Borgo Press, 1981. 64 p. index. (Borgo Reference Library, Vol. 2). LC 80-10788. ISBN 0-89370-806-2; ISBN 0-89370-906-9 (pbk.). Mallett, Daryl F., and Robert Reginald. **Reginald's Science Fiction and Fantasy Awards: A Comprehensive Guide to the Awards and Their Winners.** 2nd ed. San Bernardino, CA, The Borgo Press, 1991. 248 p. index. (Borgo Literary Guides, No. 1). LC 90-15074. ISBN 0-89370-826-7; ISBN 0-89370-926-3 (pbk.). **Reginald's Science Fiction and Fantasy Awards: A Comprehensive Guide to the Awards and Their Winners.** 3rd ed. San Bernardino, CA, The Borgo Press, 1993. 248 p. index. (Borgo Literary Guides, No. 1). LC 92-24445. ISBN 0-8095-0200-5; ISBN 0-8095-1200-9 (pbk.).

The original version of this comprehensive guide to science fiction awards was arranged alphabetically by award name (a few minor awards were inserted into conveniently blank places in the book, but these can readily be identified through the table of contents), and then chronologically by year. Two years are given for each year of presentation of a particular award, the first being the year of qualification of the award winners, the second (in parentheses) the year in which the award was actually presented; this system was necessary because there is no uniformity in the way these awards are popularly regarded or described (for example, the two major awards in the field, the Hugos and the Nebulas, are generally labeled by the year of qualification and the year of presentation, respectively, the 1980 Hugos thus being equivalent to the 1981 Nebulas).

Under each award year, the awards are listed by category, the most prestigious category being listed first, plus title and author of the winner. A "Personal Name Index" repeats the data by author name. In addition to the major and minor awards in the field, including some foreign awards, the book also includes a chronological list of the elected officers of the Science Fiction Writers of America, the major professional organization in the field; plus a chronological list of the world science fiction conventions, with formal name, site, and guests of honor—these honors are also included in the name index. Four statistical tables correlating the highest number of winners (overall, for all fiction categories, for the Hugos, and for the Nebulas), complete the book.

The second edition was updated by Daryl F. Mallett and edited by Reginald, and quadruples the data from the first version. In addition to bringing previously existing sections down to mid-1991, many new awards were added (including foreign), plus a title index, a history of each award, the rules governing the presentation of the awards, and an indication of what the presentation includes (trophy, plaque, scroll, etc.). All those awards proprietary to the science fiction world are listed in alphabetical order by name of award, then chronologically by date; however, the basic format of the book is the same as the original.

Foreign awards and those awards that have honored SF writers for accolades outside the genre of fantastic literature are grouped together into two appendices, again alphabetically by award name. Also included in the end matter are lists of the officers of the Science Fiction Writers of America, Horror Writers of America, and Science Fiction Research Association. The statistical data have also been expanded (by Reginald). The amount of data in this volume (covering 126 separate awards) far exceeds anything available on SF awards even in the major reference tools, and the detailed tables provide prime material for further sociological study.

The third edition, published early in 1993, is organized similarly to the second, but brings the data down through the end of 1992. The statistical tables were dropped from this edition for lack of space.

DeVore's guide (see #45) is more current (by four years), and includes the nominees omitted from Mallett and Reginald, but the latter features far more awards. A newly updated version would be welcome.

PSEUDONYM LISTS

SCOPE NOTE: Included herein are monographs consisting primarily of lists of science fiction pseudonyms and their real authors. Partial lists can be found in many other general guides and bibliographies.

48. Bates, Susannah. **The PENDEX: An Index of Pen Names and House Names in Fantastic, Thriller, and Series Literature.** New York & London, Garland Publishing, 1981. xii, 233 p. index. LC 80-8486. (Garland Reference Library of the Humanities, Vol. 237). ISBN 0-8240-9501-4.

The PENDEX includes pseudonyms used by authors working in both fantastic literature and in the mystery and detective genre. After a brief introduction by Bates, the book is broken into five sections.

"Real Names" includes the author's real name in capital letters, with middle names and years of birth and death (where known), followed by the writer's pen name(s) in regular type, indented two spaces. Some pseudonyms include the following letter codes after the name: "CPN" = Collaborative Pen Name; "HN" = House Name; "SSN" = Stratemeyer Syndicate Name. The second section includes "Pen Names," in which the *noms de plume* appear in all caps, with real names in regular letters indented two spaces, preceded by the letters "RN" (*i.e.,* "real name"). The third chapter lists "Collaborative Pen Names," that is, a pseudonym used by two or more authors in collaboration, listed by name (in all caps), with the real names of the authors in ordinary letters, indented two spaces.

The fourth section includes "House Names," with a similar arrangement, listing all known author(s) using the name. The final section covers the Stratemeyer Syndicate, which produced adolescent series novels under house pseudonyms. Two appendices cover "Pulps & Digests: Some Working Definitions," and "Round Robin Serials," in which each author contributes one or more chapters to an ongoing story. A brief bibliography of sources consulted is followed by a complete index to real names (in capital letters) and pseudonyms (in regular type).

Bates covers roughly 1,700 pseudonyms of some 950 authors, a figure appreciably smaller than McGhan (see #49), particularly when one realizes that she is also attempting to include the pen names of mystery writers. Her source list demonstrates that she has missed most of the major reference tools of fantastic literature published in 1979-80, thereby losing many identifications first made in those publications; for example, she only catches half of R. Lionel Fanthorpe's many names. More disturbing by far than this lack of focus or understanding of the genre is the large number of outright errors: Frank Aubrey is consistently listed as "Aubray"; Fanthorpe's pseudonym is given as "Ziegfried," when it should be "Zeigfreid," and it is *not* a house name (but Karl Zeigfried, which is not listed, *is*); several well-known names of Don Pendleton, particularly Dan Britain, are not included in his entry; only one pen name is listed for Lauran Paine, when he has used dozens on his SF, mystery, and western novels; Greye La Spina is misspelled "Greya"; Frederic Arnold Kummer is listed as "Frederick"; Edmond Hamilton is misspelled "Edmund"; Harlan Ellison's pseudonym Cordwainer Bird is spelled "Cortwainer"; Fairman did indeed write five Lester del Rey novels, but not all were juveniles, and not all were published by Scholastic; Bruce Elliott is misspelled Elliot, "Julain" (actually Julian) Chain is *not* a pseudonym of May Dikty (Bates confuses Julian May, or "Judy" Dikty, with real-life author Julian Chain, a mistake also made by McGhan); and so on, in endless permutations.

The proliferation of omissions and commissions is inexcusable, particularly given the large number of resource persons and volumes readily available; it reflects a carelessness and inattention to detail that must inevitably damn this book to the Bibliography Hall of Shame. Such errors also make the work completely untrustworthy; although McGhan's production values and binding are shoddy by comparison, his book (and Robinson's) are 100% more reliable (see #49-#50).

49. McGhan, Barry. **Science Fiction and Fantasy Pseudonyms.** Dearborn, MI, Misfit Press, 1979. vi, 77 p. LC 72-176242 [1971 ed.]; LC 74-161774 [1973 ed.] (pbk.). At least seven editions of this book were published between 1971-79, but the earlier versions have not been listed here.

McGhan provides a comprehensive list of 1,581 SF pen names and the roughly 1,000 real authors behind them in one alphabet, real names being given in boldface, house pseudonyms being indicated with the letters "*h ps*" prior to the name. Following each name is a number in parentheses, referencing a bibliography of seventy-one items at the front of the book, indicating every source used to verify a pseudonym (roughly a quarter are marked "private communication" from a specified individual). This list enables the researcher to follow in McGhan's scholarly footsteps.

The 1979 version is identical to the 1976 edition through page 70, save for the addition of further sources on introductory pages v-vi and a separate alphabetical "1979 Supplement" on pages 71-77; some pages were faint in the three editions examined, and the book uses a loose, saddle-stitched binding. Only SF authors are included in this book, but some of the pen names listed were used solely for non-SF publications, although McGhan makes no distinction between them; it is also impossible to determine which names were used on monographs and which on stories. A new edition taking into account the many major reference works published in the past several decades would certainly be welcome.

50. Robinson, Roger. **Who's Hugh? An SF Reader's Guide to Pseudonyms.** Harold Wood, Essex, England, Beccon Publications, 1987. 173 p. LC 89-146783. ISBN 1-870824-01-6; ISBN 1-870824-02-4 (pbk.).

Who's Hugh is the most current and comprehensive guide to SF pen names, covering roughly 3,200 *noms de plume* of an unknown number of real-life authors (Robinson's format makes an estimate impossible). Like McGhan, Robinson documents his work by citing ninety-nine previously published (or oral) sources (including McGhan as the ninety-ninth, but missing both Bates and Mossman's *Pseudonyms and Nicknames Dictionary*), as noted in a four-page bibliography at the front of the book; unlike Bates and McGhan (see #48-#49), Robinson's work takes into account the numerous SF reference works published in the late 1970s and early 1980s.

Robinson uses a somewhat complicated format, perhaps unduly so, running his data in three columns on facing pages, pseudonyms on the left-hand page, "usual names" on the right; by "usual," he means either the author's real name or the name under which he or she is best known, even if this is itself a pseudonym. The information is arranged so that the same sections of the alphabet are covered on both pages, even if this means that one page's copy will be very short.

The pseudonym list, running on left-hand pages only, is arranged in alphabetical order by surname or by the last element of the name (*e.g.,* The Lord Commissioner is filed under "C"); the pseudonyms occupy the first left-hand column position on the page. Pen names used on books are printed in all caps; those used on short fiction or nonfiction are listed in lower case letters, with initial capitalizations. The second column on the left-hand page includes the "usual name" by which the author is known or under which he or she commonly writes. Those names that are in themselves pen names are prefixed with an asterisk; a question mark prior to a name indicates the attribution was unverifiable; a question mark without a name indicates the real name of the writer is unknown; a " + " following a (list of) name(s) means that other authors also used the pen name; a name or publisher name in parentheses means the pseudonym was employed as a house pen name. The third column provides a list of numbers referring the user to the bibliography of sources at the front of the book.

The right-hand page lists the "usual name" by which the author is known in the first column, with a list of the pseudonyms the writer has employed in the second column, followed by a third column citing references from the bibliography of sources in the book's introduction. If the author's "usual name" is itself a pen name, an asterisk appears before the name. In the second column, book pseudonyms run in all caps, house pseudonyms are enclosed by parentheses, and a " + " before a name indicates others have used it as well. A "#" sign on either page indicates the name is not really a pseudonym but results from a publisher's typographical error.

This enormously complicated system results in much paging back and forth through the volume to locate data. For example, Rex Gordon is the usual name of British writer Stanley Hough, who also wrote under the name Bennett Stanley. Both facing pages have entries for Rex Gordon: on the left-hand page, we learn that his real name is Stanley Hough; on the right-hand page the entry for Gordon mentions his pseudonym, Bennett Stanley. Elsewhere in the book, on a right-hand page, we find Hough's real name listed, with a "See" reference to Rex Gordon. Under Bennett Stanley, however, we find a reference only to Rex Gordon. Is this *really* necessary? Could not the arrangement have been simplified into one alphabet?

There are the usual errors and omissions here: Robinson also misidentifies Julian May with Julian Chain (as do Bates and McGhan), and he lists A. A. Glynn consistently as Glyn, and Don Pfeil as Pfiel. The identification of David Wright O'Brien with David O'Brien, a British paperback writer of the early 1950s, is questionable. Ballantine Books is misspelled "Ballentine." As might be expected, Robinson's sources for modern British writers are stronger than for their American counterparts, but his work is generally sound throughout and certainly more complete and up-to-date by far than the two volumes mentioned above. Unfortunately, the book is virtually unavailable in America and only had a small printing in England. A second edition was promised, but has never appeared.

BIOGRAPHICAL AND LITERARY DIRECTORIES

SCOPE NOTE: This chapter includes who's who-type publications, bio-bibliographical directories, and literary dictionaries arranged alphabetically by author, whose focus is as much biographical as it is critical. Readers' and critical guides to SF authors and their books can be found in a later section of this book.

51. Ash, Brian. **Who's Who in Science Fiction.** London, Elm Tree Books, 1976. 220 p. LC 77-361941. ISBN 0-241-89383-6. New York, Taplinger Publishing Co., 1976. 220 p. LC 76-11667. ISBN 0-8008-8274-1; ISBN 0-8008-8279-2 (pbk.).

Ash provides biographical and critical evaluations of about 400 writers listed in alphabetical order by surname. The biographies have been adapted in very abbreviated form from previously published books and other sources, particularly Tuck's *Encyclopedia of Science Fiction and Fantasy* (see #18) and Reginald's *Science Fiction and Fantasy Literature* (see #212), as acknowledged in the author's introduction. Typical entries run between 50-1,000 words, averaging 100-200. While his biographical material is clearly derivative, Ash's comments on the writers' major works (book titles and dates are provided, but no bibliographical data) typically include pithy one-line annotations, with some attempt at appraisal. A "Select Bibliography of Books on Science Fiction" completes the book.

Ash's purpose, to provide a brief guide to the major SF writers and their works, is a worthy one, but his book suffers by comparison with the many other biographical and critical tools released during the late 1970s and early 1980s, particularly *The Encyclopedia of Science Fiction* and its update (see #12), *Science Fiction and Fantasy Literature* (see #212), *Twentieth-Century Science-Fiction Writers* (see #58), and *The New Encyclopedia of Science Fiction* (see #8). His work has also generally been dismissed by the critics as weak and secondhand and is now, of course, lamentably out-of-date. A title index would have been helpful.

See also the companion book on horror (see #52).

52. Ashley, Mike. **Who's Who in Horror and Fantasy Fiction.** London, Elm Tree Books, 1977. 240 p. LC 78-309133. ISBN 0-241-89528-6. New York, Taplinger Publishing Co., 1978. 240 p. LC 77-4608. ISBN 0-8008-8275-X; ISBN 0-8008-8278-4 (pbk.).

This companion volume to *Who's Who in Science Fiction* (see #51) is based upon Ashley's original research and is much less derivative, both in biographical details and critical comments, than the Ash work.

Following a brief introduction by Ashley, the book includes a chronological list of the genre's major works by year, title, and author; biographies of major and minor writers in the field, arranged alphabetically by surname; and five appendices: "An Index to Key Stories and Books," arranged by title, with selected annotations; "Selected Weird Fiction Anthologies," by title, with selected contents listings; "Weird and Horror Fiction Magazines," by title, with dates of publication, editors, nationality, and listings of major authors and stories published; "Awards" (the August Derleth Award and the World Fantasy Award), with winners listed chronologically by year. A short bibliography of nonfiction sources (now out-of-date) completes the book.

Ashley frequently includes biographical details and other tidbits not found in any other source, and his inclusion of a large number of classic horror writers of the eighteenth, nineteenth, and early twentieth centuries makes his book valuable even now, long after its original publication, unlike the Ash volume on SF writers. He also manages to mention and intelligently evaluate thousands of books and stories while commenting on the authors' lives and careers. A title index would have been helpful.

This concise and authoritative guide is a good example for would-be compilers of "popular" reference works to follow.

53. Cowart, David, and Thomas L. Wymer, eds. **Twentieth-Century American Science-Fiction Writers.** Detroit, A Bruccoli Clark Book, Gale Research Co., 1981. xv, 306, ix, 346 p. in 2 v. (Dictionary of Literary Biography, Vol. 8). LC 81-4182. ISBN 0-8103-0918-1 (set).

Cowart and Wymer's volume follows the standard *DLB* format, featuring critical essays by forty-one contributors on the lives and works of ninety-one American SF writers, arranged alphabetically by surname.

A typical entry includes: author's name, critic's name and academic affiliation, brief biographical data on the author, awards received by the author, a selected bibliography of the author's books, and the essay itself, followed by a selected list of secondary sources. Most entries also contain at least one author photo (some have several), and many include a sample page from one of the writer's manuscripts or reproduction(s) of one or more magazine or paperback covers featuring the author's work.

At the end of Volume Two are six Appendices: "I. Trends in Science-Fiction," including essays on "The New Wave" and "Science Fantasy"; "II. The Media of Science Fiction," including "The Iconography of Science-Fiction Art," "Paperback Science Fiction," and "Science-Fiction Films"; "III. Fandom and SFWA," including "Science-Fiction Fandom and Conventions," "Science-Fiction Fanzines: The Time Binders," "Science Fiction Writers of America and the Nebula Award," and "Hugo Awards and Nebula Awards" (a chronological checklist); "IV. A World Chronology of Important Science-Fiction Works (1818-1979)," a brief list by year, title, and author; "V. Selected Science-Fiction Magazines and Anthologies," including three sections: "Magazines," listing selected titles by title, with dates published, editors and years served, and major works published; "Reprint Anthologies," by title, giving editor(s), publisher, place, year of publication, and brief annotation (only sixteen titles are listed); "Original Anthologies," by title, with the same information as the previous section (listing just seventeen titles); "VI. Books for Further Reading," with four pages of secondary sources but no annotations. Most of these mini-essays have short secondary bibliographies attached.

The critical essays range in size from 1,500-15,000 words (averaging 2,500) and focus primarily on the author's work, although biographical details are often incorporated into the beginning paragraphs of each piece. The critiques touch upon the author's major fictions, covered roughly chronologically, with plot summaries and individual evaluations plus a one-paragraph summation. The longer essays, relatively few in number, have the space to comment at length on the author's *oeuvre,* and are distinctly superior to their 1,500-word counterparts (the bulk of those included); all, however, are at least readable and seem sound and balanced in their perceptions, well within the mainstream of SF critical thought. The appendices provide roughly 5,000 words each of illustrated comments by different critics on specific SF themes and movements; these too are at least interesting, if not particularly deep. One wonders, however, why certain topics were selected for this section and other subjects that could just as easily have been included were not. The chronology is too brief to be useful, and a general author/title index would have been appreciated.

This volume's chief rival, Bleiler's *Science Fiction Writers* (see #69), covers sixteen fewer writers but has a better mix of nationalities and time periods (Cowart and Wymer, following the series format, deliberately restrict their coverage to twentieth-century American writers). The essays in the former volume are generally longer and more illuminating, although certain essays in Cowart/Wymer (the piece on Robert A. Heinlein, for example), are considerably longer (and therefore touch upon more works in greater depth) than their Bleiler counterparts. Bleiler uses fifteen fewer critics, and as a group, they are generally better known and more authoritative than those in Cowart/Wymer; curiously, there is not one overlap between the two lists. Both are equally current in their coverage of the same writers; the addition of photographs and illustrations in *Twentieth-Century American Science-Fiction Writers* is a nice embellishment but unnecessary for the serious reader. On balance, both are worthy additions to the body of SF critical literature, and while each has its strong points, neither set has any significant advantage over the other.

54. Green, Scott E. **Contemporary Science Fiction, Fantasy, and Horror Poetry: A Resource Guide and Biographical Directory.** New York, Westport, CT, Greenwood Press, 1989. xviii, 216 p. index. LC 89-16966. ISBN 0-313-26324-8.

Green's volume is the first guide to the prominent persons and publications of a subgenre that grew rapidly in popularity during the 1980s.

A preface defines the different categories of SF and fantasy poetry and cites major sources for the book. The front matter also includes a brief acknowledgments list and an introduction, "A Brief History of Science Fiction, Fantasy, and Horror Poetry Publishing in America," all by Green.

The primary text is divided into three major sections: "I. Poetry in Magazines"; "II. Poetry in Genre Anthologies"; and "III. Biographical Directory of Poets." Part I is further subdivided into "Commercial and Newsstand Genre Magazines" and "Small-Press Genre Magazines," each organized in alphabetical order by magazine title. A typical entry provides: title (in bold italics), brief history and market orientation, editorial personnel, and a comprehensive listing of the poets who have appeared in each publication, in alphabetical order by surname, with specific dates and issues in which their poems were published. Those poets who have appeared in SF prozines that did not normally feature verse are listed in a catch-all section at the end of the first chapter, in alphabetical order by poet, with the magazine title and specific date ("3/56" = March 1956) of each appearance.

Part II is divided into four chapters: "Key Anthologies and Anthology Series," "Historical Anthologies," "Additional Anthologies," and "Single-Author Collections." The "Key" and "Historical" chapters are arranged alphabetically by book title, a typical entry providing: title (in bold italics), editor, place of publication, publisher, year of publication, annotation

(100-250 words summarizing and evaluating the contents), and a complete checklist (in alphabetical order by author's name) of the poems and poets appearing in each anthology.

The "Additional Anthologies" section provides skeletal lists (in alphabetical order by anthology title) of anthologies including one or two poems amid other material (usually short stories); the "Single-Author Collections" section, arranged alphabetically by author of the collection, similarly lists those books containing a handful of verse contributions embedded among short stories by one author.

The "Biographical Directory of Poets" comprises half the text, listing SF and fantasy poets currently active in the field alphabetically by surname, giving name (in boldface), address, a summary of the author's career as a poet (50-300 words), with lists of the major magazines and anthologies that have printed the writer's verse. An appendix provides a chronological list of the Rhysling Awards for SF poetry. Two very comprehensive general and poem title indexes complete the book. The volume is well-designed, typeset, and bound to library standards.

Green's directory will undoubtedly become the standard guide to its field, particularly if maintained through regular future editions. The only significant data lacking here are paginations, both for books and periodicals, and while enough material is provided to enable even the casual user to locate specific poems and publications, the addition of complete bibliographical information would be helpful in a second edition. Despite this minor *caveat,* Green is both authoritative and definitive, and his guide can be recommended without reservation to any library with an interest in twentieth-century American verse.

55. Pringle, David, ed. **St. James Guide to Fantasy Writers.** Detroit, St. James Press, 1996. xvi, 711 p. index. LC 95-48783. ISBN 1-55862-205-2. Contributing editors: Mike Ashley and Brian Stableford.

Contents: "Editor's Note"; "Advisers and Contributors"; "List of Entrants"; "Fantasy Writers"; "Foreign-Language Authors"; "Reading List"; "Nationality Index"; "Title Index"; "Notes on Advisers and Contributors."

Pringle's book provides commentary on the best known modern fantasy writers. The focus is on British and American authors, though there are a few of their Australian, Irish, Canadian, and New Zealander counterparts included, along with a handful (eleven) of the most important foreign-language writers. A few children and young adult authors, such as Baum and Carroll, are also featured.

414 entries are arranged alphabetically by surname. The Editor's Note makes clear that the book chooses to cover "pure" fantasy, defined as "tales of magic, heroic fantasy, sword and sorcery, humorous fantasy, adult fairy tales, animal fantasy, time-slip romance, Arabian-Nights tales and *chinoiserie,* fantastic allegories, and fabulations," pointedly avoiding horror authors, even those who have written some fantasy fiction, leaving that task for Pringle's companion volume, *St. James Guide to Horror, Ghost, and Gothic Writers* (see #56).

The typical entry includes: name (boldfaced, surname in bold caps), brief biographical information (nationality, birth place and date, family description, awards won, current address), a complete list of the author's works, in descending order by publication year, with title, publisher, and place and date of publication (divided into two categories, "fantasy" and "other"), and a signed essay commenting on the writer's major works (averaging 1,000-1,500 words).

As necessary or available, other information is added, including comments from other living authors, series titles or characters, and notations for film adaptations and secondary sources. The reading list found in the back of the volume is a bibliography of critical and reference works. There are several indexes to help the user pinpoint specific data. The nationality index lists the authors by country of origin. The title index lists all fantasy publications from the author bibliographies, whether novel or short story, giving the author's name (in parentheses), and the date of original publication.

The essays vary in quality, as is usual with such publications, consisting mostly of plot summaries plus a general overview of the author. The material does provides a good introduction to each author's works, however, which is all that one can expect. Separating the foreign-language authors into their own ghetto at the rear of the volume, where they are easy for the user to miss, is an unfortunate choice perpetuated by the St. James series format. The book is nicely typeset and bound to library standards.

In spite of such small failings, Pringle's guide is a very good addition for any reference department serving readers of fantasy fiction, and is especially recommended for public and undergraduate libraries.

56. Pringle, David, ed. **St. James Guide to Horror, Ghost & Gothic Writers.** Detroit, St. James Press, 1998. xvi, 746 p. index. LC 98-164553. ISBN 1-55862-206-3 (acid free paper).

Contents: "Preface", "Editor's Note"; "Advisers and Contributors"; "List of Entrants"; "Horror, Ghost and Gothic Writers"; "Foreign-Language Writers"; "Name Index"; "Nationality Index"; "Title Index"; "Reading List"; "Notes on Advisers and Contributors."

Pringle's book provides commentary on the best-known horror, ghost, and gothic writers, both classic and living. The focus is on British and American writers, though a few Australian, Irish, Scottish, and Canadian writers are covered, plus a handful (twenty-five) of the most important foreign-language writers, gathered with brief entries into a section of their own.

The 425 entries are arranged alphabetically by surname (except for the foreign writers). Adult writers dominate, but the book includes those children and young adult authors who continue to be popular among adults, including Roald Dahl and E. Nisbet.

The book was explicitly constructed as a companion volume to *St. James Guide to Fantasy Writers* (see #55), and avoids duplicating authors that were covered in the previous work. The Editor's Note states that this book "concentrates instead on those types of fiction which may be labelled as horror novels, dark fantasies, ghost stories, gothic novels, tales of terror, supernatural fictions, occult fantasies, black-magic stories, psychological thrillers, tales of unease, grand-guignol shockers, creepy stories, shudder-pulp fictions, *contes cruels,* uncanny stories, macabre fictions and weird tales."

A typical entry includes: name (boldfaced type, surname in bold caps), brief biographical information (nationality, birthplace, and date, with very brief descriptions of family, career, memberships, awards, address, date of death [if appropriate]), all listed together in a single paragraph; a complete list of the author's works, in descending order by publication year, giving title (italics), place of publication, publisher, and year of publication, and sometimes further broken into categories, including, irregularly, major short stories; and a signed essay commenting on the author's genre works (averaging 1,000-1,500 words in length).

The entries may also include, as necessary or available, comments from living authors, series titles or characters, notations for film adaptations, and secondary critical studies. The Reading List, the last section of the volume, features a bibliography of general and specific critical analyses and reference works, arranged alphabetically by critic surname. The book also includes several indexes.

The nationality index lists the authors by nation of origin, alphabetically by nationality, and then by author surname. The title index lists all of the publications recorded in the author bibliographies, whether long or short, alphabetically by title, giving the author's surname only (in parentheses), and the year of the original publication of the item; the inclusion of page number references would have been desirable in this section.

The essays vary in quality, but generally provide fairly sound and middle-of-the-road short critical analyses of the author's output in the horror genre, even when the individual is better known for something else (for example, Sir Arthur Quiller-Couch). It is unfortunate indeed that the poor foreign-language authors have been sequestered off into their own little literary ghetto at the rear of the volume, a hallmark of the St. James Guide series, which announces to everyone in no uncertain terms exactly how important the literary establishment in the United States and Great Britain considers these interlopers. They should have been given equal treatment with the rest.

In spite of these small failings, Pringle's guide is a good addition for any reference department serving readers of fantasy fiction, and is especially recommended for public and undergraduate libraries.

57. Reginald, R. **Stella Nova: The Contemporary Science Fiction Authors.** Los Angeles, Unicorn & Son, 1970. [358] p. index. LC 79-282012. (pbk). As: **Contemporary Science Fiction Authors, First Edition.** Rev. ed. New York, Arno Press, 1975. 365 p. index. LC 74-16517. ISBN 0-405-06332-6.

Reginald was a college student at Gonzaga University when he put together the original version of this book in 1968, compiling it from direct-mail questionnaires and his own research. *Stella Nova* incorporates bibliographies of 483 SF writers active between 1960-68, with biographies of the 308 who responded to his queries.

A typical entry includes: author's name (all caps); bibliography of the writer's science fiction books in descending chronological order by date of publication (giving book number in order of publication [*i.e.,* 1, 2, 3, etc.], publisher, year of publication, book title, and a code letter indicating format [paper or cloth] and type [collection, anthology, etc.]); first professional sale (with bibliographical data); works in progress (in 1969/70); biography (including information on the author's careers and a list of awards won); and (occasionally) an original statement by the author responding to the compiler's questions.

The original edition included a quirky and largely unusable title index keyed to the author's entry number; the Arno edition reworked this into a more normal title/author format, added a list of pseudonyms cross-referenced with the authors' real names, substituted a new introduction and abbreviations list (the latter was accidentally omitted from the first printing of the revised edition but was added to all subsequent printings), and made several other minor corrections. Most of the biographical data remained untouched, although a few additional "See" references were included where appropriate. The book eventually evolved, with a much different format, into *Science Fiction and Fantasy Literature* (see #212).

Both bibliographical and biographical entries are a bit too cryptic or concise to work very smoothly, although the format becomes somewhat clearer when one reads the introduction and actually uses the material. It is not always obvious, for example, that a particular piece of data is a marriage record, or a list of children, or some other, similar detail, without checking its position in the entry.

Despite such amateurish format problems, this first attempt at producing a "who's who" of science fiction and fantasy includes an amazing amount of original, primary data, the collaborative result of the authors' own contributions and responses and Reginald's tenacious research; one can understand this better by examining *Stella Nova*'s influence on later biographical directories of SF authors, all of which borrow from this seminal work to a greater or lesser degree (some shamelessly and without acknowledgment). In a number of key cases, such as "John Norman," the only "hard" data available on the author's life is the material in the original *Stella Nova,* endlessly repeated elsewhere, including other works of Reginald himself.

58. Smith, Curtis C., ed. **Twentieth-Century Science-Fiction Writers.** London, Macmillan, 1981. xviii, 642 p. index. ISBN 0-333-31945-1. New York, St. Martin's Press, 1981. xviii, 642 p. index. LC 81-8944. ISBN 0-312-82420-3. **Twentieth-Century Science-Fiction Writers.** 2nd ed. Chicago & London, St. James Press, 1986. xviii, 933 p. index. LC 87-180709. ISBN 0-912289-27-9. Watson, Noelle, and Paul E. Schellinger, eds. **Twentieth-Century Science-Fiction Writers.** 3rd ed. Chicago & London, St. James Press, 1991. xxvi, 1,016 p. index. LC 93-113211. ISBN 1-55862-111-3. Pederson, Jay P., ed.; Robert Reginald, bibliographic ed. **St. James Guide to Science Fiction Writers.** 4th ed. Detroit, St. James Press, 1996. xxiv, 1175 p. index. LC 95-36181. ISBN 11-55862-179-2 (acid free paper).

This bio-bibliographical and critical guide to science-fiction authors, a companion volume to similarly titled volumes on mystery, western, and romance writers, is divided into three sections: English-language writers (532 authors in the first edition, 571 in the second), foreign-language writers (thirty-five authors in the first, thirty-eight in the second), and major fantasy writers (the same five authors in both), and then alphabetically by surname. Some writers covered in the first edition were dropped from the second, and many others (especially newer authors) were added. In both editions, Smith relied upon a board of advisors (the same twenty writers and critics were used in both books, with one additional name in the revised version) to suggest a basic list of writers to be covered. The critical essays were then assigned to a long list of contributors (146 in the first book, 173 in the second).

A typical entry includes author's name (in boldface, including middle or real name[s]), nationality, brief biographical and career data (in one paragraph); a complete bibliography of the author's books, science fiction publications being listed first, then all other books (the entries provide book titles in italics, with series information, places of publication, publishers, years of publication, and corresponding data on the first U.K. or U.S. edition), as well as all uncollected short stories (including magazine or anthology of publication, place of publication, and date of issue or year of publication [for an anthology]), lists of monographic works about the author (including critiques and bibliographies), plus an indication if the author's manuscripts are housed in a library collection; commentary by the author himself (for about a third of the modern entries); plus a critical essay by a contributing critic. The critiques range in size from 300-2,500 words (most average 500-1,000) and include a short summation of the author's contributions to the genre, with commentary on the principal works, including a paragraph of plot summary and a sentence or two of critical analysis. With so many critics involved in the project, the quality of the material varies widely from essay to essay, as might be expected, but is always at least readable; the limitation on length does not allow for any serious examinations of the writers in question, but for many lesser-known writers, the brief commentaries in these volumes are the only analyses currently available.

Although the title suggests a modern focus, in fact the volumes include all major SF writers (and many lesser-known ones) who lived and/or died in the twentieth century; however, a number of historical figures were dropped from the revised edition to make room for newer authors, so both books should be retained by libraries and researchers. The biographies were compiled through direct-mail questionnaires and from other previously published sources; the authors' comments are original to these volumes, although many were repeated verbatim in the second edition; at least one-third of the entries have minimal (or no) biographical data. The bibliographies were updated where necessary in the 1986 version, and some (but not all) of the essays for active writers were either reworked by the original critics or rewritten from scratch by completely different contributors. Both editions include an introduction by the editor giving a brief background history of the genre plus a general "Reading List" of nonfiction works that unfortunately includes a few "ghost" titles. This is followed by lists of each book's advisers, contributors, and authors covered. There are brief biographies of the critics at the end of each volume, and the revised version includes a much-needed title/author index.

Smith left the series after the second edition was published, and was replaced by two in-house editors at St. James Press, Noelle Watson and Paul E. Schellinger. The format of the third edition is similar to the previous two editions, as is the overall layout of the volume. The five fantasy authors have been integrated into the primary alphabetical listing, but the foreign-language authors are still relegated to a separate section in the back that many users might miss, a sad state of affairs indeed for such prominent authors as Borges, Kafka, and Verne. The list of advisors, those who suggested the authors for this edition, also has a few new members, and this might explain the fifty-plus writers who were removed from the third edition, while over seventy new SF authors were added.

In addition, although critical essays on some writers remained identical in this new version, others were completely rewritten by new contributors. The 602 English-language authors and thirty-eight foreign-language authors covered were assigned to 187 critics.

After the sale of St. James Press to the Gale Group in the 1990s, the St. James literary guides were reworked, and outside editor Jay Pederson was given the task of revamping several volumes in the series. The overall format of the books has always remained the same, but the layout of the entries was enhanced for better readability, the bibliographies completely reworked, the foreign writers integrated into the main alphabetical sequence (and their entries expanded to the same size as the others), and a new index added.

Pederson's guide focuses primarily on American writers, with a sprinkling of major British, Australian, Irish, Canadian, New Zealander, and foreign-language writers (thirty-nine in this edition). Adult writers dominate, as usual, but major children and young adult writers of SF are also represented. There are 651 entries arranged alphabetically by author's surname.

The preface defines science fiction as fiction of the possible and "the major nonrealistic mode of imaginative creation of our epoch." Although the focus remains on science fiction writers, those fantasy and horror authors who have had an impact on the genre are also included. Thus, there is some crossover with the *St. James Guide to Fantasy Writers* (see #55), but the discussion and emphasis varies widely between the two volumes.

A typical entry includes: author's name (boldfaced, surname in bold caps), brief biographical data (nationality, birthplace and date, family description, awards, current address) in one paragraph, a complete list of the author's works, in descending order by year of publication, with title, publisher, and place and date of publication (divided into categories such as "science fiction" and "other"), and a signed critical essay (1,000-2,100 words). As necessary or available, other information may be included, such as comments from living authors, series titles/characters, and notations for film adaptations and secondary critical studies. The reading list, now gathered at the back of the volume, is a bibliography of critical analyses and reference works.

Unlike previous editions, Pederson's volume sensibly integrates all of the writers covered, whether foreign-language authors or fantasy crossovers, into one alphabetical sequence. The appearance and readability of the entries has been greatly improved by enlarging the font of the author's name, so that the beginning of each entry can be more readily distinguished by the casual user. Distinct biographical information has been highlighted by headings now rendered in boldfaced type ("Nationality," "Born," "Education," etc.), making them much more distinctive and legible. The nationality index arranges the authors by country, so the user can easily find foreign-language authors. Many of the entries from the third edition have not been revised, and the authors' own comments have also remained largely unchanged.

The bibliographies of the writers' works, which had become increasingly cluttered and uncertain as this series progressed through the three earlier editions, have been completely revamped in the fourth, removing many errors and duplications, and adding considerable new information to the data for each entry.

Forty-four authors were excised from this edition and another fifty-six new entries added, as has been the general pattern of this series, so all of the old editions should be retained by libraries.

Pederson has made a good product even better. Together with its two companion volumes (see #55-#56), *St. James Guide to Science Fiction Writers* provides the most current information available on SF, fantasy, and horror authors and their works. This is a fine addition for any reference department serving readers of science fiction and students of popular literature, and is especially recommended for public libraries and for university collections largely serving undergraduates.

59. Weinberg, Robert. **A Biographical Dictionary of Science Fiction and Fantasy Artists.** New York and Westport, CT, Greenwood Press, 1988. xvi, 346 p. index. LC 87-17651. ISBN 0-313-24349-2.

The first biographical directory specifically devoted to SF artists, Weinberg's book includes two short introductions; an abbreviations list; a thirty-one-page essay by Weinberg, "Science Fiction Art: A Historical Overview"; a biographical directory of roughly 250 artists arranged alphabetically by surname; a closing essay by Weinberg, "Science Fiction Art: What Still Exists," on the collecting of SF artwork; a chronological checklist of the Hugo and World Fantasy awards for best artist by year awarded; a bibliography; an index of biographical entries; and an author/title index, which does not, however, include books listed in the bibliographical sections of the artist biographies, but does mention the artists themselves (duplicating somewhat the previous section).

A typical entry includes: the artist's name in bold caps; date of birth, if known (a question mark appears if the date is unknown); nationality; an account in narrative form of the artist's life and career; and a selected bibliography of published works, primarily paperback covers, hardcover dustjackets, and magazine covers (the book titles appear in italics with two-digit terminal years of publication in parentheses [*e.g.*, "80" = 1980] arranged alphabetically by title, while the magazine publications are keyed to a two- to four-digit letter code [*e.g.*, "GXY" = *Galaxy Magazine*], with the years of publication written out and the months of publication indicated in numerical form in parentheses thereafter [*e.g.*, "11" = November]). Weinberg states in his introduction that the listings of magazine cover lists are nearly complete for most artists, but acknowledges that the bibliographies of book covers are often incomplete.

The essays, many of them penned by Weinberg himself (Richard Dalby wrote most of the British and French entries with the assistance of Mike Ashley and Philip Harbottle; their contributions, amounting to one-fourth to one-third of the total, are signed), normally include some brief biographical data and a lengthier career assessment, although many of the entries on artists from the pulp period provide few details about the artist's life. The critiques range in size from 50-1,500 words, and are readable and authoritative, and appear conversant with standard art techniques, forms, and media, with the science fiction world in general, and with pulp and paperback publishing in particular.

Some of the essays include much more information than others, however, depending on Weinberg's ability to contact the artist or to locate other source materials; compare, for example, the entry on modern SF artist Gray Morrow (weak and derivative at 150 words) with that for Rowena Morrill (which discusses in a 600-word essay her unique style of painting and provides much background material on her interesting life). References to other artists covered in the book are noted with asterisks following each name as they are mentioned in an entry, often as influences on the style or work of the artist being critiqued. Several reviewers have noted some errors of fact in the book, but this was probably inevitable given the pioneering nature of the work.

Although SF artists are covered to a limited degree in other major references tools (Nicholls's *Encyclopedia of Science Fiction* [see #12] mentions about fifty names), Weinberg touches upon so many more artists, at much greater length, that his volume is sure to become the standard guide to the subject.

60. Yntema, Sharon K. **More Than 100: Women Science Fiction Writers.** Freedom, CA, The Crossing Press, 1988. [vi], 193 p. LC 88-3600. ISBN 0-89594-301-8. Cover title reads: *More Than 100 Woman [sic] Science Fiction Writers: An Annotated Bibliography.*

Yntema's bio-critical directory includes entries for 104 mostly twentieth-century, mostly English-speaking, female writers of the fantastic.

A typical entry provides: name, date of birth, place of birth (country, state, city, in that order), pseudonyms, annotation, awards won by the author, a very limited bibliography of secondary sources (absent for many entries, and often consisting of just a handful of book reviews), a list of the author's fictional books in chronological order by publication year (series are grouped together under the series title), a chronological checklist of significant short stories (with publication dates plus magazine titles and/or anthology titles and editors where appropriate), and nonfiction (or other genre) monographs.

Eight appendices list "170 Additional Names of Women Science Fiction and Fantasy Authors with Titles and Dates of Their Books" (an alphabetical list of women SF writers with a chronological checklist of their books); "Authors of Science Fiction and Fantasy for Children and Young Adults" (a barebones list of thirty-three authors); "Where Were They Born?" (a checklist of the authors by country of birth); "When Were They Born?" (a chronological checklist of the authors by year of birth); "Which Authors Are No Longer Alive?" (a chronological checklist of the authors by their years of death); "Who Are Their Literary Agents?" (a very brief register of thirty authors and their agents, with agents' addresses, now outdated); "Recommended Science Fiction Books by Women" (an alphabetical list by author and title); and "Other Resources" (an annotated list of fourteen secondary sources plus nine additional undescribed books).

The textual part of each entry ranges from one to three short paragraphs, and provides brief biographical data and a summary of the writer's career, including passing mention of the author's major stories and books. Yntema's style is populist rather than literary, and her comments are often thin and unilluminating. No less than seventy-one of her entries (68.3%), for example, begin with the words "[author's name] is a/an . . . ," with many of the other entries substituting "was" for "is." Unfortunately, the book is also filled with numerous factual and typographical errors: Evangeline Walton's fantasy series should be "Mabino-gion," not "Mabinagian"; Thea Von Harbou is actually Thea von Harbou, and her name (befitting her German origin) should be filed under "H"; C. L. Moore's middle name is spelled with one "L"; Zoë Fairbairns uses an umlaut over the "e" in her first name; Jessica Amanda Salmonson's original given name (unmentioned here) was Amos; and so on.

Yntema's bibliographical data are nonexistent, her so-called list of secondary sources for each writer woefully incomplete, her biographical material very scanty. Her selection criteria must also be questioned, since she seems to have included only those writers on whom information was readily available, relegating the rest to the limbo of her appendices; such well-known women SF writers as Julian May are unmentioned in either section. On the plus side, the book is well-designed and typeset and bound to library standards.

Yntema's inspiration, to provide a bio-bibliographical directory of female writers of the fantastic, is an excellent one, particularly given the fact that women authors virtually dominated the genre during and after the 1980s, but her execution leaves much to be desired, and the resulting hodgepodge can scarcely be called a "reference" book of any kind. Compare Roger C. Schlobin's *Urania's Daughters* (see #272), which provides far more bibliographical entries, but fails to include biographies, annotations, or critical commentaries. Not recommended.

READERS' AND CRITICAL GUIDES

SCOPE NOTE: This section includes literary and critical guides whose intent is to recommend or criticize a selected list of authors, titles, or groups of authors in one or more subgenres of fantastic literature. Bibliographies intended to record an *entire* genre or subgenre or national SF literature in some systemic way are listed in the bibliographies chapters, even when extensively annotated.

61. Allen, L. David. **Science Fiction: An Introduction.** Lincoln, NE, Cliffs Notes, 1973. 187 p. index. ISBN 0-8220-1169-7 (pbk.). As: **Science Fiction Reader's Guide.** Lincoln, NE, Centennial Press, 1974. 299 p. index. ISBN 0-8220-1611-7 (pbk.).

These two nearly identical versions of the same book were originally published in the Cliffs Notes series, with their typical orientation toward plot summary rather than exegesis.

The first section includes detailed analyses of fifteen classic SF novels, followed by the chapters, "Toward a Definition of Science Fiction," "A Way of Reading Science Fiction: Another Look at *'Dune',*" "Guidelines for Reading Science Fiction," "Verisimilitude in Science Fiction," "Awards for Science Fiction," "A Selected Bibliography of Science Fiction," "A Selected Bibliography of Works About Science Fiction" (the latter three sections now badly out-of-date), and an author/title index.

Mediocrely written and of marginal interest, Allen's book is included here only because the title of the reprint promises something more than it can actually deliver. Avoid this one.

62. Barron, Neil, ed. **Anatomy of Wonder: Science Fiction.** New York, R. R. Bowker Co., 1976. xxi, 471 p. index. LC 76-10260. ISBN 0-8352-0884-2. **Anatomy of Wonder: A Critical Guide to Science Fiction.** 2nd ed. New York, R. R. Bowker Co., 1981. xiv, 724 p. index. LC 81-4391. ISBN 0-8352-1339-0; ISBN 0-8352-1404-4 (pbk.). **Anatomy of Wonder: A Critical Guide to Science Fiction.** 3rd ed. New York, R. R. Bowker Co., 1987. xvii, 874 p. index. LC 87-9305. ISBN 0-8352-2312-4. **Anatomy of Wonder 4: A Critical Guide to Science Fiction.** 4th ed. New Providence, NJ, R.R. Bowker Co., 1995. xxiv, 912 p. index. LC 94-42363. ISBN 0-8352-3288-3.

Contents (Fourth Edition): "How to Use This Guide Effectively"; "Preface"; "Contributors"; "Introduction: The Strange Journey," by James Gunn; "Primary Literature": "1. The Emergence of Science Fiction: The Beginnings Through 1915," by Thomas D. Clareson; "2. Science Fiction Between the Wars: 1916-1939," by Brian Stableford; "3. From the Golden Age to the Atomic Age: 1940-1963," by Paul A. Carter; "4. The New Wave, Cyberpunk, and Beyond: 1963-1994," by Michael M. Levy and Brian Stableford; "The Speculative Muse: An Introduction to Science Fiction Poetry," by Steve Eng; "5. Young Adult Science Fiction," by Francis J. Molson and Susan G. Miles. "Secondary Literature and Research Aids": "6. Science Fiction Publishing and Libraries," by Neil Barron; "7. General

Reference Works," by Neil Barron; "8. History and Criticism," by Gary K. Wolfe; "9. Author Studies," by Michael A. Morrison and Neil Barron; "10. Science Fiction in Film, Television, and Radio," by Michael Klossner; "11. Science Fiction Illustration," by Walter Albert and Neil Barron; "Science Fiction Comics," by Peter M. Coogan; "12. Science Fiction Magazines," by Joe Sanders; "13. "Teaching Science Fiction," by Dennis M. Kratz; "14. "Research Library Collections of Science Fiction," by Randall W. Scott; 15. "Listings: Best Books; Awards; Series; Series Index; Translations; Organizations; Conventions," by Neil Barron; "Author/Subject Index"; "Title Index"; "Theme Index."

Barron's *Anatomy* has generally been accepted as the standard readers' guide to science fiction literature. The four editions follow the same general format, with coverage of fiction broken into three or four chapters, each dealing with a specific, somewhat arbitrarily defined period of the genre's development, plus additional chapters on juvenile SF, nonfiction, and (in some editions) foreign-language SF. Each section is authored by a different critic who contributes a lengthy introductory essay framing the subject, and then provides brief annotations of each work covered, in alphabetical order by author and title.

A typical entry includes: item number (*e.g.,* "4-551," item 551 in Chapter 4), author, title (boldfaced type), publisher of the first edition, year of publication, annotation (averaging 100 words), mention of book(s) with similar themes, and a letter code indicating whether the work has been nominated for or has won an award. Alternate titles or original titles (for translations), with translators, are given as part of the collation, as are middle names (or real names) of the authors, but not on any consistent basis. The annotations are descriptive and sometimes evaluative, and tend to be somewhat longer for acknowledged classics of the field, but are generally very brief. The item numbers begin with the number one in each new chapter and are completely different from edition to edition.

The evolution of *Anatomy* can be seen in the contents pages of each version. The first edition includes, with front matter, the following chapters: "Science Fiction: From Its Beginnings to 1870," by Robert M. Philmus; "The Emergence of the Scientific Romance, 1870-1926," by Thomas D. Clareson; "The Gernsback Era, 1926-1937," by Ivor A. Rogers; "The Modern Period, 1938-1975," by Joe De Bolt and John R. Pfeiffer; "Juvenile Science Fiction," by Francis J. Molson. Also included are sections by Barron, "History, Criticism, and Biography," "Bibliographies, Indexes, and Teaching Aids," "Magazine and Book Review Indexes," "Periodicals," "Literary Awards," and "Core Collection Checklist," and a final section that includes "Library Collections of Science Fiction and Fantasy," by H. W. Hall, and "Directory of Publishers," "Author Index," and "Title Index." The indexes in this edition *only* are keyed to page number; in all later editions, they refer to item number.

The second edition includes the following sections: "The Emergence of Science Fiction: The Beginnings to the 1920s," by Thomas D. Clareson; "Science Fiction Between the Wars: 1918-1938," by Brian Stableford; "The Modern Period: 1938-1980," by Joe De Bolt and John R. Pfeiffer; "Children's Science Fiction," by Francis J. Molson; chapters on German, French, Russian, Italian, Japanese, and Chinese science fiction by experts from those countries; plus the chapter "Research Aids," most by Barron: "Selection, Acquisition, and Cataloging of Science Fiction," "Indexes and Bibliographies," "History and Criticism," "Autobiography, Biography, and Author Studies," "Science Fiction on Film and Television," "Science Fiction Illustration," "Classroom Aids" by Marshall B. Tymn, "Science Fiction

Magazines" by H. W. Hall, "Library and Private Collections of Science Fiction and Fantasy" by Hall, and "Core Collection Checklist," with author and title indices.

The third edition includes five chapters on English-language SF: "The Emergence of Science Fiction: The Beginnings to the 1920s," by Thomas D. Clareson; "Science Fiction Between the Wars: 1918-1938," by Brian Stableford; "The Early Modern Period: 1938-1963," by Joe De Bolt and John R. Pfeiffer; "The Modern Period: 1964-1986," by Brian Stableford; and "Children's and Young Adult Science Fiction," by Francis J. Molson. The foreign-language chapters are much expanded, including sections on German, French, Russian, Japanese, Italian, Danish, Swedish, Norwegian, Dutch, Belgian, Romanian, Yugoslav, and Hebrew SF, all by experts on those literatures. Research aids (most by Barron) include "Science Fiction Publishing and Libraries," "General Reference Works," "History and Criticism," "Author Studies," "Science Fiction on Film and Television," "Science Fiction Illustration," "Teaching Materials" by Muriel R. Becker, "Science Fiction Magazines" by H. W. Hall, "Library and Private Collections of Science Fiction and Fantasy" by Hall and Barron, and "Core Collection Checklist," with author/subject and title indices.

The fourth edition annotates 2,100 works of fiction and 800 works of nonfiction, with coverage now extending through early 1994. The foreign-language science fiction list has been eliminated, which is a great loss, but the core collection checklist, now called simply "Best Books," has been considerably expanded. This is followed by a chronological listing of all award winners of seven major science fiction awards (British Science Fiction Association Awards, John W. Campbell, Jr. Memorial Award, Arthur C. Clarke Award, Philip K. Dick Memorial Award, Hugo Award, Locus Award, and Nebula Award).

Another nice addition to this version is included in the "Author Studies" chapter: a chart correlating almost 600 SF authors with their coverage in ten major biographical reference books (*Contemporary Authors,* Clute's *Encyclopedia of Science Fiction* [see #12], Bleiler's *Science Fiction Writers* [see #69], and others), indicating which authors can be found in which books. The new Theme Index is also a very useful tool, aiding the book's function as a reader's advisory.

Because different critics contributed sections covering different periods of time in each edition, access to all four versions is highly desirable. For example, Clareson's section on the beginnings of SF was trimmed from 182 listings in the Second Edition to 108 books in the Third, making it much less comprehensive than comparable chapters in previous versions; while Stableford's second chapter, on the period from 1918-38, was expanded by sixteen books, with some entries being recast but many remaining exactly the same. The somewhat arbitrary breaking of the modern period into two sections for the Third Edition results in many well-known authors' works being split between the two chapters, making an overall critical perspective difficult for the user. However, despite a slight British bias in the Stableford chapters, most of the evaluations seem fair, balanced, and current.

Coverage of untranslated foreign-language SF was extensive and unrivaled in the Third Edition, but was completely dropped in the Fourth; alas and alack, because, for most of the works and authors evaluated, *Anatomy 3* was (and remains) the only critical source in English. The comments on secondary sources and research aids tend to be learned but occasionally quirky, sometimes focusing on such extraneous elements as cost instead of content; and it is here that the lack of specific bibliographical data (particularly paginations) is most heavily felt, since comparisons between similar critical works or bibliographies do not always mention their lengths. The core collection lists are useful for libraries and critics with limited budgets and are generally well-chosen and well-balanced, with a good mix of basic authors and themes.

However, Barron almost seems at times to be losing control of his numbering system in *Anatomy 4* in an effort to keep it mostly consistent with previous editions, making for rather odd bibliographical bedfellows. The New Wave/Cyberpunk section is joined with the science fiction poetry section in Chapter Four, but the entire Secondary Literature Section is off by one from the previous edition (the Third Edition's Chapter Seven: Science Fiction Publishing and Libraries thus becoming Six in the Fourth Edition).

Unlike many of the works evaluated herein, *Anatomy of Wonder* has continued to grow and evolve through four successive editions, each version larger than the last, making it perhaps the most useful single-volume guide to science fiction literature, with fair, current, comprehensive coverage of all the major books in the field. However, the rationale for breaking coverage of English-language fiction into chronological sections that vary in scope and size with each edition is unclear beyond the immediate need to pay each contributor for his or her chapters; a more logical and useful arrangement for future editions might be a single alphabetical sequence for English-language authors, excepting juvenile fiction, or a grouping of authors (rather than titles) into specific periods of development acknowledged by the critical experts, so that one writer's works would not be spread over more than one section.

Despite these rather small *caveats, Anatomy of Wonder* remains a vital and essential reference tool for every library collection, as well as for every SF critic's personal library. Libraries should maintain copies of all four editions in their collections.

63. Barron, Neil, ed. **Fantasy and Horror: A Critical and Historical Guide to Literature, Illustration, Film, TV, Radio and the Internet.** Lanham, MD, Scarecrow Press, 1999. xii, 816 p. index. LC 98-46564. ISBN 0-8108-3596-7 (cloth: alk. paper).

Contents: "How to Use This Guide Effectively"; "Preface"; "Introduction: The Return to Fantasy," by David G. Hartwell; "The Primary Literature": "1. The Early and Later Gothic Traditions, 1762-1896," by Frederick S. Frank; "2. The Development of the Fantastic Tradition through 1811," by Dennis M. Krantz; "3. Fantasy in the Nineteenth Century, 1812-1899," by Brian Stableford; "4. Early Modern Horror Fiction, 1897-1949," by Brian Stableford; "5. From Baum to Tolkien, 1900-1956," by Brian Stableford; "6. Contemporary Horror Fiction, 1950-1998," by Stefan Dziemianowicz; "7. Contemporary Fantasy, 1957-1998," by Darren Harris-Fain; "8. Fantasy and Horror Poetry," by Steve Eng; "The Secondary Literature and Research Aids": "9. Fantasy and Horror Literature in Libraries," by Neil Barron; "10. Reference Sources and Online Resources," by Neil Barron and Michael E. Stamm; "11. History and Criticism," by Gary K. Wolfe; "12. Author Studies," by Richard C. West, Fiona Kelleghan, and Michael A. Morrison; "13. Horror, Fantasy, and Animation in Film, Television and Radio," by Michael Klossner; "14. Fantasy and Horror Art and Illustration," by Walter Albert and Doug Highsmith; "15. Teaching Fantasy and Horror Literature," by Dennis M. Kratz; "16. Fantasy and Horror Magazines," by Robert Morrish and Mike Ashley; "17. Library Collections," by Neil Barron; "18. Listings: Best Books, Awards, Series, Young Adult and Children's Books, Translations, Organizations, Conventions," by Neil Barron; "Appendix A: Sources of Information on Fiction and Poetry Authors," by Neil Barron; "Author/Subject Index"; "Title Index"; "Theme Index"; "About the Contributors."

This book is an extensive revision of *Fantasy Literature: A Reader's Guide* (see #64) and *Horror Literature: A Reader's Guide* (see #65), both edited by Barron, now combined into one volume and updated; and also serves as a companion volume to *Anatomy of Wonder* (see #62).

Fantasy and Horror is organized into broad, chronological categories contributed by individual critics, then further arranged alphabetically by author's surname. "Chapters 1-7 are devoted to fiction for adults, young adults and children and are arranged chronologically. Chapter 8 is devoted to poetry. Chapters 9-17 provide thorough coverage of nonfiction examining the multiple topics shown on the table of contents."

Each chapter includes an introductory essay by the major contributor, and is followed by a list of annotated entries, arranged alphabetically by author and then by title. A typical entry includes: entry number (*e.g.*, "6-93" for the 93rd entry of Chapter 6), the author (boldfaced type), title (bold italics), publisher, year of publication, an evaluative summary (averaging 100 words), suggestions for further reading (using entry numbers), awards or nominations received, reading level (if not written for adults), sequels, and cross-references for authors mentioned in other chapters. Some entries include indicators of "best books" status (an asterisk placed before the entry number), or the age level of the suggested reader (*e.g.*, YA = young adult, placed at the end of the annotation).

Some 2,500 entries are covered in this book, almost 1,800 of them being fiction or poetry, with 700 from secondary sources; however, there is some duplication of entries in the different sections. The Author/Subject Index lists all of authors and titles covered in the fiction sections of the book, arranged alphabetically by author and then title, and citing specific entry numbers within the text, plus subject entries in the Author Studies section, again correlated by entry number. The Theme Index consists of a list of ninety-one subject categories (*i.e.*, "Angels"), followed by a list of item numbers only. The Title Index includes titles of periodicals as well as books, but excludes film titles and television programs; titles are arranged in alphabetical order, and correlated with entry numbers and page numbers (when necessary to refer to the general introductory essays).

Appendix A provides a chart of 14 major reference sources, correlating the biographical and critical information appearing in these sets with the names of all of the fantasy and horror authors covered therein. This is an extremely useful addition to this combined version of these guides.

The reviews themselves are fair and balanced, and often do a good job of "selling" a recommended book, or at least placing it within the generally considered context of genre criticism. The overall coverage includes all of the classics of these two fields, plus representative titles from some lesser-known writers. The selection criteria is not always clearly defined. Some prolific authors, such as Stephen R. Donaldson or Lois Duncan, are represented by one or two titles, though many more could have legitimately been added.

Still, this is an essential addition to all library collections and to all personal libraries of researchers of fantastic literature. Highly recommended. Another Barron triumph.

64. Barron, Neil, ed. **Fantasy Literature: A Reader's Guide.** New York & London, Garland Publishing, 1990. xxvii, 586 p. index. (Garland Reference Library of the Humanities, Vol. 874). LC 89-23693. ISBN 0-8240-3148-2.

Intended as both a companion to *Anatomy of Wonder* (see #62) and *Horror Literature* (see #65) and as a replacement for Tymn/Zahorski/Boyer's guide (see #101), this volume is organized very similarly to the other two books in the series, into broad chapters contributed by individual critics, each covering successive stages of the genre's development, then further subarranged alphabetically by author's name and by his or her individual works.

Contents: "Preface" (by Barron); "Contributors" (brief biographical squibs); Introduction, "Children Who Survive," by Michael Bishop; "Fantasy Literature": "1. Development of the Fantastic Tradition Through 1811," by Dennis M. Kratz; "2. The Nineteenth Century, 1812-99," by Brian Stableford; "3. From Baum to Tolkien, 1900-56," by Stableford; "4A. Modern Fantasy for Adults, 1957-88," by Maxim Jakubowksi; "4B. Modern Fantasy for Young Adults, 1950-88," by Francis Molson and Susan G. Miles; "Research Aids": "5. Fantasy and Horror Fiction and Libraries," by Barron; "6. General Reference Works," by Barron; "7. History and Criticism," by Gary K. Wolfe; "8. Author Studies," by Richard C. West; "9. Fantasy on Film and Television," by Michael Klossner; "10. Fantastic Art and Illustration," by Walter Albert; "11. Fantasy and Horror Magazines," by Mike Ashley; "12. Library Collections," by Randall W. Scott; "13. Core Collection, Awards, Organizations, Series," by Barron; "Author Index"; "Title Index"; "Theme Index."

The five major chapters on the literature comprise 350 pages (out of 586), and cover 1,129 items as compared to 222 books in Tymn *et al.* (see #101), providing vastly greater (and ten years more current) coverage; however, it should be noted that the focus of Tymn's work is on core collection materials only, that the annotations in Tymn are much longer (averaging nearly a full page each as compared to three sentences for Barron), and that Tymn generally contains much more analysis of the individual works, the authors of those works, and their place in the history of fantastic literature.

As with *Anatomy of Wonder,* authors whose works fall into more than one period will have their works split into two chapters without cross-references, making an overview of a particular writer's fantastic fiction sometimes difficult. The reviews themselves are fair and balanced, and the overall coverage includes all the recognized classics of the field, plus representative titles from some lesser-known writers, and a few books that are relatively little-known. A new and very attractive feature of both *Fantasy Literature* and *Horror Literature* (as compared to *Anatomy of Wonder*) is the inclusion at the head of each author's entry of a series of two- to three-letter codes referencing twenty of the best-known bio-bibliographies and readers' guides in the field; however, the abbreviations list is somewhat awkwardly buried in the middle of the preface when perhaps it would have been more obvious to casual users if listed on a separate page prior to the introductory material. The indices reference item numbers only, but in general provide ready access to all materials listed.

Now partially superseded and updated by *Fantasy and Horror* (see #63), although this earlier edition does contain material not found in the later version, and should thus be retained on library shelves.

65. Barron, Neil, ed. **Horror Literature: A Reader's Guide.** New York & London, Garland Publishing, 1990. xxvii, 596 p. index. (Garland Reference Library of the Humanities, Vol. 1220). LC 89-27454. ISBN 0-8240-4347-2.

The resurgence of weird and supernatural fiction in the 1980s, beginning with the enormous popularity of author Stephen King, resulted in the establishment of a separate paperback genre with its own packaging format and its own group of proprietary authors (who in turn formed their own writers' organization). Thus, it is highly appropriate that this readers' guide, a companion volume to Barron's *Anatomy of Wonder* (see #62) and *Fantasy Literature* (see #64), and intended partially as a replacement to Tymn's *Horror Literature* (see #102), was published.

Horror Literature is arranged similarly to its two companions, with chapters contributed by individual critics, each covering successive stages of the genre's development, then further subarranged alphabetically by author's name and by his or her individual works.

Contents: "Preface" (by Barron); "Contributors"; Introduction: "Children Who Survive," by Michael Bishop; "Horror Literature": "1. The Early Gothic, 1762-1824," by Frederick S. Frank; "2. The Later Gothic Tradition, 1825-96," by Brian Stableford; "3. Early Modern Horror Fiction, 1897-1949," by Stableford; "4. Contemporary Horror Fiction, 1950-88," by Keith Neilson; "Research Aids": "5. Libraries and Fantasy/Horror Publishing," by Barron; "6. General Reference Books," by Barron; "7. History and Criticism," by Michael A. Morrison; "8. Author Studies," by Morrison; "9. Horror on Film and Television," by Michael Klossner; "10. Fantastic Art and Illustration," by Walter Albert; "11. Fantasy and Horror Magazines," by Mike Ashley; "12. Library Collections," by Randall A. Scott; "13. Core Collections, Awards, Organizations, Series," by Barron; "Author Index," "Title Index," "Theme Index."

The four major chapters on the literature comprise 326 pages (out of 596) and cover 792 items as compared to 1,094 books in Tymn (see #102). Barron provides a thorough coverage of the vast explosion of the field during the past decade, describing books and authors unknown in 1981, while Tymn's work includes a far greater examination of the roots of the field in the gothic horror movement of the late 1700s and early 1800s, and in general covers more books in somewhat greater depth. The disparity becomes even larger when one realizes that as many as *half* of the entries in Tymn are not described in Barron.

As with *Anatomy of Wonder,* authors whose works fall into more than one period will have their works split into two chapters without cross-references, making an overview of a particular writer's horrific fiction sometimes difficult; however, *Horror Literature* evinces far less such overlapping than its two companion works, perhaps because the period divisions in *Horror* better reflect the actual development of the genre, and not just an arbitrary splitting of the literature into more digestible units.

The reviews themselves are fair and balanced, and the overall coverage includes all the recognized classics of the field, plus representative titles from some lesser-known writers, and a few books that are relatively little-known. A new and very attractive feature of both *Fantasy Literature* and *Horror Literature* (as compared to *Anatomy of Wonder*) is the inclusion at the head of each author's entry of a series of two- to three-letter codes referencing twenty of the best-known bio-bibliographies and readers' guides in the field; however, the abbreviations list is somewhat awkwardly buried in the middle of the preface when perhaps it would have been more obvious to casual users if listed on a separate page prior to the introductory material. There is considerable overlapping between the nonfiction chapters in these two guides (*Fantasy* and *Horror*), as might be expected; many entries are identical, although each book includes some unique references. The indexes refer to item numbers only but in general provide thorough access to all materials listed.

Now partially superseded and updated by *Fantasy and Horror* (see #63), although this earlier edition does contain material not found in the later version, and should thus be retained on library shelves.

66. Barron, Neil, ed. **What Fantastic Fiction Do I Read Next?: A Reader's Guide to Recent Fantasy, Horror and Science Fiction.** Detroit, New York, Toronto, London, Gale Group, 1998. xix, 1679 p. index. LC 97-33418. ISBN 0-7876-1866-7. **What Fantastic Fiction Do I Read Next?: A Reader's Guide to Recent Fantasy, Horror and Science Fiction.** 2nd ed. Detroit, New York, Toronto, London, Gale Group, 1999. xx, 1954 p. index. LC 97-33418. ISBN 0-7876-4476-5. Contributors: Stefan Dziemianowicz, Scott Imes, Don D'Ammassa (Second Edition only).

Contents (both editions): "Introduction"; "Key to Story Types"; "Award Winners"; "What Fantastic Fiction Do I Read Next? (Fantastic Fiction Titles)" [the main index]; "Series Index"; "Time Period Index"; "Geographic Index"; "Story Type Index"; "Character Name Index"; "Character Description Index"; "Author Index"; "Title Index."

Designed as a reader's advisory for the science fiction, fantasy, and horror genres, *What Fantastic Fiction Do I Read Next?* is organized similarly to the other books in this Gale series. The Second Edition completely supersedes the First Edition, covering 6,090 works of fantastic literature (as compared to 4,856 in the previous version), all of them published in the United States between 1989-98. The entries were selected from recently published books considered the most representative of the genres covered, and also from bestseller lists and from the recommended lists of librarians and other experts.

The bulk of the book consists of the "Fantastic Fiction Title" section (through page 1274). Entries are listed alphabetically by author surname and then by title, and are numbered sequentially from the number one (the books are completely renumbered in the Second Edition).

A typical entry includes: reference number (printed on white within a black box at the head of the entry), author or editor's name(s) (centered), book title (centered bold italics), place of publication, publisher, year of publication, series name (where appropriate), story type, list of major characters (where appropriate), time period(s), locale(s), plot summary, and a brief list (averaging five) of similar books the reader might enjoy, organized alphabetically by author and then by title. Most of these cross-referenced titles were originally published between 1940-98, and include both classics and currently featured recommendations from elsewhere in the text. Anthologies are mentioned along with the rest, entered with a main entry under editor's name, including either a list of some of the authors whose stories are included within the book, and/or a complete or partial story contents register; none of the shorter pieces are indexed elsewhere in the text.

Fortunately, the Title Index lists both the recommended titles as well as the main entry books, providing another venue for locating similar books. The reference numbers are used consistently in all the indices.

The front matter includes the "Key to Genre Terms" and a brief list of major genre award winners. The first section comprises almost a mini-dictionary defining each genre's (fantasy, horror, science fiction) individual story types or sub-genres, in great detail. These types are also referenced in the Story Type Index. The awards list covers the World Fantasy Award (winners and runners-up), the Mythopoeic Society Fantasy Award (winners only), the Bram Stoker Award (with runners-up), the John W. Campbell Memorial Award (winners plus second- and third-place finishers), the Nebula Award (winners with runners-up), and the Arthur C. Clarke Award (winners only). Awards are listed only for the period from 1989-98.

This book is, first and foremost, a stupendous readers' guide to modern fantastic literature of the 1990s, covering all of the major works published during that period, and many of the minor publications as well. The coverage of characters, locales, and time settings is largely unique to this volume. The indexing and cross-referencing are superbly done, although there are the usual "misses" that one might expect with such a large and complex work full of contributions from outside critics (*e.g.*, Robin McKinley's *Beauty* is not a recommended title under another McKinley novel, *Rose Daughter*). The eight indices make finding works similar to the one under discussion a very simple and straightforward process. The content of this volume is also available online, together with the other guides from this Gale series, in the electronic database, *What Do I Read Next?*, as a electronic subscription through Galenet, updated quarterly.

The volume is nicely typeset and durably bound to library standards. Another of the quality publications that we have come to expect from Neil Barron, *What Fantastic Fiction Do I Read Next?* is highly recommended for all libraries.

67. Bleiler, Everett F. **The Guide to Supernatural Fiction: A Full Description of 1,775 Books from 1750 to 1960, Including Ghost Stories, Weird Fiction, Stories of Super- natural Horror, Fantasy, Gothic Novels, Occult Fiction, and Similar Literature, with Author, Title, and Motif Indexes.** Kent, OH, Kent State University Press, 1983. ix, 723 p. index. LC 82-25477. ISBN 0-87338-228-9.

Well-known critic, editor, and bibliographer Bleiler attempts nothing less than a comprehensive annotated survey to the supernatural in fiction through 1960, and he succeeds magnificently.

Materials are organized in alphabetical order by main entry (usually by author but under title for anonymous works), then chronologically by publication date. Works are listed under the byline appearing on the book, with appropriate "See" or "See Also" references for pseudonyms; this sometimes results in a particular writer's work being split between two or more pen names.

A typical author entry includes: author's name (all caps, with middle names in brack- ets), years of birth and death, a one-paragraph critical biography (when known, mentioning nationality and summarizing the author's career), and a chronological list of the writer's supernatural fictions followed (where applicable) by a chronological list of the author's edited volumes of supernatural stories.

A typical book entry includes: item number, title (all caps, underlined), publisher of first edition, place of publication, year of publication, format (*e.g.*, "paperbound"), but no paginations, and an annotation. Entries are numbered consecutively throughout the volume from 1-1,774 (one less than the title indicates). The summaries are both descriptive and evaluative, and range in size from 50-2,700 words, 250 being average. The annotations follow a standard format, with a prompt at the beginning of the entry indicating its content (*e.g.*, "what-would-happen-if," "semiallegorical short novel set in 4th century Rome"), a mention of alternative or original titles (if translated), followed by a detailed plot summary and a brief evaluation. Bleiler does not hesitate to trash poorly-written fictions, or to praise those that deserve kudos, or to label run-of-the-mill books "routine." A few works published in the 1960s are included.

Most significantly, the author also covers in great detail the hundreds of anthologies and single-author collections produced in this genre, annotating and evaluating *every story* with supernatural content; stories are lettered in order of appearance from "a-z," "aa-zz," etc.; those reprinted in more than one publication (a not uncommon occurrence) are annotated once, with all other appearances being referenced back to the first. Thousands of tales are thus summarized, providing an immeasurably rich treasure trove for future scholarship.

Finally, Bleiler includes at the end of his book an "Index of Motifs and Story Types," enabling the researcher to gain access to the material (both novels and stories) through very detailed subject breakdowns correlated to item numbers. The Author Index references authors, titles (novels in all caps, stories in lower case letters), and item numbers for all appearances; the Title Index correlates titles and authors only, requiring the user to refer back to the Author Index. A brief closing essay, "The Phenomenology of Contranatural Fiction," completes the work. The book is shot from legible but occasionally light two-column typed copy (in 8.5" x 11" format), and bound to library standards.

Bleiler's coverage is remarkably thorough, delineating works from the gothics of the late eighteenth and early nineteenth centuries (but only those with supernatural elements) to the early modern period. As usual, his work is authoritative, his research sound, his judgments middle-of-the-road and generally supported by both the history of the literature and by the prevailing critical opinions on each writer.

The principal problem with the book is its internal layout: Bleiler provides one-line breaks between author entries but none whatever between monographic records; for prolific writers, this tends to create page after page of somewhat light, massed-together copy, with only the occasional two-line left indent of the item number to break the mass of text. On many pages one is hard pressed to distinguish specific items in the body of the material without reading the sometimes lengthy entries in their entirety.

It is also unfortunate that the title index lacks entry numbers, and that paginations were omitted. These are small *caveat*s, to be sure. The data themselves, the lifelong effort that has gone into producing this labor of love, everywhere speak to us of the knowledge, the sympathy, and the understanding that the author has brought to this book. *The Guide to Supernatural Fiction* is a great achievement, even for Everett Bleiler, and that is saying a great deal indeed. See also the companion volume on early science fiction (see #68).

68. Bleiler, E. F., with Richard J. Bleiler. **Science-Fiction, the Early Years: A Full Description of More than 3,000 Science-Fiction Stories from Earliest Times to the Appearance of the Genre Magazines in 1930, with Author, Title, and Motif Indexes.** Kent, OH, and London, Kent State University Press, 1990. xxiii, 998 p. index. LC 90-4839. ISBN 0-87338-416-4.

Bleiler (and son) have once again produced a magnificent reference tool, one which is unlikely to be duplicated by any other researcher. The author examined every prose work of science fiction (periodical as well as monographic) with a publication date prior to 1930, which Bleiler uses as the demarcation point for the beginning of SF as a modern publishing genre.

Materials are listed alphabetically by author's name, then chronologically by title. A typical author entry includes: author (all caps boldfaced), years of birth and death (if known), brief biography (if known, giving nationality, career summation, and other notable accomplishments).

A typical fiction entry provides: item number, title (boldfaced, all caps), publisher, place of publication, year of publication, pseudonym (where applicable), illustrator, plus similar data for other significant editions, and annotation. Periodical entries (interfiled with the books) give magazine title (italics) and month and year of publication, but otherwise are similarly handled.

The annotations range in size from fifty-word paragraphs for short fiction to several pages of text (roughly 2,500 words) for major works, and are largely plot-oriented, with a single-line summation/evaluation at the end and occasional bibliographical notes added on. Short SF stories within a collection are each covered individually. Completing the text are two additional sections, the "Addenda" and "Background Books" chapters. The materials are numbered consecutively throughout the book (including the "Addenda" section, but not the "Background Books") from 1-2,475.

Five indices cover every conceivable access point: "Motif and Theme Index," "Date Index," "Magazine Index," "Title Index," "Author Index," all keyed to item numbers. The first of these provides extraordinarily detailed analyses of the works, listed alphabetically by subject (*e.g.*, "Islam, sacred objects stolen. 679" or "Mercury, geography of," further subdivided into "Hot and cold zones, but habitable: 524, 1979," etc.). Would that such access were available for more recently published works of fantastic literature!

The "Date Index" records first publication dates of the works keyed to item number; one must examine the item to determine the author and title. The "Magazine Index" is arranged alphabetically by periodical title, then chronologically by year and item number. The "Title Index" lists titles (books in all caps, short stories with initial caps only) and authors, but (curiously) no item numbers. The "Author Index" correlates authors, titles (using the same style as the "Title Index"), and item numbers. A two-page bibliography at the end of the book features reference works recorded alphabetically by author's name. The book is shot from very clear word-processed copy and bound to library standards.

There are several design problems with this bibliography that were perhaps inevitable given the amount of material included. The volume is arranged in an 8.5" x 11" double-column format, with one line break between each author, but only a three-space paragraph indentation delineating new entries (for those authors who have more than one). This layout works well on those pages where there are three or more author entries and where the entries are relatively frequent and short; the single-line spacing that separates each writer also breaks up the text as the eye runs down the page.

However, the entry for Jules Verne runs a dozen pages, with several more pages of collaborative entries, many of the entries occupying a full column or more; and it is here that the reader experiences problems. The absence of running heads and the lack of any paragraph indentations except at the start of a new entry combine to run the text together into one indivisible mass on the page, making the delineation of individual entries (or even the determination of the author's name) unnecessarily difficult.

However, in this particular instance the quality of the material clearly overrides the format quirks. Simply stated, there is no other work available or likely to become available in the future that provides so much important source material on the beginnings of science-fiction literature. Many of the books and stories covered here are now totally inaccessible to modern scholars; some are known to exist in only ten or twenty copies, and many others will soon vanish with the oxidation of paper and bindings. This is not just an important reference tool; any future researcher investigating the origins of science fiction as a genre *must* have access to Bleiler's guide or forever be damned to a literary Hades. Copies should be held by all academic libraries. A companion volume on horror fiction (see #67) is also available.

69. Bleiler, E. F., ed. **Science Fiction Writers: Critical Studies of the Major Authors from the Early Nineteenth Century to the Present Day.** New York, Charles Scribner's Sons, 1982. xv, 623 p. index. LC 81-51032. ISBN 0-684-16740-9. Bleiler, Richard, ed. **Science Fiction Writers: Critical Studies of the Major Authors from the Early Nineteenth Century to the Present Day.** 2nd ed. New York, Charles Scribner's Sons, 1999. xxvii, 1009 p. index. (Scribner Writers Series). LC 98-54321. ISBN 0-684-80593-6.

E. F. Bleiler is best known for his bibliographies and critiques of fantastic and criminous literature, but this book demonstrates his further abilities as an editor. *Science Fiction Writers* is divided into seven major sections: "Early Science Fiction," "Primitive Science Fiction: The American Dime Novel and Pulp Magazines," "Mainstream Georgian Authors," "American Science Fiction: The Formative Period," "The Circumbellum Period," "The Moderns," and "Continental Science Fiction."

The book consists of seventy-five full-length essays by twenty-six contributors (including Bleiler himself) ranging in size from 4,000-8,000 words (most in the lower range), arranged in alphabetical order by surname of the author being critiqued (for chapters five and six), and in no discernible order for the rest. Each entry includes a brief biography, extensive commentary on the author's works (specifically and generally), a critical summation, an assessment of the author's place in the history of science fiction literature, and a selected bibliography of primary works (in chronological order) and secondary works (in alphabetical order by author), often including brief annotations. The focus here is on "classic" writers, the youngest author included (Samuel R. Delany) having been born in 1942. Bleiler contributes a brief introduction, and an extensive author/title index completes the book.

The essays reflect the abilities of the individual critics, but are generally authoritative, well-considered, and longer than those available in any other reference set. The arrangement by chapters, each reflecting a specific period or movement, is the only major flaw in the book, since more than half of the entries (forty) fall into "The Moderns," and three chapters (four through six) out of seven account for fifty-eight of the seventy-five entries. Also, many of the primary bibliographies are deliberately incomplete, an unfortunate choice given the ready accessibility of this information in other published sources.

Many of these problems have been fixed in the Second Edition, edited by E. F. Bleiler's librarian son, Richard Bleiler. Half-again as large as the previous volume, this bio-bibliography contains new articles on twenty-three modern SF writers not previously covered. In addition, all the former entries are included, most with minor revisions and/or additions, some with supplements following the original entry. Richard Bleiler has written a new introduction, but the introduction to the first edition is present too.

Forty-two critics (including Bleiler himself) contribute a total of ninety-eight entries on "almost entirely English and American writers of [adult] science fiction," from Edgar Allan Poe and Mary Shelley through David Brin and Lucius Shepard. Crossover authors, such as Arthur Conan Doyle, are discussed only in relation to their science fiction.

The arrangement in the new version has been redesigned for simplicity, with entries being ordered alphabetically by author's last name. However, the chronological classification from the 1982 table of contents is maintained in a new chronology section at the front of the book. While useful for providing context, some parts of this chart cannot help but appear arbitrary when highly productive authors such as Asimov, Bradbury, and Clarke are all assigned solely to 1930-1940 and 1940-1950 sections.

The typical entry consists of the author's name, years of birth and death, and a bio-critical essay averaging 7,000 words, which includes a brief biography, extensive commentary on the author's works (specifically and generally), a critical summation, and an assessment of the author's place in the history of science fiction literature. A selected bibliography of primary and secondary works follows, with title (italics), place of publication, publisher, and year, followed by a list of critical and biographical studies. Occasionally, other information is provided, such as the institutional location of the author's manuscripts, and citations to published interviews or full-length bibliographies. Many of the internal bibliographies have been expanded for the Second Edition, although some of the primary listings from the older authors still remain incomplete. A black-and-white photograph of the author now accompanies almost all entries.

The essays themselves are authoritative, having been penned by some of the most significant names in science fiction criticism (Brian W. Aldiss, E. F. Bleiler, John Clute, Brian Stableford, etc.). The next edition should include the contributor's name next to his or her contribution(s) in the table of contents, as the 1982 edition did. The index is superb, including authors, short works, novels, series, and all of the people discussed in the main entry, showing the author's name in parentheses with each of the works he or she has authored, cross-referenced with the appropriate page number in the text. Bold numbers indicate the primary entry for an author.

This volume completely supersedes the earlier edition, and makes an excellent addition for all private, public, or academic libraries, being an essential purchase for anyone even marginally interested in the field. See also Bleiler's companion volume on supernatural writers (see #70), and Cowart and Wymer's *Twentieth-Century American Science-Fiction Writers* (see #53).

70. Bleiler, E. F., ed. **Supernatural Fiction Writers, Fantasy and Horror.** New York, Charles Scribner's Sons, 1985. xix, 1,169 p. in 2 v. index. LC 84-27588. ISBN 0-684-17808-7 (set).

This companion volume to *Science Fiction Writers* (see #69) is similarly arranged and presented. 147 essays by sixty-two critics are organized into fifteen chapters representing specific periods and nationalities.

Contents: Volume One: "Early Writers," "French Writers," "German Writers," "British Gothic and Romantic Writers," "British Victorian Writers," "British Fin-de-Siècle Writers," "British Early-Twentieth-Century Writers"; Volume Two: "British Writers of the Interbellum Period," "British Postwar Writers," "American Early-Nineteenth-Century and Victorian Writers," "American Fin-de-Siècle Writers," "American Mainstream Writers of the Early to Middle Twentieth Century," "Early American Pulp Writers," "American Pulp Writers of the Circumbellum Period," and "British and American Modern Writers."

Each entry ranges in size from 3,000-7,000 words (averaging 4,000), and typically includes a brief biography, an extensive commentary on the author's major works, a critical summation, an assessment of the writer's place in the history of fantastic literature, and a selected primary and secondary bibliography. Bleiler himself contributes a brief introduction and thirteen of the critical essays; a detailed author/title index and brief general bibliography complete the book. Coverage is considerably broader than in *Science Fiction Writers,* with one-third of the essays covering nineteenth-century writers of the supernatural, many known only to experts and literary historians, and the inclusion at the other end of the scale of several writers born in the late 1940s.

As in *Science Fiction Writers,* the quality of the material varies with the abilities of the many individual critics, but is generally high. The short author bibliographies, which include only the writers' more important books with selected nonfiction sources and occasional one-sentence annotations for the latter, are at best of limited usefulness; they could easily have been expanded into more complete (and more valuable) listings.

The arrangement by individual chapter and thereafter alphabetically by author surname (for the last two chapters, the modern period, only; the other, smaller chapters have no discernible internal arrangement) is unnecessarily confusing; a more logical arrangement for a second edition might be one alphabetical sequence for the entire book. This problem is exacerbated by the failure of the publisher to repeat the table of contents at the beginning of Volume Two.

Even with these difficulties, however, Bleiler's book is a major modern source for critical evaluations of writers of the fantastic; in particular, his coverage of little-known but important nineteenth- and early twentieth-century authors of weird and supernatural literature is unparalleled. Bleiler's firm editorial hand is evident throughout, the judgments of the critics generally fair and balanced, the book well designed, bound, and presented. A necessary addition to the library of any would-be researcher of horror literature.

71. Bloom, Harold, ed. **Classic Fantasy Writers.** New York, Chelsea House Publishers, 1994. xii, 187 p. (Writers of English: Lives and Works). LC 93-8346. ISBN 0-7910-2204-8; ISBN 0-7910-2229-3 (pbk.).

Contents: "User's Guide"; "The Life of the Author," by Harold Bloom; "Introduction," by Harold Bloom; "L. Frank Baum"; "William Beckford"; "James Branch Cabell"; "Lewis Carroll"; "Lord Dunsany"; "Kenneth Grahame"; "H. Rider Haggard"; "Lafcadio Hearn"; "Rudyard Kipling"; "Andrew Lang"; "George MacDonald"; "William Morris"; "Beatrix Potter"; "Oscar Wilde."

"This volume provides biographies, critical, and bibliographical information on the fourteen most significant fantasy writers up to the early twentieth century. Each chapter consists of three parts: a biography of the author; a selection of brief critical extracts about the author; and a bibliography of the author's published books."

The biographies average 500 words, and each entry has at least six critical excerpts (Lord Dunsany has eleven), averaging 400 words each. Often Bloom includes commentary from the author who is the subject of the entry. The excerpts are not high criticism, but thoughtful and useful commentary taken (sometimes out of context) from other sources. The complete citation for the original publication from which the excerpt is taken is provided at the end of each entry. The bibliographies are ordered chronologically by date, displaying title (italics) and year of publication only, and exclude foreign-language publications unless the author himself or herself performed the translation.

Of interest is Bloom's commentary, "The Life of the Author," which appears in all of the books in the series, as well as Bloom's brief individual introduction for this volume. With such a wonderful collection of excerpts by authors such as H. G. Wells, Northrop Frye, J. R. R. Tolkien, and others, an index to these snippets would be highly welcome, and is lamentably absent here. Recommended for public library collections.

72. Bloom, Harold, ed. **Classic Horror Writers.** New York, Chelsea House Publishers, 1994. xi, 180 p. (Writers of English: Lives and Works). LC 93-13020. ISBN 0-7910-2201-3; ISBN 0-7910-2226-9 (pbk.).

Contents: "User's Guide"; "The Life of the Author," by Harold Bloom: "Introduction," by Harold Bloom; "Ambrose Bierce"; "Charles Brockden Brown"; "Henry James"; "Joseph Sheridan Le Fanu"; "Matthew Gregory Lewis"; "Charles Robert Maturin"; "Edgar Allan Poe"; "Ann Radcliffe"; "Mary Shelley"; "Robert Louis Stevenson"; "Bram Stoker"; "Horace Walpole."

This volume provides biographies, critical, and bibliographical information on twelve of the most significant writers of horror fiction from the late eighteenth century to the end of the nineteenth century. Each chapter consists of three parts: a biography of the author; a selection of brief critical extracts about the writer; and a bibliography of the author's published books. The biographies average 500 words, and each entry has at least ten critical excerpts (Poe has eighteen), averaging 400 words each.

Often Bloom includes commentary from the author who is the subject of the entry. The quotes are not high criticism, but thoughtful and useful commentary. The complete citation is provided at the end of each excerpt. The bibliographies are ordered chronologically in descending order by year of publication, with title (italics) and year only, and exclude foreign-language publications unless the author performed the translation. Of interest is Bloom's commentary, "The Life of the Author," which appears in all books in the series, as well as Bloom's brief introduction for this volume.

With such a wonderful collection of excerpts by authors such as Virginia Woolf, William Hazlitt, Joyce Carol Oates, and others, an index to the excerpts would have been welcome, and is sorely missed at times. Easy to use, with informative and entertaining selections, this is a fine and useful addition to a personal or public library, and a "must" buy for academic libraries.

73. Bloom, Harold, ed. **Classic Science Fiction Writers.** New York, Chelsea House Publishers, 1995. xii, 186 p. (Writers of English: Lives and Works). LC 94-5901. ISBN 0-7910-2211-0; ISBN 0-7910-2236-6 (pbk.).

Contents: "User's Guide"; "The Life of the Author," by Harold Bloom; "Introduction," by Harold Bloom; "Edward Bellamy"; "Edgar Rice Burroughs"; "Sir Arthur Conan Doyle"; "Aldous Huxley"; "C. S. Lewis"; "Jack London"; "H. P. Lovecraft"; "George Orwell"; "Edgar Allan Poe"; "Mary Shelley"; "Olaf Stapledon"; "H. G. Wells."

"This volume provides biographies, critical, and bibliographical information on the twelve most significant classic science fiction writers. Each chapter consists of three parts: a biography of the author; a selection of brief critical extracts about the author; and a bibliography of the author's published books."

The biographies average 900 words in length, and each entry contains at least eight critical excerpts (Burroughs, Stapledon, and Wells each have thirteen), averaging 400 words apiece. Often Bloom includes commentary from the author who is the subject of the entry. The excerpts are not always high criticism, but thoughtful and useful commentary. The complete bibliographical citation is provided at the end of each excerpt. The bibliographies are ordered chronologically by date of publication, with book title (italics) and year only, and exclude foreign-language publications unless the author actually performed the translation.

Of interest is Bloom's commentary, "The Life of the Author," which appears in all books in the series, as well as Bloom's brief introduction for this volume, although neither adds much to the literature. With such a wonderful collection of excerpts by authors such as Charles Baudelaire, George Orwell, Gore Vidal, and others, an index to the excerpts would have been helpful. This slim volume will be a useful addition to a personal, public, or academic library.

74. Bloom, Harold, ed. **Modern Fantasy Writers.** New York, Chelsea House Publishers, 1995. xii, 194 p. (Writers of English: Lives and Works.) LC 94-5890. ISBN 0-7910-2223-4; ISBN 0-7910-2248-X (pbk.).

Contents: "User's Guide"; "The Life of the Author"; "Introduction," by Harold Bloom; "Ray Bradbury"; "John Collier"; "L. Sprague de Camp and Fletcher Pratt"; "E. R. Eddison"; "Robert E. Howard"; "Fritz Leiber"; "C. S. Lewis"; "David Lindsay"; "A. Merritt"; "Mervyn Peake"; "M. P. Shiel"; "Clark Ashton Smith"; "J. R. R. Tolkien"; "Charles Williams."

"This volume provides biographies, critical, and bibliographical information on the fifteen most significant modern fantasy writers. Each chapter consists of three parts: a biography of the author; a selection of brief critical extracts about the author; and a bibliography of the author's published books."

The biographies average 500 words, and each entry has at least eight critical excerpts (L. Sprague de Camp and Fletcher Pratt have eighteen) averaging 400 words each. Often Bloom includes commentary from the author who is the subject of the entry. The excerpts are not high criticism, but provide thoughtful and useful commentary. The complete bibliographical citation is provided at the end of each entry. The bibliographies are ordered chronologically by publication date, with title (italics) and year only, and exclude foreign-language publications unless the author actually performed the translation.

Of interest is Bloom's commentary, "The Life of the Author," which appears in all books in the series, as well as Bloom's brief introduction for this volume. With such a wonderful collection of excerpts by authors such as Stephen King, Brian Stableford, T. S. Eliot, and others, an index to the text would have been appreciated. Easy to use, with informative and entertaining selections, this is a fine and useful addition to a personal or public or academic library.

75. Bloom, Harold, ed. **Modern Horror Writers.** New York, Chelsea House Publishers, 1995. xii, 185 p. (Modern Horror Writers: Lives and Works). LC 94-5884. ISBN 0-7910-2224-2; ISBN 0-7910-2249-8 (pbk.).

Contents: "User's Guide"; "The Life of the Author," by Harold Bloom; "Introduction," by Harold Bloom; "Robert Aickman"; "E. F. Benson"; "Algernon Blackwood"; "Robert Block"; "Walter de la Mare"; "L. P. Hartley"; "William Hope Hodgson"; "Shirley Jackson"; "M. R. James"; "H. P. Lovecraft"; "Arthur Machen"; "Richard Matheson."

"This volume provides biographies, critical, and bibliographical information on the twelve most significant horror writers of the first half of the twentieth century. Each chapter consists of three parts: a biography of the author; a selection of brief critical extracts about the author; and a bibliography of the author's published books."

The biographies average 500 words, and each entry has at least eight critical excerpts (de la Mare has twelve), averaging 400 words each. Often Bloom includes commentary from the author who is the subject of the entry. The excerpts are not high criticism, but thoughtful and useful commentary. The complete citation is provided at the end of each entry. The bibliographies are ordered chronologically by date, listing title (italics) and year only, and exclude foreign-language publications unless the author actually performed the translation.

Of interest is Bloom's commentary, "The Life of the Author," which appears in all books in the series, as well as Bloom's introduction for this volume. With such a wonderful collection of excerpts by authors such as Stephen King, James Blish, S. T. Joshi, and others, an index to the text would have been helpful. Of use primarily to public or community college libraries.

76. Bloom, Harold, ed. **Science Fiction Writers of the Golden Age.** New York, Chelsea House, 1995. xii, 203 p. (Writers of English: Lives and Works). LC 94-4322. ISBN 0-7910-2199-8; ISBN 0-7910-2198-X (pbk.).

Contents: "User's Guide"; "The Life of the Author," by Harold Bloom; "Introduction," by Harold Bloom; "Poul Anderson"; "Isaac Asimov"; "Alfred Bester"; "James Blish"; "Ray Bradbury"; "Arthur C. Clarke"; "Robert A. Heinlein"; "Fritz Leiber"; "C. L. Moore and Henry Kuttner"; "Frederik Pohl"; "Theodore Sturgeon"; "A. E. van Vogt."

This volume provides biographic, critical, and bibliographic information on thirteen of the most significant writers of the "Golden Age" of science fiction. Each chapter consists of three parts: a biography of the author; a selection of brief critical extracts about the author; and a bibliography of the author's published books. The biographies average 650 words, and each entry has at least nine excerpts, in one case as many as fourteen, averaging 400 words each. Most entries also include a previously-published comment from the author under discussion. The complete citation for each short critique is provided at the end of the quotation.

It is a pity that someone, either Bloom or the editorial staff at Chelsea House, didn't make a minimal effort to index this slim volume and the others in the Writers of English series, or at the very least compile an A-Z list of the critics whose words provide the bulk of the material Bloom used for each entry. All the other information, both biographical and bibliographical, has been provided more comprehensively and more completely in other publications.

Bloom's opening piece, "The Life of an Author," talks about such admittedly superior beings as Shakespeare, Joyce, Dante, *et al.*, but the editor has made no effort to connect his thoughts with the subject at hand. Yes, indeed, Asimov, Bradbury, and Clarke are writers too, but how do they, as purveyors of science fiction in a hypothetical "Golden Age," relate to the earlier literary masters whom Bloom discusses here?

Similarly, in his three-paragraph "Introduction," Bloom systematically tears apart the reputation and writing ability of Arthur C. Clarke (one of his chosen subjects), yet concludes somewhat lamely that " . . . it would be difficult to overestimate the pragmatic influence of Clarke's work. . . . "

This has all been done better before. Bloom's little book is an unnecessary extravagance that fails to provide even the minimal requirements of such an effort, to instruct, enlighten, and entertain. Not recommended.

78. Budrys, Algis. **Benchmarks:** *Galaxy* **Bookshelf.** Carbondale, IL, Southern Illinois University Press, 1985. xxvi, 349 p. index. (Alternatives). LC 84-10518. ISBN 0-8093-1187-9.

Budrys, a well-known science fiction writer, produced this series of fifty-four book review columns for the February 1965-November/December 1971 issues of *Galaxy Magazine,* covering 161 books released during this particularly fertile and energetic period in SF publishing, and touching peripherally upon many other books and authors. The columns are reproduced in the same order as originally published, with little editing but occasional sidenotes to explain particular references or to comment further on the book(s) being reviewed. Introductions by Frederik Pohl, former editor of *Galaxy,* by Catherine L. Mc-Clenahan, and by Budrys himself frame the material; and a comprehensive author/title index and a separate "List of Books Reviewed Index" complete the volume and provide complete access to the material covered.

Budrys shines while pointing out the literary deficiencies of the giants of the genre, as in his review of Frank Herbert's *Dune,* generally considered a modern classic of science fiction:

> But we are not yet the omnipathetic departed, and we have to simply read the words. What we find, dulling the fine creation and shrouding it as surely but not as stingingly as the storms of Paul's Arrakis, are the words—the twisting, subplotted, ravelled edge of unhemmed selvage at the margins of the strong whole cloth. Herbert has chucked MacLeanism, he has chucked Kipling's mistake; but instead of seeing his own mistake he has elaborated it. Being intelligent and sophisticated, he

has made the elaboration most enjoyable. But if he thinks—if you think—that the reason *Dune* turns flat and tails off at the end is because even four hundred pages cannot encompass it properly, please consider instead the possibility that 200 pages would have sufficed even for an epic. *The Odyssey* is not that long. Nor *Beowulf,* nor the narrative of the New Testament.

The critic's pointed, pithy remarks, never intended to be anything but opinionated, rarely fail to illuminate and are always entertaining and enlightening. And while this collection is not a readers' guide in its organization or original intent, Budrys touches on so many important writers and books in his six years of commentary that *Benchmarks* achieves very near the same purpose.

79. Cawthorn, James, and Michael Moorcock. **Fantasy: The 100 Best Books.** London, Xanadu Publications, 1988. 216 p. index. ISBN 0-947761-24-1. New York, Carroll & Graf, 1988. 216 p. index. LC 88-9510. ISBN 0-88184-335-0.

The second in the "100 Best Books" series includes a hundred 800-word essays on classics of fantastic literature, arranged chronologically by date of first publication (with some anomalies), beginning with *Gulliver's Travels* in 1726 and including books published as recently as 1987. Several of the pieces cover more than one item, bringing the total number of books actually discussed to 110.

Each entry includes: author, title, publication data (publisher, place of publication, and year of publication) for both the first edition and the first U.S. or U.K. edition (depending on where the book was originally published), plus critical commentary consisting in roughly equal measures of background data (often mentioning the author's other prominent works), plot summary, and evaluation and summation. A brief pair of introductions by the editors and an author/title index complete the book.

This type of work stands or falls on the validity of its selections, as well as the soundness of the authors' critical judgments. "Fantasy" is loosely interpreted here to include horrific, gothic, fantastic, surrealistic, and science fictional literature; several of the choices, such as Herman Melville's *Moby-Dick,* are only marginally fantastic under the widest possible definition of the field. The blurring of genre lines is somewhat unfortunate given the fact that two companion books in this series already cover horror and science fiction (see #96 and #85); and, in fact, several titles overlap between the horror and fantasy volumes.

Still, the eighty-four books listed prior to 1960 are all acknowledged classics of fantastic literature, with few exceptions, over whose merits no critic could much quibble. The selections for the modern period (1961-87) remain much more controversial, however, demonstrating a clear pro-British bias (eighteen out of twenty-six volumes covered), and including several books and authors little known in the United States, while omitting other acknowledged classics that should perhaps have been included (Stephen R. Donaldson's *The Chronicles of Thomas Covenant the Unbeliever,* for example).

The essays themselves are pointed, sure, illuminating, always transcending the need to include plot summations without becoming either dreary or bogged down in philosophical ruminations. One is left with a real desire to read or revisit these books, a true measure of Cawthorn and Moorcock's ability to delineate their essences. Thus, even with its selection problems, *Fantasy: The 100 Best Books* remains one of the more readable and enlightening of the four published volumes in this series. Compare Pringle's *Modern Fantasy* (see #95).

80. Crawford, Joseph H., Jr., James J. Donahue, and Donald M. Grant. **"333": A Bibliography of the Science-Fantasy Novel.** Providence, RI, The Grandon Co., 1953. 80 p. index. LC A55-8667 (pbk.). New York, Arno Press, 1975. 80 p. index. (Science Fiction series). LC 74-15959. ISBN 0-405-06324-5.

The Grandon Company was a short-lived SF specialty imprint that presaged the later and much better-known company, Donald M. Grant, Publisher. This guide includes plot summaries of 333 gothic, horror, science fiction, fantasy, lost race, and associational novels published through 1950. The book is arranged alphabetically by author, then by title.

A typical entry includes: author (surname in all caps), title (italics), place of publication, year of publication, publisher (in parentheses), an indication whether the book is "illustrated," category (*e.g.*, "lost race," "oriental," "fantastic adventure"), and summary. The annotations range from 75-150 words in length, and are descriptive rather than analytical. A title/author index completes the book. The text is typeset (an unusual feature for reference works of this period), and both printings are clear and legible.

Crawford *et al.* emphasize "classic" works of fantastic literature, and indeed, very few of the works described will be unknown to serious researchers, most also being covered in Barron's guides (see #62, #63, #64, #65) and in other reference works. However, the very lucid plot summaries in *"333"* (some of which are longer and more detailed than those found in any other source) still make this a useful guide for scholars interested in early fantasy, horror, and science fiction. The original version is now scarce, and the Arno reprint was withdrawn shortly after publication in a dispute over rights, with only a handful of copies being distributed, making it even harder to find than the Grandon edition.

81. Fletcher, Marilyn P., ed.; James L. Thorson, consulting ed. **Reader's Guide to Twentieth-Century Science Fiction.** Chicago and London, American Library Association, 1989. xiv, 673 p. index. LC 88-7815. ISBN 0-8389-0504-8.

In the first sentence of her introduction, Fletcher rhetorically poses the question, "What prompts the need for yet another science fiction reference book?" and it is her failure adequately to answer her own query that defines the problems with this book.

Fletcher offers 130 bio-critical essays on 131 writers contributed by thirty-eight critics. Entries range in size from 1,000-3,000 words, averaging 2,000, and generally are divided into four sections: "Life and Works" (250-750 words), "Themes and Style" (150-500 words), "Plot Summaries of Major Works" (the bulk of each entry), and "Biographical/Bibliographical Readings" (a short paragraph of secondary sources, without annotations, including articles, interviews, critical studies, and bibliographies, usually comprising no more than two to ten entries total). An acknowledgments page, three-page introduction, list of contributors, two appendices ("A: Science Fiction Magazines and Critical Journals"; "B: Nebula and Hugo Award Winners"), a half-page list of sources, and a title index complete the book.

All of the major SF authors are covered, of course, but it is in her selection of secondary writers, those who have yet to attain generally acknowledged fame outside of genre circles, that Fletcher begins to go awry. The focus of the book is stated to be twentieth-century writers, the earliest figure included being H. G. Wells, and Fletcher limits her coverage to no more than six items per author (although even this rule is fudged with specific entries). Fair enough. But in what sense is Anatoly Dneprov the equal, say, of Thomas M. Disch, either as craftsman or *littérateur* or science-fiction writer? How, precisely, does the career of horror writer H. P. Lovecraft fit into a book ostensibly about SF authors? Are we to presume, by virtue of the fact that her entry is equal in length to those of Heinlein and Wells, that the life and works of Marta Randall are of *equal* significance? These are troubling issues, scarcely satisfied by the introductory material.

The quality of the material also varies widely. Some of the critics—Sam Moskowitz, Michael Collings, Stephen Potts, Jay Rawlins, Richard Bleiler—are well-known researchers and acknowledged experts on the history of fantastic literature, or at least on specific writers and/or movements. The vast majority, however, are not; included among their number are a graduate student, many librarians, an environmental water specialist, several lecturers, etc. This is not to impugn any specific critic's profession, but only to suggest that Ms. Fletcher failed to draw extensively upon a well-established stable of academics and other experts who are readily available to contribute to this type of publication.

As a result, while some of the critics transcend the format limitations, weaving summaries of the author's major books into critical mosaics illuminating the major themes of the writer's career, all too many are constrained into producing potboiled plot summaries that scarcely tell us more than "so and so" did "such and such."

Also, the secondary-source lists at the end of each entry are vastly incomplete, as is the source bibliography on page 663, which misses the standard genre biblios as well as major biographical sources.

Yet even mediocre reference books sometimes have their uses, and this particular volume does contain commentaries on some specific works at lengths that might be difficult to locate elsewhere, at least in a one-volume guide. Also, Fletcher might well prove useful in the small or medium-sized public library, where resources are limited and only a few books can be purchased on specific subjects. One wonders, however, why the major American library organization, which has done so much good work in the field, continues to churn out so many half-baked reference guides. Perhaps too many cooks spoil the broth.

82. Fonseca, Anthony J., and June Michele Pulliam. **Hooked on Horror: A Guide to Reading Interests in Horror Fiction.** Englewood, CO, Libraries Unlimited, 1999. xxiii, 332 p. index. (Genreflecting Advisory Series). LC 99-31441. ISBN 1-56308-671-9.

Contents: "Foreword: Horror Fiction in Library Collections," by Stine Fletcher; "Acknowledgments"; "Preface: The Appeal of Horror"; "Introduction: Purpose and Goal of This Book" ("General Information," "Scope of This Guide," "Horror and Film," "Final Note"); "Part 1: Introduction to Horror Fiction": Chapter 1: "A Definition of Horror"; Chapter 2: "How to Use This Book"; Chapter 3: "The Appeal of Horror Fiction"; Chapter 4: "A Brief History of the Horror Genre and Its Current Trends"; "Part 2: An Annotated Bibliography of Horror Short-Story Collections": Chapter 5: "Anthologies and Collections by Multiple Authors"; Chapter 6: "Collections by Individual Authors"; "Part 3: An Annotated Bibliography of Horror Novels and Films": Chapter 7: "Ghosts and Haunted Houses"; Chapter 8: "Golems, Mummies, and Reanimated Stalkers"; Chapter 9: "Vampires and Werewolves"; Chapter 10: "Demonic Possession, Satanism, Black Magic, and Witches and Warlocks"; Chapter 11: "Mythological Monsters and 'The Old Ones'"; Chapter 12: "Telekinesis and

Hypnosis"; Chapter 13: "Small Town Horror"; Chapter 14: "Maniacs and Sociopaths, or the Nuclear Family Explodes"; Chapter 15: "Technohorror"; Chapter 16: "Rampant Animals and Other Eco-Monsters"; Chapter 17: "Psychological Horror: It's all in Your Head"; Chapter 18: "Splatterpunk: The Gross-Out"; Chapter 19: "Comic Horror"; "Part 4: Ready Reference, Criticism, and Other Helpful Information": Chapter 20: "Stretching the Boundaries: Cross-Genre Horror Fiction"; Chapter 21: "Bibliographies of Notable and Important Horror-Fiction Authors"; Chapter 22: "History and Criticism"; Chapter 23: "Periodicals: Journals, Magazines, and E-Zines"; Chapter 24: "Ready Reference Sources"; Chapter 25: "Horror-Related Organizations"; Chapter 26: "Major Awards"; Chapter 27: "Publishers and Publisher's Series"; Chapter 28: "Horror on the World Wild Web"; "Short Story Index"; "Subject Index"; "Index of Authors and Titles."

Hooked on Horror is designed for librarians as a readers' advisory text devoted solely to the horror genre. It provides a list of annotated novels, anthologies, and collections, including approximately 1,000 entries. All items are either currently in print or were published between 1994-98, being recorded in the "union catalogs of various state library systems and a few public library online catalogs." Included in spite of these general rules are "virtually every work by benchmark bestselling or most popular authors in the genre, such as Stephen King, Dean Koontz, Anne Rice, Ira Levin, and John Saul" (whether in print or not), classic works such as *Frankenstein* or *Dracula,* and selected critical and reference texts. All young adult horror, including works by such popular writers as R. L. Stine and Christopher Pike, is excluded. There is limited information provided on films.

The book is organized into thirteen sub-genres, then alphabetically by author or editor. A typical entry includes: author's name (bold type), title (bold type), place of publication, publisher, year of publication, pagination, a non-evaluative plot summary that usually ends with reading suggestions for similar titles, and (often) several subject headings assigned by the authors (not taken from the Library of Congress). The subject index utilizes these headings to point the reader to other books with similar headings. Each section ends with a few film recommendations, arranged alphabetically by title, each currently available on VHS, and an "Our Picks" section listing favorite books selected by each of the two authors. The authors employ two icons, representing the Bram Stoker Award and the Horror Guild Award, to highlight winners of those honors throughout the text.

A certain lack of focus here weakens the text in some sections, and gives the lie to its claim of completeness. Sometimes only one or two books from a well-known series are noted, with no reason given for the lapse. Also disconcerting are the frequent "See" references encountered, when a novel is listed in more than one chapter. Only one annotation actually appears, but the reader is left having either to rely on the index, or to page through the text looking for the appropriate entry. In some chapters this is less of a problem than others, but on page 147, for example, seven out of ten entries are references to coverage elsewhere in the volume, and the entire Chapter 21 consists of nothing but references. Tsk, tsk, tsk.

Still, this could be very useful guide in some public library collections.

83. Harris-Fain, Darren, ed. **British Fantasy and Science-Fiction Writers Before World War I.** Detroit, A Bruccoli Clark Layman Book, Gale Research, 1997. xvi, 363 p. index. (Dictionary of Literary Biography, v. 178). LC 97-8790. ISBN 0-8103-9941-5 (alk. paper).

Contents: "Plan of the Series"; "Introduction"; "Edwin A. Abbott"; "Grant Allen"; "F. Anstey"; "Edwin L. Arnold"; "John Davis Beresford"; "Algernon Blackwood"; "Lewis Carroll"; "G. K. Chesterton"; "Sir Arthur Conan Doyle"; "George du Maurier"; "E. M. Forester"; "Kenneth Grahame"; "George Griffith"; "H. Rider Haggard"; "William Hope Hodgson"; "Charles Kingsley"; "Vernon Lee"; "Joseph Sheridan Le Fanu"; "Matthew Gregory Lewis"; "George MacDonald"; "Arthur Machen"; "Charles Robert Maturin"; "William Morris"; "E. Nesbit"; "Ann Radcliffe"; "Mary Wollstonecraft Shelley"; "Bram Stoker"; "H. G. Wells"; "Appendix: Documents in British Fantasy and Science Fiction"; "Books for Further Reading"; "Contributors"; "Cumulative Index."

Part of Gale's excellent *Dictionary of Literary Biography* series, this book includes the standard features of that series. The text is organized alphabetically by the authors' surname, and includes career biographies "tracing the development of the author's canon and the evolution of his reputation." Reproductions of title pages and dust jackets are often included, as are specimens of the writers' manuscripts and letters, when feasible. Each entry begins with a black-and-white photograph or other image of the writer, and a bibliography of his or her book publications, including: title (in italics), place of publication, publisher, and year of publication, before turning to the critical biography proper (2,500-8,000 words).

Each essay has been contributed by a well-known critic in the field, and covers the basic elements of the author's life and career as a writer, and his or her contributions to fantastic literature. The quality of these pieces is uniformly high, with the critical assessments generally following prevailing critical opinion. Each entry concludes with a secondary bibliography of letters, bibliographies, biographies, and further references about the author (arranged in each subsection alphabetically by surname of the critic), plus a note describing any collections housing major archives of the writer's papers.

The appendix provides a small collection of documents significant to British fantasy and science fiction, such as Mary Wollstonecraft Shelley's preface to *Frankenstein,* G. K. Chesterton's essay, "The Ethics of Elfland," and an excerpt from E. M. Forster's *Aspects of the Novel.* The index merely lists all of the writers and subjects covered by the entire *DLB* series; a detailed index to this particular volume would have been welcome.

Researchers and librarians have long recognized the value of the *DLB* series as a whole; all academic libraries and major public libraries should have the entire set.

84. Holdom, Lynne. **Capsule Reviews.** Lake Jackson, TX, Joanne Burger, 1977. 51 p. index. (pbk.). San Bernardino, CA, The Borgo Press, 1980. 51 p. index. LC 80-20445. ISBN 0-89370-056-8.

This amateurishly produced guide covers roughly 450 science fiction and fantasy novels from the 1950s-'70s, arranged alphabetically by author, then by title. A typical entry includes: title (all caps), author, summary, and series notation (where applicable). The annotations range from one to three sentences and are mostly descriptive, with occasional one- or two-word analytical comments. The title index lists titles and authors only. The book is shot from typed copy. The vast majority of these books can be found in Barron's guides (see #62, #63, #64, #65) and in similar works with better annotations and bibliographical data (none of which are provided in Holdom's work). Now largely useless.

85. Jones, Steve, and Kim Newman, eds. **Horror: 100 Best Books.** London, Xanadu Publications, 1988. x, 256 p. ISBN 0-947761-37-3. New York, Carroll & Graf, 1988. x, 256 p. LC 88-7351. ISBN 0-88184-417-9.

The editors of the third volume in the "100 Best Books" series, unlike its two companions, invited the world's leading horror writers to select their favorite books in the genre and then provide a 700-word essay on each item. Several previously published critical pieces by Edgar Allan Poe and M. R. James were also reprinted. The entries are arranged chronologically from the earliest (*Doctor Faustus,* 1592) to the latest (1987). Each entry provides a 150-word plot summary in italics, including brief background material on the author followed by the critic's commentary. The contributors are mostly well-known horror and fantasy writers in their own right. Two brief introductions by the editors and by Ramsey Campbell, biographies of the contributors, and a six-page chronologically arranged "List of Recommended Reading" complete the volume.

Although the editors restricted the selections to a previously prepared list of "classics," many of these titles were perforce not chosen by the participants and therefore not included in this book except in the recommended reading section. Thus, *Horror: 100 Best Books* does not really include the *best* books of the genre under any set of criteria, but 100 individual selections of a *best book,* reflecting the idiosyncrasies of the critics, and including a number of items that are questionably fantastic or which have already been covered in the science fiction and fantasy volumes in this series. There is also a much greater focus in this book on the modern period to the detriment of truly time-tested "classics"—of the 100 selections, more than half were published after World War II, more than a third after 1970, and almost a fifth in the 1980s. One must question how so many "classics" could have appeared among us so quietly unheralded.

The quality of the essays also varies widely, from "gee whiz, that's great!" meanderings to profound literary insights from the likes of Brian W. Aldiss, Colin Wilson, and Brian Stableford. Most are at least entertaining, however, which is all this quasi-guide can be. The absence of an index is dismaying.

86. Kies, Cosette. **Supernatural Fiction for Teens: 500 Good Paperbacks to Read for Wonderment, Fear, and Fun.** Littleton, CO, Libraries Unlimited, 1987. xii, 127 p. index. LC 87-3228. ISBN 0-87287-602-0 (pbk.). **Supernatural Fiction for Teens: More than 1300 Good Paperbacks to Read for Wonderment, Fear, and Fun.** 2nd ed. Englewood, CO, Libraries Unlimited, 1992. ix, 267 p. ISBN 0-87287-940-2.

This handy guide selectively annotates works of horror and fantasy suitable for the young adult reader, most of them originally published as paperbacks.

Kies's introduction explains her criteria and includes a short seven-item list of secondary sources (all dealing specifically with the literature of horror and the supernatural). The main bibliography includes 463 novels and collections, arranged alphabetically by author. An additional thirty-seven items are included in a separate anthologies section, alphabetically by editor's name. The appendices include: a list of books in series (by series name, with author and title); an index to movies (motion pictures mentioned in the primary bibliography, by film title and item number); a directory of paperback publishers, with addresses; "Title Index" (title and item number); and "Subject Index" (by broad subject—*e.g.*, Fairies, Zombies, Paranormal Abilities, etc.—and item number).

A typical entry includes: item number, author, title (boldface), place of publication, publisher, year of publication, pagination, ISBN number, original publisher and date if previously published, series, category (a single, boldfaced letter: "**A**" = Written for Teens; "**B**" = Written for Younger Teens; "**C**" = Written for Adults; "**D**" = Classic [tales of the supernatural from nineteenth- and early twentieth-century sources]), "Other works" of interest by the author, information on movie adaptations (with title [if different], production date, director, and major stars), brief annotation, and subject (keyed to the subject index). The annotations consist of one- to three-sentence plot descriptions.

Short story collections (in the main section) and anthologies include complete contents listings (story titles and authors), except for series anthologies (*The Year's Best Horror Stories,* for example), where only the latest published volume is annotated. The text is well designed and typeset, easy to read, and well indexed.

The 1992 edition increases coverage to 1,304 paperbacks, but otherwise is organized very similarly to the first version. More "See" references have been added to existing entries, and there are more mentions of motion pictures adapted from works by the author.

Compared to Lynn's *Fantasy Literature for Children and Young Adults* (see #89), *Supernatural Fiction* surprisingly includes a great many titles annotated in no other source. Kies covers a few books that might more appropriately be categorized as "high fantasy," but the vast majority of the titles covered are original or reprint horror paperbacks published for the adult and young adult markets. Authors such as William W. Johnstone, Shaun Hutson, John Halkin, William Schoell, J. N. Williamson, and other rising stars of modern horror are scarcely mentioned elsewhere; also unique is her coverage of Bantam's Dark Forces Series, Dell's Twilight Series, Ballantine's Find Your Fate books, and Pacer's The Zodiac Club, all designed as original fantasy/horror adventure novels published only in paperback.

Kies's work should become a standard guide for public librarians.

87. King, Betty. **Women of the Future: The Female Main Character in Science Fiction.** Metuchen, NJ & London, Scarecrow Press, 1984. xxi, 273 p. index. LC 83-20130. ISBN 0-8108-1664-4.

King provides a historical and critical guide to female characters in science fiction (written by both male and female writers), the primary emphasis being on twentieth-century fantastic literature. The book is broken into seven main sections plus three appendices: "1. Historical Perspective—1818 Through 1929"; "2. The 1930s"; "3. The 1940s"; "4. The 1950s"; "5. The 1960s"; "6. The 1970s"; "7. The 1980s"; "Appendix A: Collections and Anthologies of Stories about Women Characters"; "Appendix B: Women Characters in Erotic Science Fiction"; "Appendix C: Amazon Women."

The thirty-seven-page first chapter includes, in narrative form, a chronological summary of the major works of the pre-modern period in fantastic literature. The remaining sections each provide a brief summary paragraph for the decade, and then list, in alphabetical order by author's name, the major works of short and long fiction published during that ten-year period. A typical entry includes author (in all caps, with middle names in parentheses and real names in lower case in parentheses, where applicable), story title (in quotes if a short story, underlined if a novel), and bibliographical data.

For shorter works, King provides: magazine where first published (underlined), month and year of publication, and a list of the collections or anthologies in which the story has appeared, with title (underlined), place of publication, publisher, and year of publication. Only those stories that have been reprinted in book form are included. For novels, King includes place of publication, publisher, and year of publication, plus similar information on known reprints in English. No paginations are provided.

The annotations include: main characters, with their physical characteristics and mental/emotional characteristics, and "story particulars" (*i.e.*, plot summaries) ranging in size from 300-700 words, averaging 500; even short stories are covered in great depth, and most of the descriptions include at least a one-sentence summation of the work's effectiveness. Each of the six later chapters includes an "Additional Reading List" in alphabetical order by author, then by title, giving author, title (underlined), place of publication, publisher, and year of publication, but no annotations.

104 works are annotated in the main sections, with many hundreds of other titles being mentioned in the end pieces. The first appendix lists seven anthologies of stories with women characters, arranged alphabetically by editor's name, with bibliographical data as above, plus a one-sentence annotation. The second appendix provides a few paragraphs of very incomplete and largely irrelevant text (in narrative form) on so-called erotic female SF characters. The last appendix lists novels and stories featuring "amazon"-type SF characters, in alphabetical order by author, then by title, with bare-bones bibliographical data.

King also provides a two-page bibliography of sources; an "Index of Physical and Mental/Emotional Characteristics of Characters in the Synopses," in alphabetical order by characteristic, then by page number; an "Index of Story Particulars in the Synopses," by location, societal structure, themes, and time setting, then subdivided by topic and page number; and an "Index of Titles and Authors," not cross-referenced, which lists title or author and page number(s) only, with an asterisk following the page numbers of title records indicating an annotated entry; none of the appendices are indexed, however. The book is shot from clearly reproduced typed copy and bound in library cloth.

The structural arrangement of *Women* makes it unnecessarily difficult to use, artificially dividing authors and stories into ten-year segments that sometimes make very little sense. Thus, works by Andre Norton, for example, are referenced (in the author/title index) to four sets of page numbers, including one annotated work from the 1960s (on pages 126-27), one unannotated book from the same period (on page 139), eight unannotated novels from the 1970s (on pages 195-96), and two unannotated works from the 1980s (on page 234); but there is no way to tell from the index exactly how many works by Norton are covered, what they are, or whether or not they are annotated. Further, while King covers a great many works, one wonders about her selection criteria; how could any modern researcher of women SF characters miss, for example, D. G. Compton's highly acclaimed novel, *The Continuous Katherine Mortenhoe?* Nor are there comparisons between one work and another, or one author and another, and no easy way to make such evaluations, even though the clear intent of this work is to cover a very selective list of stories and novels.

Yet, even with these *caveats* King does provide a treasure trove of descriptive and analytically indexed material found in no other source in this form, and researchers and library collections specializing in the study of women characters and authors in fantastic literature will find this book a useful starting point.

88. Lewis, Naomi. **Fantasy Books for Children.** London, National Book League, 1975. 46 p. LC 76-357468. ISBN 0-85353-240-0. **Fantasy Books for Children.** Rev. ed. London, National Book League, 1977. 61 [actually 55] p. LC 78-312430. ISBN 0-85353-260-5 (pbk.).

This slim British paperback annotates 214 fantasy novels, collections, and novel series suitable for pre- and early-teen readers. Books are arranged alphabetically by author's name and book title. A typical entry includes: item number, author or editor, title (bold caps), translator (where appropriate), (British) publisher, year of publication, price (in 1977), pagination, illustrator, ISBN number, and description. Annotations typically run 50-375 words in length, averaging 150, and include both plot description and evaluation. There is also a list of then-current publishers' addresses, now wholly outdated.

The books selected by Lewis include many nineteenth-century "classics" and well-known twentieth-century works, in equal measure, plus a scattering of 1970s titles (twenty to thirty volumes) which have had little circulation in the United States. Many of the latter are missing from Lynn's work (see #89). Lewis's annotations are also considerably longer and more evaluative than Lynn's, making her brief guide worth consulting by children's librarians and students of juvenile fantasy.

89. Lynn, Ruth Nadelman. **Fantasy for Children: An Annotated Checklist.** New York & London, R. R. Bowker Co., 1979. ix, 288 p. index. LC 79-21401. ISBN 0-8352-1232-7. **Fantasy for Children: An Annotated Checklist and Reference Guide.** 2nd ed. New York & London, R. R. Bowker Co., 1983. xiv, 444 p. index. LC 83-11868. ISBN 0-8352-1732-9. **Fantasy Literature for Children and Young Adults: An Annotated Bibliography.** 3rd ed. New York, R. R. Bowker, 1989. xlvii, 771 p. index. LC 88-8162. ISBN 0-8352-2347-7. **Fantasy Literature for Children and Young Adults: An Annotated Bibliography.** 4th ed. New Providence, NJ, R. R. Bowker Co., 1995. lxxix, 1092 p. index. LC 94-42549. ISBN 0-8352-3456-8.

Since the first three editions of this continuing work were almost completely subsumed into the much expanded fourth edition, only the latter will be considered here. *Fantasy Literature for Children and Young Adults* has quickly become the standard guide to its field.

Contents (Fourth Edition): "Preface"; "Guide to Use"; "Abbreviations of Books and Review Journals Cited"; "Introduction"; "Outstanding Contemporary Fantasy"; "Award-Winning Fantasy Literature"; "Part One: Annotated Bibliography" (includes: "1. Allegorical Fantasy and Literary Fairy Tales"; "2. Animal Fantasy"; "3. Fantasy Collections"; "4. Ghost Fantasy"; "5. High Fantasy"; "6. Humorous Fantasy"; "7. Magic Adventure Fantasy"; "8. Time Travel Fantasy"; "9. Toy Fantasy"; "10. Witchcraft and Sorcery Fantasy"); "Part Two: Research Guide" (includes: "11. Bibliographical and Reference Sources on Fantasy Literature"; "12. Critical and Historical Studies of Fantasy Literature"; "13. Educational Resources on Fantasy Literature"; "14. Fantasy Literature Author Studies"); "Author and Illustrator Index"; "Title Index"; "Subject Index."

The fourth edition of this standard reference is made up of "4,800 fantasy novels and story collections for children and young adults in grades 3 through 12, as well as a research guide to more than 10,500 articles, books, and Ph.D. dissertations about the authors who write fantasy literature for children and young adults." This represents an increase of nearly

1,500 books in Part One from the 3,300 books covered in the Third Edition, and an increase of almost 4,000 resources in Part Two. Fifty-eight titles from the previous volume were deleted in the Fourth Edition (because they have been out of print for more than fifty years); these are listed in the preface, with the abbreviated citations as they appeared in the previous edition (p. xi).

Lynn's introduction provides a broad history of the fantasy genre. "Outstanding Contemporary Books and Series" includes those publications considered by library reviewers (and by Lynn) to be particularly noteworthy, arranged by subject category and then alphabetically by author. Added to this edition is a new chunk of text providing a "Historical Overview of Children's and Young Adult Fantasy" from the nineteenth century to the present, with the twentieth century being covered decade-by-decade. The author has also provided a new list of award-winning fantasy literature taken from thirty-four awards honoring fantastic literature and children's literature.

The main section of the book, comprising 550 pages, lists 3,148 numbered fantasy volumes (novels, collections, anthologies) suitable for children, teenagers, and young adults, arranged by subject chapter and then by author (note: many of these numbered entries cover other titles by the same author, bringing the overall title count to the 4,800 works total mentioned above).

A typical entry includes: item number (bold type; left margin), author (bold), title (bold italics), grade level, original publication date and title (if any), recommendation checks (bold type; left margin), brief annotation (averaging 50 words), illustrator, publisher of first American edition, year of publication of American edition, pagination, ISBN, in-print status (noted as "o.p." if out-of-print), reviews of the book (citing an abbreviated title for the journal [*e.g.*, BL = *Booklist*], volume, and page number(s), the volume and page being separated by a colon). The annotation mentions all known sequels or associated titles (giving publisher and year of publication); these are generally not covered as separate entries. Books that fall into more than one subject category are described in the chapter considered by Lynn to be the most appropriate, with copious "See" references back from all other related chapters.

This format represents a dramatic improvement from the earlier versions of this book. Boldfaced type has been added to the author's names, making them stand out, and the left margin has been justified for the entries. The entry numbers (new) and the recommendation symbols (a graphic of either one or two checkmarks) also now rest in the left-hand margin. The new layout makes it much easier to distinguish between individual entries. Cross-referencing, too, has been greatly improved. Books that could appear in more than one section are listed alphabetically in the alternative sections, indicating the chapter where the main entry will be found. This does not completely solve the problem of authors' works being spread all over the book, but it does help. The indices have also been improved by using entry numbers rather than page numbers; this is especially true of the title index. Previously, a certain amount of scanning was needed to find the title in question on the page, but entry numbers make access by the casual user much more efficient.

The second half of the book, the "Research Guide," is vastly expanded from the previous editions, incorporating 353 pages of unannotated secondary sources, also arranged by general subject chapter, then alphabetically by main entry. Included in these sections are reference books, critical monographs, and published articles on children's literature, on children's fantasy, and on fantastic literature written by and for more adult readers.

The "Author Studies" include interviews, feature articles, bibliographies, critiques, and reference sources on 600+ authors, arranged by the name of the writer being covered, then alphabetically by main entry. Lynn provides (for monographic works): author, title (in italics), place of publication, publisher, year of publication, and pagination (but only if mentioning coverage in a section of a book); for shorter pieces, the following bibliographical data are noted: author, title (in quotes), book or magazine title (in italics), editor, place of publication, publisher, and year (for anthologies), or volume number, year, and pagination (for journal articles). These entries seem both complete and current. The indexes correlate authors/illustrators, titles, and subjects with item numbers.

The introduction states that *Fantasy Literature* focuses primarily on twentieth-century fantasy published in the United States; a few nineteenth-century classics of children's fantasy are covered if still in print, and some foreign and British titles with American editions are also listed, but these are by no means complete (Lewis's guide to children's fantasy [see #88] includes a number of British fantasies published from 1960-75 that are simply not listed in Lynn). While Lynn eschews science fiction and horror, in fact her book covers many works that traditionally have been classed in those genres, including time travel fiction, ghost stories, alternate histories, and "science fantasy."

The fourth edition also adds a great many works suitable for older teens, including novels published for the adult market and authors (in the "Research Guide" section) generally considered "adult" writers of fantastic literature; at the same time, a number of books suitable only for very young readers (grades 1-4) are also annotated in some sections, making real comparisons between works difficult, if not impossible. The line between juvenile and adult fantasy has become increasingly blurred as Lynn's volumes have progressed, marking a similar change in the publishing and critical world at large (books released in cloth for young adults are now often reprinted for the adult mass market audience).

The primary problem with Lynn's book continues to be its awkward format, although various changes made in bibliographical entry and display, as well as the introduction of item numbers, have helped to ameliorate the impact of the subject breakdown. The primary bibliography is broken into ten sections, each with its own alphabetical sequence; the works of one author are frequently spread over two, three, or more chapters, making any correlation difficult without constant reference to the author index. Undeniably, access by subject can sometimes be useful, particularly for the young reader, but this could have been accomplished more easily through a general category index. A more utilitarian arrangement might have been one general alphabetical sequence or a breakdown by age levels. Another difficulty is the absence of grade level access, something that users of this type of reference source find very desirable, because of the radically different levels of readers from early elementary through high school.

With all of these *caveats*, Lynn remains the most comprehensive and current guide to juvenile fantasy now available, including such a large number of both primary and secondary sources that it perforce must be the first stop for any librarian or researcher even marginally interested in this subgenre. Highly recommended.

90. MacNee, Marie J. **Science Fiction, Fantasy, and Horror Writers.** New York, London, UXL, 1995. xxiv, 432 p. in 2 v. index. illus. LC 94-32459. ISBN 0-8103-9865-6 (set); ISBN 0-8103-9866-4 (v. 1), 0-8103-9867-2 (v. 2).

Contents: "Advisory Board"; "Preface"; "Picture Credits"; "Biographical Listings" (v. 1: A-J; v. 2: K-Z); "List of Hugo Award Winners"; "List of Nebula Award Winners"; "Index." The latter three sections are repeated at the end of both volumes.

Science Fiction, Fantasy, and Horror Writers contains "eighty biographical entries covering the best-known, highest-praised, scariest, funniest, and most promising authors of [fantastic] tales." The entries are ordered alphabetically by author, and include: date of birth, date of death, place of birth and death (where applicable), a black-and-white photograph of the author, a biographical and critical sketch of some 500-1000 words (with one additional black-and-white illustration, usually copied from the cover of one of the author's books), "Best Bets" (a selected, chronological list of the writers' best-known works), and "Sources" for further reading.

The essays are aimed at the young adult market, and tend to focus on writings suitable for that level of reading. The biographies feature brief excerpts (usually no more than a sentence or two) from commentary by other writers and critics. Sometimes, the "Best Bets" listings of the author's better-known publications do indeed conform to general critical opinion; but often MacNee picks books that represent less than the authors' best efforts.

For example, the entry for William Kotzwinkle notes his novelizations of *E.T., the Extra-Terrestrial* and *Superman III* as major works by the writer, when clearly they are derivative works adapted from the motion picture screenplays of the same names. Similarly, the entry for Ursula K. Le Guin highlights her works *Rocannon's World* (her first novel), A *Wizard of Earthsea,* and *A Ride on the Red Mare's Back,* and mentions other, more important writings only in passing. The awards listings are complete through mid-1994. The index references titles and writers' names to specific page numbers, with main author entries being indicated by boldfaced type. The books are nicely designed and typeset, and generally pleasing to the eye, being bound to library standards.

Science Fiction, Fantasy, and Horror Writers is a rather wobbly construct, even for the market for which it is intended. It will prove most suitable for media centers in middle and high schools, as well as for children's reference collections in public libraries. It also makes a nice doorstop, but the heft of these two volumes does not at all correlate with the lesser mass of their prose.

91. Magill, Frank N., ed.; Keith Neilson, assoc. ed. **Survey of Modern Fantasy Literature.** Englewood Cliffs, NJ, Salem Press, 1983. xviii, 2,538, li p. in 5 v. index. LC 83-15189. ISBN 0-89356-450-8 (set).

This companion set to *Survey of Science Fiction Literature* (see #92) was actually edited by Neilson in the standard Magill series format. Neilson used a board of six consulting editors to determine the initial list of titles to be surveyed, then assigned the approximately 500 essays to 102 critics. "Fantasy" is loosely interpreted here to include weird and supernatural fiction, surrealistic literature, traditional fantasy, sword-and-sorcery adventures, juvenile works, and even a few books that are arguably not fantastic (for example, *Camino Real,* a play by Tennessee Williams).

As with all the Magill volumes, this book is arranged in alphabetical order by the title of the work being critiqued; the essays range in size from 1,000-10,000 words, 2,000 being average. Series are often covered under the series title, rather than individual book title; also, there are many entries grouped together under the heading "The Short Fiction of [author's name]," covering those writers who have made major contributions to the genre with less than novel-length fictions.

A typical entry includes: title, author's name, year of birth, year of first book publication, type of work (*e.g.,* "novel"), the time or era in which the book is set, the locale where the plot is set, a brief single-sentence plot summary in italics, a list of principal characters, with brief descriptive annotation; the critical essay itself; and a brief bibliography of secondary sources relevant to the work in question.

The quality of the pieces varies widely, but most are usually at least readable, and, although the series format demands much attention to plot description, many are surprisingly perceptive, the overall level of these volumes being much higher than the standard Magill fare. This particular set also includes several noteworthy innovations: at the end of Volume 5 are an additional nineteen general essays on specific aspects of fantastic literature (*e.g.,* "Arthurian Legend and Modern Fantasy" and "Modern Fantasy and Marvel Comics"), plus a year-by-year "Chronology of Modern Fantasy Literature," listing major authors and titles, a short annotated bibliography of secondary sources, a bibliography of major fantasy anthologies (by editor), and a detailed author/title index covering every reference in the entire five-volume set, an unusual bonus for a Magill book (most Magill sets index the major essays only, by author and title).

Coverage is extensive and comprehensive, touching upon almost every work ever labeled a "classic" in this genre and many others besides; however, the Magill format makes an overall evaluation of any one author's works difficult if that author has penned more than one "classic" fiction (this is a somewhat lesser problem with fantasy writers, many of whose works are covered under general series titles, than with authors included in other Magill sets). Also, although the mini-bibliographies of secondary sources at the end of each essay are somewhat more comprehensive in this set than in the SF volumes, they still seem rather scanty, with many entries listing no sources whatever. Coverage of foreign-language titles hitherto untranslated into English is much less extensive in this set as compared to the *Survey of Science Fiction Literature.* The high price tags on these sets limit their potential market largely to libraries, but they should be standard purchases for any academic institution worthy of the name.

Some of the essays from this set were carried over to *Magill's Guide to Science Fiction and Fantasy Literature* (see #100), which provides an abridged, updated continuation of the volumes.

92. Magill, Frank N., ed.; Keith Neilson, assoc. ed. **Survey of Science Fiction Literature: Five Hundred 2,000-Word Essay Reviews of World-Famous Science Fiction Novels with 2,500 Bibliographical References.** Englewood Cliffs, NJ, Salem Press, 1979. xxv, 2,542, vii p. in 5 v. index. LC 79-64639. ISBN 0-89356-194-0 (set).

The Survey, although credited to Magill, was actually edited by Neilson in the standard Magill series format. Neilson used a board of thirteen consulting editors to determine the initial list of titles to be surveyed, then assigned the approximately 500 essays to 131 critics, including sixteen from non-English-speaking countries. As with all the Magill volumes, this book is arranged in alphabetical order by the title of the work being critiqued; the essays range in size from 1,000-10,000 words, 2,000 being average. Series are sometimes covered under the series title rather than individual book title; also, there are many entries grouped together under the heading "The Short Fiction of [author's name]," covering those writers who have made major contributions to the genre with less than novel-length fiction.

A typical entry includes: title (plus original foreign language title if the work is a translation or a translated title if the book has never been published in English), author's name, year of birth, year of first book publication, type of work (*e.g.*, "novel"), the time or era in which the book is set, the locale where the plot is set, a brief single-sentence plot summary in italics, a list of principal characters, with brief descriptive annotation; the critical essay itself; a brief bibliography of secondary sources relevant to the work in question.

The quality of the pieces varies widely, as might be expected with contributed essays, but most are at least readable, although the series format demands much attention to plot description; the list of critics was drawn from a small number of academics working actively in the field, and their contributions are often surprisingly perceptive, much better than the usual Magill fare, but generally not as good as those in the *Survey of Fantasy Literature*. Essays contributed by foreign critics not fluent in English were specially translated into English for this set. The standard Magill index at the end of Volume 5 references the major essays only, by author and title; a more comprehensive index, covering every author and title mentioned in the book, would have been preferable.

Coverage is extensive and comprehensive, touching upon almost every work considered a "classic" in this genre and many others besides; however, the Magill format makes an overall evaluation of any one author's works difficult if that author has penned more than one "classic" volume, as is often the case here. This set is unique in its coverage of many older science fiction titles from foreign countries, most of which have never been translated into English. The mini-bibliographies of secondary sources at the end of each essay, consisting mostly of book review citations, were widely criticized for their lack of comprehensiveness, being generally worthless for further study; subsequently, a *Bibliographical Supplement* compiled by Marshall B. Tymn was later issued as a separate companion volume (see #129). The high price tags on these sets limit their potential market largely to libraries, but they should be standard purchases for any academic institution and all large public libraries. See also the companion set on fantasy (see #91).

Some of the essays from this set were carried over to *Magill's Guide to Science Fiction and Fantasy Literature* (see #100), which provides an abridged, updated continuation of the volumes.

93. Pfeiffer, J. R. **Fantasy and Science Fiction: A Critical Guide.** Palmer Lake, CO, Filter Press, 1971. iv, 64 p. index. LC 73-159397. ISBN 0-910584-25-7 (pbk.).

Pfeiffer's poorly presented and organized bibliography of primary and secondary sources in fantastic literature includes a brief introduction, "An Annotated Critical Bibliography of Authors and Works After 1900," "Fantasy and Science Fiction Before 1900," "Selected Periodicals Publishing Fantasy and Science Fiction," "Special Anthologies," "Bibliographical Works," "History and Criticism," "Special Periodicals ('Fanzines')," and "Title Index." The main section, focusing on SF after 1900, constitutes half of the book and is arranged alphabetically by author.

Each entry provides: author, author's pseudonyms (in parentheses), years of birth and death, nationality, representative book titles (all caps), year of publication, number of known printings (in parentheses), and a series of letter codes indicating subject content. Coverage is spotty, with no obvious system for selection of titles other than the fact the author has read the book. The second chapter, which includes representative titles before 1900, is arranged roughly chronologically by century and then alphabetically by author; these titles are not categorized. The nonfiction sections sometimes include brief annotations (no more than one phrase) that tell the reader virtually nothing about the book in question; and these chapters are, of course, long since out-of-date. The book is reproduced from barely legible typed copy.

Execrably rendered.

94. Pflieger, Pat; Helen M. Hill, advisory ed. **A Reference Guide to Modern Fantasy for Children.** Westport, CT & London, Greenwood Press, 1984. xvii, 690 p. index. LC 83-10692. ISBN 0-313-22886-8.

This curious volume is a combination readers' guide, character dictionary, gazetteer, and biographical and critical directory to thirty-six nineteenth- and twentieth-century American and British authors of fantasy books for children.

The main section of the book consists of 622 pages of material interfiled into one alphabet. The thirty-six bio-critical entries run one to two pages each in length, and typically begin with a one-paragraph biographical summary. Most of the author entries, however, focus on the writer's juvenile fantasy works, each annotation intermingling plot summary with exposition, plus a one-paragraph final summation of the writer's contributions to the history of children's and fantastic literature. A brief checklist of the author's books (adult as well as juvenile) and a selected bibliography of secondary sources (books and articles) complete the record.

The remaining entries cover a wide variety of topics, including individual novels, major characters, races (elves, for example), principal places, objects (*e.g.*, magical swords), and virtually everything else of interest to the reader and student of these writers' works. Asterisks provide internal "See" references throughout the text to related entries (titles, characters, etc.). The several appendices include a short (three-page) checklist of books and articles about fantasy; a brief chronology of the authors and works included; and an index of principal illustrators of the books mentioned. A thorough index to all names, entries, and topics mentioned completes the book. The volume is well designed and typeset and bound to library standards.

This type of work stands or falls on the selection of authors and topics to be covered and the thoroughness and authoritativeness of the annotations. The earliest of the writers in Pflieger, Charles Kingsley, was born in 1819, and the latest, Jill Paton Walsh, in 1939. Most of the remaining authors produced at least a few works that are acknowledged classics of children's and young adult fantasy, although some are better known than others. One may quibble, for example, over the inclusion of Penelope Lively, Philippa Pearce, or Jane Louise Curry in the company of J. R. R. Tolkien, George MacDonald, and Edith Nesbit, but in the end the argument doesn't really seem to matter. All of these writers have a sufficient body of work (and sufficient claim) to merit inclusion in such a directory, and one finally regrets only those authors who perforce had to be excluded.

The entries themselves are learned without becoming didactic, readable while remaining informative, and display a knowledge, sympathy, and understanding rare in this type of work. Perhaps this is due to the unified viewpoint expressed throughout and the clear and elegant language in which the book is written.

Helen Hill's foreword states: "Few reference works can be read just for pleasure, but this guide to modern fantasy for children is a book that can give pleasure to the general reader as well as to the specialist." Amen amen. Highly recommended.

95. Pringle, David. **Modern Fantasy: The Hundred Best Novels: An English-Language Selection, 1946-1987.** London & Glasgow, Grafton Books, 1988. 278 p. index. ISBN 0-246-13214-0; ISBN 0-246-13420-8 (pbk.). New York, Peter Bedrick Books, 1989. 278 p. index. LC 89-33072. ISBN 0-87226-328-2; ISBN 0-87227-219-7 (pbk.).

When Xanadu (U.K.) and Carroll and Graf (U.S.) chose to use Cawthorn and Moorcock's *Fantasy: The 100 Best Books* (see #79) rather than Pringle's own sequel to his earlier *Science Fiction: The 100 Best Novels* (see #96), perhaps due to Moorcock's name-recognition value, they did themselves a disservice, for while Cawthorn and Moorcock produced an interesting (if quirky) volume, Pringle consistently maintains a more balanced and readable effort.

As with his earlier selection, Pringle focuses on the postwar period, listing one hundred novels published from 1946-87 in chronological order by publication date. A typical entry includes: author, title, the critique (averaging 700 words each), bibliographical data (giving place, publisher, and year for the first British and American appearances, plus an indication of the most recent edition available [in 1987]).

The essays themselves each provide brief background material on the author and his *oeuvre,* but quickly focus on the works being discussed. Pringle weaves plot summaries with quotations from the authors' own hands to provide intelligent, readable, and always interesting comments that not only tell us what the book is about, but why it is significant to the history of fantastic literature. All of the acknowledged classics are covered, as are many other interesting works; few will be unknown to the informed reader, and even these may be deserving of further attention. The list is nicely balanced between U.S. and British writers, and includes some books traditionally considered to fall into the horror or supernatural genre (Shirley Jackson's *The Haunting of Hill House,* for example).

Pringle's editorial and critical balance is superior to Cawthorn and Moorcock's (see #79), although both books are readable and illuminating. The latter tends to be somewhat quirky in its choices of books to be covered, with a decided pro-British bias, but covers the entire history of fantasy literature (beginning in 1726), providing a much wider scope. There is surprisingly little overlap between the two books: of the thirty-seven entries in Cawthorn/Moorcock that fall into the period from 1946-87, only fifteen coincide with Pringle. Pringle invariably includes those books *acknowledged* to be modern classics, while Cawthorn and Moorcock tend to focus on items that they *personally found interesting.*

Thus, the average reader is much more apt to locate the modern classics with which he or she is familiar in Pringle, but Cawthorn/Moorcock remains the better overall survey of the genre simply because it covers a much greater period of time. Both should be purchased by public and academic libraries.

96. Pringle, David. **Science Fiction: The 100 Best Novels: An English-Language Selection, 1949-1984.** London, Xanadu Publications, 1985. 224 p. index. ISBN 0-947761-11-X;

ISBN 0-947761-10-1 (pbk.). New York, Carroll & Graf, 1985. 224 p. index. LC 85-32532. ISBN 0-88184-259-1. New York, Carroll & Graf, 1997. 224 p. LC index. 97-28181. ISBN 0-7867-0481-0.

The first in the "100 Best Books" series is also the most consistent, thematically as well as in execution. The idea for these books came from *99 Novels: The Best in English Since 1939: A Personal Choice,* by Anthony Burgess (London: Allison & Busby, 1984). In similar fashion, Pringle focuses on a hundred SF classics from the postwar period.

The entries are arranged in chronological order by date of original publication in book form; each includes: author, title, publishing data (place of publication, publisher, year of publication) for the first edition and first American or British edition (depending on where the book was originally issued), plus a 600- to 800-word critique consisting largely of plot summary with background material and critical summation. Introductions by Pringle and Michael Moorcock, a brief general bibliography, and a good author/title index complete the book.

Virtually every title on Pringle's list is deserving of attention, having been critically acclaimed in many other fora; his coverage is comprehensive, fair, and balanced, including a broad range of authors and themes, both British and American. His highly readable annotations often provide short, illuminating passages from the books themselves to buttress his arguments and are intended for the general reader, not the scholar.

As a one-volume popular introduction to the best of modern science fiction, *Science Fiction: The 100 Best Novels* is unsurpassed among readers' guides currently available. Note also Pringle's companion volume, *Modern Fantasy* (see #95), and compare with Searles *et al.* (see #99).

97. Pringle, David. **The Ultimate Guide to Science Fiction.** London, Grafton Books, 1990. xx, 407 p. index. ISBN 0-246-13215-9; ISBN 0-246-13635-9 (pbk.). New York, Pharos Books, 1990. xx, 407 p. index. LC 90-7968. ISBN 0-88687-537-4; ISBN 0-88687-536-6 (pbk.). **The Ultimate Guide to Science Fiction: An A-Z of Science-Fiction Books by Title.** 2nd ed. Aldershot, England, Scolar Press, 1995. xix, 481 p. index. LC 94-19564. ISBN 1-85928-071-4.

Contents (Second Edition): "A Note on How This Book Is Arranged"; "Introduction"; "Acknowledgments and Bibliography"; "A-Z of Science Pringle"; "Author Index."

The author of two previous readers' guides to fantastic literature (see #95 and #96) has here produced evaluations of roughly 3,000 novels, collections, and anthologies, most of them published since 1950.

Entries are arranged alphabetically by title, typically including: title, date of first book publication (in brackets), star rating (on a scale of 0-4 asterisks, four being best), classification (novel, collection or anthology), author's name and nationality or the country in which each has settled (in brackets), and the body of the entry, which normally consists of two-to-three sentences of brief description and evaluation. Sequels or other related works are listed at the end of each entry, as appropriate. The copious use of "See and "See Under" references, page guides, and a clear layout, makes this a very straightforward, easy-to-use volume.

The vast majority of titles covered derive from the modern period, although there is a scattering of important early classics (Wells's *The Time Machine,* for example) that have remained consistently in print or that are significant for other reasons. Pringle focuses his attention primarily on English-language authors, emphasizing science-fiction works; fantasy authors such as Katherine Kurtz are not covered, nor are individual fantasy titles by pre-dominantly SF authors (for example, Poul Anderson's *The Broken Sword*). Coverage extends through 1989. The index correlates authors and titles only. The book is nicely typeset and designed, and the cloth versions are bound to library standards.

In the second edition, Pringle has "revised much of the old material and added about 40,000 words of new entries." He covers about 4,000 science fiction books (1000 more than in the previous version), and provides brief, fifty-word evaluations for each item. Included in the new work are more scientific romances of the late nineteenth and early twentieth centuries, additional anthologies, and some novelizations and spin-off novels linking movies, television, and radio to fiction. Pringle focuses on English-language books, with an emphasis on those published within the past twenty-five years, including anthologies; but excludes fantasy and children's books and most paperback originals. Coverage is provided to the end of 1993, with a few entries from 1994.

In comparing Pringle's original guide to Wingrove's similar volume, *Science Fiction Source Book* (see #106), the latter rates some 2,500 works (including individual short stories) published through the early 1980s in four categories: readability, characterization, idea content, and literary merit, but with only moderate success. Wingrove includes a broader range of titles, including some works of pure fantasy and a wider range of years, but generally covers fewer works per author. His guide is also significantly out-of-date.

All of the major books—and most of the minor ones—by well-known SF writers are included in Pringle, and on this basis alone, plus the larger number of titles covered and the relative currency of his book, *The Ultimate Guide to Science Fiction* is probably a better buy. There is a slight British bias evident in both books. On the whole, however, Pringle's conclusions seem sound, and his ratings tend to conform with prevailing critical opinion in the field (always a good sign).

The next edition might consider including a more complete index. Recommended for all libraries.

98. Searles, Baird, Beth Meacham, and Michael Franklin. **A Reader's Guide to Fantasy.** New York, Avon, 1982. 217 p. LC 82-7364. ISBN 0-380-80333-X (pbk.). New York, Facts on File, 1982. xvi, 196 p. ISBN 0-87196-772-3.

The second book in a two-volume set of reader's guides to science fiction and fantasy written by the employees of the New York specialty bookstore, The Science Fiction Shop, is organized similarly to the companion volume on SF (see #99). An introduction by Poul Anderson and a brief guide to using the book precedes an A-Z listing of 171 major fantasy authors (including some known for their juvenile fiction), a suggested basic reading list, fantasy awards and their winners, listings of fantasy series and sequels, six lists of books arranged by rough subject type, and a brief, ten-page history of the genre.

As with the science fiction guide, the 100-1,000-word critiques are written for a popular audience, focusing on the author's contributions to the field with brief one-line annotations of the writer's major works. Some entries overlap with the previous reader's guide, but the focus here is always on the writer's fantasy output, "fantasy" being loosely defined to include some horror fiction as well as "high fantasy." Light and readable, but not to be mistaken for serious literary criticism. Even with the popular orientation, an index should have been included. Now out-of-date.

99. Searles, Baird, Martin Last, Beth Meacham, and Michael Franklin. **A Reader's Guide to Science Fiction.** New York, Avon, 1979. xv, 266 p. LC 79-51729. ISBN 0-380-46128-5 (pbk.).

The first of a two-part series of reader's guides on fantastic literature produced by the employees of New York's The Science Fiction Shop, a specialty bookstore, includes a brief introduction by Samuel R. Delany, a short guide to using the book, 202 pages of guides to the major SF authors and their works, twenty-five pages of lists of well-known SF series and sequels, a section on Hugo and Nebula Award winners, a suggested basic reading list of fifty books, and a closing, twenty-page essay outlining the history of science fiction.

The main section of the book includes short essays (ranging in size from 80-1,100 words) on the 200 best-known authors in the genre arranged alphabetically by surname of the writer. Each entry summarizes the author's contribution to SF with one- or two-sentence annotations of the major books and suggestions for further reading.

The orientation here is popular, not scholarly, the comments generally approbatory, skin-deep, and easy to read. Coverage is now largely out-of-date, however, severely limiting the volume's usefulness, as does its ephemeral, mass market paperback format. An index would also have been helpful.

This is a book to be read just for fun; it doesn't take itself too seriously and shouldn't be taken seriously in turn. See also the companion book on fantasy (see #98).

100. Shippey, T. A., consulting ed., and A. J. Sobczak, project ed. **Magill's Guide to Science Fiction and Fantasy Literature.** Pasadena, CA, Englewood Cliffs, NJ, Salem Press, 1996. lv, 1126, xxxii p. in 4 v. index. LC 96-26261. ISBN 0-89356-906-2 (set); ISBN 0-89356-907-0 (v. 1); ISBN 0-89356-908-9 (v. 2); ISBN 0-89356-909-7 (v. 3); ISBN 0-89356-910-0 (v. 4).

Contents: "Publisher's Note"; "Contributing Reviewers"; "Introduction," by Shippey; "List of Genres"; "List of Titles" [volume by volume]; "Bibliography Introduction," by Len Hatfield and W. A. Senior; "Bibliography"; "Selected Science-Fiction and Fantasy Awards," by Robert Reginald; "Genre Index"; "Title Index"; "Author and Title Index."

This four-volume set provides "descriptions of hundreds of famous and well-regarded works of science fiction and fantasy, summarizing plots and analyzing the works in terms of their contributions to literature and the effectiveness of various literary devices employed." The 791 entries are arranged alphabetically by title, with 155 entries discussing pairs of books, trilogies, or longer series. The single book discussions are about 1,000 words in length, while discussions of two or works average 1,500 words.

The typical entry includes: title (boldfaced caps), sentence synopsis (italics), author's name and dates of birth and death (where applicable), genre and sub-genre (the first volume provides a list of the thirty-seven sub-genres identified, with a brief definition of each), type of work (novel, novelette, etc.), time period of the plot, setting, year the book was first published, detailed plot summary, and critical analysis. Each entry is signed by the contributor.

Volume Four includes "a selected, annotated bibliography of critical commentary and literary theory concerning fantasy and science fiction in narrative and film; annotations provide brief comments on content and orientation, designed to aid teachers and scholars, especially newcomers, in the field. The bibliography is arranged in three sections, with works ordered alphabetically by author within each. The first section, 'Fantasy and Science Fiction,' covers works discussing both sides of the sometimes contested division between fantasy and science fiction. The remaining sections focus separately on works mainly about fantasy and mainly about science fiction."

Also included at the end of Volume Four is a selected list of science fiction and fantasy awards and their winners, alphabetically by award name and then chronologically by winner; a genre index arranged alphabetically by sub-genre and then by book title, with the author's last name in parentheses, cross-referenced to the page number where the work is covered in the text; a title index, arranged alphabetically by title, giving author surname in parentheses, cross-referenced to the page number where the work is covered in the text; and an Author and Title Index, arranged alphabetically by author, with a list of his or her works alphabetically by title, cross-referenced to the page number where each work is covered in the text.

The volumes are attractively typeset and bound to library standards, although the double-column format (obviously used to save space) can be irritating at times, particularly when the header for the main entry appears (in part) at the bottom right-hand column of one page, with the major portion of the text on one or more following pages.

Magill's Guide was intended to replace and update two previous Salem Press publications, *Survey of Science Fiction Literature* and *Survey of Modern Fantasy Literature* (see #91 and #92), which together included roughly a thousand essays. However, less than half of the works covered in the two original sets are analyzed in the new *Guide,* and almost all of the entries that have been carried from the earlier sets have been rewritten in their entirety by other critics, often in shorter, somewhat less analytical essays. The lists of characters and critical works specific to each entry that accompanied the pieces featured in the *Survey* volumes have vanished here.

The essays themselves vary considerably in quality. Some have been penned by well-known SF critics, who clearly know whereof they speak; but others have been contributed by the usual Salem Press scholars, who, although they may possess a very thorough grounding in standard litspeak, fail at times to catch connections that might have been obvious to those with a sounder background in the literature of science fiction, fantasy, and horror. Thus, the average level here remains no better than average.

Still, *Magill's Guide* will generally be useful for its many plot summaries and analyses of relatively modern works in fantastic literature, and will also serve as a general readers' advisory for public and academic libraries. Libraries should retain all three sets.

101. Tymn, Marshall B., Kenneth J. Zahorski, and Robert H. Boyer. **Fantasy Literature: A Core Collection and Reference Guide.** New York & London, R. R. Bowker Co., 1979. xiii, 273 p. index. LC 79-1533. ISBN 0-8352-1153-3.

Intended as a companion book to Barron's *Anatomy of Wonder* (see #62), *Fantasy Literature* is actually organized very differently, perhaps due to the influence of Zahorski and Boyer, well-known academic critics of fantastic literature.

Contents: "Foreword," by Lloyd Alexander; "Preface"; "Acknowledgments"; "Part I. The Literature": "1. On Fantasy" (thirty-six-page introductory essay on the definition of fantastic literature); "2. Core Collection" (subdivided into two sections: "a. Novels and Short Story Collections," and "b. Anthologies," each arranged alphabetically by authors' or editors' names); "Part II. Research Aids": "3. Fantasy Scholarship" (subdivided into two sections: "a. History, Criticism, and Author Studies," and "b. Reference Works," arranged alphabetically by authors' names); "4. Periodicals"; "5. Fantasy Societies and Organizations"; "6. Literary Awards"; "7. Fantasy Collections in U.S. and Canadian Libraries"; "Core Collection Titles Available in the United Kingdom"; "Directory of Publishers"; "Index" (author and title in one alphabet).

A typical entry in the Core Collection sections includes: author or editor (boldfaced type), title (italics), place of publication, publisher of the first edition, year of publication, and similar data on the latest paperback edition available (in 1979), plus an annotation ranging in size from 60-1,250 words (300 being average). The essays provide a brief historical content, plot summaries, and critical summation, with mentions of other authors or books of a similar nature. The anthology section is unique in its detailed coverage of these important (but often neglected) materials, usually including complete contents listings as well as evaluative annotations of specific stories. The lengthy essay "On Fantasy" is an excellent general introduction to the study and history of fantastic literature, from its beginnings to modern times. The index correlates authors/titles to page numbers. The end matter is largely out-of-date at this point.

Barron's guide of the same title (see #64) covers vastly more titles (1,129 to 222) than Tymn and is a decade more current; but the more specific focus of Tymn/Zahorski/ Boyer, on a core collection of undisputed fantasy classics, ensures its validity far longer than most reference works of this kind (except for those lists of reference materials, awards, etc., which are clearly *passé*). Moreover, Tymn's book is far more readable than Barron's, more informative on the books it covers, and not as staid. *Fantasy Literature* has been in no way superseded by the newer work and should be retained by both scholars and libraries.

102. Tymn, Marshall B., ed. **Horror Literature: A Core Collection and Reference Guide.** New York & London, R. R. Bowker Co., 1981. xviii, 559 p. index. LC 81-6176. ISBN 0-8352-1341-2; ISBN 0-8352-1405-2 (pbk.).

The third of the Bowker readers' guides to fantastic literature (see also #62 and #101) is organized very similarly to Barron's *Anatomy of Wonder* and to Barron's later work, *Horror Literature* (see #65), which was intended to replace Tymn. Like Barron, Tymn acted as overall editor of the work, with each chapter being contributed *en masse* by an outside critic.

The book is divided into three main sections: "Foreword," by Peter Haining; "Preface," by Tymn; "Contributors"; "Part I. Fiction": "1. The Gothic Romance, 1762-1820," by Frederick S. Frank; "2. The Residual Gothic Impulse, 1824-1873," by Benjamin Franklin Fisher IV; "3. Psychological, Antiquarian, and Cosmic Horror, 1872-1919," by Jack Sullivan; "4. The Modern Masters, 1920-1980," by Gary William Crawford; "5. The Horror Pulps, 1933-1940," by Robert Weinberg; "Part II. Poetry": "6. Supernatural Verse in English," by Steve Eng; "Part III. Reference Sources" (all by Mike Ashley): "7. Biography, Autobiography, and Bibliography"; "8. Criticism, Indexes, and General Reference"; "9. Periodicals"; "10. Societies and Organizations"; "11. Awards"; "12. Research Collections"; "Core Collection Checklist"; "Directory of Publishers"; "Author and Title Index."

Each of the fiction chapters includes an introductory essay, ranging in size from ten to thirty-five pages, followed by coverage of individual titles arranged alphabetically by authors' names. A typical entry provides: item number (in boldface; "1-254" = item number 254 of Chapter 1), author, title (in boldface), nationality of author (if other than American), publisher and year of publication of the first editions in the U.S. and Britain (however, without cities of publication, one is left to guess which is which), but no paginations. The annotations range in size from 25-500 words (averaging 75-100 in the chapters covering twentieth-century works), and tend to focus on plot summaries with very brief critical evaluations, although the coverage of classic antecedents is very extensive in some instances. The critics are all well-known experts in their fields, and their introductions and annotations are generally unbiased and balanced. Much of the end matter is now outdated. The index correlates authors and titles with item numbers only.

Compared to Barron, Tymn covers many more titles (1,094 to 792 entries), and they are much more heavily concentrated toward the earlier periods in the history of horrific literature. While the chapter breakdown between the two works is not exactly comparable, a few examples may still prove illuminating: Barron's first two chapters, covering through 1896, occupy ninety-two pages of text; Tymn's initial two sections, through 1873, cover 220 pages, more than twice the wordage in Barron. Conversely, Tymn devotes less than 100 pages to the period from 1920-80, while Barron uses 166 pages (and provides considerably more annotations) in covering the growth of the modern horror genre from 1950-88. Barron's coverage of secondary sources and reference materials is also far superior (and far more current) than Tymn's.

Thus, while Tymn's book has undeniably been supplanted as a *readers' guide* by Barron, ironically his material still retains enormous worth and validity as a synthesis of eighteenth-, nineteenth-, and early twentieth-century horror and gothic literature, and should be retained by both libraries and scholars for that purpose. Many of the books covered in the earlier sections in Tymn are analyzed in no other source.

103. Tymn, Marshall B., ed. **The Science Fiction Reference Book: A Comprehensive Handbook and Guide to the History, Literature, Scholarship, and Related Activities of the Science Fiction and Fantasy Fields.** Mercer Island, WA, Starmont House, 1981. ix, 536 p. index. LC 80-28888. ISBN 0-916732-49-5; ISBN 0-916732-24-X (pbk.).

This laudable attempt at producing a readers' guide of interest to both a general audience and the scholar contains much of value but also much that could be improved. Following an introduction by Frederik Pohl and a brief preface by the editor are four sections: "Backgrounds," "Fandom," "Academe," and "Appendices," followed by a chapter on the contributors and a detailed author/title index. Each section includes four or five chapters, each contributed by a different critic (Tymn himself penned five of the eighteen chapters). The contributors are well-known critics who clearly know their subjects well.

The "Backgrounds" section includes: "Toward a History of Science Fiction," by Thomas D. Clareson; "Children's Fantasy and Science Fiction," by Francis Molson; "Science Fiction Art: Some Contemporary Illustrators," by Vincent DiFate; "The Fantastic Cinema," by Vincent Miranda; and "Critical Studies and Reference Works," a bibliography by Tymn.

The "Fandom" section includes: "Science Fiction Fandom/A History of an Unusual Hobby," by Joe Siclari; "Writing Awards," by Harlan McGhan; "Literary Awards in Science Fiction," by Howard DeVore; and "Science Fiction and Fantasy Periodicals," by Tymn.

The "Academe" section includes: "From the Pulps to the Classroom: The Strange Journey of Science Fiction," by James Gunn; "Masterpieces of Modern Fantasy: An Annotated Core List," by Roger C. Schlobin; "Outstanding Science Fiction Books: 1927-1979," by Joe De Bolt; "Science Fiction and Fantasy Collections in U.S. and Canadian Libraries," by Elizabeth Cummins Cogell; and "Resources for Teaching Science Fiction," by Tymn. The "Appendices" include: "Doctoral Dissertations in Science Fiction and Fantasy, 1970-1979," by Douglas R. Justus; "Science Fiction Organizations and Societies," by Tymn; "Directory of Specialty Publishers," by Tymn; and "Definitions of Science Fiction and Fantasy," by Schlobin.

The Science Fiction Reference Book contains a large amount of data, some of it now out-of-date, and also suffers from a certain lack of focus, alternating between reference volume and critical history without ever centering on either. This kind of problem seems inherent in a reference work penned by many hands. For example, two central chapters by Schlobin and De Bolt provide annotated guides to classic fantasy and science fiction. Schlobin includes forty pages of annotations arranged by author and title (anthologies being grouped together in their own section after the novels and collections), while De Bolt arranges his eighty pages of annotations by year through 1979, and then seemingly randomly under each year. Why? Schlobin gives middle names of authors in brackets, clearly indicating the preferred byline of each writer; De Bolt gives full names without such indications. Why?

There are similar problems with other sections. The chapter on science fiction collections in libraries, while detailed and complete, uses a silly prefix code (*e.g.,* MN1 for the first Minnesota library covered) that is meaningless and unnecessary; it is also badly outdated. The critical essays on children's F&SF and fantastic cinema are too cursory in their coverage to provide much information; the four introductory chapters in this section should perhaps have been organized in reference-book fashion rather than essay form, except possibly for Clareson's excellent short history.

There is some overlap, of course, with Barron's *Anatomy of Wonder* (see #62), but there is also some information yet unique to this volume, and a second, updated edition would certainly be warranted, particularly with firmer editorial control. The seeds of a worthy rival volume to Barron have been planted; it remains to be seen if they will ever be harvested.

104. Waggoner, Diana. **The Hills of Faraway: A Guide to Fantasy.** New York, Atheneum, 1978. x, 326 p. index. LC 76-900. ISBN 0-689-10846-X.

Waggoner provides a curious hybrid between literary guide and bibliography, a kind of personal odyssey through the realms of fantasy literature.

Contents: Chapter One: "Theory of Fantasy" (twenty-five page introductory essay); Chapter Two: "Some Trends in Fantasy": "1. Mythopoeic Fantasy," "2. Heroic Fantasy and Adventure Fantasy," "3. Ironic Fantasy," "4. Comic Fantasy," "5. Nostalgic Fantasy and Sentimental Fantasy," "6. Horrific Fantasy"; "Appendix A: A Timeline of Fantasy, 1858-1975"; "Appendix B: Some Fantasy Award-Winners"; "Appendix C: Fantasy Illustration";

"Appendix D: Subgenres of Fantasy"; "Sources; A Bibliographical Guide to Fantasy" (the main part of the text); "Index of Names and Terms"; "Index of Titles."

The introductory essays are rather thin histories of each subgenre, intended for a popular rather than a scholarly audience, and lacking any real critical perspective. The first appendix provides a brief, two-and-one-half-page chronology of the history of fantasy literature by year, listing year, author, and book title. "Appendix B" is now completely outdated. "Appendix C" reproduces twenty pages of fantasy illustrations, poorly selected and reflecting no unified vision or understanding of this specialized field. "Appendix D" rearranges the books covered in the "Bibliographical Guide" by specific subjects (*e.g.,* "Faerie Magic"), listing item number, author, and title only. The bibliography of sources includes five-and-one-half pages of nonfiction materials with author, title, and collation; this section is also now badly outdated. These introductory materials cover 124 pages of text (out of 326).

The major portion of the book is an A-Z guide to the major fantasy authors and 996 of their better-known works of fiction. A typical entry includes: author (centered, all caps, with dates of birth [and death] if known), item number (consecutively from 1-996), title (italics), city of publication, publisher of the first edition, year of publication, pagination, and a one-paragraph annotation. The latter range in size from 10-300 words (averaging 30-50), and tend to be very brief plot descriptions followed by a few pithy comments. A great many works originally published for the young adult and children's markets are included, although Waggoner claims to have prepared her book for an adult audience. The indexes correlate authors and titles to item numbers only.

Almost all of these materials are covered just as completely and competently in other sources, particularly in Lynn (see #89) and Barron (see #64), and Waggoner's mediocre effort now seems more dated than many of the other older guides covered in this section. It should be retained only by larger library collections and reference completists, but is utterly dispensible for anyone else.

105. Wehmeyer, Lillian Biermann. **Images in a Crystal Ball: World Futures in Novels for Young People.** Littleton, CO, Libraries Unlimited, 1981. 211 p. index. LC 80-26892. ISBN 0-87287-219-X.

Wehmeyer describes some 150 novels in this combination literary and teachers' guide to juvenile fiction dealing with future life. Contents: "Foreword"; "Part I. Working with Futuristic Fiction: Why and How"; "Part II. Futuristics and Futuristic Novels"; "Part III. Futuristic Novels Annotated"; "Part IV. Index of Themes and Motifs"; "Appendix: Novels Annotated in Part III"; "General Index."

The first chapter provides background information for teachers interested in the study of futuristic literature, including classroom and literary approaches. The second section describes general themes, ideas, and inventions common to the SF novel—*i.e.,* the literary conventions of the genre. Wehmeyer contends "that teachers and librarians must insure a balance between optimism and pessimism in future-oriented units of study and in library collections of futuristic fiction."

The main section of the book, the annotations proper, occupies 110 pages of text arranged alphabetically by author, then by title. A typical entry includes: author, title (bold-faced), place of publication, publisher, year of publication, pagination (haphazardly), grade level, summary, and notes. The annotations are both descriptive (in the "Summary" section) and evaluative (in the somewhat misnamed "Notes" section), and emphasize in the latter parts of each annotation major themes and their application to young people. The combined Summary/Notes range in size from 50-600 words, with the "Notes" part of the annotation occupying about one-third of each description.

The first index provides very detailed access to the books by subject, author surname, and title only, including geographical subjects (*e.g.,* "U.S.—Southwest (Setting)), genre categories ("Utopias"), time periods ("Twenty-Third Century"), and many others ("Vehicles, Electric-Powered," "Weather Control," "Slavery," etc.). The second index lists the novels covered in the guide by author, title, and page number. The "General Index" provides access to Parts I-II by subject, person, and title, and to Part III by author, illustrator, title, and publisher, correlated with page number(s). The indexing in this volume is among the most comprehensive of any of the readers' guides covered in this section.

Images in a Crystal Ball only covers books published from 1964-79 (and still in print in the latter year), intended for readers in grade 8 or below, with no indication in the introductory material of why these limits were chosen. This choice creates such obvious lacunae as the complete absence of the Heinlein juveniles, considered classics of their kind, as well as the earlier adolescent SF novels by Andre Norton, and others. Most of the books and authors included *are* well known, and many (but not all) are mentioned in Barron's *Anatomy of Wonder* (see #62), with, however, fewer plot details.

Thus, Wehmeyer's book remains a useful guide for grade and high school teachers and librarians alike, although it is now out-of-date and should be upgraded (and its coverage expanded backwards) with a second edition.

106. Wingrove, David, ed. **The Science Fiction Source Book.** Harlow, England, Longman, 1984. 320 p. index. LC 86-672322. ISBN 0-582-55592-2. New York, Van Nostrand Reinhold Co., 1984. 320 p. index. LC 83-27338. ISBN 0-442-29255-4.

A strange conglomeration that never seems able to decide what it wants to be, *The Science Fiction Source Book* includes: "Foreword," by Brian W. Aldiss; "A Brief History" of the genre, by Aldiss (eleven pages); "The SF Sub-Genres," by Brian Stableford, broken into the mini-essays, "Man and Machine," "Utopia and Dystopia," "Time Travel," "Aliens," "Space Travel," "Galactic Empires," "ESP," "Disasters," "Religion and Mythology," "Parallel Worlds and Alternate Histories," "Sex and Sensuality," "Alien Ecologies," "Magic," "The Media," and "Inner Space" (averaging three pages each); "The Science Fiction Writer at Work," one-page essays by twelve major SF writers on their own working methods; "Science Fiction Writers: A Consumers' Guide," with contributions by twelve British critics (185 pages); "First Magazine Publication of Leading Authors" (a one-page table); "Science Fiction Publishing" (eighteen pages), with essays on "The Science Fiction Magazines," by David Wingrove and "SF Publishing: The Economics," by Malcolm Edwards, and a six-page magazine checklist, listing editors and dates published (incomplete); "SF Criticism," with an introductory essay by Wingrove (three pages), and a checklist of reference and critical works (twelve pages); a brief "Afterword," by Kingsley Amis; and a detailed author/title index.

The center section of the book lists 880 science fiction authors arranged alphabetically by surname, including the following data: author's name (including middle names and real name if a pseudonym), years of birth and death (if known), photograph (for one writer in ten), nationality, a brief general appraisal of the author's contributions to the genre, with very short mentions of major works or series, and separate listings of the writer's major fictional works, including short fiction (comprising 2,500 analyzed entries for the entire chapter), each being categorized by a five-star system (0-5, 5 being best), separately for readability, characterization, idea content, and literary merit.

Most authors have at least one work analyzed; none has more than four. The critical summations range in size from 20-600 words, averaging about 80 words, and seem fair, if rather brief. Virtually every writer publishing a SF book in the twenty-five years prior to 1984 is included (SF being broadly defined to include fantasy), plus many other authors whose books had been out-of-print for decades. The selection criteria for the analyzed works is unclear, however, covering a hodgepodge of novels and shorter works without any clear indication why story "X" was chosen over book "Y," or which of the twelve critics participated in evaluating each title (it seems exceedingly unlikely that all dozen read all 2,500 items). This results in the evaluation of many obscure and second- or third-rate books, often penned by writers who had no more than one book published in their entire careers, while major books from better-known authors are omitted.

The "Criticism Checklist" contains no annotations, and includes "ghost" titles never actually published. The magazine annotations list title, nationality, number of issues published, dates published, and editors with dates of service, but the chapter omits many lesser publications. The front sections of the book, while readable, interesting, and authoritative (both Stableford and Aldiss know whereof they speak), seem markedly out of place, literary orphans flung willy-nilly into the front of a reference volume to make it more "interesting." This section also includes a number of illustrations from representative books and films, added without any attempt to make them relevant to the text.

The Science Fiction Sourcebook suffers from a lack of focus and editorial control; future editions, if there are any, should expand the author/book listings and dump much of the rest. Compare with Pringle's much superior *Ultimate Guide* (see #97).

107. Winter, Douglas E., ed. **Shadowings: The Reader's Guide to Horror Fiction, 1981-1982.** Mercer Island, WA, Starmont House, 1983. xi, 148 p. (Starmont Studies in Literary Criticism, No. 1). LC 83-21326. ISBN 0-916732-86-X; ISBN 0-916732-85-1 (pbk.).

Intended as the first of a series of annual or biennial guides to horror literature, this was the only volume actually published, for good reason: *Shadowings* is a hodgepodge of reviews, film critiques, and other miscellanea that never really gels as a reference work.

A lengthy twenty-four-page introduction by Winter provides a summary of the major literary events of the two-year period. This is followed by thirteen essays by different hands on twenty-three major horror books published during 1981-82. Part II includes essays on four rising stars of the horror genre, and Part III follows with another four pieces on "Things That Go Bump in the Movies" (major films of the period), an essay on film director David Cronenberg, a forum on "Horror and the Limits of Violence" with seven horror writers, and an article by Winter on the movie *Creepshow* and its relation to E.C. Comics. The final section, "The Year in Review," provides an unannotated list of major books, stories, films, and miscellanea published during 1981-82. "Notes on the Contributors" completes the book.

The essays vary widely in form and content, some being serious attempts to analyze the works in questions, others being sufficiently "airy" to float right off the page; most are at least entertaining, if not particularly deep. The text is poorly reproduced, many pages being faint and difficult to read. The absence of an index is unpardonable. A worthy failure, but a failure nonetheless.

108. Wolf, Leonard. **Horror: A Connoisseur's Guide to Literature and Film.** New York & Oxford, Facts on File, 1989. 262 p. index. LC 88-11126. ISBN 0-8160-1274-1; ISBN 0-8160-2197-X (pbk.).

Wolf gives us a personal guide to his favorite novels, stories, verse, and movies in the horror and supernatural genre, stating (in his six-page introduction):

> In this book, the reader will find a partial record of my own lis-
> tening. Let me say at once that the entries that follow do not constitute
> a list of the best stories and films ever made. Then, why were they
> chosen? For three reasons: historical spread, thematic variety and fun. I
> have tried, as I made my selections, to keep in mind that my readers are
> connoisseurs, people who have, or are acquiring, a wide and an instructed
> experience of horror literature. But there is no connoisseur worthy of the
> name who is not also having fun.

And this is really the sum of Wolf's eclectic guide: a potpourri of good, mediocre, and bad (but entertaining) films and fiction, each covered in very well-written annotations ranging in size from 100-1,000 words (averaging 300). Wolf has a certain panache that deftly combines plot summary, historical background, and criticism into 380 scintillating mini-essays that clearly define a very personal vision of what the horror genre is, and what it should be. Short stories, novels, films, even poetry, are all intermingled into one alphabetical sequence.

A typical fiction entry provides: title (bold caps), category (*e.g.,* "short story," "novel"), author's name, nationality of author, year of first publication (for short stories) and (for the latter) an anthology in which it has recently been reprinted, or (for novels) year, place of publication, and publisher of first edition, plus similar information for a recent reprint edition, and the annotation.

A typical film entry gives: title (bold caps), alternate titles, year of production, a code indicating color or black-and-white ("C" or "B&W"), nationality, running time, production company, director, producer, screenwriter, photographer, special effects technician, music, chief cast members (and the names of the characters they played), and annotation. The book is attractively illustrated throughout with black-and-white stills and author photographs. The index correlates authors and titles with page numbers, and a six-page bibliography provides a list of fiction and nonfiction for further reading.

Wolf's book cannot really be criticized as a reference work, since he makes no pretention of it being anything more than a personal selection of some of his favorite works. Thus, quibbling over the inclusion (or omission) of specific novels, short stories, or motion pictures would be fruitless. Nor can *Horror* be compared to other reader's guides on the subject. One can only react personally to this work: Wolf's coverage of specific short stories is unparalleled, his knowledge and range (from the Gothic period to modern times) are impressive, and his guide is among the most entertaining and readable such works this critic has yet encountered.

GUIDES TO SECONDARY SOURCES

SCOPE NOTE: Herein can be found general bibliographies and literary guides of critical materials, book reviews, and reference monographs specific to the study of fantastic literature. Bibliographies of secondary materials on individual writers can be found in the "Author Bibliographies" section.

109. Anthony, Piers. **Index to Book Reviews in Science Fiction Magazines, 1926-1963.** Gainesville, FL, Phyrne Bacon, 1966 (?). xvi, 119 p. (pbk.).

Intended as an adjunct to the Day/Metcalf/Strauss indexes to SF magazines (see #149, #156, #168), Anthony's guide includes: "Abbreviations Used in the Index"; "Introduction"; "Reviewer Supplement" (*i.e.,* alphabetical list of reviewers); "Partial Listing of Review Column Titles and Page Numbers"; and a 119-page printout of the books reviewed.

A typical entry includes: author of the book being reviewed, book title, single-letter subject code (*e.g.,* "V" = science fiction novel), month and year of publication of magazine, and three-letter magazine code (*e.g.,* "ASF" = *Astounding/Analog*), the latter adapted from Strauss's index (see #168). Anthony indexes reviews on all kinds of monographs, including general nonfiction works about science and cartoon books, in addition to SF materials.

This book was photocopied or mimeographed in a very limited edition, and is now virtually impossible to find. Wholly superseded by Hall (see #153), and of interest only because Anthony has since become a well-known SF and fantasy writer.

110. Briney, Robert E., and Edward Wood. **SF Bibliographies: An Annotated Bibliography of Bibliographical Works on Science Fiction and Fantasy Fiction.** Chicago, Advent:Publishers, 1972. ix, 49 p. index. LC 72-86150. ISBN 0-911682-19-8 (pbk.).

This guide to bibliographies and indexes of science fiction and fantasy published through 1971 includes a brief introduction, with the text being divided into four sections: "I. Magazine Indexes," arranged in alphabetical order by book title (thirty-two titles covered); "II. Bibliographies of Individual Authors," with four general bibliographies arranged alphabetically by book title, followed by thirty-one single-author bibliographies arranged by surname of the author being covered; "III. General Indexes and Checklists," including general and subject bibliographies arranged by book title (twenty-seven titles); and "IV. Foreign Language Bibliographies," including six volumes arranged by book title. An author/title index completes the book.

A typical entry includes: title, author/editor, publisher, place of publication, year of publication, pagination, format (*e.g.,* quarto), type of printing, type of binding, price (or an indication the book is out of print), and edition limitation, followed by a one- or two-paragraph essay. The annotations are brief (ranging from 20-200 words), descriptive, and evaluative.

While Briney and Wood's judgments are sound, *SF Bibliographies* is so far out-of-date as to render it almost useless, except as a guide to older small-circulation fan publications that are now almost impossible to find in any collection.

111. Clareson, Thomas D. **Science Fiction Criticism: An Annotated Checklist.** Kent, OH, Kent State University Press, 1972. 225 p. index. LC 71-181084. ISBN 0-87338-123-8.

The late Tom Clareson's work was the first major attempt to identify and describe the many works of SF criticism that were starting to appear in the 1960s and '70s covering works published between 1926 and 1971. The book is divided into nine subject areas: "General Studies"; "Literary Studies"; "Book Reviews"; "The Visual Arts"; "Futurology, Utopia, and Dystopia"; "Classroom and Library"; "Publishing"; "Specialist Bibliographies, Checklists, and Indices"; and "The Contemporary Scene."

Each section is arranged alphabetically by main entry (usually the author's surname, but by title if no author is shown). A typical entry includes: item number (assigned in consecutive order from the number one with each new chapter), author, title (books are listed in italics, short essays in quotations), collation (for books, this includes place of publication, publisher, and year of publication, but no paginations; for articles, Clareson lists the magazine or book in which the essay appeared [in italics], volume number, date [in parentheses], and page number); plus an annotation.

Clareson's comments range from 10-150 words, and are almost wholly descriptive rather than evaluative, often in a kind of telegraphed English; for example, he notes that Bleiler's *Checklist of Fantastic Literature:*

> Lists 5,000 titles, British and American, from medieval period to 1947. Main listing by author is indexed by title. An "annotated list of critical and historical reference works," some sixty-five titles, focuses upon the Gothic and 19th century.

This gives us basic information on how Bleiler's is organized and what it purports to contain, but it fails to indicate whether the book succeeds in its mission.

An "Author Index of Entries" and an "Index of [other] Authors Mentioned" complete the book; both indices cite name, chapter, and item number only, but since there are no running chapter heads, the indices are virtually useless without constant referrals to the table of contents, a major flaw in this volume.

Dr. Clareson, one of the "grand old men" of science fiction criticism, founded *Extrapolation,* the first journal devoted to the study of fantastic literature (in which the early version of this book originally appeared as a series of articles in 1970-71); he clearly knows his sources well and has employed that knowledge fully here. While no book of this type is ever complete, *Science Fiction Criticism* includes a remarkably large number of entries for its period, including many studies that would prove difficult to locate even today. The work was supplemented by the several volumes of Tymn and Schlobin's *Year's Scholarship in Science Fiction and Fantasy* (see #130).

112. Crawford, Gary William, Frederick S. Frank, Benjamin Franklin Fisher IV, and Kent Ljungquist. **The 1980 Bibliography of Gothic Studies.** Baton Rouge, LA, Gothic Press, 1983. ii, 20 p. (The Gothic Chapbooks, No. 1). ISBN 0-913045-00-4 (pbk.).

Two previous versions of this annual guide to gothic criticism were published in the periodical *Gothic* (in the December 1979 issue [for 1978 materials] and in December 1980 [for 1979]), but this was the first (and last) volume in the series to appear as a separately published monograph.

Entries are broken into several sections: "I. Bibliographical and Textual Studies"; "II. General Studies"; "III. Author and Comparative Studies." Within these chapters materials arranged alphabetically by author's surname. A typical periodical entry includes: author, title (in quotes), magazine title (italics), volume number, pagination, brief (one- to two-sentence) annotation). A typical monograph entry provides: author, title (italics), place of publication, publisher, and a two- to three-sentence annotation, but no paginations. The annotations are descriptive rather than evaluative. "Gothic" is here broadly defined to include modern horror fiction.

Now completely superseded by Fisher (see #113) and Frank (see #114 and #115).

113. Fisher, Benjamin Franklin IV. **The Gothic's Gothic: Study Aids to the Tradition of the Tale of Terror.** New York & London, Garland Publishing, 1988. xix, 485 p. index. (Garland Reference Library of the Humanities, Vol. 567). LC 88-18059. ISBN 0-8240-8784-4. Includes a loose errata page.

Fisher, a well-known critic and bibliographer of mystery and gothic fiction, here contributes an annotated guide to secondary sources on gothic writers and literature.

The book is divided into two major sections: "1. Authors" and "2. Subjects," the "Authors" section comprising the majority (299 pages) of the text. Part One is arranged by the name of the author being critiqued, in chronological order by the approximate date when the writer became known (these dates are never stated, only implied), and then alphabetically by main entry. A typical author entry gives: writer's name (centered, boldfaced head in inverse order with dates and nationality; *e.g.,* "Leland, Thomas (1722-1785): British"), followed by a list of books and periodical articles about the author or his or her writings.

A typical critical citation includes: entry number, critic's name (uncredited materials are filed under "Anon.," in alphabetical order by title), title (in quotes for periodical articles, in italics for books), bibliographical data, and a one- to two-sentence descriptive annotation (*e.g.,* "Scattered analyses of blending horror with humor."). Bibliographical data include (for articles): magazine title (in italics), volume number, month and year of publication, pagination; and for monographs: place of publication, publisher, year of publication, and pagination only for those items where specific page numbers are referenced within the text (for those monographs that deal with the author's corpus *in toto,* no paginations are given).

Entries are numbered consecutively throughout the book from 1-2614. Part One also includes three small "dump" categories at the end of the section: "Miscellaneous American Gothics, Chronologically Arranged"; "Miscellaneous Later British Gothics, Chronologically Arranged"; "Miscellaneous Foreign Gothics, Chronologically Arranged."

Part Two (134 pages of text) is broken into broad and specific subject categories, including "Historical, General Critical, and Bibliographical Accounts: British and Continental"; "Historical, General Critical, and Bibliographical Accounts: American and Canadian" (these two sections occupy forty pages of text); and other miscellaneous categories such as "Orientalism," "Anti-Gothic Materials," "Faust," "Science Fiction and Fantasy," "Doubles," etc. (twenty-eight categories in all).

Each of these chapters is arranged in alphabetical order by main entry, with data elements similar to those in Part One. Some foreign-language authors and critical materials are included, although the general focus throughout remains on British and American literature. The book includes three very comprehensive indices, all referencing item numbers: "Author, Artist, Subject Index"; "Title Index"; and "Critic Index." The volume is attractively typeset and bound to library standards.

Despite the thorough indexing, there are some obvious problems here, both with organization and selection criteria. In Part One, the organization of the 110 separate author sections is not obvious even to the most sophisticated of users, despite the fact that a complete list of the writers is provided in the table of contents. Nor is it clear why some writers were separated into their own categories, and others of potentially equal merit were dumped into the three miscellaneous categories at the end of the section.

All of this makes access to information in the book unnecessarily difficult. For example, Ann Radcliffe's chapter runs from pages 16-27, including entries #86-158; the subject index lists over 200 other references, with no indication what subjects or aspects these items may contain, requiring the reader to examine each one individually to determine content. An alphabetical arrangement of the authors in Part One would have been much clearer: the user should have been able to go directly to the section on Radcliffe without searching either the contents page or index, and should have been able to determine from the index specifically what subjects the other references to Radcliffe's work might cover.

One must also question the choice of authors and subject entries for twentieth-century materials. In precisely what sense, for example, is Carson McCullers a "gothic writer," or John Hawkes, Margaret Atwood, Truman Capote, William Faulkner, and Stephen King? Fisher includes King and H. P. Lovecraft, both well-known horror writers, but excludes most other twentieth-century writers of the supernatural. Why?

Again, why does Fisher include subject chapters on "Detective/Mystery Fiction," "Science Fiction and Fantasy," or "Racial Issues"? None of these questions are answered, none of the author's choices explained.

It is also within these modern sections that one spots the most obvious lacunae in coverage: Fisher's coverage of Stephen King is laughable, consisting of two wholly minor entries from *People* magazine and *The New York Times Book Review,* and ignoring dozens of widely available critical articles and monographs. Similarly, if Fisher includes Bleiler's *The Checklist of Fantastic Literature* (see #208), how can he ignore Reginald's *Science Fiction and Fantasy Literature* (see #212)?

The Radcliffe entries provide a good comparison between Fisher's guide and his four major competitors, since all include individual sections on this seminal gothic writer. Fisher includes seventy-three entries, Frank's *Gothic Fiction* (see #114) 123 entries, Frank's *Guide to the Gothic* (see #115) 121 entries, McNutt's *The Eighteenth-Century Gothic Novel* (see #123) 117 entries, and Spector's *The English Gothic* (see #125) 129 entries, with the second Frank volume and Spector also providing annotations that are generally longer than Fisher's. Overall, Fisher provides more entries than the largest of these other works, particularly the two Frank volumes, but exceeds these volumes only by a couple hundred items. All five books include at least a few entries in their Radcliffe sections not found in the other four.

Fisher's strongest point is his coverage of materials on the early gothic, especially references to materials on a particular author contained in larger works on other writers or subjects: there are literally hundreds of such items here, many not caught in Frank's two works. For further comparisons, see the Frank entries (#114 and #116).

Nota bene: although Fisher's was the latest published of these five bibliographies, his coverage ceases with 1978, apparently on the theory that the annual volumes of *The Bibliography of Gothic Studies* (see #112) would provide sufficient coverage thereafter. Since these slim booklets are virtually unobtainable in university libraries, and in any case ceased publication in 1980, one must question this editorial decision, along with so many others, and defer to Frank's books, which operate under no such self-imposed limitations, particularly with the release of *Guide to the Gothic II.*

114. Frank, Frederick S. **Gothic Fiction: A Master List of Twentieth Century Criticism and Research.** Westport, CT, Meckler, 1988. xv, 193 p. index. (Meckler's Bibliographies on Science Fiction, Fantasy and Horror, 3). LC 87-24705. ISBN 0-88736-218-4.

Frank is an acknowledged expert on the history of the gothic, particularly the classic gothic of the late eighteenth and early nineteenth centuries, so it is no surprise that his latest book, a comprehensive guide to secondary sources, is authoritative and complete; unfortunately, this is also one of its major problems.

Gothic Fiction includes a brief introductory history of gothic criticism and bibliography, including analyses of all previous attempts to list secondary sources on the gothic. The bibliography itself is organized into (appropriately enough!) thirteen chapters: "English Gothic Fiction: Primary and Secondary Bibliographies, Special Collections, Research and Reference Works"; "English Gothic Fiction: Literary Histories, Theories and Formal Definitions, Genre Studies"; "English Gothic Fiction: Individual Author Studies," including fourteen subsections on specific writers arranged by surname of the author being covered; "English Gothic Fiction: Special Subject Areas," with nine subsections such as "Gothic Parodies and Parodists" and "Pre-Gothic Tendencies and Graveyard Verse"; "American Gothic Fiction: General Histories, Critical Surveys, Definitions of Genre"; "American Gothic Fiction: Individual Author Studies," broken into ten subsections on specific writers, plus an eleventh section on "Later American Gothic (1820-1985), including Faulkner, Flannery O'Connor, Stephen King and the Popular American Gothic"; "The French Gothic Novel or Roman Noir"; "The German Gothic Novel or Schauerroman"; "Other National Gothics and Comparative Gothicisms"; "Special Gothic Themes: The Evil Eye, Spontaneous Combustion, Science Fiction Gothic, Prominent Gothicists, Writing the Gothic Novel"; "The Wandering Jew and the Double Figure"; "Werewolfery and Vampirism"; and "The Gothic Film: A Selective Listing." A brief addenda of two items, and indices of critics and of authors and artists, complete the book.

The 2,491 entries are numbered consecutively from the number one, the indices referencing critics and authors with item numbers only. Entries are arranged in alphabetical order by main entry (usually author or editor), by section and/or subsection, depending on the chapter (as indicated above). A typical entry includes: author, title (underlined for books, in quotes for articles), and bibliographical data (complete paginations for articles or essays included in anthologies, but no paginations for books). There are no annotations. Many foreign sources are listed in addition to the standard English-language works. The book was shot from word-processed copy but is generally clear and legible throughout. Entries as late as 1987 are included.

Frank is very thorough in his coverage of the early gothic novel; indeed, *Gothic Fiction* will undoubtedly become (with Fisher's work, #89) a standard source for secondary materials on this era. Frank's bibliography is better organized than Fisher's, with the author studies section being arranged more logically, but Frank also has the same problem as Fisher in defining twentieth-century materials and writers.

One can make a legitimate case for including materials on the modern gothic, which was developed as a paperback genre (with a very specific cover package) by Donald A. Wollheim and Evelyn Grippo at Ace Books in 1960 and was virtually dead by 1980, even though there is a vast difference in style, content, and intent between the two. The modern version at least hearkened back to the original literary tradition, although it basically followed the precepts and forms of the popular women's romance genre. But in what sense is H. P. Lovecraft, the twentieth-century American horror writer, a gothicist, or Stephen King, William Faulkner, Flannery O'Connor, or Russell Kirk?

Like Fisher, Frank includes a few modern horror writers and ignores the rest, and as with his competitor's volume, his coverage of materials for the modern writers that he *has* chosen is lamentably incomplete, missing major and minor sources obvious to any real student of modern horror literature.

Frank also makes the same unfortunate choices as Fisher in several other sections. In the first chapter, which includes bibliographies of gothic fiction, Frank lists such works as Bleiler's *The Checklist of Science-Fiction and Supernatural Fiction* (see #208), Hubin's *The Bibliography of Crime Fiction, 1749-1975,* and Tymn's *Horror Literature* (see #102), but omits Reginald's *Science Fiction and Fantasy Literature* (see #212), which parallels and exceeds Bleiler in coverage, as well as the second, much expanded edition of Hubin's bibliography (1984) and other similar works. Questions such as "Are all vampire and werewolf stories *per se* gothics?" are never answered, or even asked.

Similarly, the admittedly incomplete listing of materials on the "gothic film" includes a wide variety of books and essays on Frankenstein films, vampire films, horror films in general, Dracula films, and werewolf films. Are these also gothics? What exactly *is* a gothic? Frank's (and Fisher's) responses to such questions seem to rely more on serendipitous encounters than on any reasoned definition of this genre. Finally, although the author indexes are comprehensive, the absence of a title listing in Frank is most unfortunate.

Frank's coverage of secondary sources for the classic gothic is about the same as Fisher's bibliography. Although both books include unique entries, and neither has any significant advantage over the other, the deficiencies of one cancel out those of its competitor. For the record, Fisher has a few hundred more entries and brief annotations, while Frank includes an extra decade of coverage without annotations (but Frank's earlier bibliography [see #115] *is* annotated). Scholars (and academic libraries) will need to maintain copies of all three bibliographies.

A second edition of Frank should include a title index, and both authors need to rethink their basic definitions of the field before embarking on newer versions of their books.

115. Frank, Frederick S. **Guide to the Gothic: An Annotated Bibliography of Criticism.** Metuchen, NJ & London, The Scarecrow Press, 1984. xvi, 421 p. index. LC 83-24507. ISBN 0-8108-1669-5. **Guide to the Gothic II: An Annotated Bibliography of Criticism, 1983-1993.** Lanham, MD, Scarecrow Press, 1995. xvii, 523 p. index. LC 94-39101. ISBN 0-8108-2968-1.

Frank's interest in the bibliographical control of secondary gothic literature dates to at least 1973, when his article, "The Gothic Novel: A Checklist of Modern Criticism," appeared in the *Bulletin of Bibliography.* Much of the *Guide* overlaps with his later volume, *Gothic Fiction* (see #114), although this book does include annotations.

The *Guide* is broken into several major sections: "Previous Guides to the Gothic"; "English Gothic"; "Canadian Gothic"; "American Gothic"; "French Gothic"; "German Gothic"; "Other National Gothics"; and "Special Subject Areas." The Second Edition has a similar but slightly expanded arrangement: "Previous Guides to the Gothic: Research and Reference Works"; "English Gothic Fiction: General Histories, Definitions, Theories"; "English Gothic Fiction: Individual Authors"; "American Gothic Fiction: General Histories and Critical Studies"; "American Gothic Fiction: Individual Authors"; "Other National Gothics: Individual Nations and Authors"; "Special Subject Areas."

Most of these sections are further divided into chapters on specific writers (for the national gothics) and/or subjects. Under each subdivision, entries are arranged alphabetically by main entry. A typical entry includes: item number, critic's name, title (periodical articles in quotes, books underlined), bibliographical data (for periodical articles: journal title [underlined], volume number, year of publication, and pagination; for monographs: place of publication, publisher, year of publication, but no paginations), and a one-paragraph descriptive annotation averaging fifty words in length.

Entries are numbered consecutively in the first book from 1-2,508, and from 0001-1547 in the second; some items are repeated in more than one section and are renumbered with each appearance, making a total entry count problematical. End matter in Volume I includes a "List of Journals" (now largely useless), an "Index of Critics" (keyed to item number), and an "Index of Authors, Artists, and Actors" (also referenced to item number), but, astonishingly, no title index. The supplemental volume includes an "Index of Critics, Editors, Illustrators, and Translators," keyed to item number, and an "Index of Authors, Titles, Artists, and Actors," also referenced to item number. A boldfaced number sequence in the latter index indicates an entire section devoted to that particular author or title. It should be noted, however, that the critical works covered in these volumes are *not* indexed, a major lapse.

The arrangement of the authors is chronological, as in Fisher's book (see #113), making access occasionally difficult for the casual user; this is mitigated, however, by the detailed contents page and indexes. As with Fisher's works, there are some problems with definition, scope, and coverage for the modern period (see the discussion in #114). The several Frank bibliographies contain very close correspondences in certain chapters, as one might expect; for example, the coverage of German gothics in *Gothic Fiction* includes seventy entries in one unbroken alphabetical sequence without annotations; in *Guide* the coverage is broken into nine subsections, seven dealing with an individual writer, also totalling seventy entries, but twenty-nine of these are "See" references to entries elsewhere in the book, although they are also numbered in sequence here.

Since none of the unreferenced entries are missing from *Gothic Fiction,* the later book is clearly more comprehensive (and easier to use), but *Guide to the Gothic* does provide annotations longer than those in Fisher's bibliography, and its internal references, although occasionally irritating, could also be useful to the scholar by providing additional subject access while bypassing the index. The first *Guide* is shot from occasionally faint typed copy, but the second is typeset.

The second *Guide* is considered an "autonomous bibliography, reflecting acute shifts in Gothic novel scholarship." It includes some material missed from the first volume, plus a great many new entries published during the decade 1983-93. A typical entry contains: reference number (assigned sequentially throughout the book from the number 0001), author, book title (italics) or article (quotation marks), publication information, and a usually non-evaluative annotation ranging from a brief sentence to four pages, with very helpful detailed contents notes for anthologies and major reference works. Frank will occasionally provide a brief evaluative remark, such as "a superlative collection" or "fascinating."

The section titled "Other National Gothics: Individual Nations and Authors" covers primarily French and German works, with some mention of Russian, Spanish, and Portuguese publications. "Special Subject Areas" cover Romantic Poets, Victorian Gothic, Vampirism and Werewolfery, Popular Culture, Recent Anthologies, Special Collections, and Gothic Film Criticism.

The second edition exceeds its predecessor both in total pagination, scope, range, and depth of coverage, without supplanting it, reflecting the growth of modern criticism on and interest in gothic literature; but this vast increase in new material has created a few other problems with the *Guide.* A quick examination of the new Stephen King section in *Guide II,* for example, reveals at least one "ghost" title, *The Stephen King Concordance,* and another critique recorded under an erroneous title, *The Reader's Guide to Stephen King.*

Similarly, the contents of Schweitzer's 1985 critical anthology, *Discovering Stephen King,* are not recorded in the entry for that book (as is usual), but the essays are covered individually throughout the King section; however, a second anthology, *Discovering Stephen King II,* is listed with just the brief description, "Second volume of critical essays, again, of uneven quality." Alas and alack, we should pity poor Mr. Schweitzer: the material in his books is so untrustworthy (in Frank's considered opinion) that it's roundly condemned here without ever having been seen, either by Frank or by anyone else, since Schweitzer's volume was never actually published or even compiled, merely contemplated.

Still, with all their attendant faults, both in structure and content, the two *Guides* together form the best single source of information now available to the scholar of gothic literature and film; and must be thus abided, like some scruffy cousin from the sticks with whom one would prefer not to associate, but whose inherent wealth or position makes the occasional meeting regretably necessary.

Recommended for major university library collections.

116. Hall, Hal W. **Science Fiction Book Review Index, 1923-1973.** Detroit, Gale Research Co., 1975. xvi, 438 p. index. LC 74-29085. ISBN 0-8103-1054-6. **Science Fiction Book Review Index, 1974-1979.** Detroit, Gale Research Co., 1981. xx, 391 p. index. LC 81-1490. ISBN 0-8103-1107-0. Hall, Hal W., and Geraldine L. Hutchins. **Science Fiction and Fantasy Book Review Index, 1980-1984: An Index to More Than 13,800 Book Reviews**

Appearing in Over 70 Science Fiction, Fantasy, and General Periodicals from 1980 to 1984 and Containing "Science Fiction and Fantasy Research Index," an Index to Secondary Literature, Providing Nearly 16,000 Subject and Author Access Points to Articles, Essays, and Books Featuring the History of, or Criticism on, Science Fiction and Fantasy Literature, Television Programs, Motion Pictures, and Graphic Arts. Detroit, Gale Research Co., 1985. xxi, 761 p. index. LC 85-25219. ISBN 0-8103-1646-3. **Science Fiction and Fantasy Book Review Index, Volume 16, 1985.** Bryan, TX, SFBRI, 1988. 69 p. index. LC 72-625320. ISBN 0-935064-20-6 (pbk.). San Bernardino, CA, The Borgo Press, 1988. 69 p. index. ISBN 0-89370-531-4. Previous annual editions were published beginning in 1970 by SFBRI in paperback, often with the title *SFBRI: Science Fiction Book Review Index,* and in 1980 in simultaneous library cloth editions by Borgo Press (including those released during the preceding decade). *Volumes 17-19* were published by SFBRI in paper and by Borgo Press in cloth in 1992, and *Volume 20* by SFBRI and Borgo in 1993, bringing coverage up to 1989.

Hall's is the only work that attempts systematically to record book reviews on works of fantastic literature (and associated primary and secondary publications) in fan, professional, and library journals worldwide. Originally conceived as a series of annual volumes published by Hall himself under the SFBRI imprint, the first four books were cumulated and extended into a retrospective volume extending back to the beginnings of the field as an identifiable genre. From the very beginning Hall included all reviews appearing in the SF professional magazines, scholarly journals, and major fan publications, with selected coverage of SF books reviewed in the major library serials, particularly *Library Journal, Horn Book, Choice, Booklist,* and *Kirkus Reviews,* such major English literary journals as *English Journal* and *Elementary English,* and such popular magazines as *Time* and *Newsweek.* The set is arranged alphabetically by author of the book being reviewed, then alphabetically by book title under each author, where more than one book by the writer has been reviewed.

A typical entry includes: author or editor (in boldface beginning with the third Gale volume), title (underlined), place of publication, publisher, year of publication, pagination, LC card number (sporadically, in the first two volumes only), and a list of the reviews arranged alphabetically in descending order by one- to five-letter abbreviations identifying each publication in which the review appeared, with volume number (or issue number if the magazine issues are numbered consecutively without volume), issue number in parentheses (if the publication has a volume number), pagination (following a colon), date of issue, and reviewer (in parentheses, with the first name of the reviewer abbreviated to an initial letter). The abbreviations lists are provided in the front of each volume and also on the endsheets of the second and third Gale books; many of the initials will be obvious to anyone familiar with library and SF publications. A title/author index completes each work.

The second half of the third Gale cumulation is an early version of the *Science Fiction and Fantasy Reference Index* (see #117), and thus will not be annotated separately here. The first two Gale volumes were shot from typed copy, the third (and the more recent annuals) from word-processed copy; all are legible and easy to follow, although boldfacing the authors' names in the more recent books does help make the entries stand out better.

It's difficult to imagine how any scholar even remotely interested in fantastic literature could bypass these volumes. Hall has gradually increased his coverage over the years to include a number of foreign publications difficult to find in the United States, some additional fanzines, and scholarly journals that rarely review SF materials. While no book of this type is ever complete, it is hard to see where large numbers of additional sources may be found. This is one of the major reference tools of fantastic literature.

117. Hall, Hal W. **Science Fiction and Fantasy Reference Index, 1878-1985: An International Author and Subject Index to History and Criticism.** Detroit, Gale Research Co., 1987. xviii, xx, 1,460 p. in 2 v. index. LC 87-173. ISBN 0-8103-2129-7 (set). **Science Fiction and Fantasy Reference Index, 1985-1991: An International Author and Subject Index to History and Criticism.** Englewood, CO, Libraries Unlimited, Inc., 1993. xxii, 677 p. index. LC 92-43531. ISBN 1-56308-113-X. **Science Fiction and Fantasy Reference Index, 1992-1995 : An International Subject and Author Index to History and Criticism.** Englewood, CO, 1997. xxi, 503 p. index. LC 97-10057. ISBN 1-56308-527-5. Previous annual editions were published beginning in 1981 as *Science Fiction Research Index, Volume 1,* and *Science Fiction and Fantasy Research Index, Volumes 2-3,* by SFBRI (paper) and Borgo Press (cloth), *Volume 4* (by Hall and Geraldine Hutchins) by SFBRI and Borgo, *Volume 5* (by Hall and Hutchins) by Borgo only in cloth, *Volume 6* (by Hall alone) by Borgo only in cloth, *Volume 7* (by Hall and Jan Swanbeck) by Borgo only in cloth, *Volumes 8-10* by Borgo only in cloth; all were later incorporated into the cumulated volumes.

Contents (for the two Libraries Unlimited volumes): "Preface"; "Books Analyzed"; "Magazines Indexed"; "Acknowledgments"; "Subject Index"; "Author Index."

Hall's continuing reference series has become the standard guide to secondary sources in the field of fantastic literature (including science fiction, fantasy, and horror). Hall divides his material into two sections: "Subject Index" or "Subject Entries" and "Author Index" or "Author Entries."

In the original set, the first division arranges the data alphabetically by critic or bibliographer, and typically includes: author (as a boldfaced head), title (articles in quotes, books underlined), and bibliographical data. The latter include, for books: place of publication, publisher, year of publication, and pagination; for articles appearing in journals: magazine title (underlined), volume number, issue number (in parentheses), pagination, month and year of publication; for articles appearing in books: editor of book, book title (underlined), place of publication, publisher, year of publication, specific pagination of article within the volume.

The second section rearranges the material by subject, then alphabetically under each header by title. A typical entry includes: subject heading (bold caps), author, title (articles in quotes, book titles underlined), author (where appropriate; many of the entries were anonymously contributed), and the same bibliographical data included in the Author Entries section. Entries may be indexed very specifically by proper name, and/or into such broader topics as "Science in SF," "Definitions," and "Romanticism." In general, the subject indexing seems at least adequate to allow the user access to the most obviously desired points of each essay. Also included in the Gale volumes are a "Thesaurus of Science Fiction and Fantasy Indexing Terms (Proper Names and Movie Titles Excluded)" and "Lists of Sources" (with title [in italics], author, place of publication, publisher, year of publication, pagination).

The first supplement (1985-1991) adds more than 16,250 of the most significant secondary materials (books, articles, and news reports) in the science fiction, fantasy, and horror genres in the English language. "Coverage of European material is representative, not comprehensive." The magazines *Locus, Fantasy Times/Science Fiction Times,* and *Science Fiction Chronicle* are almost completely indexed, as well as many other publications.

Both Libraries Unlimited supplements reverse the order of information presentation from the original volumes, placing the subject section first. A typical subject entry includes: subject heading (all caps), and a complete citation, including pagination. Subject entries are subdivided alphabetically under each subject by author's surname; works without authors are listed in alphabetical order by title prior to the author listings. A subject may have as many as 50 records attached to it, but many have only one or two.

A typical author entry includes: author's name (inverted, all caps), plus the essays, essays within books, edited books, and monographs that person has written, arranged in alphabetical order by title. Full citations are provided, with complete paginations and using no abbreviations, which greatly facilitates the user's access to the material. Book titles are listed in bold type in both sections.

The second supplement (1992-1995) adds coverage of another 10,625 titles, including some retrospective materials not found in any earlier volume. The nature of these publications is serial, requiring libraries to retain all of the books for complete coverage.

Although the Clareson/Tymn volumes (see #111) include some older entries not found in Hall, there is in fact a huge disparity in the number of entries that Hall lists as compared to all other published sources combined. His coverage of secondary materials for fantastic literature is quite simply unsurpassed, including thousands of entries from U.S. and foreign sources that are mentioned nowhere else. It is thus difficult to imagine how any researcher worthy of the name could possibly begin a critique or bibliography without first doing a literature search through these volumes. Also, the very specific subject indexing and the descriptive nature of the titles themselves somewhat alleviate the absence of annotations and the lack of an index, both of which would be desirable additions to future versions.

These are necessary purchases for all academic libraries and all large public libraries, and for the personal libraries of all serious SF researchers.

118. Haschak, Paul G. **Utopian/Dystopian Literature: A Bibliography of Literary Criticism.** Metuchen, NJ, Scarecrow Press, 1994. viii, 370 p. index. LC 93-30232. ISBN 0-8108-2752-2 (acid free paper).

Contents: "Preface"; "Listings"; "Appendix"; "Title Index"; "Critic Index"; "About the Author."

This checklist is devoted exclusively to listing general literary criticism of individual utopian and dystopian plays, short stories, novels, novellas, and prose writing.

The book is arranged alphabetically by the name of the author being covered, and then by subsection, covering "General Criticism" of each writer, and then the individual works, alphabetically by title (short stories are flanked by quotation marks). Authors' names are listed in all caps, surnames given first; titles are recorded in boldfaced type. The book includes approximately 3,600 entries covering ancient and modern authors.

The typical criticism entry includes: critic's name (surname listed first), title of the item (in quotation marks), periodical title in which it appeared (italics), volume number, date and year of publication, and specific pagination. Entries that comprise chapters from larger monographs include: publisher and place of publication and pagination. The critical monographs covered are included in the appendix, which lists anthologies by title, and single-authored works by the name of the critic, providing: author (or editor), book title (in italics), place of publication, publisher, and date of publication, but no overall paginations.

The title index lists the primary works covered in the bibliography, plus the author's surname in parentheses and the page number referenced in this book; the critic index cross-references the secondary material by author and page number.

One small drawback of the volume is its layout. The eye can easily miss the major headings for the primary authors (all-caps), because the sub-headings for the primary works (in bold italics) tend to stand out much more. There are no page headings to guide the reader through the alphabetical list. Certainly this could be improved in a subsequent edition.

Another question that always arises with a book of this type is the issue of comprehensiveness, but there is no easy way that this can be measured. One can say with certainty that the number of essays listed herein on SF writer Ursula K. Le Guin is far less than the body of criticism known to exist about that author; however, since Haschak is only including materials dealing with the utopian or dystopian aspects of each writer's work, this *per se* reduces the overall coverage considerably.

However, on the whole the material seems comprehensive and sound, and provides a good starting point for the researcher. Recommended for academic libraries.

119. Justice, Keith L. **Science Fiction, Fantasy, and Horror Reference: An Annotated Bibliography of Works about Literature and Film.** Jefferson, NC and London, McFarland & Co., Publishers, 1989. xiii, 226 p. index. LC 89-2841. ISBN 0-89950-406-X.

It is difficult to do justice to this work. On the one hand, the main title suggests a comprehensive bibliography of SF reference works, while on the other, the subtitle and contents actually provide something very different indeed. This curious dichotomy is symptomatic of a basic flaw at the heart of this work, an absence of focus and a certain muddiness in concept that combine to strangle this book before it ever achieves life.

Some of the problems become clear in Justice's introduction. He states:

> This bibliography was compiled to help librarians, collectors, researchers, and others with an interest in SF/fantasy/horror reference materials determine what books might be of use or interest to them or their library's patrons. The book is not comprehensive; however, it is the first book ever published which is devoted exclusively to listing and evaluating secondary materials (books) for the SF, fantasy, and horror genres.

The latter statement is not quite true, even in the sense that Justice intends, for while there indeed exists no other book *exactly* like his, there are in fact many other sources that evaluate SF secondary materials to a greater or lesser degree. But even if we accept his statement at face value, we soon begin wondering what exactly is included here, and why.

Justice annotates 305 books in nine sections: "1. General History & Criticism"; "2. Author Studies"; "3. General Bibliographies"; "4. Author Bibliographies"; "5. Biography, Autobiography, Letters & Interviews"; "6. Encyclopedias, Dictionaries, Indexes & Checklists"; "7. Television, Film & Radio"; "8. Comics, Art & Illustration"; "9. Anthologies,

Collections & Annotated Editions." Three appendices include "I. Evaluations of Critical and Bibliographical Book Series"; "II. Critical and Bibliographical Book Series Title Listings"; "III. Suggested Core Collection Checklist." Three indices, by subject, title, and author/editor/compiler/major contributor, provide quick and easy access to specific item numbers only.

In each section, entries are arranged alphabetically by main entry (author, editor, or compiler); entries are numbered consecutively from 1-305. A typical entry includes: item number and author (boldface type), title (italics), place of publication, publisher, year of publication, pagination, and a three-letter reference code to a basic list of five publications providing other annotations or sources (the master index to codes is buried in the introduction rather than on a separate page, making access more difficult than it should have been). The annotations are both descriptive and evaluative, and range in size from 150-400 words, averaging 250.

There is very little correlation here between inherent value and size of annotation: a six-page checklist on little-known British author Barrington Bayley receives as much notice as Aldiss and Harrison's major anthology of autobiographical essays, *Hell's Cartographers*. Justice's comments also vary widely in scope and content: he correctly analyzes some of the structural problems with Holdstock's *Encyclopedia* (see #9) and Ash's *Who's Who* (see #51), but completely misses the second and third Editions of Barron's standard guide, *Anatomy of Wonder* (see #62), which should be readily accessible to any researcher in the field, and thus also misses the many important changes in the evolution of that publication. Justice provides a good summary of Jakubowski and Edwards's *SF Book of Lists* (see #43), but clearly has no knowledge of Ashley's competing volume, which appeared virtually simultaneously.

This hit-or-miss anarchy pervades the entire volume: major and minor reference tools and other sources may or may not be covered, unpredictably and completely at random. Justice's haphazard selectiveness becomes even more apparent as it progresses, for, although this book was published in 1989, it misses many of the major works of the 1980s, particularly those published after 1985; and also fails to take into account numerous new editions, new developments in publishers' series, and significant new titles in general.

For example, Starmont House had produced thirty-seven titles in its Starmont Reader's Guides (not Readers' Guides, as Justice has it) series of SF critiques through the end of 1988; Justice provides annotations for just ten, missing the very first book in the series, on Arthur C. Clarke, which went through two separate editions, while covering volumes 2-8, 18, 20, and 22. Where are the others? Similarly, Justice covers just twenty books (out of forty-one) produced in The Milford Series through 1988, and virtually misses coverage of the Masters of Science Fiction and Fantasy Series (which had ceased by 1984; see #300), reviewing just one title of these major author bibliographies (out of fourteen produced) on Robert Silverberg, and even there his few general comments on the Masters Series and on the Silverberg bibliography demonstrate a woeful lack of understanding of how and why and for what audience these books were produced.

Justice's volume also has a few structural problems. The format (alphabetically by main entry) works well for the general chapters, but surely must be questioned in "Section 2: Author Studies" and "Section 4: Author Bibliographies," where the average reader would reasonably expect to find the material arranged by name of the author *being covered* instead of the author producing the book. The appendices seem dated and largely irrelevant, although the brief core collection list will be useful for public libraries.

One must not dismiss this book completely out-of-hand, however. Justice does provide annotations for some critical materials at lengths available in no other source, and his comments are generally fair and competent, if not particularly deep. If reworked into a general readers' guide to critical materials, his volume has some future possibilities. Otherwise, it can be employed (with caution) as no more than a supplemental adjunct to the SF reference collection.

120. Justice, Keith L. **Science Fiction Master Index of Names.** Jefferson, NC and London, McFarland & Co., Publishers, 1986. vi, 394 p. index. LC 85-42533. ISBN 0-89950-183-4.

Justice indexes personal name references in 132 SF critical and reference works published between 1953-84, putting them into one alphabet arranged by surname, and keying each entry to a three-letter code representing the book title of the work cited, plus page numbers where appropriate.

The book includes: several introductions by Justice explaining how the book is organized, a list of the works cited arranged in alphabetical order by each book's three-letter code, the index itself (367 pages), and two checklists of the works cited by author and by title, the latter also including place of publication, publisher, and year of publication. Roughly 18,000 names are covered, with citations ranging from one reference to several hundred for a writer such as Robert A. Heinlein, averaging five per writer. There are copious "See" and "See Also" references to and from other pseudonyms used by each author; slight variations of one name are centralized under the most common variation. Middle names and years of birth and death are included when known.

Justice's index is a handy guide to many of the books annotated in this volume and, although it was shot from typed copy, is both legible and easy to use. Unfortunately, it suffers from a certain overzealousness, since not all of the works cited are comparable to the others, either in design, function, status, or worth; and there is often no easy way to determine what the citation represents without looking at the original work. For example, the entry for Robert Reginald cites two reviews of a Reginald work, fourteen essays by Reginald on other writers, a contents list of an anthology edited by Reginald, a biography of author Robert Silverberg in a work compiled by Reginald, two biographies and one bibliography of Reginald, and a passing reference to a Reginald book. One might wish to have access to all of these citations, if one were doing an extensive biography or bibliography of Reginald; however, the casual user who just wants a biography or other brief data would have a difficult time wading through these entries and discerning which is which.

This situation is compounded a hundredfold with such major SF authors as Isaac Asimov, whose entry occupies nearly a full page of double-column text. The problem may be endemic to a work of this type, but could have been helped with some annotations of the books themselves, indicating generally what each contains (this is not always obvious from the work's title). Also, there is no indication (other than the ready availability of the work to Justice) why certain titles were analyzed and others presumably just as worthy were not. Major reference tools lie side by side with slim critical texts, each given equal weight here.

Despite these *caveats,* the *Master Index of Names* can be an extremely useful shortcut to the researcher or student who understands its limitations and who already has some basic familiarity with the major reference works in the field. It should certainly be continued and expanded with supplements or future editions.

121. Lerner, Fred. **An Annotated Checklist of Science Fiction Bibliographical Works.** East Paterson, NJ, Fred Lerner, 1969. [7] p. (pbk.).

A brief selected annotated bibliography of SF reference tools arranged in alphabetical order by title, with an appendix covering five additional titles. A typical entry includes: author, title, bibliographical data (including paginations), and annotation. The essays are one paragraph in length, descriptive, with occasional evaluations. Lerner, a librarian and bibliographer, produced this now outdated but laudable effort as a library school project.

122. McGhan, Barry. **An Index to Science Fiction Book Reviews in** *Astounding/Analog,* **1949-1969,** *Fantasy and Science Fiction,* **1949-1969,** *Galaxy,* **1950-1969.** College Station, TX, SFRA, 1973. vii, 88 p. index. (SFRA Miscellaneous Publication No. 1). LC 74-152723. (pbk.).

McGhan focuses on three of the better-known prozines of the 1950s and '60s, omitting brief mentions of SF books and reviews of non-book materials.

Following a short preface, "On Book Reviewing," by Damon Knight, McGhan includes: an introduction explaining the book's guidelines, a general guide to the review columns arranged by magazine title, then chronologically by major period, covering the chief reviewers, the name of the column, exceptions to the standard reviewers, and issues not covered in this index. The major part of this book (63 pages) comprises an alphabetical list of the authors of the books being reviewed, with their publications listed alphabetically under each writer, referenced to the magazine title (a three-letter code: ASF, FSF, GAL) and date (in the form 10/62 for October, 1962). The title index correlates titles and page references to the first part of the book only; one must refer back to the author index to find complete bibliographical data. The book is shot from very legible typed copy.

Mediocre mush, now completely superseded by Hall (see #116).

123. McNutt, Dan J. **The Eighteenth-Century Gothic Novel: An Annotated Bibliography of Criticism and Selected Texts.** New York & London, Garland Publishing, 1975. xxii, 330 p. index. (Garland Reference Library of the Humanities, Vol. 4). LC 74-22490. ISBN 0-8240-1058-2.

This was the first attempt to provide a systematic, comprehensive bibliography on the secondary literature of the classic gothic novel, and it remains a credible effort, if now out-of-date.

McNutt organizes his book into thirteen chapters and an appendix: "1. Bibliographies and Research Guides"; "2. Aesthetic Background"; "3. Literary Background"; "4. Psychological, Social, and Scientific Background"; "5. Eighteenth-Century Gothic, in General Studies"; "6. Studies Devoted to Eighteenth-Century Gothic"; "7. The Gothic Legacy"; "8. Horace Walpole, 4th Earl of Orford (1717-1797)"; "9. Clara Reeve (1729-1807)"; "10. Charlotte (Turner) Smith (1749-1806)"; "11. Ann (Ward) Radcliffe (1764-1823)"; "12. Matthew Gregory Lewis (1775-1818)"; "13. William Beckford (1760-1844)"; "Appendix: Selected Foreign

Language Items." Each of the main chapters is further subdivided into additional sections; Chapter 3, for example, is broken into four units: "a. Early Literary Theories"; "b. Verse Precursors"; "c. Prose Precursors"; "d. The Continental Background."

In each subdivision, materials are arranged alphabetically by main entry (usually author or editor). A typical entry includes: author, title (periodical articles in quotes, books underlined), bibliographical data (for articles: magazine title [underlined], volume number, year of publication, pagination; for monographs: title [underlined], place of publication, publisher, year of publication, but no paginations), item number, and a descriptive annotation averaging sixty words in length, but sometimes exceeding 200 words.

The entry numbers run down the right-hand margin of each page, sometimes pushing the numbers on the left-hand (*i.e.*, even-numbered) pages close to the gutter, making them unnecessarily difficult to read; entries are numbered consecutively from one in each chapter, in the form 12/1, 12/2, 12/3, etc., for the first few items in Chapter 12. The brief foreign language section (sixty-four entries) is unannotated. The index references authors' names and item numbers only, the authors' first names being abbreviated to initials (something wholly unnecessary and absolutely irritating); the absence of a title index is unfortunate. The book is shot from occasionally faint typed copy.

McNutt covers 1,154 items, less than Fisher (see #113) and Frank (see #114 and #115), but his range is deliberately more restrictive. Unusually, he also lists and evaluates the major modern editions of the primary works of the several authors covered in Chapters 8-13, something that only Spector (see #125) among his competitors does on any systematic basis, and then only scantily. McNutt's annotations are also longer and more descriptive than those found in any of the books mentioned above, and his overall focus is sharper and more distinctive.

Thus, despite the fact that his coverage only extends through 1974, McNutt's bibliography remains a very useful guide to the rapidly growing critical resources in this genre.

124. Science Fiction Book Reviews, 1969-1972. Sydney, Australia, Australian Science Fiction Association, 1973. 60 p. LC 77-354986. (pbk.).

No author is indicated for this book, but well-known Australian librarian and indexer Graham Stone may well have participated in its compilation. The index is broken into two sections: "Books Reviewed" by title and "Index" by author. The main section is arranged alphabetically by title of the book being reviewed, a typical entry including: title (all caps), author, magazine title, month and year of magazine publication, pagination of review, reviewer's name; multiple reviews are arranged alphabetically by magazine title underneath the book title. The author index gives authors and titles only.

Now largely superseded by Hall (see #116), whose sets do not, however, include book reviews from *Science Fiction News* and the *ASFA Journal,* two fanzines that are covered in this index.

125. Spector, Robert Donald. **The English Gothic: A Bibliographic Guide to Writers from Horace Walpole to Mary Shelley.** Westport, CT & London, Greenwood Press, 1984. xiii, 269 p. index. LC 83-1443. ISBN 0-313-22536-2.

Spector's guide to the secondary literature of the classic gothic is presented in narrative form, very much akin to the style and format of *The Year's Work in English Studies.*

Following a preface, abbreviations list, and a critical/historical introduction to the genre, the book is arranged into five broad chapters: "1. Gothic, Gothicism, and Gothicists"; "2. The Beginnings: Horace Walpole and Clara Reeve"; "3. Sentimental Gothicism: Charlotte Smith and Ann Radcliffe"; "4. Schauer-Romantik: Matthew Gregory Lewis and William Beckford"; "5. The Inheritors: Charles Robert Maturin and Mary Shelley."

Spector follows the same format in each chapter: in narrative style, he analyzes the major and minor works of the field, including the fictions of the gothic writers themselves, showing the development of each writer's career and the critical response to it, both contemporaneously and subsequently. The narrative text is followed at the end of each chapter by a list of references arranged in alphabetical order by critic, and broken into two divisions, each corresponding to one of the authors being covered. A typical bibliographical entry includes: author, title (in quotes for journal articles, in italics for book titles), publication data (for periodical entries: magazine title or abbreviation [in italics], volume number, month and year of publication, pagination; for monographs: place of publication, publisher, year of publication, but no paginations). The index references both authors and titles to page numbers. The book is beautifully typeset and bound to library standards.

Spector covers a more restricted range of materials than his competitors, Fisher (see #113), Frank (see #114 and #115), and McNutt (see #123), but his intelligent, perceptive evaluations, which place both the authors and the criticism about them in historical perspective, make his bibliography far more useful to the scholar.

When, for example, he writes of John Garrett's *Gothic Strains and Bourgeois Sentiments in the Novels of Mrs. Ann Radcliffe and Her Imitators,* he notes that "his major contribution is to distinguish between Radcliffe's attachment to eighteenth-century didacticism—her concern for the triumph of virtue over vice—and the often indulgent play upon the emotions exhibited by other Gothicists." We know immediately what Garrett says and, more importantly, how he says it and in what context. This type of evaluative commentary of secondary sources is badly needed in the related field of science fiction and fantasy, which has in recent years overflowed with an effluence of second-rate critical monographs.

Spector is both knowledgeable and credible, and his guide is highly recommended to all libraries.

126. Tymn, Marshall B. **A Basic Reference Shelf for Science Fiction Teachers.** Monticello, IL, Council of Planning Librarians, 1978. 13 p. (Exchange Bibliography, No. 1523). LC 78-105377 (pbk.).

This work and its companion volume on fantasy (see #127) were the result of two conferences on teaching science fiction held at Eastern Michigan University (where Tymn was a Professor of English) in 1975 and 1976. Both works were designed to provide the teacher of fantastic literature with a core list of reference and critical works that might be useful in preparing classes, or to which students could be referred for further study.

This 8.5" x 11" booklet is divided into basic categories (*e.g.,* "Preliminary Sources," "General Bibliographies," etc.), then arranged alphabetically by author. The annotations range from one to five sentences, and are primarily descriptive rather than evaluative. All of the information included herein was later incorporated into *The Year's Scholarship* volumes (see #130).

127. Tymn, Marshall B. **Recent Critical Studies on Fantasy Literature: An Annotated Checklist.** Monticello, IL, Council of Planning Librarians, 1978. 21 p. (Exchange Bibliography, No. 1522). LC 78-105385 (pbk.).

Unlike its companion volume on science fiction (see #126), this selective bibliography focuses primarily on critical materials about fantasy fiction and its authors and includes more articles than books. Tymn attempts to provide a basic list of materials suitable for the beginning teacher of fantastic literature.

The arrangement here is by general category (*e.g.,* "Critical Studies: Articles and Essays") and then alphabetically by author. Tymn's annotations are short (one brief sentence) and descriptive rather than evaluative. As with *A Basic Reference Shelf* (see #126), all of the data were later incorporated into Tymn and Schlobin's annual guide to secondary sources (see #130).

128. Tymn, Marshall B., Roger C. Schlobin, and L. W. Currey. **A Research Guide to Science Fiction Studies: An Annotated Checklist of Primary and Secondary Sources for Fantasy and Science Fiction.** New York & London, Garland Publishing Co., 1977. ix, 165 p. index. (Garland Reference Library of the Humanities, Vol. 87). LC 76-52682. ISBN 0-8240-9886-2.

Tymn/Schlobin/Currey cover much of the same territory as Clareson (see #111), albeit with an additional five years of data (through 1976). This new book is somewhat better organized, however, being broken into six major sections: "I. Preliminary Sources"; "II. Sources for Primary Materials"; "III. Sources for Secondary Materials"; "IV. Author Studies & Bibliographies"; "V. Periodicals"; "VI. Sources for Acquisition," followed by a thirty-six page checklist of "Doctoral Dissertations in Science Fiction and Fantasy" by Douglas R. Justus (arranged alphabetically by author), and author and title indices.

Each of the first three chapters is broken into two sections: "General" (sources outside the science fiction field [*Dissertation Abstracts International,* for example]), and "Science Fiction" sources. These latter sections are further subdivided into five or six other divisions. For example, the chapter "Sources for Primary Materials" includes the subdivisions: "1. General Bibliographies"; "2. Subject Bibliographies"; "3. Anthology Indices"; "4. Magazine Indices" (General and Individual); "5. Film." The materials are numbered consecutively from 1-404 (the doctoral dissertations are not numbered or indexed, however); the author and title indices refer to item number only.

In each section, materials are arranged alphabetically by main entry (usually author or editor), except for the long forty-page section on authors' studies, which is appropriately organized by name of the writer being covered, then alphabetically by name of critic or bibliographer. A typical entry includes: item number, author, title (in italics), place of publication, publisher, year of publication, pagination, format ("paper" = paperback), and place of publication, publisher, and year of publication for any reprints. The annotations range in size from one short sentence to 300 words, averaging about seventy-five words, and are primarily descriptive, not evaluative, although occasional summations or pithy comments may be included.

The separate checklist of dissertations remains a very thorough and useful starting point for these hard-to-locate, largely unpublished materials, although it is unfortunate that no attempt was made to index them with the rest of the items. Chapters 5-6 are now wholly out-of-date and useless.

Tymn's book differs from Clareson (see #111) in both coverage and arrangement: the latter includes hundreds of additional essays and articles broken into many more sections (not a benefit in this case), while *A Research Guide* restricts itself to separately published monographs (including chapbooks), is better organized, provides longer and more evaluative annotations, and includes five years more data. Neither really supplants the other. A new version of Tymn providing a current, up-to-date, completely annotated synthesis of the many critical monographs available in the field is badly needed; until one appears, this book, supplemented by Hall (see #116), Justice (see #120), and Tymn's annuals on SF scholarship with their cumulations (see #130), will have to do.

129. Tymn, Marshall B. **Survey of Science Fiction Literature: Bibliographical Supplement.** Englewood Cliffs, NJ, Salem Press, 1982. xiv, 183 p. index. LC 79-64639. ISBN 0-89356-185-1 (pbk.).

When the *Survey of Science Fiction Literature* (see #92) first appeared in 1979, it was criticized for the relatively poor "Sources for Further Study" sections appended at the end of each essay (and not contributed by the authors of those essays). Subsequently, well-known critic Tymn was commissioned to produce this supplemental volume (a unique occurrence in the history of the Salem Press guides), providing much greater access to secondary materials for each of the works covered in the original five-volume set.

The arrangement is the same as the original: by title of the work being covered, exactly reproducing the top matter at the beginning of each of the original essays (title, author, years of birth and death, type of work, one-sentence summation), followed by each mini-bibliography arranged alphabetically by name of critic. A typical entry includes: critic, title of book or article, bibliographical data, and (inconsistently) specific paginations for the material within the book covering the specific work targeted in the original critical essay, plus a one-sentence descriptive annotation. Both books and magazine articles are included, as well as essays included in anthologies, but in general, Tymn's coverage of critical monographs and anthologies seems superior to his comprehension of the much vaster array of journal articles. An author index is included, but references only those SF authors (and titles) on whom essays were written in the original set, correlated to the page number references in this new volume; none of the secondary materials are specifically indexed. The proprietary arrangement makes this book relatively useless without access to the *Survey* itself.

130. Tymn, Marshall B., and Roger C. Schlobin. **The Year's Scholarship in Science Fiction and Fantasy, 1972-1975.** Kent, OH, Kent State University Press, 1979. xvi, 222 p. index. (The Serif Series, Bibliographies and Checklists, No. 36). LC 78-21976. ISBN 0-87338-222-6. **The Year's Scholarship in Science Fiction and Fantasy, 1976-1979.** Kent, OH, Kent State University Press, 1982. ix, 251 p. index. (The Serif Series, Bibliographies and Checklists, No. 41). LC 82-16190. ISBN 0-87388-257-9 [*sic*]. Tymn, Marshall B. **The Year's Scholarship in Science Fiction, Fantasy, and Horror Literature 1980.** Kent, OH, Kent State University Press, 1983. viii, 110 p. index. ISBN 0-87338-279-X (pbk.). **The Year's Scholarship in Science Fiction, Fantasy, and Horror Literature 1981.** Kent, OH,

Kent State University Press, n.d. [1984]. viii, 103 p. index. ISBN 0-87338-301-X (pbk.). **The Year's Scholarship in Science Fiction, Fantasy, and Horror Literature 1982.** Kent, OH, Kent State University Press, n.d. [1985]. x, 107 p. index. ISBN 0-87338-302-8 (pbk.). Continued by annual supplements in *Extrapolation,* and (beginning in 1989) by *Journal of the Fantastic in the Arts.*

Tymn's was intended directly to supplement Clareson (see #111) by providing comprehensive annotated coverage of all books and essays published in the fields of science fiction and fantasy for the specific years covered. Following two conferences that were held at Tymn's home instititution, Eastern Michigan University, in 1975 and 1976, Tymn and Schlobin prepared the first of their annual surveys for publication in *Extrapolation* and also simultaneously began work on the first of their cumulated volumes (1972-75). Beginning with the 1980 volume, Schlobin dropped out of the project to pursue other interests, and Tymn carried on the annual supplements himself (the last of these was published in the Fall 1988 issue of *Extrapolation,* covering 1987 publications).

The first of the cumulations, covering the years 1972-75, is something of a hybrid, containing elements of both Clareson and the later format that Tymn eventually developed. It organizes the book into four major sections: "I. General Studies"; "II. Bibliography and Reference"; "III. Author Studies and Bibliographies"; "IV. Teaching and Visual Aids," followed by author and title indexes. The major divisions are organized alphabetically by main entry (usually author or editor); the section on author studies is subdivided into "Collective Studies" and "Individual Studies" (eighty pages), the latter arranged by name of the author being covered.

Each chapter or subchapter is numbered from the number one to the end; this arrangement works well enough except in the author studies chapter, where each individual subsection (the name of the author being covered) is also numbered from one. Since the indices correlate item numbers only, this results in the very cumbersome reference III-B-xxxiii-1 for the sole interview on L. Sprague de Camp.

A typical book entry includes: author, title (in italics), place of publication, publisher, year of publication, but no paginations. A typical essay entry includes: author, title (in quotes), magazine title (in italics), volume number, year, and paginations (for a journal article), or book title, editor, place of publication, publisher, year of publication, and paginations (for an essay published in a book). A number of the books that could have been further analyzed were not: *Hell's Cartographers* is covered in the "Collective Studies" section of Chapter 3, but the individual autobiographical pieces are not mentioned under the respective authors' names in the "Individual Studies" subchapter. The annotations are generally very brief (one to three sentences, averaging one), and usually descriptive rather than evaluative.

Beginning with the 1976-1979 cumulation, Tymn began using a more standard format. The contents for that volume include "Foreword"; "Preface"; "A. General Studies"; "B. Bibliography and Reference"; "C. Collective Author Studies"; "D. Individual Author Studies"; "E. Art and Film"; "F. Teaching Resources"; author and title Indexes. In each of these chapters, materials are numbered from one to the end, preceded by the key letter for each chapter, and are organized alphabetically by main entry. As before, individual author studies are arranged by name of the author being covered; this section also includes numerous "See" references to materials analyzed elsewhere in the volume. The indices correlate item numbers only.

Later annuals added still more subject chapters as the field continued to expand. The 1982 annual, for example, includes the following divisions: "A. Bibliography and Reference"; "B. General Surveys and Histories"; "C. Theoretical and Critical Studies"; "D. Subject Studies"; "E. Collective Author Studies"; "F. Individual Author Studies"; "G. Art; Media: Film, TV, Radio";"H. Writing and Publishing"; "J. Teaching Resources." Otherwise it follows the same general format.

Hall (see #117), Tymn's chief rival, has always had a far greater reach than Tymn and his main set (covering 1878-1985) is unrivaled as an initial source for further study, including thousands more entries than the Clareson/Tymn sets for a comparable period, with many more specific subject analyses. However, Tymn/Schlobin and Clareson's annotations provide a dimension not available in Hall, and include a few dozen items missed by Hall, for no apparent reason. Also, Tymn's arrangement is more accessible for certain kinds of research. Thus, scholars should consult both sets if they wish to conduct a thorough literary search.

Unfortunately, none of the later Tymn volumes have been cumulated or (after 1982) even published in book form, rendering access increasingly difficult. Tymn had been discussing the possibility of doing a completely new cumulation of the entire data base, but his near-fatal car accident in 1989 has put that project on indefinite hold. The 1989 annual was edited by his colleagues for publication in Tymn's *Journal of the Fantastic in the Arts,* and subsequent volumes may also be compiled by other hands.

LIBRARY CATALOGS
AND COLLECTION GUIDES

SCOPE NOTE: This section includes published catalogs of library collections specifically devoted primarily to fantastic literature.

131. Hall, Hal W., ed. **Science/Fiction Collections: Fantasy, Supernatural & Weird Tales.** New York, Haworth Press, 1983. 181 p. LC 82-21355. ISBN 0-917724-49-6.

This interesting collection of essays focuses on nine special libraries of fantastic literature, seven public and two private, and was previously published as an issue of the journal *Special Collections.*

Hall's introduction outlines the major SF collections known to exist in the world today. This is followed by contributed essays on the collections of fantastic literature at the Library of Congress, the University of California, Riverside, Texas A&M University, Eastern New Mexico University, Syracuse University, the Toronto Public Library, and the M.I.T. Science Fiction Society, plus the private collections of the late Sam Moskowitz and Forrest J Ackerman. The pieces focus both on the history and the scope of the analyzed libraries, ranging in size from thirty-two pages (Moskowitz) to four pages (Syracuse), and have all been contributed by current or past employees of the libraries or by the owners (in the case of the two private collections).

Several additional essays are also included: "Science Fiction Specialty Publishers," by Robert Weinberg; "Bibliographical Control in Fantastic Literature: An Evaluation of Works Published, 1941-1981," by Marshall B. Tymn; "The Cataloging and Classification of Science Fiction Collections," by Fred Lerner (annotated separately in this volume in the "Cataloging Manuals" chapter [see #23]); "A Checklist of Science Fiction and Fantasy Book Dealers," by David Aylward and Robert Hadji; and "A Brief Directory of Science Fiction Research Collections," by Hall.

These latter sections are all now out-of-date, but provide some useful information (particularly Lerner and Hall). The same is true to a lesser degree of the library histories, but their broader scope still provides the potential researcher with a real feel for what each library contains, its primary emphases, and how well each collection is being maintained, facts that are unlikely to have altered very much in the intervening years (UC Riverside is still the only academic collection that makes any real attempt to acquire all currently published materials in the field).

This is one volume that should be read and studied by any scholar intending to do intensive research on a particular SF writer or movement.

132. Lewis, Arthur O. **Utopian Literature in the Pennsylvania State University Libraries: A Selected Bibliography.** University Park, PA, Pennsylvania State University Libraries, 1984. xxx, 230 p. index. (Bibliographical Series, No. 9). (pbk.).

This catalog, like the Negley work (see #133), is arranged alphabetically by author, then by title. A typical entry includes: author's name (that under which he or she is best known), title (italics), place of publication, publisher, year of publication, and similar data for the various editions held by the library. Since the bibliography describes only those books actually located in the library collection, the first edition of the work may not be included. No paginations are given, but brief descriptive annotations are included for most entries, ranging in size from one sentence to 500 words (averaging seventy-five).

In addition, a few entries (for Sir Thomas More, Plato, Aldous Huxley, etc.) feature major bio-critical essays on the author, his life, and works, ranging up to 2,300 words in length. Many foreign-language books are covered. Lewis's fourteen-page introduction provides a brief but well-written history of the utopia genre. The title index references book titles and page numbers only. *Utopian Literature* also includes a one-page addendum, a pseudonym list, and reproductions of sixteen title pages and woodcuts from some of the books annotated. The book is shot from legible typed copy.

Lewis covers about 1,700 works, compared to 1,200 in the Negley catalog (see #133), and his sometimes lengthy annotations provide descriptions and other background material not found in the Negley or Sargent utopian bibliographies (see #266 and #267). His catalog is sufficiently important in its own right that it should be collected by the larger university libraries.

133. Negley, Glenn. **Utopia Collection of the Duke University Library.** Durham, NC, Friends of Duke University Library, 1965. iii, 83 p. LC 66-95608. (pbk.). Folcroft, PA, Folcroft Library Editions, 1970. iii, 83 p. LC 72-194356. Norwood, PA, Norwood Editions, 1975. iii, 83 p. LC 75-34123. Philadelphia, R. West, 1976. iii, 83 p. LC 76-45655.

Negley arranges this collection catalog alphabetically by author, then by title. A typical entry includes: author's name, title, place of publication, year of publication, year of publication of the edition held by Duke University, but no publishers or paginations. Known pseudonymous works are referenced to the authors' real names.

Completing the book is an eleven-page chronological checklist of the works by date of the first edition, irrespective of the printing held by Duke, referencing author's name only (no titles). The book is shot from legible typed copy. Roughly 1,200 titles are included, including many rare English- and foreign-language editions. This catalog was later subsumed into Negley's larger bibliography of utopian literature (see #266).

134. University of California, Riverside. **Dictionary Catalog of the J. Lloyd Eaton Collection of Science Fiction and Fantasy Literature.** Boston, G. K. Hall, 1982. v, 558, 575, 568 p. in 3 v. ISBN 0-8161-0379-8 (set).

This catalog of the Eaton Collection at the University of California, Riverside Library is the only volume of its kind ever published in the field, barring several dealers' catalogs generated for the sale of specific private collections (and these vary greatly both in scope and in the kind of information they provide).

Following a brief three-page introduction by Dr. George Edgar Slusser, former curator of the collection, touching upon its history and outlining the types of materials the collection contains, the bulk of this oversized three-volume set is an exact reproduction of the shelflist cards in the Eaton Collection's card catalog in main-entry order (usually by author). Any errors of cataloging, typographical, or otherwise included on the original cards are faithfully reproduced here; also, many books have more than one edition listed, since the intent of the library is to acquire all printing variations of any particular publication.

The Eaton Collection is the largest *cataloged* library of fantastic literature anywhere in the world, public or private; this volume includes card entries generated through 1981, covering about 20,000 volumes. Although some of this information is now available on a restricted or proprietary basis through OCLC and other sources, the value of this set should not be minimized, since it provides extensive bibliographical data on the books, and organizes into one finding list the many obscure or hard-to-locate titles of this broadly based collection. Some of the volumes included herein have no other holdings records either in the *National Union Catalog* or in OCLC. All major academic libraries should acquire this set.

135. Wurfel, Clifford. **An Introduction to the J. Lloyd Eaton Collection of Science Fiction and Fantasy.** Riverside, CA, University of California, Riverside Library, 1979. 13 p. (pbk.).

A short, in-house guide to the major authors and works held by the Eaton collection by the librarian formerly in charge of Special Collections at UC Riverside, Wurfel's history of the collection notes that its core of 7,500 early volumes of fantastic literature was acquired from the estate of J. Lloyd Eaton, a medical doctor, in 1969, and that this early segment of the collection included many rare and obscure titles, as well as all the standard works in the field, through about 1956.

The UCR Library has made significant efforts through the purchase of other collections (particularly the Douglas Menville library) to bolster its holdings for the "gap" between 1956-69, to maintain the collection through ongoing purchases of all new SF publications, and to acquire large foreign-language holdings, particularly of French and other European SF. This basic introductory guide to the world's largest publicly accessible collection of science fiction and fantasy literature, now exceeding 100,000 cataloged items, should definitely be expanded and brought up-to-date.

MAGAZINE AND ANTHOLOGY INDEXES

SCOPE NOTE: This chapter includes indexes and checklists of science fiction, fantasy, and weird fiction professional magazines, scholarly journals, and fanzines, plus indexes to monographic collections and anthologies and general cyclopedic guides to SF periodicals. Guides to specific publications are arranged in alphabetical order by periodical name at the end of this section.

CYCLOPEDIAS OF SF MAGAZINES

136. Bleiler, Everett F., with Richard J. Bleiler. **Science-Fiction: The Gernsback Years: A Complete Coverage of the Genre Magazines** *Amazing, Astounding, Wonder,* **and Others from 1926 Through 1936.** Kent, OH, and London, Kent State University Press, 1998. xxx, 730 p. index. LC 98-13374. ISBN 0-87338-604-3.

Contents: "Preface"; "Acknowledgments"; "Introduction"; "Story Descriptions"; "Anthologizations"; "Authors' Letters"; "Poetry"; "Reprint Sources"; "The Science-Fiction Solar System"; "Magazine Histories and Contents"; "Magazine Illustrators"; "Motif and Theme Index"; "Title Index"; "Author Index"; "Bibliography."

Well-known SF historian and bibliography E. F. Bleiler and son attempt to "provide complete coverage of the genre magazines *Amazing* [*Stories*], *Astounding* [*Stories*], *Wonder* [*Stories*], and others from 1926 through 1936." The bulk of the book (to page 522) includes extensive story descriptions, with 1,835 entries ordered alphabetically by author's last name, followed by each writer's publications arranged chronologically by magazine date. The header for each main entry includes: brief biographical information about the author (where known; some entries just include the note "no information"), with name in inverted order (boldfaced type), a brief biography (10-100 words), usually including country of origin and year of birth and death, but sometimes merely speculating about the real identity of the more obscure contributors.

The story entries each include: reference number (numbered consecutively throughout the book, starting from the number "1"), story title (bold caps), magazine in which it was published, month and year of publication, illustrator (if known), type of fiction (short story, novelette), indication of the story's time and place (if appropriate), and plot summary, averaging 200 words. Following the synopsis, there is often a brief review by Everett Bleiler of the piece's worthiness as science fiction. Running author headers throughout this large section of the bibliography make following the sometimes dense text relatively easy, even for unsophisticated users.

Scholars will also be interested in the analytical essay that makes up the introduction, which includes a three-and-a-half-page table tracking forty-eight important story motifs and their use in the three periodicals covered during the ten-year period from 1926-36. A second table follows six important story formulas employed during the same period of time. A great deal of information about early publishing is provided in the section called Magazine Histories, which is broken down by the three magazines covered, each being prefaced by an essay covering the magazine's development. This section also includes names and dates of the various publishers of each periodical, the staff, publication schedule, physical appearance of the magazine, issue price, number of issues published in the target years, usual pagination, departments, miscellaneous comments, and specific contents by issue.

The Magazine Illustrators section includes a selection of thirteen black-and-white reproductions of magazine covers. The three indices (title, author, and motif/theme) are straightforward and easy to use, correlating all of the information in the book with the page numbers where it appears.

As usual with the Bleilers' guides, *Science-Fiction: The Gernsback Years* is both authoritative and well-written, being based upon more than half a century of reading and analysis in the field. When the Bleilers make an identification of an obscure writer or state an inference about the development of fantastic literature, one can be certain that their sources have been thoroughly checked and verified.

Nicely typeset and durably bound to library standards, this excellent reference volume will be useful both to scholars and to students of pulp magazines and early science fiction. A veritable treasure trove of detailed information on a formative period of the genre, *Science Fiction: The Gernsback Years* is recommended for all research libraries.

137. Tymn, Marshall B., and Mike Ashley, eds. **Science Fiction, Fantasy, and Weird Fiction Magazines.** Westport, CT & London, Greenwood Press, 1985. xxx, 970 p. index. (Historical Guides to the World's Periodicals and Newspapers). LC 84-11523. ISBN 0-313-21221-X.

Tymn and Ashley have compiled a comprehensive, authoritative, and exceptionally well researched A-Z guide to the major and minor professional periodicals in fantastic literature. The preface succinctly states: "Our purpose in compiling this volume is to provide scholars, researchers, and the general reader with a useful tool for evaluating the science fiction, fantasy, and weird fiction magazines as a historical and literary phenomenon, and to furnish a bibliographical apparatus for documenting the appearance of these magazines in all their various phases." And what a good job they do!

Thirty-eight well-known scholars in the field, including a number of the old-time editors themselves, have contributed hundreds of essays ranging in size from 200-20,000 + words (averaging 1,000). The magazines are listed in alphabetical order by title. A typical entry includes: title, narration, footnotes, and two entry appendices: "Information Sources" and "Publication History." "Information Sources" may include the following items: "Bibliography" (reference sources specific to the magazine), "Index Sources" (places where the magazine is indexed, keyed to a set of letter codes referenced in an abbreviations list at the front of the book), "Reprint Sources" (derivative books and periodicals), "Location Sources" ([mostly academic] libraries currently holding substantial runs of the periodical).

The "Publication History" section may include: title (all title changes or variations, with subtitles), volume data (volume and issue sequence numbering, noting all errors, with magazine schedule and changes in schedule, and total number of issues published), publisher (publisher's name and place of publication, including locations of executive or other offices), editors (all editorial personnel responsible for selection of stories), format (the size and shape of the magazine, and the usual number of pages), price (cover price at the time of sale, with variations).

The essays vary widely in size, depending on the importance of the publication in question, the entry on *Astounding/Analog* running over 20,000 words, and generally include background history (how and why the publication was founded and its principal owners), some biographical and historical information on the editors, mention of the major authors and artists and stories featured in the magazine's run, reasons for decline and failure (where the publications have ceased), and a final summation of the periodical's importance to the history of fantastic literature.

Some of the material differs in quality, as might be expected with such a large number of contributors, but there is a sure editorial hand at work here, and the pieces never stray too far from their avowed purpose. Many of the histories include anecdotes, personal data, or other material that clearly derives from correspondence or interviews with the principals of the publications (and these sources are carefully cited). On the whole, the critiques seem fair, reliable, and historically sound. There are numerous internal "See" references to other titles covered in this volume.

End matter includes a section on "Associational English-Language Anthologies" (covering the hybrid "paperback magazine" series); "Academic Periodicals" and "Major Fanzines" (both of these chapters are arranged in separate alphabetical sequences by title); "Non-English-Language Magazines, by Country" (by country name, then alphabetically by title); "An Index to Major Cover Artists," alphabetically by artist name, showing major cover assignments (listing the magazine title and specific cover date of the artist's first SF cover assignment, then the total numbers of his covers for each magazine in descending order by number of assignments), followed by a list of the top fifty-five cover artists in descending order by total number of assignments; a general "Chronology" of the development of the SF magazine, showing years of birth for each publication listed herein; a "Bibliography" of all sources consulted, with author title and bibliographical data; and a comprehensive every-name index.

Tymn and Ashley have produced the standard guide to the SF magazines, one that is likely to stand the test of time for generations to come. It is difficult to imagine any serious researcher of these publications beginning his or her work without first consulting this volume. It should be on the shelves of every academic library.

GENERAL INDEXES AND CHECKLISTS

138. Ashley, Mike, and William G. Contento. **The Supernatural Index: A Listing of Fantasy, Supernatural, Occult, Weird, and Horror Anthologies.** Westport, CT, London, Greenwood Press, 1995. xii, 993 p. LC 95-6290. (Bibliographies and Indexes in Science Fiction, Fantasy, and Horror, Number 5). ISBN 0-313-24030-2.

Contents: "Preface"; "Introduction"; "Abbreviations"; "Editor List"; "Author Index"; "Story Index"; "Book Contents"; "Appendix I: Associational Books"; "Appendix II: Late Arrivals."

This volume attempts to index the contents of all English language anthologies of supernatural horror and fantasy fiction. The book covers over 2,100 volumes containing some 21,300 different stories by roughly 7,700 writers, from an 1813 publication (*Tales of the Dead*) to volumes published as late as 1993.

The Editor List is arranged alphabetically by editor surname, and includes: editor's name (all caps), edition code (* = first edition, + = first U.S. edition), title (bold type), co-editors (if any), publisher, ISBN, month and year of publication, original price, pagination, type of binding, and an 8-12 word description of the contents.

The Book List is arranged alphabetically by title, and includes: title (bold), editor(s), and book type code (an = reprint, oa = original, om = omnibus).

The largest part of the book (p. 65-601) comprises the Author Index, arranged alphabetically by contributor surname, which includes: author (all caps), pseudonym (if any), story title, co-author (if any), story type code (vi = vignette, ss = short story, nv = novelette, na = novella, n = novel), original publication information (including magazine title [italics] and month and year of publication), a list of reprints in chronological order by publication date, giving anthology title (italics), book editor, publisher, year of publication, and version notes.

The Story Index is arranged alphabetially by story title, and lists all of the stories indexed in the volume, including: story title, author(s), and story type.

The Book Contents section is arranged alphabetically by editor, and details the contents of each anthology. A typical entry includes: editor (caps), edition code, book title (italics), publisher, ISBN, publication date, price, pagination, binding, general description of contents, and a detailed story listing, in descending order by the place each piece occupies in the volume, giving: starting page number for that story, story title, story author, and story type code. Birth and death dates, along with pseudonyms, are provided for more than 7,700 authors, when known.

The first Appendix lists associational titles that the editors decided to exclude, for the various reasons cited (however, they often give partial or detailed contents listings even for these titles). The second Appendix adds seven books that arrived too late to be listed in the main index, using the format of the Book Contents section.

This is another first-rate index from two well-known bibliographers in the field. The various sections are clearly labeled and not at all difficult to navigate, and the authors do a wonderful job in the preface of explaining exactly how to use their book, and providing sample entries for each type of entry recorded. The volume is nicely typeset and organized, and durably bound to library standards.

Highly recommended for the reference collections of all academic libraries and for all major public libraries.

139. Bell, John. **The Far North and Beyond: An Index to Canadian Science Fiction and Fantasy in English-Language Genre Magazines and Other Selected Periodicals of the Pulp Era, 1896-1955.** Halifax, Nova Scotia, Canada, Dalhousie University School of Library and Information Studies; London, Vine Press, 1998. v, 62 p. index. LC 91-658651 (Occasional Papers Series, No. 61). ISBN 0-7703-9774-3 (pbk.).

Contents: "Introduction"; "Abbreviations"; "Author Index"; "Title Index"; "Artist Index"; "Magazine Index"; "Series Index"; "Appendix: English-Language Science-Fiction and Fantasy Magazines Published in Canada During the Pulp Era"; "Bibliography."

This text attempts to identify Canadian publications in English-language SF pulp magazines. Of the 76 periodicals indexed, all are American except for six British titles (*Authentic Science Fiction, Fantasy, Nebula Science Fiction, New Worlds, Science Fantasy,* and *Tales of Wonder*), and two Canadian ones (*Eerie Tales* and *Uncanny Tales*). Excluded are Canadian and British facsimile reprints of American pulp magazines. Canadians are defined as native-born residents of Canada, foreign-born residents who lived in Canada at least ten years or more during their adulthood, and all native-born expatriates.

The material is presented in five indices. The Author Index alphabetically lists the seventy Canadian writers and their pseudonyms. A typical entry includes: name (bold caps), birth and death dates (if available), story or stories, arranged alphabetically by title, type of fiction (*e.g.,* ss = short story, n = novel), abbreviation of the magazine title in which the story appeared, and month and year published. Stories published under pseudonyms appear under the author's main entry, alphabetically by pen name and then by story title; "See" references in the main text refer the user back to the author's real name.

The Title Index lists 513 works alphabetically by title, cross-referenced to the author's name (if a pseudonym, his or her real name is listed in brackets). The Artist Index alphabetically lists eleven Canadian SF artists, giving name (bold caps), birth and death dates (if available), type of art (cover or interior), abbreviation of the magazine title, and the month and year published.

The Magazine Index lists the periodicals featuring works by Canadian writers or artists, alphabetically by magazine title, and then chronologically by publication date; 599 issues are covered. A typical entry includes: magazine title (bold caps), dates of overall publication run, specific month and year of issue, story title, type of fiction (in brackets), and author (real name in brackets). The Series Index lists 21 series, arranged alphabetically by series name, including: title of the series (bold caps), the author as listed (real name in brackets), individual story titles, arranged chronologically by publication date, magazine abbreviation, and month and year of publication.

This is a useful beginning point for research on Canadian science fiction and fantasy, although there is much that could be added to any future edition, including more complete biographical data on these (mostly) little-known writers of the fantastic. Of specialized interest only.

140. Boyajian, Jerry, and Kenneth R. Johnson. **Index to the Science Fiction Magazines: 1977-1984.** Cambridge, MA, Twaci Press, 1981-85. 8 v. LC 82-641836. ISSN 0732-0655 (pbk.). **Index to the Semi-Professional Fantasy Magazines: 1982-1983.** Cambridge, MA, Twaci Press, 1983-84. 2 v. LC 84-642059. ISSN 0743-4103 (pbk.).

The Twaci Press series of magazine indexes ceased with the 1984 annual, but until that time was a well-established rival to the NESFA series (see #159). A typical annual includes a "Magazine Index" comprising two lists, both organized alphabetically by magazine title.

The first index provides a chronological checklist of the issues, giving month, year, volume number, issue number, whole number, format (*e.g.,* "D" = Digest sized), pagination. The second list is an issue-by-issue rendering of the magazine contents, giving magazine title, month and year of publication, title of each selection in the order presented in that issue, type when not a piece of short fiction (*e.g.,* "art" or "verse" or "pt 1 of 3" for the first part of a serialized novel), author, page number where the selection begins.

The "Author Index" gives author, title of individual selections, magazine title, and month of publication, and is followed by a "Title Index" listing author and title only, and an "Artist Index," which provides artist, magazine, paginations where the artwork appeared (or "cover" if the contribution was a cover illustration). Increasingly as the series developed more attention was paid to SF published in periodicals not generally regarded as genre publications (*Playboy,* for example, or *Omni*), and separate "Author Indexes" to these are provided in the later annuals.

The companion *Index to the Semi-Professional Fantasy Magazines* covers in identical format the many borderline fiction magazines that were founded in the 1980s (*Whispers,* for example), which published professional-level SF, fantasy, or horror without mass market distribution.

The Twaci series provided some minor information not found in the NESFA guides (the detailed listings of artists' contributions, for example), but not enough to justify its continued existence in the face of its better-established competitor.

Now mostly subsumed into Miller/Contento's CD-ROM (see #157).

141. Cockcroft, T. G. L. **Index to Fiction in *Radio News* and Other Magazines.** Lower Hutt, New Zealand, T.G.L. Cockcroft, 1970. 12 p. index. (pbk.). Based in part on two previous compilations: Evans, William H. **The Gernsback Forerunners.** Brooklyn, NY, Julius Unger, 1944. 5 leaves. (pbk.). And: Engel, Theodore. **Evolution of Modern Science Fiction.** New York, Hugo Gernsback, 1952 (?). 12 p. (pbk.).

New Zealand fan Tom Cockcroft produced over a two-decade period a series of small but worthy indexes to fantastic literature in the early pulp magazines. This booklet is based on a series of issue-by-issue checklists of the early Hugo Gernsback magazines previously produced by Evans' and Engel (as noted above).

Gernsback, who founded the first professional SF magazine, *Amazing Stories,* in 1926, had begun his career in publishing during World War I by inaugurating a group of popular science and radio periodicals, some of which published science and other speculative fiction, including his own seminal novel, *Ralph 124C41+*. Cockcroft's index covers six of these titles: *Modern Electrics, Practical Electrics, The Experimenter, Radio News, The Electrical Experimenter,* and *Science & Invention.*

The basic index is arranged alphabetically by author surname, then by title, giving: author (all caps), title, magazine abbreviation, month and year of publication, but no paginations. The title index includes: title (all caps), author, magazine abbreviation, and month and year of publication. There is a separate guide on page 2 to American writer Clement Fezandié's series of stories, Dr. Hackensaw's Secrets, plus an index of those stories later reprinted in *Amazing Stories* and the other professional science-fiction magazines.

As with all of Cockcroft's works, the book is shot from photoreduced but legible typed copy. Although difficult to locate, these brief indexes do provide a service to scholars and should ultimately be gathered into some more permanent form.

142. Cockcroft, Thomas G. L. **Index to the Verse in *Weird Tales,* Including *Oriental Stories,* and the *Magic Carpet Magazine,* and *The Thrill Book*.** Lower Hutt, New Zealand,

Thomas G. L. Cockcroft, 1960. 16 p. + 1 unnumbered page on the inside back cover. index. (pbk.).

Cockcroft's booklet was a precursor to his *Index to the Weird Fiction Magazines* (see #143), covering many of the same titles. The major part of this guide is devoted to *Weird Tales,* indexing the poems appearing in that publication first by title, then by author, with months and years of publication but no paginations. Page 10 includes a brief guide to "Virgil Finlay's Poetry Series" in *WT,* plus a brief index to verse published in *Oriental Stories* and *The Magic Carpet Magazine.* The inside back cover provides an index to the verse appearing in the sixteen issues of *The Thrill Book.* The book is shot from legible typed copy.

Although the *Index* is still useful as a one-volume guide to verse in the early fantasy pulps, much of this information is available in the more detailed indexes to *The Thrill Book* (see #201) and *Weird Tales* (see #206) covered elsewhere in this volume.

143. Cockcroft, T. G. L. **Index to the Weird Fiction Magazines.** Lower Hutt, New Zealand, T. G. L. Cockcroft, 1962-64 (and 1967). 100 p. in 2 v. index. (pbk.). New York, Arno Press, 1975. 100 p. index. (Science Fiction). LC 74-15955. ISBN 0-405-06322-9.

Since Day's index of the science fiction magazines (see #149) failed to include those pulps devoted to weird or supernatural fiction (specifically, *Weird Tales*), Cockcroft produced this supplemental index as a labor of love to record the stories published in these periodicals between 1923-54 (when *Weird Tales* ceased publication).

The first volume provides a brief introduction, a checklist of magazines indexed (giving an issue-by-issue rendering of whole number published, year and month of publication, volume and issue number, cover artist, title of story featured on the cover), a list of editorial staff, a checklist of cover artists and the issues they illustrated, some general editorial notes, and a comprehensive index to the fiction published in these periodicals, alphabetically by title of each story, plus author and month and year of publication. Seven magazines are indexed other than *Weird Tales,* although the latter comprises the vast majority of the entries; the *WT* listings are uncoded, while entries for fiction appearing in other publications are noted with a two- or three-letter code preceding the date (*e.g.,* "GF" = *Golden Fleece*).

The second volume, issued in 1964 (and slightly updated in 1967), reworks the same material alphabetically by author, and also provides a brief story series index and a note on "Translators and Translations." Both books were shot from typed copy; some pages in some copies are faint. The Arno Press reprint was shot facsimile from the original booklets and produced as a one-volume amalgamation.

Cockcroft has now largely been superseded by Parnell and Ashley (see #160), except that the latter fails to include a title index; also, three of the relatively minor magazines covered by Cockcroft (*Oriental Stories, The Magic Carpet Magazine,* and *Golden Fleece Historical Adventure*) are *not* indexed in Parnell, although some issues are covered haphazardly in Robbins (see #163) and Day (see #149), and the first two are mentioned in Jaffery/Cook's index to *Weird Tales* (see #206).

Now mostly subsumed into Miller/Contento's CD-ROM (see #157).

144. Cole, W. R. **A Checklist of Science-Fiction Anthologies.** Brooklyn, NY, W. R. Cole, 1964. xvi, 374 p. index. LC 65-1442. New York, Arno Press, 1975. xvi, 374 p. index. (Science Fiction). LC 74-15956. ISBN 0-405-06323-7.

This was the first guide to stories in SF anthologies ever attempted, and as with many fan-produced indexes, a few organizational and production problems frame its large mass of data.

Following brief introductions by the author and by Theodore Sturgeon, we find a two-page "How to Use the Checklist," an "Abbreviations List," a brief list of the anthologies included in the *Checklist,* alphabetical by title (correlated with editor's names and the page numbers within this book on which the contents of each anthology are delineated), then the main "Alphabetical Listing by Editor."

The latter section includes: editor's name(s), anthology title, publisher, place of publication, number of stories included, pagination, price, date of publication (in most instances, to the month or day), and a list of the stories in the same sequence as they were published in the anthology. Each story listing includes: story title, author, magazine in which the story was originally printed (where applicable), and month and year of original magazine publication. No paginations are provided for the stories within the anthology.

There are separate indices by story author and title, correlated with anthology title, magazine issue in which the story was originally published, and month and year of original periodical publication. Supplemental sections covering those anthologies produced in 1962-63 appear on pages 298-374 in their own alphabetical sequences. The book is shot from generally legible typed copy on strangely textured glossy paper.

The major problem with Cole's book lies in its initial section, the index by anthology, where the editor's name, anthology title, and story contents listings are all listed in capital letters, with the anthology title (but nothing else) indented five spaces from the left margin. The major entries are separated only by one full line break flanking the editor's name and title, making discernment of individual anthology listings difficult at first glance, particularly on pages where the anthologies are broken into two or more sections, each with their own half-titles. The author and title indexes do not share this defect, the data in these sections being clearly delineated through the use of hanging indents.

The Arno reprint reduced the physical size of the book from 8.5" x 11" to 5" x 8", with many pages appearing much fainter than the original (apparently the glossy paper did not reproduce well). Virtually all of the data in Cole have now been subsumed into Contento's continuing indices (see #145) and Miller and Contento's CD-ROM (see #157), but it should be noted that Contento does not provide quite as much bibliographical detail for the anthologies themselves, omitting total paginations for the books, and including only a skeletal series of codes for publisher and publication information.

145. Contento, William G. **Index to Science Fiction Anthologies and Collections.** Boston, G. K. Hall & Co., 1978. xii, 608 p. index. (A Reference Publication in Science Fiction). LC 78-155. ISBN 0-8161-8092-X. **Index to Science Fiction Anthologies and Collections, 1977-1983.** Boston, G. K. Hall & Co., 1984. xvi, 503 p. index. (A Reference Publication in Science Fiction). LC 78-155. ISBN 0-8161-8554-9.

Contento's continuing series has become the standard guide to SF stories printed in anthologies, supplanting Cole's index (see #144); he was among the first researchers in the field to utilize the possibilities of the computer age. This is both the strongest and weakest point of the set.

Both volumes are organized similarly. The introduction provides a general description of what the books contain, and is followed by a bibliography of sources consulted (including some, but not all, of the major SF reference tools, plus a few individual author bibliographies). This is followed by a brief "How to Use the Index" and an extensive abbreviations list (using two-letter codes for format and type, three-letter codes for publishers and periodicals, and seven-letter codes for anthology titles). There are almost 2,000 abbreviation codes in the second volume alone, requiring constant reference to and from the list.

The "Checklist of Books Indexed" is arranged by title in the first volume, and by main entry (usually editor, although at least one of the titles is referenced under the entry "Anonymous") in the second, and provides the following data: primary editor (second volume only), anthology title, primary editor (first volume only), type code (*e.g.,* "AN" = anthology, "AC" = single author collection), format code (*e.g.,* "Pa" = paperback), publisher code (*e.g.,* "GOL" = Gollancz), year (or sometimes month/season and year) of publication.

The major section of each book, the "Author Index," provides a list of the stories anthologized, arranged alphabetically by name of author, including: author's name, story title, type code (*e.g.,* "SS" = short story), publisher/magazine code and date of original publication (*e.g.,* "FSF" = *The Magazine of Fantasy & Science Fiction*), anthology title, anthology editor, type code (*e.g.,* "OA" = original anthology [an anthology comprised of stories published for the first time]). The "Story Index" rearranges the same data alphabetically by individual story title.

The final section, "Book Contents," is arranged alphabetically by anthology title, and includes: title, editor, type code, format code, publisher code, date of publication, followed by complete contents listed in the same sequence as in the anthology (data include story title, author, type code, publisher code for the magazine or anthology in which the story first appeared, and the date of that original appearance). No paginations, either of the anthologies themselves or of the contents within those collections, are provided, making bibliographical citation of the stories impossible without actually viewing the books in question.

There's no doubt Contento correlates an enormous amount of data in these 8.5" x 11" volumes covering thousands of anthologies (including a few foreign-language volumes), including tens of thousands of individual stories, essays, and poems. But measuring the level of his completeness is extraordinarily difficult. Contento excludes some (but not all) collections of fantasy and horror fiction, depending on the background of the authors (if they are associated with the science fiction field, he may include them); judging whether or not he has omitted an item because of content or because he is unaware of the volume is impossible to determine. Undoubtedly, he covers 95% or more of publications produced by the major trade and mass market firms; however, his coverage of lesser-known items appears more haphazard (for example, of nine anthologies produced by Menville/Reginald in the 1970s for the academic publishing house Arno Press, only one is indexed).

The physical appearances of these volumes and their basic organization also leave much to be desired. Both are produced from old-style, computer-generated copy that has been substantially photoreduced in size to produce a double-column format. The copy is often difficult to read and follow, with the type all being in one face, and the extreme use of abbreviation codes is not just intrusive, but frequently irritating and counterproductive. One can understand the need to conserve space in massive compilations of this kind, but when such conservation itself becomes a restriction on the average reader's ability to use these volumes successfully, one must question the utility of this kind of overcoded bibliomania. The use of codes should be severely restricted in any future editions.

Fortunately, the editor himself seems to have realized some of the problems with his format, because in the Brown/Contento annuals (see #33), he has provided a partial continuation of this series in the section entitled "Book Contents." Here the anthologies are arranged in alphabetical order by main entry (usually editors' names), providing: editor (all caps), book title (boldface type), publisher, ISBN, date of publication, price, pagination, format (*e.g.,* "hc" = hardcover), brief description ("Collection of 18 stories set in West Virginia"), and complete contents listings (these include the page numbers where each story begins, story title, author, type [*e.g.,* "ss" = short story], and publisher and publishing date of the story's first appearance [if any]).

The individual stories and their authors are then indexed in the "Title List: Stories" and "Author List: Stories" sections, respectively, together with stories and authors from the "Magazine Contents" chapter of the annuals. This is a much more readable and usable format than that employed in the original Contento indexes; since the Brown/Contento books (see #33) extended from 1984, being followed by the cumulated CD-ROM version of the data, there is no gap in coverage.

As for the original two-volume set, even with its structural defects it remains a wholly necessary tool for the serious SF scholar and should be acquired by all large university libraries.

Continued on an annual basis by Brown and Contento's annual volume, *Science Fiction, Fantasy and Horror,* and then cumulated with an updated index on the CD-ROM version of that product (see #33).

146. Cook, Frederick S. **Fred Cook's Index to the Wonder Group.** Grand Haven, MI, Fred Cook, 1966. 239 p. [but some pages do not follow in sequence, and others are missing altogether]. index. LC 70-14090 (pbk.).

Cook's guide indexes a group of SF pulp magazines originally founded by entrepreneur Hugo Gernsback and later incorporated into the "Thrilling" pulp group after Gernsback lost control of his own creations. The index covers *Air Wonder Stories, Science Wonder Quarterly/Wonder Stories Quarterly, Science Wonder Stories/Wonder Stories/Thrilling Wonder Stories, Wonder Stories Annual, Startling Stories, Captain Future, Fantastic Story Quarterly/Fantastic Story Magazine,* and *Space Stories.*

Each of the publications is treated separately, in four sections: a one-page history of the magazine with a checklist of the publication dates of each issue (by year), physical description, price, and number of pages; a chronological checklist of each issue showing month and year of publication, volume and issue number, cover artist, and a list of the stories and authors appearing in each issue in the same order as they originally ran, but no paginations; an author index giving author's name (all caps), title, month and year of publication; a second author index showing the total number of stories written by each. The book is shot from very clear typed copy.

The absence of an overall index severely limits the usefulness of this publication, and there is very little here (other, perhaps, than some of the brief historical data) that cannot be found in the general periodical indexes covered elsewhere in this section (see particularly Don Day's index, #149).

Now mostly subsumed into Miller/Contento's CD-ROM (see #157).

147. Day, Bradford M. **The Complete Checklist of Science-Fiction Magazines.** Woodhaven, NY, Science-Fiction & Fantasy Publications, 1961. 63 p. LC 61-19464 (pbk.).

Day lists all known professional science-fiction, fantasy, horror, and some peripheral magazines published in the United States, Canada, Great Britain, and Australia, plus a few foreign-language publications from continental Europe and Mexico. The periodicals are listed in alphabetical order by title, then chronologically by date of publication. Day uses a gridbox system, twelve boxes across (corresponding to the months of the year, with appropriate single-letter initials as running heads), each box down the page representing one year. Normally, two sets of numbers appear in each box (representing each issue of the magazine actually published); the top number is the volume number, the bottom number the issue number of that particular release. Quarterly publications are marked with single-letter codes next to these numbers indicating the season (*e.g.,* "A" = Autumn). Bimonthly periodicals are so indicated by extending a series of hyphens across two boxes. In general, the schematic should be obvious at a glance even to the inexperienced user. The book is shot from clearly reproduced typed copy.

Day lists data through the end of 1960; his work was continued by Desmond (see #150), and has now largely been superseded by Hall *et al.* (see #153), but Day does include some peripheral publications not indexed in other sources in quite this fashion.

Now mostly subsumed into Miller/Contento's CD-ROM (see #157).

148. Day, Bradford M., [and William H. Evans]. **An Index on the Weird & Fantastica in Magazines.** S. Ozone Park, NY, Bradford M. Day, 1953. 162 p. (pbk.).

One of the many bibliographies and indexes produced by this Long Island author during the period 1950-63, Day's guide is divided into three sections.

Part I provides an issue-by-issue contents guide to eight pulp horror magazines of the 1920s-50s (*Weird Tales, Golden Fleece, Strange Tales, Oriental Stories, Magic Carpet, Tales of Magic & Mystery, Thrill Book, Strange Stories*), derived largely from an untitled series of magazine checklists produced in looseleaf format by William H. Evans in 1950. A typical entry provides: editor's name (if it has changed from the previous issue), month and year of publication, size (if it has changed from the previous issue), volume and issue number, and a list of the material published in each issue with author names as they appeared in the original. Day has updated the *WT* list through the end of 1953 (the magazine died in 1954).

A second section reproduces Evans's indexes to fantastic fiction published in the general adventure pulps (*The Argosy, Blue Book Magazine, Complete Stories, Romance Magazine, Popular Magazine, The Idler, All-American Fiction, All-Story Magazine, The Cavalier, Live Wire, Munsey's Magazine, Ocean,* and *Scrap Book,* with incomplete listings from thirteen other periodicals). The third section, "A Checklist of Fantastic Magazines," was a precursor to *The Complete Checklist* (see #147) published by Day in 1961 and follows the same format. The book is shot from generally clear typed copy, with the usual Day production problems (poor binding and proofreading).

Now partly superseded by Parnell/Ashby (see #160) and Robbins (see #163), and almost wholly by Miller/Contento's CD-ROM (see #157).

149. Day, Donald B. **Index to the Science-Fiction Magazines, 1926-1950.** Portland, OR, Perri Press, 1952. xv, 184 p. index. LC 52-41880. **Index to the Science Fiction Magazines, 1926-1950.** Rev. ed. Boston, G. K. Hall & Co., 1982. xv, 289 p. index. ISBN 0-8161-8591-3.

The *Index to the Science-Fiction Magazines* was the first serious attempt to produce a unified one-volume guide to the fiction published by the professional SF periodicals of the pulp era, and it marked an early high point in fan scholarship.

The main index is arranged alphabetically by author's name, then alphabetically by story title. A typical entry provides: author (all caps), title, type (*e.g.,* "s" = short story), a two- or three-letter abbreviation for the magazine title (*e.g.,* "ASF" = *Astounding Science Fiction*), month and year of publication (in the form "Aug 42" for August 1942), and beginning page number.

The title index gives: story title (all caps), author, type, month and year of publication, and page number. A third section provides an issue-by-issue checklist of each magazine, chronologically in descending order by date, giving month and year of publication, volume and issue number for each issue published, physical page size (in inches), number of pages in each issue, and cover artist for each issue. A brief, two-page list of "Back Cover Pictures" completes the book; later issues also included a tipped-in errata sheet after the last page of text.

Day does not include *Weird Tales,* ostensibly because he lacked access to a complete set, but otherwise he covers all the major and minor professional magazines of fantastic literature from the founding of *Amazing Stories* in 1926 through the end of 1950. Some story series listings are embedded in the author entries. There are numerous "See" and "See Also" references to and from known pen names and house pseudonyms to the real authors; in general, however, Day lists each story under the names actually used for publication. Day also indexes artists and magazine editors in the general alphabetical author sequence. The book is shot from sometimes faint typed copy.

G. K. Hall has done the SF world a service by completely resetting the book and updating the text from Day's own notes and from other corrections and addenda published in a wide variety of fan and professional sources. The result is an attractive, easy-to-use, authoritative guide to the nascence of the science fiction field. No serious student of the genre should be without it.

Now mostly subsumed into Miller/Contento's CD-ROM (see #157).

150. Desmond, William H. **The Science-Fiction Magazine Checklist, 1961-1972.** South Boston, MA, Archival Press, 1973. 16 p. (pbk.).

Desmond's booklet was intended directly to supplement Day's *Checklist* (see #147), and uses a very similar format with slightly higher production values. Magazines are arranged alphabetically by title, then chronologically by year of issue. A boxed grid occupies each page, twelve boxes wide (corresponding to the months of the year), each descending box representing one year of issue. Desmond includes only those titles published between January 1961 and the end of 1972.

Largely superseded by Hall *et al.* (see #153) and Wysocki (see #173).

151. Evans, William H. **Index of Science Fiction.** [Denver, CO, Robert C. Peterson], 1949. 148 leaves. index. (pbk.).

Evans was an early indexer of the field whose work appeared in a variety of rather amateurish formats (this index was issued in looseleaf format); some of his work was later reworked into more professional guise by Brad Day (see #148).

This guide indexes roughly thirty pulp SF magazines, providing complete contents listings on an issue-by-issue basis, and covering issues produced through 1947/48. Although most of his material has been superseded by Donald Day (see #149), Evans did attempt to classify the subject matter of each story through the Speer Decimal System, providing a unique subject access unavailable in any other source. Unfortunately, this index is itself virtually unobtainable, and most of Evans's pioneering work is now almost completely lost.

152. Frank, Howard, and Roy Torgeson. **The 1977 Science Fiction & Fantasy Magazine Checklist & Price Guide, 1923-1976.** Port Washington, NY, Science Fiction Resources, 1977. 50 p. index. ISBN 0-918364-00-0 (pbk.).

This checklist of SF and fantasy magazines is arranged alphabetically by title, then chronologically by year, noting each issue produced by year and by month, the latter being designated by its numerical equivalent (*e.g.,* "12" = December). The booklet also provides general prices for copies of the issues in "good" condition. The checklist part of this booklet has been completely superseded by Hall *et al.* (see #153), and the pricing information is so far out-of-date as to be utterly useless, except possibly as a general guide to value ratios.

153. Hall, H. W., Kenneth R. Johnson, and George Michaels. **The Science Fiction Magazines: A Bibliographical Checklist of Titles and Issues Through 1982.** Bryan, TX, SFBRI, 1983. iv, 89 p. index. ISBN 0-935064-10-9 (pbk.). San Bernardino, CA, The Borgo Press, 1985. iv, 89 p. index. LC 84-11192. ISBN 0-89370-772-4.

Hall's checklist generally replaces all earlier efforts of this type, including Day (see #149), Desmond (see #150), Frank/Torgeson (see #152), and Robinson (see #164), with a few exceptions (Day lists some very peripheral titles not covered in Hall).

The main section includes a complete alphabetical list of the professional science fiction and fantasy magazines published in English from 1924-82, excluding comic books and the broadly-based adventure pulp magazines. Under each entry, Hall provides the following information: magazine title (all caps), total volumes published (*e.g.,* "v.1-7 no.2," indicating that the magazine published issues from volume 1 through volume 7, issue 2), total years published, place of publication and publisher (either primary publisher, or the latest publisher for active titles), a historical list of editorial personnel (by date), a historical list of publishers (by date), historical notes of interest, the two- or three-letter code commonly used for the magazine in the published indices, a list of publications that have indexed the periodical, plus a comprehensive checklist of each issue published, in descending order by publication date, including volume number, issue number, and month and year of publication. Hall notes title changes as interpolated line breaks when they occur, and similarly records numbering errors (a frequent occurrence in the pulps) and other bibliographical data of interest.

End matter includes an "Editor Index," alphabetically by editor name, with a listing of the publications and years the editor served; "Indexes to the Magazines," a bibliography of published index sources; and an "Appendix: Non-English Language Magazines," which presents a skeletal listing of foreign prozines, arranged alphabetically by country, then by publication.

Hall's research is both sound and meticulous, and his checklist is a handy synthesis of the history of magazine publication in the field of fantastic literature. Note that Wysocki's checklist (see #173), although not as complete, does include several years' more data.

154. Index to Fantasy & Science Fiction in Munsey Publications. [S.l., s.n., n.d.]. 36 p. (pbk.).

This uncredited fan index, produced from mimeographed 8.5" x 11" copy circa 1950-55, provides a useful guide to fantastic stories and novels published in the following Munsey pulps: *Argosy Monthly, All-Story Magazine, The Cavalier, Munsey's Magazine, The Scrap Book, The Live Wire, Argosy All-Story Weekly, Argosy Weekly, All-Story Weekly,* and *All-Story Cavalier Weekly.*

The volume indexes the material alphabetically by author's name, then by story title. A typical entry includes: author (all caps), title, type (*e.g.,* "ss" = short story), subject code (*e.g.,* "A" = Atlantis), magazine title abbreviation (*e.g.,* "AS W" = *All-Story Weekly*), month (and day, where applicable) and year of publication. There is no title index. The booklet is shot from generally legible typed copy, although the publication itself is now yellowing with age. The subject codes, which are not universally applied, are still useful in determining what each story is about. Now virtually unobtainable.

155. Lewis, Al, [with various co-editors]. **Index to the Science Fiction Magazines: 1961-1963.** Los Angeles, CA, Al Lewis, 1962-64. 3 v. index. (pbk.).

These three annual indexes to the SF magazines published during each calendar year include complete contents for each issue, in chronological order by publication date, plus author, title, and illustrator indices. The 1962-63 volumes also include an "Index to Book Reviews," a feature not incorporated into most other guides of this kind. However, virtually all of this data has now been subsumed into Metcalf (see #156), Strauss (see #168), and Miller/Contento's CD-ROM (see #157), and the book review material into Hall's guide (see #116), making these laudable early efforts now obsolete. Al Lewis should not be confused with Anthony R. Lewis, who edited many of the NESFA annuals (see #159).

156. Metcalf, Norm. **The Index of Science Fiction Magazines, 1951-1965.** El Cerrito, CA, J. Ben Stark, Publisher, 1968. ix, 249 p. index. (pbk.).

Metcalf intended his index as a direct sequel and supplement to Donald Day's pioneering effort (see #149), and his guide follows much the same format as the earlier book.

Following a brief introduction on how to use the book, plus an abbreviations list (arranged two ways, by magazine title and inversely by abbreviation), the main section of the index is organized in alphabetical order by author's name or pseudonym, then alphabetically by individual story title. A typical entry includes: author's name (all caps), story title, word count (in the form "14.4" for 14,400 words), magazine title abbreviation (*e.g.,* "ASF" = *Astounding Science Fiction*), and month and year of publication (in the form "Sep 61" for September 1961).

As with Day, many story series listings are interpolated into the text, and the book is filled with "See" and "See Also" references to other pen names of the authors. Editorial staff are indexed along with the rest, with appropriate periods of service; also included are references to photographs and biographical material. Finally, Metcalf also provides a general reference to authors covered in the earlier Day index (in the form "26-50" following the author's name).

The title index records: story title (all caps), author (including mention of the author's real name where appropriate), word length, magazine title abbreviation, and month and year of publication. A separate index to illustrators (cover and interior) lists: artist's name (all caps), magazine abbreviation, and cover and interior credits (by month and year of publication). An index to editorial staff provides a list of personnel by magazine, editor's name, and dates of service. A checklist correlating magazine titles, dates and years of publication, volume and issue numbers, and cover illustrators, completes the main text. An unpaged, two-page corrigenda to Donald Day's earlier index is appended at the end of the book. The book is reproduced from very clear typed copy.

Metcalf's work is far more readable and legible than the computer-generated copy of Strauss (see #168), and is generally to be preferred; however, Strauss includes initial page numbers for all entries, data not found in Metcalf, while Metcalf includes series and pseudonym information and story lengths not in Strauss. Therefore, the avid bibliographer (and the academic library) may wish to retain copies of both books.

Most of this material has now been subsumed into Miller and Contento's CD-ROM (see #157).

157. Miller, Stephen T. and William G. Contento. **Science Fiction, Fantasy, & Weird Fiction Magazine Index (1890-2000).** Oakland, CA, Locus Press, 2001. CD-ROM. Index. Updated annually and produced on demand.

Contents (2001 version): "Preface," by Stephen T. Miller; "Introduction," by Sam Moskowitz; "Acknowledgments"; "Magazines, Listed by Title"; "Author Index"; "Stories, Listed by Author"; "Stories, Listed by Title"; "Works About Specific Authors"; "Chronological List"; "Series List"; "Cover Artists"; "Magazine Checklist"; "Abbreviations"; "Bibliography"; "Known Missing Issues"; "Notes: Using the Index"; "To Find an Issue of a Magazine"; "To Find an Author"; "To Find a Story"; "To Find a Cover Artist"; "Series Annotations"; "Future Plans"; "To Contact the Authors."

This CD-ROM indexes some 82,000 stories by 23,000 authors from 1,022 different English-language periodicals in 14,559 individual issues, even including data from some magazines that were never actually published, but whose issues were assembled.

The organization and layout is identical to the *Locus Index to Science Fiction* (see #33), using plain text, little formatting, and a series of alphabetical menus for easy navigation through the menus. The links to magazine titles provide a list of issues, including: volume and issue number, date, cover price, pagination, cover artist name (linked), and contents (linked). The author index links to a list of story titles that provide magazine title and date only, but are further linked to the table of contents for that issue. The individual tables of contents provide: volume and issue number, date, cover price, pagination, cover artist (linked), and a list of the contents by page, with article title, author (linked), and an abbreviation for the type of material (ss = short story, nv = novelette, etc.).

There is little direct help for those users unfamiliar with the abbreviations employed in the text, but a link to the abbreviations guide in the index's table of contents does provide some assistance. Unlike *The Locus Index to Science Fiction and Index to Science Fiction Anthologies and Collections* (see #33), this index is not available free on the Locus Press website. There is only an excerpted magazine checklist (http://www.sff.net/locus/chklst/0chklst.htm) to give users a taste of the material, and this has not been kept up-to-date.

However, since the index is updated annually in new editions, Miller and Contento's guide is by far the largest repository of information on SF, fantasy, and horror magazines and their publications, basically superseding all other previously-published print indices, some of which, however, may selectively include small pieces of data not covered on the CD-ROM.

For genre collectors, fans, researchers, and all of the libraries serving them, this is an inexpensive, "must have" reference purchase.

158. Murray, Terry A. **Science Fiction Magazine Story Index, 1926-1995.** Jefferson, NC, and London, McFarland & Company, 1999. ix, 627 p. index. LC 98-532290. ISBN 0-7864-0691-7 (library binding: alkaline paper).

Contents: "Acknowledgments"; "Introduction"; "Bibliography"; "User's Guide"; "The Magazines"; "Appendix: Prolific Authors, with Titles"; "Title Index"; "Author Index."

"The book is arranged in four parts: an issue-by-issue listing for each magazine (with the magazines appearing alphabetically), an appendix listing the story titles of prolific authors, a title index, and an author index."

The magazine header for each periodical title is listed in boldfaced type, flush left to the gutter in a two-column format, under the best-known title of the publication. Alternative titles are listed underneath in italics, with the dates those title variations were in effect.

Each individual magazine issue entry includes: issue item number (numbered consecutively from 1-4943 throughout the book); publication date (in the form of 10/86 for October 1986); issue number; and the fiction contents for each issue, arranged alphabetically by title, with the author name listed first in inverted order (bold caps), followed by the title of that author's story in regular type. No paginations or volume information are provided. 134 separate periodicals are indexed in the book, with 4,943 separate issues actually being covered, with an average of six stories per issue.

The Appendix: Prolific Authors, with Titles is arranged alphabetically by the authors' last name (bold), and includes an alphabetical listing of stories written by the author listed in the index. Only authors with 25 or more stories are included in this section. However, no item numbers are provided, forcing the the user to go to the title index to locate the listing for a particular work. The title and author indexes refer to the entry numbers found in the magazine listing, but are not cross-referenced: the Author Index simply gives a list of authors in alphabetical order, plus the item numbers assigned to each, in numerical order, while the Title Index lists titles (mostly) without authors, except where two or more titles are identical and need to be differentiated, all cross-referenced to the appropriate item numbers. This is an unnecessarily clunky, clumsy system that makes this book exceedingly difficult to use for the average user.

Murray's index defines science fiction very broadly, making no attempt to separate fantasy from science fiction. The book excludes poetry, nonfiction articles, columns, letters, contests, cover art, interior art, and information on editorial staff, publisher, physical size, page count, price, or story series. It also makes no attempt to identify pseudonyms, and most of the well-known British magazines are not included, evidently because he had no access to them. Thus, such classic SF periodicals as *New Worlds, Science Fantasy, Nebula, Interzone, Impulse, Authentic Science Fiction, Science Fiction Adventures* (British version), and *Vision of Tomorrow,* to mention but a few, are completely missing here.

It is exceedingly depressing to note what could have been done with this guide to make it the standard reference of its type. Lamentably, however, Murray's book is useful only as a finding tool, and fails even that test through its lackadaisical indexing. Prefer the far superior Miller and Contento CD-ROM (see #157), which is more current, more complete, provides much more information, and is much easier to access.

159. New England Science Fiction Association, Inc. (some volumes edited by Anthony R. Lewis). **Index to the Science Fiction Magazines, 1966-1970.** Cambridge, MA, New England Science Fiction Association, 1971. ix, 82 p. index. **Index to the Science Fiction Magazines, 1966-1969.** Cambridge, MA, New England Science Fiction Association, 1968-70. 4 v. index. LC 75-650102. ISSN 0579-6059 (pbk.). **The N.E.S.F.A. Index [to] Science Fiction Magazines and Original Anthologies, 1971/1972-1986.** Cambridge, MA, New England Science Fiction Association, 1973-88. 14 v. index. LC 75-646017 and LC 84-643001. ISSN 0361-3038 and ISSN 0747-7546 (pbk.). **The N.E.S.F.A. Index to Short SF, 1987-1988.** Cambridge, MA, New England Science Fiction Association, 1989-1990. 2 v. index. (pbk.). **The N.E.S.F.A. Index to Short Science Fiction for 1989.** Cambridge, MA, New England Science Fiction Association, 1992. 1 v. index. (pbk.).

The NESFA volumes were intended directly to supplement Strauss (see #168). The 1966-69 annual volumes were cumulated (and added to) in the 1966-70 hardcover version; the later series evolved both in title and content through several permutations, gradually becoming more elaborate with the passing of years. Three of these volumes were published as two-year sets: 1971/72, 1977/78, and 1979/80.

The 1966-70 cumulation is virtually identical in style and format to Strauss, providing an abbreviations list, magazine checklist, and three indexes to the contents (by magazine issue, title, and author). A typical entry includes: author, title, page number on which the piece begins, type (*e.g.,* "S" = short story), month and year of publication (in the form "FEB 70" for February 1970), and a three-letter magazine code (*e.g.,* "FSF" = *The Magazine of Fantasy & Science Fiction*). The book is shot in all capital letters from photoreduced, computer-generated copy.

The latter annuals, beginning with the 1971/72 two-year cumulation, gradually began indexing, in addition to the dwindling number of professional magazines in the field, the many anthologies of original science fiction stories that began proliferating in the 1970s, assigning them six-letter abbreviation codes. The later volumes also include somewhat more elaborate formats, featuring some indentations of title data in the author section of the indexes and typeset introductory material (including expanded descriptions of the format and contents of the original anthologies), although the basic arrangement has stayed the same throughout. The books also continued to increase in size, finally passing the 100-page mark with the 1987 annual (which further expanded coverage to *all* short SF fiction published in the year).

The NESFA indices supplemented Donald Day's guide (see #149) and the later Strauss and Metcalf indexes (see #168 and #156), but the last volume published was 1989. Now mostly subsumed into Miller/Contento's much more complete, much more searchable CD-ROM (see #157).

160. Parnell, Frank H., and Mike Ashley. **Monthly Terrors: An Index to the Weird Fantasy Magazines Published in the United States and Great Britain.** Westport, CT & London, Greenwood Press, 1985. xxvii, 602 p. index. (Bibliographies and Indexes in World Literature, No. 4). LC 84-19225. ISBN 0-313-23989-4.

This generally sound guide focuses on professional and semi-professional horror and fantasy magazines published in English from 1919-83. Following brief introductions by Peter Haining and Parnell, Ashley contributes a six-page historical survey of the weird fantasy magazines. The "User's Guide" then provides a detailed summary of how the book is organized.

The major part of the book (300 of 602 pages), the "Issue Index," is arranged alphabetically by magazine title, each magazine's listings starting on a new page. A typical entry includes: magazine title (centered in all caps), a brief historical summary, including publisher(s), publisher addresses, editor(s), title changes, and other vital data (all in italics), plus an issue-by-issue contents listing (giving month and year of publication, volume and issue number, cover artist, and contents). The contents listings include: title, type (if longer than short story length), and author. Major title changes are noted with appropriate "See" references at the end of the contents listings to the magazine's new title.

The other major section, the "Author Index," includes the following data: author's name (all caps), years of birth and death (if known), brief italicized description of the author's nationality and occupation (if known), and an alphabetical listing of the author's stories and other contributions (giving title, magazine title abbreviation, month [and/or issue number] and year of publication); stories under pseudonyms are listed under the author's real (or best-known) name, alphabetically by pen name and then by title, with "See" references from the bogus name to the real one. Middle or additional names of authors are provided in parentheses.

A separate "Artist Index," also arranged alphabetically by name, notes the artists' cover and interior illustrations alphabetically by name of magazine (listed by abbreviations code), with year and month (or issue number) of publication. The "Editor Index" similarly lists each publication's editorial staff, correlated with position and time served, and name of the periodical.

The several appendices include an "Index to Series and Connected Stories," "Honorable Mentions" (borderline publications summarized in one or more paragraphs), "Chronological Checklist of Magazines" (by date of initial publication, showing entire range of publication dates), and a "Geographical Listing of Magazines," by state and country, then alphabetically by publisher, with name(s) of magazines issued by that publisher and publishing address. Completing the book is a two-page bibliography and an errata page. *Monthly*

Terrors is reproduced from legible word-processed copy and is well bound in a library cloth edition.

As always with Ashley's publications, the historical notes and biographical squibs are thoroughly researched and indisputably sound. The book is well organized, clearly and logically laid out, and well indexed. However, the absence of a title index to the individual stories flaws what is otherwise a virtuoso performance, and makes access to Miller and Contento's index (see #157) absolutely necessary.

161. Pavlat, Robert, and Bill Evans. **Fanzine Index, Listing Most Fanzines from the Beginning Through 1952, Including Titles, Editors' Names, and Data on Each Issue.** Flushing, NY, Harold Palmer Piser, Worldfare Publications, 1965. 141 p. LC 89-832232 (pbk.). Originally issued about 1953 by Pavlat and Evans as a series of fascicles.

Pavlat and Evans have provided an important checklist of the science fiction field's important but highly ephemeral fan publications, most of which are now impossible to find.

The index is arranged in alphabetical order by title of the periodical. A typical entry includes: magazine title (with occasional "See" references to alternate titles), editor's name, and a chronological list of all known issues. For each issue, the authors have noted: volume and/or issue number, month and year of publication (in the form "Jul 39" for July 1939), and a series of codes indicating (in order) page size, number of pages, and printing medium. All of this is valuable information, although an index of the editors would also have been desirable.

The *Index* was shot from legible typed copy and mimeographed in paper covers (the paper is now highly oxidized), and has itself become very difficult to locate. A comprehensive contents index of SF fanzines is badly needed, since so many SF professionals got their start with these publications.

NOTE: the largest collection of science fiction fan magazines accessible to scholars is located at the Eaton Collection, Rivera Library, University of California, Riverside, which purchased the 20,000-volume Terry Carr collection in the late 1980s.

162. Plum, Claude D., Jr. **The Terratoid Guide: A Checklist of Magazines Dealing with Fantasy, Science-Fiction and Horror Films.** Hollywood, CA, Claude D. Plum, Jr., 1973. 18 p. (pbk.).

This A-Z guide lists professional and amateur magazines dealing with fantastic films. A typical entry includes: title (all caps), publisher (or editor), and a list of known issues published (in the form "#1 to #30"), plus an additional notation if the magazine had "ceased publication" by 1973. A few foreign-language publications are listed. A second section provides publishers and their addresses (with the name[s] of the periodicals they produce) in alphabetical order by publisher name. The book is shot from very legible typed copy.

Now out-of-date, although no comparable publication exists to supplant it.

163. Robbins, Leonard A. **The Pulp Magazine Index, First Series.** Mercer Island, WA, Starmont House, 1988. x, 460, 882, 810 p. in 3 v. index. LC 88-20056, LC 91-658651. ISBN 1-55742-111-0 (set). **The Pulp Magazine Index, Second Series.** Mercer Island, WA, Starmont House, 1990. viii, 583 p. index. LC 89-34752. ISBN 1-55742-162-5. **The Pulp Magazine Index, Third Series.** Mercer Island, WA, Starmont House, 1990. xii, 639 p.

index. ISBN 1-55742-204-4. **The Pulp Magazine Index, Fourth Series.** Mercer Island, WA, Starmount House, 1991. xi, 567 p. ISBN 1-55742-241-9.

This massive attempt to index all known surviving pulp magazines includes many references to the SF, weird, fantastic, hero, and supernatural pulps, in addition to those published in other genres.

Robbins employs a unique format that sometimes mitigates against any quick or logical access to his material. Each magazine indexed has been assigned an arbitrary one- to two-letter code (*Doctor Death,* for example, is "AT"), which is thereafter used to refer to that publication throughout the index. Since none of the codes are mnemonic, one must refer constantly back to the code list to determine a particular publication's title: they are not at all obvious.

The individual volumes/sets are all arranged similarly: the first section, "Special Remarks," lists discrepancies or variations in the data, reported in alphabetical order by magazine code, listing code letters, volume and issue numbers, and remarks (*e.g.,* "Magazine TOC [*i.e.,* Table of Contents] reflects B-3 in error"). These notes are themselves largely incomprehensible without reference to the main text. Following the remarks are lists of the magazines indexed, in alphabetical order by title, including title, price, page size, customary pagination, frequency, publisher's name, editor, and magazine code. The "Code Index" re-works the same information in alphabetical order by code.

The main index is arranged alphabetically by magazine code (not title), and provides the following data: code letter, issue date (in the form "04-1934" for April 1934), volume and issue number, initial pagination for the piece indexed, title of story or article, author of story or article, remarks (referring the user back to the "Remarks Index" at the front of the volume). Each issue of a particular periodical is indexed chronologically in order of publication, stories being recorded consecutively in ascending order by page number. The title and author indices reorder the same data by title and author name, respectively.

In addition, a separate "Artists File Report" indexes all known artwork used in these publications, alphabetically by artist name, giving: artist, magazine code, volume and issue number, two columns labelled "Cover" [art] and "Int"[erior art] (an "X" is placed in the appropriate column), and the title of the story being illustrated.

Finally, the "Character File Report" provides a list of chief characters associated with the stories, alphabetically by character name, including: character, magazine code, volume and issue number, and story title. Following the character index is a short alphabetical guide to the characters' aliases and chief associates, referred back to their original names. The books are clearly reproduced from computer-generated copy, and sturdily bound in library cloth editions.

There is a wealth of material here on a facet of American publishing that has now almost completely vanished. The first series alone indexes almost two hundred pulp titles, and the two additional volumes add another seventy periodicals. The huge bulk of the material, however, combined with its division into four units, and the arbitrary arrangement of the main indexes in all three sets, make access much more difficult than it should have been. Also, not all issues of all of the periodicals covered may be indexed in one particular series, requiring the user to check all four sets to see if the missing issues have been picked up elsewhere (not all have been completed).

Even with these *caveats*, *The Pulp Magazine Index* provides a major new reference source for future scholarly research into American popular and SF literature, one that should be acquired by all large university libraries. Only a few hundred copies of each set were produced, and have now become exceedingly difficult to locate.

164. Robinson, Roger. **Science Fiction and Fantasy Magazines, 1923-1980.** Harold Wood, Essex, England, Beccon Publications, 1984. 28 p. (Beccon Publications Collector's Checklist). (pbk.).

Robinson provides a brief checklist of all known professional SF and fantasy magazines published between the inception of *Weird Tales* in 1923 through the end of 1980, arranged alphabetically by magazine title.

A typical entry includes: title, nationality (*e.g.,* "US" = United States), span of publication (*e.g.,* "Mar52-Dec74" for March 1952 through December 1974), total number of issues published, and format (*e.g.,* digest). Beneath this summary material is a chronological checklist of every issue published, by volume and issue number, in block paragraph format (*e.g.,* "19/1,2,3,4" for volume 19, numbers 1-4), without correlation to months or years of publication. Similar data are provided for overseas editions.

Compared to Robinson, Hall's guide (see #153) includes considerably more data on the periodicals themselves (including editors' names, index references, publishers' names, and an exact correlation between months of publication and specific issue numbers) in a much more readable format with two extra years of material. Both volumes include titles not featured in the other, although there is considerable overlap, as might be expected. Robinson's smaller page size, however, makes his checklist much more convenient for actual use as a buying guide by collectors at conventions and book fairs.

Libraries will prefer Hall.

165. Siemon, Fred(erick). **Ghost Story Index: An Author-Title Index to More Than 2,200 Stories of Ghosts, Horrors, and the Macabre Appearing in 190 Books and Anthologies.** San Jose, CA, Library Research Associates, 1967. 141 p. index LC 67-30345.

Very similarly organized to the author's *Science Fiction Story Index* (see #166), Siemon's book indexes collections and anthologies of weird supernatural fiction.

The first index correlates story authors and titles with anthology code numbers. The middle section of the book lists anthologies in alphabetical order by main entry (usually editor's name), including the following data: code number (in the form "A572" for an anthology by Pierre Andrezel), source code (*e.g.,* "F" = *Fiction Catalog*), editor, title (underlined), place of publication, publisher, year of publication, and pagination. The final section gives story titles and authors only (last names and first initials).

As with the author's companion volume on science fiction, the anthology codes are so arbitrary that the user must constantly recheck the code/anthology index, and the absence of the codes from the title index requires the referencing of no less than three different sections of Siemon's book to locate the anthology in which a particular story appears. Such a remarkably poor design for a reference guide undoubtedly required much cogitation to devise. Siemon also misses nearly as many anthologies in this book as he did with his SF guide four years later.

Completely superseded by Ashley and Contento's much superior production (see #138).

166. Siemon, Frederick. **Science Fiction Story Index, 1950-1968.** Chicago, American Library Association, 1971. x, 274 p. index. LC 70-162470. ISBN 0-8389-0107-7 (pbk.). Fletcher, Marilyn P. **Science Fiction Story Index, 1950-1979.** 2nd ed. Chicago, American Library Association, 1981. xi, 610 p. index. LC 80-28685. ISBN 0-8389-0320-7 (pbk.).

Siemon's index is not so much a bad book as a mediocre one, which often amounts to much the same thing in reference terms. The author attempts to index SF short stories published in monographic collections and anthologies from 1950-68.

The first section of the book indexes the stories alphabetically by author and then by title, correlating each entry with a series of code numbers referring to the anthology title (but with no paginations). The anthologies themselves are indexed in the middle part of the volume alphabetically by main entry (usually by editor's name, although some anonymously edited works are filed by title, and a few collections derived from magazines are listed under that periodical's name).

A typical entry includes: code number (*e.g.,* "M275"), reference code (*e.g.,* "F" = indexed in the *Fiction Catalog*), editor's name, title (underlined), subtitle (*not* underlined), author's statement (repeated), place of publication, publisher, year of publication, and pagination. The code numbers are generated from the main entry (the "M" in "M275," for example, corresponding to the first letter of the editor's name [in this case, Robert *M*agidoff]), each number interpolating the title in alphabetical order by main entry. There are often large gaps in the number sequences ("M455" is followed by "M570"), and the whole numbering system is so arbitrary that the user must refer constantly back to the code/anthology section to check references from the author and title indexes.

The title index correlates story titles and authors' names only; no references are made to the code numbers, requiring the reader to check *three* sections to locate a specific anthology from a story title; also, the author references only include the first *initial* of an author's name. Anthology titles are also interfiled in the title index with a reference to entry number (but anthologies are not otherwise readily distinguishable from the other titles listed).

Siemon himself acknowledges in his introduction missing almost a hundred anthologies or collections known to him, and indeed there are major lacunae in his volume; both Cole (see #144) and particularly Contento (see #145) cover many more anthologies in much more usable formats with considerably more information (Contento, for example, lists original places of publication for all reprinted stories). Unfortunately, Fletcher's reworking of the *Index* does not help matters much.

Fletcher has placed the anthology list at the beginning of her book, which *is* a helpful move, and has expanded the code list from four digits to six (*e.g.,* "BL0250" for an entry by Robert Bloch). Anthologies are again listed usually by main entry, although magazine-generated titles appear under the magazine name, and some titles, for no obvious reason, are filed by book title. The title index correlates story titles, authors, and code numbers; the author index lists authors, story or anthology titles (the latter followed by the appellation [anthology]), and code numbers. The book is reproduced from generally legible computer-generated copy, all entries running in all-capital letters. Again, Fletcher is far from complete, missing, for example, volumes 10-18, 20-25, and 27-30 out of the *New Writings in SF* series, and including only the American edition of #7 (which has very different contents from the British original).

Both of these books have been superseded by the better-organized, far more complete volumes of Contento (see #145), which will be preferred by libraries. Evidently, the American Library Association itself acknowledged the ephemeral nature of these mighty tomes by releasing them only in paperback.

167. Stone, Graham. **Index to British Science Fiction Magazines, 1934-1953.** Canberra City and Sydney, Australia, Australian Science Fiction Association, 1977-80. 3 v. index. LC 74-491122. ISBN 0-9598342-2-2 (v.1), ISBN 0-9598342-4-9 (v.2), ISBN 0-9598342-3-0 (v.3) (pbk.). Originally issued in fascicles beginning in 1968, and also issued in a preliminary book version that year. Volume 2 of the 1977-80 set was issued after Volume 3.

Stone provides a necessary adjunct to Donald Day's index (see #149), Metcalf (see #156), and Strauss (see #168), which generally cover the major independent British magazines (such as *New Worlds*), but often miss the British editions of the major American SF periodicals, versions which usually had vastly different contents from their U.S. counterparts.

Volume 1 provides an issue-by-issue contents guide to the magazines, typically including: magazine title (all caps), volume and/or issue number, month and year of publication, physical size (if it has changed from the preceding issue), total page count of the issue, an arbitrarily assigned consecutive issue number running from 1-503 (the total number of issues indexed in these volumes), and cover artist.

The contents listings themselves record titles and authors in the same order as they appeared in each magazine issue; book review features include listings of the books (and their authors) being reviewed. Volume 2 indexes the material alphabetically by story author, including: title, magazine, issue number appearing on the publication itself, and Stone's consecutive issue number. Volume 3 reworks the same data alphabetically by title, then author, magazine, issue number, and Stone's ID number, divided, however, into the following sections: "Fiction," "Verse," "Nonfiction," "Editorials," "Features," and "Reviews."

Since Volume 1 was originally issued in seven parts, individual magazines being covered as Stone was able to locate them, the cumulated version, which maintains the original order of the fascicles, follows no discernible arrangement, except that most (but not all) of the journals are indexed in complete, consecutive runs. Individual periodicals can, however, be located through alphabetical tables of contents reproduced at the beginning of each volume. The books are shot from stenciled copy, which is faint on some pages of some copies; and the volumes themselves have rather amateurishly been gathered into signatures, side-stapled, and glued into flimsy paper covers. The 1953 cutoff date is not always followed, with some (but not all) of the individual periodical runs arbitrarily being continued down through 1955.

Librarian Stone has shown with other volumes that he has the talent to do better than this "*faanish*" effort; a reworked, updated second edition, with better organization, production values, and a continuation of the data to modern times, would be highly desirable. In the meantime, this set is useful only as an adjunct to the major SF periodical indexes mentioned above, and has now been largely superseded by Miller/Contento (see #157).

168. Strauss, Erwin S. **The MIT Science Fiction Society's Index to the S-F Magazines, 1951-1965.** Cambridge, MA, MIT Science Fiction Society, 1966. iii, 207 p. index. LC 73-174981. Cover title.

The MIT index was the first serious attempt to supplement Donald Day's pioneering 1926-50 index of SF magazines (see #149), and was among the first publications in the field to make use of computer technology to automate the indexing process. The result, although esthetically displeasing, is at least functional.

A brief introduction by the compiler is followed by an abbreviations list and a checklist by magazine, giving: magazine title, abbreviation code, month and year of publication, volume and issue number, physical size, total page count, and cover artist. The main section of the book consists of the same data reorganized into three different indexes: by magazine issue, by title, and by author.

The magazine issue index includes: author, title, the page number on which the piece begins, content code (*e.g.,* "S" = short story), month and year of publication (in the form "MAR 52" for March 1952) and a three-letter magazine code (*e.g.,* "AMZ" = *Amazing Stories*). The title index reworks the same data by title, with the title listings being reproduced in the *second* column of text. The author index reorganizes the same data by author.

All of the material is shot from all-capital computer-generated copy with no running heads or indentations to set off the text; while the multiple-column format does aid in identifying specific pieces of information (the authors are always listed in the first column and the titles in the second, etc.), the photoreduced typeface tends to run the copy together, and some of the copy is faint and difficult to read. Were it not for Strauss's inclusion of page numbers, Metcalf (see #156), which covers virtually the same material (but lacks this particular data), would be much preferred; as it is, however, both books are necessary adjuncts to the library of the serious researcher.

Now largely superseded by Miller/Contento's CD-ROM (see #157).

169. Sween, Roger D. **Fanzine Publishing Record.** Kalamazoo, MI, The Index Company, 1974-75 (?). 12 p. each. (pbk.). At least two trial issues and one regular issue were produced of this index.

Sween attempted to provide a complete contents listing for every fanzine issue being published in the United States in the mid-1970s. Entries are consecutively numbered from one in the first issue recorded for each year, apparently continuing until the final issue of that year. In each issue, fanzine issues are listed alphabetically by title. A typical entry provides: item number, title (all caps), volume and issue number, editor, address, pagination, frequency, price, method of reproduction, and a complete contents listing (including artwork). The absence of indexes in the issues viewed makes access extremely difficult.

Sween's idea is a worthy one, but his aborted attempt to provide bibliographical access to these hard-to-find publications is now itself just a footnote in the history of SF bibliography.

170. Tymn, Marshall B., Martin H. Greenberg, L. W. Currey, and Joseph D. Olander. **Index to Stories in Thematic Anthologies of Science Fiction.** Boston, G. K. Hall & Co., 1978. xiii, 193 p. index. (A Reference Publication in Science Fiction). LC 78-14287. ISBN 0-8161-8027-X.

This curious little guide indexes 181 anthologies of science-fiction stories by broad theme or subject category. The fifty categories include such chapters as "Alien Encounter," "Corruption," "Ethics," "Sports," "Women," and many others. In each chapter anthologies are listed chronologically by publication date (a rather strange choice for organization). The collections are numbered consecutively from 1-181.

A typical entry provides: entry number, title (underlined), editor, place of publication, publisher, year of publication, pagination, format ("paper" = paperback), and a list of the stories and authors included in each book in the same descending order as they appear within the anthology. No specific paginations are listed. An author index references both story authors and anthology editors in one alphabetical sequence, with the code numbers for the books in which their stories appear (code numbers for anthology editors are under-lined), but no specific list of stories. The title index correlates story and anthology titles to the code numbers (the numbers for anthology titles are underlined), but no authors. The volume is shot from legible typed copy.

All of this material is available in Contento (see #145), and while the latter does not attempt to categorize anthologies by subject, most of the subject assignments are fairly obvious from the book titles. The indexing in Tymn *et al.* also leaves much to be desired; readers seeking stories by such prolific writers as Isaac Asimov are left with a list of forty-four code numbers, all of which must be individually searched to determine the actual story titles. This is a particularly unfortunate choice for a guide that purports to index *stories.* Similarly, without appropriate author information the title index is virtually useless.

A poor excuse for a reference volume.

171. McKinstry, Lohr, and Weinberg, Robert. **The Hero-Pulp Index.** Hillside, NJ, Robert Weinberg, 1970. 54 p. index. LC 70-24788 (pbk.). Weinberg, Robert, and Lohr McKinstry. **The Hero Pulp Index.** [2nd ed.]. Evergreen, CO, Opar Press, 1971. 48 p., [16] p. of plates. index. (pbk.).

The first version of this guide to the hero pulps (magazines that were named for a continuing character appearing in the lead novel-length story featured in each issue—*e.g., Doc Savage*) was an 8.5" x 11" mimeographed production rather amateurishly produced and distributed and difficult to read in spots. The second version was reduced in size to 5.5" x 8.5", shot from completely reworked typed copy, and illustrated throughout with sixteen full-page reproductions of the original magazine covers; despite its lesser page count and size, it actually contains more text.

The main section of the book is arranged alphabetically by magazine title (*i.e.*, char-acter name). A typical entry includes: magazine title (all caps), author (usually a house pseudonym followed in parentheses by the major author[s] known to have written under that name), and a chronological list of the issues published, giving: consecutive issue whole number, volume and issue number, month and year of publication, and title of the lead character novel for that issue. Title changes are also noted, as well as the title of the novel announced in the final issue of the magazine for publication in the next issue that never appeared.

A brief author index lists the main house pen names in alphabetical order, with the authors known to have contributed entries under those names, plus an alphabetical list of the real authors and the hero pulps they contributed to (with the total number of such novels that have been attributed to them). A third section lists later reprints in book form from the hero pulps by character (*i.e.,* title) name. The final section, "A Guide to the Hero Pulps," provides detailed summaries of the histories, backgrounds, associates, characteristics, enemies, and careers of the heroes themselves. The book is shot from legible typed copy; the second edition also has a loose errata page slipped into some copies.

Weinberg and McKinstry have produced a very worthwhile guide to these now vanishing monuments to American popular culture, and a third edition with better production values and an individual title index would definitely be warranted. It should be noted that, although many of the hero pulps were fantastic in nature, very few of these periodicals are indexed in other sources; this book also covers a number of mystery and western heroes not indexed elsewhere, although some are found in Robbins (see #163) and Miller/Contento (see #157), but without the additional historical and background material.

172. Wood, Edward. *Journal of Science Fiction* **Magazine Index, 1951-1952.** Chicago, Edward Wood, 1952-53. 2 v. index. (pbk.). Wood, Edward, and Earl Kemp. **The *Destiny* Index of Fantasy—1953.** Chicago, Edward Wood, 1954. 64 p. index. (pbk.).

Intended to supplement Donald Day's 1926-50 index (see #149), Wood's three annuals were published as entire issues of the fanzines indicated (Vol. 1, No. 3 and Vol. 1, No. 4 of the *Journal,* and the Fall 1954 issue of *Destiny*). In both instances, Wood merely provided issue-by-issue contents lists of the SF magazines published in each calendar year; however, the third annual also included a brief five-page list of SF monographs published in 1953, plus "White Paper: 1953-1954," providing detailed statistics on the history of SF periodical publishing. All data except the latter have now been subsumed into other publications, particularly Strauss (see #168), Metcalf (see #156), and especially Miller/Contento (see #157).

173. Wysocki, R. J. **The Science Fiction, Fantasy, Weird, Hero Magazine Checklist.** Westlake, OH, R. J. Wysocki with cooperation from The Cleveland Science Fiction Connection, 1985. iv, 90 p. index. (pbk.).

Raymond Wysocki employs the same block format used by Brad Day in his 1961 checklist (see #148). Magazines are arranged throughout the guide alphabetically by title. Under each periodical, issues are listed chronologically, year by year, each year comprising one line of fourteen boxes across the page. The first box is reserved for the year itself, in the form "28" for 1928, the next twelve boxes for specific issue numbers, and the fourteenth box for running totals (total issues published during that year and total issues published through the end of that year for the entire run of the periodical); the empty space beyond the fourteenth box is reserved for notes. Across the top of each page are running heads listing the months of the year.

In each box for which a corresponding issue was published, Wysocki puts the volume and issue number of that specific issue; quarterly publications also have added a one-letter code (*e.g.,* "W" = Winter) for the season. Issues are recorded through January 1985. A brief magazine title index for publications with variant titles is located on page 90, followed by a tabular recapitulation on page 91 showing the total number of titles and issues published for each year from 1919-84.

Wysocki's guide is the most current box-style checklist of SF magazine issues available, but lacks the detailed historical, bibliographical, and other information provided by Hall's list (see #153), which is generally to be preferred.

INDEXES TO SPECIFIC MAGAZINES

Adventure

174. Bleiler, Richard. **The Index to *Adventure Magazine*.** Mercer Island, WA, Starmont House, 1990. xii, 1,085 p. in 2 v. index. LC 90-10407. ISBN 1-55742-189-7 (set). **The Index to *Adventure Magazine*.** [rev. ed.]. Oakland, CA, Locus Press, 2000. CD-ROM.

This magnificent guide surely must rank as among the most thorough indexes of one magazine ever compiled. Bleiler's forty-page introduction provides an excellent history of the founding and development of *Adventure,* which was possibly the best known (and one of the highest paying) of the "slick" pulp magazines from its founding in 1910.

The main part of Volume One is an issue-by-issue contents guide, from November 1910-April 1971 (881 issues). A typical entry includes: month and year of publication, volume and issue number, editor for that issue, cover artist, interior artist(s), and a complete list of stories/articles and their authors in alphabetical order by author's name, plus continuing departments ("The Camp-Fire," for example). The first volume also includes an index of illustrators, arranged alphabetically by name, giving: artist's name, years of birth and death and brief bio squib (when known), and a list of the specific issues for which the artist produced cover and/or interior art (so specified).

Volume Two includes a 400-page author index, alphabetical by name, listing: author, middle names (if known), years of birth and death and brief bio squib (if known), and an alphabetical list of the stories and/or articles appearing in *Adventure,* with the specific issues in which they appeared. The title index correlates titles and authors only. A four-page bibliography lists sources for the biographical material. This 8.5" x 11" set is shot from very clear word-processed copy, and is bound in sturdy library cloth.

Adventure included all kinds of fiction by major authors, including fantastic, mystery, western, and general adventure, which are now made accessible to scholars and fans for the first time. It's a shame, however, that Bleiler did not choose to list the stories in the order in that they appeared in the magazines, with initial paginations, something which could easily have been added. On the other hand, the biographical material is unparalleled for a guide of this kind, reflecting a considerable amount of secondary and primary research by the author. This set was produced in a very short print run (several hundred copies) for the pulp collectors' market, and is now very difficult to locate.

However, the Locus Press CD-ROM, which fills in a dozen or so issues of *Adventure* that could not be located in time to include in the print version, is an inexpensive, easy-to-use alternative. Recommended for all research libraries.

Air Wonder Stories

175. Okada, Masaya. **Illustrated Index to** *Air Wonder Stories* **(Vol. 1, No. 1-Vol. 1, No. 11, July 1929-May 1930) = Kuchu Kyoi Monogatari e-i Sakuin.** Nagoya, Japan, Masaya Okada, 1973. 79 p. index. (pbk.).

Okada's tribute to this well-known Hugo Gernsback pulp SF magazine includes: "I. *Air Wonder Stories*" (introduction in Japanese); "II. How to Use the Index" (in Japanese); "III. Index of Issues"; "IV. Index of Titles (Fiction)"; "V. Index by Authors (Fiction)"; "VI. Index by Authors" (nonfiction and miscellaneous); "VII. Aviation Forum"; "VIII. Aviation News of the Month"; "IX. Book Reviews"; "X. The Reader Airs His Views"; "XI. Front Covers by Frank R. Paul"; "XII. Principal Illustrations by Ruger, Leonard, Frank R. Paul"; "Postscript" (in Japanese). Except where noted, the text is in English with Japanese and English chapter heads.

The index of issues lists: story number (each fiction piece is numbered in order, from #1 in the first issue to #50 in the last), title (all caps), serial note (*e.g.,* "1/4" = first part of four), author; nonfiction pieces are listed in normal case letters with initial capitals (*e.g.,* "Future Aviation Problems"), and cover stories are so indicated by an asterisk following the story title. The title and author indexes provide similar data, plus issue and initial page number of the story (serialized pieces include such information only for the first part of the serial).

In addition to the bibliographical material, much of which can be found in Donald Day's index (see #149) and Miller/Contento (see #157), Okada reproduces (in black-and-white) all of the eleven front cover illustrations and many of the major interior drawings, plus selected advertisements and small features that appeared in the magazine. Also included are twenty-four of the black-and-white drawings of the authors that ran in each issue, many of them of very obscure writers of whom little is known today. The book is shot from typed copy.

Okada's guide to the magazine, which many collectors regard as the best *looking* of the fantastic pulps, is itself difficult to find, but certainly of value to scholars seriously interested in the history of the early pulp era.

Analog/Astounding Science Fiction

176. Ashley, Mike, with the assistance of Terry Jeeves. **The Complete Index to** *Astounding/Analog,* **Being an Index to the 50 Years of** *Astounding Stories—Astounding SF & Analog:* **January 1930-December 1979, Together with the** *Analog Annual,* **the** *Analog Yearbook,* **& the** *John W. Campbell Memorial Anthology.* Oak Forest, IL, Robert Weinberg Publications, 1981. [vi], 253 p. index. LC 80-53784. ISBN 0-934498-07-5. Jeeves, Terry. **A Checklist of** *Astounding Stories of Super Science, Astounding Stories, Astounding Science Fiction, Analog Science Fiction—Science* Fact. Sheffield, England, ERG Publication, 1965-70. 3 vols. LC 84-125630 (pbk.).

The self-published Jeeves checklist is included here because it was largely incorporated into the later work. Ashley and Jeeves's *Complete Index* is perhaps the best single-magazine index yet produced in the genre, providing every possible access point that the reader or reseacher might desire to search in this most significant of science fiction prozines.

Contents: "Introduction"; "How to Use the Index"; "*Astounding* Analyzed" (title variations, publishers, schedule, format, page counts, cover prices, by issue date); "The People that Brought You *Astounding/Analog*" (list of editorial staff); "Issue Index"; "Author Index—Fiction"; "Author Index—Nonfiction"; "Title Index—Fiction"; "Title Index—Nonfiction"; "Series Index"; "Artist Index"; "Letter Index"; Appendices: "I. Total Number of Contents in ASF"; "II. Most Prolific Contributors"; "III. The Analytical Laboratory: A) Top Writers, B) Top Novels, C) Top Stories"; "IV. Most Prolific Artist"; "Errata" and "Addenda."

The main index lists each issue in order published, giving: date, volume and issue number, whole issue number, cover artist (and story illustrated), and each issue's contents in order by internal pagination. Included are: item number (each story or essay has been assigned a consecutive number from 1-4,239, beginning with the first piece in the first issue of the magazine to the last story in the *Analog Yearbook,* the last "issue" covered in the index); title; format (*e.g.,* "s" = short story); author; initial page number; internal story artist (if any).

Ashley has not numbered items mentioned at the end of each issue, including the subjects of the "Biolog" Department (which provided a one-page biography of one of the authors featured in the magazine issue), and the title (and author, if not a regular columnist) of the "Reference Library" monthly book review column. Coverage is complete through the end of 1979; Ashley and Jeeves also list three original book anthologies that included "*Analog*" in their titles: these appear after the last magazine issue (December 1979) covered.

The author index lists: author (all caps), years of birth and death (if known), brief description (*e.g.,* "US linguist and writer"), story number, story title (in alphabetical order), format, month and year of publication. The title index lists: title (all caps), author, format, month and year of publication. The series index references series title and author(s) only. The artist index includes: artist name (all caps), years of birth and death (if known), list of credits separated into covers and interiors, listed chronologically by year and month. The letter index lists persons who contributed missives to the monthly letter column, alphabetically by surname, with state or country of origin and a chronological list of years and months of contributions. The appendices include a complete breakdown of the periodical's output by year, plus lists of the most prolific authors, most popular contributors, and most prolific artists. The book is shot from legible typed copy, and bound in sturdy library cloth.

Ashley and Jeeves's guide is complete, accurate, well organized, and full of interesting details. The only additional data that might be of value to some future researcher are annotations; given the number of stories published in *Astounding/Analog,* such a guide is unlikely, and, if ever produced, would be immense. A supplement covering the 1980s or a revised, updated second edition of this exceptionally well-produced index would certainly be justified.

177. Boggs, D. W. *Astounding* **Story-Key, 1930-1951.** Minneapolis, MN, D. W. Boggs, 1952. 18 p. (pbk.).

This brief alphabetical checklist indexes stories published in *Astounding Science Fiction* from its inception in 1930 through the end of 1951, citing story titles only, authors being cited by surname alone. Completely superseded by Ashley/Jeeves (see #176).

178. Diviney, Jim, and Shirl Diviney. **Index** *Astounding Analog,* **British Edition, Nov. 53-Aug 63.** Brampton, Huntington, England, [s.n.], [1963?]. 41 p. index. (pbk.).

This guide to the British edition of *Astounding Science Fiction* (later *Analog Science Fiction/Science Fact*), which selected stories from various issues of the U.S. parent magazine, includes three indexes by issue number, author, and story title. Since the British editions of American SF magazines are *not* included in the standard indexes, and the years indexed are not covered in Stone's guide (see #167), fan publications such as Diviney's provide a useful service for bibliographical completists. [not seen].

179. Lorenzen, Jan A. **"20 Years of** *Analog/Astounding Science Fiction*Science Fact,* **1952-1971."** Avon Lake, OH, Locomotive Workshop, 1971. 40 leaves. (pbk.). Cover title.

The basic index in this brief guide to the premier American SF magazine of the period is by author (all caps), with each author's stories listed in chronological order by publication date under the main entry. There is no attempt to identify pseudonyms or to provide other biographical data, and no title index. Also included is a chronological list of editorials, a similar index of cover symbols, a chronological checklist of nonfiction pieces and the "Department of Diverse Data," and a list of cover artists and the dates of the paintings they contributed to the magazine. Wholly superseded by Ashley/Jeeves (see #176).

180. Weinberg, Robert. **An Index to** *Analog* **(January 1960 to June 1965).** [Chicago?, Robert Weinberg, 1966?]. [10] p. index. (pbk.).

Well-known SF historian and book dealer Weinberg analyzes six years of *Astounding/Analog* in chronological order by issue, with complete contents listings and an index by author. No title indexing is provided. Now wholly superseded by Ashley/Jeeves (see #176).

Authentic Science Fiction

181. Burgess, Brian. **Authentic Science Fiction.** [England: s.n., 1960?]. 32 p. (p. 25-57). index. (pbk.).

Produced for a fanzine mailing, this index provides a complete guide to this little-known British SF magazine, with contents listings issue-by-issue and indexes by title and author. Now virtually unobtainable, Burgess's index has largely been subsumed into the cumulative magazine indexes produced by Strauss (see #168), Metcalf (see #156), and Miller/Contento (see #157).

Doc Savage

182. Clark, William J. **The Author Index to the** *Doc Savage Magazine.* Los Angeles, M & B Publishers, 1971. 21 p. (pbk.).

Just as it says, Clark's brief guide provides access to the fiction published in this fantastic hero pulp magazine by author only, individual stories being listed in chronological order under each main entry. He also gives issue date and total pagination of each piece, identifications of pseudonyms (where known), and some cross references. *Doc Savage Magazine,* in addition to running one novel per issue featuring that superhero, also included three or more short stories per issue; Clark provides a valuable service in indexing this scarce pulp, but title, issue, and artist indexes would also have been helpful.

However, much of this data is covered in McKinstry and Weinberg's index (see #171).

ERB-dom

183. Roy, John F., John Harwood, and Camille Cazedessus, Jr. ***ERB-dom:* A Guide to Issues No. 1-25.** Evergreen, CO, Opar Press, 1964. 23 p. (pbk.).

A brief index to the first twenty-five issues of this fanzine devoted to the works of Edgar Rice Burroughs. [Not seen].

Fantastic Adventures

184. Gallagher, Edward J. **The Annotated Guide to *Fantastic Adventures*.** Mercer Island, WA, Starmont House, 1985. xxi, 170 p. index. (Starmont Reference Guide, No. 2). LC 84-16228. ISBN 0-916732-71-1; ISBN 0-916732-70-3 (pbk.).

Fantastic Adventures, a companion magazine to *Amazing Stories,* published 129 pulp issues between May 1939 and March 1953, including primarily fantasy stories with some science fantasy and weird supernatural tales tossed in.

Contents: "Introduction"; "Annotated Story Guide"; "Appendix I—List of Issues"; "Appendix II—List of Departments"; "Appendix III—List of Biographies"; "Appendix IV—List of Illustrators"; "Appendix V—Story Motifs"; "Appendix VI—Editorial Personnel"; "Author Index"; "Title Index."

Gallagher's introduction provides an eighteen-page historical and critical overview of the periodical and its chief editors. The main index (139 pages) lists 852 fictional pieces included in the magazine, numbered in chronological order by date of publication. Each magazine issue includes volume and issue number, and month and year of publication (as centered heads), followed by a list of the stories included in each issue.

A typical fiction entry includes: item number, title (in quotes if a short story, under-lined if a novel), author, real name (if the byline is a pseudonym), format (*e.g.,* "novelette"), and a one-paragraph descriptive annotation. No paginations are provided for the individual stories. The appendices include: lists of editorial staff, artists and item numbers of the stories they illustrated, a complete list of the 129 issues, including year, month, volume and number, total pagination, and cover artist(s), a motif index broken into seventeen general categories such as "war" (keyed to item number), and a list of the author biographies that appeared in the "Introducing the Author" department.

The indices coordinate authors and item numbers or titles with item numbers only, making it impossible to get a list of the stories penned by any one writer without constantly referring back to the main text. The book is shot from legible word-processed copy.

This very thorough guide to a rather mediocre magazine provides plot summaries for many hard-to-find fictions and much background information on the Ziff-Davis SF magazines; it should be of interest to both fans of the fantastic pulps and serious students of the SF pulp period. This was the first volume in a series of four magazine guides produced by Starmont House (see also #200, #201, #202).

Fantastic Novels

185. Dard, Roger. *Fantastic Novels:* **A Check List.** Perth, Australia, Dragon Press, 1957. 11 p. index. (pbk.).

Dard provides a chronological issue-by-issue contents guide to a well-received pulp magazine published between 1940-51, which featured one reprint per issue of an often abridged classic novel of the fantastic. Superseded by Miller/Contento (see #157). [not seen].

Fantasy Review

186. *Fantasy Review:* **1984 Index to the Reviews, Volume 7, No.'s 1-11, Whole Numbers 64-74.** Boca Raton, FL, College of Humanities, Florida Atlantic University, 1985 (?). 14 p. (pbk.). Cover title.

Originally called *Fantasy Newsletter, Fantasy Review* served during the mid-1980s as the principal review medium for science fiction books and related materials. This brief index (which may have been edited by Robert A. Collins) is arranged alphabetically by name of the author being reviewed, then by book title.

A typical entry includes: author's name (surname in all caps), title (boldfaced), re-viewer's initials, and the review citation (in the form "68-24" for issue #68, page 24). The title index references titles (boldfaced) and authors' surnames only. The final page includes an alphabetical directory of reviewers' initials correlated with their complete names. All of this material has been subsumed into Hall's *SFBRI* (see #116).

Fiction

187 Valery, Francis. *Fiction:* **Domaine Français.** Cavignac, France, Auto Édition A&A, 1979 (?). 14 p. (Bibliographie des Revues Spécialisées, Volume 1). (Collection Documents SF). (pbk.).

The French magazine *Fiction,* started in the 1950s as a reprint vehicle for *The Magazine of Fantasy & Science Fiction,* soon began cultivating its own school of writers, which eventually formed the core of the developing literature of French science fiction, a very different style of SF than that popular in the United States. Well-known bibliographer Valery here provides a brief index of the original French-generated science fiction and fantasy published in this long-running prozine.

The book is arranged alphabetically by author's name. A typical entry provides: name (surname in reverse order, all caps, entire name underlined), and a chronological list of that writer's contributions, with issue number, date (in the form "6/61" for Juin 1961), and title. Materials are included through Janvier 1979 (issue #297). A title index would have been helpful, and a comprehensive index to all of the stories and articles reproduced in this premier continental European SF magazine is badly needed.

Foundation

188. James, Edward. **Index to *Foundation*, 1-40.** Dagenham, Essex, England, Science Fiction Foundation, North East London Polytechnic, 1988. 108 p. index. (pbk.).

James's index covers the first forty issues (1972-87) of this well-known British scholarly journal, in eight sections: "A. Dates of Issue"; "B. The Editorial Team"; "C. Author Index"; "D. Title Index"; "E. The Profession of Science Fiction series"; "F. Books Reviewed"; "G. Lists of Books Received"; "H. Subject Index."

The main author index lists the writers in alphabetical order by surname, then alphabetically by title, giving author, title, issue number, pagination. The title index rearranges the same data by title, author, issue number, and pages. The index to book reviews is arranged alphabetically by author of the material being reviewed, and includes: author reviewed, title reviewed (in italics), reviewer's name, issue number, and pages. The subject index is organized alphabetically by topic (author, book title, movie title, subject) in one alphabet, giving topic and issue and page numbers (*e.g.,* "22.49" = issue #22, page 49), with authors or topics receiving extended treatment (the focus of a full-length article, for example) listed in boldface, together with boldfaced issue and page numbers for the piece in question.

Section A provides a complete list of the magazine issues in release order, with publication dates; and Section B lists the editorial personnel who have worked on the journal, in alphabetical order by name, with titles and dates of service. The book is shot from generally clear word-processed copy (a few pages are fainter than others).

This is a very thorough and well-designed guide to this important academic publication, the only periodical of its type in Britain. All large university libraries should order a copy, and should subscribe to *Foundation.*

G-8 and His Battle Aces

189. Carr, Nick. **The Flying Spy: A History of *G-8*.** Chicago, Robert Weinberg, 1978. 160 p. LC 78-106443. (pbk.). Mercer Island, WA, Starmont House, 1989. 160 p. (Starmont Pulp and Dime Novel Studies, No. 3). LC 85-26231. ISBN 0-930261-72-0; ISBN 0-930261-75-5 (pbk.).

Carr's work is more a guide than an index, although a checklist of titles and dates published in this hero pulp magazine is also provided on pages 153-55.

Contents: "The Author," by Sid Bradd (biography of *G-8*'s author, Robert J. Hogan); "The Author," by Carr (another biography of Hogan); "Warrior of the Clouds" (a biography of the character "G-8," including a checklist of the wounds he received); "The Two Gladiators" (biographies of two of G-8's compatriots); "Portrait of an Extraordinary Englishman" (a biography of G-8's manservant); "The Necessities of Life" (implements used by G-8); "The Supporting Characters" (biographies of various characters appearing in the 110 G-8 novels); "A Bunch of Deceitful Rascals" (biographies of the principal villains [mostly German] opposing G-8, including a checklist of the issues in which they appeared); "The Little Fiend" (biography of another villainous character, Herr Doktor Krueger); "The Inventions of Madmen" (a list of the often fantastic inventions, machines, and devices used by G-8's opponents); "The War" (a history of World War I from G-8's perspective); "The Novels" (a checklist of G-8's 110 adventures); "Conclusion."

The book is illustrated throughout with reproductions of magazine covers and drawings of the G-8 characters and is reproduced from usually legible typed copy (a few pages are faint). An index would have been helpful.

Galaxy Magazine

190. Dollner, Karl. **The *Galaxy* Checklist, Covering the Period October 1950 to December 1958.** Cheltenham, Gloucester, England, British Science Fiction Association, 1961. 60 p. index. (pbk.).

One of a series of such booklets produced in the late 1950s and early 1960s by the BSFA, Dollner's guide analyzes *Galaxy Magazine* on an issue-by-issue basis, providing complete contents listings, including: month and year of publication, volume and issue number, story title (all caps), type (*e.g.,* "Nvt" = novelette), and author. The author index is arranged alphabetically by name, then by title, giving: author (all caps), title, type, month and year of publication, with "See" references to co-authors. The title index rearranges the same data by title, type, author, and publication date. Largely subsumed by Metcalf (see #156), Strauss (see #168), and Miller/Contento (see #157).

191. The Only Eleven-Year Cumulative Index to *Galaxy Magazine,* by Author and by Title, Oct. 1950-Dec. 1961, Complete, Including a Listing-by-Subject of Willy Ley's Science Articles. [S.1., s.n., 1962?]. [22 leaves]. (pbk.). Cover title. Limited to 100 copies.

This uncredited index is arranged alphabetically by author, then by title. A typical entry includes: author's name (all caps), title, and month and year of publication (in the form "10/58" for October 1958). The title index contains title, author, and month and year of publication. A detailed listing of the articles in Willy Ley's monthly science column is provided in the title section under the general heading "For Your Information" (the title of the feature), then arranged alphabetically by subject (*e.g.,* "Greek Fire," "Dinosaurs," etc.).

The 8.5" x 11" booklet was mimeographed and stapled through the spine, each copy being numbered in ink on the bottom right corner of the front cover. All of these data *except* the material on Ley's long-running nonfiction series are available in Metcalf (see #156), Strauss (see #168), and Miller/Contento (see #157).

Ghost Stories

192. Sieger, James R. *Ghost Stories:* **Stories of Ghosts.** Evergreen, CO, Opar Press, 1973. [29] p. index. (pbk.). The author's name is given as "Seiger" on the cover and title page, but is consistently mentioned as "Sieger" numerous times in the introduction and index credit.

This somewhat amateurishly produced booklet includes a brief introduction by Camille Cazedessus, a historical essay by Sam Moskowitz, a complete index of *Ghost Stories* by Sieger (fifteen pages), a reprint of a Robert E. Howard story (published in *GS* under the pen name John Taverel), and reproductions of other minor pieces and ads from the publication.

Sieger indexes his material alphabetically by author, providing: author (all caps), years of birth and death and one- to three-word bio squib (if known), and a list of the stories/ articles each writer has contributed, alphabetically by title, with months and years of publication. There are also supplemental lists of editorial staff, continuing "departments" and other features, cover artists, and reprint editions in book form, but no title index.

Ghost Stories is covered in Parnell/Ashley (see #160), but Sieger's guide does provide some minor biographical material not found elsewhere. Peripheral and unnecessary except for the most specialized collections.

The Magazine of Fantasy & Science Fiction

193. Durie, A. J. L. **Index to the British Editions of the '***Magazine of Fantasy and Science Fiction***', with a Cross-Reference to the Original American Edition.** Wisbech, Cambs., England, Fantast (Medway) Ltd., 1966. 44 p. index. LC 66-71451 (pbk.).

Durie indexes the first (1953-54) and second (1959-64) series of the English versions of *Fantasy & Science Fiction,* which were actually selections from various issues of the American parent publication and not facsimile reproductions. Complete contents listings on an issue-by-issue basis are provided, plus indices by author and title, and an indication of when the story was published in the American edition of *F&SF.* These data are *not* available in the standard magazine indexes.

Nebula Science Fiction

194. Jakubowski, Maxim. *Nebula:* **An Index.** [England], British Science Fiction Association, 1963. 18 p. index. (pbk.).

One of a series of indexes to British SF magazines issued by the BSFA, this guide provides an issue-by-issue contents guide to *Nebula,* which was published between 1952-59. Well-known historian and editor Jakubowski also provides a brief history of the periodical and an author index. A title index would have been appreciated. Now largely subsumed by Metcalf (see #156), Strauss (see #168), and Miller/Contento (see #157).

New Worlds

195. Burgess, Brian. **A History and Checklist of *New Worlds*.** [England], British Science Fiction Association, 1959. 33 p. index. (pbk.).

Burgess indexes the first eleven years of the premier British SF magazine (from 1946 to January 1957), with an introduction by founding editor John Carnell detailing its history and development. Complete contents guides are provided on an issue-by-issue basis, with author and title indexes. Although largely superseded by Metcalf (see #156), Strauss (see #168), and Miller/Contento (see #157), Carnell's brief essay does add some small significance to this booklet.

Operator #5

196. Carr, Nick. **America's Secret Service Ace: The *Operator 5* Story.** Chicago, Robert Weinberg, 1974. 63 p. (pbk.). Mercer Island, WA, Starmont House, 1985. 63 p. (Starmont Pulp and Dime Novel Studies, No. 2). LC 85-26269. ISBN 0-930261-70-4; ISBN 0-930261-73-9 (pbk.).

One of a series of "pulp classics" published by Weinberg in the mid-1970s, Carr's literary guide to this fantastic hero pulp magazine includes a chronology of the life of

Operator 5 (Jimmy Christopher), a biography of the character, biographies of "Alter Egos & Major Characters," biographies of the chief villains, guides to the supporting characters, a history of the fictitious invasion of America by the Purple Empire, biographies of the real-life authors of the novels, fantastic inventions and weapons used by the invading legions, and a chronological checklist of the feature novels correlated with issue dates. Also included are numerous reproductions of the magazine covers, of varying quality.

Carr provides a thorough introduction to this bizarre forty-eight-issue pulp, which featured a long-running invasion of the United States by a Germanic state and the Aztec Empire. As with the other volumes in this series, the book is shot from sometimes faint typed copy, and production values are low. The Starmont edition is a facsimile of the original. The absence of an index and the generally loose organization of the book (the chapter on villains, for example, lists them in no apparent order) hamper what could have been a worthwhile tribute to this most imaginative pulp.

Perry Rhodan

197. Lewis, Anthony R. **Index to *Perry Rhodan*, U.S. Edition 1-25.** Boston, New England Science Fiction Association, 1973. 12 p. (pbk.). **Index to *Perry Rhodan*, U.S. Edition 25-50.** Boston, New England Science Fiction Association, 1975. 18 p. (pbk.).

Produced in the same format as the NESFA magazine indexes (see #159), these two slight indexes provide author/title access to the fiction published in the first fifty volumes of the paperback magazine *Perry Rhodan* published in the United States by Ace Books. One wonders why this material was not incorporated into the NESFA annuals. Very peripheral.

Science Fiction Adventures

198. Peyton, Roger G. **A Checklist of *Science Fiction Adventures* (British Edition).** [England, s.n., 1962?]. [13] p. index. (pbk.).

Peyton provides a brief, issue-by-issue contents guide to the English version of the American SF magazine, which carried different contents from its U.S. parent publication (for issues #1-5), with indexes by title and author. After its first five issues, the British *SFA* began running original stories by British and American writers. Now subsumed into Metcalf (see #156), Strauss (see #168), and Miller/Contento (see #157).

The Shadow

199. Eisgruber, Frank, Jr. **Gangland's Doom: *The Shadow* of the Pulps.** Chicago, Robert Weinberg, 1974. 64 p. (pbk.). Mercer Island, WA, Starmont House, 1985. 64 p. (Starmont Pulp and Dime Novel Studies, No. 1). LC 85-26069. ISBN 0-930261-71-2; ISBN 0-930261-74-7 (pbk.).

The first in a series of guides to the major hero pulp magazines, their characters, and authors, Eisgruber's work includes: a historical preface by Robert Weinberg, a discussion of The Shadow's "true" identity, biographies of his aliases, biographies of his major allies and associates, a description of the Sanctum, guides to the chief villains, the locales of the novels, a response to Philip José Farmer's theory of The Shadow's background, biographies of the real-life authors of The Shadow stories, and a checklist of the 325 Shadow novels, chronologically by publication date, with months and years of publication and identification of the authors (when not by Walter Gibson).

Eisgruber's information seems generally sound, but the book as a whole is poorly printed, shot from sometimes faint typed copy and atrociously proofread. The numerous reproductions of *Shadow* magazine covers are also badly reproduced. The Starmont edition is an exact facsimile of the original.

As with the other two books in this series (see #189 and #196), *Gangland's Doom* is a useful guide to a vintage American hero, synthesizing much information unavailable elsewhere (although some of the narrative is speculative). A revised edition that is typeset, better organized, with additional details on the various later reprints in paperback and cloth, would definitely be warranted.

Startling Stories

200. Gammell, Leon L. **The Annotated Guide to *Startling Stories*.** Mercer Island, WA, Starmont House, 1986. 90 p. (Starmont Reference Guide, No. 3). LC 86-6012. ISBN 0-930261-51-8; ISBN 0-930261-50-X (pbk.).

The second of Starmont's magazine guides (see also #184, #201, #202) provides much hard-to-find information embedded in a rather strange format.

The first section indexes the novels published in *Startling Stories,* chronologically by publication date. A typical entry includes: author, title (all caps), month and year of publication, and an annotation ranging in size from 50-500 words (averaging 200). The summaries tend to be descriptive rather than evaluative, although the closing sentence sometimes includes critical remarks. Also mentioned are reprints in book form, with titles, publishers, dates, and motion picture versions of the novels.

The second part indexes short stories, again chronologically by issue date, giving: month and year of publication, volume and issue number, author (underlined), title (all caps), type (*e.g.,* "novelette"), and a one- to two-sentence annotation. At the end of each issue's entry Gammell lists the cover artist and featured story for that issue and the editor's name. The appendices provide contents listings of two anthologies derived from *Startling Stories* fiction, and a series listing for Jack Vance's Magnus Ridolph stories, many of which first appeared in this periodical. The book is shot from very clear word-processed copy.

There are two problems with this guide: Gammell unnecessarily divides the novels from the other contents of each issue, making a double reference necessary for the researcher who wants to examine the continuity of the periodical's publication; the absence of any indices, either author or title, forces the user to page through the book to locate specific fictions, and is utterly appalling in a purported reference guide.

Hokum and humbug!

The Thrill Book

201. Bleiler, Richard J. **The Annotated Index to *The Thrill Book:* Complete Indexes to and Descriptions of Everything Published in Street and Smith's *The Thrill Book*.** Mercer

Island, WA, Starmont House, 1991. vii, 256 p. index. (Starmont Reference Guide, No. 18). ISBN 1-55742-206-0; ISBN 1-55742-205-2 (pbk.).

Academic librarian Bleiler, author of a previous guide to *Adventure Magazine* (see #174), here provides a comprehensive index to *The Thrill Book,* one of the rarest of the pulp magazines. This fourth volume in the Starmont magazine guide series includes a lengthy historical introduction by Bleiler, an issue-by-issue checklist, annotations, a title index, a subject/motif index, an illustrator index, and sixteen selected black-and-white cover reproductions.

Bleiler's authoritative twenty-eight-page introductory essay puts the periodical in perspective, and provides what will surely become the standard critical view of this magazine. The contents list is a straightforward, issue-by-issue index to everything published in *The Thrill Book* in the order in which the pieces appeared in the original issues, including: date of publication (boldfaced), volume and issue number (boldfaced), price (boldfaced), editor, cover artist, interior artists, and complete contents (in descending order as published, with author, title [all caps], and specific paginations). So detailed are these listings that they even include advertisements!

The third section of the book provides annotations for every story, article, and verse, editorials, fillers, and departments that appeared in the magazine, in alphabetical order by main entry (usually author). Items are numbered throughout the section, consecutively from the number one.

A typical entry includes: author's name (including middle name and dates, if known), biographical details (one paragraph of varying size, depending on the status of the author and on the availability of information), and a detailed descriptive annotation of each piece published (plus a skeletal listing of stories announced for publication). Materials are listed alphabetically by title under each author's name; anonymous items are filed under title. Each entry also includes the issue date and specific pagination where it appeared.

The title index references titles, authors, and item numbers; titles are listed consistently throughout all parts of Bleiler's book in all caps. The subject/motif index correlates situations, locations, and specific subjects with item numbers. The illustrator index is arranged alphabetically by artist name, with a chronological list of the artwork each contributed to the magazine in order by issue date; biographical details for the artists are also provided where known. The cover reproductions add a touch of class to what is already a quintessential reference guide.

Bleiler has contributed another superlative effort, the perfect example of what a literary guide should be—and rarely is. Richard Bleiler is well on the way to establishing the same kind of reputation for quality and reliability as his father has already garnered as a bibliographer of fantastic literature. Highly recommended for all research libraries.

Unknown/Unknown Worlds

202. Dziemianowicz, Stefan R. **The Annotated Guide to *Unknown* and *Unknown Worlds*.** Mercer Island, WA, Starmont House, 1990. 212 p. index. (Starmont Reference Guide, No. 13). ISBN 1-55742-141-2; ISBN 1-55742-140-4 (pbk.).

The third of Starmont's magazine guides (see also #184, #200, #201) focuses on the classic Street & Smith pulp *Unknown* (later *Unknown Worlds*), edited by John W. Campbell,

Jr. as a fantasy companion to the better-known *Astounding Science Fiction*. (*Unknown* ironi-cally helped launch the career of Scientology founder L. Ron Hubbard, who was a regular contributor to the magazine from its second issue.)

Dziemianowicz provides a lengthy introduction, giving the history of *Unknown* dur-ing its thirty-nine-issue run from its founding in 1939 to its ultimate demise in 1943, a victim of wartime paper shortages; this is the longest critical evaluation of this seminal fantasy periodical yet published. The main part of the book is an issue-by-issue index of *Unknown*'s fiction, nonfiction, and verse, in chronological order by date of publication.

A typical entry includes: (for the first story in each issue) cumulative issue number (in brackets, from 1 to 39), month and year of publication, volume and issue number, cover artist (individual cover art was discontinued with the July 1940 issue). For the individual pieces the entries include: item number (numbered from one to the end), title, author, initial page number on which the story begins, word count (derived from Street & Smith's payment receipts), name of the artist who illustrated the story, original title of the story (if changed for publication), and an annotation.

The material is arranged in the same order as originally published in each issue of the magazine; an asterisk before the title indicates the story was originally purchased for use in *Astounding*. The summaries range in size from 500 words (for some of the novels) to fifty words for short fiction, and are both descriptive and evaluative (particularly for the longer works), providing much historical background and some indication of each piece's significance.

The eight appendices include: "Unpublished Manuscript Inventory," "Stories Trans-ferred to *Astounding Science Fiction*," "Inventory Dates of Purchase," "Story Index," "Au-thor Index," "Letters Index," "British Edition," and "Reprints." The "Story Index" is arranged alphabetically by title, including author, date of publication, and item number. The "Author Index" rearranges the data alphabetically by surname, then by title, mentioning known pseu-donyms, dates of publication of the stories, and item numbers. The "Letters Index" lists correspondents and the months and years of the issues in which their letters appeared. The book is produced from very legible word-processed copy, and includes reproductions of a number of covers and interior illustrations from the periodical itself.

Unknown was among the most influential of all the pulp magazines despite its short run, with roughly half of the stories published in this periodical eventually being reprinted in book form; many of the major writers of modern science fiction cut their literary teeth on this publication and its sister magazine, *Astounding Science Fiction*. Dziemianowicz's guide is a superb work of research, much of it original to this book, well organized and presented, clearly a labor of love that every serious scholar of SF and fantasy will welcome. Highly recommended.

203. [Hoffman, Stuart]. **An Index to *Unknown* and *Unknown Worlds*, by Author and by Title.** Black Earth, WI, The Sirius Press, 1955. 34 p. (pbk.). Cover title.

This uncredited publication is among the most professionally produced of the early fan indexes.

The first section of the book indexes *Unknown*'s fiction by author, giving: name (boldface caps), title, type ("short" = short story), initial page number, volume and issue number (but no dates). The title index gives: title (bold caps), author, type, page, volume and issue number, and a short annotation listing "Locale" and "Principal Characters." A third section indexes the principal characters by character name (bold caps) and story title.

Unusually for this period, the book is typeset and housed in hard paper boards held together with a spiral plastic binder. A loose addenda page provides the otherwise missing correlation between volume/issue numbers and months and years of publication.

Most of this material has been subsumed into Dziemianowicz (see #202), but the character index still has some value (very few such guides are available in the field).

204. Metzger, Arthur. **An Index & Short History of** *Unknown.* Baltimore, MD, T-K Graphics, 1976. [27] p. (pbk.).

Metzger provides a four-page historical introduction followed by an author index (in alphabetical order by writer's name, then by title, with months and years of publication), a title index (the same data reorganized by title, author, and publication date), a list of important reprints in book form, and brief lists of the cover artists for the first eight issues (after which pictorial cover art was discontinued). Now wholly superseded by Dziemianowicz (see #202).

Venture Science Fiction

205. Bishop, Gerald, and Bob Leman. *Venture Science Fiction Magazine:* **A Checklist of the First American Series, and the British Reprint Series, with an Index to Both of These by Author and Title; Also, an Index of the First Three Issues of the Second American Series.** Exeter, England, Aardvark House, 1970. [28] p. (pbk.).

This brief guide indexes the American and British series of the short-lived companion to *The Magazine of Fantasy & Science Fiction.* The first section provides an issue-by-issue contents list, beginning with the first American series (1957-58), continuing with the British series (1963-65), and ending with the first three issues of the second American incarnation (1969; the publication actually continued for three more issues into 1970 before folding a second time). It should be noted that the British series reprinted stories from various issues of the earlier *Venture* and *F&SF* and occasionally from other sources.

A typical entry includes: cumulative issue number (beginning from one with each series, except that the second American series is properly considered an extension of the first); month and year of publication, cover artist, title, author, type (*e.g.,* "short" = short story, with wordages indicated for any length beyond the short story level [for example, "16.5k" = 16,500 words]). The second section indexes the material alphabetically by author's name, then by title, giving author, title, and publication dates (in two columns, one for the American series, the second for the British incarnation). The third part rearranges the same data by title, author, and publication dates. A two-page introduction by Bishop places the magazine in its historical perspective and provides a short publication history. The booklet is reproduced from generally clear typed copy.

Since neither Metcalf (see #156) nor Strauss (see #168) nor Stone (see #167) cover the British version of *Venture,* Bishop's index is a useful (though peripheral) guide to this reprint publication.

Weird Tales

206. Jaffery, Sheldon R., and Fred Cook. **The Collector's Index to *Weird Tales*.** Bowling Green, OH, Bowling Green State University Popular Press, 1985. 162 p. index. LC 85-71020. ISBN 0-87972-283-5; ISBN 0-87972-284-3 (pbk.).

Jaffery and Cook's index provides a handy one-volume guide to this influential horror fiction magazine.

The main section is an issue-by-issue contents listing. A typical entry includes: month and year of publication, volume and issue number, cover artist, and a list of the stories, verse, and features in the order in which they appeared in each issue, with authors and illustrators. The author index lists the authors (bold caps) in alphabetical order by surname, with their stories organized in chronological order by publication date. A third section indexes poets and their verse, also in descending order by date.

The fourth part lists cover artists with their artwork, in descending order by publication date, and the names of the stories illustrated (if known) or a description of the cover art (if no obvious attribution is made in the magazine issue). An appendix provides contents and author indices for two *Weird Tales* competitors, *Oriental Stories* and *The Magic Carpet*. The second appendix includes a two-and-one-half-page essay, "Why *Weird Tales?*" A third appendix lists "Virgil Finlay's Poetry Series," a pictorial feature that ran from 1937-40. The last appendix delineates in skeletal form the British and Canadian editions of the magazine. The book is attractively typeset and bound. A few amateurish, black-and-white illustrations by current artists (not from the original publication) fail to capture the flavor of the original.

There are two design problems with this book: the subsidiary indexes list their materials chronologically by publication date, not alphabetically, which is not a problem for short entries, but can become irritatingly burdensome for a writer like Seabury Quinn, who contributed more than a hundred stories to the magazine; this defect is compounded by the absence of a title index.

Much of Jaffery and Cook's material can be found in Parnell (see #160), which also lacks a title index, although Jaffery/Cook *is* more detailed and explicit in its contents listings, and uses a larger, more attractive, and much more readable typeface. *The Collector's Index* is a disappointment more for the expectations raised—and dashed—than anything else, because the authors clearly know their material and have done their research well, and could have produced *the standard* guide to *Weird Tales*. And didn't.

GENERAL BIBLIOGRAPHIES

SCOPE NOTE: Included herein are all general bibliographies of fantastic literature. Bibliographies on specific national literatures, subjects, publishers, authors, or artists may be found in those sections, arranged alphabetically by topic. General literary guides are listed in the Reader's Guides chapter of this book.

207. Allard, Yvon. **Paralittératures.** Montréal, Canada, La Centrale des Bibliothèques, 1975. 728 p. index. (Sélections Documentaires, no. 2). LC 75-509636. ISBN 2-89059-000-3.

Allard has compiled a bibliography of French-language genre literatures in ten categories: "Mythe et Merveilleux," "Le Récit Fantastique," "Le Roman d'Aventures," "Le Roman Sentimental," "Le Roman Historique," "Le Roman d'Espionnage et de Politique Fiction," "Le Roman Western," "Le Roman Policier," "La Science-Fiction," "L'Humour."

Each chapter includes an introduction with a brief history of the genre, critical definitions, and a guide to what is included in that section's bibliography. Every bibliography is divided into several sections (using "Le Récit Fantastique" chapter as an example): "Études Historiques et Critiques," in turn broken into "Volumes" (*i.e.,* books) and "Articles de Revues et Extraits de Volumes"; "Petit Dictionnaire d'Auteurs," giving biographical squibs (one paragraph) on each author mentioned; "Collections" (a list of major publishing series, with one-paragraph summaries of their programs); "Anthologies" (of fantastic literature), with complete bibliographical data and one-paragraph annotations; "Choix de Récits Fantastiques," an A-Z bibliography of major works listed alphabetically by author, then by title, with complete bibliographical data, original titles (if translated from English or other languages), and one-paragraph annotations; "Le Fantastique Occulte" (a bibliography of occult fiction), in the same format as the preceding section; "Annexes," broken into sections "Arts Fantastiques," "Cinéma Fantastique," "Les Meilleurs Nouvelles et Contes Fantastiques," and "Les 25 Chefs-d'Oeuvre du Roman Fantastique."

Similarly, the science fiction chapter is broken into "Ouvrages de Référence"; "Périodiques Spécialisés"; "Études Historiques et Critiques"; "Petit Dicionnaire d'Auteurs"; "Collections"; "Anthologies"; "Choix de Romans de Science-Fiction"; "Annexes."

A typical entry includes: author, title, original title (if translated), translator (where appropriate), place of publication, publisher, year of publication, pagination, an indication of whether the book is illustrated, series data, ISBN, price, and Canadian National Library card number. The annotations average two to three sentences of commentary, and tend to be evaluative. Concerning David Lindsay's *A Voyage to Arcturus,* for example, Allard states: "Plus qu'un simple roman de science-fiction; il s'agit d'une allégorie métaphysique aux multiples interprétations, qui semblerait avoir inspiré C.S. Lewis pour sa fameuse trilogie. Un classique, vu sa date et son contenu."

Each entry also features rating codes at the end of the annotation, as explicated on page three; these include symbols for age level suitability, knowledge level required (for the science fiction section only), and overall rating (on a scale of 3-5, 5 being best). Thus, the rating "J**A4" indicates that the novel is suitable for young adults as well as the general public, and is "recommended." The Author Index correlates authors, titles, and page numbers; the title index includes titles and page numbers only.

Only a third of the volume deals with fantastic literature, but Allard's coverage of French-language materials, translations as well as original works, is unparalleled elsewhere, making this an important bibliographical source. A second, updated edition would definitely be warranted.

208. Bleiler, E. F. **The Checklist of Fantastic Literature: A Bibliography of Fantasy, Weird, and Science Fiction Books Published in the English Language.** Chicago, Shasta Publishers, 1948. xix, 455 p. index. LC 48-6709. Naperville, IL, FAX Collector's Editions, 1972. xix, 455 p. index. **The Checklist of Science-Fiction and Supernatural Fiction.** [2nd ed.]. Glen Rock, NJ, Firebell Books, 1978. xxii, 266 p. index. LC 79-101446.

Bleiler's book was the first attempt to provide a comprehensive bibliography of science fiction and fantasy literature, and it set the standards for its successors.

A lengthy introduction describes how the book was compiled. The bibliography itself is arranged alphabetically by author and then title, using the name of the primary author or editor as it appears on the title page; secondary authors appear throughout the bibliography with "See" references back to the main entries of the books they co-authored. Anonymously published books are gathered together in alphabetical order by title under the general heading "Anonymous." Authors writing under more than one name have their works split under each name, with appropriate "See" references.

Each main entry provides: title, publisher, place of publication, year of publication, pagination, and an indication whether the book contains illustrations. The title index cross-references short title and author only. Back matter includes: "Notes," "Annotated List of Critical and Historical Reference Works," "A Few Associational Items," and "Bibliographical Sources."

The *Checklist* was started as a fan project prior to World War II; Bleiler took the notes and card files compiled by others and added considerable research of his own, as well as checking some bibliographical data on the original cards; no effort was made, however, to verify first editions. The communal nature of the project resulted in the inclusion of many books with questionable fantasy content, and in some bibliographical errors that have been noted in subsequent reviews and fan articles. Nonetheless, Bleiler's original work was good enough to make it the standard guide to the field for over thirty years before it was finally supplanted by the deluge of bibliographies that began appearing in the late 1970s, including a revision by Bleiler himself (covered below). The original edition remains a valuable if somewhat idiosyncratic guide to pre-World War II fantastic literature (and, being the first book issued by the SF specialty publisher, Shasta Publishers, is itself highly collectible).

The revised edition follows the same general format as the original, except that subject codes have been added after the pagination. Bleiler notes in his introduction that the data have been systematically rechecked whenever possible, with proper first-edition information being inserted; that 600 entries from the original work have been removed; and that roughly 1,150 new books have been added. The coverage has also been extended slightly through the end of 1948 (the original included only a few titles from that year). Altogether, approximately 5,600 books are listed, 5,300 of them subject coded.

The ninety subject categories range from the general ("science fiction") to the very specific ("revolt of animals"), and are often combined in the text to indicate more than one subject. Since the codes are not obvious or alliterative, using them requires constant referencing back to the front matter. The absence of an overall subject index requires the user to examine entries individually to locate books with themes or subjects of a similar nature.

Yet, these are minor quibbles. Bleiler's knowledge of fantastic literature prior to the modern era is unsurpassed (he personally examined 95% of the titles included), and his bibliographical sense rates near the top of the field. This is a superb piece of scholarship, one that should be included in every collection of popular literature and on every SF scholar's bookshelf. Even though much of this material (although not the subject categorizations) now resides in Reginald's larger bibliography (see #212), this volume is still a "must" acquisition for research collections.

209. Day, Bradford M. **The Supplemental Checklist of Fantastic Literature.** Denver, NY, Science-Fiction & Fantasy Publications, 1963. ii, 155 p. index. LC 64-46968. (pbk.). New York, Arno Press, 1975. ii, 155 p. index. LC 74-15962. ISBN 0-405-06327-X.

Day intended this volume as a direct supplement to Bleiler's pioneering checklist (see #208), organizing it very similarly.

The main sequence lists titles alphabetically by author's name, then by title, providing: author, title (all caps), publisher, place of publication, and pagination. The title index correlates titles and authors only. Anonymous works of fiction are grouped together under the heading "Anonymous"; anonymously edited anthologies appear under the heading "Anonymous Anthologies." Juvenile works are so indicated with the word "juv" after the pagination, verse with the appellation "poetry" after the pagination, and other notes or edition limitations noted in the same part of the entry.

The book is shot from typed copy, being generally legible but with occasional broken letters or faint spots, and stapled through the side in flimsy paper covers. The Arno reprint reproduces the original version exactly, faint spots and all, in a much more permanent library cloth binding.

Day is less careful than Bleiler, and his book lacks the numerous "See" references and precise bibliographical data that the revised Bleiler contains. *The Supplemental Checklist* does attempt, however, to fill in lacunae in the original version of the Bleiler checklist (many of which have now been added to Bleiler's second edition), without noting the many items that should have been removed therefrom.

Day restricts his supplement only to cloth editions, reserving paperbound books to a companion volume (see #234); *The Supplemental Checklist* itself includes roughly 3,025 volumes. Now largely (but not wholly) superseded by the revised Bleiler *Checklist* (see #208) and by Reginald (see #212).

210. Locke, George. **Ferret Fantasy's Christmas Annual for 1972.** London, Ferret Fantasy, 1972. 76 p. (pbk.). **Ferret Fantasy's Christmas Annual for 1973.** London, Ferret Fantasy, 1974. ii, 54 p. (pbk.).

These two booklets by a well-known British OP book dealer were intended as additional supplements to the Bleiler (see #208) and Day (see #209) checklists. The main index in both booklets is organized alphabetically by author's name, then by title. A typical entry includes: author's name (underlined [in 1972 only]), title (all caps), place of publication, publisher, year of publication, pagination, plus an annotation.

The summaries for collections and anthologies generally consist of complete contents listings analyzed by brief subject appellation (*e.g.,* "Maori legend," "murder story," "ghost story," etc.), although not all such volumes are analyzed. The annotations for the novels average one to two sentences in length, summarizing the fantastical elements of each narrative (*e.g.,* "Space opera of an inhabited solar system, set in the year 3020AD"). Both annuals also provide indices to illustrators (if known), and a very useful index to themes by general category (*e.g.,* "Future War," "The Interplanetary Theme"), then alphabetically by main entry.

In addition to the checklist additions, both books also include articles on various bibliographical mysteries or puzzles, such as "The Christopher Blayre Trail," "British Paperback Fantasy, 1941-6," "Ghost Stories a la Mode." There are no overall indices to the volumes and no title indices to the bibliographies. Much of the content of these checklists has been subsumed into the revised Bleiler (see #208) and Reginald (see #212), and some (but not all) of the entries into Locke's *A Spectrum of Fantasy* (see #211), but the annotations, subject guides, and miscellaneous articles will still be of interest to the SF scholar and collector.

211. Locke, George. **A Spectrum of Fantasy: The Bibliography and Biography of a Collection of Fantastic Literature.** London, Ferret, 1980. vi, 246 p. LC 84-137321. Issued in limited edition cloth and pbk.

Partially reflecting Locke's earlier research on early SF and fantasy (see #210, #245, #262), *A Spectrum of Fantasy* provides an A-Z annotated guide of roughly 3,600 works from the author's personal collection of science fiction, horror, and fantasy monographs.

The book is arranged alphabetically by author; a typical entry lists: author (boldface type), type code (*e.g.,* "N" = novel), title (all caps), place of publication, publisher, year of publication, pagination, mention of illustrations or plates, illustrator's name, a description of the binding cloth and known bibliographical variations, and an annotation. The latter include a brief two- or three-sentence description of the book's fantasy elements, an indication of where and when Locke purchased the book, and sometimes why he regarded the acquisition as significant.

The result is a very personal view of fantastic literature as seen from the perspective of a sensitive and informed collector and bibliophile. Some of the books described date from as late as the 1970s, but the overall focus of the collection (and this bibliography) is on the pre-1950s period of fantastic literature, with a heavy emphasis on British authors and publications. Since this is this very period that includes much "hard-to-find" bibliographical data, Locke's descriptions are extraordinarily valuable additions to the literature of the field, even though many of the bibliographical listings themselves can be found in Bleiler's revised *Checklist* (see #208) or in Reginald's bibliography (see #212).

212. Reginald, R. **Science Fiction and Fantasy Literature, a Checklist, 1700-1974; with, Contemporary Science Fiction Authors II.** Detroit, Gale Research Co., 1979. xi, 1,141 p. in 2 v., [28] p. of plates. index. LC 76-46130. ISBN 0-8103-1051-1 (set). Reginald, Robert; Associate Editors: Mary A. Burgess; Daryl F. Mallett. **Science Fiction and Fantasy Literature 1975-1991: A Bibliography of Science Fiction, Fantasy, and Horror Fiction Books and Nonfiction Monographs.** Detroit, Washington, DC, London: Gale Research Inc., 1992. xii, 1512 p. index. LC 92-28219. ISBN 0-8103-1825-3. Editorial Assistants and Advisors on the second set: Scott Alan Burgess; John Clute; William G. Contento; John Hansen Gurley; Douglas Menville; Paul David Seldis.

Contents (1975-1991 supplement): "Introduction"; "How to Use This Book"; "Abbreviations and Definitions"; "Author Index"; "Title Index"; "Series Index"; "Doubles Index"; "Major Awards"; "About the Author."

This is the largest bibliography of fantastic literature published to date.

The major part of Volume 1 (583 of 786 pages) contains the bibliography proper, comprising 15,884 individually numbered monographs of fantastic literature in roughly 16,500 distinct entries (retitled entries are not renumbered, nor are co-authored entry numbers repeated a second or third time; such entries maintain the numbering of the original listing), arranged alphabetically by main entry (usually by name of author, but occasionally [for anonymous works] by title or author appellation), then alphabetically by title.

A typical entry includes: author's name (all caps), with middle names and years of birth and death (or real names if the author is pseudonymous), with a "See Also" reference to the biographical volume, where appropriate (*e.g.,* "biography included"); entry number (numbered consecutively from 1-15,884); book title (in italics), publisher, place of publication, year of publication, pagination, format (cloth or paper), type (*e.g.,* Novel, Coll.[ection], Anth.[ology], etc.), series information (in brackets). An author's work is centralized under the name by which he or she is best known, with appropriate "See Also" references throughout the text. Pseudonymous or co-authored works are listed after each author's individually-authored books. Retitlings of books are listed under the original title in descending chronological order, numbered with the original entry number followed by "a," "b," etc., with "See" references embedded at the point where that title would normally appear in the author's alphabetical title sequence.

The title index correlates titles and authors only; a series index is arranged alphabetically by series name, then chronologically by number (if the books are numbered) or date of publication, with titles, years of publication (in parentheses), and authors' names. End matter also includes an awards index, listed alphabetically by name of award and then chronologically by award date (through 1978), and an Ace and Belmont Doubles Index. A list of the nine abbreviations used in the text (all fairly obvious even to the casual user) appears on page xi at the front of the book.

The 1,443 biographies in Volume 2 of the first set are arranged alphabetically by author's surname, then organized in the standard *Contemporary Authors* format, with some minor modifications. In general, a typical entry is broken into several distinct paragraphs corresponding to the following data: personal details (full name, date and place of birth, parents' names, spouse and date of marriage, children's names); education, including degrees and honors; career, with details and dates of positions held; first professional sale, with bibliographical data; literary agent, with current address; honors, with names of works honored and dates of awards; memberships; avocations and interests; and direct comments by the writers. Inserted between pages 972-973 are twenty-eight pages of plates representing "A Short Pictorial History of Science Fiction and Fantasy Publishing," which is the weakest part of the entire set.

The supplement is similarly organized, listing new works published from 1975-91, and older works missed in the first set, plus corrections. Some works by house pseudonyms are completely relisted in the new volume, providing additional attributions of the real authors behind the collective pen names. Some barebones author headers from the first set are repeated with additional personal information, such as death years and/or middle names. The use of typeset copy and boldfaced entries for the main entries makes this new book much more legible and easier to follow than the original set. Bibliographical data are arranged as before, with some minor changes: publisher information is now presented first in each entry (thereby corresponding with Library of Congress usage), and "Anonymous Works" have been gathered together into one sequence near the front of the book, alphabetically by title, under that header inserted in the main text. New entries are numbered from #15885-#38181, adding 22,296 works to the overall bibliography, more than was recorded as being published in the first 275 years of the genre.

A book of this type stands or falls on the completeness and veracity of the data and on the strengths or weaknesses in the organization of that data. The published reviews on Reginald's checklist were generally approbatory, and the set has generally been accepted by many scholars as the standard bibliography of fantastic literature in both scope and completeness. Both Reginald's book and Bleiler's revised edition (see #208), which covers a more limited time period (monographs published through 1948), list works from comparable eras not found in the other. Part of the discrepancy is due to differing definitions of fantastic literature, Bleiler being slightly more liberal than Reginald in what he regards as "fantastic"; and part is undoubtedly due to the use of different source libraries, Bleiler's major sources being located on the East Coast and Reginald's in the West. Bleiler provides subject coding not found in Reginald's book, while Reginald generally has more data on title changes, authors' names and dates, and series. The best that can be said is that both books represent major bibliographical efforts on the part of their authors (Bleiler examined at least 95% of the entries included in his work, Reginald 98%), each supplementing the other while providing unique and valuable data.

Some criticism was leveled at Reginald's biographical volume, *Contemporary Science Fiction Authors II* (Volume 2 of the original set), which was partially adapted from his earlier work, *Contemporary Science Fiction Authors* (aka *Stella Nova;* see #57), and reworked using the format established by Gale Research Company's well-known continuing set, *Contemporary Authors.* Reginald compiled the work largely from primary sources— the authors themselves—via direct-mail questionnaires supplemented with a few biographies taken (with permission) from *CA.*

Some critics called the data "dry," while others decried the content or volume of the personal comments supplied by the authors as not being matched by the author's so-called literary importance. However, this ignores the way this volume (and the *Contemporary Authors* set after which it was patterned) are actually compiled. The sole criterion for inclusion was the publication of a single monographic work with fantastic content during the modern period. Comments were solicited from all the writers known to be living at the time:

some responded, others didn't. Those who provided sidelights had them included in their entries, irrespective of the author's importance. Perhaps the true measure of the validity of Reginald's data can be seen in the extent to which later purported biographical directories of SF authors have often liberally borrowed material (often without credit) from this volume and its predecessor, *Stella Nova*.

Science Fiction and Fantasy Literature is a necessary purchase for all academic and large public libraries, and for any serious SF researcher. A unified, updated version of the work is reportedly underway for production on CD-ROM.

213. Tuck, Donald H. **Author's Works Listing.** Hobart, Tasmania, Australia, Donald H. Tuck, 1960-62. 121 p. (pbk.). **Authors' Books Listing.** Lindisfarne, Tasmania, Australia, The Compiler, 1975. 32 p. (pbk.).

In the early 1960s Tuck, author of *The Encyclopedia of Science Fiction and Fantasy* (see #18), compiled a series of author bibliographies issued as fascicles, which were later cumulated into this guide, and then reworked and updated as a brief bibliography of the works of seven science fiction writers (John Brunner, A. Bertram Chandler, Edmund Cooper, Philip José Farmer, Ursula K. Le Guin, Michael Moorcock, A. E. van Vogt) for the 33rd World Science Fiction Convention (held at Melbourne in 1975), at which Tuck was Australian Guest-of-Honor.

Each writer's monographic works are arranged alphabetically by book title. A typical entry includes: author (all caps) with middle names and dates of birth, book title (underlined), publisher of the first edition, place of publication, year of publication, and similar data for all subsequent editions (paperback versions being indicated with the letters "pa" after the date), plus occasional annotations indicating earlier magazine publications, alternate titles, etc. Collections include complete contents listings.

These booklets are shot from typed copy (and stapled into limp paper covers), and the reproductions are occasionally faint and hard to read. There are no title indexes. All of the author's books are listed, including those falling outside the SF genre; thus, although most of these data are available in Reginald's bibliography (see #212), a few items are not.

214. Wells, Stuart W. III. **The Science Fiction and Heroic Fantasy Author Index.** Duluth, MN, Purple Unicorn Books, 1978. xxi, 185 p. LC 79-119071 (pbk.). ISBN 0-931998-00-X; ISBN 0-931998-01-8 (pbk.). Page 186, although numbered, is blank.

In the introduction to this volume, Wells states that his book

> . . . is intended to be a compilation of every science fiction and heroic fantasy title published in America since 1945. It covers every novel and collection initially published or reprinted during this period in hardcover or paperback. Many earlier titles are included so that complete information is given for most authors. Anthologies are beyond the scope of this work as are pulp or magazine appearances of the various titles. Weird and horror stories are also omitted.

In fact, Wells includes skeletal checklists of roughly 5,000 titles by 1,000 authors. British and other foreign authors are listed along with their American counterparts, but only when editions of their works have been published in the United States. Thus, many of the bibliographies of major English writers are incomplete and/or lack proper first-edition information, while many very minor American writers are listed when perhaps they should have been dropped—if this volume is intended for the collectors' market. And if this bibliography is not aimed at the SF collector, then for whom is it intended? Wells never seems to have asked—or answered—this vital question.

The authors are listed alphabetically by surname. A typical entry includes: author's name (very large caps), title (small caps), type code (*e.g.,* "N" = novel), publisher's abbreviation (*e.g.,* "Pinn" = Pinnacle Books), stock number (for paperbacks), year of publication of the first American edition of the book, publisher codes and stock numbers (but no years of publication) for subsequent reprint editions in the U.S., but no paginations or other bibliographical data.

Most of the books are listed alphabetically by title under each author's name; however, novels issued in series are listed in descending order under the blanket series title, chronologically by publication date; the author's other books then appear in alphabetical order by title after the series listings have been completed. The real names of pseudonymous authors appear after their pen names (*e.g.,* "Peters, L. T. = Albert & Jo Ann Klainer"). All of the type in the checklist is in boldface, making discernment of individual data sometimes difficult, the pages tending to lump together before one's eyes.

Front matter includes a quick reference table of types of works excluded and included, an explanation of the symbols used, abbreviations of hardcover publishers, abbreviations of paperback publishers, author and co-author cross index (some "See" references are provided in the text, but not consistently), and thirteen bibliographical notes. End matter includes novel winners for the International Fantasy, Hugo, and Nebula Awards (through 1978), comments, more notes, "Partial Bibliography of Recommended [nonfiction] Works" (ten items only), and an addendum. There is no title index.

Wells includes paperback stock numbers not listed in Reginald's bibliography (see #212). The list of reprints could be of interest to bibliographical historians, but is presented in such sketchy form as to be almost useless. The hit-or-miss nature of this mediocre effort makes one realize how truly useful an abridged checklist of modern fantastic *authors* and their works would be for the collector, and just how far Wells's *Index* misses the mark.

NATIONAL BIBLIOGRAPHIES

SCOPE NOTE: This section includes monographs that attempt to record all science fiction and fantasy books and/or fan and professional magazines published in a particular country, with occasional limitations by time period or broad genre.

AUSTRALIA

215. Stone, Graham. **Australian Science Fiction Index, 1939-1962.** Sydney, Australia, Futurian Society, 1964. 113 p. index. (pbk.). **Australian Science Fiction Index, 1925-1967.** Canberra, Australia, Australian Science Fiction Association, 1968. viii, 158 p. index. LC 72-367644 (pbk.). **Australian Science Fiction Index, Supplement, 1968/1975.** Sydney, Australia, Australian Science Fiction Association, 1976. vii, 48 p. index. LC 78-305781 (pbk.).

Well-known librarian Stone, author of an index to British science fiction magazines (see #167), has attempted in these volumes to provide complete bibliographical control over all SF books and periodicals published in Australia.

There are four major sections: "Magazines," "Numbered Series," "Unnumbered Series," and "Books." The magazines chapter includes seven titles, arranged by founding date, then chronologically, with issue-by-issue contents listings. A typical entry gives: magazine title (underlined), issue number, month and year of publication, pagination, physical size, cover and interior artists, and a list of the stories and authors in each issue, arranged as they appeared in the original publication. For the book series, Stone provides: months and years of publication, authors and titles, and contents (where applicable).

The books chapter includes all known monographs of fantastic literature published in Australia, both original and reprint, arranged alphabetically by author name, then by title, including: author's name (surname in all caps), title (all caps, indented), publisher, year of publication, series title and number (if any), pagination, physical size. Middle names and years of birth and death of the authors are provided where known. The author index lists authors and titles with either magazine title and issue number (for short stories) or with publisher, publishing series and number, and year of publication (for books). The title index rearranges the same data by title and author. The eight-year *Supplement* is similarly arranged and produced.

The Australian Science Fiction Index is shot from generally legible but occasionally faint typed copy, and bound with staples in flimsy paper covers. The data seem complete as presented, but the primitive production values sometimes make proper distinction of the material listed in the indexes difficult for the casual user. A revised, cumulated edition would definitely be useful.

CANADA

216. Colombo, John Robert, Michael Richardson, John Bell, and Alexandre L. Amprimoz. **CDN SF & F: A Bibliography of Canadian Science Fiction and Fantasy.** Toronto, Hounslow Press, 1979. viii, 85 p. LC 80-511063. ISBN 0-88882-036-4 (pbk.).

This annotated bibliography lists some 600 SF books by Canadian authors, including fiction titles with fantastic content, nonfiction books dealing with some aspect of Canadian SF or fantasy, plus fantastic literature by non-Canadian authors with Canadian settings.

The book is arranged by subject, then by author and title. Chapters include: "Science Fiction," "National Disaster Scenarios," "Polar Worlds," "Fantasy and Weird Tales," "French-Language Science Fiction and Fantasy," "Children's Literature," "Non-Fiction" (including poetry, plays, prose, collections, criticism, and coverage of two fanzines), and "Canadian Interest" (*i.e.,* books with Canadian settings). A typical entry includes: author, title (in italics), place of publication, publisher, year of publication, all known reprints, and annotation. The latter are often very brief, but occasionally quite helpful; references to previous editions under different titles, and to other titles of interest (by the author or by others) are sometimes included. The section on French-language materials is particularly valuable, since information on these books is often hard to find.

Many of the annotations provide plot information found nowhere else, and for this reason alone, the devoted scholar of Canadian SF will want access to this volume. However, a title index would have been quite useful, and the book definitely needs a supplement or revised edition.

CZECHOSLOVAKIA

217. Olša, Jaroslav, Jr. **Bibliografie Českých a Slovenských Fanzinů do Roku 1987.** Praha, Czechoslovakia, Ústřední Kulturní dům Železničářů-Klub Vědecké Fantastiky R.U.R., 1988. 4 v. index. (pbk.).

The *Bibliografie Českých* is included in this section because it amounts to a partial national bibliography of short Czech SF, both translations and original works, as published in Czech fanzines (the only medium during the Communist era for both professional and amateur fiction). The first two volumes (the only ones examined) are an A-Z index to the authors and their works. Volume 3 was announced as a guide to reviews and Volume 4 to criticism.

The first volume includes an introduction in Czech, English, and Russian, followed by the main index to prose, in alphabetical order by author, then title. A typical entry includes: author (large type), nationality (a two- to three-letter abbreviation), title, original title (for translations), translator's name, magazine title (a two- to three-letter, all-caps abbreviation), issue number, and pagination. Volume One covers the authors whose surnames begin with the letters A-K, Volume Two those from L-Z, plus an A-Z listing of poets, a list of anonymously written poetry and prose (in alphabetical order by title), a general abbreviations list, and a list of magazine abbreviations. There is no title index.

Data are included through 1987, although the author acknowledges that some of the more ephemeral publications may have been missed. The book is shot from legible word-processed copy. A great many Western authors are included in the *Bibliografie* (British writer Brian W. Aldiss, for example, has a half dozen prose entries), making this index useful as both a contemporary portrait of one aspect of modern Czech literature, and as a guide to translations of foreign SF authors into Eastern European languages.

DENMARK

218. Guld, Jens. **Bibliografi over Litteratur på Dansk om Science Fiction Indtil 1976.** København, Denmark, Science Fiction Cirklen, 1977. 37 p. (Tangentserien, no. 5). LC 78-342552. ISBN 87-87662-08-6 (pbk.).

[Not seen.]

219. Schiøler, Carsten, and Erik H. Swiatek. **Dansk Science Fiction Guide 1974.** København, Denmark, Science Fiction Cirklen, 1975. [unknown] p. **Dansk Science Fiction Indeks, 1741-1976.** København, Science Fiction Cirklen, 1977. [125] p. (Tangentserien, No. 2). LC 78-376683. ISBN 87-87662-00-0 (pbk.?).

[Not seen.]

GREAT BRITAIN

220. Bishop, Gerald. **New SF Published in Great Britain, 1968, 1969.** London, British Science Fiction Assocation; Lake Jackson, TX, Joanne Burger, 1970. 15 p. index. (pbk.). **New British Science Fiction and Fantasy Books Published During 1970 & 1971.** Lake Jackson, TX, Joanne Burger, 1972?. 40 p. index. (pbk.). **Science Fiction Books Published in Britain, 1972 & 1973.** Winchester, England, Aardvark House, 1975. v, 33 p. index. LC 76-353013. ISBN 0-904756-10-6 (pbk.). **Science Fiction Books Published in Britain, 1974-1978.** Exeter, England, Aardvark House, 1979. vi, 82 p. index. LC 80-145464. ISBN 0-904756-11-4 (pbk.). Quarterly supplements were published through at least Vol. 7, No. 6 (January, 1985).

For over a decade Bishop produced a series of annual and cumulated indexes of fantastic literature published in England, some published under his own imprint, others released solely or jointly by Joanne Burger, publisher of a similar series on American SF books (see #230).

Using the last volume as a guide, the main section indexes authors alphabetically by surname, then by title. A typical entry includes: author, title (indented), publisher, price, year and month of publication (in the form "77.09" for September 1977), edition (*e.g.,* "ne" = new edition), format (*e.g.,* "pb" = paperback), and ISBNs, but no paginations. Anonymous works are listed after the letter "Z" in alphabetical order by title. This section is followed by a chronological checklist of publications issued by the Science Fiction Book Club (British version), and a separate author index to nonfiction works. The title index correlates title and author only.

Bishop cast his net widely in an attempt to list all printings and editions of every SF book published in Britain, and generally succeeded very well; the absence of his publication has been keenly felt by all bibliographers in the field. In later years another British bibliographer, Phil Stephensen-Payne, produced a monthly checklist of English publications in

Locus that partially replace Bishop; these were cumulated in Charlie Brown's annual publication, *Science Fiction, Fantasy, & Horror* (see #33).

221. Harbottle, Philip, and Stephen Holland. **British Science Fiction Paperbacks and Magazines, 1949-1956: An Annotated Bibliography and Guide.** San Bernardino, CA, The Borgo Press, 1994. 232 p. index. (Borgo Literary Guides, No. 7). LC 87-752. ISBN 0-89370-821-6 (cloth); ISBN 0-89370-921-2 (pbk.). **British Science Fiction Paperbacks and Magazines, 1949-1956: An Annotated Bibliography and Guide.** Rev. ed. San Bernardino, Borgo, 1995. 232 p. index. (Borgo Literary Guides, No. 7). LC 95-19142. ISBN 0-8095-0204-6 (cloth); ISBN 0-8095-1204-1 (pbk.).

Contents: "Dedication"; "Acknowledgments"; "How To Use This Book"; "Introduction"; "A. Original Science Fiction Paperbacks, 1949-1956"; "B. Paperback Books from Established Houses, 1949-1956"; "C. A Checklist of British Science Fiction Magazines, 1949-1956"; "D. A Complete Author Index to the Stories in the British Science Fiction Magazines, 1949-1956"; "Book Title Index"; "Short Story Title Index"; "About the Authors."

This annotated bibliography to the post-World War II British SF boom covers hundreds of ephemeral paperbacks published mostly under house pseudonyms during a period when paper restrictions were still in effect throughout the British Isles.

The How to Use This Book section states: "The first section of this book contains a complete listing of all original paperback SF books published in Great Britain between January 1949 and February 1956. The books are alphabetically listed by author name, and cross-referenced to pseudonyms. Biographical data is given where known, and each book entry includes: a reference number for use within this volume, title of the work, author's real name (where appropriate), city of publication, publisher, date of publication, number of pages, release price, and interior and cover artist (where known). Also included is a plot precis of each book, and occasional critical comments whereby the best and the worst stories can be identified by the discerning reader. The second section of this book comprises reprint paperbacks published during the same period, listed by publisher and date of publication. The original source and first book edition is given, along with page count, price, and cover artists (where known)."

The third part lists all SF magazines published in Britain during this period, giving: date of each issue, volume number, size, page count, and cover artist (where known). The first column contains an identifying code for each issue to use in finding the magazine in the fourth section. "The fourth section of the book is a complete index to all the magazine stories and articles. Also included are stories that appeared in two anthologies listed in section one, and 'filler' short stories that cropped up in original novels." Finally, there is a complete title index in two parts, the first covering the books, the second the short stories.

The Revised Edition provides corrections and updates to thirty-two pages of text, but is otherwise identical to the original.

This is a companion volume to the authors' critical history, *Vultures of the Void: A History of British Science Fiction Publishing, 1946-1956* (Borgo Press, 1992). Dealers and researchers will find herein a treasure trove of hard-to-find bibliographic information for these older, largely unknown publications. Every book and magazine has been physically examined by either Harbottle or Holland, and they have endeavored to make the information as complete as possible for those who cannot handle (or even locate) the books themselves.

Suitable for large academic libraries, or for smaller libraries with a special collection of science fiction materials.

222. Slater, Kenneth F. **British Science Fiction Book Index 1955.** Wisbech, Cambs., England, Fantast (Medway) Ltd., 1956. 14 p. index. (pbk.). **A Checklist of Science Fiction, Fantasy, and Supernatural Stories Available in Paperback in Britain, January, 1966.** Wisbech, Cambs., England, Fantast (Medway) Ltd., 1966. 30 p. index. LC 66-78086 (pbk.).

The first publication is a bibliography of monographs with fantastic content issued in Great Britain in 1955, arranged alphabetically by author surname, with a title/author index. The second publication, a legal-sized booklet, is directly adapted from the catalogs issued periodically by Slater's book operation, Fantast (Medway) Ltd. (which specializes in new SF and fantasy materials), and amounts to a cumulative stocklist of works available at the time of issue.

Unusually, Slater includes brief plot summaries and other information of note, plus complete bibliographical data (including paginations) and contents listings for anthologies. Thus, although much of this material has been subsumed into Reginald's checklist (see #212), the supplementary material still provides valuable descriptions of (primarily British) books now long out-of-print. A peripheral acquisition for all but the most specialized libraries and research collections.

HUNGARY

223. Csiszár, Jolán. **Utópisztikus Tudományos-Fantasztikus Művek Bibliográfiája.** Miskolc, Hungary, [s.n.], 1970. 159 p. index. (pbk.). Bezerédy, Ágnes, and Jolán Csiszár. **Tudományos-Fantasztikus, Utópisztikus Fantasztikus Művek Bibliográfiája.** [2nd ed.] Miskolc, Hungary, Rákóczi Ferenc Könyvtár, 1979. 434 p. index. LC 81-126692. ISBN 963-7571-32-9 (pbk.).

The standard guide to fantastic literature published in Hungary covers translations from foreign literature, as well as original fiction and nonfiction. Csiszár and Bezerédy's bibliography is prefaced by introductions in Hungarian, English, and Russian, and then divided into three main sections: "Szépirodalom" (*i.e.,* Fiction and Literary Works), "Szakirodalom" (*i.e.,* Nonfiction), and "SF Konferenciák, Klubok, Szövetségek."

The first part is itself subdivided into four sections: "Regények" (books), "Elbeszélések" (short fiction), "Versek" (poetry), and "Egyéb Műfajok"; and the second part into five sections: "Anticipáció, Fantasztikus Hipotézisek," "Tanulmányok az SF Témaköréből," "Életrajzok, Könyvismertetések, Kritikák," "Biliográfiák," and "Fantasztikus Művészet," which is further subdivided into "Filmművészet" and "Képzőművészet."

In each section, materials are arranged alphabetically by main entry (usually author, although occasionally title in the nonfiction chapters), then by title. A typical book entry includes: item number, author (all caps), title, series (in brackets), translator's name (in parentheses), place of publication, year of publication, publisher, pagination. A typical short fiction entry gives: item number, author (all caps), title, type (*e.g.,* "novella"), translator, magazine title (often *Galaktika*), issue number, place of publication, year of publication, publisher, and the specific pagination of that story. Items are numbered consecutively from 1-2,644. The author index references authors and item numbers only, and the title index correlates titles, author surnames (in parentheses), and item numbers only. The book is shot from very clear typed copy. Data are included from the 1800s through 1977.

There is no way to determine how comprehensively this bibliography covers its subject except to note that 2,600 + items are an extraordinary number of publications to be recorded from a small, Eastern European country. However, future editions should include the original titles of translated literature following the Hungarian titles, since the user presently has no way of knowing for certain exactly what "Odakint," a story by Brian W. Aldiss, is; translations often undergo metamorphoses in titles as well as content, and access to dictionaries from the country in question will sometimes not help to identify a particular work's original incarnation. For very large research collections.

JAPAN

224. Ishihara, Fujio. **S-F Tosho Kaisetsu Somokuroku: 1946-70-nen.** Kamakura, Japan, S-F Shiryo Kenkyukai, 1982. 1624 p. in 2 v. index. LC 83-169920. (pbk.). **S-F Tosho Kaisetsu Somokuroku: 1971-80-nen.** Kamakura, Japan, S-F Shiryo Kenkyukai, 1989-91. 2338 p. (2 v. in 5). index. LC 92-129788. (pbk.). Title translates as: *SF Grand Annotated Catalogue.*

Dr. Ishihara, a well-known Japanese science-fiction writer and engineer, has compiled a masterful bibliography of all science fiction published in Japan between 1946-80, in great and copious detail.

Both sets follow the same format: "1. Description of This Bibliography"; "2. Comprehensive List by Publishers and Series"; "3. Comprehensive List by Juvenile Publishers and Series"; "4. Photograph Collection of Book Covers"; "5. List in Order of Publishing Date"; "6. Title Index"; "7. Author Index" (including: Nationality, Birth Date, Original English Spelling); "8. Translator Index"; "9. Original Works" (English Titles); "10. Authors of Original Works" (English Spelling); "11. Appendices" (including statistical tables and graphs); "12. References and Acknowledgments."

Entries in the two main sections are arranged by publisher and series number, and typically include the following data: publisher, title, author, date of publication (month and year, in the format 7503 for March, 1975), page count and size of book (keyed to seven different sizes, using letter codes), subtitle, title and author in English (if translated), name of series or collection and series number, cover artist, illustrator, annotator, titles of other novels or shorter works included in the volume, with their respective authors and translators, plus a one-line description of each book's content.

Sections 4-10 include: photographs of the book covers (where available), a table of titles arranged by publication date, and comprehensive indices by title, author, translator, and original title and author in English (where appropriate). The title index includes both titles of the books plus titles of any contents of those volumes, in alphabetical order by Japanese title. The author index includes the author's nationality, years of birth and death, name in the language of national origin, and pseudonyms.

Section 11 includes a number of statistical tables, including year-by-year publication data for the production of SF monographs in Japan. Section 12 includes a detailed explanation on how the book was compiled, plus a bibliography of works consulted. The formats for entries, meanings of symbols, and guides for use are clearly described at the beginning of each section, in addition to a comprehensive explanation given as Section 1 of the first volume.

Dr. Ishihara has spent an enormous amount of time compiling this work, and it is difficult to imagine how any future researcher studying the publication or history of SF in Japan could possibly conduct his or her investigations without access to these volumes. Recommended for purchase by all research libraries.

NETHERLANDS

225. Spaink, A[rnold], G[eorges] Gorremans, and R[inus] Gaasbeek. **Fantasfeer: Bibliografie van Science Fiction en Fantasy in het Nederlands.** Amsterdam, Nederland, Meulenhoff, 1979. [viii], 279 p. index. ISBN 90-290-1261-7 (pbk.).

This bibliography lists 5,600 SF works by 1,200 authors, original fictions as well as translations, published in The Netherlands through 1978, but organized in a somewhat difficult format to access.

The main index is arranged alphabetically by author's name, then by title. A typical entry includes: item number (items are numbered consecutively from one in each chapter, corresponding to each letter of the alphabet), author, title (the numbers, authors, and titles are slightly boldfaced; titles are preceded by a double hyphen), total page count (both for books and short stories), original title and original year of publication (for translations), and either bibliographical data (for books, including publisher, year of publication, series and series number, and pagination [in parentheses]), or a "See" reference to the publication (and to the item number elsewhere in the bibliography) in which the story or novel appears. There are hundreds, even thousands, of such references (in the form "B255" for item number 255 in the "B" section). In the entry for American author Alfred Bester, for example, we find the novel *De Grote Onttakeling* (*The Demolished Man*) listed both as a separate publication (entry #B259) and referenced as part of the anthology *Science Fiction-Omnibus 2* (entry #S106).

The title index lists titles, authors' surnames, and item numbers only. End matter includes a chronological checklist of Dutch SF publishing series by series number, author surname, and title, and a brief, one-page pseudonym/real name list. The book is shot from fairly legible typed or word-processed copy, with occasional faint spots.

There are two obvious structural problems with this book: although each page carries a boldfaced running head for the letter of the alphabet in which that chapter falls ("H," for example), the numbers themselves do not include the letter prefixes used as "See" references throughout the work. Thus, it is very easy for the user to lose his or her place when skipping from section to section.

Also, the text is apportioned throughout the book in double-column format, resulting in very tight internal columnar margins (for a 5.5" x 8.25" page size). These have forced the compilers to display the titles without obvious indentation, except for the double hyphen that precedes each. Since the titles and authors are shown in exactly the same typeface and size, and since the authors' names only appear once, it is very difficult on many pages to determine easily what portion of the alphabet one has reached, or, indeed, what author's works one is examining. The name of a prolific author may actually occur a page or two before the page being examined. The result is a mass of severely photoreduced text (to roughly an eight-point level) that tends to bunch together on the page. In their haste to save space, the compilers have produced a reference work that approaches the unreadable and unusable.

For those who wish to spend the time to dig them out, the data are here. The rest of us must wait for a (*mirabile dictu!*) completely redesigned second edition.

NEW ZEALAND

226. Rowe, Nigel. **The History of Science Fiction Fandom in New Zealand, Volume 3.** Auckland, New Zealand, Nigel Rowe, 1981. [21] p. (pbk.).

Volume Three of this multi-part work focuses on New Zealand fanzines, providing a complete chronological checklist of issues known to have been produced through May 1981. A typical entry includes: year and month of publication, fanzine name, issue number, number of pages, size, reproduction medium, and editor(s) [surnames only]. The periodicals are listed in chronological order by publication date. The absence of any indices severely limits the usefulness of this booklet. Reproduced from somewhat faint typed copy.

RUSSIA

227. Kerr, Stephen T. **A Bibliographical Guide to Soviet Fantasy and Science Fiction, 1957-1968.** New York, [Stephen T. Kerr], 1969. vi, 92 leaves. LC 78-20634 (pbk.).

Kerr adapted this bibliography of Soviet science fiction from his master's thesis (Columbia University, 1969).

The main section of the book is arranged alphabetically by author's name, then by title. A typical entry includes: author (surname in all caps), Russian title (stories in quotes, novels underlined), English-language translation (in brackets), bibliographical data (for monographs: place of publication, publisher, year of publication, and total pagination; for stories: anthology or collection name, volume number [where applicable], and specific paginations), with similar information on known reprints (both of stories and novels).

Kerr also occasionally includes contemporaneous review citations. Anonymous anthologies are interfiled with the rest under title. Items are numbered consecutively from 1-1,485 throughout the book. Abbreviations are employed heavily for place of publication, publishers, and recurring book titles (most Soviet short stories were first published in original anthology series). A section at the end of the index lists "Special Bibliographical Sources on Soviet S.F." Appendix A provides a checklist of anthologies, alphabetically by English title (for translated anthologies), then a separate listing by Russian title. There is no overall title index. The book is shot from generally clear typed copy.

Compared to Suvin (see #228), Kerr includes short stories that Suvin does not separately mention, but Suvin covers an additional seven years of data, and provides a much broader list of Russian-language secondary sources. Both works will be necessary for the serious scholar.

228. Suvin, Darko. **Russian Science Fiction Literature and Criticism, 1956-1970: A Bibliography.** Toronto, "Secondary Universe 4" Conference, 1971. 35 p. LC 74-183207 (pbk.). **Russian Science Fiction, 1956-1974: A Bibliography: Original Books, Translated Books, and an Annotated Checklist of Criticism; with an Appendix on Criticism of Russian SF Before 1956.** Elizabethtown, NY, Dragon Press, 1976. vi, 73 p. LC 76-151334.

Yugoslavian academic Suvin (now a permanent resident of Canada) has produced a now-standard bibliography of Russian-language science fiction, divided into three sections: "Science Fiction Books in the Russian Language, 1956-1974"; "Russian Science Fiction in English and French Books"; "Criticism of Soviet Science Fiction, 1956-1970"; with an "Appendix: Selective Bibliography of Critical Works on Russian Science Fiction to 1956," plus addendum.

The first section lists works alphabetically by author, then by Russian title. A typical entry includes: author, title (underlined), place of publication (often abbreviated to "M" = Moscow or "L" = Leningrad), publisher, year of publication, and pagination. Anonymous works are interfiled by title with the rest. The second chapter includes a similarly arranged list of translated titles in English and French, alphabetically by author, giving: author, title (underlined), place of publication, publisher, and year of publication, but no paginations or original titles. Contents listings are also provided for anthologies (something not done in the first section).

Part Three is a chronological (by year), annotated bibliography of criticism on Russian science fiction and its authors, in all languages; paginations are listed only for articles, not monographs. The Appendix lists pre-1956 criticism by subject and main entry, broken into the following categories: 18th Century, 19th Century (subdivided into sections, "To 1860," "Chernyshevsky," "Dostoevsky"), 1890-1956 (subdivided into "Tsiolkovsky," "Bryusov," "Bogdanov," "Mayakovsky," "Zamyatin," "A. Tolstoy," "A. Belyaev," "Others, 1890-1930," and "Others, 1931-1956"). The book is shot from clearly reproduced typed copy.

A major problem with the work is the inconsistency in bibliographical format between the sections: why, for example, provide paginations in the first part and not in Chapters 2-3? If the data are worth capturing for one, should they not be worth recording for all? Also, the absence of a title index and the utter failure to record the original Russian-language titles for the translations seriously hampers the potential researcher. The immense body of Russian SF, one of the largest such literatures outside the U.S. (and among the most important), cries out for an updated version of this book, one with full annotations and complete bibliographical data, and an accurate, comprehensive guide to secondary sources. Until such a work appears, this somewhat lame bibliography will have to do.

SWEDEN

229. Lundwall, Sam J. **Bibliografi över Science Fiction och Fantasy, 1830-1961.** Stockholm, Sweden, Lundwall, 1962. 58 p. index. (pbk.). **Illustrerad Bibliografi över Science Fiction & Fantasy, 1741-1973.** [2nd ed.]. Stockholm, Sweden, Lindqvists, 1974. 338 p. index. LC 75-574749. ISBN 91-7090-115-5 (pbk.?).

Well-known SF writer and critic Lundwall has produced the standard guide to fantastic literature in Sweden (original works as well as translations) in this well-illustrated and presented bibliography.

Authors and titles are indexed together in one alphabetical sequence. Authors' names appear in boldfaced caps (quite distinguishable from the rest of the text). A typical author entry includes: author, years of birth and death (if known), single-paragraph critical evaluation (one to three sentences), and a list of the author's books in alphabetical order by title. Title entries throughout the main text contain "See" references back to their authors. Title entries within author entries include: title (indented, in boldfaced type), original title (if translated), translator's name, series and series number, place of publication, publisher, year of publication, pagination, price, and ISBN.

Also included in the main alphabetical sequence are publishers' series listings arranged by publisher name, then numerically by series number, with author and title, but no bibliographical data (which are included with the author entries). The book is attractively typeset and illustrated throughout with author photographs and cover reproductions.

Lundwall's guide is one of the best organized and presented national bibliographies/ cyclopedias yet produced, and should definitely be updated to reflect the nearly many decades of data that have cumulated since this volume was published.

UNITED STATES

230. Burger, Joanne. **SF Published in 1967-[1977].** Lake Jackson, TX, Joanne Burger, 1968-79. 11 v. index. LC 71-10701 (pbk.).

The late Joanne Burger began producing these bibliographies of all SF and fantasy books published in the United States as monthly and bimonthly checklists of forthcoming titles, including reprints and original works, which were then cumulated into annual indices of those works that had supposedly appeared.

The main listing is alphabetically by author, then by title. A typical entry includes: author, title (in italics in later volumes), publisher, stock number or ISBN, price, copyright date (if different from original publication date), type code (if not a novel; *e.g.,* "a" = anthology), series number. Not all of the books listed were viewed by Burger, and some were never actually published as scheduled. The title index lists title and author only.

The 1977 annual also includes "Address[es] of Small Publishers," "Juvenile Books" (authors and titles only), "Art Books" (authors and titles only), "Non Fiction Books" (authors and titles only), and "Series Listings" (by author, with titles listed in chronological order). The books were produced somewhat amateurishly, reproduced from typed copy, and photocopied or mimeographed into stapled paper covers.

Burger was not always reliable, but her lists were brief, useful guides to the SF books scheduled to appear in the U.S. during each year. They now have been partially superseded by Reginald's bibliography (see #212) and have been continued by the monthly checklists of published SF works in *Locus* and by Charlie Brown's annuals and CD-ROM (see #33) since 1984.

231. Clareson, Thomas D. **Science Fiction in America, 1870s-1930s: An Annotated Bibliography of Primary Sources.** Westport, CT & London, Greenwood Press, 1984. xiv, 305

p. index. (Bibliographies and Indexes in American Literature, Number 1). LC 84-8934. ISBN 0-313-23169-9.

The late Thomas D. Clareson is well known in the SF field for his essays and critical work, and for having founded (and edited for three decades) the first academic journal devoted to science-fiction criticism, *Extrapolation*. Indeed, the first issue of that periodical, dated December 1959, featured Clareson's nineteen-page article, "An Annotated Checklist of American Science-Fiction, 1880-1915," obviously the precursor to this larger work.

The book is organized in alphabetical order by author's name, then by title. Clareson uses the name by which the author is best known, even if it is a pseudonym, with no "See" references; thus, the works of "Harris Burland" and J. B. Harris-Burland (both the same man) are split, although the entry for the former does mention the author's real name. The entries are numbered in consecutive order from 001-838.

A typical entry includes: item number, author's name, title (underlined), place of publication, publisher, year of publication, but no paginations. The annotations are descriptive rather than evaluative, and range in size from 10-300 words (100 being average). The author index lists authors and item numbers only; the "Short-Title Index" lists titles (but no subtitles) and item numbers only. The book is shot from very clear word-processed copy and bound in library cloth.

Clareson's 1959 article focused entirely on U.S. authors, and while the emphasis in this expanded version is still on writers of American descent, he also adds (somewhat randomly) works by British and other foreign authors, if their works were regarded as influential in the history of American fantastic literature. Thus, nine works each by Wells and Verne are annotated, seven by George Griffith, and eleven by H. Rider Haggard (only one of which could be considered SF by the furthest stretch of the definition). Clareson's stated rationale for this decision, "to give a detailed and comprehensive overview of the field during the period from the 1870s to the 1930s," is a laudable one, but in so doing he opens a bibliographical barn door, in and out of which may wander all kinds of literary oddities, including many works with fantasy elements. One is left asking why some books were included while others were omitted, with no obvious answers except to say that they were.

Still, Clareson provides a gold mine of information on a period that is not well known or understood in the history of fantastic literature, and his annotations cover in detail a great many works described nowhere else. One might have wished for a better title index, a motif or subject index, and volume paginations, but these are relatively minor carpings. *Science Fiction in America* will undoubtedly become a prime source book for further research on these antecedent fictions, and should be acquired by all academic libraries.

232. Tymn, Marshall B. **American Fantasy and Science Fiction: Toward a Bibliography of Works Published in the United States, 1948-1973.** West Linn, OR, FAX Collector's Editions, 1979. ix, 228 p. index. LC 76-55151. ISBN 0-913960-15-2 (pbk.).

This little volume (4" x 7") was intended directly to supplement Bleiler's pioneering *Checklist* (see #208), following the same general format as that work, and covering cloth hardcovers published in the United States between January 1948 and the end of 1973 (Bleiler's original edition includes some works published in 1948; his second edition covers through the end of 1948).

The main part of the bibliography is arranged alphabetically by author's surname, then by title. A typical entry provides: author (all caps), title (italics), place of publication, publisher, and year of publication, but no paginations (unlike Bleiler). Middle names and pseudonyms are listed for some authors, with appropriate "See" references scattered throughout the text; illustrations, juvenile works, collections, and anthologies are so noted with abbreviations after the bibliographical data (*e.g.,* "ill, juv" for an illustrated juvenile work). The title index lists titles and authors only.

End matter includes fifty-four bibliographical notes, a thirteen-page list of "Borderline Titles" (arranged and presented in the same way as the main bibliography), and a list of first editions published by the Science Fiction Book Club (also alphabetically by author, although no mention whatever is made of the fact that first-edition SFBC books from this period bore the imprint "Nelson Doubleday"). The book is typeset, but the type has been photoreduced to about a six-point level, making it hard to read for middle-aged eyes.

About 2,250 books are listed in the main sequence, only a fraction of those published during the twenty-five year period that this bibliography ostensibly covers; and there are problems even with these data. Many of the books by British authors had English first editions not noted or acknowledged here; and many books that could or should have been listed are not mentioned. Well-known fantasy writer Robert Nathan, for example, has five works listed between 1951-72, when he actually published fifteen novels with fantasy content between 1948-73, plus two new omnibuses of previously published books issued for the first time under those titles; by any accounting, Tymn has missed two-thirds of Nathan's relevant works.

He is more certain (and complete) with well-known SF writers, but by omitting paperbacks, he deliberately ignores many first editions even from these authors. Finally, why provide a list of so-called "borderline titles"? If one cannot locate specific titles—or determine their fantastic content—then they should be omitted; dumping them into a miscellanea file simply trumpets one's own bibliographical shortcomings, of which, alas, there are too many in *American Fantasy and Science Fiction.* All of these books, with complete bibliographical data, are listed in Reginald (see #212), which is much to be preferred.

233. Whyte, Andrew Adams. **The New SF Bulletin Index to SF Books 1974.** Boston, Spike MacPhee, Publisher, Paratime Press Publications, 1974. 42 p. (pbk.).

This one-shot was intended to rival Burger's bibliography (see #230) but failed for lack of a second—volume, that is.

The first section, "Comprehensive Listings: Original U.S. Novels—1974," is arranged alphabetically by author, then by title. A typical entry includes: author's name (surname in all caps), title (indented), type code (the abbreviations list at the front of the book is incomplete, making identification of the codes problematical at best), publisher (one word only), month of publication (in the form "04" for April). The rest of the index is broken into sixteen other mini-sections, each devoted to a very limited area ("Posthumous One-Author Collections," for example). Without an author or title index, the entire bibliography is essentially unusable unless one particularly enjoys reading such works word for word just before bedtime.

Amateurish mishmash/trash.

SUBJECT BIBLIOGRAPHIES

SCOPE NOTE: Included herein are bibliographies dealing primarily with specific subjects or themes, where the main intent is to provide a comprehensive list, annotated or not, of the books relating to that particular category. Books whose primary purpose is to provide readers with evaluative guides to broad genre categories (*e.g.,* Barron's *Anatomy of Wonder*) may be found in the "Readers' and Critical Guides" section of this book. Background articles on specific subgenres of science fiction and fantasy literature may also be found in such works as Nicholls's *Science Fiction Encyclopedia.*

ADVENTURE FICTION

234. Day, Bradford M. **Bibliography of Adventure: Mundy, Burroughs, Rohmer, Haggard.** Denver, NY, Science-Fiction & Fantasy Publications, 1964. 125 p. LC 64-56055 (pbk.). **Bibliography of Adventure: Mundy, Burroughs, Rohmer, Haggard.** Rev. ed. New York, Arno Press, 1978. 125 p. (Lost Race and Adult Fantasy Fiction). LC 77-84282. ISBN 0-405-11019-7.

Well-known fan researcher Day here contributes the collected bibliographies of four writers of fantasy adventure, the first three of which were previously published by Day under his S-F&F imprint and updated for this edition (see #342, #441, #460).

The Mundy, Burroughs, and Rohmer sections are similarly organized. Day provides brief, two-page biographical introductions to each writer, then lists the first editions of his books in alphabetical order by title, followed by the short fiction in chronological order by publication date. A typical book entry includes: title (all caps), publisher, place of publication, year of publication, pagination, brief mention of known reprint publishers (with, however, no bibliographical data), a one-line quotation taken from the book, data on previous magazine serializations, if any (giving original title of the story, magazine title, and issue dates in which the piece appeared, but no paginations), and a description of the binding color and style on the first edition (*e.g.,* "Cover red—black letters").

A typical short fiction entry provides: title (all caps), magazine title, year of publication, month of publication, but no paginations. Also included in the short fiction section are serializations of the novels, thus recording double entries for some works later collected in book form. The Mundy bibliography also includes an appreciation and series listing by Dr. J. Lloyd Eaton, and the Burroughs section has an afterword delineating known newspaper serializations of Burroughs's works, a summary of comic strip appearances, a listing of Big Little Books adaptations, selected foreign-language translations, and a list of ephemera.

The Haggard bibliography, original to the 1964 edition, lists first editions of Haggard's books only, in chronological order by publication date. A typical entry includes: title (all caps), publisher, place of publication, year of publication, pagination (the exact numbered page count—*e.g.,* 3-242), description of binding style and cloth, number of copies printed, exact publication date (if known), and similar information on the first U.S. (or first British) edition. At the end of the checklist Day provides two other lists: the reading sequence of the Allan Quatermain series, and a correlation between U.S. and U.K. title variations. There are no indices.

As usual with Day's publications, the original book was reproduced from typed, mimeographed copy and bound in flimsy covers, and the first edition copies are now yellowed and brittle. The Arno reprint, which includes minor bibliographical corrections to the original, is bound to library standards.

The Burroughs section has now been superseded by Heins's more complete bibliography (see #344), the Haggard by Whatmore (see #385), and the Mundy by Grant (see #441). No complete or current bibliography of Rohmer exists, however, leaving Day's guide the most recent work available.

ALTERNATE HISTORIES

235. Hacker, Barton C., and Gordon B. Chamberlain. **"Pasts that Might Have Been, II: A Revised Bibliography of Alternative History,"** in *Alternative Histories: Eleven Stories of the World As It Might Have Been,* edited by Charles G. Waugh and Martin H. Greenberg. New York & London, Garland Publishing, 1986. p. 301-363. LC 85-45130. ISBN 0-8240-8659-7.

Although it is not the intent of this book to cover works within works, Hacker and Chamberlain's bibliography is so unique and well executed that omitting it would itself be a bibliographical crime.

Originally published in *Extrapolation* in 1981, this revised and expanded version of "Pasts That Might Have Been" provides an annotated guide to alternate histories, imaginative variations on real-life historical events (for example, what might have happened if Germany had won World War II). Entries are arranged in alphabetical order by author, then by title. A typical item includes: author (surname in all caps), title (stories in quotes, novels in italics), bibliographical data (for short stories: magazine title, and month and year of publication, or book title [if the first appearance was in an anthology] and editor's name [the anthology is usually also covered in a separate entry]; for monographs: publisher and year of publication, but no paginations for either category). Information is provided haphazardly on subsequent editions and reprintings. Each entry is accompanied by a one-sentence annotation (up to forty words) giving a brief description of where the history of the story varies from real-world events. There are also copious "See" references to related works in the bibliography.

Hacker and Chamberlain make too much use of publisher/periodical abbreviations, and probably should have provided title and subject indices, but the latter may have been beyond the scope of the two publications in which this bibliography appeared. Separate book publication of this very comprehensive guide, with additional bibliographical data, would definitely be warranted.

ARCHITECTURE

236. White, Anthony G. **Science Fiction and Architecture: A Selected Bibliography.** Monticello, IL, Vance Bibliographies, 1979. 12 p. (Architecture Series: Bibliography, no. A-74). LC 79-120247 (pbk.).

White's brief annotated guide deals with architectural structures, particularly the depiction of futuristic cities, in fantastic literature.

His booklet is divided into two sections: "Non-Episodal Literature" (nonfiction and art books) and "Episodal Literature" (*i.e.,* fiction), and arranged in alphabetical order by author's name in each section. A typical entry includes: author's name, title (shorter works in quotes, books not otherwise marked), bibliographical data (for short works: magazine title, volume and issue number, month and year of publication, and pagination; for monographs: place of publication, publisher, year of publication, but no paginations). No data are provided for subsequent reprints.

Each entry also includes a descriptive annotation ranging from single-sentence notes in section one to 30-100 words in part two. Sixteen works are described in the first bibliography, forty in the second. There is no title index. The book is shot from generally clear typed copy. *Science Fiction and Architecture* provides a beginning point for studies on this very specialized topic, but it is hardly definitive and badly needs updating and expansion.

ARTHURIAN FICTION

237. Mediavilla, Cindy. **Arthurian Fiction: An Annotated Bibliography.** Lanham, MD, and London, Scarecrow Press, 1999. xvi, 157 p. index. LC 99-12199. ISBN 0-8108-3644-0 (pbk.: alk. paper).

Contents: "Acknowledgments"; "Introduction"; "Chapter One: Romance of Camelot"; "Chapter Two: Arthur, the Roman Leader"; "Chapter Three: The Women of Camelot"; "Chapter Four: Merlin, Kingmaker and Mage"; "Chapter Five: Unlikely Heroes of Camelot"; "Chapter Six: The Holy Quest"; "Chapter Seven: Return of the King"; "Chapter Eight: The Legacy Continues"; "Appendix A: Books Listed by Reading Level"; "Appendix B: Arthurian Fiction: Recommended Core List"; "Appendix C: Recent Short Story Anthologies"; "Index"; "About the Author."

Mediavilla provides a clear, informative introduction that defines both Arthurian fiction and the eight divisions she employed to organize coverage of fiction suitable for teenagers and young adults based on the Arthurian legend (excluding "older books written in archaic or pedantic prose" and "novels that contain overly explicit sexual content intended for a more mature audience"). 227 novels are annotated.

Each subject chapter is arranged alphabetically by author, with the books being numbering consecutively throughout the volume from the number one. A typical entry includes: reference number, author, title (in italics), place of publication, publisher, year of publication, pagination, illustration notation, reading level, and an evaluative summary averaging 250 words in length. The critiques are both descriptive and evaluative, and generally follow accepted literary opinions on the books and authors in question.

Three appendices are featured: a list of novels by reading level (*e.g.,* "high school level"), arranged in alphabetical order in each section by author and then by title, and also giving item number; a core reading list of 58 titles, arranged alphabetically by author and title, with item numbers; and a list of thirteen Arthurian-oriented fantasy anthologies published from 1986-98, giving editor, title (in italics), place of publication, publisher, and year of publication, but no contents.

Items were included in the bibliography if they were currently in print or generally available at larger public libraries. "Titles cited are American first editions, though British editions appear if they are considered significant."

The index combines themes, character names (with numerous "See" references), authors, titles, and item numbers to give users good access to the materials, although book titles are not cross-referenced to their authors, and the author names only provide lists of item numbers, not titles. Thus, one must go back to the entry number in the main text to find specific data.

There is also an unusual amount of crossover between Mediavilla's three assigned reading levels: "Middle School Level" for grades six through eight; "Junior High School Level" for grades seven through nine; and "High School Level" for older teens and adults. The book is nicely designed and typeset.

This is an excellent addition for middle school and high school libraries, public libraries, and university library collections catering to teaching education departments.

ATLANTIS

238. Eichner, Henry M. **Atlantean Chronicles.** Alhambra, CA, Fantasy Publishing Co., Inc., 1971. [x], 230 p., [16] p. of plates.

The first half of this posthumously published book (through page 132) is a rather amateurish rehash of legends, myths, tales, and speculations relating to the Atlantis story in history. Of much more importance are the several bibliographies compiled by Eichner on the Atlantis theme in literature, divided into two sections: "English Literature" (eighty-three pages) and "Foreign Literature" (twenty-five pages).

The English Literature section is organized in alphabetical order by author surname, then by title. A typical entry provides: author's name, title (all caps), publisher, year of publication, but no paginations, and a one- to two-paragraph descriptive annotation. At the end of the main section are several subsidiary bibliographies: "Addenda," "Pocketbook Novels on Atlantis," "Pocketbook Novels on Lemuria," a list of books whose titles suggest they might be about Atlantis (but are not), "Motion Pictures of Atlantis," "Magazine Stories on Atlantis and Lemuria" (in alphabetical order by magazine title, then chronologically by issue date).

The "Foreign Language" section is unannotated and arranged haphazardly by language, then alphabetically by author's name. A typical entry includes: author, title, English-language title (occasionally), publisher, place of publication, and year of publication. There is a separate bibliography of works consulted. The book is professionally typeset, although not very well proofread, and includes a sixteen-plate set of glossy reproductions of well-known Atlantis-oriented book and magazine covers.

Eichner's comments are occasionally cutesy, and he is far from a polished writer, but his lifelong obsession with the Atlantis theme is evident in this book, which is by far the most complete compilation of such materials ever gathered into one source. A more professional reworking and updating of this bibliography would certainly be justified.

BRAILLE AND LARGE PRINT BOOKS

239. Science Fiction: A Selected List of Books that Have Appeared in *Talking Book Topics* **and** *Braille Book Review.* Washington, DC, Library of Congress, 1979. 61 p. index. LC 79-15071. ISBN 0-8444-0287-7 (large print pbk.). Also available in computer disk and braille formats.

This nonbylined bibliography lists science fiction novels, anthologies, and young adult discs, cassettes, and braille books published for the blind and reviewed in the publications listed in the title (as well as being housed in the collection of the National Library Service for the Blind and Physically Handicapped).

Each of the three sections is divided into three parts, corresponding to the medium in question, with materials listed in each alphabetically by title. A typical entry includes: title (boldfaced), order number (boldfaced), author, narrator (where appropriate), number of discs, cassettes, or volumes, a one-paragraph descriptive annotation, and year of original publication. The index correlates authors, titles, and editors with page numbers in one alphabet and also includes order numbers. A library order blank is provided at the end of the book.

This type of work is intended more as a service to its library customers than as a literary guide, but it is astonishing to see the popularity of the genre reflected in the numerous SF titles (over 550 works) that had been made available to the blind and visually handicapped through 1979. An updated version is badly needed.

DRUGS

240. Silverberg, Robert. **Drug Themes in Science Fiction.** Rockville, MD, National Institute on Drug Abuse, 1974. vii, 55 p. index. (Research Issues, 9). LC 75-601268 (pbk.).

Well-known SF writer Silverberg produced many nonfiction books in the earlier stages of his career, this bibliography being among the last such works before the author turned his talents exclusively to writing more lucrative fantastic fiction.

A six-page introduction provides an overview of drug themes in science fiction. The bibliography proper is broken into three sections: "Primitive Period" (1900-1935), "Predictive Period" (1935-1965), and "Contemporary Period" (1965-date). Within each section stories and novels are listed chronologically by publication date. A typical entry includes: author, title, publisher and place of publication (for books) or magazine title (underlined), volume and issue number, pagination, and publisher (for short stories), date of publication, format (*e.g.,* novel or short story), descriptor (*e.g.,* "drugs as intelligence enhancers"), and a one-paragraph descriptive annotation (averaging 100 words). Eight items are listed in the first section, twenty-five in the second, and forty-two in the third. Materials are dated as late as 1973. An author/title index referencing page numbers completes the book. The monograph is shot from very clear typed copy.

It's impossible to determine the completeness of this work, although the small number of total citations (seventy-five) may signify a less than comprehensive survey. Still, Silverberg's inherent intelligence and literacy shine through *Drug Themes,* and it does provide a sound starting point for future scholarship. This would be a good project for some budding bibliographer to rework and bring up to date.

DYSTOPIAN LITERATURE

241. Booker, M. Keith. **Dystopian Literature: A Theory and Research Guide.** Westport, CT, Greenwood Press, 1994. xiii, 408 p. index. LC 93-40173. ISBN 0-313-29115-2.

Contents: "Introduction"; "Part One: A Guide to Selected Modern Cultural Criticism with Relevance to Dystopian Literature"; "Part Two: A Guide to Selected Utopian Fictions"; "Part Three: A Guide to Dystopian Fictions"; "Part Four: A Guide to Selected Dystopian Drama"; "Part Five: A Guide to Selected Dystopian Films"; "Bibliography"; "Index."

Designed to be an introduction to dystopian literature and criticism, this book is arranged into five parts, which are structured very similarly. Part One looks at significant critics (Adorno, Althusser, Bakhtin, Benjamin, Foucault, Freud, Marx, and Nietzsche), gives a brief overview of their work, and examines how it relates to utopian and dystopian literature.

Part Two (eight titles) and Part Three (sixty-five titles) discuss utopian and dystopian fiction, and are arranged by the author's last name, then alphabetically by book title. These two sections make up the bulk of the volume. Part Four examines fourteen dystopian dramas, being arranged by author's surname. Part Five discusses twelve dystopian films, being arranged alphabetically by motion picture title.

Each section begins with an overview on the topic in question. A typical entry includes: author (bold caps), title (bold italic caps), year of original publication, and a summary-*cum*-analysis (1,000-1,500 words). The critiques are well-written and -presented, summarizing both the plots of the pieces covered, and the general critical reactions of the literary world at large, and citing other major coverage of these pieces both at the end of each individual essay, and in the general bibliography. The selection of works covered by Booker is solidly balanced, with only a few questionable choices (James Joyce's *Dubliners,* for example); however, few can quibble with the vast majority of the works included. Overall, the commentary is exceedingly well done for a work of this type.

Bound to library standards, this is an excellent purchase for academic libraries serving upper-division undergraduates and graduate students in English, Film Studies, and Popular Culture. Highly recommended.

FANTASY FICTION

242. Schlobin, Roger C. **The Literature of Fantasy: A Comprehensive Annotated Bibliography of Modern Fantasy Fiction.** New York, Garland Publishing Co., 1979. xxxv, 425 p. index. (Garland Reference Library in the Humanities, Vol. 176). LC 78-68287. ISBN 0-8240-9757-2.

Schlobin's book is the first and thus far only attempt to compile a complete bibliography of modern adult fantasy, a category virtually created in paperback form by Ballantine Books during the 1960s and '70s, with its publication of the Tolkien Trilogy and the Adult Fantasy Series edited by Lin Carter.

The twenty-page introduction provides a critical and historical summary of the genre's development from publication of George MacDonald's *Phantastes* in 1858 through May of 1979. 721 novels, 244 collections, 100 anthologies and the 3,610 short stories collected in those volumes, and 165 author bibliographies are cited and indexed.

The main part of the bibliography (268 pages) records novels and collections, arranged alphabetically by author, then by title. A typical entry includes: author's name (centered, all caps), item number, title (italics), place of publication, publisher, year of publication, similar data for noteworthy recent reprints, and an annotation, but no paginations. The summaries range in size from a sentence to 300 words, averaging sixty words, and are primarily descriptive, with occasional critical comments.

Schlobin also makes an effort to note special apparatus that might enhance reprint editions (new introductions, for example), and cites bibliographies consulted at the end of each author's overall entry. Short stories are mentioned only as parts of book collections or anthologies, and are not separately annotated. Entries are numbered consecutively throughout the book from 1-1,249. Anthologies are listed in a separate section at the end of the volume, being arranged alphabetically by primary editor and then by title; similar data are provided for these publications, but without annotations. Two indices complete the book, both correlated with entry numbers: "Author, Compiler, Editor, and Translator Index" and "Title Index." The book is reproduced clearly from legible typed copy, and bound to library standards.

If we compare Schlobin with his chief rival, Barron's *Fantasy Literature* (see #64), we see that the latter work covers 945 items published through 1988, with annotations of roughly comparable size contributed by three different critics, while Schlobin's bibliography lists 300 more books with nine years' less data. Barron includes many early mythical or antecedental works not found in Schlobin, although Schlobin is more complete in his coverage of the modern period. *Fantasy Literature* provides copious "theme" references to books of a similar nature, even when they're not penned by the same writer, and also cites vastly more references to nonfiction sources about the authors and their literature. However, both books include numerous listings not found in the other, thus requiring libraries and researchers to have access to both.

One problem with Schlobin's work is his insistence on using the real names of pseudonymous writers as the major reference point for their entries, thus putting, for example, Piers Anthony's books under Piers Anthony Dillingham Jacob, with an appropriate "See" reference. This creates irritation for both the casual and heavy user, since one is constantly having to flip back and forth through the book looking for writers in places where one does not expect to find them. Barron's work also provides such information, but files entries under the names commonly used by the writers, a much more logical arrangement.

Still, *The Literature of Fantasy* is a worthy initial effort at establishing bibliographical control over a rapidly growing and extremely popular genre, and should be expanded into a second edition with paginations included.

FIRST EDITIONS

243. Bell, Joseph. **First Editions: "A Thousand and One Nights of Reading."** Toronto, Canada, Soft Books, 1988. 82 p. in 2 v. (pbk.). 200 numbered copies.

Canadian book dealer Bell here provides bibliographical descriptions of some 1,050 first-edition monographs of fantastic literature, including science fiction, fantasy, and horror.

Items are arranged in alphabetical order by author, and then by title; nonbylined works are grouped together in volume one under the label "Anonymous." A typical entry includes: author, title (boldfaced), imprint, stock number (where applicable), description of binding (if a cloth edition), format (*e.g.,* "dw" = dust wrapper), edition statement, year of publication, type (*e.g.,* "coll" = collection), price, but no paginations. Bell reproduces the title of each work as given on its title page, in capital or small letters, and similarly lists the edition statement (on the title or copyright page) exactly as printed in the original book. Pseudonymous works are unfortunately noted under the real names of the authors, with appropriate "See" references. The 8.5" x 11" volumes are shot from legible word-processed, laser-generated copy, and bound in paper covers stapled to the text. The set also includes seven full-page black-and-white reproductions from dust jackets and paperback covers. There is no title index.

The major problem with these volumes is the utter absence of any selection criteria beyond the author's personal tastes. Old and new authors, major and minor works, paper-bound and cloth editions, are all intermingled willy-nilly, with nary a thought as to why or how. As one might expect, the majority of the books covered were published during the three decades leading up to 1988; but even these newer writers have only a fraction of their works delineated. For example, just six works of Isaac Asimov are covered, and only two of these could be considered "major" first editions.

Thus, while Bell's data seem sound (although there are a number of typographical and other minor errors), the eclectic nature of his selections render this work almost useless. Although Currey's guide (see #244) is much to be preferred, Bell includes many books and authors, older and newer, not mentioned in the former.

244. Currey, L. W., with the editorial assistance of David G. Hartwell. **Science Fiction and Fantasy Authors: A Bibliography of First Printings of Their Fiction and Selected Non-fiction.** Boston, G. K. Hall & Co., 1979. xxix, 571 p. LC 79-18217. ISBN 0-8161-8242-6.

Currey's guide has become the standard bibliography of science fiction first editions since its initial release, with good reason: it is precise, authoritative, and complete for the authors and books listed. Currey is, like his two competitors, Bell and Locke, a dealer in science fiction and fantasy books, and his knowledge of first editions and points, particularly in the modern period, is unsurpassed.

The author's introduction discusses purpose, scope and coverage, arrangement, and terms of description. The bibliographies proper are listed in alphabetical order by the author's real name, and although the front matter includes a master pseudonym/real name index, this format still can create problems for the casual user (for example, well-known author Piers Anthony is filed under his legal name, Piers Anthony Dillingham Jacob).

Each writer's monographs are broken into several sections: fiction, edited fiction, nonfiction (dealing with the fantasy genre only), edited nonfiction (dealing with the fantasy genre only), prose adaptations, associational, letters, and reference (*i.e.,* monographic critiques and bibliographies about the author). In each subsection, books are listed in alphabetical order by title. A typical author entry provides the author's full name and years of birth and death.

A typical book entry includes: title (small caps), place of publication, publisher, year of publication (but no paginations), binding style (*e.g.,* "wrappers" = paperback; cloth bindings are described in detail), printing format, dustjackets, identification of printing and edition (including edition, printing, state, and issue), priority of issue, mass-market paperback book stock number and price, numbered series, and serial publications. The intent here is to enable the collector, scholar, and bibliographer to properly identify the first printing states of a particular title's first edition.

No contents listings are provided for collections or anthologies, and no general nonfiction books are included for very prolific authors like Asimov and Silverberg (but associational books about fantastic literature *are* covered); however, fictional works outside the genre (mystery novels, for example) are listed with the rest of the author's novels and collections. With few exceptions, later reprints of the same title are unmentioned unless they must be distinguished from the original, or unless they represent first hardcover appearances of the works. There are no indices. The book is beautifully typeset and bound to library standards. Books published through 1977 are included.

Currey covers every major writer of the genre (215 authors) from H. G. Wells through Vonda N. McIntyre and Stephen King, who became prominent in the mid-1970s. His work has generally been accepted, by both collectors and dealers, as definitive for the period covered. However, the omission of page numbers from monographic listings was an unfortunate bibliographical choice, since the presence of such information is one of the ways a collector, for example, may readily distinguish between a first edition of a novel and the book club reprint.

An updated edition adding a title index and paginations is badly needed.

245. Locke, George. **Science Fiction First Editions: A Select Bibliography and Notes for the Collector.** London, Ferret, 1978. 96 p. LC 80-483930 (pbk.).

Like Bell (see #243), Locke is a well-known dealer specializing in out-of-print science fiction and fantasy books, and his bibliographical knowledge was derived from years of handling and vending scarce first-edition materials. Unfortunately, this book also shares the major shortcoming of Bell's bibliography, being little more than a potpourri of bibliomania mixing old works with new, with no apparent selection criteria other than the fact that Locke possessed them at the time this book was prepared and was simultaneously offering copies for sale.

The data are arranged alphabetically by author surname, then by title. A typical entry includes: author, title (all caps), place of publication, publisher, pagination, number of illustrations, illustrator, and a detailed description of first edition points; at the end of each entry is a one-line description of the copy or copies actually being offered for sale, with an item number attached for ordering purposes. 247 such items are recorded, and perhaps fifteen less records are actually described (several of the entries have two or three copies for sale). The books covered by Locke do tend to have more importance than those recorded in Bell's work (see #243), and Locke is more precise and more bibliographically correct in his discernment and description of points. Some of the books and authors covered in Locke are not mentioned in Currey's definitive work (see #244).

More important perhaps than the bibliography proper are the two addenda: "Notes for the Collector" and "The Bookcase of Morlock Tomes." The first section discusses the collecting and identification and pricing and importance of Ace Books and "Ace Doubles," Avalon Books, Ballantine Books, Doubleday, dustwrappers, film and television linked books, first hardcover editions, Grosset & Dunlap and A. L. Burt, letters, limited editions, manuscripts and typescripts, modern science fiction, proof copies, remainders, science fiction book club [editions], science fiction speciality publishers, signed copies, and single author short story collections. This twenty-two page essay should be reproduced and distributed by the thousands to every OP book dealer in the Western world, for it succinctly and precisely summarizes Locke's genuine bibliographical knowledge of these materials and his philosophy of the art of collecting.

"The Bookcase of Morlock Tomes," a Sherlock Holmes pastiche, is a witty fictional account of the ratiocinative processes necessary to delineate the priorities or printing states of five major works of fantastic literature, including H. G. Wells's *The Time Machine*. Step by step the art of bibliographical detection is revealed clearly and precisely. A virtuoso performance, one which makes this book, now a hard-to-find collector's edition of its own, well worth reading.

FUTURE TALES

246. Clarke, I. F. **The Tale of the Future, from the Beginning to the Present Day.** London, Library Association, 1961. 165 p. index. LC 63-4922 (pbk.). **The Tale of the Future, from the Beginning to the Present Day: An Annotated Bibliography of Those Satires, Ideal States, Imaginary Wars and Invasions, Political Warnings and Forecasts, Interplanetary Voyages and Scientific Romances—All Located in an Imaginary Future Period—That Have Been Published in the United Kingdom Between 1644 and 1970.** 2nd ed. London, Library Association, 1972. 196 p. index. LC 73-157454. ISBN 0-85365-046-2 (pbk.). **Tale of the Future, from the Beginning to the Present Day: An Annotated Bibliography of Those Satires, Ideal States, Imaginary Wars and Invasions, Coming Catastrophes and End-of-the-World Stories, Political Warnings and Forecasts, Interplanetary Voyages and Scientific Romances—All Located in an Imaginary Future Period—That Have Been Published in the United Kingdom Between 1644 and 1976.** 3rd ed. London, Library Association, 1978. xvii, 357 p. index. LC 79-310478. ISBN 0-85365-550-2 (U.S. ISBN 0-8389-3225-8) (pbk.).

Each of the three editions of this bibliography have built upon the previous, adding new entries throughout the text and correcting older entries, and each has been organized identically, so only the most recent version will be considered here. The intent of Clarke's work is to record any fictional titles published in England with a futuristic setting or background.

The books are arranged in chronological order by year of publication, then alphabetically (within each year) by author, then by title. A typical entry includes: year of publication (running down the left-hand margin), author's name (boldfaced, with initials only given for first and middle names), title (italics), publisher, pagination, and a one-phrase annotation (*e.g.,* "Mysterious spaceships invade earth."). Single-author collections and multi-author anthologies are also included, with contents not otherwise delineated save to list the total number of stories. Books previously published in the United States are so noted with the appellation "[U.S., {date}]" after the annotation. Books with a publication date through 1976 are included in the third edition.

A comprehensive short title index references book titles, authors' surnames (in parentheses), and years of publication, and the author index lists complete authors' names (unlike the main text), short titles, and years of publication for the third edition only (previous editions listed authors' first names as initials, identically with the main bibliography). Roughly 4,000 books are covered in the 1978 edition. The book is professionally typeset, but is only available in an impermanent trade paperback binding.

There are several problems with Clarke's work. His annotations are at times so cryptic ("a young Russian tells the truth") that they provide little indication of why they were selected; and the selection criteria themselves seem at times to question Clarke's basic definition of the "tale of the future." In what way, for example, is Stephen King's horror tale *Carrie* futuristic? Many political thrillers are also included whose premises are at best open to interpretation, and whose background settings may not be definitively future-oriented. Clarke frequently seems to opt *for* rather than *against* such borderline cases, thereby tainting the very foundations of his bibliography.

Also, one must question his decision to limit the scope of his work to monographs published in the British Isles. Many mid-level American SF titles are no longer reprinted in the declining British book market, both for cultural and financial reasons, and by omitting such works, Clarke deliberately shortens his bibliography by at least a third, possibly more, leaving out thousands of works at least as significant as some of the very obscure paperbacks and vanity press items included herein.

Finally, this reader, at least, finds the use of initials in place of author's first names both irritating and occasionally obfuscating. A new edition building upon Clarke's original work, but correcting some of its structural flaws, would definitely be warranted.

FUTURE WAR FICTION

247. Clarke, I. F. **Voices Prophesying War, 1763-1984.** London, Oxford University Press, 1966. x, 254 p. index. LC 66-77284. London, Panther Arts, 1970. x, 254 p. index. ISBN 0-586-03278-9 (pbk.). **Voices Prophesying War, 1763-3749.** 2nd ed. London, New York, Oxford University Press, 1992. x, 268 p. index. LC 92-8583. ISBN 0-19-212302-5.

Clarke's interest in futuristic fiction has already been seen in his continuing *Tale of the Future* (see #246). This bibliocritical text examines the "future war" genre from its inception in 1871 with the publication of *The Battle of Dorking,* Sir George Chesney's xenophobic reaction to the establishment of the German Empire (a few seminal works prior to this date are also covered). Chesney's influential work sparked discussions in Parliament and a flood of sequels, responses, and counterscenarios, culminating in a rash of publications leading up to the outbreak of World War I. Thereafter, matched against the horrors of real-life battle, the genre declined somewhat but has never been wholly extinguished, with new popular successes (*The Third World War*) appearing through modern times.

Clarke provides a narrative analysis and description of the major future war scenarios published through 1990 (in his Second Edition), including reproductions of a number of illustrations from the original publications. Three major bibliographies are included in the First Edition: "A. Principal Works Consulted"; "B. Select List of War Studies, 1770-1964";

and "C. Check List of Imaginary Wars, 1763-1965." Only one of these, "Checklist of Imaginary Wars, 1763-1990," is included in the 1992 edition.

The latter bibliography is arranged chronologically by year of publication, then alphabetically by main entry. A typical entry includes: year of publication, author's name, title, and place of publication of the first edition, but no bibliographical data. The list is noteworthy for its inclusion of many European publications (particularly French and German) not found in any other source, although the lack of publishing information could limit the ability of researchers to locate actual copies of the volumes. The text is indexed in one alphabet, but the index fails to include entries from the bibliography, making them unsearchable save by serendipitous encounter.

Although the bibliography proper lacks annotations, in effect Clarke does the same thing, at least for the better-known works, through his extensive analyses in the main part of the text. In general his book has been accepted as authoritative, clearly reflecting a broad-based knowledge of the subject. Clarke lists more works than Newman/Unsworth (see #248), but the latter book provides more discussion of individual titles. No serious scholar of the future war genre could even contemplate beginning their researches without access to this seminal text.

248. Newman, John, and Michael Unsworth. **Future War Novels: An Annotated Bibliography of Works in English Published Since 1946.** Phoenix, AZ, Oryx Press, 1984. x, 101 p. index. LC 83-43245. ISBN 0-89774-103-X.

Newman and Unsworth describe 191 future war novels produced in the post-World War II period, arranged chronologically by year of publication, then alphabetically by author's name.

A typical entry includes: item number, author's name, title (italics), place of publication, publisher, pagination, LC card number, ISBN, and a one-paragraph description averaging 150 words in length. Books are numbered consecutively throughout the volume from the number one. Bibliographical data are provided for both the original editions and all known reprints (including paperbacks) in the U.S. and England. The annotations (written by Newman only) are largely descriptive, with occasional one-sentence summations or commentary. Author and title indexes, referencing item numbers only, complete the book. The text is nicely typeset and the book is bound to library standards.

Clarke's guide (see #247) covers more works than Newman and Unsworth's, but the latter volume does provide more coverage of individual novels; thus, both will be required by serious researchers in this field. By whatever definition, this book seems to miss a great many titles that could justly have been included (see the comments on Brians's *Nuclear Holocausts* [see #255]), and one must ask if the net was cast widely enough. Perhaps an expanded future edition of *Future War Novels* will settle the conflict.

GOTHIC FICTION

249. Frank, Frederick S. **The First Gothics: A Critical Guide to the English Gothic Novel.** New York & London, Garland Publishing, 1987. xxxi, 496 p. index. (Garland Reference Library of the Humanities, Vol. 710). LC 86-27092. ISBN 0-8240-8501-9.

Frank, author of several bibliographies of secondary resources on the literature of the gothic revival (see #114, #115), here provides an annotated bibliography to 500 of these extraordinarily rare novels of terror and the supernatural, all from the classic period of gothic literature (1758-1832).

Materials are arranged alphabetically by author, then by title (but nonbylined novels, of which there are many, are interfiled in the main sequence by title). A typical entry includes: item number, author, title (all caps), place of publication, publisher, and year of publication of first edition, plus similar data on modern reprints, "Gothic Type" (*e.g.*, "Gothified history"), biographical and research data, and an annotation. The secondary sources mentioned in the "biographical and research data" reference the "Selected Bibliography of Critical Sources on the English Gothic Novel" in Appendix Two, citing authors, titles, and specific page numbers, and generally adding a very useful dimension to the entries. The annotations are both descriptive and evaluative and range in size from 50-1,500 words, averaging 300. Frank makes some comparisons between similar works, and his comments are informed, literate, and to the point.

End matter includes: "Appendix One: Glossary of Gothic Terms" (very useful); "Appendix Two" (noted above); "Appendix Three: Annual Chronology of the First Gothics, 1758-1832" (giving years, titles [all caps], and item numbers); "Index One: Index of Gothic Authors" (referencing authors and item numbers, but no titles, with primary records [*i.e.*, those annotated] underlined); "Index Two: Index of Gothic Titles" (giving titles and item numbers only, with primary entries underlined); "Index Three: Index of Critics" (citing critics and item numbers only). The book is shot from legible typed copy and bound to library standards; fourteen full-page reproductions of illustrations from the gothics themselves add a touch of spice to the text. Frank's twelve-page historical introduction provides a good general introduction to the history of the literature.

The First Gothics covers 500 titles, while Tracy's *The Gothic Novel* (see #252) annotates just 208 books. Only a few titles are unique to Tracy's volume (perhaps twenty items), and Frank makes some attempt at evaluating the titles, while Tracy just supplies straightforward plot summaries. Thus, while serious scholars will probably want access to both books, most libraries can satisfy the needs of their patrons, academics included, with copies of Frank's more authoritative bibliography.

Locating copies of the gothics themselves is almost an impossible task, of course, since the vast majority have never been reprinted; most exist in less than ten or twenty copies, and some survive with just one known example; other titles mentioned in various contemporaneous lists and in Summers's bibliography (see #251) apparently no longer survive. Frank estimates that as many as 4,500-5,000 gothic novels may actually have been published in the seventy-year period between 1760-1830.

250. Radcliffe, Elsa J. **Gothic Novels of the Twentieth Century: An Annotated Bibliography.** Metuchen, NJ & London, The Scarecrow Press, 1979. xix, 272 p. LC 78-24357. ISBN 0-8108-1190-1.

In 1960 the late Donald A. Wollheim and Evelyn Grippo, editors of the paperback house Ace Books, created the modern gothic as a mass market category by developing a distinctive series package for several romance novels they had recently purchased for reprinting. This unique cover design, later adopted by many rival companies who published gothic lines of their own, featured a young woman fleeing from a castle or old house at night, a look of horror or fear frozen on her face, and one lone light flickering at the window of the decaying manse. The popularity of these first few releases sparked the rapid development of the category from the mid-1960s through the early '70s, when the genre rapidly began to wane. The aptly named Radcliffe has published the first bibliographical guide to this modern publishing phenomenon.

Gothic Novels is organized alphabetically by author surname, then by title. A typical entry includes: author's name (all caps), biographical data (one brief paragraph; data are present for only about a third of the authors), entry number, title (underlined), rating (using the grade school letter grades of A, B, C, D, F), place of publication, publisher, year of publication, LC card number, paperback stock number (haphazardly), with similar data for all known reprints, and a descriptive annotation (for about half of the entries) averaging forty words in length. No paginations are provided.

Books by one writer are unified under the best-known pseudonym (or real name) of that author, with "See" references scattered throughout the text, and an indication after each title which name was employed on that book. Thus, the writings of Canadian writer W. E. D. Ross, who produced at least a hundred gothics, are centralized under his real name, with references from his thirteen gothic pen names to his real name. The entries are numbered consecutively from 1-1,973. Works are included through at least 1977. The title index references titles and item numbers only. There is also a list of works consulted at the beginning of the book. As usual with older Scarecrow Press volumes, the bibliography is shot from very legible typed copy and bound to library standards.

Some of Radcliffe's comments are overly cute, and her bibliographical data are far from definitive; most of the novels she cites, for example, are known to have been pseudonymous (many were written by male writers under female names), with only a partial list of identifications being provided here. There are similar questions about the comprehensiveness of this volume (Radcliffe herself mentions in passing works by authors already included in her book that appear to be gothics, but that she has been unable to verify; these novels are not included in the number count), as well as about the compiler's selection criteria (in what way are the two fantasies by Peter S. Beagle gothics?), and about the uniformity of the application of these criteria to the works at hand.

On the other side, however, the gothic genre was itself so ill-defined (and bibliographical data on these books so difficult to find) as to present major problems to any potential bibliographer, since the paperback publishers, in their initial desperate search for material, threw into this category any work that could be even remotely construed as fitting the idea of the "gothic mystique." Radcliffe does adequately cover a majority of the books produced during the fifteen-year rise and fall of the modern gothic revival, providing some initial basis for future scholarship; perhaps her bibliography, as mediocre as the fiction it indexes, is the best we can hope for under the circumstances.

251. Summers, Montague. **A Gothic Bibliography.** London, Fortune Press, 1941. xx, 621 p. LC a41-3676. New York, Russell & Russell, 1964. xx, 620 p. LC 64-8918.

Summers was a well-known critic and bibliographer with a particular interest in the gothic and horror novel. His guide to the classic gothic was so well produced that it has never really been supplanted.

A Gothic Bibliography is divided into two major sections: "Index of Authors" and "Title Index," with a brief addendum similarly subdivided. The author index is arranged alphabetically by author surname. A typical entry includes: author's name (surname in large caps, remainder of the name in small caps), biographical information (ranging from nothing [more than half of the entries] to mini-essays of 400 words), and a chronological list of the author's gothics, giving title (italics) and year of publication, but no other data.

The title index is actually the major focus of the volume, listing works in alphabetical order by title and giving: title (italics), author, year of publication, place of publication, publisher, variant titles, number of volumes or pagination, size (*e.g.,* "8vo" for octavo), price, and an occasional one-line descriptive annotation. Not all of the entries have the same level of data, due to lack of sources (some of these books no longer survive with any known examples); many items lack paginations, for example. Similar information is provided on all known reprints. An extraordinary number of French, German, and other foreign gothics are included in the bibliography, some with English-language translations.

Summers's work is both authoritative and definitive; indeed, it is difficult to imagine any current researcher redoing his work or having sufficient resources even to begin such a project. This bibliography should be owned by all university libraries.

Frank's guide (see #249) provides a worthy supplemental text.

252. Tracy, Ann B. **The Gothic Novel, 1790-1830: Plot Summaries and Index to Motifs.** Lexington, KY, The University Press of Kentucky, 1981. vii, 216 p. index. LC 79-4013. ISBN 0-8131-1397-0.

Given the difficulty in locating surviving copies of the novels produced during the classic gothic period of the early 1800s, one marvels at the plethora of literature available on the topic. Tracy provides a valuable service to the scholarly world by summarizing the plots of 208 of these rare and extraordinarily intricate fictions.

The Gothic Novel is arranged in alphabetical order by main entry (usually author, but occasionally title if no author is known), and then by title. A typical entry provides: item number, author, title (all caps), number of volumes or pagination, place of publication, publisher, year of publication, and an annotation. Tracy's summaries are descriptive rather than evaluative, ranging in size from thirty words (for several of the pamphlets) to 750 words, and are very detailed and explicit. The items are numbered consecutively throughout the book from the number one. The title index references titles and page numbers. Tracy also provides two other valuable indices, to motifs and to characters, both referenced, curiously, to item numbers (it seems illogical and unnecessarily confusing to index titles one way and everything else another way). The book is shot from legible typed copy.

Students of the gothic revival will welcome this guide to the major gothic authors and their works. Although Tracy makes no attempt to evaluate the works in question or even to suggest a reading list, all of the major gothics are here, and many of the minor ones; the only useful addenda that could conceivably be added in the future are summaries of other novels not heretofore covered. Compare with Frank's more complete bibliographical guide (see #249).

IMAGINARY VOYAGES

253. Gove, Philip Babcock. **The Imaginary Voyage in Prose Fiction: A History of Its Criticism and a Guide for Its Study, with an Annotated Checklist of 215 Imaginary Voyages from 1700 to 1800.** New York, Columbia University Press, 1941. xi, 445 p. index. (Columbia University Studies in English and Comparative Literature, No. 152). LC 41-6604. New York, Arno Press, 1975. xi, 445 p. index. (Science Fiction). LC 74-15972. ISBN 0-405-06328-8.

Gove's book deals with a now defunct subgenre of fantastic literature, the imaginary voyage to a mythical (and often fantastical) island, continent, or country (*Gulliver's Travels* is the best-known example), which became the rage of early eighteenth-century literature, then gradually faded into oblivion as the farther reaches of the world were actually explored (a later offshoot is the lost race novel, now also consigned to the ashheap of literature).

The first half of this book (178 pages) is "A History of the Criticism of the Imaginary Voyage," in which Gove succinctly and carefully summarizes critical reactions to the genre. Part Two, an "Annotated Check List of Two Hundred and Fifteen Imaginary Voyages from 1700 to 1800," is arranged chronologically by year of publication.

A typical entry includes: year of publication, author (with years of birth and death, if known), title, place of publication, publisher, and similar data for all known reprints through the year 1800 (but no paginations), a list of libraries in the United States known to have copies of the items in question (using the library symbols from the *Library of Congress* [later *National Union*] *Catalog*), and an annotation. The descriptions vary widely in length, some being very perfunctory, others providing much background data on editions, history, and other details; very few contain actual plot summaries or any literary evaluation of the texts.

Gove also provides a separate bibliography of works consulted, and a detailed author/title index correlated to page numbers. Works from all languages are covered (including almost as many original French and German editions as those in English) in almost a thousand separate printings. The book is attractively typeset, and both editions are bound to library standards (the Arno version is a facsimile reprint of the original).

The widespread acceptance of Gove as the standard work on the subject can be seen by the fact that no significant revision or upgrade of *The Imaginary Voyage* has ever been undertaken, despite the passage of half a century. While his standards are undoubtedly high, it would have been helpful to have had paginations for these very rare publications, and some indication of plots or motifs. These are minor points, however. This well-wrought critical bibliography should be available in all academic libraries.

MACHINES

254. Erlich, Richard D., and Thomas P. Dunn. **Clockworks: A Multimedia Bibliography of Works Useful for the Study of the Human/Machine Interface in SF.** Westport, CT, Greenwood Press, 1993. xvi, 324 p. index. (Bibliographies and Indexes in World Literature, No. 37). LC 93-1069. ISBN 0-313-27305-7 (alk. paper).

Contents: "About this Volume"; "Abbreviations"; "Introduction"; "A List of Works Useful for the Study of the Human/Machine Interface in SF" (1. Reference Works; 2. Anthologies and Collections; 3. Fiction and Poetry; 4. Literary Criticism; 5. Stage, Screen, and Television Drama; 6. Stage, Screen, and Television Drama Criticism; 7. Graphic and Plastic Arts; 8. Music; 9. Background Reading); "Author Index"; "Title Index"; "Keyword and Theme Index."

A selected bibliography and filmography of works in all media concerning the "human/machine interface in SF," Erlich and Dunn's volume covers books, stage, screen, and television drama; graphic and plastic arts; and music on records and audiotapes. The emphasis is on works produced in English from 1895-1990.

The 2,059 entries are divided into nine chapters by type of material, and organized by author's last name. The referencing system combines the chapter number and item number (*e.g.*, "1.048" indicates the forty-eighth entry of the first chapter). A typical book entry includes: reference number (bold type), author, title (underlined), place of publication, publisher, and year of publication, but no paginations, and a brief (20-100 words) descriptive annotation.

A typical short fiction entry (making up almost half of the book) includes: reference number (bold), author, title (in quotation marks), periodical or anthology in which the item appeared, and publication data. Publications appearing first in magazines include: magazine title (underlined), volume and issue number (in the form "1:3" for Volume 1, Number 3), month and year of publication (in parentheses), and a short description (50-100 words). Shorter works appearing originally in anthologies give the anthology title (underlined), and refer the user to that section of the bibliography for more complete data. Paginations are haphazardly mentioned for shorter works.

The author and title indices do a very good job of cross-referencing materials with their reference numbers. The Keyword and Theme Index is sometimes helpful in providing additional access by subject, but some of the keywords have so many items attached, without further division, as to make them almost useless.

This highly specialized bibliography would be most helpful to those scholars interested in this particular subgenre of science fiction. For larger academic libraries only.

NUCLEAR WARFARE

255. Brians, Paul. **Nuclear Holocausts: Atomic War in Fiction, 1895-1984.** Kent, OH & London, The Kent State University Press, 1987. xi, 398 p. index. LC 86-10685. ISBN 0-87338-335-4.

This critical bibliography is divided into two sections. The first half (ninety-four pages) provides a history of nuclear warfare in literature in five chapters: "1. The History of the Holocaust"; "2. The Causes of Nuclear War"; "3. The Short-Term Effects of Nuclear War"; "4. The Long-Term Consequences of Nuclear War"; and "5. Avoiding the Holocaust." These sections evaluate and compare (through the broad categories into which they fall) the fictions mentioned in the bibliography. A six-page intermediate section, "Sources," discusses and compares in narrative form the many secondary sources, both books and articles, on atomic energy and warfare in modern fiction.

The major part of the book (350 pages) is an annotated guide to the literature of nuclear warfare, arranged alphabetically by author, and then by title. A typical entry includes: author's name (boldfaced), title (italics), place of publication, publisher, and year of publication, but no paginations; similar data are provided for known reprints. Both novels and short stories are covered. The entry annotations range in size from one brief sentence (ten words) to 1,500 words, 100 being average, and tend to be descriptive, with occasional one-line evaluations.

End matter includes: "Timeline," a chronological checklist of the materials covered by year, giving author and title; and "Supplementary Checklists" of closely-related books and stories, including "Near-War Narratives," "Doubtful Cases," "Nuclear Testing," and "Reactor Disasters." Each of these brief sections is arranged alphabetically by author, then by title, the entries providing authors, titles, and years of publication only. There are also title and detailed subject indices keyed to page number (the title index notes the authors after each title). The book is very professionally and attractively designed and typeset and bound to library standards.

In comparing Brian's guide to Newman/Unsworth's *Future War Novels* (see #248), one would expect to find all of the works mentioned in *Nuclear Holocausts* for the years 1946-83 included in the latter, but in fact at least half are missing. It is difficult to make exact comparisons, but Brians includes roughly 780 titles, not all of them with full-length entries; of these, perhaps 40% are short fiction, and another sixty or so were published before Newman/Unsworth's 1946 cutoff date, leaving about 400 novels in Brians compared to 191 in *Future War Novels*. Brians's reach is clearly much longer and his knowledge of the literature much broader.

There are also, however, a few problems with the selection criteria employed in *Nuclear Holocausts:* a very small number of entries (for example, Mitchell Wilson's *Live with Lightning*) deal realistically with the development of the atomic bomb in the 1940s, or with some other aspect of nuclear physics, and are not clearly futuristic or fantastic by any stretch of the imagination. They seem out-of-place in the midst of so much fictional over-destruction. Barring such minor quibbles, Brians's bibliography is a thoroughly good piece of work, and should be continued with subsequent editions.

For research libraries.

PAPERBACKS

256. Day, Bradford M. **The Checklist of Fantastic Literature in Paperbound Books**. Denver, NY, Science-Fiction & Fantasy Publications, 1965. 128 p. index. LC 66-342. (pbk.). New York, Arno Press, 1975. 128 p. index. (Science Fiction). LC 74-15961. ISBN 0-405-06326-1.

Day intended this book as a companion volume to his *Supplemental Checklist of Fantastic Literature* (see #209), which included only cloth volumes, and ultimately as a supplement to Bleiler's *Checklist of Fantastic Literature* (see #208), and it is organized very similarly to both.

The main section of the book organizes the literature in alphabetical order by author, then by title, anonymous works being centralized under the headings "Anonymous" or "Anonymous Anthology." A typical entry includes: author, title (all caps), publisher, year of publication, pagination, and an indication (using the words "Book: same" or "Book: [original title]" beneath the entry) whether the work was previously published in cloth (original paperbacks have no such appellation). The title index cross-references titles and author surnames only.

As is usual with Day's self-published works, the text is reproduced from sometimes faint typed copy and bound through the side with staples; the edges of some pages are beginning to yellow. The Arno Press edition is a facsimile of the original, photoreduced from 8.5" x 11" to 5" x 8" (which does help concentrate the text into a more legible format), and bound to library standards.

Day includes materials largely from the period 1948-64, although some earlier original paperbacks missed by Bleiler in his 1948 *Checklist* have been added. Now largely superseded by Reginald's *Science Fiction and Fantasy Literature* (see #212), which does not, however, include reprints.

257. Stephens, Christopher P. **The Science Fiction and Fantasy Paperback First Edition: A Complete List of Them All (1939-1973).** Hastings-on-Hudson, NY, Ultramarine Publishing Co., 1991. 143 p. index. ISBN 0-89366-162-7 (pbk.).

Chris Stephens, author of twenty-five other short bibliographies on topics as diverse as science fiction, the literature of the Vietnam War, and the writings of P. C. Wren, was very active in the late 1980s and early 1990s. This bibliography attempts to list all SF paperback first editions published from the inception of the mass market paperback in June of 1939 to the end of 1973.

Materials are arranged alphabetically by author's surname, then chronologically by title. A typical entry includes: author (surname in all caps), item number, title (underlined), publisher, stock number, price, year of publication, pagination, cover illustrator, information on later cloth editions (where applicable), and other bibliographical notes. Materials are numbered consecutively from 1-1,655. Authors are listed under their real names when known, with "See" references from their pseudonyms to their birth names; this can create confusion for users attempting to find authors who have only written under one very well-known pen name. The index correlates titles with authors and years of publication, not item numbers. Books that the author has not actually seen are so indicated by an asterisk placed before the item number. The book is shot from typed copy and stapled through the spine into stiff paper covers.

Much of these data can already be found in Reginald's more complete bibliography (see #212) or in Tuck's *Encyclopedia* (see #18); however, Stephens does include information on stock numbers, cover illustrators, and subsequent cloth editions for the period 1969-73 that are not readily found elsewhere, and his guide will prove useful for bibliographers and researchers studying the golden age of paperback originals.

PSEUDONYMOUS AUTHORS

258. Rock, James A. **Who Goes There: A Bibliographic Dictionary, Being a Guide to the Works of Authors Who Have Contributed to the Literature of Fantasy and Science Fiction, and Who Have Published Some or All of Their Work Pseudonymously.** Bloomington, IN, James A. Rock & Co., 1979. viii, 201 p. LC 79-125345. ISBN 0-918736-04-8; ISBN 0-918736-05-6 (pbk.).

This is a strangely realized bibliography, its basic premise being the listing of all fantastic literature written by authors who have penned at least one work pseudonymously in whatever forum.

The main section of *Who Goes There* is arranged alphabetically by author's name, then alphabetically by pen name, then chronologically under each name by title. A typical entry includes: author's name (bold caps), years of birth and death and place of birth (if known), author's pseudonym (boldface), the first story published under this name in a periodical (plus magazine title [italics] and month and year of publication), then a chronological checklist of the author's science fiction and fantasy books under this name, giving titles (italics), places of publication, publishers, years of publications, paginations, an indication of illustrations, and binding ("paper" = paperback).

This arrangement is repeated for each pen name in alphabetical order by pseudonym. Rock also provides a representative selection of the authors' nonfiction and non-SF fiction monographs, if such exist, and references other known or unverified pseudonyms outside the field, without, however, providing examples of works under those names. The index coordinates pen names (boldfaced) to real names and page numbers, but does not index titles. The book also includes a source bibliography and a six-page illustrated essay, "Notes on Collecting." The text is clearly typeset in double-column format and printed in an over-sized 9" x 12" format.

There's a great deal of data here, but Rock's book is filled with inconsistencies, stretched examples, and skewed logic. For example, author Leo P. Kelley is included solely on the basis of a typographical error on the cover of one of his paperback novels, which misconstrued his middle initial as "F." *This* is a pseudonym? Chad Oliver is included because the fuller form of his name, Dr. Symmes C(had) Oliver, appeared on an anthropological text. Andy Offutt is listed because some half-stewed magazine editor left the second "T" off his last name, another clear instance of "typo-slipping." One can play such games, of course, but ultimately one must ask what purpose this bibliography serves. The only answer is irretrievably stuck between a bibliographical Rock and a hard place.

RECURSIVE SCIENCE FICTION

259. Lewis, Anthony R. **An Annotated Bibliography of Recursive Science Fiction.** Cambridge, MA, NESFA Press, 1990. 56 p. index. ISBN 0-915368-47-1 (pbk.). The running title throughout the book is *Recursion!: Science Fiction Stories About Science Fiction.*

Lewis, one of the principals behind the NESFA magazine indexes (see #159), here provides an annotated bibliography of SF and other fictions using science-fiction authors, SF fandom, or other science-fictional backgrounds or settings as an integral part of their stories.

The main part of the book is organized alphabetically by author's name, then by title. A typical entry includes: author (boldfaced), title (boldfaced, in quotes for short stories, in bold italics for novels), genre for works that are not in themselves fantastic (boldfaced, run to the righthand margin), annotation, and bibliographical data (publisher or magazine title, series, ISBN number [where appropriate], month and year of publication [with paginations provided on an inconsistent basis for short story appearances only] for all known editions and reprints). The annotations are descriptive rather than evaluative, focusing on the recursive elements in each story and averaging about eighty words each. The introduction incorporates a bibliography of "References" consulted.

Included at the end of the book are separate sections on "Graphics" (comic books); "Performing Arts" (plays, musicals, teleplays, and films); a two-page addendum of "Items That Didn't Quite Make It Into the Bibliography" (all three sections are arranged in similar format to the main bibliography); "Cross Reference by Title," giving titles and authors only (plus, inconsistently, a few appellations such as "[film]," referencing titles in the three addendum sections); and a "Listing by Date of First Appearance," arranged by year, month (where known), author, title, and magazine title or publisher. Materials are covered through October 1990. The book is reproduced from excellent laser printer-generated copy on 8.5" x 11" sheets and stapled through the spine.

Lewis's coverage seems reasonably thorough (roughly 220 items), his list of reprintings valuable, and his annotations very readable; one might have wished, however, for complete paginations for all items included, instead of the hodgepodge actually provided. Moreover, the title index does not always distinguish between books, graphic publications, and media productions, and the books in the borderline chapter are not indexed at all. These inconsistencies need to be resolved in any future edition. Despite the book's title, Lewis also includes mysteries, romances, and other works with settings in the SF field (for example, Anthony Boucher's *Rocket to the Morgue*), interfiled with the rest but distinguished by category tags; these add a valuable adjunct to the main listings.

For specialized collections only.

SERIES

260. Cottrill, Tim, Martin H. Greenberg, and Charles G. Waugh. **Science Fiction and Fantasy Series and Sequels: A Bibliography, Volume 1: Books.** New York & London, Garland Publishing Co., 1986. xix, 398 p. index. (Garland Reference Library of the Humanities, Vol. 611). LC 85-45121. ISBN 0-8240-8671-6.

Cottrill *et al.* provide a very useful guide to the seemingly interminable spate of sequels and series that have plagued all genre literatures from their very beginnings.

The basic arrangement of the book is alphabetically by author's name (or by series name if more than one author has contributed separate items to the series—for example, "*Star Trek*"), then by series title. A typical entry includes: author (all caps), years of birth and death (if known), series title (underlined), and a numbered list of the novels in the order of their publication (although additional numbering is sometimes provided if there are major sequential problems), coordinated with years of initial publication and publishers' names (often abbreviated). Multi-authored series volumes such as "*Star Wars,*" "*The Man from U.N.C.L.E.,*" and "*Star Trek*" may incorporate several numbering sequences for different subseries; these sections also include the names of each author after the titles they authored, in parentheses.

A second part of the book lists anthology series arranged by editor, then by title, in chronological order by issue date, with the same data as above. Two indices, to series titles and book titles, cross-referenced to author surnames and page numbers, complete the book, with brief addenda and corrigenda sections, and a bibliography of sources consulted. The book is shot from very clear typed copy and bound to library standards. A detailed abbreviations list appears at the front of the book.

Cottrill's reach is vast, and he and his co-authors cover every major (and most minor) SF series published in the English language through 1985. Roughly 5,200 books are covered. The only problem with the bibliography is the extensive use of publisher abbreviations, which are totally unnecessary (the book has plenty of white space running down the middle of each page), and often obtrusive and irritating, or occasionally misleading for lesser-known publishing firms. This problem should be fixed in any future edition.

A second volume devoted to short fiction was announced, but has not been published, and the basic volume itself now badly needs updating. For all academic collections.

SEXUALITY

261. Garber, Eric, and Lyn Paleo. **Uranian Worlds: A Reader's Guide to Alternative Sexuality in Science Fiction and Fantasy.** Boston, G. K. Hall & Co., 1983. xxvi, 177 p. index. (A Reference Publication in Science Fiction). LC 82-21198. ISBN 0-8161-8573-5. **Uranian Worlds: A Reader's Guide to Alternative Sexuality in Science Fiction and Fantasy.** 2nd ed. Boston, G. K. Hall & Co., 1990. xxvi, 286 p. index. LC 90-37434. ISBN 0-8161-1832-9.

Garber and Paleo here contribute a very interesting series of bibliographies on homosexuality and other alternative sexual lifestyles mentioned in fantasy and science fiction stories and novels.

The main part of the book is organized alphabetically by author, then by title. A typical entry provides: item number, author's name (all caps), title (italics), place of publication, publisher, year of publication (but no paginations), subject code letter (*e.g.,* "F" = "Lesbianism or female bisexuality is a major component within a work"), and a brief descriptive annotation ranging in size from one sentence (ten words) to 200 words, fifty being average.

Short story entries typically include: author, story title, magazine or anthology title (italics), month and year of publication (for periodical appearances), or place of publication, publisher, and year of publication (for appearances in books), but no paginations. Interpolated throughout the text are biographical notes on the major writers, set off from the rest of the text by line rules, and printed in smaller boldfaced type; these sections include author's name, year of birth (and death, if appropriate), career highlights as a writer, and an assessment of the writer's contributions to alternative sexuality in fantastic literature. Also listed in these sections are sources for additional information (bibliographies, critiques, etc.).

The annotations include plot summaries, plus the rationale for the work's inclusion in the bibliography (sometimes the alternative lifestyle is a very minor part of the fictional framework of the novel or story, sometimes it dominates the narrative). Entries are numbered consecutively throughout each volume from the number one: the first edition contains 568 items, the second edition 935. Garber and Paleo also cover in the main sequence a handful of nonfiction articles about homosexuality and lesbianism in fantastic literature.

The second edition adds three appendices: "Selected Anthologies," listed alphabetically by title, giving: title (italics), editor, place of publication, publisher, year of publication, and a one-sentence annotation that mentions the stories featuring alternative sexualities (which in turn are covered as separate items in the main text); "Selected Films," also alphabetically by title, giving: title (italics), director's name, country of origin, year of production, subject code (as above, for the main part of the book), and a two-sentence annotation summarizing plot elements, mentioning the homosexual aspects of the motion picture, and giving the names of the chief characters (and the actors/actresses who play them); and "Selected Fan Organizations," noting organization name (all caps), description and purpose, and address.

Both books also include a chronological index rearranging the data year by year, then alphabetically by author, a typical entry including: year of publication, author's surname, title (italics), and item number; and an alphabetical title index correlating titles, author surnames, and item numbers only. The first volume is shot from typed copy, while the second is attractively typeset, providing a great improvement in general readability; both are bound to library standards.

Uranian Worlds represents one of the few instances where an effort has been made to maintain and expand an existing bibliographical data base. The original volume was a worthy effort; the 1990 version expands these listings by almost forty percent, including both the great and very obscure, and certainly covering the vast majority of works published. The only modifications that might be desirable for future editions would be the addition of paginations to the bibliographical data, and of full author names to the two indices.

Note also Donald Palumbo's edited volume, *Erotic Universe: Sexuality and Fantastic Literature* (New York & Westport, CT, Greenwood Press, 1986), which includes a short annotated bibliography of fiction, nonfiction, and film SF and fantasy featuring sexual themes on pages 257-89, among them some works not mentioned in Garber/Paleo (but falling outside of their stated parameters).

For all research collections. A third edition would be welcome.

SPACE VOYAGES

262. Locke, George. **Voyages in Space: A Bibliography of Interplanetary Fiction, 1801-1914.** London, Ferret Fantasy, 1975. 80 p. index. (Ferret Fantasy's Christmas Annual for 1974). LC 76-365519 (cloth and pbk.).

Two earlier, more general bibliographies by Locke bore the title *Ferret Fantasy's Christmas Annual for 1972* and . . . *1973* (see #210), but this particular volume was the first in the series to have a specific title and focus.

Locke's learned introduction discusses definitions and format. This is followed by a nineteen-item preliminary list, "What Had Gone Before: A Chronological Survey and Select Bibliography of Interplanetary Fiction up to 1800," which, except for the chronological arrangement, includes the same type of data as the main section.

The primary bibliography is itself divided into two sections: "1. Books" and "2. Periodicals, Boys' Novelettes, Etc." In each section materials are arranged alphabetically by author, then by title (nonbylined works being filed under the appellation "Anonymous"). A typical entry provides: item number, author's name, title (all caps), place of publication, publisher, year of publication, pagination, illustration note, and a brief descriptive annotation ranging in size from twenty-five to seventy-five words (averaging forty), followed by a detailed bibliographical description of the first edition of the publication, including binding cloth, priority points, notes on reprint editions, etc. Items are numbered consecutively from 001-019 in the preliminary section, and from 1-263 in the main bibliography (both parts together).

The short stories mentioned in section two include: story title (in quotes), place of publication, magazine title (italics), month and year of publication, and occasionally total (but no specific) paginations. A postscript includes statistic tables and graphs (*e.g.,* "Flights to and from Earth"), and a brief checklist of further secondary reading sources. The index correlates authors with titles and item numbers, but there is no separate title index; since the main organization of the book is by author, including an author index seems a fruitless waste of space. The book is shot from attractive and legible typed copy, and the cloth edition is sewn to library standards.

Locke's immense knowledge of early science fiction is clearly reflected here; his book is filled with rare, seminal works, many of them described for the first (and only) time in this volume. Researchers interested in the antecedents of modern SF would find their time well spent examining Locke's very authoritative bibliographies, and all major research collections should own copies.

263. Smith, Lynn S. **Space Voyages, 1591-1920: A Bibliography of Works Held in the Library of the University of California, Riverside.** Riverside, CA, University of California, Riverside Library, 1979. 45 p. (pbk.).

This very brief guide was produced to highlight books held in the J. Lloyd Eaton Collection of Science Fiction and Fantasy housed in the Rivera Library at the University of California, Riverside, whose complete collection catalog is covered elsewhere in this volume (see #134).

Librarian Lynn S. Smith lists 131 mostly fictional voyages to outer space dated from 1591-1920, with a heavy emphasis on the pre-industrial era. A typical entry includes: call number, author, title (underlined), place of publication, publisher, year of publication, a one- to two-sentence descriptive annotation, and a reference citation to one of three works: Locke (see #262), Bleiler (see #208), or Majorie Hope Nicolson's classic historical survey, *Voyages to the Moon* (New York, Macmillan, 1948). The book is shot from typed copy and includes several full-page illustrations taken from the works annotated.

For scholars interested in this very limited topic, and wishing to examine copies of the works in question, this is a useful introductory guide; students of the very early antecedents of the science fiction genre may also find this bibliography of interest.

STAR WARS FICTION

264. Sheldon, Lita. **An Author List of Star Wars Fan Fiction.** Tsaile, AZ, Lita Sheldon, 1984. [i], 33p., 4 leaves. index. (pbk).

The three *Star Wars* films spawned a rabid fan following that reached almost the level of the *Star Trek* fandom before suddenly dissipating after *Return of the Jedi* was released (it reappeared again in the late 1990s). During its heydey, *Star Wars* fans, like their *ST* counterparts, produced reams of amateur stories, novellas, novels, and plays. Some of these were published in *SW* fanzines; others appeared as separate monographs or in *SW* anthologies. Such publications are technically violations of the copyright law, of course, since both created universes are proprietary properties owned and leased by the film companies that produced the original motion pictures and television programs. However, this has not stopped the fans, who have produced scores of derivatory fictions distributed in small numbers of copies to other fans.

Sheldon's guide is arranged alphabetically by author/illustrator's name, and then by title. A typical entry provides: author/illustrator, title, type (*e.g.,* "story," "play," etc.), universe (*e.g.,* "SW" = *Star Wars*), fanzine/book title, page numbers. A separate section indexes fanzine/book editors and addresses. The book is photocopied from sometimes faint computer-generated printout and bound with two staples through the side (without covers).

Although useful as a guide to these very ephemeral materials, Sheldon's bibliography is necessary only for the most specialized collections, and now badly needs updating.

TITLE CHANGES

265. Viggiano, Michael, and Donald Franson. **Science Fiction Title Changes: A Guide to the Changing Titles of Science Fiction and Fantasy Stories Published in Magazines and Books.** Seattle, WA, National Fantasy Fan Federation, 1965. 47 p. LC 66-6551 (pbk.).

This straightforward guide lists variant titles of SF stories and novels correlated with author names. The basic arrangement is alphabetically by title; a typical entry lists the first title and second title (all caps, separated by slashes), followed by a [—] and the author's name. The second title appears in reverse order later in the index. The book is shot from legible typed copy.

One problem with the guide is the absence of any indication of which title was used first or in what forum: magazine and book titles are jumbled together willy-nilly without distinction. Also, an author index would have been useful.

Now badly out-of-date, although the data remain valid for the period prior to 1965; a revised edition would be welcome.

UTOPIAN FICTION

266. Negley, Glenn. **Utopian Literature: A Bibliography, with a Supplementary Listing of Works Influential in Utopian Thought.** Lawrence, KS, The Regents Press of Kansas, 1977. xxiii, 228 p. index. LC 77-8265. ISBN 0-7006-0164-3.

Negley's bibliography derived in part from his earlier guide to the *Utopia Collection of the Duke University Library* (see #133).

The main section of the book is arranged alphabetically by author, then by title. A typical entry lists: item number, author's name, title (italics), place of publication, year of publication, pagination (*but no publishers!*), and a very useful list of codes (the abbreviations list appears on page xxiii) noting libraries at which copies of the books may be found. This is followed by a bibliography, "Works Influential in Utopian Thought," similarly organized; "Short-Title Index" (referencing titles and entry numbers only); and a "Chronological Index" (listing works by years and item numbers only). Books are numbered consecutively throughout the book from 1-1,608; however, it should be noted that the numerous "See" references scattered throughout the bibliography are *also numbered* with the rest, as are subsequent editions, making an assessment of the real number of items included utterly impossible; 1,200 are mentioned in the introduction. The latest book covered is dated 1963.

There are some major problems with this book. The deliberate omission of publishers' names, while perhaps appropriate for books published in the seventeenth century, is a serious error for later periods, as is the decision to number the reprint editions and name references in the same sequence as the main entries. One must also question the index formats, particularly the chronology, which fails to include either authors or titles, but lists only the item numbers, requiring the user to refer constantly back and forth to different sections of the text. This type of amateurish mishmash severely reduces the integrity of the work.

For a comparison with Sargent's competing work (see #267), see below. For major research libraries only.

267. Sargent, Lyman Tower. **British and American Utopian Literature, 1516-1975: An Annotated Bibliography**. Boston, G. K. Hall & Co., 1979. xxvi, 324 p. index. (A Reference Publication in Science Fiction). LC 78-11086. ISBN 0-8161-8243-4. **British and American Utopian Literature, 1516-1986: An Annotated, Chronological Bibliography.** 2nd ed. New York & London, Garland Publishing Co., 1988. xix, 559 p. index. (Garland Reference Library of the Humanities, Vol. 831). LC 88-2546. ISBN 0-8240-0694-1.

These two volumes represent the development of a continuing bibliography on English-language utopian literature.

Sargent's books are arranged chronologically by year of publication, then alphabetically by author name, then by title. A typical entry includes: year of publication, author's name, title, place of publication, publisher (but no paginations), library location symbols, and a one-line annotation (*e.g.,* "machine dystopia," "aliens bring eutopia to earth through conscience gas," "communist takeover of the U.S."). Sargent also includes short fiction, listing: year, author, title (in quotes), magazine title, volume and issue numbers, month and year of publication, and specific pagination. Similar data are presented for all known reprints in English. Short stories appearing originally in anthologies give: publication year, author, title (quotes), anthology title, editors, place of publication, publisher, and specific pagination. Materials are filed under the authors' real names, with both real and pen names being referenced in the author index. The author index correlates authors with titles and years of publication; the title index lists titles, author surnames, and years.

There are major differences between the two editions: the original version provides a 124-page bibliography, "Secondary Sources on Utopian Literature," subdivided into three sections, "Books," "Articles," and "Unpublished Materials" (usually dissertations). Each section is arranged alphabetically by author's name, then by title. A typical book entry includes: author's name (boldfaced), title (italics), place of publication, publisher, year of publication, but no paginations. The "Articles" section provides: author (boldfaced), title (in quotes), magazine title (italics), volume number, month and year of publication, and pagination.

The third part of the secondary sources bibliography lists: author (boldfaced), title (in quotes), and description (usually the name of the university and year the thesis was approved). All of these materials were dropped from the second edition, an extremely unfortunate choice. Also, this is the first time this critic has encountered a revised version of a reference work from a major publisher in which the production qualities have significantly declined. The first edition is attractively typeset and designed; the Garland version is shot from much less readable typed copy; both books are bound to library standards.

Negley's utopian bibliography (see #266) includes foreign-language utopias, while Sargent only lists English-language materials (many [but not all] of the foreign works were translated into English, however). Sargent's work is much more current, the second edition extending the data base through 1985; the latest book in Negley is dated 1963, and his bibliography contains very few works published after 1949 (forty-five monographs), while Sargent lists hundreds. Negley also appears to use a much more restrictive definition of "utopia" than Sargent, thereby limiting his scope to more traditionally accepted forms, while Sargent includes "dystopias" and many other somewhat peripheral items. Sargent also includes short fiction, while Negley restricts his coverage to monographs. Finally, Sargent provides at least a brief annotation, while Negley has no indication of content other than the title. *British and American Utopian Literature* includes roughly 1,650 records published through 1975 in the 1979 version, and approximately 2,580 in the 1988 edition. All three books will be needed by utopian scholars; this includes Sargent's first edition, which possesses a vital secondary sources index not found in any other work.

The guide to secondary materials should be restored with any third edition, or, if this is not possible, should be updated and separately published. The addition of paginations to the bibliographical data would also be appreciated. If a choice must be made, libraries should prefer Sargent's second edition.

VAMPIRE FICTION

268. Altner, Patricia. **Vampire Readings: An Annotated Bibliography.** Lanham, MD, Scarecrow Press, 1998. x, 163 p. index. LC 98-33693. ISBN 0-8108-3504-5 (pbk.).

Contents: "Acknowledgments"; "Foreword," by Thomas P. Ofcansky; "Introduction"; "Novels"; "Anthologies and Novellas"; "Young Adult"; "Additional Readings"; "The Unread Undead" ("Unread Novels"; "Unread Anthologies and Novellas"; "Unread Young Adult Fiction"; "Unread Additional Readings"); "Author/Editor Index"; "Title Index"; "About the Author."

This annotated bibliography of vampire fiction focuses on materials published since 1987. The guide does not claim to be comprehensive, though it does include selected older works. The 779 entries are divided into the following five categories, each arranged alphabetically by author, and then by title: novels, anthologies and novellas, young adult fiction, additional readings, and the "Unread Undead." Entries are numbered consecutively from the number one throughout the book.

A typical entry includes: reference number, author (bold type), title (italics), year and place of publication, publisher, year, and format (hardcover or paperback). Each entry contains a non-evaluative plot summary, notes indicating graphic sexuality and/or violence, and an "Element" section that defines the nature of the book: *i.e.,* romance, Dracula, history, humor, mystery, and science fiction/fantasy (SF/F). The annotations are short (averaging three sentences) and descriptive. Series notations are provided where appropriate.

Anthology and short story entries are arranged alphabetically by editor name, typically mentioning: item number, editor (boldfaced), book title (italics), place of publication, publisher, year of publication, brief annotation, and a list of the stories included in the volume, in descending order, alphabetically by contributor surname. Many of these short story entries lack the plot summaries common to other sections of the bibliography. The author/editor and title indices cross-reference the materials to item numbers only.

The amateurish cartoons used to illustrate the beginning of each chapter seem grossly inappropriate, giving the volume the feel of a fannish or juvenile guide, and the limited, ten-year coverage of the work reduces its usefulness for the blood-sucking *littérateur*.

Cox's guide (see #270) is more complete for its period, but Altner's book will provide a useful supplement.

269. Carter, Margaret L. **The Vampire in Literature: A Critical Bibliography.** Ann Arbor, MI & London, UMI Research Press, 1989. viii, 135 p. index. (Studies in Speculative Fiction, No. 21). LC 89-31932. ISBN 0-8357-1998-7. **Vampire Bibliography Annual Update No. 1 (January, 1990).** Annapolis, MD, [Margaret L. Carter]. 1990. 18 p. (pbk.). **Vampire Bibliography Annual Update No. 2 (January, 1991).** Annapolis, MD, [Margaret L. Carter]. 1991. 30 p. (pbk.).

The lowly vampire continues to exert an uncanny influence on modern readers, film-goers, and scholars, resulting in the publication of numerous bibliographies on vampire fiction in the past few decades.

Carter's guide is both a critical introduction to vampiric literature and a bibliography of primary and secondary sources. Chapter One, "The Study of Vampirism in Literature," examines and evaluates in narrative form the major critical and bibliographical studies of the literature (both essays and monographs). The second chapter, "The Vampire in Legend, Lore, and Literature," contributed by the late Dr. Devendra P. Varma (a well-known expert on the gothic revival), discusses the folklore of vampirism and major early literary contri-butions. Chapter Three, "An Anatomy of Vampirism," delineates the major physical char-acteristics of fictional vampires as revealed in some of their fictional depictions. These narrative chapters occupy forty-four pages of text.

The remainder of the book (eighty-eight pages) contains the bibliography, broken into the following sections: "Chapter 4. Key to Annotations"; "5. Vampire Fiction in En-glish"; "6. Anthologies of Vampire Fiction and Verse"; "7. Non-English Vampire Fiction in Translation"; "8. Dramatic Works on Vampires in English"; "9. Nonfiction: Books"; "10. Nonfiction: Articles."

In each section, materials are arranged alphabetically by author's name, then by title. A typical novel entry includes: author, title (italics), place of publication, publisher, year of publication (but no paginations), and subject code(s). A typical short fiction entry includes: author, title (quotes), magazine title (italics), volume and issue number, month and year of publication (but no paginations), and subject code(s). A short fiction piece appearing orig-inally in a collection or anthology lists: title of the book (italics), author or editor, place of publication, publisher, and year of publication, but no paginations. First appearances only are noted.

The subject codes, as delineated in Chapter 4, analyze the stories into very specific categories (*e.g.,* "Rob" = robot, android, or cyborg vampire; "Pl" = blood-drinking or energy-draining plant); more than one code may be attached to any particular item. The anthologies are arranged in alphabetical order by editor's name, then by title, and typically include: editor, title (italics), place of publication, publisher, year of publication, but no paginations or attempts at coding.

Chapter 7, on translations, similarly does not attempt to code the entries, but does try to provide the original foreign-language title (and original publication data), wherever known, in addition to the first known translation into English. The "Drama" section lists plays in alphabetical order by playwright, then by title, with similar publication data and subject codes. The two chapters on secondary sources are arranged similarly to the fiction sections, and provide the same kinds of data (except that Chapter 10 *does* include paginations), without coding.

The index covers the narrative chapters only; astonishingly, there is no title index (however, a separately printed title index is available from the author). Roughly 1,150 titles are listed in the forty-eight-page main bibliography (Chapter 5); perhaps a third of these are short stories. Fifty-four secondary monographs are listed in Chapter 9, and seventy-nine articles in Chapter 10. The book is attractively typeset and bound to library standards.

Carter's bibliography on vampire literature is the most complete available; the self-produced annual supplements (beginning in 1990) are organized similarly to the original work. Any second edition should include an author/title index, paginations for all bibliographical citations, and a record of all known reprints for stories and novels alike. *The Vampire in Literature* is a necessary starting point for all scholars interested in these most fascinating of fictional creatures. Compare with Riccardo's *Vampires Unearthed* (see #271) and Cox (see #270).

270. Cox, Greg. **The Transylvanian Library: A Consumer's Guide to Vampire Fiction.** San Bernardino, CA, The Borgo Press, 1993. 264 p. index. (Borgo Literary Guides, No. 8). LC 88-36553. ISBN 0-89370-335-4; ISBN 0-89370-435-0 (pbk.).

This comprehensive annotated guide to vampire fiction arranges materials chronologically by year of publication, then alphabetically by author.

A typical entry includes: item number, author, title (italics), place of publication, publisher, year of publication, pagination, and a lengthy annotation. The summaries range in size from 50-1,500 words, averaging 300, and are light, pithy, and heavily opinionated, filled with witticisms and comparisons to other novels or stories. All items are rated at the end of each entry on a scale from "one bat" to "four bats," four being best. Monographs and short fictions are interfiled without distinction, save for the bibliographical data; all entries are numbered consecutively throughout the text from the number one. 258 fictions are described, evaluated, and rated.

End matter includes: "Appendix I: The Un-Read" (items not viewed by Cox); "Appendix II: The Blood Countess on Film"; "Bibliography of Works Consulted"; "Author Index"; "Title Index." The indices refer the user to item numbers only.

Cox provides the first extended examination of individual vampire fictions, and his work is sure to be welcomed by scholars and fans alike. While not as comprehensive as Carter's bibliography (see #269), *The Transylvanian Library* does cover all the major (and many minor) works, and includes paginations that Carter's guide lacks. Since the books complement each other, researchers should have access to both.

271. Riccardo, Martin V. **Vampires Unearthed: The Complete Multi-Media Vampire and Dracula Bibliography.** New York & London, Garland Publishing, 1983. viii, 135 p. index. (The Unexplained, the Mysterious, and the Supernatural, Vol. 2; Garland Reference Library of Social Science, Vol. 177). LC 82-49261. ISBN 0-8240-9128-0.

Riccardo attempts to record all known references to vampires in "Fiction" (Section One), "Dramatic Media and Performing Arts" (Section Two), "Nonfiction" (Section Three), and "Journals and Clubs" (Section Four).

Each of the four major sections are further subdivided into chapters: Section One: "1. Vampire Anthologies"; "2. *Dracula*," by Bram Stoker; "3. Vampire Novels in a Series"; "4. Vampire Novels"; "5. Short Stories of Vampires"; 6. "Children's Literature on Vampires"; "7. Vampires in Comic Books." Section Two: "8. Written Works on Vampires in the Dramatic Media: Movies, Theater, and Television"; "9. American Television Series with a Vampire"; "10. Vampire Plays"; "11. Vampire Movies"; "12. Vampire Records and Recordings"; "13. Vampire Poetry and Songs." Section Three: "14. General Nonfiction Works on the Vampire Mythos"; "15. The Vampire as an Unearthly Reality"; "16. Human Blood-Drinking (Hematomania)"; "17. Vlad Tepes, the Historical Dracula"; "18. Biographies of Figures Connected with Vampirism"; "19. Vampire Bats"; "20. Vampire Jokes and Humor"; "21. Vampire Cookbooks"; "22. Other Miscellaneous Vampire Material." Section Four: "23. Magazines and Periodicals with Vampire Material"; "24. Clubs and Organizations with Interests in Vampires"; "25. Sources for Further Research."

Most sections are organized alphabetically by author, then by title. A typical book entry includes: item number, title (italics), place of publication, publisher, year of publication, paginations (lacking for some paperback entries), format (*e.g.,* "p" = paperback), and similar data on known reprints. A typical shorter work entry gives: item number, author, title (quotes), magazine title (italics), issue number (irregularly), month and year of publication, but no paginations; stories and essays first appearing in collections or anthologies give, in addition to the first three elements: editor's name, title (italics), place of publication, publisher, year of publication, and total page count for the book (but not of the individual piece). Items are numbered consecutively throughout the book from 1-1,116.

The movie listings are arranged alphabetically by title, and include: item number, title (italics), director's name, nationality, year of production, and principal characters and the actors who play them. Three indices, "Alternate and Foreign Film Titles," an authors and editors index, and a very brief one-page guide to selected subjects and characters, all cross-referenced to item numbers, complete the book. There is, however, no overall author/title index. The book is shot from legible typed copy and bound to library standards.

Riccardo's scope is much larger than Carter's (see #269), including film media and nonfiction works on vampire folklore, but he records (proportionately) far fewer items. Carter focuses specifically on vampires as literary characters, including works published through 1988; Riccardo lists titles with dates as late as 1982. Riccardo lists 106 vampire novels, plus another sixty-four novels in series, 172 short stories, and twenty-three juvenile pieces, for a total of 365 fictional works; Carter lists some 1,150 items in the same categories, and while some small measure of the increase is due to another six years of data, such a wide variation suggests to even the most casual observer that Carter has cast a much wider net. Also, Carter's listings are subject coded, providing much assistance to the researcher.

However, Riccardo does include monographic paginations (which Carter's book lacks) and much data on peripheral vampiric infestations outside of Carter's scope.

Both books will therefore be required for most library collections.

WOMEN WRITERS

272. Schlobin, Roger C. **Urania's Daughters: A Checklist of Women Science-Fiction Writers, 1692-1982.** Mercer Island, WA, Starmont House, 1983. xiii, 79 p. index. (Starmont Reference Guide, No. 1). LC 83-2467. ISBN 0-916732-57-6; ISBN 0-916732-56-8 (pbk.).

Well-known critic Schlobin, former editor of the Starmont Reader's Guide series of critical monographs, here contributes a generally sound guide to science fiction and fantasy novels and story collections produced by female writers.

The basic arrangement of the book is alphabetically by author surname, then by title. A typical entry includes: author (boldfaced), title (underlined), place of publication, publisher, year of publication, but no paginations. Series entries under each author are listed in descending chronological order under the boldfaced series title. The title index gives titles and author surnames only. Authors are listed under their legal names; a "Directory of Pseudonyms, Joint Authors, and Variant Names" at the front of the book refers the user to the proper heading. The book is shot from legible word-processed copy.

Schlobin's bibliography seems reasonably complete for its period; most of the roughly 950 titles included were published in the modern period (since World War II), and there are no obvious omissions. Any future edition should consider the addition of paginations, brief biographical details on the writers (at least years of birth and death), and a more complete title index.

Even in this somewhat skeletal form, *Urania's Daughters* should prove a useful starting point for scholars interested in researching the influence of women writers on modern fantastic literature or on modern American literature in general. Compare with Yntema (see #60).

PUBLISHER BIBLIOGRAPHIES

SCOPE NOTE: This section includes bibliographies that delineate the science-fiction publications of one specific publishing company or works that focus on a group of SF specialty houses. Excluded are publishers' stock lists or catalogs. Additional information on SF publishers and their books may be found in such works as Nicholls's *The Science Fiction Encyclopedia* (see #12), Tuck's *The Encyclopedia of Science Fiction and Fantasy* (which includes dozens of SF paperback lists arranged by publisher, year of publication, and stock number; see #18), the many general bibliographies of science fiction and fantasy included herein, Robert Reginald and Michael Burgess's *Cumulative Paperback Index, 1939-1959,* and Kevin Hancer and Robert Reginald's *The Paperback Price Guide* (through three editions).

GENERAL WORKS

273. Owings, Mark, and Jack L. Chalker. **Index to the Science Fantasy Publishers.** Baltimore, MD, The Anthem Series, 1966. 78 p. (pbk.). **The Index to the Science-Fantasy Publishers: A Bibliography of the Science Fiction and Fantasy Specialty Houses.** 2nd ed. Baltimore, MD, The Anthem Series, 1966. viii, 74 p. cloth and pbk. Chalker, Jack L., and Mark Owings. **The Science Fantasy Publishers: A Critical and Bibliographic History.** 3d ed. Westminster, MD, Mirage Press, 1991. xxviii, 744 p. index. ISBN 0-88358-204-X. The first printing [edition] was rejected, and very few copies were actually circulated. Updated with printed and on-line supplements.

Owings and Chalker compiled this bibliography as a guide to the SF specialty publishers that began with Arkham House in 1939, and that rapidly expanded following World War II to produce cloth editions of publications that had previously only been available in magazine form. Most of these publishers were forced out of business starting the mid-1950s by the entrance of the large, New York-based trade publishers into the regular production of science-fiction novels.

The book is arranged alphabetically by publisher, with each firm's books listed chronologically by date of production under that company's main entry. A typical publisher entry includes an historical survey of the house, with a list of the principals and dates of founding and cessation, and much additional information (when known); some of these histories are very brief, but the history of Arkham House runs a full seven pages, and provides much background data.

A typical book entry gives: title (all caps), author, year of publication, pagination, number of copies printed, price, plus similar data for all known reprints by the same publisher, detailed contents (for collections and anthologies), jacket and/or interior illustrator, and a brief (one-paragraph) annotation, which often includes much peripheral information of interest. To qualify for inclusion, the publisher had to have issued at least one cloth volume and to have specialized only in fantastic literature.

End matter includes: "Appendix A: Fellow Travelers," listing houses and publications that just failed to meet the authors' definition, but providing similar information on their histories and publications; "Appendix B: Almost-Rans," ventures that failed even before they even began; "Appendix C: Ordering Directly from a Specialty Publisher"; "Appendix D: Where to Find Them" (addresses; now outdated); "Appendix E: 'But What's It Worth?': Notes on Pricing and Availability"; "Appendix F: The Essential SF Reference Shelf" (a very selective bibliography of reference sources, omitting some of the major tools in the field); "Appendix G: Where They Are: Geographic Breakdown"; "Glossary of Terms Used"; "Author & Artist Index"; "Index by Title"; "Oops! Supplemental Information & Corrections"; "About the Authors." The Third Edition is nicely typeset in two-column format, and bound to library standards.

The Science-Fantasy Publishers has been criticized for occasional historical or bibliographical inaccuracies and for a number of outright errors, but many of these were fixed in the latest version of the guide, although others were apparently newly introduced, according to several reviewers. The third edition is vastly expanded over any previous incarnations of the bibliography. There is simply no other work even roughly comparable to this guide, or containing such an enormous amount of bibliographical data about these specialized publications, and Chalker and Owings's volume should be purchased by all research libraries. Any scholar of the science fiction field will find this history-*cum*-bibliography invaluable in tracking the development of fan-based publishing operations.

BIBLIOGRAPHIES OF INDIVIDUAL PUBLISHERS

Ace Books

274. Corrick, James A. **Double Your Pleasure: The Ace SF Double.** Brooklyn, NY, Gryphon Books, 1989. 85 p. index. ISBN 0-936071-13-3 (pbk.).

Well-known paperback historian Corrick here focuses specifically on the Ace Doubles, a publishing gimmick developed by Ace in 1952, in which two separate category novels (usually by different writers) were bound upside down to each other, with two covers. The first SF Double was published in 1953, the last original title in 1973, almost twenty years later.

Corrick provides a brief historical introduction to the series, then lists the books in chronological order by publication date. A typical entry includes: Ace stock number, month and year of publication, first book title (all caps), author, second book title (all caps), second book author, cover artist(s), and a summary of all known previous magazine serializations and cloth publications and subsequent printings of the books in English. No paginations are given. There are separate author and title indices, both referring the user to Ace stock numbers. The book is shot from generally clear type and illustrated throughout with partial and full-page illustrations from the book covers.

This is the best single guide to the Ace SF Doubles yet published; a second printing would benefit from better typography and a more professional appearance.

275. Dillon, Peter C. **An Ace Alpha-Numeric Annotated Science Fiction Checklist.** Richmond, CA, Peter C. Dillon, 1973. 29 p. (pbk.).

Dillon lists Ace SF double and single novels through the early 1970s, in order by stock number, with a separate record of the Edgar Rice Burroughs reprints published by Ace in the 1960s. A typical entry includes: stock number, title, author (surname only), year of publication, former title (in parentheses), plus any previous magazine serialization (with months and years of original publication, and a two- to four-letter abbreviation for the periodical; the abbreviations list appears at the end of the book).

This amateurishly produced volume is shot from legible typed copy. However, the absence of full author names, paginations, exact months of issues, and indices of any kind severely limit the usefulness of this index.

276. Massoglia, Marty. **Checklist of Ace SF Through 1968.** East Lansing, MI, Marty Massoglia, 1969 (?). 11 leaves. (pbk.).

Ace Books seems to have attracted more amateur bibliographers than any other publishing line. This checklist lists Ace SF books in numerical order by price series and stock number. A typical entry includes: year of publication (*e.g.,* "55" = 1955), stock number, author's name, title, and references to previous stock numbers under which the volume may have been issued by Ace. An erratum page is tacked on to the end.

Poorly edited, and produced on faint legal-sized sheets stapled together through the corner. Prefer Corrick (see #274).

277. Robinson, Roger. **Ace Science-Fiction Double Books.** Harold Wood, Essex, England, Beccon Publications, 1987. 16 p. index. (Beccon Publications Collectors' Checklists). (pbk.).

British fan Robinson provides a simple checklist of the Ace SF Doubles, two books bound upside down to each other, with two separate covers. The books are listed chronologically by publication date and stock number. A typical entry includes: stock number, authors' surnames only, and book titles. The author index correlates authors and stock numbers only; there is no title index. The final page of this brief guide also covers three other "double" series: the Belmont Doubles, the Dell Binary Star series, and Galaxy Magabooks.

Prefer Corrick's more detailed bibliography (see #274).

278. Spelman, Dick. **Science Fiction and Fantasy Published by Ace Books (1953-1968).** North Hollywood, CA, Institute for Specialized Literature, 1976. [ii], 62 p. index. (pbk.).

One of a series of checklists issued by Spelman in the mid-1970s, this particular volume is typical of the lot.

The main index organizes Ace's science-fiction and fantasy publications in chronological order by stock number, arranged alphabetically by the letter preceding each number (after 1960 Ace assigned a letter code signifying price to each number; all books with that price and letter code were numbered in order in each separate series).

A typical entry includes: stock number, author(s), title(s), a reference to any previous Ace stock numbers, note code (*e.g.,* "*" = Ace Special Edition, "1" = Ace Double Novel, etc.), and year of publication. The author index correlates authors, titles, and stock numbers (more than one for some titles), while the title index provides titles, authors, and numbers. The book is shot from very clear typed copy.

Spelman's ignorance of Ace's numbering system is shown by the fact that he lists the handful of novels published in the 1950s with an "S" prefix separately, when in fact they were issued as part of the "D" series. A definitive guide to Ace's science fiction publications has yet to be issued.

Arkham House

279. Derleth, August. **Arkham House: The First Twenty Years, 1939-1959: A History and Bibliography.** Sauk City, WI, Arkham House, 1959. liv p. (pbk.). **Thirty Years of Arkham House, 1939-1969: A History and Bibliography.** [2nd ed.]. Sauk City, WI, Arkham House, 1970. 99 p., [8] p. of plates. LC 76-121892. Joshi, S. T. **Sixty Years of Arkham House: A History and Bibliography.** Sauk City, WI, Arkham House Publishers, 1999. viii, 281 p. index. LC 99-047946. ISBN 0-87054-176-5 (alk. paper).

Contents (Joshi edition): "Preface"; "Arkham House: 1939-1969," by August Derleth; "Arkham House: 1970-1999," by S. T. Joshi; "Bibliography" (includes "Arkham House," "Mycroft & Moran," and "Stanton & Lee"); "Appendix: The 'Lost' Arkhams"; "Reference Bibliography"; "Index of Names"; "Index of Titles."

August Derleth founded Arkham House, the oldest continuously-operated publishing house specializing in fantastic literature, in 1939 to publish a collection of tales by the late H. P. Lovecraft. During his life Derleth prepared two bibliographies of Arkham's publications, the second building on the first. In both books entries are arranged chronologically by date of publication, with the books of the associated imprints, Mycroft & Moran and Stanton & Lee, being listed separately at the end of each volume.

A typical entry includes: item number, title (all caps), author, publisher, place of publication, year of publication, pagination, price, number of copies printed, contents (for collections or anthologies), and cover artist. Books are numbered consecutively in order from the number one, separately for each imprint; the 1970 edition lists ninety-eight Arkham House books and fourteen each from the associated imprints. There are no indices. The books are professionally typeset, and the second edition was bound to library standards in typical black AH cloth.

Derleth's sixteen-page introduction to the second edition provides much background and historical details about the founding and maintenance of the imprint, and includes eight glossy pages of photographs of Lovecraft, Derleth, and other authors associated with the imprint tipped in to the center of the book.

Joshi's *Sixty Years* is an expanded and updated edition of Derleth's volumes. The historical essay by Derleth is reprinted from the earlier edition, supplemented with a new historical essay by Joshi covering the period from 1970-99.

The bibliography proper is divided into three sections reflecting Arkham's three imprints: Arkham House Publishers, Mycroft & Moran, and Stanton & Lee. As in the early editions, books are arranged chronologically by issue date. There are 228 main entries (193 in part one, 19 in part two, and 16 in part three, respectively). A typical entry includes: entry number (numbered consecutively from the number one in each section), title (all caps), author, editor or compiler, publisher, year of publication, pagination, marked price, complete contents, and notes, which include jacket artist, number of copies printed, and "brief accounts of some of the more significant features" of the publication. Also included is any reprint information (publisher, place of publication, and year only).

In addition, Joshi appends a list of 56 "lost" publications, items announced by Arkham House, but never actually published by them, with an indication of whether the items ever appeared elsewhere. The index of names is very thorough, including "every author, editor, cover artist, or other name found in the table of contents of each title or in [the] notes." The index of titles includes titles of all books listed, as well as the shorter works included within a given book. Both indices cross-reference their materials with item numbers, the numbers for the second and third sections being preceded by the letter "M" for Mycroft & Mycroft and "S" for Stanton & Lee. The index numbering system is not immediately obvious to the casual user.

This is a remarkably thorough, well-organized, and knowledgeable bibliography, as we have come to expect from Mr. Joshi's capable hands, and is highly recommended for Arkham collectors, scholars, and larger research libraries. *Sixty Years of Arkham House* now completely supersedes Jaffery's less current guide (see #280), as well as the two previous editions of Joshi's bibliography by Derleth himself.

280. Jaffery, Sheldon. **Horrors and Unpleasantries: A Bibliographical History & Collectors' Price Guide to Arkham House.** Bowling Green, OH, Bowling Green State University Popular Press, 1982. 142 p. LC 82-73849. ISBN 0-87972-219-3; ISBN 0-87972-220-7 (pbk.). **The Arkham House Companion: Fifty Years of Arkham House: A Bibliographical History and Collector's Price Guide to Arkham House/Mycroft & Moran, Including the Revised and Expanded Horrors and Unpleasantries.** [2nd ed.]. Mercer Island, WA, Starmont House, 1989. xv, 184 p. index. (Starmont Reference Guide, No. 9). LC 89-31701. ISBN 1-55742-005-X; ISBN 1-55742-004-1 (pbk.).

Both of these bibliographical guides are organized similarly, except that the revised version, in addition to its extended data base, also includes a detailed index.

The basic arrangement of both books is chronologically by publication date, generally following the format established by Derleth and Joshi in their three bibliographies on Arkham House (see #279). A typical entry includes: item number, title (italicized in the original, boldfaced in the second edition), author's name, publisher, place of publication, year of publication, pagination, price, number of copies printed, cover artist, contents, annotation, and current estimated value on the OP book market (at the time these guides were published; now outdated).

The annotations average 300 words in length, and include background information on the authors and their books, bibliographical tidbits, and other ephemera of interest. Items are numbered consecutively throughout the second book from 1-180. Unlike the Derleth guides, Jaffery interfiles Mycroft & Moran titles with regular Arkham House productions, but strangely does not mention the other AH imprint, Stanton & Lee.

End matter includes: "Appendix I: The Unpublished Titles"; "Appendix II: Sponsored Books"; "Appendix III: Horror Literature Core Collection, Arkham House Entries," taken from Marshall B. Tymn's *Horror Literature* (see #102); "Appendix IV: The Illustrated Lovecraft"; "Author/Title Index," correlating major entry authors and their books with entry numbers; and a very thorough "General Index," also referencing item numbers. The books are shot from very clear word-processed copy; the 1982 version was produced in 5" x 8" format, the 1989 volume in 8.5" x 11" style.

Jaffery's work will be of interest to collectors and researchers alike, but has now been superseded in its coverage by Joshi's more current guide (see #279).

281. Spelman, Dick. **Science Fiction and Fantasy Published by Arkham House and Mycroft & Moran (1939-1976).** North Hollywood, CA, Institute for Specialized Literature, 1977. 10 leaves. index. (pbk.). **Science Fiction and Fantasy Published by Arkham House and Mycroft & Moran (1939-1976).** Rev. ed. North Hollywood, CA, Institute for Specialized Literature, 1978. 10 leaves. index. (pbk.).

The final volume in Spelman's publisher checklist series is arranged very similarly to the others. The main part of the book organizes the data by imprint, then alphabetically by author's name and title. A typical entry includes: author, title, year of publication, page count, number of copies printed, and price. The title index lists: titles, authors, and imprint codes (*e.g.,* "AH" and "MM") only. The book is shot from typed copy. The revised edition adds a few titles, but otherwise is the same as the original.

Now completely superseded by Joshi's much more detailed and complete guide (see #279).

Avalon Books

282. Spelman, Dick. **Science Fiction and Fantasy Published by Avalon Books and Bouregy & Curl.** North Hollywood, CA, Institute for Specialized Literature, 1977. 10 leaves. index. (pbk.).

One of a series of publisher indexes prepared by SF fan Spelman in the mid-1970s, this brief guide indexes the 136 books produced by Thomas Bouregy & Co. under the imprints Avalon Books (the vast majority of the titles) and the earlier Bouregy & Curl. The main part of the book arranges the data alphabetically by author's name, then by title. A typical entry includes: author, title, date of publication (in the form "12-56" for December 1956), page count, dust jacket artist, and price. The title index lists titles, authors, and imprints only. The book is shot from typed copy.

Although this is a very simple checklist, it does include the entire SF output of this collectible imprint, and provides a useful guide to this important publisher.

Ballantine Books

283. Aronovitz, David. **Ballantine Books: The First Decade: A Bibliographical History & Guide of the Publisher's Early Years.** Rochester, MI, Bailiwick Books, 1987. x, 107 p. index. LC 87-11504. ISBN 0-9618295-0-8.

Although Aronovitz's bibliography is not limited to science-fiction works, the early history of Ballantine Books is so intertwined with the SF genre, and its publications were of such importance to the development of fantastic literature as a *book* category in the 1950s, that this excellent guide to the Ballantine dual editions (produced simultaneously in paper and cloth editions) will become a necessary adjunct to studies of this most vital period.

The bibliography is arranged alphabetically by author, then by title. A typical entry includes: author's name, title (all caps, boldfaced), publisher of the cloth edition (usually Ballantine, but occasionally other houses), year of publication, price of the cloth edition, stock number, but no paginations; some entries also include bibliographical notes. Aronovitz's sixteen-page "Introduction" and "History" provide necessary background data on the development of Ballantine Books between 1952-61 (the period covered by this guide).

Two indices, by genre (then alphabetically by main entry) and by publishing imprint (then alphabetically by main entry), both correlating entries with page numbers, complete the volume. The book is attractively typeset, printed in a small 4" x 7" format, and bound to library standards.

Nicely done, although a complete guide to this major publisher's SF and fantasy publications has yet to be countenanced.

284. Spelman, Dick. **A Preliminary Checklist of Science Fiction and Fantasy Published by Ballantine Books (1953-1974).** North Hollywood, CA, Institute for Specialized Literature, 1976. 42 leaves. (pbk.). **A Preliminary Checklist of Science Fiction and Fantasy Published by Ballantine Books (1953-1977).** [Rev. ed.]. North Hollywood, CA, Institute for Specialized Literature, 1977. 76 p. index. (pbk.).

Spelman's guide to the SF published by Ballantine Books is arranged chronologically by stock number. A typical entry provides: number, edition (*e.g.,* "1st"), author, title, publication date (in the form "12-54" for December 1954), price. The book is shot from sometimes faint typed copy. The first version of this checklist is unindexed. The revised edition extends the data base through February 1977 and includes an author index giving authors, titles, and stock numbers for each Ballantine printing.

Prefer Aronovitz's more detailed guide (see #283) for the early years of Ballantine Books; a definitive index to the science fiction and fantasy publications of this important paperback house has yet to be produced.

Borgo Press

285. Reginald, Robert, and Mary A. Burgess. **BP 250: An Annotated Bibliography of the First 250 Publications of the Borgo Press, 1975-1996.** San Bernardino, CA, Borgo Press, 1996. 190 p. index. (Borgo Literary Guides, Vol. 10). LC 96-1744. ISBN 0-8095-0206-2 (cloth); ISBN 0-8095-1206-8 (pbk.). Limited to 110 signed, numbered copies in all bindings.

Contents: Introduction; "A. Borgo Press Books, 1976-1996"; "B. Xenos Books, 1986-1990"; "C. Brownstone Books, 1981-1989 (1991)"; "D. Starmont Contemporary Writers Series, 1988-1989 (1991)"; "E. Sidewinder Press (Sun Dance Press), 1971 (1991)"; "F. St. Willibrord's Press, 1985-1991 (1991)"; "G. Starmont House & FAX Collector's Editions, 1973-1992 (1993)"; "H. Miscellaneous Publications, 1973-1994"; "Series Index"; "Author Index"; "Title Index"; "About the Authors"; Limitation Page.

This is an annotated bibliography of the first 250 publications of Borgo Press and affiliated imprints, plus lists of titles acquired from other firms. Each section represents the listings of a different imprint, and each section is arranged in chronological order by publication date. There are 389 main entries, plus detailed information on all reprints. The entries follow the Borgo bibliographical standard as it appears in their other publications, with minor changes.

A typical entry includes: item number (section letter plus cardinal number, *i.e.*, A3, A4, etc.), title (bold italics), author(s), series and volume number (as necessary), pagination,

Library of Congress card number, OCLC number, ISBN, binding, price, notes on the cover (cover artist, design, etc.), month and year of first edition, and a note whether the book was out of print at the time of this bibliography's publication (in brackets). This is followed by a summary of the book's contents, usually no more than a sentence, and a listing of the table of contents of the publication, with paginations for each section. There are three indices cross-referencing item numbers, for series, author, and title.

Borgo Press shut down its operation in 1999 after publishing another fifty titles, so this bibliography provides a potentially significant chronicle for those researchers interested in SF and other genre bibliographies and critiques, not just those issued by Borgo, but also by Starmont House, FAX Collector's Editions, and the mystery house, Brownstone Books, lamentably all now consigned to the publishers' graveyard.

DAW Books

286. Covell, Ian. **An Index to DAW Books.** Leeds, West Yorkshire, England, Galactic Central Publications, 1989. 58 p. index. (Galactic Central Publisher Checklists, Vol. 1). ISBN 1-871133-15-7 (pbk.).

The main part of this bibliography indexes DAW Books publications in chronological order by date/stock number, giving: stock number, date of publication (in the form "0472" for April 1972, the first month of DAW's publication), DAW book number (in addition to the standard stock number, DAW also assigned each of its releases a consecutive "collectors" number beginning at "1"), price, author, title (all caps).

An asterisk before the first stock number signifies an original DAW publication, and a "@" before the author indicates an anthology. Reprints with the same stock numbers are also indicated, with printing information (*e.g.,* "3" = third printing) and the symbols "RP" after the DAW book number. Personal names in quotes are pseudonyms; the handful of titles not assigned individual DAW book numbers are so indicated with the symbol "+ + +." No paginations are included.

Books are recorded through DAW collectors' #781, published in May, 1989. Also provided is an author (but no title) index, giving: author's name, book titles, DAW number, date of issue, and stock number; authors are listed under their real names, with appropriate "See" references. The final page of the book also includes a brief checklist of the four DAW hardcovers and trade paperbacks issued through mid-1989. The guide is shot from very clear word-processed copy, and stapled through the spine.

Compare with Jaffery's more thorough bibliography (see #287), which is, however, not quite as current in its coverage.

287. Jaffery, Sheldon. **Future and Fantastic Worlds: A Bibliographical Retrospective of DAW Books (1972-1987).** Mercer Island, WA, Starmont House, 1987. xiii, 297 p. index. (Starmont Reference Guide, No. 4). LC 87-9901. ISBN 1-55742-003-3; ISBN 1-55742-002-5 (pbk.).

DAW Books was founded in 1972 by the late editor Donald A. Wollheim (hence the name) as the first exclusive science-fiction paperback house. Well-known critic Jaffery, author of a previous guide to Arkham House publications (see #280) and other reference works, arranges the main part of this guide in chronological order by DAW book number and issue date.

A typical entry includes: DAW book number (boldfaced), author's name, title (italics), stock number, edition and printing data, month and year of publication, pagination, cover artist, price, mentions of previous or subsequent printings from other publishers, annotation, and series or other bibliographical notes (where appropriate). The annotations are descriptive rather than evaluative, and heavily plot oriented, with occasional light, pithy, even flippant comments; entries for collections and anthologies include complete contents listings. Items are included through #707, published in May 1987. The book is shot from very clean word-processed copy, and attractively printed, designed, and bound.

Jaffery has produced another definitive and very useful publisher bibliography, one which should be maintained with future supplements or newly updated editions. All major research libraries should acquire this book. Covell's guide (see #286) is less complete but more current.

288. Robinson, Roger. **DAW Science-Fiction Books.** Harold Wood, Essex, England, Beccon Publications, 1987. 20 p. index. (Beccon Publications Collectors' Checklist). (pbk.).

One of a series of checklists produced by British fan Robinson, this booklet indexes DAW Books in chronological order by issue date and book number. A typical entry includes: DAW book number, author, and title, but no other bibliographical data (including publication dates). Books are listed through #710 (1987); the fifteen Cap Kennedy novels, which were not numbered in the main sequence, are listed after the principal bibliography and numbered from CK1-CK15. The index correlates authors and book numbers only; there is no title index. The guide is shot from legible word-processed copy.

Prefer Jaffery's definitive bibliography (see #287), although Covell (see #286) is more current.

Editrice Nord

289. Editrice Nord. **Editrice Nord: Quindici Anni di Fantascienza in Italia: Catalogo Ragionato delle Opere Pubblicate Fino al Dicembre 1985.** Milano, Italy, Editrice Nord, 1985. [116] p. index. (pbk.).

One of the larger popular publishing houses in Italy, Editrice Nord issued this bibliographical catalog to celebrate the fifteenth anniversary of its SF program.

The book is arranged by publishing series and number. Each section includes a *précis* of the series as a whole, its intent and content. An individual book entry gives: series code and number (*e.g.,* "CA1" = volume one of the Cosmo Collana di Fantascienza series), title (bold caps), author (boldfaced), and a hundred-word plot summary of the book. There are occasional "See" references at the end of some entries to other works of interest, but most of the bibliographic data are included in the detailed author index, which is almost a separate guide in itself.

A typical index entry gives: author (bold caps), title (small bold caps), original title (if a translation), date and place of original publication, series number, month and year of publication by Editrice Nord, translator, and a list of awards (American and Italian) the work has received, but no paginations. The book is nicely typeset.

Information on European translations of English-language SF (which constitute the majority of entries here) is always hard to find; bibliographers will welcome this catalog, and hope that other companies will follow suit.

Robert Hale Ltd.

290. Robinson, Roger. **Hale & Gresham Hardback Science Fiction.** Harold Wood, Essex, England, Beccon Publications, 1988. 16 p. index. (Beccon Publications Collectors' Checklist). (pbk.).

Robert Hale Ltd. published (and still publishes) several series of category novels for the public library market in Great Britain, including a lengthy SF line produced between 1968-82. Many of these books were original publications featuring authors not well known in the United States. This booklet indexes the "Hale SF" line alphabetically by author, then by title. A typical entry provides: author's name (all caps), year of publication, and title. Also included are a pseudonym guide and a brief addendum. The pamphlet is shot from legible word-processed copy and stapled through the spine. This is the latest of the four collectors' guides produced by British fan Robinson.

Morrigan Press/Kerosina Press

291. Stephens, Christopher P. **A Checklist of Morrigan Press and Kerosina Press.** Hastings-on-Hudson, NY, Ultramarine Publishing Co., 1991. 18 p. index. ISBN 0-89366-165-1 (pbk.).

One of a series of checklists by Stephens on collectible publishing houses (see also #292 and #296), including four bibliographies on publishers not associated with the SF field, this new guide is broken into two sections corresponding to the imprints covered.

In each section materials are arranged by publication date. A typical entry includes: year of publication (as a running head), item number, author (surname in all caps), title (underlined), pagination, number of copies issued, description of binding, price, and similar data on all known variant issues. Materials are numbered from 1-8 (Morrigan) and 1-14 (Kerosina); variant editions are numbered in order under the main entry (for example, 2b, 2c, 2d). The index correlates authors/titles to years of publication, not item numbers. The booklet is shot from very legible typed copy, and bound with staples into stiff paper covers.

Although these two British imprints are not well known in the United States, the quality of their lists makes them future targets for the collector's market.

Phantasia Press

292. Stephens, Christopher P. **A Checklist of Phantasia Press.** Hastings-on-Hudson, NY, Ultramarine Publishing Co., 1991. 19 p. index. ISBN 0-89366-201-1 (pbk.).

Phantasia Press has become one of the more collectible SF specialty publishing houses since its inception in 1978. Stephens's bibliography lists Phantasia's books chronologically by publication date in entries numbered from 1-49.

A typical entry includes: year of publication (as a running head), item number, author (surname in all caps), title (underlined), series, number of copies issued, pagination, description of binding, cover illustrator, price, and similar data for all known variant issues (which are numbered, for example, 16b, 16c, 16d). The index correlates authors and titles (in one alphabet) to years of publication, not to item numbers. The book is shot from typed copy and bound with staples into stiff paper covers.

Collectors will appreciate this succinct and well-organized guide. Future editions should reference index entries to the existing item numbers; an introduction giving a brief history of Phantasia Press, its styles and practices, would also be useful to the target audience.

Soft Books

293. Bell, Joseph. **Soft Book Publications: First Five Years, 1981-1986.** Toronto, Canada, Soft Books, 1986. 7 p. (pbk.).

This small Canadian house, the publishing arm of Bell's out-of-print bookselling operation, specializes in producing books, pamphlets, and broadsides relating to the modern horror genre. Bell's brief checklist lists twenty-one items in chronological order by publication date. A typical entry includes: item number, title (boldfaced), publisher's address, pagination, physical size, binding style, cover style, paper color, limitation notice, in-print status (with month and year when the book went out-of-print, if it did), series note, price, month and year of publication (boldfaced), and a complete contents listing, with bibliographical notes. Of interest primarily to collectors of modern horror fiction.

John Spencer & Co.

294. Ashley, Michael. **A Complete Index and Annotated Commentary to the John Spencer Fantasy Publications (1950-66).** Wallsend, England, Cosmos Literary Agency, 1979. 54 p. index. (Fantasy Readers Guide, No. 1). (pbk.). Cover title.

John Spencer & Co. Ltd. produced several series of paperbound genre books during the period from 1950-70, including both science fiction and supernatural horror short stories and novels. Among their publications were several supposed magazines that were actually collections penned by one writer per issue contributing stories under a variety of pseudonyms; two writers, Robert Lionel Fanthorpe and John Glasby, produced 95% of this publisher's SF and horror paperbacks between 1958-67, when the last "issue" of *Supernatural Stories* appeared.

Well-known bibliographer and literary historian Ashley provides a brief history of Spencer, and then lists each series and "magazine" in chronological order by series number and publication date. A typical entry gives: series number, month and year of publication, book title (all caps) and author (for monographs), and complete contents and authors (for magazine issues). There are also brief guides to books reprinted by other publishers and to story series. The author index gives: authors, titles, and book numbers, together with brief biographies of the principals. Ashley also provides a brief statistical chart and more extended biographies of Fanthorpe and Glasby, plus sample stories by E. C. Tubb and John Glasby. Reproduced from typed copy.

This should be the last word on the subject (we hope).

Roy A. Squires

295. Squires, Roy A. **The Private Press of Roy A. Squires: A Checklist of Imprints.** Glendale, CA, [Roy A. Squires], 1970. [4] p. (pbk.). **The Private Press of Roy A. Squires: A Descriptive Listing of Publications, 1962-1979.** [2nd ed.]. Glendale, CA, [Roy A. Squires], 1987. [24] p. LC 88-113413 (pbk.).

The late Roy Squires was a well-known California collector and book dealer who in his spare time served as publisher and proprietor of the SF field's only true modern private press. In a shed in his back yard, Squires would spend hundreds of hours carefully hand setting the type for his distinctive booklets of poetry and prose, imprinting each sheet individually, then tying copies together with his distinctive flair, often housing them in specially imprinted envelopes. Squires's authors included Ray Bradbury, Clark Ashton Smith, H. P. Lovecraft (previously unpublished letters and poems), and many others.

Unusually, none of his books bore an imprint of any kind, only a place of publication (Glendale, California) on the bottom of each title page. Squires printed his first booklet in December 1960 in an edition of ninety-six copies; few of his publications ever reached runs higher than 300 copies, and none, of course, were ever reprinted, since the type was reused and reset after each series of impressions was finished. His booklets have been highly collectible from their first issue, and will continue to appreciate in value as bibliophiles everywhere appreciate the care with which they were prepared.

The first of these checklists lists each of the works in order of publication. A typical entry includes: item number (the materials are numbered consecutively from 1-30, number 30 being the bibliography itself), title (small caps), author, date of publication, number of copies produced. There is no index. The second version is believed to be the last work produced from Squires's press, issued long after the publisher had ceased to print works regularly. The format is identical to that of the original guide. No indices are provided.

These lists will themselves become collectors' items, having been produced and typeset to the same high standards as the rest of the printer's publications. What a shame that we will see no more of these books.

Tor Books

296. Stephens, Christopher P. **A Checklist of the Tor Doubles.** Hastings-on-Hudson, NY, Ultramarine Publishing Co., 1991. 18 p. index. ISBN 0-89366-194-5 (pbk.).

Like Ace Books before it, Tor began issuing a series of "double books" in 1988 (with a preliminary volume published in 1985), packaging the stories back-to-back and upside down to each other. Stephens lists the books in order by series number and year, giving the following information: publication year (as a running head), series number, author (surname in all caps), title (underlined), pagination, previous publication particulars, cover artist, plus similar data on the second short novel, and price. Discrepancies in the series numbering are also noted. The author/title index correlates each with series number. The pamphlet is shot from typed copy and stapled into stiff paper covers.

This is a handy short guide to a popular publisher's series, one that fans and collectors will appreciate.

AUTHOR BIBLIOGRAPHIES

SCOPE NOTE: This section includes bibliographies of one author published in one monograph, or up to three authors where all of the authors covered are mentioned in the book title, and where each of the writers is covered individually within the book in his or her own section. Arrangement is by name of the author being covered. Bibliographies published in magazine format are included only where an entire issue (or some significant portion) of the journal consists of the bibliography of one author. Other potential sources for bibliographical data on science fiction and fantasy authors include author directories, encyclopedias, readers' guides, general bibliographies on fantastic literature or any of its many subgenres, and critical monographs about one or more SF authors. At the beginning of this section are listed series of author bibliographies consisting of at least five published volumes packaged under a common series title with standardized formats. Books included in these series are also covered individually.

BIBLIOGRAPHY SERIES

297. Bibliographies of Modern Authors. Boden Clarke, Series Editor. San Bernardino, CA, The Borgo Press, 1984-97. 31 v. indexed. cloth and pbk. ISSN 0749-470X.

The intent of this series was to provide complete, comprehensive, current guides to the authors' lives and works. The books were designed to be upgraded into new editions every three to five years for active writers. Paginations range in size from 60-500 pages in 5.5" x 8.5" format (Vol. 29 was issued in 6" x 9" size), with the books gradually increasing in length and sophistication as the series advanced. The volumes were edited to strict series guidelines, and the series editor was directly and intensively involved in the preparation of individual monographs, sometimes adding data or reworking the manuscripts.

Thus, each work in the series closely resembles the others in format. Each author's works are divided into separate subject categories, the first of which is always Chapter A., the writer's "Books." Subsequent sections may include (in this order): "Short Fiction," "Short Nonfiction," "Poetry," "Drama," "Editorial Credits," "Other Media," "Screenplays," "Teleplays," "Radio Plays," "Unpublished Works," "Interviews," "Secondary Sources," "Miscellanea," "Quoth the Critics" (selected critical opinions on the author's work), "Title Index," with additional chapters being generated as necessary to fit each writer's interests.

Works in each section are listed chronologically, from the earliest to the latest, and numbered consecutively item by item, beginning at the number one and continuing to the end of each chapter; since each section is assigned a key letter in alphabetical order, the author's books will always be numbered "A1," "A2," "A3," etc., in publication order, his short stories "B1," "B2," etc., and so forth. Complete bibliographical data are provided, both for the primary edition and all known reprints, new editions, or anthologizations, including foreign-language publications. Annotations are provided for all books and any other noteworthy stories or materials.

There are two distinct stylistic periods in the development of this series. The first series, running from 1984-87, originated the basic series format, but the absence of line breaks combined with the somewhat primitive computer-generated printout make some entries sometimes hard to read or find on the rather crowded pages.

Beginning with the first edition of *The Work of William F. Nolan* (October 1988), the basic format was upgraded to include lists of book reviews on individual monographs, and the overall internal and external design of the volumes was improved with the interpolation of line breaks and the use of near typeset quality (laser printer-generated) copy. All of the later volumes also feature detailed biographical chronologies and critical introductions, and many have afterwords by or interviews with the authors themselves commenting on their lives and careers. Most of the books lack illustrations, the bibliography on Nolan being the one exception (it included eight pages of cover reproductions). The cloth editions are bound to library standards.

The first of the second editions of previously published works in the series appeared in late 1990 with the publication of revised bibliographies on George Zebrowski and Charles Beaumont; both of these volumes were extensively upgraded, the page count virtually doubling in size from the earlier versions.

This was by far the most comprehensive series of author bibliographies and literary guides produced in the genre, but with the demise of Borgo Press in 1999, the series came to an abrupt end, the last volume, the second edition of the Nolan bibliography, having appeared in 1997.

298. Drumm Bibliographies. Chris Drumm, Series Editor. Polk City, IA, Chris Drumm Books, 1983-DATE. 8 v. indexed. (pbk.).

These very basic chronological checklists of science fiction and fantasy authors, most of them written by Drumm himself, are primarily intended for a fan audience. Materials are organized chronologically by publication year, all of the author's works being interfiled into one straightforward list. Some bibliographical data are provided, plus an index keyed to title and page number. The books range in size from 8 to 63 pages (averaging 30 p.), and are produced inexpensively in 4" x 7" stapled paperback editions. The earlier books in the series were shot from somewhat primitive typed copy; later volumes employ much more legible laser-generated text. These are skeleton guides to the authors' work only; secondary materials are mentioned only in the most recent books in the series.

299. Galactic Central Bibliographies for the Avid Reader. Gordon Benson, Jr. and Phil Stephensen-Payne, Series Editors (and publishers). Leeds, West Yorkshire, England, Galactic Central Publications, 1982-DATE. 52 v. ISSN 1049-6386 (pbk.).

This long series of copublished author checklists has been produced in three distinct styles. The earliest editions were shot from very cramped typed copy, with text tightly compressed into a small number of pages and often extending into the inner and outer margins, making many of the books difficult to read and use and (for libraries) impossible to rebind without losing text.

Beginning in 1989, the books were progressively reworked as newer editions and volumes were released, by increasing the use of line breaks, white space, and margins and by using clearer and more legible word-processed copy as opposed to typed text; this has resulted in longer, roomier bibliographies, much more pleasing to the eye, with some attempt in the British-generated editions (constructed by Stephensen-Payne) to add secondary sources and other peripheral data. Also added was a nine-page standardized series introduction, identical in each book, providing a guide to the series format, section by section, and listing a two-page bibliography of works consulted.

A later innovation, beginning in the mid-1990s, reduced the physical size of the volumes from 8.5" x 11" to a standard 5" x 8" format. This coincided with the death of the founder of the series, Gordon Benson, Jr., in 1996, and the consolidation of the production of these bibliographies in England, under the careful guiding hand of editor Phil Stephensen-Payne.

The editor/publisher has also added some retrospective volumes on major fantastic writers of the past, beginning with nineteenth-century writer Grant Allen in 1999, greatly enhancing the overall value of the series, and adding, for the first time, a title page, contents page, a distinguishable spine, and perfect (glued) binding.

The arrangement of these books is alphabetically by title, the author's works being broken into specific subject sections; these have been standardized in the revised format to the following sections: "A. Stories"; "B. Fiction Books"; "C. Series"; "D. Poems, Songs, and Plays"; "E. Poem, Song, and Play Volumes"; "F. Articles"; "G. Miscellaneous"; "H. Non-Fiction Books"; "I. Books and Magazines Edited"; "J. Media Presentations"; "K. Articles on [the author]"; "L. Reviews"; "M. Books About [the author]"; "N. Phantom and Forthcoming Titles"; "O. Related Books by Other Authors"; "P. Textual Variations"; "Q. Chronological Index." The volumes lack title indexes.

The earlier books range in size from 5-50 pages, the later editions from 20-150 pages. Each biblio is updated about every five years (sometimes more frequently). This series includes about the same level of material as the Drumm Booklets, but in greater bibliographical detail; the books have never attempted to approach the depth of the Bibliographies of Modern Authors (see #297) or Masters of Science Fiction and Fantasy (see #300) series, although they have become increasingly more elaborate and valuable with the passage of time.

Originally intended primarily for the fan market, these checklists provide concise, up-to-date starting points for scholars and researchers interested in the work of the authors in question, and should be acquired by all major research collections.

Note: only the latest editions of these frequently revised bibliographies are covered herein.

300. Masters of Science Fiction and Fantasy. L. W. Currey, Series Editor. Boston, G. K. Hall & Co., 1980-84. 14 v. cloth.

This excellent series of fourteen bibliographies on eighteen writers (two of the books cover three writers each, in separate sections) was edited by a well-known SF bibliographer and book dealer who extensively reworked (and added material to) many of the books.

Each volume is divided into four sections: "A. Fiction"; "B. Miscellaneous Media"; "C. Nonfiction"; "D. Critical Studies," with comprehensive indexes keyed to title and item number. Materials are arranged chronologically, from the earliest publications to the latest, each work being numbered by chapter and item in the same manner as the Bibliographies of Modern Authors series (see #297), except that a couple of the books also number reprints of the writer's monographs in the same sequence as the rest. Many of the volumes also include excellent extensive biocritical introductions to the writer's work. Physically, the books range in size from 100 to 400 pages, in 5.5" x 8.5" or 6" x 9" cloth format; most were shot from typed copy, include no illustrations, and are bound to library standards.

As with the Borgo series, these are primarily literary guides and do not include first-edition points. The Masters series was well edited and soundly based, by far the best set of SF bibliographies published through the mid-1980s, covering many of the classic SF authors; the individual volumes contain few factual errors, are current through the late 1970s, and provide much useful information on the authors' lives and works. However, none of these books has been revised, which is a great pity, and most are now out-of-date.

301. Ultramarine Checklists. Christopher P. Stephens, Editor. Hastings-on-Hudson, NY, Ultramarine Publishing Co., Inc., 1987-1994? 20 v. (pbk.).

Stephens has authored or co-authored all of the books in this series of author check-lists, of which fifteen have been compiled on science-fiction authors, and another half dozen on other writers.

All of the books follow the same basic format, materials being organized in chro-nological order by publication date and numbered anew from the number one in each section. Complete bibliographical data are provided for all English-language editions and printings of the author's monographs, and similar data for the short works (except that Stephens does not include paginations for any of the shorter work entries). A brief index at the end of each volume correlates titles and years of publication only. The books are all shot from typed or word-processed copy, and bound with staples into stiff paper covers. The booklets were frequently updated, approximately once every two years, but no new editions have been seen since the mid-1990s.

These are very basic guides, of use primarily to collectors, but a number of the books cover authors for whom no other bibliography is available.

BIBLIOGRAPHIES OF INDIVIDUAL AUTHORS

Brian W. Aldiss

302. Manson, Margaret. **Item Forty-Three: Brian W. Aldiss: A Bibliography, 1954-1962.** Birmingham, England, Dryden Press, 1962. [24] p. (pbk.). Aldiss, Margaret. **Item Eighty-Three: Brian W. Aldiss: A Bibliography, 1954-1972.** Oxford, England, SF Horizons, 1973. 40 p. LC 79-10344 (pbk.).

This pair of basic checklists of Aldiss's work by his wife (the first done before she married the author) are similarly arranged into three sections: "A. Fiction"; "B. Nonfiction and Miscellanea"; "C. Edited Volumes," with materials being organized alphabetically by title in each part.

A typical entry includes: entry number (List A only, numbered in order); title; de-scription (*e.g.,* "novel," "8 story collection"; the short fiction section includes an estimated word count for each story); publication data (magazine, issue number, and date for short fiction; contents for collections; publisher, city [foreign only], year of publication, and pag-ination for books); and similar data for all known reprints. It is clear from both of these books that Aldiss has always been exceptionally careful in keeping track of his own work. All of these data except the word counts have been subsumed into Margaret Aldiss's later, definitive bibliography (see #303).

303. Aldiss, Margaret. **The Work of Brian W. Aldiss: An Annotated Bibliography & Guide,** by Margaret Aldiss. San Bernardino, CA, The Borgo Press, 1992. 360 p. index. (Bibliographies of Modern Authors, No. 9). LC 87-746. ISBN 0-89370-388-5; ISBN 0-89370-488-1 (pbk.).

Preliminary guides to this important British author's works were published by the bibliographer (the author's wife) in 1964 and 1972 (see #302). This new work completely updates and revises the earlier books and rearranges the data in a more logical, legible, and easier-to-use format.

Contents: "Foreword"; "Introduction: 'Map and Territory'," by David Wingrove; "A Brian W. Aldiss Chronology"; "A. Books" (with Annotations by Brian W. Aldiss); "B. Short Fiction"; "C. Nonfiction"; "D. Poetry"; "E. Other Media"; "F. Editorial Credits"; "G. Secondary Sources"; "Papers"; "G. Editorial Credits"; "H. Honors and Awards"; "I. Miscellanea"; "Quoth the Critics"; "A Walk in the Glass Forest: Autobiographical Reflections," by Aldiss; "Afterword: Slaves of the Megamachine," by Aldiss; "Title Index"; "Index to Secondary Sources"; "About Margaret Aldiss."

In each section, materials are arranged chronologically and numbered consecutively, chapter by chapter, beginning at the number one (for example, Aldiss's second published book is "A2," his third short story "B3," etc.). All titles are boldfaced. A typical entry includes: item number, title, byline, place of publication, publisher, year of publication, pagination, format, type of publication, and full bibliographical data on reprint editions, translations, republications, anthologizations, and anything else of interest.

The books are annotated by Brian Aldiss himself, and the entries also include complete contents listings, plot summaries, and other pertinent data; entries from other sections are selectively annotated as needed. Each of the books also includes a list of "Secondary Sources and Reviews," listed alphabetically by main entry (critic, title, or magazine), with as much bibliographical data as are known. Wingrove's introduction provides background material on Aldiss's life and works. The chronology provides a year-by-year account of the author's professional and personal life in descending, block paragraph format.

"Secondary Sources" includes all known works about the author. "Miscellanea" includes information on pen names, book dedications, memberships, Library of Congress cataloging data, career highlights, and similar information. "Quoth the Critics" includes selected excerpts of reviews and other comments by leading critics on the author's work. The index correlates titles and item numbers only. Aldiss's contributed essays provide much insight on his own life and creative work.

Aldiss's bibliography is one of the most impressive published in this series, containing over a hundred published books, 300 short stories, and many other works, with huge numbers of subsidiary editions listed in every section. For example, Aldiss's well-known short story, "Who Can Replace a Man?," records two pages of reprints in languages as diverse as Polish and Estonian. Much of the material in this bibliography, as with Margaret Aldiss's two earlier checklists (see #302), derives from her husband's extensive personal library, which includes copies of the vast majority of the known foreign-language editions of his own works. The book is well designed and typeset, and the cloth edition is bound to library standards. Coverage is complete through mid-1991.

This bibliography must surely be *the* major starting point for all future scholarship on this important writer's work, and is recommended for all research libraries. Alas, with the 1997 death of Margaret Aldiss, a second edition of this volume is unlikely.

304. Stephensen-Payne, Phil. **Brian W. Aldiss, a Man for All Seasons: A Working Bibliography.** 2nd rev. ed. Leeds, West Yorkshire, England, Galactic Central Publications, 1990. 9, 138 p. (Galactic Central Bibliographies for the Avid Reader, Vol. 26). ISBN 1-871133-21-1 (pbk.). Later reprints divide this book into two volumes, labelled "Part 1: Fiction" and "Part 2: Non-Fiction," although the same pagination is maintained throughout.

This basic checklist of primary and secondary works is arranged similarly to Margaret Aldiss's *Item* volumes (see #302). The nine-page standard series introduction (numbered separately from the rest) provides a general description of categories, organization of the bibliography, and a bibliography of works consulted. The first page gives the author's full name, date and place of birth, pseudonyms, and a chronological checklist of Aldiss's awards by year, award name, and work being honored.

The bibliography proper is divided into subject categories, materials being listed in alphabetical order by title in each section. Contents include: "A. Stories"; "B. Fiction Books"; "C. Series"; "D. Poems, Songs, and Plays"; "E. Poem, Song, and Play Volumes"; "F. Articles"; "G. Miscellaneous"; "H. Non-Fiction Books"; "I. Books and Magazines Edited by Brian Aldiss"; "J. Media Presentations"; "K. Articles on Brian Aldiss"; "L. Reviews" (in alphabetical order by book being reviewed, then by publication in which the review appeared); "M. Books About Brian Aldiss"; "N. Phantom and Forthcoming Titles"; "O. Related Books by Other Authors" (none—this is an empty category); "P. Textual Variations"; "Q. Chronological Index" (listed in order by year and month [but month is not listed], with books and stories interfiled).

A typical shorter work entry gives: item number, title, category ("ss" = short story, "nt" = novelette, etc.), magazine or book in which the item appeared, month and year of publication and issue number (British serials only) for materials published in magazines, or editor's last name, publisher, and year of publication (for anthology listings), plus similar data for all known reprints, including some foreign-language materials. No paginations are included.

A typical monograph entry includes: item number, title (all caps), contents (for story collections, giving a list of item numbers correlated to the other sections of the bibliography), publication data (publisher, LC or British Library card number [inconsistently], stock number, month and year of publication [in the form "10-59" for October 1959], pagination, and price), plus similar data on all known reprints and reissues, including some foreign-language editions (with the foreign titles). Entries are numbered anew from one in each separate chapter, prefixed by the identifying chapter letter (*e.g.,* A1, A2, A3, etc., for the "Stories" section). There is no general title index.

Some 960 entries are included, although reprint information makes the total much greater. 174 secondary sources are noted, of which 80 consist of book review categories; the reviews themselves number in the hundreds. The book is shot from very clear word-processed copy and stapled through the spine. Data are complete through 1989.

Although never intended to be more than a checklist, this volume provides a surprising amount of information in compact form. There are a few problems, however: Stephensen-Payne's book does not provide complete paginations for shorter works, and the series' "shorthand" style, which makes copious use of abbreviations to save space, could cause problems for the casual user. Nonetheless, this is an attractive, inexpensive alternative to Margaret Aldiss's more complete and detailed work (see #303); the latter will be preferred by serious scholars and academic libraries, but Aldiss's many fans will find this shorter guide perfectly adequate.

Lloyd Alexander

305. Zahorski, Kenneth J., and Robert H. Boyer. **Lloyd Alexander, Evangeline Walton Ensley, Kenneth Morris: A Primary and Secondary Bibliography.** Boston, G. K. Hall, 1981. xvi, 291 p. index. (Masters of Science Fiction and Fantasy). LC 81-6219. ISBN 0-8161-8055-5.

These bibliographies of three highly regarded fantasy authors provide a great deal of new information for the student and researcher.

Contents: "Preface" (discussing the book's arrangement); "Acknowledgments"; [individual bibliographies on] "Lloyd Alexander," "Evangeline Walton Ensley," and "Kenneth Vennor Morris"; "Indexes."

In each section, the authors provide a lengthy critical and biographical introduction to the writer's work (averaging 25-30 pages), the bibliography proper being subdivided into four chapters: "Part A: Fiction"; "Part B: Miscellaneous Media"; "Part C: Nonfiction"; "Part D: Critical Studies." Completing the book are two indices, "Works by the Authors" and "Works About the Authors."

Each of the author bibliographies is separated into its own section of the book, being arranged chronologically from the earliest published material to the latest, and numbered consecutively by section from the number one (*e.g.,* A1, A2, for each author's fictional works, these numbers being repeated in each of the separate bibliographies).

Books and shorter pieces are interfiled; reprints of books and stories are grouped as subsidiary entries under their first edition or appearance, chronologically by year of reprint. Reprint editions of short stories include: editor of anthology, title, place of publication, publisher, year, format (*e.g.,* "paper"), but no paginations. Book entries give: title (underlined), place of publication, publisher, but no paginations.

Each shorter work entry lists: title (in quotes), magazine, volume number, issue number, date, pagination; or, for those published originally in books: book title, book editor, place of publication, publisher, format, and paginations. Story collections include complete contents listings, plus the years in which the original stories were published. A few entries in Sections A-C include bibliographical notes, but no other annotations.

"Part B: Miscellaneous Media" includes screenplays, teleplays, interviews, recordings, poetry, and other material that does not specifically fit the other three categories; only one item total is noted among the three authors. "Part C: Nonfiction" includes all the author's nonfiction publications arranged chronologically by publication date. "Part D: Critical Studies" includes: author, title, bibliographical data, and extensive subject annotations for book reviews, fan commentaries, critiques, bibliographies, and other secondary works. The indices cite title and item number only, or author or title plus item number for the indices to critical studies, with small letters prefixing the number to cross-reference the entries from each of the three individual author sections (*e.g.,* "kmC12" = item "C12" in the Kenneth Morris bibliography). The book is reproduced from legible typed copy and bound to library standards. Foreign language reprint editions are mentioned when known, but, curiously, none of the foreign-language titles are given.

Of the fourteen volumes published in this series, Zahorski and Boyer's is one of the best, and certainly the least likely to become outdated: all three authors had essentially completed their careers by the time the book was published, with two of them (Morris and Walton) having undergone significant rediscoveries of their work in the 1970s. The critical introductions provide readable, authoritative, even important summaries of the writers' lives and contributions to fantastic literature, as valuable in their own right as the bibliographies themselves. It is difficult to imagine how any future researcher of these writers' works could ignore this excellent volume.

Grant Allen

306. Stephensen-Payne, Phil, and Virgil Utter. **Grant Allen, Hill-Top Philosopher: A Working Bibliography.** Leeds, West Yorkshire, England, Galactic Central Publications, 1999. vii, 106 p. (Bibliographies for the Avid Reader, Vol. 52). ISBN 1-871133-51-1 (pbk.).

This bibliography represents a new departure for this series, both in content and format. Grant Allen (1848-1899) was a nineteenth-century British writer who penned some science fiction in a career that produced hundreds of other publications. Also, this volume introduces a title page and contents page, and is among the first books in the Galactic Central line to be perfect-bound.

Contents: "Introduction"; "Awards and Pseudonyms"; "A. Prose Fiction"; "B. Prose Fiction Books"; "C. Series"; "D. Poetry & Drama"; "E. Poetry & Drama Books"; "F. Articles"; "G. Miscellaneous"; "H. Non-Fiction Books"; "I. Publications Edited by Grant Allen"; "J. Other Media"; "K. Articles on Grant Allen"; "L. Reviews"; "M. Items Devoted to Grant Allen"; "N. Phantom and Forthcoming Titles"; "O. Related Items by Other Authors"; "P. Textual Variations and Other Notes"; "Q. Chronological Index of Prose Fiction."

The introduction is almost identical throughout the series, and clearly explains the many different sections of the bibliography. Stephensen-Payne and Utter's basic checklist is arranged by subject category, then alphabetically by title; materials are numbered consecutively from one in each chapter (for example, B1, B2, B3, etc., for the author's books).

Shorter work entries include: item number, title, category ("ss" = short story, "nt" = novelette, etc.), magazine or book in which the item appeared, month and year of publication (for magazines in the form "2-68" for February 1968) or year of publication (for books), a list of subsequent reprints (for which title, publisher, year, and editor's last name are given), but no paginations.

For book-length works, Stephensen-Payne and Utter provide: item number, title, contents (if a collection, by item number), publication data (publisher, stock number, month and year of publication [if known, in the form "10-59" for October 1959], pagination, price), cover artist, plus similar data for known reprints. There is no title index. The book includes over a thousand entries, many of them short non-fiction works by Allen, although reprint information makes the total even greater. There are some 154 secondary sources mentioned, forty-five of which are book review categories, further subdivided into hundreds of actual review listings. An index would have been helpful, as would the addition of paginations for the short fiction.

However, Stephensen-Payne and Utter's bibliography is a substantial, well-researched contribution to the literature about Allen, and should be included in all major research library collections.

Poul Anderson

307. Benson, Gordon, Jr., and Phil Stephensen-Payne. **Poul Anderson, Myth-Master and Wonder-Weaver: A Working Bibliography.** 5th ed. Leeds, West Yorkshire, England & Albuquerque, NM, Galactic Central Publications, 1989. 9, 123 p. (Galactic Central Bibliographies for the Avid Reader, Vol. 1). ISBN 0-912613-03-3 and 1-871133-11-4 (pbk.). San Bernardino, CA, The Borgo Press, 1990, 9, 123 p. (Galactic Central Bibliographies for the Avid Reader, Vol. 1). LC 90-1934. ISBN 0-8095-4700-7 (cloth). The later printings from Galactic Central divide the book into two volumes, labelled "Part 1: Fiction" and "Part 2: Non-Fiction," but continue the same consecutive paging throughout.

Benson and Stephensen-Payne's basic checklist of this well-known American science-fiction writer's works is arranged by subject category, then alphabetically by title.

Contents: Author's name, date and place of birth, lists of awards won by the author (in chronological order, giving year, name of award, and title of work being honored), and his pseudonyms; "A. Stories"; "B. Fiction Books"; "C. Series" (including separate chronologies of the Technic Civilization and the Psychotechnic Series); "D. Poems"; "E. Poem & Song Collections" [blank section]; "F. Articles"; "G. Miscellaneous" (including introductions and afterwords by Anderson, letters, and interviews with the author); "H. Non-Fiction Books"; "I. Edited Books"; "J. Media Presentations"; "K. Articles on Poul Anderson"; "L. Reviews" (of Anderson's books, alphabetically by title of the book being reviewed, then by magazine title, giving date and reviewer); "M. Books About Poul Anderson"; "N. Phantom and Forthcoming Titles"; "O. Related Items by Other Authors"; "P. Textual Variations" [blank section]; "Q. Chronological Index" (by year and month [but months are not actually listed here], and title).

In each section the material is arranged in alphabetical order by title; materials are numbered consecutively from one in each chapter (for example, B1, B2, B3, etc., for the author's books). Shorter work entries include: item number, title, category ("ss" = short story, "nt" = novelette, etc.), magazine or book in which the item appeared, month and year of publication (for magazines in the form "2-68" for February 1968) or year of publication (for books), a list of subsequent reprints (for which title, publisher, year, and editor's last name are given), but no paginations.

For book-length works, Benson and Stephensen-Payne provide: item number, title, contents (if a collection, by item number), publication data (publisher, stock number, month and year of publication [if known, in the form "10-59" for October 1959], pagination, price), cover artist, plus similar data for known reprints. There is no title index. The series listings are especially helpful for Anderson, who has based so much of his work around a very detailed "history" of the future. The book is shot from very clear word-processed copy and stapled through the spine; the Borgo facsimile reprint is bound in library cloth. An index should be added to any future editions.

Benson and Stephensen-Payne's bibliography is the most current and accurate guide to this important author's fiction yet produced; their work is a necessary starting point for all future scholarship on Anderson's many publications. The death of Poul Anderson in 2001 means that any subsequent edition of this volume is likely to mark a definitive closure to this prolific writer's career.

308. Owings, Mark. **Poul Anderson: Bibliography.** Baltimore, MD, Balticon VII, T-K Graphics, 1973. [15] p. (pbk.).

Owings was a major bibliographer of the field during the late 1960s and early '70s before dropping out of fandom. His brief checklist of Anderson's work, produced for distribution at a science fiction convention, arranges the author's writings in one straight alphabetical list.

For short fiction, Owings gives: story title (in quotes), magazine title, publication date (in the form of "6/65" for June of 1965), and a basic list of subsequent reprints, but no paginations. Book entries include: book title (underlined), publisher, place of publication, date, pagination, price, and known reprints, including some foreign-language editions (information on which is very difficult to find).

Owings is both careful and accurate: foreign cities of publication, for example, are listed exactly as they appear in their original languages. The book is shot from usually legible typed copy, mimeographed on 8.5" x 11" sheets, and stapled through the spine. This is a sound piece of work despite the limited production values, but it is now very much out-of-date and has mostly been superseded by Benson and Stephensen-Payne (see #307), who do not, however, include the foreign-language reprints.

309. Peyton, Roger G. **A Checklist of Poul Anderson.** Birmingham, England, [Roger G. Peyton], 1965. 26 p. (pbk.).

Peyton provides a brief checklist of Anderson's science-fiction publications, omitting works in other genres. Now superseded by Benson/Stephensen-Payne (see #307).

[Not seen].

Piers Anthony

310. Stephensen-Payne, Phil. **Piers Anthony: Biblio of an Ogre: A Working Bibliography.** Leeds, West Yorkshire, England, Galactic Central Publications, 1990. 9, 45 p. (Galactic Central Bibliographies for the Avid Reader, Vol. 35). ISBN 1-871133-23-8 (pbk.).

This guide to popular SF and fantasy writer Piers Anthony is arranged by subject category, then alphabetically by title.

Contents: Author's complete real name, date and place of birth, lists of awards won by the author (by year of award, also listing award name and title of work being honored), and Anthony's pseudonyms (including "Piers Anthony" itself); "A. Stories"; "B. Fiction Books"; "C. Series" (keyed to entry number from the B section; no titles or years are listed, forcing the user to refer back to the previous chapter for hard data); "D. Poems, Songs & Plays"; "E. Poem, Song and Play Volumes" [blank section]; "F. Articles"; "G. Miscellane-

ous" (including author's notes, book reviews by Anthony, forewords, introductions by Anthony, letters, and interviews with the author); "H. Non-Fiction Books"; "I. Books Edited
by Piers Anthony"; "J. Media Presentations" [blank section]; "K. Articles on Piers Anthony";
"L. Reviews" (of Anthony's books, alphabetically by title of the book being reviewed, then
by magazine title, giving issue number, date of publication, and reviewer); "M. Books About
Piers Anthony"; "N. Phantom & Forthcoming Titles"; "O. Related Items by Other Authors";
"P. Textual Variations"; "Q. Chronological Index" (by year and month [but months are not
actually listed], and title).

In each section the material is arranged in alphabetical order by title; materials are
numbered consecutively from one in each chapter (for example, A1, A2, A3, etc., for the
author's stories). Shorter work entries include: item number, title, category ("ss" = short
story, "nt" = novelette, etc.), magazine or book in which the item appeared, month and
year of publication (for magazines in the form "2-68" for February 1968) or year of publication (for books), a list of subsequent reprints (for which title, publisher, year, and editor's
last name are given), but no paginations.

For book-length works, Stephensen-Payne provides: item number, title, contents (if
a collection, by item number), publication data (publisher, stock number, month and year
of publication [if known, in the form "10-59" for October 1959], pagination, price), cover
artist, plus similar data on all known reprints. There is no title index. 333 entries are included,
though reprint information inflates the figure far beyond that number; of these, some 117
numbers consist of secondary sources, 52 of which are book review categories, with hundreds of reviews actually being listed. The book is shot from generally clear word-processed
copy and stapled through the spine.

Given Anthony's enormous popularity in the 1980s and '90s, it's strange that Stephensen-Payne's bibliography is the first separately published guide to the author's many
novels and stories. Future editions should incorporate an overall title index and add specific
paginations for those sections that do not have them. However, this is a well-constructed if
occasionally cryptic bibliography, one that will be very useful to all students of Piers Anthony's work, and welcomed by his many fans.

Isaac Asimov

311. Miller, Marjorie M. **Isaac Asimov: A Checklist of Works Published in the United
States, March 1939-May 1972.** Kent, OH, Kent State University Press, 1972. xiii, 98 p.
index. LC 72-76948. ISBN 0-87338-126-2.

Miller's straightforward bibliography lists Asimov's works in chronological order by
publication date. A typical entry provides: title, place of publication and publisher (for
books), or magazine title, volume number, month of publication, and paginations (for shorter
works), followed by a list of all known reprints in the U.S., England, and Canada. No
foreign-language editions are shown, and no paginations are provided for books. An "F" in
front of an entry designates a fictional title. Some abbreviations are used to designate magazines ("*F&SF*" = *The Magazine of Fantasy and Science Fiction*); an abbreviations list is
located at the front of the book. Coverage is complete through May 1972.

The second section of the book, "Selected Criticism and Works about Asimov,"
consists of just over six pages of entries arranged in alphabetical order by author, providing

bibliographical data similar to that included in the main section, plus a two- to five-sentence evaluative annotation. This chapter is noticeably *passé*.

The title index correlates titles and dates only, making location of specific items difficult for the average user, particularly in those years where Asimov produced a great many titles (which, for this particular author, is *most* of them). Miller's coverage seems thorough, but her book is now so seriously outdated (Asimov died in 1992) that it can be no more than a starting point for future scholarly research. Clearly, a more detailed and expanded bibliography of the author's work is long overdue.

312. Tepper, M. B. **The Asimov Science Fiction Bibliography.** Santa Monica, CA, The Chinese Ducked Press, 1970. [89] leaves. index. LC 79-21922 (pbk.).

This amateurishly produced fan checklist of Asimov's works includes: "Adult Science Fiction Novels," "Juvenile Science Fiction Novels," "Straight Mystery Novel," "Collections," "Omnibuses," "Science Fiction Stories," "Straight Mystery Stories," "Poems," "Spoof Articles," "Plays," "Comic Strip Continuity," "Notes," "Alternate Title Index."

Each section is arranged chronologically by publication date, with book entries restricted to one a page. A typical monograph entry provides: title, publisher, year of publication, and complete contents (either a list of the stories included or a reproduction of the chapter heads). The short stories are grouped one year to a page, then listed by title, listing: magazine, month of publication, and size (*i.e.,* novel, novella, novelette, short story, short-short story). No other bibliographical data are provided.

Tepper omits Asimov's many hard science articles and the few anthologies he had then edited. Coverage is complete through 1969, with a few titles with 1970 dates. Now superseded by Miller (see #311), whose bibliography does not, however, include Tepper's size categorizations, and by Stephensen-Payne (see #310).

J. G. Ballard

313. Pringle, David. **J. G. Ballard: A Primary and Secondary Bibliography.** Boston, G. K. Hall, 1984. xxxvi, 156 p. index. (Masters of Science Fiction and Fantasy). LC 83-18528. ISBN 0-8161-8603-0.

Pringle, editor of the British magazines *Interzone* and *Million* and an acknowledged authority on Ballard's work, here provides the first comprehensive guide to the works of this highly regarded English writer of the fantastic.

Contents: "Preface" (discussing the book's arrangement); "Introduction" (twenty-three pages of critical and biographical background on Ballard); a chronological "Checklist of Books" by the author; an original "Interview with J. G. Ballard"; the bibliography proper, divided into several sections: "Part A: Fiction"; "Part B: Miscellaneous Media"; "Part C: Nonfiction"; "Part D: Critical and Bio-Bibliographical Studies."

Two appendices list all known foreign-language editions of Ballard's books by language, in chronological order by date of publication. Three indices at the end of the book cover: "The Writings of J. G. Ballard" (by title and item number), "Critics, Reviewers, and Interviewers" (by surname and item number), and "Persons Referred to by Ballard and His Critics" (by surname and item number).

Each section of the bibliography is arranged chronologically by publication year, and numbered consecutively by section and item (*e.g.,* A1, A2, A3, etc., for the author's fiction). Books and shorter works are interfiled together; reprints of books and stories are grouped as subsidiary entries under their first editions or appearances, chronologically by year of reprint.

Each book entry provides: title (underlined), place of publication, publisher, but no paginations. Each shorter work entry gives: title (in quotations), magazine, volume number, issue number, date, pagination; or, for works published originally in books: book title, book editor, place of publication, publisher, format, and paginations. Reprint editions of short stories include: anthology editor, title, place of publication, publisher, year, format (*e.g.,* "paper"), but no paginations. Story collections include complete contents listings, plus the years in which the original stories were published. Some entries, particularly in Sections B-C, include bibliographical or descriptive notes, but no other annotations; all of the entries in Part D are extensively annotated.

"Part B: Miscellaneous Media" largely consists of a listing of Ballard's published verse. "Part C: Nonfiction" covers the author's nonfiction publications, arranged chronologically by publication date. The "Critical Studies" section includes major reviews and all known articles and books about Ballard, arranged chronologically by publication date, with author, title, bibliographical data, and summaries. Coverage is complete through 1982. The book is reproduced from generally legible typed copy, and bound to library standards.

Pringle's book was one of the last two volumes published in this series, and while his work is now out-of-date (missing Ballard's most successful novel [and movie], *Empire of the Sun*), it remains a sound, thoroughly comprehensive, well-framed guide to the writer's *oeuvre*. The critical introduction is an excellent starting point for future scholarly studies, and the interview conducted in 1979 reveals much of Ballard's unique personality and character. In particular, the coverage of secondary sources in this volume is among the best in the series, including 167 references, many of them difficult to locate, with particularly thorough and analytic annotations. This is a first-class bibliographical effort that should be maintained with future editions.

Clive Barker

314. Bell, Joseph. **The Books of Clive Barker.** Toronto, Canada, Soft Books, 1988. [18] p. (pbk.).

Canadian book dealer Bell provides a collector's bibliography of the works of this well-known British horror writer, arranged in chronological order by publication date.

A typical entry includes: title (large bold type), publisher, address, exact collation, first edition statement, number of copies printed, edition priority states, price, cover artist, exact date of publication (as close as possible), contents, and similar information on all known reprintings and subsequent editions. Bell also provides a one-page chronological checklist of all Barker's editions (including reprints), but no overall index. A one-page addendum is inserted into the basic bibliography. The book is nicely designed and typeset, printed in 8.5" x 11" format, and stapled through the spine.

This checklist is clearly intended for collectors, and does provide much data of interest to the bookman; however, one might hope that a future edition would also feature more information about the *content* of the books, plus an index and some basic biographical information on the author.

Barrington J. Bayley

315. Ashley, Mike. **The Writings of Barrington J. Bayley: A Bibliography Prepared Specially for Beccon.** [Harold Wood, Essex, England: Beccon Committee], 1981. [7] p. (pbk.).

Ashley is a well-known British bibliographer. This brief checklist of Bayley's work was originally prepared for distribution at Beccon, the major annual English science fiction convention.

Data are organized into three sections: "A. Books"; "B. Short Fiction"; and "C. Of Further Interest." The first two parts are each arranged alphabetically by title. A typical book entry includes: item number (*e.g.,* A1, A2, A3), title, notes (*e.g.,* "collection of 13 stories"), publisher, place of publication, year of publication, pagination, format ("pb" and "sc" = paperback, "hb" = cloth); similar data are provided for all subsequent reprints. Short story collections also include complete contents listings, plus references to the short fiction section.

A typical "Short Fiction" entry includes: item number, title, magazine or book title, pseudonym (where appropriate), issue number and date (for magazines); or publisher, place of publication, and year (for books); similar data are provided for all known reprints. No paginations are listed for short fiction. "Of Further Interest" mentions an article by Bayley and an essay *on* Bayley's work by another writer. Coverage is complete through 1980. A photo of the author appears on the front cover.

Complete and thorough, if somewhat condensed in format, *The Writings of Barrington J. Bayley* would benefit from a more elaborate and attractive physical format in an updated second edition.

Charles Beaumont

316. Nolan, William F. **The Work of Charles Beaumont: An Annotated Bibliography & Guide.** San Bernardino, CA, The Borgo Press, 1986. 48 p. index. (Bibliographies of Modern Authors, No. 6). LC 85-460. ISBN 0-89370-385-0; ISBN 0-89370-485-7 (pbk.). **The Work of Charles Beaumont: An Annotated Bibliography & Guide.** 2nd ed., rev. and exp. San Bernardino, CA, The Borgo Press, 1990. 92 p. index. (Bibliographies of Modern Authors, No. 6). LC 90-15043. ISBN 0-8095-0517-7; ISBN 0-8095-1517-2 (pbk.).

Charles Beaumont burst like a shooting star on the science fiction world, beginning his brief career in 1950, then quickly moving to the high-paying slick magazines, and finally finding an outlet for his enormous energies in such award-winning television programs as *The Twilight Zone.* Sadly, after a brilliant ten-year career, Beaumont contracted Alzheimer's disease, prematurely dying at the age of thirty-eight. Nolan was Beaumont's close friend and frequent collaborator, and because they so often wrote in tandem, kept meticulous notes on Beaumont's publications.

Contents (second edition): "Preface to the Second Edition"; "Introduction to the First Edition"; "Chronology"; "A. Books"; "B. Short Fiction"; "C. Nonfiction"; "D. Screenplays";

"E. Teleplays"; "F. Comics"; "G. Letters"; "H. Unpublished Works"; "I. Verse"; "J. Honors and Awards"; "K. Artwork"; "L. Editorial Credits"; "M. About the Author"; "N. Miscellanea"; "Quoth the Critics"; Afterword: "My Grandmother's Japonicas," by Charles Beaumont; "Index"; "About William F. Nolan."

Materials are arranged chronologically, section by section, and numbered consecutively from one in each chapter (*e.g.,* Beaumont's sixth book is numbered "A6," his first short story "B1," etc.). A typical book entry includes: item number (boldfaced), title (boldfaced), byline, place of publication, publisher, month and year of publication, pagination, format (*e.g.,* "paper"), type of publication (*e.g.,* "anthology"), and full bibliographical data on all known reprint editions and translations. The second edition also lists book reviews for each monograph, arranged alphabetically by main entry (usually critic's name), with complete bibliographical data. The books are fully annotated, with complete contents listings and/or plot summaries; entries in the other sections are selectively annotated, mentioning television adaptations, awards, or signficance.

A typical shorter work entry provides: item number (boldfaced), title (in quotes, boldfaced), byline (if a pseudonym was used), magazine title (italics), volume number, month and year of publication, and pagination. Stories appearing first in collections or anthologies also include: book title (italics), editor, place of publication, publisher, month and year of publication, format (*e.g.,* "cloth"), and pagination; similar data are provided for all known reprint editions and translations. Nolan's introduction gives a brief history of Beaumont's life and career, and the six-page chronology in the second edition provides a detailed survey of Beaumont's life, publications, and his brief career.

"About the Author" includes all known secondary works arranged chronologically by publication date, with complete bibliographical data. The title index correlates titles and item numbers only. The media sections include such details as air and production dates, director, major actors (for motion pictures), production company, etc. Nolan acknowledges that the section on Beaumont's television work is incomplete and likely to remain so, since neither he nor Beaumont's family have complete records on his work outside *The Twilight Zone.*

Appreciation for Beaumont's legacy has been growing in recent years, and Nolan's bibliography is probably the most complete record now possible of his many writings. This well-organized and -presented publication will be an essential starting point for all future research on this fantasy writer's life and career.

Michael Bishop

317. Nee, Dave. **Michael Bishop: A Preliminary Bibliography.** Berkeley, CA, The Other Change of Hobbit, 1983. ii, 34 p. (+4-page supplement). index. (pbk.).

Nee, proprietor of the science-fiction bookstore The Other Change of Hobbit, has compiled a short checklist of this author's work, arranged by category, and then alphabetically by title.

Major sections include: "Preface and Acknowledgments"; "B. Books"; "C. Anthologies Edited"; "F. Fiction"; "N. Non-Fiction/Criticism" (*i.e.,* secondary sources); "P. Poetry"; "R. Reviews" (of Bishop's works); "X. Source Books" (for stories of Bishop reprinted in other volumes); "Title Index"; "Chronological Index."

Materials are numbered consecutively in each section from the number one. Works in the "Books" section include: item number, title, the author's dedication in each book (reprinted verbatim), complete bibliographical data for all editions, including place of publication, publisher, ISBN, price, pagination, size in centimeters, cover artist, and exact date of publication (when known).

The short fiction section lists: item number, story title, magazine, date, pagination, plus all known reprints, with title of the reprint anthology, date of publication, and pagination. The "Non-Fiction/Criticism" section includes: articles, biographies, and review essays on Bishop, and interviews with the author, but does not mention the book(s) being reviewed; reviews *by* Bishop are included in the "Reviews" chapter.

Section X, "Source Books," gives complete bibliographical data (in a format similar to Section B) on the anthologies and other works *not* actually authored by Bishop but mentioned elsewhere in the bibliography. The indices cite title and item number only. The book is reproduced from 8.5" x 11" computer printout, using hanging indents to set off specific data, and stapled through the spine into paper covers. A four-page supplement, also dated 1983, was inserted in some copies.

Nee's volume includes a surprising amount of data for this type of checklist, particularly on reprint editions; however, the volume numbers of periodicals are omitted. A revised edition was announced but never published. See also the companion volume on Thomas M. Disch (see #375). Prefer Stephensen-Payne and Benson's more current guide (see #318), which does not, however, include short fiction paginations.

318. Stephensen-Payne, Phil, and Gordon Benson, Jr. **Michael Bishop, a Transfigured Talent: A Working Bibliography.** 3rd rev. ed. Leeds, West Yorkshire, England, Galactic Central, 1992. 9, 38 p. (Bibliographies for the Avid Reader, Vol. 33). ISBN 1-871133-32-7 (pbk.).

Science fiction writer Michael Bishop has won numerous awards during the past few decades.

Contents: Author's name, date and place of birth, list of awards won by the author (in chronological order, giving year, name of award, and title of work being honored) and his pseudonyms [blank section]; "A. Stories"; "B. Fiction Books"; "C. Series"; "D. Poems, Songs & Plays"; "E. Poem, Song & Play Volumes" ; "F. Articles"; "G. Miscellaneous" (including introductions and afterwords by Michael Bishop, letters, and interviews with the author); "H. Non-Fiction Books" [blank section]; "I. Books Edited by Michael Bishop"; "J. Media Presentations"; "K. Articles on Michael Bishop"; "L. Reviews" (of Bishop's books, alphabetically by title of the book being reviewed, then by magazine title, giving date and reviewer); "M. Books About Michael Bishop"; "N. Phantom & Forthcoming Titles"; "O. Related Items by Other Authors" [blank section]; "P. Textual Variations"; "Q. Chronological Index" (by year and title).

The introduction is almost identical throughout the series, and clearly explains the many different sections of the bibliography. Stephensen-Payne's and Benson's basic checklist is arranged by subject category, then alphabetically by title; materials are numbered consecutively from one in each chapter (for example, B1, B2, B3, etc., for the author's books).

Shorter work entries include: item number, story title, category ("ss" = short story, "nt" = novelette, etc.), magazine or book in which the item appeared, month and year of publication (for magazines in the form "2-68" for February 1968) or year of publication (for books), a list of subsequent reprints (for which title, publisher, year, and editor's last name are given), but no paginations.

For book-length works, Stephensen-Payne and Benson provide: item number, title, contents (if a collection, by item number), publication data (publisher, stock number, month and year of publication [if known, in the form "10-59" for October 1959], pagination, price), cover artist, plus similar data for known reprints. There is no title index. 292 entries are included, although reprint information makes the total greater; forty-eight of these are secondary sources, of which nineteen consist of book review categories. Hundreds of actual book reviews are noted in these sections. No attempt has been made to include foreign language publications. The book is shot from clear word-processed copy, and stapled through the spine.

Although an index would have been helpful, as would the addition of paginations for the short fiction, this is an excellent beginning place for all scholarship on this popular writer's work. Nee's book (see #317) is much less current, but includes the story paginations that Stephensen-Payne and Benson's guide lacks.

Algernon Blackwood

319. Ashley, Mike. **Algernon Blackwood: A Bio-Bibliography.** New York, London, Greenwood Press, 1987. xx, 349 p. index. (Bio-Bibliographies in World Literature, No. 1). LC 87-17808. ISBN 0-313-25158-4.

This absolutely superb work on a classic British writer of the supernatural is a paradigm of what a bibliography should be: well-organized and comprehensive, with virtually everything that one might want to know about the author.

Contents: "Foreword," by Ramsey Campbell; "The Why and the Wherefore: An Introduction"; "Acknowledgements"; "User's Guide"; "The Biography"; "The Bibliography." The biographical section contains a thirty-four-page essay by Ashley giving many little-known details about Blackwood's life and career; a chronology summarizes the salient points into a four-page table.

The bibliography proper is organized into four major sections: Part I. "Works by Blackwood"—"A. Books"; "B. Short and Serial Fiction"; "C. Non-Fiction": "CA. Essays and Sketches," "CB. Book Reviews"; "D. Poetry and Songs"; "E. Plays and Dramas": "EA. Stage Plays," "EB. Radio Plays"; "F. Radio Broadcasts": "FA. Stories," "FB. Talks," "FC. Interviews and Discussions"; "G. Television Broadcasts": "GA. Stories and Talks," "GB. Interviews and Discussions"; "H. Films"; "I. Recorded Works"; "J. Unpublished or Unbroadcast Manuscripts"; "K. Untraced Items."

Part II: "Adaptations by Others," includes the following chapters: "L. Stage Plays"; "M. Radio Broadcasts": "MA. Stories, Talks and Poetry," "MB. Radio Plays"; "N. Television Adaptations"; "O. Recorded Works and Editions for the Blind": "OA. Stories," "OB. Poetry and Songs," "OC. Plays," "OD. Books in Braille." (Note: there is no Section P.)

Part III: "Works About Blackwood" includes chapters on: "Q. Selected Secondary Bibliography"; "R. Reviews of Blackwood's Books"; "S. Radio Documentaries About Blackwood"; "T. Portraits and Photography."

Part IV: "Source Indexes" includes: "U. Index to Books by Publisher"; "V. Index to Magazines and Periodicals"; "W. Index by Anthologist"; "X. Index to Books Reviewed by Blackwood"; "Y. Index to Secondary Bibliography by Periodical."

Appendices: "I. Translated Books and Foreign Editions"; "II. Library Holdings": "A. By Library," "B. By Book"; "III. Archive Holdings"—"Manuscripts and Letters."

Indexes: "I. Index to Locale and Theme"; "II. Chronological Index to All Works"; "III. Alphabetical Index to All Works"; "IV. Index to Personal Names": "1. Actors and Narrators"; "2. Artists and Designers"; "3. Writers and Critics"; "4. Friends and Acquaintances."

Each section is arranged chronologically by date of original publication. Materials are numbered consecutively from one in each new section, in the left-hand margin of the page; further printings of books are numbered from one (*e.g.,* "A.1.4" is the fourth British edition of Blackwood's first book). A typical book entry includes: title (in boldface), description (novel or collection), total wordage for the book, contents (for a collection) or three- to four-sentence plot description (for a novel), the author's dedication (verbatim), a list of the British editions of the book in chronological order, a list of the American editions in chronological order, and see references. Bibliographical data include: place of publication, publisher, year of publication, month of publication, format, physical size (in centimeters), exact pagination, description of binding and other "points," price, date of contract between author and publisher, and description of reissues by the same publisher.

The "Short and Serial Fiction" section and similar chapters include: title (in boldface), total wordage, one- to two-sentence plot description, bibliographical data (magazine, volume number, issue number, date, pagination, mention of illustration and illustrator's name), subsequent reprints (stories in Blackwood's own collections are cross-referenced by title and year; those appearing in other anthologies include title, editor, place of publication, publisher, date, and pagination).

The media sections include all details known about the production companies, writers, actors, air times, etc. The indices are enormously thorough, reworking the data through a wide variety of access points keyed to item number. The book is shot from occasionally faint word-processed copy.

Ashley is to be congratulated on producing perhaps the finest—certainly the most comprehensive—bibliography ever compiled on an individual writer of fantastic literature, organized into a very accessible and logical format. Future researchers will find a literary gold mine in these pages. Highly recommended, not just to students of Blackwood's life and literary career, but also to potential bibliographers everywhere.

320. Colombo, John Robert. **Blackwood's Books: A Bibliography Devoted to Algernon Blackwood.** Toronto, Canada, Hounslow Press, 1981. 119 p. index. LC 83-128835. ISBN 0-88882-055-0 (pbk.).

Colombo, best known for his checklist of Canadian science fiction (see #216), originally prepared this bibliography of Blackwood's books to assist in the compilation of a new collection of the author's horror stories.

Blackwood's monographs are arranged alphabetically by title. A typical entry includes: book title (boldfaced), place of publication, publisher, year of publication, author's dedication (reproduced verbatim), edition statement, other material of interest, and a complete contents list (for story collections) recording the fictions in the same order in which they appeared in the book. Also mentioned are place of publication, publisher, and year of publication for all known reprints and subsequent editions. Each of Blackwood's books is recorded on a separate page.

Appendices include: "I. List of Books by Year of Publication"; "II. Alphabetical List of [152] Stories with Locations" [in Blackwood's collections]; "III. Brief Life of Blackwood"; "IV. The Canadian Years" (*i.e.,* Blackwood's adventures in Canada); "V. Theatre, Radio, and Television" [productions]; "VI. Master of Horror" by Walter Gillings (a critical essay on Blackwood's life and fiction); "VII. Select Bibliography" [of works consulted].

Colombo's arrangement may sometimes seem more quickly accessible for the casual user than that in *Algernon Blackwood: A Bio-Bibliography* (see #319), but there is very little here that Ashley does not subsume into his masterful bibliography.

James P. Blaylock

321. Stephens, Christopher P., and Tom Joyce. **A Checklist of James P. Blaylock.** Hastings-on-Hudson, NY, Ultramarine Publishing Co., 1991. 17 p. index. ISBN 0-89366-199-6 (pbk.).

Stephens and Joyce's guide is organized chronologically by publication date, materials being numbered consecutively from one in two sections covering the author's books (A1-15) and stories (B1-13).

A typical book entry provides: year (as a floating head), item number, title (underlined), pseudonym, publisher, stock or ISBN number, pagination, format (*e.g.,* "paperback original"), cover illustrator, price, and similar data for all known reprints (which are numbered, for example, A2a, A2b, A2c, etc., in descending order by publication date). The chapbook is shot from legible typed copy and bound with staples in stiff paper covers.

The index correlates titles with years of publication only. Blaylock is a well-known writer in the science-fiction field; this brief guide will be of interest primarily to his fans.

James Blish

322. Blish, Judith Lawrence. **"Bibliography of the Works of James Blish,"** in *The Tale That Wags the God,* by James Blish, edited by Cy Chauvin. Chicago, Advent:Publishers, 1987, p. 197-290. index. LC 88-162246. ISBN 0-911682-29-5.

This final collection of essays on science fiction was originally penned by SF author James Blish under his academic pseudonym, William Atheling, Jr.; it also includes a nearly definitive bibliography of his works by his widow, J. A. Lawrence (Judith Blish), in a separate section following the index to the main text.

Materials in the bibliography are arranged into twelve subject categories: "Books," "Short Stories," "Anthologies," "Short Story Collections," "Science Fiction Criticism" (subdivided into "The Issue at Hand," "Column and Books"), "Literary Criticism," "Book Reviews," "Articles and Interviews," "Introductions," "Poetry," and "*Star Trek* Books."

In each section materials are sorted alphabetically by title. A typical book entry includes: title (italics, all caps), series title, original magazine serialization (where applicable, giving title, volume and issue number[s], months and years of publication, and publisher), publisher, nationality of publisher, year of publication, and similar data on all known reprints, listed in order by nationality, then by date, with variant and foreign-language titles. No paginations are listed.

A typical short fiction entry includes: title (in quotes), total wordage, pseudonym (where applicable), magazine title (italics), volume and issue number, publisher, nationality of publisher, month and year of publication, but no paginations. Similar data are provided for all known reprint editions, including anthology appearances and translations. Shorter works in other sections do not include word counts. There are separate title and name indices referencing the page numbers on which the titles or persons are mentioned. The book is attractively typeset and bound to library standards.

This will obviously be the first stopping point for all students of Blish's work; among others, the data on the author's numerous translations are virtually unobtainable in any other source. However, it would have been helpful to have had paginations for all entries (and they should be added to any future edition) placed in a somewhat more standardized format. Lawrence's bibliography will likely remain current almost indefinitely; Blish's 1975 death means that any future additions to this guide will probably be rehashes or reprintings of old work. However, Stephensen-Payne's guide (see #323) can serve as a supplement to the secondary sources.

323. Stephensen-Payne, Phil. **James Blish, Author Mirabilis: A Working Bibliography.** Leeds, West Yorkshire, England, Galactic Central Publications, 1996. ix, 161 p. (Bibliographies for the Avid Reader, Vol. 46). ISBN 1-871133-46-7 (pbk.).

The late American writer SF James Blish authored such classic works in the field as *Cities in Flight* and *A Case of Conscience.*

Contents: "Introduction"; "Awards and Pseudonyms"; "A. Prose Fiction"; "B. Prose Fiction Books"; "C. Series"; "D. Poetry & Drama"; "E. Poetry & Drama Books"; "F. Articles"; "G. Miscellaneous"; "H. Non-Fiction Books"; "I. Publications Edited by James Blish"; "J. Other Media"; "K. Articles on James Blish"; "L. Reviews"; "M. Books about James Blish"; "N. Phantom and Forthcoming Titles"; "O. Related Items by Other Authors"; "P. Textual Variations and Other Notes"; "Q. Chronological Index of Prose Fiction."

The introduction is almost identical throughout the series, and clearly explains the many different sections of the bibliography. Stephensen-Payne's basic checklist is arranged by subject category, then alphabetically by title; materials are numbered consecutively from one in each chapter (for example, B1, B2, B3, etc., for the author's books).

Shorter work entries include: item number, title, category ("ss" = short story, "nt" = novelette, etc.), magazine or book in which the item appeared, month and year of publication (for magazines in the form "2-68" for February 1968) or year of publication (for books), a list of subsequent reprints (for which title, publisher, year, and editor's last name are given), but no paginations.

For book-length works, Stephensen-Payne provides: item number, title, contents (if a collection, by item number), publication data (publisher, stock number, month and year of publication [if known, in the form "10-59" for October 1959], pagination, price), cover artist, plus similar data for known reprints. There is no title index.

Some 1,113 entries are noted, although reprint information makes the overall total much larger. Of these, some 294 secondary sources mentioned, of which fifty consist of book review categories; the reviews themselves number in the hundreds. There was an attempt to include some foreign language publications, but the information noted here is sparse. An index would have been helpful, as would the addition of paginations for the short fiction sections.

This was one of the first volumes in the Galactic Central series issued in the revised format for the series, which includes title and content pages and perfect (*i.e.*, glued) binding. The book is attractively produced from word-processed copy. Since Blish died in 1975, the volume is essentially complete save for new reprintings of the author's work, and additional secondary works. Recommended.

See also Judith Blish's bibliography on her husband (see #322), which is slightly less current, but includes data not found in Stephensen-Payne's guide. Careful researchers will require both volumes.

Robert Bloch

324. Flanagan, Graeme. **Robert Bloch: A Bio-Bibliography.** Canberra City, A.C.T., Australia, Graeme Flanagan, 1979. 63 p. (pbk.).

Flanagan provides a tribute to the late horror writer, Robert Bloch, together with a checklist of his works.

Contents: "Introduction"; "Robert Bloch: A Few Words of Friendship," by Harlan Ellison; "Biography"; "The Robert Bloch Collection" (describing the collection of his manuscripts at the University of Wyoming Library); "Mr. Weird Tales," by Robert Weinberg; "Interview One: Mostly Concerning Weird Tales"; "'When Screwballs Meet . . . ,'" by Fritz Leiber; "Interview Two"; "Bibliography"; "Radio, Television and Motion Pictures"; "My Weird Little Brother," by Mary Elizabeth Counselman; "Acknowledgments."

The miscellaneous articles and interviews provide much background material on Bloch and his work. The bibliography proper is organized into the following sections: "A. Short Stories—First Magazine Printings"; "B. Non-Fiction Published in Magazines"; "C. Novels"; "D. Collections—Short Stories"; "E. Collections—Non-Fiction"; "F. Short Stories and Non-Fiction Published in Anthologies"; "G. Short Stories and Non-Fiction Reprinted in Magazines"; "H. Foreign Translations"; "I. Miscellanea," including "Introductions/Afterwords," "Speeches," "Interviews," and "Biographies" (secondary sources in magazines).

Sections A and B are arranged in chronological order, listing: title, magazine, and date only, but no paginations. Most of the remaining parts are listed in alphabetical order by title. A typical book entry includes: title, publisher, place of publication, year of publication, pagination, and price for all known editions. The secondary sources are scanty at best. The other media section includes works by Bloch as well as screenplays and teleplays adapted by others from his work. The volume is shot from typed copy, and is illustrated throughout with photographs of the author and a few book and magazine cover reproductions.

While some of the background material remains interesting—and unique to this volume—the bibliography itself has been almost totally subsumed into Larson's book (see #326).

325. Hall, Graham M. **Robert Bloch Bibliography.** Tewksbury, England, Graham M. Hall, 1965. 32 p. index. (pbk.).

This mimeographed checklist of Bloch's publications lists titles in straight chronological order by publication date. Reprints reappear as new entries throughout the list, making any kind of correlation between items unnecessarily difficult. The shorter works in the list are indexed at the end of the book by title of the magazine in which they were originally published, and also by anthology name (neither of these provide particularly helpful access points).

There is also the usual guide to the Lefty Feep stories (a lengthy series of humorous SF tales penned by Bloch), and a short, very incomplete listing of Bloch's teleplays, radio work, and screenplays and film adaptations. Now completely outdated and superseded by Larson (see #326).

326. Larson, Randall D. **The Complete Robert Bloch: An Illustrated International Bibliography.** Sunnyvale, CA, Fandom Unlimited Enterprises, 1986. x, 126 p. index. LC 85-82410. ISBN 0-9607178-1-1 (pbk.).

This nicely illustrated bibliography was compiled by the same critic who penned several well-received critiques on Bloch for Starmont House.

Contents: "Preface"; "Introduction," by Bloch; "Robert Bloch: The Man with the Heart of a Small Boy," by Larson; "Main Bibliography"; "Fanzine Bibliography"; "Supplemental Bibliographies" (*i.e.,* indexes); "Themes and Variations: A Categorical Guide to the Short Stories and Novels of Robert Bloch." The Main Bibliography is further subdivided into: "1. Short Stories"; "2. Novels"; "3. Collections"; "4. Non-Fiction"; "5. Introductions & Afterwords"; "6. Verse"; "7. Radio, Television & Motion Pictures"; "8. Bibliographic & Biographic Material" (secondary sources); "9. Miscellany."

In each section materials are listed alphabetically by title. A typical short story entry provides: title (boldfaced), wordage, magazine title, date, and known reprints in descending, chronological order by date of publication (magazine titles are underlined, book titles are capitalized), but no paginations.

A typical book entry includes: title (bold caps), wordage, place of publication, publisher, year, format abbreviation (*e.g.,* "hb" = hardcover, "pb" = paperback), but no paginations, plus a list of all known reprint editions, American versions being listed first, with similar types of publication data. No paginations are provided.

For media presentations, Larson gives: title or program title, year, network or production company, and (for motion pictures) director. The indices rearrange the data by magazine and date of publication; also included are lists of Bloch's unanthologized short stories, the Lefty Feep series, collaborative stories, and pseudonymous stories. The themes and variations section provides a guide to Bloch's works by specific subject category.

The book also includes illustrations of book and magazine covers, title pages, and interior drawings on virtually every page plus a few stills from Bloch's screenplays and teleplays, and is generally very attractively presented. The coverage of foreign editions is particularly strong.

However, one would hope in any future edition for both a general title index and paginations, the lack of which detract from what would otherwise be *the* definitive guide to Bloch's life and works.

Still the best-maintained Bloch in town.

Anthony Boucher

327. Christopher, J(oe) R., with D(ean) W. Dickensheet and R(obert) E. Briney. **A. Boucher Bibliography.** [White Bear Lake, MN, Allen J. Hubin], 1969. [34] p. index. (pbk.). Bound with: *A Boucher Portrait: Anthony Boucher as Seen by His Friends and Colleagues,* edited by Lenore Glen Offord.

Anthony Boucher, the well-known science-fiction and mystery writer, editor, and critic, died prematurely in 1968 at the age of fifty-seven. This memorial bibliography, re-printed from its original serialization in Volume 2 (Nos. 2-4) of *The Armchair Detective,* records materials from all of Boucher's writing worlds.

Materials are organized into specific series and subject categories: "I. Alias Watson: The Memoirs of Martin Lamb"; "II. The Casebook of Fergus O'Breen" (plus a separate section of "Related Stories"); "III. The Pride of Sister Ursula, O.M.B." (plus "Related Sto-ries"); "IV. Noble Obliges: The Adventures of Detective Lt. Donald MacDonald, L.A.P.D."; "V. Usuform Robotics" (plus "Related Stories"); "VI. Non-Sequence Stories"; "VII. Col-lected Fiction"; "VIII. Holmesian Material"; "IX. Essays and Other Non-Fiction"; "X. Verse"; "XI. Items in Special Interest Publications" (subdivided into: "a. Mystery Writers of America Periodicals"; "b. Opera Periodicals and Programs"; "c. Science Fiction 'Fan-zines'"); "XII. Anthologies Edited"; "XIII. Reviewing Series"; "XIV. Magazine and Book-Series Editing"; "XV. Introductions to Non-Series Volumes"; "XVI. Translations"; "XVII. Biographical and Autobiographical Material"; "XVIII. General Addenda"; "Combined List of Subject Headings and Index" (to titles and item numbers).

In each section, materials are listed chronologically by publication date, novels and short fiction being interfiled together. A typical book entry includes: item number, title (underlined), place of publication, publisher, year of publication, but no paginations; similar data are provided for all known reprints in English. A typical short fiction entry provides: item number, title (in quotes), magazine title (underlined), month and year of publication, but no paginations, plus a list of known reprints in anthologies and collections (for which book title, editor, place of publication, publisher, and year of publication are included). Every fiction entry includes a descriptive annotation ranging in size from 50-300 words (averaging 150).

Materials are numbered in each section or subject from the number one, using small roman numerals; thus, *The Case of the Seven of Calvary,* part of the Martin Lamb series, is numbered "i." in section "I." and should have been referenced in the title index as "I.i." (but the index misses this novel); those chapters that are divided into two or three parts (Sections II. and III., for example) are numbered from the small Roman numeral "i." in each subsec-tion, preceded by an identifying letter (for example, "Mystery for Christmas" is referenced in the index as "II.b.i.," being the first item of the "Related Stories" section of Chapter II.).

If this seems overly cumbersome, consider the last entry of Chapter VI., "The Smoke-Filled Locked Room," which is numbered "VI.xxxviii." The 8.5" x 11" booklet is shot from occasionally faint typed copy and stapled through the side.

The compilers acknowledge the incompleteness of the later sections of the bibliography, which record secondary sources and peripheral items by and about the author. The fiction chapters are much more complete, but the unnecessarily confusing format and poor production values make access difficult for the casual user. Very few copies of this guide were distributed, and the early issues of *The Armchair Detective* are themselves rarities. A definitive bibliography of this influential *littérateur* of the 1950s and '60s has yet to be produced.

Leigh Brackett

328. Arbur, Rosemarie. **Leigh Brackett, Marion Zimmer Bradley, Anne McCaffrey: A Primary and Secondary Bibliography.** Boston, G. K. Hall & Co., 1982. xlviii, 277 p. index. (Masters of Science Fiction and Fantasy). LC 81-4216. ISBN 0-8161-8120-9.

This tripartite bibliography of primary and secondary sources on three American women science fiction writers of the twentieth century includes: "[About] the Author"; "Preface" (describing how the book is arranged); "Abbreviations and Other Minutiae"; "Introduction" (providing broad biographical and critical backgrounds for all three authors); the bibliographies proper, in three separate parts: "Leigh Brackett"; "Marion Zimmer Bradley"; "Anne McCaffrey"; "Indexes."

In each chapter, the author's works are subdivided into four sections: "Part A: Fiction"; "Part B: Miscellaneous Media"; "Part C: Nonfiction"; "Part D: Critical Studies." The indices grouped at the end of the book are similarly broken into six sections, one each for the writer's primary and secondary works.

Each bibliography is arranged chronologically, from the earliest published material to the latest, and numbered consecutively from one in each section (*e.g.,* A1, A2, A3, etc., for each author's fiction). Books and shorter works are interfiled; reprint editions of books appear as new entries under their respective years, with "See" references from one to the other. Reprints of stories are listed under the main entry, chronologically by year of reprint, with editor of anthology, title, place of publication, publisher, year, and format (*e.g.,* "paper" = paperback).

Each book entry lists: title (underlined), subject category (*e.g.,* "mystery"), place of publication, publisher, but no paginations. Each shorter work entry gives: title (in quotations), magazine, volume number, issue number, date, pagination; or, for those published originally in books: book title, book editor, place of publication, publisher, format, paginations. Story collections include complete contents listings, plus the years in which the original stories were published. Many entries include bibliographical notes, but few other annotations for Parts A-C.

"Part B: Miscellaneous Media" includes each author's screenplays, teleplays, interviews, recordings, poetry, etc. "Part C: Nonfiction" includes all of each author's nonfiction publications, with brief subject annotations. "Part D: Critical Studies" includes: author, title, bibliographical data, and extensive subject annotations for book reviews, fan commentaries, critiques, bibliographies, and other secondary works, arranged chronologically by publication date. The indices correlate titles and item numbers only, or authors, titles, and item numbers for the indices to critical studies. No foreign language editions are included. The book is reproduced from typed copy and bound to library standards.

The decision to list exact reprints of previously published books as new entries under the appropriate year is unfortunate, since it tends to result in endless repetitions of the same titles over and over again (Arbur does provide "See Also" references, however); it would have been more useful to include subsidiary printings under the first edition of each book, as is true with most of the other volumes in this series. Coverage is complete only through 1980, making the sections on Bradley and McCaffrey, who remained active as writers for long after this period, very much out-of-date (but Brackett's section remains fairly current, the author having died in 1978).

Finally, having six indices to one volume, one after another, is rather cumbersome, to say the least; these should have either been combined into two sequences, as with the other tripartite volume in this series (on Lloyd Alexander/Evangeline Walton/Kenneth Morris; see #305), or included in place immediately following each author's bibliography.

Even with these minor caveats, further editions of both Bradley and McCaffrey would certainly be justified.

329. Benson, Gordon, Jr. **Leigh Douglass Brackett & Edmond Hamilton, the Enchantress & the World Wrecker: A Working Bibliography.** 2nd rev. ed. Leeds, West Yorkshire, England & Albuquerque, NM, Galactic Central Publications, 1988. 25 p. (Galactic Central Bibliographies for the Avid Reader, Vol. 20). ISBN 0-912613-05-X (pbk.).

Brackett and Hamilton comprised one of several husband-and-wife writer teams in science fiction, although they rarely collaborated with each other; they died a year apart in the late 1970s. Benson's checklist is arranged by category, then alphabetically by title; Brackett's list occupies pages 1-8, Hamilton's 9-25.

Contents (for each author): author's full name, date and place of birth and date of death, lists of awards won by the author, pseudonyms, brief list of biographical sketches and obituaries. Bibliographical contents for Brackett: "A. The Stories"; "B. The Books"; "C. The Series"; "Addenda"; "Screenplays." Contents for Hamilton: "Abbreviations List"; "A. The Stories" (Excluding "Captain Future"); "B. The Series" (including the Captain Future stories and novels); "C. The Other Books"; "Additions and Corrections."

In each section the material is arranged in alphabetical order by title, items being numbered consecutively from the number one in each section. For shorter works, Benson gives: item number, title, category ("ss" = short story, "nt" = novelette, etc.), magazine or book in which the item appeared, month and year of publication (for magazines, in the form of "4-42" for April 1942) or year of publication (for books), a list of subsequent reprints (for which title, publisher, year, and editor's last name are given), but no paginations.

Typical book entries include: item number, title, contents (for collections, by item number), publication data (publisher, stock number, month and year of publication [in the form "10-59" for October 1959], pagination, price, with dates of reissues by the same publisher), cover artist. There is no index and just a minimal list of secondary sources. The series listings are very helpful, particularly for Hamilton, who produced many works for the hero and SF pulps.

The book is shot from fairly legible typed copy, and some of the text runs close to the right margins of some pages, making potential rebinding difficult for libraries. This bibliography has not yet been revised into the new format for this series. Future editions should include a title index and detailed paginations of short story appearances and their reprints, as well as more information on Brackett's screen and television work, which is given minimal play here.

Benson's book is a useful starting point for the researcher interested in the Golden Era of the pulps, but Arbur's guide (see #328) includes the paginations for Brackett that this bibliography lacks, although its coverage is not quite as current.

Ray Bradbury

330. Nolan, William F. **The Ray Bradbury Companion: A Life and Career History, Photolog, and Comprehensive Checklist of Writings with Facsimiles from Ray Bradbury's Unpublished and Uncollected Work in All Media.** Detroit, MI, A Bruccoli Clark Book, Gale Research Co., 1975. xiii, 339 p. index. LC 74-10397. ISBN 0-8103-0930-0 (boxed).

Nolan, a well-known SF writer in his own right, became interested in Bradbury's work at an early age (see also his *Ray Bradbury Review* [#331]). This magnificently designed and produced 7.5" x 10.5" book was issued as a boxed volume, and beautifully illustrated with full-page reproductions of manuscript pages, title pages, dust jackets, paperback covers, and photos of the author and his family.

Contents: "The Inherited Wish: An Introduction," by Bradbury; "Preface"; "Ray Bradbury Photolog"; "The Life and Career of Ray Bradbury—A Chronology"; "Facsimiles from Ray Bradbury's Unpublished and Uncollected Work in All Media"; "The Writings of Ray Bradbury" (the bibliography proper); "Writings About Ray Bradbury"; "Index to the Writings of Ray Bradbury."

The introductory sections, and particularly the photolog and chronology, provide extensive background material on Bradbury's life and career, the latter running thirty-one pages (through 1973). The bibliography proper is divided into the following sections: "Books and Pamphlets" (eighty out of 202 pages); "Bradbury's Magazine"; "Fiction"; "Articles and Miscellaneous Non-Fiction"; "Verse"; "Introductions"; "Reviews"; "Published Speeches"; "Published Plays"; "Stage Productions"; "Films"; "Television"; "Radio"; "Published Letters"; "Interviews"; "Anthology Appearances"; "Comic Book Appearances"; "Bradbury in Sound"; "Book Dedications"; "Bradbury Pseudonyms."

The books section is arranged in chronological order by year of publication, and includes data on all known U.S. and British first cloth and paperback editions, and all known reprints; foreign-language editions are listed only for *The Martian Chronicles*. For each first edition, Nolan provides: complete collations, contents, and bibliographical data, as well as known print runs. For subsequent editions, only place of publication, publisher, and book I.D. number are given, with occasional notes citing title or contents variations from the original. Included in this section are facsimiles of most of the title pages (and many of the covers) of the first editions.

Other sections of the book provide less detailed information. Bradbury's short stories, for example, are listed in chronological order by date of publication, with titles, magazines, and dates listed, but no paginations. Nolan uses two-letter codes (*e.g.,* "SS" = *S Is for Space*) to indicate the Bradbury book collections in which these stories have been included, noting briefly those stories anthologized elsewhere, with the title and year of the anthology (further details on these reprints are rather cumbersomely provided in the "Anthology Appearances" section, which is arranged in chronological order, with story title, anthology title, editor, place of publication, and publisher, but no paginations).

The media sections include works by Bradbury as well as adaptations of his work, with all known air dates, production companies, program titles, etc. The secondary bibliography is broken into two sections covering books and magazine/newspaper articles, both arranged in chronological order, giving: title, author, and bibliographical data, but no paginations. Nolan provides short annotations of the monographs only. The index covers Bradbury's titles and other persons and titles mentioned by page number. Data are complete through 1973.

This is one of the best-*looking* single-author bibliographies ever produced in the genre, with extraordinarily high production values, but it also includes a wealth of details on the writer and his works. One might have hoped for a few more specifics (such as paginations) on the magazine and anthology appearances of Bradbury's stories, but otherwise, Nolan's work stands as a monument to one of the most popular and enduring writers of the fantastic.

331. Nolan, William F. **"Ray Bradbury Index,"** in *Ray Bradbury Review,* edited by William F. Nolan. San Diego, CA, William F. Nolan, 1952. p. 46-63. index. (pbk.). Los Angeles, Graham Press, 1988. p. 46-63. index. A supplement (under the same title) appeared in *Shangri-LA* (Fall/Winter, 1953): 14-26.

This distant precursor to *The Ray Bradbury Companion* (see #330) is broken into eight sections: "Published Books," "Original Stories in U.S. Magazines," "Radio and Television Adaptations," "Articles," "Anthologies," "Reprints," "Scheduled Stories," "Index Addenda and Totals."

A typical book entry includes: title (all caps), publisher, year of publication, pagination, and contents. The short fiction section is arranged by magazine title, then chronologically by publication date. A typical entry includes: magazine title (all caps), story title, type (*e.g.,* "s.s." = short story), month of publication, year of publication. The "Anthologies" section is arranged in chronological order by date of publication of the anthology, giving: book title (all caps), editor, year of publication (but no publishing data), and story title(s). This 5" x 8" booklet is shot from generally clear typed copy and stapled through the spine.

The 1988 cloth edition is a facsimile of the original. Now outdated and subsumed into Nolan's later bibliography of Bradbury (see #330).

Marion Zimmer Bradley

Arbur, Rosemarie. **Leigh Brackett, Marion Zimmer Bradley, Anne McCaffrey: A Primary and Secondary Bibliography**. *See the entry of Leigh Brackett* (see #328).

332. Benson, Gordon Jr., and Phil Stephensen-Payne. **Marion Zimmer Bradley, Mistress of Magic: A Working Bibliography.** Albuquerque, NM & Leeds, West Yorkshire, England, Galactic Central Publications, 1991. 9, 51 p. (Galactic Central Bibliographies for the Avid Reader, Vol. 40). ISBN 1-871133-25-4 (pbk.).

The late Marion Zimmer Bradley has been widely acclaimed for her Darkover stories, which combine the best of science fiction with fantasy and psi elements. This checklist of her works is complete through early 1991.

Bradley's works are organized alphabetically by title within broad subject categories: "A. Stories"; "B. Fiction Books";" C. Series"; "D. Poems, Songs & Plays"; "E. Poem, Song & Play Volumes"; "F. Articles"; "G. Miscellaneous"; "H. Non-Fiction Books"; "I. Books Edited by Marion Zimmer Bradley"; "J. Media Presentations" [blank section]; "K. Articles on Marion Zimmer Bradley"; "L. Reviews"; "M. Books About Marion Zimmer Bradley"; "N. Phantom & Forthcoming Titles"; "O. Related Items by Other Authors"; "P. Textual Variations"; "Q. Chronological Index."

A typical short fiction entry includes: item number (A1-A65), title, type (*e.g.*, "NT" = novelette), magazine title and month and year of publication (*e.g.*, "9-54" = September 1954), or, for those stories first appearing in anthologies or collections: book title (all caps), editor, publisher, and year of publication, plus similar data for all known reprints. No paginations are given.

A typical book listing provides: item number, title (all caps), publisher, format (*e.g.*, "pb" = paperback), stock number, month and year of publication, pagination, price, and cover artist surname (in parentheses), with similar data on all known reprints and reissues in chronological order by issue date. The chronology groups Bradley's fiction year by year, then monthly by publication date (but the individual months are not actually listed). The book is shot from very legible word-processed copy, and is easy to read and use.

In comparing Benson/Stephensen-Payne's checklist with Arbur's bibliography (see #328), the former is a decade more current, while the latter includes many more secondary sources, all of them annotated. Arbur also provides paginations for original short story appearances, data that this guide lacks; but Arbur fails to list the paginations for Bradley's monographs that Benson/Stephensen-Payne includes.

Thus, serious scholars and libraries will need to retain both works; fans will be content to own this more recent inexpensive checklist.

Gary Brandner

333. Wood, Martine. **The Work of Gary Brandner: An Annotated Bibliography & Guide.** San Bernardino, CA, The Borgo Press, 1995. 112 p. index. (Bibliographies of Modern Authors, No. 23). LC 93-2881. ISBN 0-8095-0519-3; ISBN 0-8095-1519-9 (pbk.).

Contents: Preface: "The Hemingway of Horror," by Wood; Foreword: "Gary Brandner: 'Oh Yeah?'" by Richard Laymon; Introduction: "My Introduction to Gary Brandner," by Kim Greenblatt; "A Gary Brandner Chronology"; "A. Books"; "B. Short Fiction"; "C. Short Nonfiction"; "D. Other Media"; "E. Interviews"; "F. Secondary Sources"; "G. Speeches and Public Appearances"; "H. Miscellanea"; "Quoth the Critics"; Afterword: "Martine Wood Interviews Gary Brandner"; "Sweet Lusting Heart," by "Luranna Duchamp" [*i.e.,* Brandner]; Postscript: "How It Feels," by Brandner; "About Martine Wood"; "A Gary Brandner Cyclopedia"; "Index."

Brandner is best known as the author of *The Howling* series of werewolf books and films, and many other very popular works of modern horror fiction. This guide by his wife provides a thorough examination of the author's literary and screen work. The chronology records a year-by-year account of the author's professional and personal life in block paragraph, descending format. Each section of the bibliography is arranged in chronological order by publication date. There are 206 main entries, but the detailed reprint information, as well as secondary sources, easily double that figure.

The typical monograph entry includes: item number (section letter plus cardinal number; *e.g.*, A3, A4, etc.), title (bold italics), place of publication, publisher, date of publication, pagination, binding, ISBN (in parentheses), LC card number, marked price, series information (where applicable), and type of book (in brackets; *e.g.*, [novel, collection]). Entries often include plot summaries, either excerpted from reviews (as cited) or written by the author himself (averaging 200 words). There follows a list of subsequent reprints in all languages, with all bibliographical data in descending, chronological order by publication date, from the earliest to the latest, plus a list of secondary sources and reviews in alphabetical order by critic or magazine.

A typical short work entry includes: item number, title (boldfaced type, in quotation marks), magazine title, volume or issue number, date, pagination, and bibliographic data of all known reprints. "Quoth the Critics" includes twenty-five excerpts of reviews and other comments by leading critics on the author's work. "The Gary Brander Cyclopedia" lists characters from twenty-four novels cross-referenced with a two-letter code indicating the piece in which the character appears. The index references titles, editors, and periodical titles with their item numbers. The book is nicely designed and typeset, and remarkably thorough in its coverage.

The introductory material, the detailed interview by Wood, the snippet of romantic satire, and the afterword by Brander, all give the reader an excellent idea of the no-nonsense character and off-beat humor of this horror novelist. Indeed, one can safely say that no possible trivia about Gary Brandner has been left untouched; we discover, for example, that during the year 1936 the author's first pet dog, Friday, "loyally holds would-be rescuers at bay while little Gary is wedged into the 'v' of a tree trunk." Ahem.

Recommended for serious fans, academics, larger academic libraries, and any library collecting science fiction or dark fantasy.

Reginald Bretnor

334. Burgess, Scott Alan. **The Work of Reginald Bretnor: An Annotated Bibliography & Guide.** San Bernardino, CA, The Borgo Press, 1989. 122 p. index. (Bibliographies of Modern Authors, No. 8). LC 85-31405. ISBN 0-89370-387-7; ISBN 0-89370-487-3 (pbk.).

The late Reginald Bretnor is well-regarded as an American SF and mystery writer, military historian, and critic, although he is perhaps best known for his Feghoots, short SF pun-stories featuring that debonair space- and time-travelling adventurer, Ferdinand Feghoot.

Contents: Introduction: "The Ghosts We Share," by Judith Merril; "A Reginald Bretnor Chronology"; "A. Books"; "B. Short Fiction"; "C. Nonfiction"; "D. Feghoots"; "E. Verse"; "F. Editorial Credits"; "G. Unpublished Works"; "H. Honors and Awards"; "I. About the Author"; "J. Miscellanea"; "Quoth the Critics"; "Through Time and Space with Ferdinand Feghoot #118" (an original story by Bretnor); "On the Proper Perpetration of Feghoots" (an original essay); "Through Time and Space with Ferdinand Fedhoot #119" (an original story); Afterword: "Debts and Acknowledgments," by Bretnor (an original essay); "Index."

In each section, the author's works are arranged chronologically and numbered consecutively, chapter by chapter (*e.g.,* A1, A2, for Bretnor's first two books). A typical book entry includes: item number (boldfaced), title (boldfaced), byline (for pseudonymous works), place of publication, publisher, year of publication, pagination, format (paper or cloth), type of publication (*e.g.,* "novel"), and similar data for known reprint editions and translations. Also included are secondary sources and reviews, listed at the end of the entry alphabetically by critic or title (if no author is recorded), with full bibliographical data.

A typical shorter work entry records: item number (boldfaced), title (in quotes, boldfaced), magazine title (italicized), volume number, month and year of publication, pagination, and similar data for all known reprints, including foreign-language titles. All monographs are annotated, with complete contents listings and/or plot summaries; entries in other sections are selectively annotated as needed, providing information on award nominations, significance, etc.

Merril's introduction is a poignant look at the author's life and works. The chronology provides a year-by-year account in block paragraph format of the author's professional and personal life. Bretnor, whose original name was Alfred Reginald Kahn, was known for his reticence about the personal details of his life, some of which are revealed here for the first time.

"About the Author" includes all known secondary works. "Miscellanea" include information on pen names, book dedications, memberships, Library of Congress cataloging data, and similar data. The "Quoth the Critics" section reproduces selected excerpts of comments by the leading critics on the author's work. The index cites titles and item numbers only. Bretnor's afterword notes his debt to the literary community and to his two deceased wives, both of them writers themselves. The book is shot from very attractive word-processed copy, and the cloth edition bound to library standards.

Burgess worked very closely with Bretnor (then a neighbor in Medford, Oregon), using the author's personal collection of his own works to construct this very comprehensive bibliography. Coverage is complete through the Fall of 1989. Bretnor's humor is aptly demonstrated in the two Feghoots original to this volume, and his concluding essay (also an original work) reveals some of his personal and literary antecedents. The humanity of his fiction makes him a prime potential target for future scholars; this well-presented and -executed guide to his work will become a necessary starting point for all researchers.

Fredric Brown

335. Baird, Newton. **A Key to Fredric Brown's Wonderland: A Study and an Annotated Bibliographical Checklist.** Georgetown, CA, Talisman Literary Research, 1981. 63 p. index. LC 81-52422 (cloth and pbk.).

Baird's interesting, attractive, well-designed 8.5" x 11" tribute to this late, well-regarded SF and mystery writer and his work includes: "Preface" (about this book); "A Key to Fredric Brown's Wonderland" (biographical and critical introduction); "Chronology of

Fredric Brown"; "Fredric Brown: My Husband," by Elizabeth C. Brown; "The Early Career of Fredric Brown," by Harry Altshuler; "It's Only Everything," a short autobiographical piece by Brown himself; "An Annotated Bibliographical Checklist of Fredric Brown's Writing" (the bibliography proper); "Index."

The introductory sections provide interesting background material on the author and his work. The bibliography itself is broken into these subject sections: "A. Books"; "B. Foreign Anthologies by Brown Not Published in the U.S."; "C. Parts of Books by Brown"; "D. Short Stories"; "E. Poetry"; "F. Other Contributions to Periodicals"; "G. Radio Adaptations of Stories by Brown"; "H. Television Adaptations of Fiction by Brown"; "I. Film Adaptations of Fiction by Brown"; "J. Phonograph Recordings of Fiction by Brown"; "K. Parts of Books About Brown"; "L. Articles, Parts of Articles, and Published Letters About Brown"; "Appendix." Each of the sections other than K and L (which are organized alphabetically) are arranged in chronological order by date of publication.

A typical book entry includes: title (in italics), place of publication, publisher, year of publication, pagination, and similar data for all known reprints, including foreign editions (with foreign titles mentioned), plus a 50-100-word annotation or contents listing (for collections), and a list of contemporaneous reviews of the book. A typical story entry gives: title (in boldface), magazine (in italics), and date of publication, with no paginations. Reprint editions, including some foreign reprints, are also mentioned. For anthology listings, Baird provides editor, title, publisher, and date, but no paginations.

Section C includes the lone SF anthology edited by Brown (with Mack Reynolds), and an article penned for a writers' "how-to" book. The media listings include: title, program, broadcast dates, director, writer, cast, and other data. The secondary source listings seem complete through 1980. The appendix quotes several letters about Brown, includes a list of heroes, heroines, and anti-heroes in his fiction, tallies point-of-view methods in his novels, provides a list of his pseudonyms, and lists the stories he wrote in collaboration with Mack Reynolds. The index is comprehensive, correlating titles and authors to page numbers. The volume is nicely produced and printed, and illustrated with a score of author photos and magazine and book cover reproductions.

This is a superior tribute to this late writer's work, one that should have received wider circulation at the time (only a few hundred copies were produced). Since Brown ceased writing in the mid-1960s and died in 1972, Baird's guide is virtually complete save for the several dozen short collections of Brown's pulp mystery stories exhumed and reprinted by Dennis McMillan. A new edition or printing would definitely be warranted. Recommended.

John Brunner

336. Benson, Gordon Jr., and Phil Stephensen-Payne. **John Brunner, Shockwave Writer: A Working Bibliography.** 3rd rev. ed. Leeds, West Yorkshire, England & Albuquerque, NM, Galactic Central. 1989. 9, 79 p. index. (Galactic Central Bibliographies for the Avid Reader, Vol. 11). ISBN 0-912613-06-8 and ISBN 1-871133-18-1 (pbk.). Later (undated) 5" x 8" reprints were issued in two volumes, labelled "Part 1—Fiction" and "Part 2—Non-Fiction," with the pagination continued consecutively from one volume to the other.

The late British SF author's works are arranged by broad category, then alphabetically by title.

Contents: Author's full name, date and place of birth, lists of awards won by the author (in chronological order by year, with name of award and title of work being honored), and his pseudonyms. The bibliography proper includes: "A. Stories"; "B. Fiction Books"; "C. Series"; "D. Poems & Songs"; "E. Poem & Song Collections"; "F. Articles"; "G. Miscellaneous" (including letters, prefaces, notes, etc.); "H. Non-Fiction Books"; "I. Edited Books" [blank section]; "J. Media Presentations"; "K. Articles on John Brunner"; "L. Reviews" (on Brunner's books, alphabetically by title of the work being reviewed, then by magazine title in which the review appeared, giving month and year of publication, and reviewer's name); "M. Books about John Brunner"; "N. Phantom and Forthcoming Titles"; "O. Related Items by Other Authors" [blank section]; "P. Textual Variations" [blank section]; "Q. Chronological Index" (in order by year and month [but month is not recorded], giving titles only).

In each section materials are arranged in alphabetical order by title, items being numbered consecutively from the number one in each chapter (for example, A1, A2, A3, etc., for Brunner's stories). A typical shorter work entry provides: item number, title, category ("ss" = short story, "nt" = novelette, etc.), magazine or book in which the item appeared, month and year of publication (for magazines, in the form "6-74" for June 1974), or year of publication (for books), and a list of subsequent reprints (for which title, publisher, year, and editor's last name are given), but no paginations.

For book-length works, Benson and Stephensen-Payne give: item number, title, publication data (publisher, stock number, month and year of publication [if known, in the form "10-59" for October 1959], pagination, price), cover artist, and similar data for known reprints. There are numerous "See Also" references to Brunner's many alternate titles. Some 640 entries are included, though reprint information makes the overall total much greater. Of these, 123 are secondary sources, 66 being are book review categories (the actual number of reviews recorded, however, total well into the hundreds). There is no overall title index. The series lists include: books, articles, and short stories. The book is shot from very legible word-processed copy and stapled through the spine.

Brunner is a notoriously difficult writer on which to construct a bibliography, having produced numerous variant, rewritten, and upgraded editions of his works. Benson and Stephensen-Payne have done a great job of tracking these items through a maze of bibliographical chaos, although a general title index and short story paginations would be helpful in any future editions.

Recommended for all researchers of Brunner's work.

Algis Budrys

337. Drumm, Chris. **An Algis Budrys Checklist.** Polk City, IA, Chris Drumm Books, 1983. 16 p. index. ISBN 0-936055-03-0 (pbk.).

This 4.25" x 7" checklist of this noted American SF writer's works is organized into one chronological sequence, books and short stories being interfiled. Drumm provides a short outline of Budrys's life and a list of his pseudonyms before proceeding with the bibliography itself.

Entries are grouped by year and under each year by month; those titles for which a month is not known appear at the end of each year's listings; items are numbered in order from the number one (through 147). Books are underlined, short stories appear in quotation marks. A typical short fiction entry includes: item number, title, magazine, category code (*e.g.*, "s" = short story), month of publication (or book title, if an anthology, editor, publisher, year of publication). Subsequent reprintings are grouped under the original edition, with similar data provided. No paginations are included.

A typical book entry gives: item number, title, category code ("n" = novel), publisher, stock number, month of publication (if known), pagination, price, and format (*e.g.*, "pb" = paperback). There are numerous "See Also" references (by item number) to alternate or incorporated titles. Some major secondary materials are mentioned in passing in their appropriate years. The index correlates titles and item numbers only. Data are complete through 1982; a one-leaf corrigenda sheet was also inserted in some copies. The book is shot from typed copy; some text runs too close to the right margin to allow rebinding by libraries.

In a major omission, Drumm does not include references to Budrys's significant and long-running monthly review columns in *Galaxy Magazine* (see #78). Still, this is a useful, inexpensive starting point for research on Budrys's work. An expanded, updated version with better production values and more bibliographical details would certainly be justified.

Kenneth Bulmer

338. Robinson, Roger. **The Writings of Henry Kenneth Bulmer.** Harold Wood, Essex, England, Beccon 83. 1983. 51 p. index. (pbk). **The Writings of Henry Kenneth Bulmer.** Rev. and updated ed. Harold Wood, Essex, England, Beccon Publications, 1984. 51 p. index. ISBN 1-870824-00-8 (spiral-bound pbk.).

Robinson, author of *Who's Hugh?*, the standard pseudonym guide of the genre (see #50), here contributes a valuable checklist on the works of the prolific British writer Kenneth Bulmer.

Contents (both versions): "Editor's Notes"; "On the Pen-Name Trail," by Bulmer; "Ken Bulmer: An Appreciation," by John Clute; "Pseudonyms and Collaborations"; "Alphabetical Listing of Fiction"; "Alphabetical Listing of Non-Fiction"; "List of Edited Works and Miscellaneous Items"; "Career Schematic"; "Book Series"; "Story Series"; "Chronological Listing of All Work with Publication Details."

The latter is actually the main section of the book, listing all of Bulmer's works chronologically, year by year (novels and stories interfiled) and then month by month; items whose months of publication are unknown are grouped at the end of their respective years. Each item is numbered by year (*e.g.*, "54" = 1954) and then consecutively from one: ("54.1," "54.2," etc.).

A typical short fiction entry includes: item number, month, category code ("S" = story, "N" = novel, etc.), title (in quotes), byline (Bulmer frequently used pseudonyms, so every byline is listed verbatim), an indication whether Robinson has actually seen the item in question (" + " = seen), magazine, issue number, and other notes, but no paginations.

A typical book entry includes: item number, month (if known), category, title (all caps), byline, previous publication data, place of publication, publisher, year of publication, pagination, format ("pa" = paperback), price, with similar data for all subsequent editions and reprintings. Numerous "See" references scattered throughout the alphabetical lists and internally in the chronological list refer the user to item number.

The revised edition includes nearly two extra years of data, covering items published through October 1984 (the last item in the first edition is dated December 1982), plus corrections. Both books are shot from generally readable word-processed copy, although the typeface in the second edition is much larger and more readable. Clute's introduction provides a short but valuable guide to Bulmer's major works; Robinson's "Career Schematic" of Bulmer's work charts his literary output (some 135 books) year by year from 1952-84 (the last year of data for this bibliography).

Robinson clearly had help from Bulmer himself, particularly for his pulp publications, and his bibliography is exceedingly thorough and competent. Future editions should include short story paginations.

Edgar Rice Burroughs

339. Adkins, P. H. **Edgar Rice Burroughs Bibliography & Price Guide.** New Orleans, LA, P.D.A. Enterprises, 1974. ii, 25 p. (pbk.).

Adkins's brief checklist and price guide contains: "Editions" (information on Burroughs's publishers), "Format" (*i.e.,* how to use the bibliography), "Pricing" (how prices were determined), "Condition" (rating system used), and the bibliography proper.

Burroughs's books are listed in alphabetical order by title. A typical entry includes: publisher, year of publication, cloth color, pagination, numbers of plates or an indication that the book is illustrated, first edition indicators, and suggested prices for good, fine, etc., copies of the volumes. Similar data are provided for all subsequent editions, including paperbacks (paperback listings include stock number of first printing). Page 25 includes a series listing. This booklet is shot from dark, photoreduced (to about an eight-point level) typed copy; the pricing data are now wholly out-of-date.

Prefer Bergen's more current guide (see #340).

340. Bergen, James A., Jr. **A Reference and Price Guide to U.S. Books Written by Edgar Rice Burroughs.** Tualatin, OR, James A. Bergen, 1989. 46 p. LC 90-197302 (pbk.). **Price and Reference Guide to Books Written by Edgar Rice Burroughs.** [2nd ed.]. Beaverton, OR, The Golden Lion, 1991. vii, 214 p. (pbk.)

Bergen's guide is a synthesis of recent prices actually charged for Burroughsiana by U.S. book dealers, plus basic first (and later) edition identification data for Burroughs's books.

Contents (First Edition): "Birth Certificate" (of Edgar Rice Burroughs), "Reference and Price Guides Used," "General Information on Prices," "The Author" (on Bergen himself), "References," and "Cover Art," "Editions Published by ERB Publishers," "Big Little Books," "Biographical and Bibliographical Books on ERB," "Chronology of Tarzan Books," "Tarzan Editions" (book by book in chronological order by publication date), "Chronology of Mars Books," "Martian Editions" (book by book in chronological order by publication date), "Venus Editions" (ditto), "Earth's Core Editions" (ditto), "Unrelated Editions" (alpha-betically by title), "First Edition Paperbacks Published by Ballantine"; "First Edition Pa-perbacks Published by Ace," "First Edition Paperbacks from Other Publishers," "Authorized Professional Sequel(s)," "Authorized Amateur Sequels," "Unauthorized Amateur Sequels," "Burroughs Fanzines," "Active ERB Fanzines," "Death Certificate" (of ERB, reproduced from the original).

Contents (Second Edition): "General Information on Prices"; "Dust Jacket and Ref-erences"; "Publishers"; "Tarzan Series"; "Martian Series"; "Venus Series"; "Earth's Core Series"; "Non-Series Alphabetical Order"; "Paperbacks"; "Biographical, Bibliographical, and Related Publications"; "Big Little Books"; "Pulps and Fan Magazines"; "Active E. R. Burroughs Fanzines."

A typical entry includes a summary of edition points for each magazine appearance and monograph publication that has resale value, with the title of the piece being listed first in centered, boldfaced type. Among the data included are: magazine title (where appropriate, if the novel or story appeared first in magazine form), brief description, cover artist, date of publication, price range; and item number (the book versions of each particular title are numbered in order from the number one), publisher (boldfaced), year of publication, pagi-nation, number of plates, binding color, first edition statement (if any), cover and interior illustrations artist(s), price range (e.g., "$100 to $250"), and other bibliographical data of interest.

The Second Edition is greatly expanded, and also features reproductions of some dustjacket art, as well as interior illustrations by well-known Burroughs artists.

Although the book has no index, the contents page serves essentially the same func-tion, and the user will find navigating through this guide remarkably easy. The volume (second edition) is shot from very legible word-processed copy, and bound in 8.5 x 11" trade paperback form.

Bergen's guide, by synthesizing the actual sale prices of Burroughs's books from a variety of sources, provides a useful composite of current market values (through 1991) for fans and collectors alike. An updated edition would be most welcome, although the book is still valuable in providing comparative value ranges for a wide variety of highly-collectible Burroughsiana.

341. Cummings, David George. **An Edgar Rice Burroughs Checklist.** [s.l.], Savage Press in Association with Comma Publications, 1974. 31 p. (pbk.).

This poorly organized guide is divided into three sections covering Burroughs's hard-cover books, paperback books, and magazine serializations. The author's preface, "Hard-cover Notes," describes in very general terms, on a company-by-company basis, the main publishers of Burroughs's cloth fiction, with some information on the identification of first editions. A similar essay, "Papercover Notes," covers Ace, Ballantine, and the other Bur-roughs reprinters.

Most of the book consists of a general schematic listing Burroughs's novels by series, together with their publishers, in descending order by publication date (however, none of the dates are actually given), plus a blank chart for the collector to describe the condition of his or her own copy of that work. There is also a brief checklist of the magazine issues in which Burroughs stories appear, in alphabetical order by periodical title, giving story title, issue date, and year, but no other data. The final section of the checklist includes three pages of "story lines," one-sentence plot descriptions of each of the novels. The book is shot from barely legible typed copy.

Prefer Bergen (see #340).

342. Day, Bradford M. **Edgar Rice Burroughs Biblio: Materials Toward A Bibliography.** South Ozone Park, NY, Science-Fiction & Fantasy Publications, 1956. 28 p. (pbk.). **Edgar Rice Burroughs: A Bibliography.** [2nd ed.]. Woodhaven, NY, Science-Fiction & Fantasy Publications, 1962. 45 p. LC 62-3803 (pbk.).

Day's brief checklist of this American science fiction and fantasy author's fiction is organized similarly to his bibliographies on Haggard, Mundy, and Rohmer (see #234, #441, #460).

The book section is arranged alphabetically by title. A typical entry includes: title (all caps), categorization (*e.g.,* "stone age adventure," "Inner-Earth"), publisher, place of publication, year of publication, pagination, cover copy quote, brief mention of reprint editions (by publisher's name only) and/or magazine serialization (with magazine name and dates), plus binding color style.

The short fiction section is arranged in chronological order by date of publication and lists: title (caps), magazine title, year of publication, month of publication, list of reprints in Burroughs's books, but no paginations. There are also checklists of stories serialized in the *New York Evening World,* and books included in the Big Little Books series, plus a brief list of foreign-language editions (giving foreign-language titles only—no bibliographical data). The book is mimeographed (1956 edition) or offset (1962 version) from occasionally faint typed copy, and stapled through the spine.

The basic bibliography was slightly updated in Day's later compilation, *Bibliography of Adventure* (see #234). Prefer Heins (see #344).

343. Harwood, John. **The Literature of Burroughsiana: A Listing of Magazine Articles, Book Commentaries, News Items, and Related Items Concerning the Life and/or Works of Edgar Rice Burroughs.** Baton Rouge, LA, Camille Cazedessus, 1963. 105 p. (pbk.).

[Not seen.]

344. Heins, Henry Hardy. **A Golden Anniversary Bibliography of Edgar Rice Burroughs.** Albany, NY, [Henry Hardy Heins], 1962. 122 p. index. LC 63-336 (pbk.). **A Golden Anniversary Bibliography of Edgar Rice Burroughs.** Rev. ed. West Kingston, RI, Donald M. Grant, 1964. 418 p. index. LC 63-13900.

Both of these bibliographies quickly assumed the status of collectors' items upon publication, almost immediately going out-of-print, and now sell for hundreds of dollars each. The first edition was published by Heins himself as an 8.5" x 11" paperback (150 copies), mimeographed from typed copy on green paper and pinned through the spine. Its data (and format) were subsumed, updated, and expanded into the more elaborate 7" x 10" Grant hardcover, the first book released under that highly successful specialty imprint.

Contents (Grant edition): Part One: "1. Foreword to the Revised Edition"; "2. Editor's Preface"; "3. The Master Story-Teller: An Appreciation"; "4. How I Wrote the Tarzan

Books," by Burroughs; "5. Newspaper Appearances of Early ERB Stories"; "6. Chronology of the Stories," by Magazine Appearance; "7. Mr. Burroughs' Publishers"; "8. The A. C. McClurg & Co. Trade Lists"; "9. The Dedications of the Books"; "10. Entertainment Is Fiction's Purpose," by Burroughs; "11. The A. L. Burt and Grosset & Dunlap Catalogues"; "12. Explanation of the Format"; "13. The Bibliography"; "14. The First Book Reviews of *Tarzan*"; "15. Special Note on the Grosset & Dunlap Reprints"; "16. The Red-Cover Tarzanas"; "17. The McLeod Titles"; "18. Copyright Data on the 'Big Little Books'"; "19. The Tarzan Clans of America"; "20. One Other Tarzan Book—And a Tarzan Booklet"; "21. Tarzan Series—Recapitulation"; "22. The Tarzan Theme," by Burroughs; "23. The 1958 Fire at Edgar Rice Burroughs, Inc."; "24. Mars Series—Recapitulation"; "25. Pellucidar Series—Recapitulation"; "26. Venus Series—Recapitulation"; "27. Other Works of Fiction—Recapitulation"; "28. Who's Who in the Titles"; "29. Other Published Writings of Edgar Rice Burroughs"; "30. Burroughs' Literary Activities During World War II"; "31. Radio Scripts by Burroughs"; "32. Mr. Burroughs Describes His Publishing Methods," by Burroughs; "33. The Officers of Edgar Rice Burroughs, Inc."; "34. The Munsey Magazine Dates"; "35. Burroughs in Foreign Translation"; "36. The Literature of Burroughsiana"; "37. It Runs in the Family"; "38. The Burroughs Bibliophiles"; "39. Other Fan Magazines"; "40. Burroughs Bibliographies"; "41. Related Items"; "42. Index to the Burroughs Chapter Titles"; addenda to Part One: "43. New Book Releases"; "44. Unpublished Manuscripts"; "45. Some Unusual Titles"; "46. Pseudonyms"; "47. Poetry by Burroughs"; "48. The Burroughs Story That Was Based on a Poem"; "49. Out There Somewhere," by Burroughs; "50. The Notebook of Edgar Rice Burroughs"; "51. Supplements."

Part Two (in Grant edition only) includes "Illustrations and Advertisements" (161 pages of facsimile reproductions of book and magazine covers and of publisher catalog advertisements), plus an "Index" and an "Abbreviations List."

The bibliography proper is arranged by novel series (the Tarzan books, for example), then in chronological order by publication date. A typical entry includes: title (underlined caps), copyright registration number, dedication, one- to two-sentence annotation; cover and interior illustration artist; a list of every edition and printing known to exist, with specific printing dates, original book prices, paginations, collations, binding colors and textures, and any other information necessary to identify edition states and priorities. Similar data are provided for British editions. At the end of each series section Heins summarizes the data for the series in a table running sideways down the page, giving: page number where the book is covered in Heins's bibliography; series number; title code; title (with magazine title[s], if different); date of book publication, start of magazine serialization, and actual dates when written (as taken from Burroughs's master notebook); first edition publisher, magazine publisher, Burroughs's story number (derived from his notebook).

In addition to the bibliographical data, Heins provides a wealth of other sidenotes and details on Burroughs, his work and life, and related topics, as well as many quotations from the master's own work. The illustrations section, completely new to the Grant edition, provides very clear, black-and-white reproductions of Burroughs's book and magazine covers (some of the book covers are also reproduced in the main bibliography section), interior magazine illustrations, and catalogs featuring Burroughs novels. The index correlates titles, publishers, and other names to their appropriate page numbers. The abbreviations list includes the letter codes Heins arbitrarily assigned to each Burroughs work, which he uses throughout these books for "See" references.

At the time this book appeared, a renaissance of Burroughs's works had just begun, and while some of the soon-to-be-released "new" titles are mentioned by Heins, most, of course, are not, except in manuscript form (some of Burroughs's then-unpublished manuscripts were issued by Canaveral Press, Ace Books, and Ballantine Books between 1963-70). Thus, while Heins is remarkably complete through the early 1960s, he misses perhaps eight original Burroughs titles released after 1964. Also, few foreign-language titles are mentioned, as Heins himself admits. It should be noted that the interior production values of this early Don Grant book do not match the elaborate, beautifully designed collector's items of later years; most of the text is shot from typed copy, although the numerous illustrations are faithfully and carefully reproduced.

A Golden Anniversary Bibliography was out-of-print within two months of publication, and has curiously never been reprinted or updated since; most copies went to fans, and relatively few found their way into library collections. Copies of both versions now routinely sell for $400+ each. This means, unfortunately, that much of Heins's carefully gathered data are inaccessible to the average scholar. A new edition, updated and expanded (and reset), is badly needed.

Now partially superseded by Zeuschner (see #346).

345. McWhorter, George T. **Edgar Rice Burroughs Memorial Collection: A Catalog.** [United States], House of Greystoke, 1991. xxv, 190 p. LC 90-45383. ISBN 0-31327-696-X (lib. bdg.: alk. paper).

Contents: "Acknowledgments"; "Dedication"; "The Edgar Rice Burroughs Memorial Collection"; I: Prolegomena ("Bibliographic Overview"; "'How I Wrote the Tarzan Books'" by Edgar Rice Burroughs); II: A Catalog [alphabetical list of Burroughs's novels]; III: Burroughsiana ("Sample Items"; "A Basic Reference Library"; "Current Burroughs Fanzines").

This limited edition of 500 numbered copies is a catalog of the Edgar Rice Burroughs Memorial Collection at the University of Louisville in Kentucky, "the largest and most comprehensive of its kind in any institutional library in the world." It contains a bibliographic overview by McWhorter, an essay by Burroughs, "How I Wrote the Tarzan Books" (that originally appeared in the *Washington Post* for October 27, 1929), and the catalog proper.

The Bibliographic Overview has a simple chronological list of each of Burroughs's series, with title and date of the first hardback publication of each of the author's books, plus a short introductory essay to each series (especially the Tarzan books).

The catalog itself, the major part of the guide, includes seventy-three main entries, with a total of 1,523 citations. They are arranged alphabetically by title of the novel, giving both periodical and book editions of that title, in order by publication date, the editions for each novel being numbered from the number one in order of publication year. Both English-language and foreign editions are included. Each citation notes: title (bold caps), city of publication, publisher, date of publication (either by exact date or by whole year, in parentheses), and a two-sentence annotation. The latter describe the condition and binding of the item, plus the artist's name, the stock number, original price, and pagination.

The catalog is nicely illustrated with black-and-white reproductions of magazine and book covers, three per page, showing several dustjackets or front covers for a single title.

McWhorter's guide will prove of interest to collectors, dealers, large academic libraries, and scholars focusing on the study or acquisition of Burroughs materials, but it should be noted that it is not intended to be a comprehensive bibliography of the writer's publications.

346. Zeuschner, Robert B. **Edgar Rice Burroughs: The Exhaustive Scholar's and Collector's Descriptive Bibliography of American Periodical, Hardcover, Paperback, and Reprint Editions.** Jefferson, NC, McFarland & Co., 1996. xi, 287 p. index. LC 96-273311. ISBN 0-7864-0183-4.

Contents: "Acknowledgments"; "Foreword," by Philip José Farmer; "Preface: Edgar Rice Burroughs: His Life and His Work"; "'Edgar Rice Burroughs Tells All': An Autobiographical Sketch," by Edgar Rice Burroughs; "Part I: Bibliography of Books by Edgar Rice Burroughs (Alphabetically by Title)"; "Part II: Other Bibliographies (Unpublished and Miscellaneous Short Works by Burroughs [Alphabetically by Title]; Big Little Books Based on Burroughs' Plots or Characters [Chronologically by Publisher or Series]; Published and Unpublished Books Based on Burroughs' Plots or Characters [Alphabetically by Author]; A Selected Bibliography of Works About Burroughs [Alphabetically by Author]; A Selected Bibliography of Works About Burroughs Artists [Alphabetically by Artist]; A Selected List of Burroughs Fanzines [Alphabetically by Title])"; "Appendices: A. Values of Burroughs First Editions; B. Chronological List (by Publication Date) of Burroughs Hardback First Editions; C. Companies That Published Burroughs First Editions; D. The Two Most Popular Burroughs Reprint Publishers; E. McClurg Print Run Records; F. The House of Greystoke Publications; G. Chronological List (by Date of Authorship) of Burroughs' Stories"; "Index."

This well-organized volume is divided into two parts, consisting of a primary bibliography and "other bibliographies" (short lists of miscellaneous publications, usually based on Burroughs' work), for a total of 1,221 entries. The primary bibliography alphabetically arranges 846 entries under eighty book titles. The focus is on American publications; few foreign reprints are listed, unless they have been the source of confusion for collectors (usually British reprints).

A typical entry includes: cardinal reference number, title (articles in quotation marks; books in bold italics), publication information (articles include periodical name and date of publication; books list place and year of publication and publisher), plus an annotation. The annotations neither summarize nor review the books, but minutely describe the published condition of the monograph or magazine issue, including such details as color of binding, artwork, dust jacket, cover lettering, original (or marked) price, and pagination. First editions are recorded in even greater detail. Even the introductory sections of this volume are better than in many author bibliographies.

Burroughs's short autobiography runs twelve pages, and includes six black-and-white photographs of the writer as an adult. The appendices are made up of brief but useful lists. The only data that seem to be missing are the physical dimensions of these books, standard information in library cataloging. The index is complete, with main entries in bold type, including titles, protagonists, illustrators, periodicals, and more. Heins's bibliography (see #344) includes more peripheral details on Burroughs's early publications, and more illustrations of the books, but Zeuschner corrects several of the former's errors, and provides data on the numerous reprints (and several original editions) of Burroughs books released during the past four decades. The scholar will want to consult both works.

This well-constructed, easy-to-use volume is nicely typeset and bound to library standards, and would make a useful addition to any scholar's, collector's, or larger library's collection. Recommended.

James Branch Cabell

347. Brewer, Frances Joan. **James Branch Cabell: A Bibliography of His Writings, Biography, and Criticism.** Charlottesville, VA, University of Virginia Press, 1957. 206 p. index. LC a58-5622. Freeport, NY, Books for Libraries Press, 1971. 206 p. LC 76-157325. ISBN 0-8369-5785-7.

This book and Bruccoli's collection guide (see #348) were issued simultaneously as a matched set and cataloged as one record in the *National Union Catalogue.*

Cabell's books are listed by series name (*e.g., Biography of the Life of Manuel*), then by series number (or in chronological order by publication date, whichever is appropriate). A typical entry includes: item number, title (all caps), place of publication, publisher, year of publication, pagination, physical size (in centimeters), description of binding cloth, points, total printing number of the first edition, contents, previously published excerpts or serialization, a list of contemporaneous reviews, and mentions of subsequent American and first British editions. Revised editions are covered as part of the entries for the original versions.

Part II: "Contributions to Books and Magazines" arranges the author's shorter works by title. A typical entry provides: item number, title (small caps), magazine or book title (also in small caps), month and year of publication (periodical entries) or year of publication (book entries), but no paginations. Similar data are provided for all known reprints, including those in Cabell's own books. Cabell's works are numbered in order from 1 (the first book) through 276 (the last short piece).

The third section lists "Biography [and] Criticism" on Cabell, arranged alphabetically by author, but including data similar to that of Part II. Secondary works are numbered from A1-A257. There is also a "Chronology of Books and Contributions to Books and Magazines" (by Cabell), arranged in order by year and month, and giving: date, title, type (*e.g.,* "m" = magazine [contribution]), and item number. Supplementary material includes a complete checklist of book dedications by Cabell to other persons, cited to item number(s), and a separate listing of "Bibliographies of the Works of James Branch Cabell," in alphabetical order by author, with complete bibliographical data. The index references authors, titles, and subjects to item numbers. The book is nicely typeset and bound to library standards.

Cabell died in 1958, shortly after this volume was published, so Brewer's guide is essentially complete for primary works. One laments, however, the lack of paginations for shorter works; also, Brewer's organization of the books section is unnecessarily confusing, particularly towards the end of the chapter, where works appear almost jumbled together haphazardly (there is, in fact, some order here [miscellaneous materials are arranged chronologically by publication date], but it is not obvious to the casual user); some of these organizational problems are offset by the detailed index.

This bibliography supplements but does not supplant Brussel (see #350), who provides more detailed descriptions of individual monographs. Prefer Hall's more current guide (see #349).

348. Bruccoli, Matthew J. **Notes on the Cabell Collection at the University of Virginia.** Charlottesville, VA, University of Virginia Press, 1957. 178 p. index. (James Branch Cabell: A Bibliography, Part II). LC a58-5622 [*sic*].

Produced as a companion volume to Brewer's bibliography of Cabell's works (see #347), *Notes* is a straightforward description of the books, manuscripts, and letters by James Branch Cabell held in the Alderman Library of the University of Virginia at Charlottesville.

Books are listed in the same order as in Brewer's bibliography, with the same identification number, and indexed alphabetically by title in the table of contents. A typical entry includes: item number, title (all caps), plus detailed descriptions of any copies of the manuscripts, galley proofs, and printed copies available in the Alderman collections.

The second section, "Notes on Special Material," mentions secondary sources about Cabell and describes the Cabell manuscript collection (detailed physical descriptions of these materials are given in the first part under their respective book titles; however, a few of the manuscripts covered here are shorter works not mentioned in Section One). Also included are "Cabell's Notes on His Printed Books" (in two parts, by Cabell).

Section Three, "Notes on the Cabell Letters," provides a detailed rendering of the Cabell correspondence (to and from) held by the University of Virginia, listed chronologically by date of letter, with a one- to two-sentence description of the contents. The very complete index correlates authors and titles with page numbers. The book is attractively typeset and bound to library standards.

Since the Alderman Library remains the largest single repository of Cabelliana, all scholars seriously interested in studying this influential writer's life and works will want access to this volume. This catalog is also interesting to the student of bibliography as being one of the early works of Matthew J. Bruccoli, who later developed so many major literary reference guides for Gale Research Co. and other companies, including his own firm, Bruccoli Clark Layman Inc.

For larger academic library collections.

349. Hall, James N. **James Branch Cabell: A Complete Bibliography, with a Supplement of Current Values of Cabell Books,** by Nelson Bond. New York, Revisionist Press, 1974. xi, 245 p. index. LC 74-23476. (The James Branch Cabell Series). ISBN 0-87700-208-8. Limited to 200 copies.

Hall's bibliography was prompted by a resurgence of popular interest in Cabell's work during the early 1970s, when Lin Carter reprinted a number of JBC's novels in his Ballantine Books Adult Fantasy paperback series. His book is arranged similarly to Brewer's guide (see #347).

Part 1 separates Cabell's monographs into their respective series (for example, "The Nightmare Has Triplets"), then lists them in volume order. A typical entry includes: item number, book title (all caps), ID code (mnemonic, consisting of two or three capital letters [*e.g.,* "BL" = *Beyond Life*], followed by a hyphen and a printing ID number [*e.g.,* "BL-A2" = the second printing of the first edition of *Beyond Life*]), publisher, printing statement reproduced from the copyright page of the book, pagination, and a complete description of binding cloth and other edition and printing points. Every known printing of the book, including translations into foreign languages (with foreign-language titles), is listed. The books are numbered consecutively from 1-43.

Part 2 lists shorter works by Cabell broken into four sections: "Original Material by Cabell," "Magazine Reprints in Books," "Reprint Material in Books," and "Selected Contributions to Periodicals." Materials in each section are organized chronologically by publication date. A typical anthology entry includes: item number, book title (all caps), editor's name, place of publication, publisher (variously; not all entries include publisher's name), year of publication, and the specific item contributed by Cabell, with exact paginations and literary antecedents (previous appearances elsewhere) for all known printings of the books. Section IV, "Selected Contributions to Periodicals," includes only those items never reprinted in book form. Materials in each of these four subchapters are numbered from the number one, prefixed by the letters A, B, C, or D (corresponding to Sections I, II, III, and IV).

Part 3, "Cabelliana—About Cabell," is divided into five sections: "Books About Cabell and His Works," "Bibliographies," "Cabellian Art," "Cabellian Magazines," and "Miscellaneous," arranged chronologically by publication date and providing information comparable to the earlier chapters. Items in these sections are also numbered consecutively from one, prefixed by the letters E, F, G, H, and K, respectively.

"Appendix A: Where to Find It" correlates specific title and printing codes for Cabell's books with location symbols of libraries that have copies in their collections, followed by detailed one- to two-paragraph descriptions of academic libraries with major book and/or manuscript holdings of Cabelliana. This is a very useful tool for the scholar, although the heavy use of abbreviations, many of which require constant reference to the front of the book, is unnecessary, often irritating, and even counterproductive.

Bond's afterword on valuing Cabell's books as collectors' items uses a similar code system, but at least inserts book titles throughout the text; this section would have been better arranged alphabetically by title. The very detailed index correlates authors and titles to page numbers. The book is shot from sometimes light typed copy, and bound to library standards.

James Branch Cabell: A Complete Bibliography is not quite the definitive work that Hall obviously intended it to be. It lacks the very careful title page descriptions provided by Brussel (see #350), omits some publisher data in Part 2, and uses too many abbreviations in subsidiary sections. One might also have wished for better production values internally. However, these are minor points: Hall does record in authoritative detail every printing of every book that Cabell ever produced and the vast majority of all other works of interest, including secondary materials, and his bibliography will prove quite sufficient for the vast majority of scholars.

350. Johnson, Merle. **A Bibliographic Check-List of the Works of James Branch Cabell, 1904-1921.** New York, F. Shay, 1921. 27 p. (pbk.). Holt, Guy. **A Bibliography of the Writings of James Branch Cabell.** Philadelphia, The Centaur Book Shop, 1924. 73 p. (The Centaur Bibliographies, No. 3). LC 24-9701. Brussel, I. R. **A Bibliography of the Writings of James Branch Cabell: A Revised Bibliography.** [2nd ed.]. Philadelphia, The Centaur

Book Shop, 1932. 126 p. (The Centaur Bibliographies, No. 11). LC 32-14209. London: Folcroft Press, 1970. 126 p. All three books were issued in very limited editions averaging fewer than 500 copies each.

Cabell, whose name is accented on the first syllable, attained early notoriety with publication of his satirical fantasy *Jurgen* in 1919. His fame generated great fan interest beginning in the 1920s, resulting in these three bibliographies, each pyramided on its predecessor(s).

Both Holt and Brussel (Holt loosely based his work on Johnson's brief guide) list Cabell's books chronologically by publication date. A typical entry includes: item number (the books are numbered in order from the number one), title (all caps), exact publication date (to the day), an exact description of the title-page copy, complete collation, detailed description of the binding cloth and inscription(s), variations in later printings, original magazine publication date (where applicable), plus a brief description of the first British edition (if any).

Many of Cabell's books were heavily revised or rewritten, sometimes under new titles; these are treated as variants of the original edition in Brussel (Holt records them as separate entries), and listed after them under separate entries, numbered, for example, "1a," "1b," etc., for each significant alteration in text. Twenty-nine books are listed in Holt, and thirty-one numbered entries (through *Some of Us,* published on Oct. 10, 1930) are described in Brussel, with a thirty-second title, the eighteen-volume Storisende Edition of *The Works of James Branch Cabell,* capping the sixty-eight-page main section.

Other chapters record Cabell's "Contributions to Books," "Contributions to Periodicals," "Studies and Reviews of James Branch Cabell" (broken into two sections: "I. In Books and Pamphlets," and "II. In Periodicals"). An appendix in Brussel reproduces a one-page letter by Cabell denying authorship for the literary hoax *Poor Jack,* plus a reproduction of that play's title page and facsimiles of two pages from a pair of pirated editions of Cabell's works.

Cabell's "Contributions to Books" are also listed in chronological order by publication date of the book, giving: book title (small caps), author, place of publication (but no publisher), binding style, pagination, title of Cabell's work (in italics), and specific pagination of Cabell's contribution to the work. The "Contributions to Periodicals" chapter is much less helpful, being organized in chronological order in Holt, but in alphabetical order by magazine title in Brussel, then chronologically by publication date.

Both of these books list (in different order) story or article title, magazine title, and month and year of publication (but no paginations). Secondary sources are recorded in chronological order by publication date, with complete bibliographical data except for publisher names (a serious omission). There are no indices. Both bibliographies are beautifully typeset and designed, with a (different) photograph of Cabell pasted opposite each title page, and an original introduction by the master himself commenting on the "first edition" phenomenon.

Brussel's careful bibliographic description of Cabell's most popular novels (particularly the title-page copy) has not been totally superseded by any of the more recent works described above (see #347, #348, #349), and his bibliography retains sufficient value for scholars and researchers that it should be retained by all academic libraries. Hall's guide (see #349) remains, however, the most definitive modern bibliography of Cabell's work.

Ramsey Campbell

351. Ashley, Mike. **Fantasy Readers Guide to Ramsey Campbell.** Wallsend, Tyne and Wear, England, Cosmos Literary Agency, 1980. 62 p. (pbk.).

The second book of this two-volume bibliography series (see also Ashley's guide to the publications of John Spencer & Co. Ltd. [see #294]) focuses on well-known British horror writer Ramsey Campbell.

Contents: "Unshackled from Shadow," by Ashley (background material on Campbell's life); "As Far As I Can Recall . . . ," by Campbell (autobiographical reminiscences); "Where It All Began," by George MacDonald (an extract from *The Princess and the Goblin,* which inspired the author); "Before the Storm," by Campbell (an original short story); "Ramsey Campbell: An Appreciation," by T. E. D. Klein (a survey of Campbell's early writings); "Ramsey Campbell: Premier Stylist," by Jack Sullivan (a survey of the author's most recent work); "Ramsey Campbell: An Editor's Dream," by Hugh Lamb (profile and tribute); "The Gap," by Campbell (story); "The File on Ramsey Campbell," by Ashley (the bibliography itself).

"The File" is divided into three parts: Sections A and B, in flanking columns, give the author's fiction in order of writing, and in order of publication by year, title, and item number, entries in one column being cross-referenced to those in the other. Section C, the primary bibliography, is also subdivided into three parts: "1. Short Fiction"; "2. Books"; "3. Non-Fiction"; in each section Campbell's work is arranged alphabetically by title.

A typical short fiction entry includes: title (in caps), year of composition, magazine or anthology title, date of publication, editor and publisher (for anthologies), and similar data on known reprints. No paginations are listed. A typical book entry lists: title (in caps), date of composition, publisher, year of publication, reprints (with similar data), and complete contents (for collections). The non-fiction section includes a miscellany of items (letters, editorials, reviews). Some foreign-language editions are listed in all sections. Ashley also appends a note on Campbell's series, and Campbell himself adds a list of bowdlerized editions (with corrections!). The book is shot from generally legible typed copy and stapled through the spine.

Campbell has been very active in recent decades, making this checklist, which covers material published as late as 1980, now woefully out-of-date. A newly revised edition with paginations, better production values, and expanded details about each novel and story would certainly be warranted.

Orson Scott Card

352. Collings, Michael R. **Card Catalogue: The Science Fiction and Fantasy of Orson Scott Card.** Eugene, OR, Hypatia Press, 1987. 15 p. (pbk.).

This brief guide to the works of an established SF star was prepared as a booklet to be inserted in the signed, limited edition of Card's 1987 collection, *Cardography.* The *Catalogue* focuses on his fiction and nonfiction in fantastic literature, omitting his many religious publications but including articles, poems, and plays, and also his technical essays on computer science.

Contents: "I. Novels"; "II. Collections"; "III. Short Fiction"; "III [*sic*]. Poetry"; "IV. Edited Volumes"; "V. Non-Fiction," in two sections, "Books" and "Articles."

In each section and sub-section, Card's writings are arranged in alphabetical order by title; complete bibliographical data are provided for the short fiction and short nonfiction, but only place of publication, publisher, and year for book-length works. No reprint editions are listed for monographs. Award winners and nominees are mentioned, but few other annotations are provided. While this is a useful beginning checklist of Card's science fiction publications through 1987, it can in no way masquerade as a full-fledged bibliography. Collings is reportedly preparing a second, much reorganized, and expanded bibliography of Card's works.

A. Bertram Chandler

353. Benson, Gordon, Jr. **A. Bertram Chandler, Master Navigator of Space: A Working Bibliography.** 2nd rev. ed. Albuquerque, NM and Leeds, West Yorkshire, England, Galactic Central Publications, 1989. v, 43 p. (Galactic Central Bibliographies for the Avid Reader, Vol. 3). ISBN 0-912613-27-0 (pbk.).

Benson's checklist of this late Australian SF author's works is arranged by broad subject category, then alphabetically by title.

Contents: Author's full name, date and place of birth and date of death, his pseudonyms, and his awards (listed in chronological order by date of award, giving year, award name, and title honored); "A. The Stories"; "B. Phantom Stories"; "C. The Books"; "D. Series and Related Stories" (arranged in proper reading order); "E. Book Reviews" (of Chandler's books, listed in alphabetical order by book title, then by magazine title, giving book title [boldfaced caps], magazine title [all caps], month and year of publication, reviewer); "F. Articles"; "G. Articles and Miscellaneous about A. B. Chandler"; "H. Chronological Listing of Stories and Books (First Appearances)"; "Reference Sources" (*i.e.,* works Benson has consulted, divided into three parts: primary, secondary, tertiary).

In each section materials are arranged in alphabetical order by title, each item being numbered consecutively from the number one in each section. For shorter works, Benson gives: item number, title, category ("ss" = short story, "nt" = novelette, etc.), magazine or book in which the item appeared, month and year of publication (for magazines in the form "1-47" for January 1947), or year of publication (for books), and a list of subsequent reprints (for which title, publisher, year, and editor's last name are given), but no paginations.

For book-length works, Benson provides: item number, title (bold caps), publisher, stock number, month and year of publication (if known, in the form "10-59" for October 1959), pagination, price, cover artist, and similar data for all known reprint editions. The book lacks an index. There are 289 entries overall, though reprint information makes the total somewhat greater, with twenty secondary sources noted. As is typical of the older style in this series, the typeface is somewhat faint and unattractive, and the navigation through the volume is made more difficult than necessary without some clear visual markers to divide each section. Benson's book is shot from word-processed copy, and stapled through the spine.

Chandler died in 1984, making this volume essentially complete save for future reprintings of existing material. Benson reported at the time of publication that a definitive bibliography of Chandler was in preparation by Keith Curtis, but that book has never appeared. In the meantime, Benson's book will provide a good starting place for scholars and fans interested in researching Chandler's many space operas.

Elizabeth Chater

354. Mallett, Daryl F., and Annette Y. Mallett. **The Work of Elizabeth Chater: An Annotated Bibliography & Guide.** San Bernardino, CA, The Borgo Press, 1994. 80 p. index. (Bibliographies of Modern Authors, No. 27). LC 93-333. ISBN 0-89370-390-7 (cloth); ISBN 0-89370-490-3 (pbk.).

This is a primary and secondary bibliography to the works of Canadian-born romance-mystery-science fiction novelist and short story writer, Elizabeth Chater (better known in the SF world under her pen name, Lee Chaytor).

Contents: "Dedication"; "Acknowledgments"; "Foreword: 'Milady Elizabeth,'" by the Malletts; "Introduction: 'Bette,'" by Greg Bear; "An Elizabeth Chater Chronology"; "About the Format"; "A. Books"; "B. Short Fiction"; "C. Poetry"; "D. Nonfiction"; "E. Secondary Sources"; "F. Honors and Awards"; "G. Miscellanea"; "Five Works by Elizabeth Chater" (includes: "Just Another Wooden House . . . ," "The Week the Traveling Salesman Came to Town," "Optomendacity," "Epilogue: 'You Want to Talk About Endings . . . ?'," and "All the World's a Screen . . . "); "Index"; "About the Authors."

The chronology provides a year-by-year account of the author's professional and personal life in block paragraph format. Each section of the bibliography is arranged in chronological order by publication date. There are seventy-four main entries, but reprints and secondary sources bring the total slightly higher.

The typical monograph entry includes: item number (section letter plus cardinal number; *e.g.,* A3, A4, etc.), title (bold italics), place of publication, publisher, date of publication, pagination, binding, ISBN number (in parentheses), series information (where applicable), cover illustrator (where known), and type of book (in brackets; *e.g.,* [romance novel]). In addition, the entries include (where applicable) the marked prices on each book, the LC number, the author's dedication, a plot summary (averaging 100 words), a list of subsequent reprints in all languages, with all bibliographical data in descending order by publication date, and all known secondary sources and reviews, in alphabetical order by critic or magazine.

A typical short work entry includes: item number, title (bold type in quotation marks), pseudonym (when appropriate), magazine title, volume and/or issue number, date, pagination, illustrator (where known), and bibliographic data on all known reprints.

The five, short original works by Chater, along with the appreciation by the Malletts and the introduction by well-known SF writer Bear, give a good snapshot of Chater's style and personality. The index correlates titles, editors, illustrators, and periodical titles with item numbers. The character index indicates the novel in which the character appears, cross-referenced to item numbers in the bibliography.

The volume is nicely designed and typeset and bound to library standards. This very thorough compilation was obviously a labor of love by the authors. Recommended for large academic libraries.

C. J. Cherryh

355. Stephensen-Payne, Phil. **C. J. Cherryh, Citizen of the Universe: A Working Bibliography.** Leeds, West Yorkshire, England, Galactic Central Publications, 1992. 9, 36 p. (Bibliographies for the Avid Reader, Vol. 43). ISBN 1-871133-33-5 (pbk.).

American writer C. J. Cherryh has attained major status among science fiction writers in the past several decades.

Contents: author's name, date and place of birth, lists of awards won by the author (in chronological order, giving year, name of award, and title of work being honored); "A. Stories"; "B. Fiction Books"; "C. Series"; "D. Poems, Songs & Plays" [blank section]; "E. Poem, Song & Play Volumes" [blank section]; "F. Articles"; "G. Miscellaneous" (including introductions and afterwords by C. J. Cherryh, letters, and interviews with the author); "H. Non-Fiction Books" [blank section]; "I. Books Edited by C. J. Cherryh"; "J. Media Presentations"; "K. Articles on C. J. Cherryh"; "L. Reviews" (of Cherryh's books, alphabetically by title of the book being reviewed, then by magazine title, giving date and reviewer); "M. Books About C. J. Cherryh" [blank section]; "N. Phantom & Forthcoming Titles"; "O. Related Items by Other Authors"; "P. Textual Variations" [blank section]; "Q. Chronological Index" (by year and title).

The introduction is almost identical throughout the series, and clearly explains the many different sections of the bibliography. Stephensen-Payne's basic checklist is arranged by subject category, then alphabetically by title; materials are numbered consecutively from one in each chapter (for example, B1, B2, B3, etc., for the author's books). Shorter work entries include: item number, title, category ("ss" = short story, "nt" = novelette, etc.), magazine or book in which the item appeared, month and year of publication (for magazines in the form "2-88" for February 1988) or year of publication (for books), a list of subsequent reprints (for which title, publisher, year, and editor's last name are given), but no paginations.

For book-length works, Stephensen-Payne provides: item number, title, contents (if a collection, by item number), publication data (publisher, stock number, month and year of publication [if known, in the form "10-59" for October 1959], pagination, price), cover artist, plus similar data for known reprints. There is no title index.

Some 248 entries are included, though reprint information makes the total somewhat greater. Of these, seventy-one are secondary sources, thirty of them consisting of book review categories (the actual number of book reviews shown runs into the hundreds). A few foreign language publications are also noted. The book is shot from legible word-processed copy, and stapled through the spine. An index would have been helpful, as would the addition of paginations for the short fiction sections.

Stephensen-Payne's guide will be of interest both to researchers of Cherryh's fiction, and to her many fans.

John Christopher

356. Stephensen-Payne, Phil. **Christopher Samuel Youd, Master of All Genres: A Working Bibliography.** 2nd rev. ed. Leeds, West Yorkshire, England, Galactic Central Publications, 1990. 9, 33 p. (Galactic Central Bibliographies for the Avid Reader, Vol. 25). ISBN 1-871133-17-3 (pbk.).

This new checklist on Sam Youd, a British SF and children's book writer who writes as John Christopher, is organized by subject category, then alphabetically by title.

Contents: Author's name, date and place of birth, pseudonyms, and awards (listed chronologically, a typical entry giving year of award, award name, and title of work being honored); "A. Stories"; "B. Fiction Books"; "C. Series"; "D. Poems and Songs (All as by C. S. Youd)"; "E. Poem and Song Collections" [blank section]; "F. Articles"; "G. Miscellaneous (as by C. S. Youd Unless Otherwise Indicated)" (includes letters, interviews, etc.); "H. Non-Fiction Books" [blank section]; "I. Books Edited by C. S. Youd" [blank section]; "J. Media Presentations"; "K. Articles on C. S. Youd"; "L. Reviews" (of the author's works, listed alphabetically by title of his books, then by magazine title, giving item number, book title [all caps], magazine title, month and year of publication, reviewer's name); "M. Books about C. S. Youd"; "N. 'Phantom' Titles"; "O. Related Items by Other Authors" [blank section]; "P. Textual Variations"; "Q. Chronological Index" (arranged by year, books and other works being interfiled).

In each section Youd's works are arranged in alphabetical order by title, items being numbered consecutively from the number one in each section, prefixed by the identifying letter for that section. A typical book entry includes: item number, title (all caps), pseudonym (where appropriate), contents for collections keyed to item number, and publication data (publisher, stock number [and occasionally, Library of Congress or British Library Catalog Card Number], month and year of publication [if known, in the form "7-56" for July 1956], pagination, price, cover artist), and similar data on known reprint editions.

Each shorter work entry includes: item number, title, category (*e.g.,* "NT" = novelette), magazine or book in which the item appeared, month and year of publication (for magazines, in the form "12-54" for December 1954); or year of publication (for books), plus a list of subsequent reprints (for which title, editor, publisher, and year are given), but no paginations. There is no index. 207 entries are included, although reprint information makes the total somewhat greater. Forty-seven of these consist of secondary sources, of which twenty-two are book review categories (there are also numerous individual book reviews recorded under these categories). The book is shot from very clear word-processed copy, and stapled through the spine.

An index and magazine paginations would be worthy additions to a future edition, but given the fact that each section is arranged alphabetically, these are relatively minor quibbles. As the only current guide to this enigmatic author's work, Stephensen-Payne's bibliography is a basic resource for both student and scholar.

Arthur C. Clarke

357. Samuelson, David N. **Arthur C. Clarke: A Primary and Secondary Bibliography.** Boston, G. K. Hall, 1984. xv, 256 p. index. (Masters of Science Fiction and Fantasy). LC 84-10762. ISBN 0-8161-8111-X.

Samuelson, author of *Visions of Tomorrow* and other works, here provides a complete and well-organized bibliography of this classic British SF writer.

Contents: "Preface" (discussing the book's arrangement); "Introduction" (a very brief biographical guide to the author); "Part A: Fiction"; "Part B: Miscellaneous Media"; "Part C: Nonfiction"; "Part D: Biography, Bibliography, Criticism" (on Clarke); "Part E: Book

Reviews" (of Clarke's books). Four appendices list: "Manuscripts in Collections"; "Resources—People, Institutions, Publications"; "Honors and Awards"; "Radio and Television Broadcasts." Three indexes at the end of the book cover "Works by Arthur C. Clarke," "Works About Arthur C. Clarke," and "Register of Names."

Each section except E is arranged chronologically from the earliest published material to the latest, and numbered consecutively by section and item (*e.g.,* A1, A2, etc., for Clarke's fiction). Books and shorter works are interfiled by year; reprints of books and stories are grouped as subsidiary entries under their first edition or appearance, chronologically by year of reprint. Reprint editions of short stories include: editor of anthology, title, place of publication, publisher, year, format (*e.g.,* "paper"), but no paginations.

Each book entry gives: item number, title (underlined), place of publication, publisher, format ("paper"), but no paginations. Each shorter work entry provides: item number, title (in quotes), magazine, volume number, issue number, date, pagination; or, for those published originally in books: book title, book editor, place of publication, publisher, format, and specific pagination. Story collections include complete contents listings, plus the years in which the original stories were published, and references to the item numbers of the stories included. Some entries, particularly in Sections B-C, include bibliographical or descriptive notes but no other annotations; however, all of the entries in Part D are extensively annotated.

"Part B: Miscellaneous Media" includes a few audio tapes and recordings by Clarke, plus some video tapes; for each of these, Samuelson lists: item number, title, city of publication, publisher or production company, stock number, and description of item (*e.g.,* "32-minute audio cassette").

"Part C: Nonfiction" includes all the author's nonfiction publications (some 700 items), arranged chronologically by publishing date, undated items being grouped at the very end of the section.

Parts D and E include secondary sources: D covers all known articles and books about Clarke, arranged chronologically, with author, title, bibliographical data, and summaries; most "Who's Who" publications are omitted after the author's first appearance in them. Part E indexes all known book reviews of Clarke's books, alphabetically by title and then chronologically under each work, providing: magazine title (keyed to a letter code referenced to the abbreviations list at the front of this section), volume number and pagination, year and month of publication, and reviewer's name (when known). The indices correlate titles, names, and item numbers only. Coverage is complete through 1980. The book is reproduced from typed copy, and bound to academic library standards.

Samuelson's book was the last of the fourteen volumes published in this series, and while it lacks the critical apparatus of, say, Pringle on Ballard (see #313) and is several decades out-of-date, it remains a thoroughly good piece of work, an essential starting point for all future scholarship. Very little is missed here, with over 1,000 items in the primary bibliography alone. This is a worthy swan song of a notable set of bibliographies; kudos to both Samuelson and to series editor, Lloyd W. Currey.

Hal Clement

358. Benson, Gordon, Jr. **Hal Clement, Scientist with a Mission: A Working Bibliography.** Albuquerque, NM, Galactic Central Publications, 1989. v, 20 p. (Galactic Central Bibliographies for the Avid Reader, Vol. 4). ISBN 0-912613-08-4 (pbk.).

Benson's checklist of this American "hard" science fiction writer's works is arranged by general subject category, then alphabetically by title.

Contents: Author's full name, date and place of birth, and his awards and honors arranged chronologically by date, giving year of award, award name, and title being honored; "A. The Stories"; "B. The Science Fiction Books"; "C. Non-Fiction Books and Edited Anthologies"; "D. Articles and Miscellaneous"; "E. Biography, Criticism, and Survey"; "F. Book Reviews" (listed alphabetically by title of the work being reviewed, then by review, giving book title [bold caps], magazine title, month and year of publication, reviewer).

In each part Clement's works are arranged in alphabetical order by title, items being numbered consecutively from the number one in each section. A typical shorter work entry includes: item number, title, category ("ss" = short story, "nt" = novelette, etc.), magazine or book in which the item appeared, month and year of publication (for magazines in the form "9-68" for September 1968) or year of publication (for books), plus a list of subsequent reprints (for which title, publisher, year, and editor's last name are given), but no paginations.

Book-length works cite: item number, title (bold caps), publisher, stock number, month and year of publication (if known, in the form "6-87" for June 1987), pagination, price, cover artist, and similar material on all known reprint editions. There is no index. The book is shot from very clear word-processed copy, and stapled through the side. This volume has not been completely reworked into the new series format.

Clement (in real life, science teacher Harry Stubbs) has never been a prolific writer, but his works have long been championed as exemplars of the "hard" science fiction school. This very comprehensive checklist should stay reasonably current for quite some time. The addition of an index and magazine paginations should be considered for future editions.

359. Drumm, Chris. **A Hal Clement Checklist.** Polk City, IA, Chris Drumm Books, 1983. 8 p. ISBN 0-936055-00-6 (pbk.).

This small-sized (4.25" x 7") checklist of Clement's works is arranged in one straight chronological sequence. Entries are grouped by year and under each year by month; materials are numbered in order from the number one (through fifty-three). Books are underlined, short stories surrounded by quotation marks.

A typical short fiction entry includes: item number, title, magazine, category code (*e.g.,* "s" = short story), and month of publication (or book title, if an anthology, plus editor's name, publisher, and year of publication). Subsequent reprintings are grouped under the original edition with similar data provided. No paginations are included.

A typical book entry includes: item number, title, category code ("n" = novel), publisher, stock number, month of publication (if known), pagination, price, and format (*e.g.,* "pb" = paperback). "See" references and contents listings are keyed to item number. There are no paginations, secondary materials, or index. Data are complete through 1980; a one-leaf addendum is also available. The book is shot from typed copy, and stapled through the spine; the text runs too close to the right-hand margin to allow rebinding by libraries.

Prefer Benson's more current and complete bibliography, which also includes secondary sources (see #358).

Stanton A. Coblentz

360. Utter, Virgil, and Gordon Benson, Jr. **Stanton Arthur Coblentz, Poet and Science Fictioneer: A Working Bibliography.** Leeds, West Yorkshire, England, Galactic Central Publications, 1999. ix, 57 p. (Bibliographies for the Avid Reader, Vol. 51). ISBN 1-871133-54-8 (pbk.).

The late American pulp writer and poet Stanton A. Coblentz is best known for having edited and published the traditional poetry magazine *Wings* for almost three decades.

Contents: "Introduction"; "Awards and Pseudonyms"; "A. Prose Fiction"; "B. Prose Fiction Books"; "C. Series"; "D. Poetry & Drama"; "E. Poetry & Drama Books"; "F. Articles"; "G. Miscellaneous"; "H. Non-Fiction Books"; "I. Publications Edited by Stanton A. Coblentz"; "J. Other Media" [blank section]; "K. Articles on Stanton A. Coblentz"; "L. Reviews"; "M. Books About Stanton A. Coblentz" [blank section]; "N. Phantom and Forthcoming Titles"; "O. Related Items by Other Authors" [blank section]; "P. Textual Variations and Other Notes" [blank section]; "Q. Chronological Index of Prose Fiction."

The introduction is almost identical throughout the series, and clearly explains the many different sections of the bibliography. Utter and Benson's basic checklist is arranged by subject category, then alphabetically by title; materials are numbered consecutively from one in each chapter (for example, B1, B2, B3, etc., for the author's books). Shorter work entries include: item number, title, category ("ss" = short story, "nt" = novelette, etc.), magazine or book in which the item appeared, month and year of publication (for magazines in the form "2-68" for February 1968) or year of publication (for books), a list of subsequent reprints (for which title, publisher, year, and editor's last name are given), but no paginations.

For book-length works, Utter and Benson provide: item number, title, contents (if a collection, by item number), publication data (publisher, stock number, month and year of publication [if known, in the form "10-59" for October 1959], pagination, price), cover artist, plus similar data for known reprints. There is no title index.

Approximately 1,519 entries are featured, although reprint information makes the overall total much greater. There are also fifty-seven secondary sources, twenty-one of which are book review categories; many more reviews are themselves listed under the latter sections. Some foreign language publications are included, but are admitted to be incomplete. An index would have been helpful, as would the addition of paginations for the short fiction sections.

This series is beginning to examine several of the classic, early writers of SF and fantasy, which is much to be applauded. However, the information on Coblentz's non-SF work, which constituted the bulk of his writing effort, is somewhat sketchy, with minimal bibliographical details provided on his huge output of poetry (although the authors include in the bibliography some twenty pages listing Coblentz's poetry titles, they admit that they lack information on the original publication data of these works, and that the list itself is likely very incomplete). Still, this is a laudable effort that should be acquired by all major research libraries.

Glen Cook

361. Schlobin, Roger C., and Glen Cook. **A Glen Cook Bibliography.** [S.l., s.n.], 1983. [4] p. (pbk.).

This brief checklist by a well-known critic and bibliographer covers Cook's works through 1983, broken into discrete subject sections: "Novels," "Series Novels," "Short Fiction," "Nonfiction," "Secondary Studies & Interviews," and "Addenda." Each section is listed in chronological order or in series order for those novels and short stories that are parts of series (the majority of his works).

A typical book entry provides: title (in italics), city of publication, publisher, year of publication, but no paginations. A typical short story listing includes: title, magazine, date of publication, pagination. A few reprints are noted, several in foreign languages.

Scanty and outdated.

Ray Cummings

362. Utter, Virgil, and Gordon Benson, Jr. **Raymond King Cummings, Explorer of the Infinite: A Working Bibliography.** Leeds, West Yorkshire, England, Galactic Central Publications, 1999. ix, 85 p. (Bibliographies for the Avid Reader, Vol. 50). ISBN 1-871133-53-X (pbk.).

Ray Cummings was an American pulp SF writer active mainly during the 1920s-'40s.

Contents: "Introduction"; "Awards and Pseudonyms"; "A. Prose Fiction"; "B. Prose Fiction Books"; "C. Series"; "D. Poetry & Drama" [blank section]; "E. Poetry & Drama Books" [blank section]; "F. Articles"; "G. Miscellaneous"; "H. Non-Fiction Books" [blank section]; "I. Publications Edited by Raymond King Cummings" [blank section]; "J. Other Media"; "K. Articles on Raymond King Cummings"; "L. Reviews"; "M. Books about Raymond King Cummings"; "N. Phantom and Forthcoming Titles"; "O. Related Items by Other Authors" [blank section]; "P. Textual Variations and Other Notes"; "Q. Chronological Index of Prose Fiction."

The introduction is almost identical throughout the series, and clearly explains the many different sections of the bibliography. Utter and Benson's basic checklist is arranged by subject category, then alphabetically by title; materials are numbered consecutively from one in each chapter (for example, B1, B2, B3, etc., for the author's books). Shorter work entries include: item number, title, category ("ss" = short story, "nt" = novelette, etc.), magazine or book in which the item appeared, month and year of publication (for magazines in the form "2-68" for February 1968) or year of publication (for books), a list of subsequent reprints (for which title, publisher, year, and editor's last name are given), but no paginations.

For book-length works, Utter and Benson provide: item number, title, contents (if a collection, by item number), publication data (publisher, stock number, month and year of publication [if known, in the form "10-59" for October 1959], pagination, price), cover artist, plus similar data for known reprints. There is no title index. 742 entries are included, although reprint information makes the overall total much greater. Some sixty-seven secondary sources are also mentioned, fourteen of which are book review categories; numerous book reviews are mentioned in these latter sections. A few foreign language publications are listed. An index would have been helpful, as would the addition of paginations for the short fiction sections.

Cummings, a well-known SF pulp writer of the 1920s and '30s, is little-known today, and while Utter and Benson have produced a laudable effort, only larger library collections need acquire this guide.

Jack Dann

363. Elliot, Jeffrey M. **The Work of Jack Dann: An Annotated Bibliography & Guide.** San Bernardino, CA, The Borgo Press, 1990. 128 p. index. (Bibliographies of Modern Authors, No. 16). LC 88-34679. ISBN 0-8095-0506-1; ISBN 0-8095-1506-7 (pbk.).

Elliot's comprehensive guide to the works of this well-known SF writer, editor, and critic includes: "Introduction"; "A Jack Dann Chronology"; "A. Books"; "B. Short Fiction"; "C. Poetry"; "D. Nonfiction"; "E. Editorial Credits"; "F. About the Author"; "H. Public Appearances"; "G. Honors and Awards"; "I. Miscellanea"; "Quoth the Critics"; "Index."

In each section, the author's works are arranged chronologically and numbered consecutively from one, chapter by chapter (*e.g.,* C1, C2, C3, etc.). A typical book entry includes: item number, title (in boldface), byline, place of publication, publisher, month and year of publication, pagination, format (*e.g.,* "cloth"), type of publication (*e.g.,* "anthology), and similar data on reprint editions, translations, republications, etc. The books are fully annotated, with complete contents listings and/or plot summaries and other pertinent data, and include a list of "Secondary Sources and Reviews" filed alphabetically by main entry after the annotation; entries from other sections are selectively annotated as needed.

A typical short fiction entry includes: item number, title (in boldface quotes), magazine or anthology title, volume number, month and year of publication, and pagination, or, for stories published in anthologies, title, editor, place of publication, publisher, year of publication, format (*e.g.,* "paper"), pagination; similar data are included on all known reprints, including foreign editions.

Elliot's interesting "Introduction" provides basic background material on Dann's life and works. The chronology provides a year-by-year account of the author's professional and personal life, in descending, block paragraph format. "About the Author" includes all known secondary works arranged chronologically. The "Miscellanea" section includes information on pen names, book dedications, memberships, Library of Congress cataloging data, career highlights, and similar data. "Quoth the Critics" includes selected excerpts of reviews and other comments by leading critics on the author's work. The index correlates titles and item numbers only.

Dann had been a Nebula Award finalist eleven times before he finally won the award; his work is held in great esteem by his fellow writers. Much of the material in this book derives from his own records; coverage is complete through the summer of 1989. Complete and well-organized, this guide will be an essential beginning point for all future reseachers into the author's work.

L. Sprague de Camp

364. Laughlin, Charlotte, and Daniel J. H. Levack, with annotations by Loay H. Hall. **De Camp: An L. Sprague de Camp Bibliography.** San Francisco, CA & Columbia, PA, Underwood/Miller, 1983. 328 p. index. ISBN 0-934438-71-4; ISBN 0-934438-70-6 (pbk.).

A comprehensive, illustrated bibliography of L. Sprague de Camp's writings through mid-1982, Laughlin and Levack's work includes: "Introduction," "Annotator's Introduction," and the bibliography proper, "The Works of L. Sprague de Camp."

The major part of the book is broken into appropriate chapters: "Books," "Edited Books," "Non-Book Appearances," "Translations," "Miscellaneous." Completing the guide are a series of indices: "Fiction," "Verse," "Book Reviews," "Radio Scripts," "Other Non-Fiction"; a chronological list of "Pseudonym Appearances," "Connected Works—Continuing Characters—Series, Genres, Collaborations"; "Magazine Checklist"; "A Catherine Crook de Camp Checklist"; an alphabetical general index; "Acknowledgments."

Works are listed alphabetically by title, and numbered consecutively from the number one in each section, with over 800 items included. A typical book entry includes: item number, title (bold caps), series (when appropriate) or category (*e.g.,* "Non-Fiction"), contents (if a collection) or one-paragraph annotation in boldfaced type (if a novel), publisher, stock number (for paperback editions), place of publication (with original price for paperback versions), year of publication, cover artist (for cloth editions), edition points, and paginations. Reprints are listed in chronological order by publication date; many foreign editions are included, but few of the reprint editions provide page counts. An asterisk after a specific edition indicates it has been viewed by the compilers.

A typical shorter work entry includes: item number, title (in bold quotes), estimated wordage, type or other notes (*e.g.,* "verse"), annotation (in bold type), magazine or book title, date, volume number, issue number, and occasionally the starting page number (only of the story). All subsequent reprint editions (including some foreign-language materials with foreign-language titles) are listed with similar data. Anthology appearances note: title, editor, publisher, place of publication, price, year of publication, but no paginations.

The indices by type include titles only, greatly reducing their effectiveness: one must refer to the bibliography proper or to the alphabetical index to locate specific items. The latter is itself organized in quirky fashion, giving titles and abbreviated references to each chapter only (*e.g.,* "B" = Books, "NBA" = Non-Book Appearances, etc.). Although the various sections of the bibliography are alphabetically arranged, there are no running heads to key the user into each chapter without having to page through the book. One wonders why the compilers bothered to number each item when those numbers were not used as quick reference points for the indices.

The book is beautifully typeset and designed, and is illustrated throughout with reproductions of book and magazine covers featuring de Camp material. The addition of a mini-bibliography covering the writings of de Camp's wife (an increasingly frequent collaborator in the author's later years) is a nice touch.

However, while one can applaud the enormous labor that went into this volume, and the immense amount of material thus made available to the scholar, one must also lament the missed opportunities that would have made this one of the finest bibliographies in the field. The lack of adequate indexing, the absence of complete paginations in the shorter works section, the utter absence of secondary materials, inevitably mean that somewhere, somehow, someone must do this work over again. And that's a real shame.

Samuel R. Delany

365. Peplow, Michael W., and Robert S. Bravard. **Samuel R. Delany: A Primary and Secondary Bibliography, 1962-1979.** Boston, G. K. Hall, 1980. xiv, 178 p. index. (Masters of Science Fiction and Fantasy). LC 80-20108. ISBN 0-8161-8054-7.

Delany, the first African-American writer to attain "major-author" status in the field, has attracted a great deal of critical attention in the last decade; a detailed guide to his fiction was long overdue.

Contents: "Preface" (discussing the book's arrangement); "Magazine and Journal Abbreviations," "Introduction" (a sixty-one-page biographical and critical guide to the author's life and work); "Part A: Fiction"; "Part B: Miscellaneous Media"; "Part C: Nonfiction"; "Part D: Critical Studies." Three appendices list: "Part E. Juvenilia"; "Part F. Unpublished Speeches and Nonfiction"; "Part G. Collections of Delanyana." Two indices cover "Works by Delany" and "Works about Delany."

Each section is arranged chronologically, from the earliest published material to the latest, and numbered consecutively by section from one (*e.g.,* C1, C2, etc., for nonfiction). Books and shorter works are interfiled by year; reprints of books and stories are grouped as subsidiary entries under their first edition or appearance, chronologically by year of reprint (some foreign editions are listed, but none of the translated foreign-language titles); reprint editions of short stories include: editor of anthology, title, place of publication, publisher, year, format (*e.g.,* "paper"), but no paginations.

Each book entry gives: item number, title (underlined), place of publication, publisher, format ("paper"), but no pagination. Each shorter work entry provides: item number, title (in quotations), magazine, volume number, date, pagination, or, for those published originally in books, book title, book editor, place of publication, publisher, format, pagination. Story collections include complete contents listings, plus the years in which the original stories were published. Some entries, particularly in Sections B-C, include bibliographical or descriptive notes, but no other annotations; all of the entries in Part D are extensively annotated.

"Part B: Miscellaneous Media" includes screenplays, teleplays, interviews, recordings, poetry, and other material by the author that does not specifically fit the other three categories; for Delany, there are only a handful of comic book adaptations and amateur films recorded.

"Part C: Nonfiction" includes all the author's nonfiction publications arranged chronologically. Part D includes known secondary sources, including some book reviews arranged chronologically, with author, title, bibliographical data, and extensive annotations; most "Who's Who" publications are omitted, but the authors still note some 274 items, making this a major resource.

Parts E-G only cover twenty-eight items, but do include mentions of two Delany manuscript collections of great potential value to researchers. The indices reference titles, names, and item numbers only. The introduction by Peplow and Bravard provides extensive and little-known background material on the author's youth in New York City, and is valuable in its own right. Coverage of Delany's books is complete through 1979. The volume is reproduced from typed copy and bound to library standards.

This thoroughly professional effort is now several decades outdated, lacking all of Delany's numerous and significant publications from the 1980s and '90s (particularly the Nevèrÿon Cycle), and should be revised into a second edition. In the interim, this is a sound piece of work in its own right, one of interest both to SF scholars and those researching modern African-American literature. Stephens's checklist (see #366) can serve as a supplement.

366. Stephens, Christopher P. **A Checklist of Samuel R. Delany.** Hastings-on-Hudson, NY, Ultramarine Publishing Co., 1991. 18 p. index. ISBN 0-89366-184-8 (pbk.).

The major African-American writer in the SF field, Delany has written noteworthy criticism on fantastic literature in addition to his acclaimed novels and short stories.

This new checklist is arranged chronologically by publication date and divided into two sections: "Part One: Books Written by Samuel R. Delany"; "Part Two: Books Edited by Samuel R. Delany." Materials in each section are numbered from the number one (A1-A31 and AA1-AA5). A typical entry provides: year (as a floating head), item number, title (underlined), pseudonym, publisher, stock or ISBN number, pagination, format (*e.g.,* "cloth with dust wrapper"), cover illustrator, price, and similar data for all known reprints (which are numbered, for example, A10a, A10b, A10c, etc., in descending order by publication date). The chapbook is shot from legible typed copy and bound with staples in stiff paper covers. The index correlates titles with years of publication only.

Stephens's chapbook in no way supplants Peplow and Bravard's more extensive work (see #365), which, although now outdated, includes extensive secondary source listings, among others; however, until a newer version of that work is available, this brief guide can serve as a supplement.

August Derleth

367. Derleth, August. **August Derleth: Thirty Years of Writing, 1926-1956.** Sauk City, WI, Arkham House, 1956. 24 p. (pbk.). **100 Books by August Derleth.** [2nd ed.]. Sauk City, WI, Arkham House, 1962. 121 p. LC 63-4567 (pbk.).

These two versions of a developing personal bibliography were issued by Derleth through Arkham House, the publishing company he founded in 1939 to disseminate the writings of H. P. Lovecraft.

Contents (*100 Books*): "Foreword," by Donald Wandrei; "Biographical" (background); "Bibliographical" (a list of magazines in which Derleth's work has appeared); "A Checklist of Published Books"; "Awaiting Publication"; "Work in Progress"; "Summary" (lists of Derleth's books by series and/or subject); "Recordings" (including contents, price, and bibliographical data); "Compilations" (single-author collections edited or introduced by Derleth, with no details other than titles and dates); "Anthologies/Textbooks" (in which Derleth stories have appeared with some bibliographical details but no paginations); "Publications" (issued by Arkham House—a skeletal listing); "Films" (adaptations of Derleth stories for motion pictures and television, with no production details); "Lectures" (topics only; no actual list of appearances); "Appraisals" (short critical excerpts on Derleth books);

"From the Reviews" (more of the same); "Self-Appraisal" (Derleth's own list of his best books).

The bulk of this bibliography (sixty-one pages) is a chronological checklist of Derleth's books, numbered in order from one (strangely, original paperback editions are listed but not numbered). A typical entry includes: item number, title (all caps), byline, publisher, place of publication, year of publication, contents (for collections and anthologies), cover artist, format (*e.g.,* "paperbound"), pagination, and price; similar data are provided for all known English-language reprint editions. The remaining sections are much less bibliographically detailed, providing barebones listings of peripheral items. The book lacks a title index, making access relatively difficult for the uninitiated.

Derleth died in 1971, having produced a number of additional works not included herein; however, in the absence of any definitive bibliography, *100 Books by August Derleth* must still be regarded as an essential starting point for all future scholarship. Compare with Wilson's more recent guide (see #368), which can serve as a supplement.

368. Wilson, Alison M. **August Derleth: A Bibliography.** Metuchen, NJ & London, The Scarecrow Press, 1983. xxvi, 229 p. index. (The Scarecrow Author Bibliographies, No. 59). LC 82-24020. ISBN 0-8108-1606-7.

Derleth, a well-known American writer, editor, and publisher, founded Arkham House in 1939 to disseminate the works of H. P. Lovecraft and others.

Contents: "Preface"; "Introduction" (on Derleth's life and career); "Chronology" (two pages, year by year, in block paragraph format); "I. The Fantasy World: Mystery, Science Fiction, and Horror." "A. Short Stories"; "B. Anthologies of Derleth's Own Work"; "C. Posthumous Collaborations with H. P. Lovecraft"; "D. Collaborations with Mark Schorer"; "E. Collaborations: Books"; "F. The Pontine Canon"; "G. Judge Peck"; "H. Miscellaneous Mysteries"; "I. Books Edited by Derleth"; "J. Derleth Introductions."

"II. Sac Prairie and the Real World." "A. Sac Prairie Saga: Short Stories"; "B. Collections"; "C. Novels"; "D. Miscellaneous Prose"; "E. Steve-Sim Juvenile Mysteries"; "F. Wisconsin Saga"; "G. Other Juvenile Literature"; "H. Poetry"; "I. Nonfiction: Books"; "J. Nonfiction: Articles, Reviews, Introductions"; "K. Representative Published Letters." "Index."

In each section Derleth's works are listed alphabetically by title; entries are in the book is numbered in consecutive order from 1-736. A typical shorter work entry includes: item number, title (in quotes), one- to two-sentence annotation, magazine, volume and issue number, date, pagination, pseudonym (where appropriate), plus a list of reprints in chronological order by date of publication. Reprints in anthologies include: title (underlined), editor, place of publication, publisher, year of publication, pagination of story; reprints in collections of Derleth's own works include: title (in caps), pagination.

A typical book entry gives: item number, title (underlined), place of publication, publisher, year of publication, contents (if a collection or anthology) or three- to four-sentence annotation (if a novel), brief list of reviews (two or three maximum), list of reprint editions (with similar data), but no paginations. Omitted are Derleth's poems (an estimated 1,000 items), most book reviews written by Derleth (estimated in the hundreds), plays (none of which were ever published), and all secondary sources save for a handful of book reviews.

The index references titles and item numbers only. The book is shot from legible typed copy.

The lack of book paginations and secondary resources hamper what could have become a standard guide to the author's work. The annotations are valuable in their own right, but the book is so broken into subject-oriented sections that it is very difficult for the scholar to get an overview of Derleth's writings. The alphabetical arrangement in such circumstances can become almost irritating: one can get a chronological list of the Solar Pons stories or Judge Peck novels (surely a desirable datum!), for example, only by laboriously comparing several different sections and rearranging the data oneself. This is hardly the definitive work it should have been, and can only be considered a beginning point for the study of this prolific author's life and career.

Prefer Derleth's own, better-organized guide to his work (see #367) for materials published prior to 1962.

Philip K. Dick

369. Levack, Daniel J. H., with annotations by Steven Owen Godersky. **PKD: A Philip K. Dick Bibliography.** Columbia, PA, San Francisco, CA, Underwood/Miller, 1981. 158 p. **PKD: A Philip K. Dick Bibliography.** Rev. ed. Westport, CT, Meckler Corp., 1988. 156 p. (Meckler's Bibliographies on Science Fiction, Fantasy, and Horror, No. 1). LC 88-15597. ISBN 0-88736-096-3.

Levack, who also compiled similarly formatted bibliographies on L. Sprague de Camp, Jack Vance, and Roger Zelazny for Underwood/Miller, as well as a more recent book on Frank Herbert (see #364, #496, #519, #393), prepared this book just prior to Dick's sudden death in early 1982 (the book covers through mid-1981).

Contents: "Introduction," "Annotator's Note," "Books," "Stories," "Unpublished Manuscripts," "Other Media," "Pseudonyms," "Collaborations," "Connected Stories and Continuing Characters," "Non-Fiction Index," "Verse Index," "Chronological Order of Publication of Philip K. Dick's Work," "Magazine Checklist," "Works About Philip K. Dick," "Afterword" by Philip K. Dick, "Acknowledgements."

Works are listed alphabetically by title and numbered consecutively from one, section by section, with over 200 items included. A typical book entry includes: item number, title (bold caps), series note (when appropriate) or category (*e.g.,* "Non-Fiction"), contents (if a collection) or one-paragraph annotation (if a novel) in boldfaced type, publisher, stock number (for paperback editions), place of publication (inconsistently; the price, in parentheses, is included for paperback versions), year of publication, edition points, but no paginations. Reprints are listed in chronological order by publication date; many foreign editions are also included. An asterisk after a specific edition indicates that it has been viewed by Levack.

A typical shorter work entry includes: item number, title (in bold quotes), estimated wordage, type or other notes (*e.g.,* "verse"), one- to two-sentence annotation (in bold type), magazine or book title, date, volume number, issue number, but no paginations. All subsequent reprint editions (including some foreign-language materials with foreign-language titles) are listed with similar data. Anthology appearances include title, editor, publisher, stock number, price, year of publication, format (*e.g.,* "paper"), but no paginations. The magazine checklist is an alphabetical listing of those publications in which Dick stories appeared, keyed to issue date and to item number in the short fiction section. There is also a master chronological checklist of Dick's work, year by year, with all publications interfiled, but no index.

The book is beautifully typeset and designed, bound to library standards, and illustrated throughout with reproductions of book and magazine covers featuring Dick's fiction. The brief (two-page) secondary bibliography only lists seventeen items and is lamentably incomplete and out-of-date. *Caveat emptor!:* the Meckler edition contains only very minor revisions at the end of the book and does not update the basic bibliography beyond 1981, specifically failing to include the many Dick novels published posthumously during the 1980s; it is in no sense the revised edition it claims to be.

The lack of an index, the total absence of paginations, and the miserly list of secondary materials inevitably make this work much less than it should have been. Prefer Stephensen-Payne and Benson's more current and detailed checklist (see #371) for bibliographical data.

370. Stephens, Christopher P. **A Checklist of Philip K. Dick.** Hastings-on-Hudson, NY, Ultramarine Publishing Co., 1990. 46 p. index. ISBN 0-89366-174-0 (pbk.).

Stephens's brief bibliography of this late American writer's fiction is broken into two parts: "Books by Philip K. Dick" and "Stories by Philip K. Dick."

Materials are arranged in chronological order by publication date in each section and are numbered, respectively, from 1-55 and 1-130. A typical book entry provides: publication year (as a floating head), item number, title (underlined), pseudonym, publisher, stock or ISBN number, pagination, format (*e.g.,* "cloth with dust wrapper"), cover illustrator, price, and similar data for all known reprints (which are numbered, for example, A30a, A30b, A30c, etc., in descending order by publication date).

Short fiction entries typically include: title (in quotes), magazine title (underlined), month and year of publication, pagination (provided on a very haphazard basis), and a list of all known reprints, with brief bibliographical data (but no paginations). The book is shot from legible typed copy and bound with staples in stiff paper covers. The index correlates titles with years of publication only.

With the exception of a few story paginations for original magazine publications, there is nothing here that can't be found in Stephensen-Payne and Benson's more extensive (and current) guide (see #371).

371. Stephensen-Payne, Phil, and Gordon Benson, Jr. **Philip Kindred Dick, Metaphysical Conjurer: A Working Bibliography.** 4th rev. ed. Leeds, West Yorkshire, England, Galactic Central Publications, 1995. 9, 154 p. in 2 v. (Galactic Central Bibliographies for the Avid Reader, Vol. 18). ISBN 1-871133-42-4 (pbk.). Issued in two volumes, labelled "Part 1: Primary Bibliography" and "Part 2: Secondary Bibliography," the paginations being continued throughout both books.

In an irony that the author would surely have appreciated, Philip K. Dick attained his greatest commercial success by dying in February of 1982, at which point all of the unpublished book manuscripts that he had been unable to sell in the preceding decades suddenly became valuable commodities. His literary reputation has continued to inflate with each passing year, and this update of a standard bibliography is most welcome.

This comprehensive checklist of Dicks writings is arranged by category, then alphabetically by title. The introduction gives: author's name, date and place of birth and death, list of awards won by the author (in chronological order, giving year, name of award, and title of work being honored), and his pseudonyms.

Contents: "A. Stories"; "B. Fiction Books"; "C. Series"; "D. Poems, Songs, Plays and TV/Film Scripts"; "E. Poem, Song, Play & TV/Film Script Volumes" [blank section]; "F. Articles"; "G. Miscellaneous" (including introductions and afterwords by Philip K. Dick, letters, and interviews with the author); "H. Non-Fiction Books"; "I. Edited Books" [blank section]; "J. Other Media"; "K. Articles on Philip K. Dick"; "L. Reviews" (of Dick's books, alphabetically by title of the book being reviewed, then by magazine title, giving date and reviewer); "M. Books About Philip K. Dick"; "N. Phantom and Forthcoming Titles"; "O. Related Items by Other Authors"; "P. Textual Variations"; "Q. Chronological Listing of Fiction" (with date of submission, when known, and date of publication by year, then arranged by date and month of issue).

For shorter works, the authors provide: item number, title, category ("ss" = short story, "nt" = novelette, etc.), magazine or book in which the item appeared, month and year of publication (for magazines in the form "1-59" for January 1959) or year of publication (for books), plus similar data for all known reprints (for which title, publisher, year, and editor's last name are given), but no paginations.

For book-length works, the authors list: item number, title, contents listing of collections (keyed to item number), publication data (publisher, stock number, month and year of publication [if known, in the form "10-59" for October 1959], pagination, price), and cover artist, plus similar data for all known reprint editions. There is no general index. Secondary monographs are listed in alphabetical order by main entry (usually critic's name), including similar data as above. There are 1,052 entries, though reprint information makes the overall entry total much greater; 661 of these consist of secondary sources, 78 of which are book review categories, the reviews themselves numbering in the hundreds. Data are complete through the end of 1994. The checklist is shot from very legible word-processed copy, and bound through the spine with staples.

Although Levack's book (see #369) is somewhat more complete and more explicit for the period covered (and certainly more physically attractive), Stephensen-Payne and Benson's guide is more current, and covers far more secondary sources than Levack. Future editions would benefit from an overall index and the addition of short fiction paginations. Serious researchers should have access to both books; SF fans and most libraries will find Stephensen-Payne/Benson's bibliography quite sufficient.

Gordon R. Dickson

372. Benson, Gordon, Jr., and Phil Stephensen-Payne. **Gordon Rupert Dickson, First Dorsai: A Working Bibliography.** 4th rev. ed. Albuquerque, NM, & Leeds, West Yorkshire, England, Galactic Central Publications, 1990. 9, 62 p. (Galactic Central Bibliographies for the Avid Reader, Vol. 2). ISBN 0-912613-10-6 and 1-871133-19-X (pbk.).

The late American SF writer Dickson is best known for his Dorsai Series. This checklist of his works is arranged by category, then alphabetically by title.

Contents: Author's full name, date and place of birth, and his awards and honors; "A. Stories"; "B. Fiction Books"; "C. Series"; "D. Poems, Songs & Plays"; "E. Poem & Song Collections" [blank section]; "F. Articles"; "G. Miscellaneous"; "H. Non-Fiction Books" [blank section]; "I. Books Edited by Gordon R. Dickson"; "J. Media Presentations"; "K. Articles on Gordon R. Dickson"; "L. Reviews" [of Dickson's books]; "M. Books About Gordon R. Dickson"; "N. Phantom & Forthcoming Titles"; "O. Related Items by Other Authors"; "P. Textual Variations" [blank section]; "Q. Chronological Index."

In each section the material is arranged in alphabetical order by title, items being numbered consecutively from the number one in each section. For shorter works, the authors provide: item number, title, category ("ss" = short story, "nt" = novelette, etc.), magazine or book in which the item appeared, month and year of publication (for magazines in the form "9-60" for September 1960), or year of publication (for books), a list of subsequent reprints (for which title, publisher, year, and editor's last name are given), but no paginations.

For book-length works, the authors give: item number, title, publication data (publisher, stock number, month and year of publication [if known, in the form "10-59" for October 1959], pagination, price), cover artist, plus similar data for known reprints. There is no overall index. The book includes some 419 entries, though reprint information makes the grand total much greater; of these, 113 are secondary sources, 53 of which are book review categories; hundreds of book review citations are listed. The book is shot from readable word-processed copy and stapled through the spine. Materials are included through the end of 1989.

Although this basic checklist is not as detailed as Thompson's guide (see #373), it covers an additional decade of material, both primary and secondary, and serves quite well as a supplement. An index and magazine paginations should be added to future editions. Researchers and academic libraries should acquire both works; fans of Dickson's fiction will find Benson and Stephensen-Payne quite satisfactory.

373. Thompson, Raymond H. **Gordon R. Dickson: A Primary and Secondary Bibliography.** Boston, G. K. Hall, 1983. xix, 108 p. index. (Masters of Science Fiction and Fantasy). LC 82-12126. ISBN 0-8161-8363-5.

The late Canadian-born SF writer Dickson moved to the United States as a child; this bibliography was compiled by a well-known Canadian academic critic.

Contents: "Preface" (discussing the book's arrangement); "Introduction" (a brief guide to the author and his work); "Abbreviations List"; "Part A: Fiction"; "Part B: Miscellaneous Media"; "Part C: Nonfiction"; "Part D: Critical Studies"; plus five appendices: "A. An Overview of MSS 39, The Gordon R. Dickson Papers, Manuscript Division, University of Minnesota Libraries"; "B. Chronological Checklist of Novels, Collections, and Anthologies by Dickson"; "C. Series by Dickson"; "D. Translations of Dickson's Works"; "E. Reviews Excluded"; plus indices.

Each section is arranged chronologically, from the earliest published material to the latest, and numbered consecutively from one, section by section (*e.g.,* A1, A2, for fiction). Books and shorter works are interfiled by year; reprints of books and stories are grouped as subsidiary entries under their first edition or appearance, chronologically by year of reprint; reprint editions of short stories include editor of anthology, title, place of publication, publisher, year, format (*e.g.,* "paper"), but no paginations.

A typical book entry provides: item number, title (underlined), place of publication, publisher, format ("paper"), contents (for collections and anthologies), but no paginations. Each shorter work entry gives: item number, title (in quotations), magazine, volume number, date, pagination, or, for those published originally in books, book title, book editor, place of publication, publisher, format, and pagination. Story collections include complete contents listings, plus the years in which the original stories were published. Some entries, particularly in Sections B-C, include bibliographical or descriptive notes, but no other annotations; all of the entries in Part D are extensively annotated.

"Part B: Miscellaneous Media" include screenplays, teleplays, interviews, recordings, poetry, and other material that does not specifically fit the other three categories. "Part C: Nonfiction" includes all the author's nonfiction publications, arranged chronologically by issue date. Part D includes all known articles, reviews, and books about Dickson, arranged chronologically by publication date, typically giving: author, title, bibliographical data (in the same form as the other sections), and a one-to-five-sentence annotation; most "Who's Who"-type publications are omitted. Appendix D, "Translations," is arranged by language, and then in item number order as correlated with Section A (the original item number appears in brackets at the end of the entry). Two indices complete the book, correlating Dickson's works and secondary sources with item numbers. Coverage is complete through the first part of 1981. The book is reproduced from typed copy, and bound in sturdy library cloth.

Thompson's volume is soundly organized and constructed, the author demonstrating a clear familiarity with (and sympathy for) Dickson's work. Although now out-of-date, this will be an essential starting point for all future research on this popular writer. A new edition would be warranted, although Benson and Stephensen-Payne's checklist (see #372) provides very adequate coverage of the intervening decade.

Thomas M. Disch

374. Drumm, Chris. **A Tom Disch Checklist: Notes Toward a Bibliography.** Polk City, IA, Chris Drumm Books, 1983. [22] p. index. ISBN 0-936055-02-2 (pbk.).

Disch, an American science fiction writer, has received great critical acclaim from academic circles. Drumm's 4.25" x 7" checklist of the author's works is arranged in one straight chronological sequence. Entries are grouped by year, and under each year by month; each item is numbered in order from 1-194. Books are underlined, short stories appear in quotation marks.

A typical short fiction entry includes: item number, title, magazine, category code (*e.g.,* "s" = short story), date of completion by the writer, and month of publication; or book title, if an anthology, plus editor, publisher, and year of publication. Subsequent reprintings are grouped under the original edition, with similar data provided. No paginations are listed.

A typical book entry includes: item number, title, category code ("n" = novel), publisher, stock number, month of publication (if known), pagination, price, format (*e.g.,* "pb" = paperback), and contents of collections. The "See" references, index, and contents listings are keyed to item number. No secondary materials are included. Data are complete through 1982; a one-leaf addendum sheet is also available. The book is shot from typed copy; the text runs too close to the right-hand margin to allow rebinding by libraries.

Although Drumm's coverage is comparable to Nee's (see #375), the latter bibliography does list some secondary sources. However, Stephens's more current guide is preferable to either (see #376).

375. Nee, Dave. **Thomas M. Disch: A Preliminary Bibliography.** Berkeley, CA, The Other Change of Hobbit, 1982. ii, 30 p. (pbk.).

Nee, owner of a well-known science fiction shop in Northern California, assembled this short checklist of Disch's work, arranged by category and then alphabetically by title.

Contents: "Prefatory Note"; "B. Books"; "C. Anthologies Edited"; "F. Fiction"; "N. Non-Fiction, Reviews, Criticism" (*i.e.,* secondary sources); "P. Poetry." Materials are numbered consecutively in each section from the number one.

A typical book entry includes: item number, title, publisher, ISBN or stock number, and exact month of publication (when known). A typical short fiction entry lists: item number, story title, magazine, publication date, plus all known reprints, including (when appropriate) titles of the reprint anthology and year and month of publication. The secondary sources include articles, biographies, and reviews on Disch and his works, as well as interviews with the author, but do not mention the titles of the books being reviewed.

The volume is reproduced from rather faint 8.5" x 11" computer printout, using hanging indents to offset specific entries. Nee's guide includes considerably less data than his bibliography on Michael Bishop (see #317), overlapping to a great extent with Drumm's work (see #374); however, the addition of secondary sources makes this work slightly the more valuable of the two. Stephens's checklist (see #376), although it lacks secondary works, is far more current.

376. Stephens, Christopher P. **A Checklist of Thomas M. Disch.** Hastings-on-Hudson, NY, Ultramarine Publishing Co., 1989. 22 p. index. ISBN 0-89366-183-X (pbk.).

This checklist is arranged chronologically by publication date, covering books written by Disch and volumes edited by him, in two separate sections numbered from A1-A41 and from AA1-AA5, respectively.

A typical entry provides: publication year (as a floating head), item number, title (underlined), pseudonym, publisher, stock or ISBN number, pagination, format (*e.g.,* "cloth with dust wrapper"), cover illustrator, price, and similar data for all known reprints (which are numbered, for example, A12a, A12b, A12c, etc., in descending order by publication date).

The index correlates titles with years of publication only. The book is shot from legible typed copy and bound with staples in stiff paper covers. Disch deserves better bibliographical treatment than any of these three checklists provide; however, the currency of Stephens's guide makes it slightly preferable to Drumm (see #374) or Nee (see #375).

Lord Dunsany

377. Joshi, S. T., and Darrell Schweitzer. **Lord Dunsany: A Bibliography.** Metuchen, NJ, & London, Scarecrow Press, 1993. xxiv, 365 p. index. (Scarecrow Author Bibliographies, No. 90). LC 93-8453. ISBN 0-8108-2714-X.

Contents: "Introduction"; "Explanatory Notes and Acknowledgments"; "I. Works by Dunsany in English" ("A. Books"; "B. Contributions to Books and Periodicals"); "II. Works by Dunsany in Translation" ("A. Books by Dunsany"; "B. Contributions to Books and Periodicals"); "III. Dunsany Criticism" ("A. Dictionary and Encyclopedia Authors"; "B. Bibliographies"; "C. Books About Dunsany"; "D. Criticism in Books and Periodicals"; "E. Theses and Dissertations"; "F. Reviews"; "G. Unclassifiable Data"); "IV. Indexes" ("A. Names"; "B. Works by Dunsany"; "C. Periodicals"); "About the Authors."

The eighteenth Baron Dunsany has influenced several generations of writers with his fantasy stories and novels. This is the first comprehensive bibliography of his enormously complex output (including over 500 published short stories).

With the exception of the two sections covering letters by Dunsany and Dunsany criticism, this volume presents information in strict chronological order by date of first publication, under Dunsany's preferred title for the work (when known). The index of works by Dunsany provides a cross-reference to variant titles. In the lists of books, tables of contents are supplied where relevant, and brief explanatory notes have been added for clarity. In the contributions section, publications are listed in chronological order, whether published in a magazine, anthology, or collection; collections are referred to only by number, however, requiring the user to look elsewhere in the volume to find specific data on the book. Publications that are dated only by year are listed first, followed by those for which specific dates are known; publications dated by season are interspersed as follows: Spring precedes March; Summer precedes June; Autumn precedes September; and Winter precedes December. Collections are given precedence over all other publications for that year, unless an exact publication date for the collection is known.

Because it is sometimes difficult to distinguish between Dunsany's fiction and his essays, the index of works should be consulted when in doubt. Descriptive and evaluative annotations are provided for essays and letters. Play reviews, prefaces, and introductions appear in the essay section. Published letters are listed in chronological order by date of the letter, not by date of publication. Radio dramatizations of stories, essays, and plays are listed under the relevant sections, and works that were broadcast but not published are listed as appendices to these sections. Plays that were written but never published or produced are also noted.

Citations for works by Dunsany in translation have usually been taken from other reference works, and are listed in chronological order by date of publication of the translation, not of the original work. Where a volume has been seen, specific contents are provided.

The section on Dunsany criticism lists only the most important dictionary and encyclopedia articles, since Dunsany appears in most reference guides to fantastic literature. Important items in this section are annotated. Many newspaper articles and reviews are listed, but the authors admit that the reviews are incomplete, since "it would an heroic task to unearth them all." There is a final section of unclassifiable data that includes parodies, tributes, musical adaptations, etc.

A typical book entry lists: item number, title (in italics), with variant publications in chronological order (numbered, for example, a.1, a.2, a.3, b.1, b.2), including place, publisher, publication date (including month, where known), illustrations, contents, and other

Author Bibliographies / 293

relevant information, but no paginations. Paginations are included for shorter works, however.

The reference number assigned to each entry is based on its position in the outline, making some of the citations rather unruly (for example, "II.B.iii.86"). Although there are running heads throughout the book indicating which reference number ends a particular page, and these are certainly helpful, they become cumbersome and even irritating at times. Later editions of the bibliography should consider a more manageable numbering system.

Still, the data included here are both comprehensive and authoritative, and it is difficult to imagine any scholar worthy of the name not consulting this volume to begin his or her research on Lord Dunsany. The book is attractively typeset and bound to library standards. Recommended for all students of Dunsany and all major university libraries.

Jeffrey M. Elliot

378. Clarke, Boden. **The Work of Jeffrey M. Elliot: An Annotated Bibliography & Guide.** San Bernardino, CA, The Borgo Press, 1984. 50 p. index. (Bibliographies of Modern Authors, No. 2). LC 84-21745. ISBN 0-89370-381-8; ISBN 0-89370-481-4 (pbk.).

Although not himself a science-fiction writer, Elliot, a well-known political scientist, has been extensively involved with the genre as an SF interviewer, critic, anthologist, and bibliographer.

Contents: "Introduction," by Clarke; "Section A: Books"; "Section B: Articles"; "Section C: Book Reviews"; "Section D: Letters to the Editor"; "Section E: Speeches and Papers"; "Section F: Television Productions and Appearances"; "Section G: Radio Appearances"; "Section H: Other Media"; "Section J: Honors and Awards"; "Section K: About the Author"; "Section L: Unpublished Works"; "Quoth the Critics"; "Index."

In each section, the author's works are arranged chronologically and numbered consecutively chapter by chapter. A typical book entry includes: item number, title (underlined), place of publication, publisher, year of publication, pagination, format (*e.g.,* "paper"), and type of publication (*e.g.,* "children's story), with similar data on all reprint editions, translations, republications, etc. Book entries are fully annotated with complete contents listings and plot summaries; entries from other sections are selectively annotated as needed.

A typical shorter work entry includes: item number, title (in quotes), magazine title (underlined), volume or issue number, date, pagination. A brief introduction provides background material on the author's life and works. "About the Author" includes all known secondary works. "Quoth the Critics" includes selected excerpts of reviews and other comments by leading critics on the author's work. The index correlates titles and item numbers only.

Although listed as the second volume in the set, Clarke's was the first actually published in the Bibliographies of Modern Authors series, and was used as the pattern volume for the first half-dozen books (the style was extensively reworked in 1986 and 1988). The format used in this bibliography was somewhat cramped, employing a small typeface (word-processed copy), with minimal spacing between lines. Thus, a great deal of information is crammed into these fifty pages, much of it derived from Elliot's own records and files.

Data on this prolific author are provided through only the fall of 1984, making this publication now lamentably out-of-date.

Harlan Ellison

379. Swigart, Leslie Kay. **Harlan Ellison: A Bibliographical Checklist.** Dallas, TX, Williams Pub. Co., 1973. vi, 117 p. index. LC 74-159836 (pbk.). **Harlan Ellison: A Bibliographical Checklist.** 2nd ed. *Fantasy Research & Bibliography* no. 1-2 (December 1980-February 1981/March 1981-May 1981): 24-94. (pbk.).

Ellison, a popular fantasy and screen writer, was well treated in this early bibliography by librarian Swigart.

Contents: "Preface"; "Harlan Ellison" (biographical background); "In Re Ellison," by Isaac Asimov; "Harlan Ellison," by Ben Bova; "A Fagin Walks Among Us," by Edward Bryant; "Partners in Wonder," by Joanna Russ; "Harlan Ellison: An Appreciation," by Robert Silverberg; "Harlan Ellison: An Appreciation," by James Sutherland; "Section A: Books"; "B. Scripts"; "C. Fiction"; "D. Articles and Essays"; "E. Introductions and Afterwords"; "F. Reviews"; "G. Published Letters"; "H. Interviews with Harlan Ellison"; "I. Fanzines" edited by Harlan Ellison; "J. Titles Announced But Not Yet Published"; Afterword: "Thoughts on Turning Eighteen," by Ellison; "Index."

The introductory pieces provide insights into Ellison's character and life. The bibliography proper is arranged in chronological order, section by section, materials being numbered from one in each part. A typical book entry includes: item number, title (in caps), category (*e.g.,* "anthology"), plus complete bibliographical data for each edition and printing, in chronological order by release date. Each edition listing includes: title, subtitle, byline (as shown in the book), illustrators, city of publication, publisher, year of publication, collation, size in centimeters, series title, price, other notes, and contents listings (for the first printing only unless contents have changed).

Short fiction and nonfiction are listed by year, then alphabetically under each year by title. Each short fiction entry includes: item number, byline, title, magazine (underlined), volume and issue number, date of publication, pagination. Reprints in this and the nonfiction section are shown as new entries whenever they appear, and are numbered accordingly without "See" references (but can be accessed through the master index). Some foreign-language titles are included.

Section B lists scripts in order by air date, with item number, byline, title, TV series title, and first known air date. The index correlates all data in the bibliography, including titles, names, and non-Ellisonian publications by entry number.

Swigart's 8.5" x 11" volume is attractively illustrated with dozens of author photos and reproductions of book and magazine covers. The book is shot from typed copy with limp paper covers that cannot withstand heavy use. The constant repetition of short story titles in Section C is unfortunate, making it difficult for the casual user to trace reprints of the same story or even to determine how many stories Ellison has actually penned. Still, Swigart's guide is a remarkable bibliographical achievement for its time period, although now largely (and sadly) outdated.

Philip José Farmer

380. Knapp, Lawrence J. **The First Editions of Philip Jose [*sic*] Farmer.** Menlo Park, CA, David G. Turner, Bookman, 1976. ii, 8 p. (Science Fiction Bibliographies, 2). (pbk.).

This very brief checklist focuses on Farmer's first edition books and uncollected short stories, with a few secondary sources and a series index. The books are listed chronologically by year of publication and numbered from one; a typical entry includes: item number, title (in underlined caps), publisher, place of publication, year of publication, stock number, format (*e.g.,* "wraps"). Collections include complete contents listings; there are other occasional bibliographical notes, but no paginations. The uncollected stories are listed alphabetically by title, with magazine title and date of publication, but no paginations. The brief list of secondary sources is arranged in alphabetical order by critic. Now completely superseded by Stephensen-Payne/Benson's guide (see #381).

381. Stephensen-Payne, Phil, & Gordon Benson, Jr. **Philip José Farmer, Good-Natured Ground Breaker: A Working Bibliography.** 2nd rev. ed. Leeds, West Yorkshire, England, Galactic Central Publications, 1990. 9, 63 p. (Galactic Central Bibliographies for the Avid Reader, Vol. 23). ISBN 1-871133-22-X (pbk.).

Farmer is the highly regarded American SF author of the Riverworld stories. Stephensen-Payne and Benson's guide to his work is arranged by category, then alphabetically by title.

Contents: Author's full name, pseudonyms, date and place of birth, and his awards and honors; "A. Stories"; "B. Fiction Books"; "C. Series"; "D. Poems & Songs"; "E. Poem & Song Collections" [blank section]; "F. Articles"; "G. Miscellaneous"; "H. Non-Fiction Books"; "I. Books Edited by Philip José Farmer"; "J. Media Presentations"; "K. Articles on Philip José Farmer"; "L. Reviews" [of Farmer's books, alphabetically by book title]; "M. Books About Philip José Farmer"; "N. Phantom & Forthcoming Titles"; "O. Related Items by Other Authors"; "P. Textual Variations"; "Q. Chronological Index."

Materials are arranged alphabetically by title and numbered consecutively from the number one in each section. For shorter works, Stephensen-Payne and Benson give: item number, title, category ("ss" = short story, "nt" = novelette, etc.), magazine or book in which the item appeared, month and year of publication (for magazines in the form "12-54" for December 1954), or year of publication (for books), a list of subsequent reprints (for which title, publisher, year, and editor's last name are given), but no paginations.

For book-length works, Benson provides: item number, title, publication data (publisher, stock number, month and year of publication [if known, in the form "10-59" for October 1959], pagination, price), cover artist, and similar information on all known reprints. There is no general index. The book is shot from very legible word-processed copy and stapled into paper covers. Data are complete through mid-1990.

These checklists have developed considerably with each new edition, both in terms of content and style; the second edition is three times the size of the first (1987), and includes over seventy secondary sources, plus more than a hundred book reviews, in addition to a very comprehensive primary bibliography. An index and short story paginations would be attractive additions to future editions. Any scholar researching Farmer's work would be well advised to consult this checklist first.

John Russell Fearn

382. Harbottle, Philip. **John Russell Fearn: An Evaluation.** Wabash, IN, Coulson Publications, 1963. 10 p. (pbk.). **John Russell Fearn: The Ultimate Analysis.** [2nd ed.]. Wallsend, England: Philip Harbottle, 1965. 94 p. (pbk.). **The Multi-Man: A Biographic and Bibliographic Study of John Russell Fearn (1908-60).** [3rd ed.]. Wallsend, England, The Author, 1968. iv, 69 p. LC 68-135425 (pbk.).

Harbottle, Fearn's literary executor, has compiled three different versions of an illustrated biography, analysis, and bibliography of this prolific British pulp writer, each expanding upon the previous edition.

Contents (*The Multi-Man*): "The Ultimate Analysis" (a thirty-four-page biographical and critical background on the author); "Part One: Science Fiction and Fantasy"; "Part Two: Detective and Mystery"; "Part Three: Westerns"; "Part Four: Romances"; "Part Five: Film Magazines."

In each section and subdivision, materials are arranged by pseudonym, and then in alphabetical order by title. The major section, Part One, is subdivided into "Non-Fiction," "SF Fanzine Articles," "Fanzine Fiction," "Magazine Stories," "Miscellaneous and Associated Magazine Items," "Unconfirmed Pseudonyms," and "Science Fiction Novels." A typical short fiction entry includes: title, category code (*e.g.,* "s" = short story), magazine title, date of publication, illustrator, and one-sentence annotation, but no paginations.

A typical book entry includes: title, publisher, pagination, price, format ("pb" = paperback), reprint editions (including some foreign, with foreign-language titles and similar bibliographical details), plus a one- to five-sentence annotation. There is no index, making location of any specific title difficult for the casual user; the many textual subdivisions also tend to overwhelm the data, making an overall evaluation of Fearn's enormous output inordinately difficult. Harbottle has also included a number of generally well-reproduced black-and-white illustrations taken from the covers of Fearn's paperbacks and from the drawings accompanying his pulp stories; these are attractively reproduced.

As the only guide to Fearn's work currently available, *The Multi-Man* is a valuable introduction to a little-known period of British publishing; however, a completely revised and updated edition with better internal organization and index plus individual story paginations would certainly be justified.

Hugo Gernsback

SEE: *Science-Fiction: The Gernsback Years,* by Everett F. Bleiler (see #136).

James Gunn

383. Drumm, Chris. **A James Gunn Checklist.** Polk City, IA, Chris Drumm Books, 1984. [24] p. index. LC 84-212825. ISBN 0-936055-13-8 (pbk.).

Gunn, a respected American English professor, critic, and science fiction writer, is the featured target of this brief 4.25" x 7" checklist.

The author's works are arranged in one straight chronological sequence. Entries are grouped by year and under each year by month; each item is numbered in order from 1-

142. Books are underlined, short stories listed in quotation marks. A typical short fiction entry includes: item number, title, category code (*e.g.,* "s" = short story), magazine, and month of publication (or book title, if the first appearance is in an anthology, plus editor, publisher, and year of publication). Subsequent reprintings are grouped under the original edition, with similar data provided. No paginations are included.

A typical book entry includes: item number, title, category code (*e.g.,* "c" = collection), publisher, stock number, month of publication (if known), pagination, price, format (*e.g.,* "pb" = paperback), and contents of collections. The "See" references, index, and contents listings are keyed to item numbers. A few secondary materials are mentioned in passing in their appropriate years, but are not easily accessible. Data are complete through mid-1984. The book is shot from typed copy; the text runs too close to the right-hand margin to allow rebinding by libraries. A four-page critical essay, "Of Dreams and of Nightmares," by Stephen H. Goldman, provides a basic introduction to the author and his work.

This booklet provides a good starting point for future scholarship on this writer, but a new edition of this outdated pamphlet would now be warranted.

H. Rider Haggard

384. Scott, J. E. **A Bibliography of the Works of Sir Henry Rider Haggard, 1856-1925.** Takeley, England, Elkin Matthews, 1947. 258 p. index. LC a48-430. Limited to 500 copies.

This thorough and very carefully rendered bibliography is organized into nine chapters: "Preface"; "A Note Concerning the Late Mr. Allan Quatermain" (a detailed examination of the chronology of the Quatermain tales); "I. First Editions"; "II. Articles in Newspapers, Periodicals, Etc."; "III. Letters to *The Times*"; "IV. Letters to Newspapers, Periodicals, Etc."; "V. Reports of Haggard's Speeches"; "VI. Reviews by H. Rider Haggard"; "VII. Dramatisations of Haggard's Novels"; "VIII. Parodies, Etc., of Haggard's Books"; "IX. Interviews, Biographical Sketches, Critical Articles, Etc."; "Index."

The section on Haggard's books accounts for 132 pages (and eighty-five first editions), more than half the bibliography, and is arranged chronologically by publication date. A typical book entry includes: item number, title (boldfaced caps), year of publication, and exact transcription of title page copy, collation, description of binding cloth and style, publication date, number of copies published, contents (where appropriate), details on previous serialization (where appropriate), background information, and notes. Second editions and first American editions are described immediately following the first British versions, as separate entries, being numbered (in the case of *Mr. Meeson's Will,* for example) "9A" and "9B." Materials are numbered consecutively throughout the book from 1-732. No attempt has been made to cover the myriad reprints of Haggard's popular novels.

The remaining sections are also recorded chronologically by date of publication or filming. A typical shorter work entry provides: year of publication, item number, date of publication, title (small caps), magazine title (italics), and occasional descriptive notes, but no paginations. The chapter on dramatizations is broken into two sections covering play adaptations of Haggard's work (including date of first production, theatre name, principal stars, author, etc.), and motion picture versions of the author's work (giving production company, director, writer, date of first showing, and the names of actors and other principals). The section on parodies is notably incomplete, lacking all of the American parody novels that appeared in the late 1880s.

The valuable final chapter, on secondary sources, includes references to and descriptions of many materials that would be nearly impossible to locate today. The index correlates titles (including periodicals) and entry numbers. A few facsimiles of Haggard manuscript pages are included. The book is beautifully typeset and bound to library standards.

One very obvious omission from this otherwise excellent bibliography is a section covering Haggard's ten or twenty short stories. Some information on the previous publication of these works is buried at the end of the several collections issued in book form (*Smith and the Pharoahs,* for example), and the individual story titles do appear in the index; nonetheless, one can gain no unified overview of these materials without a great deal of flipping back and forth between different monograph entries. Compare with Whatmore's more recent guide (see #385).

385. Whatmore, D. E. **H. Rider Haggard: A Bibliography.** London, Mansell Publishing Ltd., 1987. xix, 187 p. index. ISBN 0-7201-1806-9. Westport, CT, Meckler Publishing Corp., 1987. xix, 187 p. index. LC 86-33272. ISBN 0-88736-102-1.

Whatmore generally follows Scott's format (see #384), with further divisions and amalgamations. Contents: "Preface"; "Introduction"; "Guide to the Bibliography"; "Sources and Acknowledgements"; Bibliography: "1. Principal Works [*i.e.,* books]: Fiction"; "2. Principal Works: Nonfiction"; "3. Pamphlets and Reports"; "4. The African Review"; "5. Miscellaneous Writings"; "6. Letters to Newspapers and Periodicals"; "7. Selected Reports of Haggard's Speeches"; "8. Films, Plays and Radio Broadcasts Based on Haggard's Work"; "9. Books and Articles About Haggard and His Works"; "10. Parodies and Lampoons"; "11. Theses" [about Haggard's works]; Appendixes: "1. Some Popular Editions of Note"; "2. Haggard Manuscripts in the Norfolk Record Office"; "Subject Index"; "Index to Newspapers and Periodicals."

Materials in each section are listed in chronological order by publication date and numbered anew from one, chapter by chapter. A typical monograph entry provides: item number, title, year of publisher, publisher, identification features (binding, spine, front cover, end papers, preliminaries, text, supplements, illustrations, errors), technical data (format, edges, collation), number of copies in first edition (with exact date of publication), any earlier publication in magazine form, other editions of note (chiefly the first American edition, early large paper editions, and other contemporaneous variants of significance; no later editions are described, and relatively few bibliographical details are provided in any case), "Notes," "Some Haggard Notes" (comments by Haggard himself). The two book sections account for 93 pages out of 187.

A typical short work entry includes: year of publication, item number, month (and day, where appropriate) of publication, title (in quotes), magazine title (italics), and pagination (where known). The first appendix lists fourteen series (British and American), which included significant numbers of Haggard titles, including the early unauthorized U.S. dime novel versions, with dates of publication and series number (where appropriate), but no other bibliographical data. The second appendix is a very useful guide to the major collection of surviving Haggard manuscripts in the Norfolk Record Office; included are the originals of some of his best-known novels.

The "Subject Index" correlates titles, authors, and some subjects to item numbers; the "Index to Newspapers and Periodicals" is organized by country (the United Kingdom is listed first, then all others alphabetically by country name), then alphabetically by magazine title, with a list of entry numbers following each title. The book is very clearly typeset and bound to library standards. Data are complete through part of 1986.

Both Whatmore's bibliography and Scott's (see #384) lack any specific section covering Haggard's short fiction. Scott provides more details on first American editions, while Whatmore includes somewhat more explicit data on first British editions. Whatmore also lists far more secondary sources (359 items, plus seven unpublished academic theses, versus ninety-one records for Scott), but not all of the entries from Scott are repeated in Whatmore. Whatmore is also more complete in his coverage of the Haggard parodies, and far more complete in his listings of dramatizations, movie versions of Haggard's works, and other media adaptations; but he misses the 1978 American republication (in two omnibuses) of six Haggard parodies by Arno Press, and the reprint of eight Haggard titles between 1973-80 in the Newcastle Forgotten Fantasy Library (and a half dozen books reprinted for libraries by Arno Press), among others.

Libraries will probably find Whatmore adequate for most purposes, but scholars seriously interested in researching Haggard's fiction will require both volumes, and then some.

Edmond Hamilton

Benson, Gordon, Jr. **Leigh Douglass Brackett and Edmond Hamilton: A Working Bibliography**. *See the entry for Leigh Brackett* (see #328).

Charles L. Harness

386. Koppel, T. **Chronology: A Chronological Bibliography of Books by Charles L. Harness.** Polk City, IA, Chris Drumm Books, 1992. 27 p. (Drumm Booklet #44). ISBN 0-936055-57-X (pbk.).

Contents: "Introduction"; "Notes on Arrangement of Compilation"; "Part I: Novels & Collection by Year"; "Part II: Undated Editions"; "Part III: Unpublished Novels"; "Part IV: Shorter Works in Collections"; "Part V: Index of Book Titles (published)"; "Part VI: Personal Chronology of C.L.H."

The bulk of this stapled pamphlet is Part I, covering fourteen book titles in fifty-seven entries. "Only books are listed (with original magazine appearance, where appropriate), not any short stories that have appeared solely in magazines or more general anthologies." An entry may represent the original publication, a reprint, or a foreign-language publication. Materials are organized by publication year.

A typical entry includes: title (underlined caps), country and format (*e.g.*, paper, hardback, magazine), publisher, place of publication, publication year, and pagination (in brackets). As available or appropriate, Koppel also adds notes on contents, the author of the introduction, illustrators, jacket designers, and cover artists. Questionable information is marked with a question mark or with bracketed notes to the reader.

Koppel's guide includes an index, which makes his data slightly more accessible than Stephensen-Payne's (see #387), but the latter's more complete bibliography is generally to be preferred.

387. Stephensen-Payne, Phil. **Charles L. Harness, Attorney in Space: A Working Bibliography.** Leeds, West Yorkshire, England, Galactic Central Publications, 1992. 9, 15 p. (Bibliographies for the Avid Reader, Vol. 44). ISBN 1-871133-34-3 (pbk.).

Contents: Author's name, date and place of birth, and his pseudonyms; "A. Stories"; "B. Fiction Books"; "C. Series"; "D. Poems, Songs & Plays" [blank section]; "E. Poem, Song & Play Volumes" [blank section]; "F. Articles"; "G. Miscellaneous" (including introductions and afterwords by Charles L. Harness, letters, and interviews with the author); "H. Non-Fiction Books"; "I. Books Edited by Charles L. Harness" [blank section]; "J. Media Presentations" [blank section]; "K. Articles on Charles L. Harness"; "L. Reviews" (of Harness's books, alphabetically by title of the book being reviewed, then by magazine title, giving date and reviewer); "M. Books About Charles L. Harness" [blank section]; "N. Phantom & Forthcoming Titles"; "O. Related Items by Other Authors"; "P. Textual Variations"; "Q. Chronological Index" (by year and title).

The introduction is almost identical throughout the series, and clearly explains how to use the many different sections of the bibliography. Stephensen-Payne's basic checklist is arranged by subject category, then alphabetically by title; materials are numbered consecutively from one in each chapter (for example, B1, B2, B3, etc., for the author's books). A typical shorter work entry includes: item number, title, category ("ss" = short story, "nt" = novelette, etc.), magazine or book in which the item appeared, month and year of publication (for magazines in the form "2-68" for February 1968), or year of publication (for books), a list of subsequent reprints (for which title, publisher, year, and editor's last name are given), but no paginations.

For book-length works, Stephensen-Payne provides: item number, title, contents (if a collection, by item number), publication data (publisher, stock number, month and year of publication [if known, in the form "10-59" for October 1959], pagination, price), cover artist, plus similar data for known reprints. There is no title index. Some 90 entries are mentioned, though reprint information inflates this total; of these, 34 are secondary sources, 10 of which are book review categories, the latter including many dozens of actual review citations. Some minor foreign language publication information is mentioned. The guide is shot from legible word-processed copy and stapled through the spine. An index would have been helpful, as would the addition of paginations for the short fiction sections.

American SF writer Harness is not well-known today, but his fans will appreciate the appearance of this bibliography devoted to his primary and secondary publications. Compare with Koppel's guide (see #386).

Harry Harrison

388. Benson, Gordon, Jr., and Phil Stephensen-Payne. **Harry Maxwell Harrison, a Stainless Steel Talent: A Working Bibliography.** 4th rev. ed. Albuquerque, NM and Leeds, West Yorkshire, England, Galactic Central Publications, 1989. 9, 71 p. (Galactic Central

Bibliographies for the Avid Reader, Vol. 9). ISBN 0-912613-12-2 and 1-871133-13-0 (pbk.).

Harry Harrison, author of the Stainless Steel Rat stories and the Eden series, is an American SF writer turned British émigré.

Contents: Author's full name, date and place of birth, and pseudonyms; "A. Stories"; "B. Fiction Books"; "C. Series"; "D. Poems & Songs"; "E. Poem & Song Collections" [blank section]; "F. Articles"; "G. Miscellaneous"; "H. Non-Fiction Books"; "I. Edited Books"; "J. Media Presentations"; "K. Articles on Harry Harrison"; "L. Reviews" [of Harrison's books]; "M. Books About Harry Harrison"; "N. Phantom Titles and References"; "O. Related Works by Other Authors" [blank section]; "P. Textual Variations" [blank section]; "Q. Chronological Index."

In each section materials are arranged alphabetically by title and numbered consecutively from the number one. A typical shorter work entry gives: item number, title, category ("ss" = short story, "nt" = novelette, etc.), magazine or book in which the item appeared, month and year of publication (for magazines in the form "4-64" for April 1964) or year of publication (for books), plus similar data for all known reprints (for which title, publisher, year, and editor's last name are given), but no paginations.

A typical book entry provides: item number, title (all caps), contents (where applicable, listing the item numbers of the stories recorded in Section A), publication data (publisher, stock number, month and year of publication [if known, in the form "10-59" for October 1959], pagination, price, and cover artist), plus similar information on all known reprints. There is no general index. The book is shot from very legible word-processed copy and stapled into paper covers. Data are complete through mid-1989.

Benson and Stephensen-Payne's work is a sound piece of bibliography, and will provide most students with a firm beginning point for their research.

389. Biamonti, Francesco. **Harry Harrison: Bibliographia (1951-1965).** Trieste, Italy, Printed by Editoriale Libraria, 1965. [11] p. (pbk.).

Biamonti's brief guide to Harrison's work uses the same format developed by Margaret Aldiss for her bibliographical chapbooks, *Item Forty-Three* and *Item Eighty-Three* (see #302). Forty-six items are listed (and numbered) in alphabetical order by title.

A typical entry includes: item number, title (in bold caps), estimated wordage, pen name (where appropriate), magazine title, date of publication (for short fiction), or, for books, publisher, date of publication, plus all known reprints (including some foreign-language editions, with translated titles), and occasional one- to two-sentence annotations by Harrison himself in italics at the end of the entry.

Beautifully typeset, but now outdated and subsumed by Benson/Stephensen-Payne (see #388).

Robert A. Heinlein

390. Gifford, James. **Robert A. Heinlein: A Reader's Companion.** Sacramento, CA: Nitrosyncretic Press, 2000. xxi, 281 p. LC 00-102119. ISBN 0-9679874-1-5; ISBN 0-9679874-0-7 (pbk.).

The late Robert A. Heinlein is generally acknowledged as the major science fiction writer of the genre's classical period.

Contents: "Foreword," by L. Sprague and Catherine Crook de Camp; "Introduction," by Gifford; "Sources & Acknowledgments"; "Cross-References"; "The Major Works"; "Other Works"; "Notes"; "A Selected Heinlein Bibliography"; "The New Heinlein Opus List"; "Title Index"; "General Index."

Gifford's guide is a cross between a critique and a bibliography, but it succeeds better in providing access to Heinlein's many works than in delineating their numerous appearances.

The main section of this book (comprising 172 pages) is organized alphabetically by title, interfiling both stories and books into one sequence. A typical entry includes: title (boldfaced type, short stories in quotation marks), entry number, type (*e.g.*, "Short Story"), year of composition (or year of publication if the composition date is unknown), and, for shorter works only, magazine title and publication date (in the form "5/48" for May, 1948) for the item's first appearance in print, Heinlein collections in which the story is included, and series information (*e.g.*, "Future History"). No paginations are given. Stories that were first published in anthologies include: anthology title (in italics), publisher, place of publication, year of publication, and editor, but no paginations. No bibliographical data are provided for Heinlein's books.

The entry numbers are generated from a chronological list of Heinlein's publications near the rear of the volume, giving: entry number, date the manuscript was created (in the form "5/39" for May, 1939), publication date, title, and notes. The selected Heinlein bibliography includes an alphabetical listing of the writer's published books, but adds bibliographical data (publisher, year of publication, ISBN) on just a handful of the entries. The comprehensive index covers everything mentioned in this volume, coordinated to page numbers, with boldfaced numbers indicating the main coverage herein.

Gifford's commentary is well-considered and middle-of-the-road, and he provides a basic entry into Heinlein's complex web of fictions. One might wish, however, that he had included sufficient bibliographical data to make this the definitive guide to the master's work. Prefer Stephensen-Payne's guide (see #392) for bibliographical information.

391. Owings, Mark. **Robert A. Heinlein: A Bibliography.** Baltimore, MD, Croatan House, 1973. xii, 23 p. ISBN 0-88358-000-4 (pbk.).

A seven-page critical introduction by Fred Lerner frames Heinlein's life and work. The bibliography proper is organized in one alphabetical sequence by title, book entries being underlined. Each title is flush to the left-hand margin, the remainder of the entry being indented three spaces to set it off. There are no line breaks between entries (but several lines are skipped between letters of the alphabet).

A typical short fiction entry includes: title, magazine title, month and year of publication (in the form 5/48 for May 1948), and known reprint editions, with book title, editor, publisher, place of publication, stock number (for paperbacks), year of publication, format (*e.g.*, "wpps" = paperback), total pagination of the book, price, but no specific paginations for the story.

A typical book entry includes: title, publisher, place of publication, year of publication, pagination, price, with similar data for known reprint editions. Many foreign-language editions are shown with translators and foreign-language title equivalents (such data are very difficult to locate elsewhere). The book is shot from sometimes faint typed copy. Data are included through part of 1973.

This guide is now wholly out-of-date. Prefer Stephensen-Payne (see #392).

392. Stephensen-Payne, Phil. **Robert Heinlein, Stormtrooping Guru: A Working Bibliography.** Leeds, West Yorkshire, England, Galactic Central Publications, 1993. 9, 100 p. (Bibliographies for the Avid Reader, Vol. 42). ISBN 1-871133-35-1 (pbk.).

The late American writer Robert A. Heinlein is justly considered to be one of the premier science fiction writers of the twentieth century.

Contents: Author's name, date and place of birth and death, a list of awards won by the author (in chronological order, giving year, name of award, and title of work being honored), and his pseudonyms; "A. Stories"; "B. Fiction Books"; "C. Series"; "D. Poems"; "E. Poem, Song & Play Volumes" [blank section]; "F. Articles"; "G. Miscellaneous" (including introductions and afterwords by Robert Heinlein, letters, and interviews with the author); "H. Non-Fiction Books"; "I. Books Edited by Robert Heinlein" [blank section]; "J. Media Presentations"; "K. Articles on Robert Heinlein"; "L. Reviews" (of Heinlein's books, alphabetically by title of the book being reviewed, then by magazine title, giving date and reviewer); "M. Books About Robert A. Heinlein"; "N. Phantom & Forthcoming Titles"; "O. Related Items by Other Authors"; "P. Textual Variations"; "Q. Chronological Index" (by year and title).

The introduction is almost identical throughout the series, and clearly explains the many different sections of the bibliography. Stephensen-Payne's basic checklist is arranged by subject category, then alphabetically by title; materials are numbered consecutively from one in each chapter (for example, B1, B2, B3, etc., for the author's books). A typical shorter work entry includes: item number, title, category ("ss" = short story, "nt" = novelette, etc.), magazine or book in which the item appeared, month and year of publication (for magazines in the form "2-68" for February 1968) or year of publication (for books), a list of subsequent reprints (for which title, publisher, year, and editor's last name are given), but no paginations.

For book-length works, Stephensen-Payne provides: item number, title, contents (if a collection, by item number), publication data (publisher, stock number, month and year of publication [if known, in the form "10-59" for October 1959], pagination, price), cover artist, plus similar data for known reprints. There is no title index.

Some 628 entries are included, though reprint information makes the overall total much greater. Of these, 397 consist of secondary sources, and 56 of book review categories; the actual number of review citations is much, much larger, reaching well into the hundreds. Some foreign language publications are mentioned, but the information on these books is generally sparse. Information is included through 1992 (the author died in 1988), making the coverage virtually complete for Heinlein's first editions. The volume uses very legible word-processed copy, and is stapled through the spine.

An index would have been helpful, as would the addition of paginations for the short fiction sections, but overall, this is the first serious attempt to provide a comprehensive guide to the author's works. Recommended for both fans and scholars alike.

Frank Herbert

393. Levack, Daniel J. H., with annotations by Mark Willard. **Dune Master: A Frank Herbert Bibliography.** Westport, CT, Meckler Corp., 1988. xx, 176 p. (Meckler's Bibliographies on Science Fiction, Fantasy, and Horror, No. 2). LC 87-25034. ISBN 0-88736-099-8.

Levack has authored four other similarly formatted bibliographies on de Camp, Dick, Vance, and Zelazny (see #364, #369, #496, #519); this new work contains many of the same faults and virtues as its brethren.

Contents: "Introduction," "Annotator's Introduction"; "Books"; "Edited Books"; "Non-Book Appearances" (*i.e.,* short fiction and nonfiction); "Manuscript Collection"; "Series and Connected Stories"; "Pseudonyms"; "Chronological Order of Publication of Frank Herbert's Work"; "Fiction Checklist"; "Non-Fiction Checklist"; "Verse Checklist"; "Other Media Checklist"; "Magazine Checklist"; "Works About Frank Herbert"; "Appendix: Illustrations of Covers."

Works are listed in the major sections alphabetically by title and numbered consecutively from the number one, section by section, with over 160 items included. A typical book entry includes: item number, title (bold caps), series note (when appropriate) or category (*e.g.,* "Non-Fiction"), contents (if a collection) or one- to three-page annotation (if a novel) in boldface, publisher, stock number (for paperback editions), place of publication (inconsistently), price (in parentheses), year of publication, edition points, but no paginations. Reprints are listed under the main entry in chronological order by publication date; many foreign editions are also mentioned, with the foreign-language titles. An asterisk after a specific edition indicates that it has been viewed by Levack.

A typical shorter work entry gives: item number, title (in bold quotes), category (*e.g.,* "non-fiction"), one- to fifteen-paragraph annotation (in bold type), magazine or book title, date, issue number (inconsistently), but no paginations. All subsequent reprint editions (including some foreign-language materials with foreign-language titles) are listed with similar data. Anthology appearances include: title, editor, publisher, stock number, price, year of publication, format (*e.g.,* "paper"), but no paginations. This section also includes some media publications (sound recordings, for example). The magazine checklist is an alphabetic listing of those publications in which Herbert stories appeared, keyed to issue date and to item number in the "Non-Book Appearances" section.

Levack also includes a master chronological checklist of Herbert's work, year by year, with all publications interfiled (but their titles lack the item numbers from the main bibliography). A "Fiction Checklist" (and non-fiction and verse lists) provide quick, alphabetical sequences for each category, but again fail to refer the reader to specific item numbers from the main bibliography. There is no index as such. The book includes twenty pages of well-reproduced, black-and-white book and magazine cover reproductions (four to a page), a very attractive feature. The two-page secondary bibliography includes just eleven items, five monographs and six articles, and is lamentably incomplete, even for its period. Coverage extends through early 1987, just after Herbert's death.

The absence of an index, of all paginations, of most secondary sources, is inexcusable in a production of this magnitude from a major publisher. Levack does contain a great deal of useful information, but his guide can serve as no more than a starting point for the serious researcher, being in no way "definitive." Compare with Stephensen-Payne's more current checklist (see #394).

394. Stephensen-Payne, Phil. **Frank Herbert, a Voice from the Desert: A Working Bibliography.** Leeds, West Yorkshire, England, Galactic Central Publications, 1990. 9, 48 p. (Galactic Central Bibliographies for the Avid Reader, Vol. 36). ISBN 1-871133-27-0 (pbk.).

The late Frank Herbert is best known for his six novels revolving around the planet Dune.

Contents: Author's full name and dates of birth and death; dates and names of awards received; "A. Stories"; "B. Fiction Books"; "C. Series"; "D. Poems, Songs & Plays"; "E. Poem, Song & Play Volumes" [blank section]; "F. Articles"; "G. Miscellaneous"; "H. Non-Fiction Books"; "I. Books Edited by Frank Herbert"; "J. Media Presentations"; "K. Articles on Frank Herbert"; "L. Reviews" (of Herbert's books listed alphabetically by book title, then alphabetically by magazine title); "M. Books About Frank Herbert"; "N. Phantom & Forthcoming Titles"; "O. Related Items by Other Authors"; "P. Textual Variations"; "Q. Chronological Index."

Materials are listed in each section alphabetically by title, and are numbered anew from one, prefixed by the identifying letter for that chapter (*e.g.,* P1, P2, P3, etc.). A typical book entry provides: item number, title (all caps), contents (where appropriate, by item number), publisher, format (*e.g.,* "pb" = paperback), stock number, month and year of publication (in the form "12-70" for December 1970), pagination, price, cover artist, a list of subsequent printings from the same publisher (with similar data), and all other known reprints from other publishers, listed chronologically by initial publication date. No foreign language editions are included.

A typical shorter work entry gives: item number, title, type (*e.g.,* "N-3" = a serialized novel in three parts), magazine title, month and year of publication (in the form "7-55" for July 1955), and brief bibliographical data on all known reprints. Reprints in anthologies include: book title (all caps), editor's last name, publisher, and year of publication. There are 322 entries, though reprint information makes the total greater. Of these, some 150 secondary sources are mentioned, 35 of which are book review categories (comprising well over a hundred actual review citations). Coverage is complete through mid-1990. The checklist has no overall index, but the alphabetization of individual sections makes materials relatively easy to find. The book is shot from dark, clear word-processed copy, and stapled into paper covers.

Levack's guide (see #393) includes some foreign-language editions of Herbert's books, provides minimal annotations, and reproduces numerous illustrations of paperback and magazine covers of interest to the Herbert collector, making it more attractive physically; but in virtually every other respect it is deficient to Stephensen-Payne's more concise and detailed checklist. Scholars interested in intensively researching the author's life and works should have access to both bibliographies; all others, including libraries, will find Stephensen-Payne more than adequate.

William Hope Hodgson

395. Bell, Joseph. **William Hope Hodgson, Night Pirate; Volume One: An Annotated Bibliography of Published Works, 1902-1987.** Toronto, Canada, Soft Books, 1988 (?). viii, 41 p. (pbk.).

Bell has also compiled bibliographies with similar formats on Clive Barker and H. P. Lovecraft (see #314, #417, #418). This new work covers the publications of a classic British horror writer killed in World War I.

The main section, covering the author's books, is arranged in chronological order by publication date, and includes: title (large, boldfaced type), publisher, place of publication, pagination, price, binding, date of publication, information on edition priority states, contents (for collections), other notes, and similar data on all known reprintings and subsequent editions. A second section covers periodical and anthology appearance(s) of Hodgson's stories and essays, in alphabetical order by title.

A typical shorter work entry includes: title (bold caps), category (*e.g.,* "nf" = non fantasy), magazine title, month and year of publication, but no paginations, and a list of all known reprint editions, including those in Hodgson's own books. Anthology appearances include: book title, editor, publisher, place of publication, format (*e.g.,* "paper cover" for paperback), year of publication, but no paginations. As usual with Bell's bibliographies, there is no overall title index.

This volume is intended primarily as a collectors' guide, not a literary bibliography, and contains no information on the content of the books or stories, and very little on Hodgson himself. The volume is nicely designed and typeset and stapled into 8.5" x 11" paper covers.

Note: the remaining five volumes in this series include a biography of Hodgson, three collections of stories by Hodgson, and a concluding book (not yet published) containing addenda to the first two volumes, plus a bibliography covering Hodgson's works in translation.

Robert E. Howard

396. Lord, Glenn. **The Last Celt: A Bio-Bibliography of Robert Ervin Howard.** West Kingston, RI, Donald M. Grant, Publisher, 1976. 416 p. index. LC 77-351659. New York, A Berkley Windhover Book, Berkley Books, 1976. 415 p. index. LC 77-154974. ISBN 0-425-03630-8 (pbk.).

This 7" x 10" volume was published for the fan and collectors' market to commemorate the life and works of a well-known American pulp fantasy writer who took his own life in 1936 at the age of thirty.

Contents: "Introduction," by E. Hoffmann Price; "Foreword" (by Lord); "I. Autobiography" (various pieces by Howard); "II. Biography" (essays on Howard's life and career by different hands); "III. Bibliography" (p. 103-352); "IV. Miscellanea" (reproductions of several Howard manuscripts and magazine covers featuring Howard stories, and photographs of the author and his family).

The bibliography proper includes: "Introduction"; "Books"; "Fiction"; "Verse," (with "Title Index," "First Line Index," and "Headings"); "Articles"; "Letters"; "Index by Periodicals"; "Translations: Books, Fiction, Verse, Headings, Articles, Letters"; "Unpublished

Fiction"; "Unpublished Verse" (with "Title Index" and "Headings"); "Unpublished Articles"; "Series Index"; "Lost Manuscripts"; "Unborn Books"; "Comics"; "Television Adaptations"; "The Junto"; "About the Author: Books, Amateur Publications, Robert E. Howard Press Association, Articles, Conan Pastiches."

Monographs are listed in chronological order by publication date. A typical book entry includes: title (caps), contents (for collections), publisher, place of publication, year of publication, pagination, price, in-print status, binding details, cover artist (if known), and other bibliographical notes.

Howard's short fiction is organized by pseudonym, then alphabetically by story title. Each entry provides: title, magazine title, month and year of publication, and all known reprints, but no paginations. Reprints in anthologies include: book title, editor, publisher, place of publication, and year of publication. Verse and nonfiction are arranged similarly to short fiction, by pseudonym and title; a separate index correlates the first lines of Howard's poems with their titles. Howard's letters are arranged in alphabetical order by recipient.

The index by periodicals provides magazine title, then titles of Howard stories that appeared in each, by date. Translations of books are organized chronologically by date of publication; translations of stories, however, are arranged by country, pseudonym and English-language title, with publication data and foreign-language titles. The secondary bibliography covers a paltry three books and two additional pages of articles (nineteen items), arranged by critic, including the original newspaper obituaries of the author and some rather obscure fan articles, all of them virtually unobtainable now.

The Last Celt is beautifully printed and designed, typical of Grant's fine press editions, but the absence of an index is a major flaw in a volume with so much text and so many internal subdivisions. Finding a specific title can require much paging through many non-relevant sections. One also laments the lack of page number data for anything except book publications. A revised, expanded edition is overdue.

397. McHaney, Dennis, and Glenn Lord. **The Fiction of Robert E. Howard: A Pocket Checklist.** [S.l.], D. McHaney & T. Foster, 1975. [22] p. (pbk.).

Just what it says, this small (4.25" x 5.5") checklist of Howard's short stories is alphabetically arranged by title, listing the first appearances of each in published form, either by magazine title, with month and year of publication, or by book title (in caps) and year. There is also a separate two-and-one-half-page list of Howard's "Unpublished Fiction," and eight pages of very amateurish drawings of Howard heroes. The booklet is shot from typed copy. Clearly something to carry with you wherever you go. . . .

398. Weinberg, Robert. **The Robert E. Howard Fantasy Biblio.** Newark, NJ, Mike Deck-inger and Robert Weinberg, 1969. 7 p. (pbk.).

[not seen].

L. Ron Hubbard

399. Widder, William J. **The Fiction of L. Ron Hubbard: A Comprehensive Bibliography & Reference Guide to Published and Selected Unpublished Works.** Los Angeles,

CA, Bridge Publications, Inc., 1994. vii, 373 p. index. (L. Ron Hubbard Library). LC 94-205781. ISBN 0-88404-936-1.

Widder uses a variation of the Borgo Press style to produce a comprehensive bibliography of the literary works of this American pulp writer, the founder of the Church of Scientology, specifically excluding works on the latter topic.

Contents: "Foreword," by Stephen V. Whaley; "Preface," by William J. Widder; "Introduction," by Jana Blythe; "Chronologies of L. Ron Hubbard's Life and Fiction Works"; "A. Books"; "B. Magazine Fiction"; "C. Magazine Nonfiction"; "D. Verse"; "E. Audio Tape Recordings"; "F. Plays & Screenplays"; "G. Honors and Awards for Fiction Works"; "H. Doctor of Literature Award from Moscow University"; "I. Critical Appreciation"; "J. About the Author: Selected Letters and Articles"; "K. About the Author: Biographical Entries and Awards"; "L. About the Author: Monographs, Interviews, References and Reviews"; "M. Miscellanea"; "N. Introduction to *Battlefield Earth*"; "O. L. Ron Hubbard's Writers of the Future"; "P. Photographic Reference Section"; "Q. Series Index"; "R. Index of Quotes and Critical Appreciations"; "S. Title Index."

The first section of this bibliography, dealing with the author's books, is arranged in chronological order by publication date. A typical entry includes: item number (materials are numbered in order by publication date, from the earliest to the latest, prefixed by the chapter letter; *e.g.*, A1, A2, A3, etc., for books), title (boldfaced type), place of publication, publisher, year of publication, format (*e.g.*, "cloth" or "paper"), pagination, similar data for all known reprint editions, including magazine and foreign, and (inconsistently) a non-evaluative annotation ranging in size from one sentence to several paragraphs; many of the entries have no annotations. "See Also" notes are appended in parentheses after the pagination of the first book edition to cross-reference the original magazine publication information located in the "Magazine Fiction" section. Thus, item "A2. Final Blackout," published in hardcover in 1948, is noted as having previously been published in "(1940; see B142)." Some entries include small, black-and-white reproductions of book covers, usually not of the first editions, however.

A typical short fiction entry includes: item number, title (boldfaced type, in quotes), magazine title (italics), volume and issue number, month and year of publication, pagination, similar data for all known reprint editions, including those in books, a brief, one-sentence annotation, and other notes. The other sections are organized similarly.

Each of the major chapters also appends a section of "unpublished" or "forthcoming" materials, numbered with double letters ("AA" for books, for example, "BB" for short stories, etc.). Combining these sections together, there are 139 main book entries, 422 article entries, 131 verse entries, 22 audio tapes, 3 music albums, and 15 screenplays. Black-and-white photographs from Hubbard's career decorate the Chronology, while Section O reproduces a color brochure from a 1994 celebration of the tenth anniversary of the Writers of the Future Program. The Critical Appreciations section includes quotes from authors and critics about specific Hubbard works. The indices cite page numbers only. The book is nicely typeset and bound to library standards.

Curiously, bibliographical data on the recent Author Services editions of Hubbard's work, which will eventually bring into (re)print all of his numerous short fictions written for the pulp magazines of the 1930s and '40s, is somewhat scanty, the entries for these publications generally providing no more than "bare bones" listings of publisher, date, and pagination (or contents, where appropriate). The secondary sources section provides numerous listings of "Who's Who"-type publications, but little else.

Still, this bibliography will be the last word on an author known primarily today for his dianetics writings. A very comprehensive guide suitable for any large library.

Dean Ing

400. Burgess, Scott Alan. **The Work of Dean Ing: An Annotated Bibliography & Guide.** San Bernardino, CA, The Borgo Press, 1990. 82 p. index. (Bibliographies of Modern Authors, No. 11). LC 87-827. ISBN 0-89370-395-8; ISBN 0-89370-495-4 (pbk.).

Dean Ing is best known for his tales of a post-nuclear holocaust America, and for his bestselling near-future techno-thrillers.

Contents: Introduction: "Talking with Dean Ing" (an original interview conducted by Burgess); "A Dean Ing Chronology"; "A. Books"; "B. Short Fiction"; "C. Nonfiction"; "D. Unpublished Works"; "E. Editorial Credits"; "F. Radio and Television Appearances"; "G. Honors and Awards"; "H. About the Author"; "I. Miscellanea"; "Quoth the Critics"; Afterword: "Excuse the Shouting . . . ," by Dean Ing (on his philosophy of writing and living); "Index"; "About Scott Alan Burgess."

In each section, Ing's works are arranged chronologically and numbered consecutively from the number one, chapter by chapter, prefixed by the appropriate letter code (*e.g.,* C1, C2, C3, etc.). A typical book entry includes: item number, title (in boldface), place of publication, publisher, year of publication, pagination, format (*e.g.,* "cloth"), and type of publication (*e.g.,* "novel"); full bibliographical data are also included for all known reprint editions, translations, republications, etc. The books are annotated with complete contents listings and/or plot summaries and other pertinent data; entries from other sections are selectively annotated as needed.

A typical shorter work entry includes: item number, title (in bold quotes), magazine, volume number, month and year of publication, pagination, and complete bibliographical data for all known reprints, including foreign publications. The nonfiction chapter lists over a hundred of Ing's little-known writings for survivalist magazines. The chronology provides a year-by-year account of the author's professional and personal life in block paragraph format.

"About the Author" lists all known secondary works chronologically by publication date. "Miscellanea" includes information on pen names, book dedications, memberships, Library of Congress cataloging data, career highlights, and other data. "Quoth the Critics" includes selected excerpts of reviews and other comments by leading critics on the author's work. The index correlates titles and item numbers only. The book is nicely typeset and the cloth version bound to library standards.

Much of the material in this volume was compiled directly from Ing's own files and personal library of his works. Coverage is complete through late 1990. Although Ing is not well-known outside the SF field, his reputation is growing rapidly. Burgess's guide will provide the scholar with everything he or she would ever want to know about this Oregon author. For larger academic collections only.

Carl Jacobi

401. Smith, R. Dixon. **Lost in the Rentharpian Hills: Spanning the Decades with Carl Jacobi.** Bowling Green, OH, Bowling Green State University Popular Press, 1985. 146 p. index. LC 84-72634. ISBN 0-87972-287-8; ISBN 0-87972-288-6 (pbk.).

Both a biography and bibliography of this American pulp writer's life and works, Smith's guide includes the following sections: "Acknowledgments"; "Foreword," by Robert Bloch; "Foreword," by Joseph Payne Brennan; "Lost in the Rentharpian Hills" (biography); "Notes"; "Appendix I: Carl Jacobi: A Bibliography" (p. 75-119); "Appendix II: Selected Letters to Carl Jacobi"; "Index."

The forty-five-page bibliography is organized into several sections: "I. High School and College Publications" (further divided into two parts, "A. Central High School" and "B. University of Minnesota"); "II. Magazine Publications" (the bulk of the entries); "III. Fan Magazine Publications": "A. Fiction," "B. Non-Fiction"; "IV. Book Publications": "A. [stories in] "Anthologies," "B. Collections" [of fiction by Jacobi himself], "C. Non-Fiction" [books by Jacobi]; "V. Selected Foreign Publications": "A. Magazines," "B. Anthologies," "C. Collections"; "VI. Miscellaneous Publications": "A. Interviews," "B. Autobiographical Sketches," "C. Letters to Editors," "D. Humorous Sketches," "Anecdotes," and "Poems," "E. Book Reviews," "F. Articles Written as a Reporter on the *Minneapolis Star*," "G. Other Writings"; "VII. Unpublished Works."

In each section, materials are arranged chronologically by publication date. A typical book entry includes: author (even when it's Jacobi himself!), title (italics), place of publication, publisher, year of publication, pagination, price, cover illustrator, and a list of the stories included in that volume by Jacobi, with title of the magazine where the piece originally appeared, and the year and month of original publication.

A typical short fiction entry provides: title (in quotes), magazine title (in italics), volume and issue number, month and year of publication, pagination, category (*e.g.,* "Borneo adventure"), wordage, submission and title change history, and the amount that Jacobi was paid for the sale. The book is nicely typeset and designed, featuring some reproductions of the original magazine covers and interior illustrations, and the hardcover version is bound to library standards. The bibliographical items described are indexed within the body of Jacobi's own entry in the general index at the end of the volume, and then alphabetically by title, keyed to specific page numbers throughout the entire book (not just the bibliography).

One major problem with the bibliography is the absence of any coordinated list of reprints for a particular story or collection. This is less burdensome in the book section, where the overall number of monograph titles and reissues by Jacobi are small enough that the eye can encompass virtually the entire list at a glance; but Jacobi was also responsible for the publication of many dozens of pulp stories, and tracking these items is difficult without constant references back and forth to the index.

Scholars will welcome the publication of this volume, but will lament the unnecessarily cumbersome structure of the bibliography section.

K. W. Jeter

402. Joyce, Tom, and Christopher P. Stephens. **A Checklist of K. W. Jeter.** Hastings-on-Hudson, NY, 1991. 13 p. index. ISBN 0-89366-200-3 (pbk.).

This brief guide to American SF writer Jeter's works is arranged in two sections: "Books" and "Short Stories." In both parts materials are arranged in chronological order by publication date, and numbered anew from the number one (books from A1-A14, short fiction from B1-B5).

A typical book entry includes: year (as a floating head), item number, title (underlined), publisher, stock or ISBN number, pagination, format (*e.g.,* "paper over boards"), cover illustrator, price, and similar data for all known reprints (which are numbered, for example, A9a, A9b, A9c, etc., in descending order by publication date).

A typical short fiction entry gives: year (header), item number, title (in quotes), magazine title (underlined), and month and year of publication; or book title (if an anthology; underlined), editor's name, publisher, year of publication, but no paginations. The booklet is shot from legible typed copy and bound with staples in stiff paper covers. The index correlates titles with years of publication only.

Joyce and Stephens have provided an inexpensive introduction to Jeter's work, one that will be primarily of use to fans and collectors.

Stephen King

403. Collings, Michael R. **The Annotated Guide to Stephen King: A Primary and Secondary Bibliography of the Works of America's Premier Horror Writer.** Mercer Island, WA, Starmont House, 1986. vi, 176 p. (Starmont Reference Guide, No. 8). LC 86-1854. ISBN 0-930261-81-X; ISBN 0-930261-80-1 (pbk.).

Collings, author of a half dozen critical monographs on America's premier writer of horror fiction, here has produced the first comprehensive bibliography of King's work.

Contents: "Foreword" (by Collings); "List of Abbreviations"; "Part One: Primary Bibliography": "A. Book-Length Fiction"; "B. Collections of King's Fiction"; "C. Short Fiction and Poetry"; "D. Non-Fiction, Criticism, and Reviews"; "E. The Audio-Visual King." "Part Two: Secondary Bibliography": "F. Bibliographical Studies"; "G. Book-Length Critical Studies and Newsletters"; "H. Selected Critical Articles, Reviews, and Interviews"; "List of Works Cited."

Entries are numbered anew from one in each chapter (*e.g.,* A1, A2, A3, for the first three book titles). The primary bibliography lists King's works in alphabetical order by title, section by section. A typical book entry includes: item number, title (underlined boldface), place of publication, publisher, format (*e.g.,* paperback), brief data on reprint editions and translations, plot summary, list of book reviews (by magazine title, with date and page number). No paginations are supplied for monographs. The collections also include contents listings in addition to analytical annotations.

A typical shorter work entry includes: item number, title (in bold quotes), magazine (underlined), date, pagination, and an abbreviated title of the King collection in which the piece is included (where appropriate), with year of publication of the collection, and the exact pagination of the story or article in the first edition of the collection; one-paragraph annotations are also included for all short fiction and essays. Section E includes: item number, title, production company, date, whether the film is available on tape (and in what format), number of minutes, film rating (G, R, etc.), critical evaluation, list of principals (producer, director, etc.), and cast. Also mentioned are computer games, audio tapes, calendars, with brief summaries of each.

The secondary bibliography is arranged by author or main entry, section by section, with approximately 600 secondary sources listed. A typical entry includes: item number, author, title, publication, date, pagination, and brief critical evaluation.

Collings's coverage is thorough, and his knowledge of King's work is unsurpassed; the list of secondary sources is particularly valuable for researchers. However, the book is somewhat crowded and cramped, particularly in Sections C, D, and H, where the items are jammed together with no spaces between the entries. Also, the constant use of abbreviations is both irritating and unnecessary. The absence of a comprehensive title index is very noticeable here, and one also misses having paginations for King's monographs.

Still, Collings's work, outdated as it is, remains a good beginning guide to a modern literary phenomenon, which should be owned by all academic (and all large public) libraries. Now superseded by *The Work of Stephen King* (see #404).

404. Collings, Michael R. **The Work of Stephen King: An Annotated Bibliography & Guide.** San Bernardino, CA, Borgo Press, 1996. 480 p. index. (Bibliographies of Modern Authors, No. 25). LC 93-16091. ISBN 0-8095-0520-7 (cloth); ISBN 0-8095-1520-2 (pbk.).

Stephen King has become one of the world's bestselling authors, and certainly the best-known horror writer since H. P. Lovecraft. Collings's book is a completely reorganized, updated, and expanded version of his previous bibliography, *The Annotated Guide to Stephen King* (#403).

Contents: "Introduction: 'Not So Much to Tell, as to Let the Story Flow Through,' by Collings"; "A Stephen King Chronology"; "About Michael R. Collings." Part One: Primary Works. "A. Books"; "B. Short Fiction"; "C. Short Nonfiction"; "D. Poetry"; "E. Screenplays" [those by King]: "EA. Produced Screenplays," "EB. Unproduced Screenplays"; "F. Public and Screen Appearances": "FA. Public Appearances and Speeches," "FB. Screen Appearances"; "G. Visual Adaptations of King Materials": "GA. Feature-Length Films," "GB. Teleplays and Television Adaptations," "GC. Musical Adaptations," "GD. Stage Adaptations," "GE. Videocassettes"; "H. Audio Adaptations of King Materials."

Part Two: Secondary Works. "I. Books and Book-Length Studies"; "J. Newsletters"; "K. Bibliographies and Filmographies"; "L. Profiles and Bio-Bibliographical Sketches"; "M. Interviews with Stephen King": "MA. Print Interviews," "MB. Non-Print Interviews"; "N. Scholarly Essays"; "O. Articles in Popular and News Magazines"; "P. Media Magazines, Specialty Magazines, Fan Publications"; "Q. *Castle Rock: The Stephen King Newsletter* (1985-1989)"; "R. Newspaper Articles"; "S. Articles in Professional and Trade Journals"; "T. Selected Reviews of Stephen King Works"; "U. The Stephen King Archives, University of Maine, Orono"; "V. Unpublished Works": "VA. Novels," "VB. Short Fiction"; "W. Parodies, Pastiches, Etc.": "WA. Cartoons About Stephen King," "WB. Contents and Puzzles," "WC. Parodies and Satires," "WD. Pastiches," "WE. Stories and Poems About King," "WF. Conferences," "WG. Miscellaneous Secondary Items"; "X. Honors and Awards"; "Y. Miscellanea"; "Quoth the Critics"; "Index: Primary Works"; "Index: Secondary Works"; "Index: Authors of Secondary Works and Miscellanea."

In each section and subsection materials are arranged chronologically by publication date and numbered anew from the number one, with the appropriate letter prefix (*e.g.,* MB1, MB2, MB3, etc.). A typical book entry includes: item number, title (bold italics), place of publication, publisher, year of publication, pagination, format (*e.g.,* cloth), and type (*e.g.,* collection), plus similar data on all known reprints, foreign and domestic, a plot synopsis and/or list of contents, references to motion picture or other video or audio versions of the work, and a comprehensive list of reviews and/or articles about that specific title arranged in alphabetical order by main entry (by critic, if known, or by title or magazine, in that order, if no byline is credited).

A typical shorter work entry gives: item number, title (boldfaced, in quotes), magazine title, volume number, month and year of publication, and pagination, or, if the publication has first appeared in an anthology or collection: book title (in italics), editor or author, place of publication, publisher, month and year of publication, format, and specific pagination. Similar data are provided for all known reprints. The media sections give: title (bold italics), production company, producer, director, screenwriter, running time, rating (*e.g.,* "R"), cast, and a comprehensive list of reviews. The two title indices (primary and secondary) correlate titles and item numbers only; the secondary author index correlates names and item numbers only. The book is beautifully typeset and the hardcover version is bound to library standards.

Collings has assembled an incredibly large number of citations, carefully arranged and logically organized. Some 2,388 main entries are noted, plus 1,521 secondary sources, with more than a thousand reviews of King's novels and film adaptations of his work, all made easily accessible through the index. The complete content notes for books in section I, "Books and Book-Length Studies," is a nice touch. Data are complete through early 1995.

However, the renumbering within a section is occasionally inconsistent and sometimes confusing (*e.g.*, Section G starts renumbering with GB, while Section I starts with IA), and sometimes gets out of control (G renumbers subsections through GE, while W is divided through WG). This renumbering reflects slight differences in the types of material being addressed; however, some material could perhaps be incorporated into already existing groups, such as the motion picture *Carrie,* which is now covered in three different sections, for the original film (G1), the videocassette version (GE1), and the musical (GC1). The primary index does address this issue by correlating the item numbers of all three entries.

Such minor problems, which may be inherent in a particularly large and complex bibliography (this is the longest and most detailed volume in the Bibliographies of Modern Authors series), do not detract from the wealth of information included in this book. Indeed, it is difficult to imagine how any serious researcher of Stephen King's fiction could bypass this extremely comprehensive and detailed guide, although it is already in need of an update. Recommended for all university and large public library collections.

Dean R. Koontz

405. Stephens, Christopher P. **A Checklist of Dean R. Koontz.** Hastings-on-Hudson, NY, Ultramarine Publishing Co., 1987. 14 p. index. ISBN 0-89366-133-3 (pbk.). **A Checklist**

of Dean R. Koontz. [3rd ed.]. Hastings-on-Hudson, NY, Ultramarine Publishing Co., 1990. 19 p. index. ISBN 0-89366-133-3 (pbk.) [sic].

Koontz has achieved wide popularity in recent years with his horror and suspense novels, although his beginnings as a writer were deeply rooted in the science-fiction field. Stephens's checklist (both editions) is organized in chronological order by publication date, books being numbered from A1-A61.

A typical entry provides: year (as a floating head), item number, title (underlined), pseudonym, publisher, stock or ISBN number, pagination, format (*e.g.,* "cloth with dust wrapper"), cover illustrator, price, and similar data for all known reprints (which are numbered, for example, A40a, A40b, A40c, etc., in descending order by publication date). The chapbook is shot from legible typed copy and bound with staples in stiff paper covers. The index correlates titles with years of publication only.

Koontz deserves fuller treatment than this brief guide provides, but until a complete bibliography is available, Stephens's checklist will suffice for most fans.

C. M. Kornbluth

406. Stephensen-Payne, Phil, and Gordon Benson, Jr. **Cyril M. Kornbluth, the Cynical Scrutineer: A Working Bibliography.** 2nd rev. ed. Leeds, West Yorkshire, England, Galactic Central Publications, 1990. 9, 39 p. (Galactic Central Bibliographies for the Avid Reader, Vol. 29). ISBN 1-871133-03-3 (pbk.).

Kornbluth, who died tragically young in 1958, left over a hundred vivid stories and novels as an abiding literary legacy. Stephensen-Payne and Benson arrange this new bibliography by subject category, then alphabetically by title.

Contents: Author's full name, date and place of birth and date of death, awards, and pseudonyms; "A. Stories"; "B. Fiction Books"; "C. Series"; "D. Poems"; "E. Poetry Collections" [blank section]; "F. Articles"; "G. Miscellaneous"; "H. Non-Fiction Books" [blank section]; "I. Edited Books" [blank section]; "J. Media Presentations"; "K. Articles on C. M. Kornbluth"; "L. Reviews"; "M. Books About C. M. Kornbluth" [blank section]; "N. Phantom Titles"; "O. Related Books by Other Authors"; "P. Textual Variations"; "Q. Chronological Index."

In each part the material is arranged in alphabetical order by title, the author's works being numbered anew from the number one in each. For shorter works, the authors give: item number, title, category ("ss" = short story, "nt" = novelette, etc.), pseudonym (where appropriate), magazine or book in which the item appeared, month and year of publication (for magazines in the form "7-50" for July 1950), or year of publication (for books), a list of subsequent reprints (for which title, publisher, year, and editor's last name are given), but no paginations.

For book-length works, they provide: item number, title (in caps), pseudonym, contents for collections (keyed to item number), and publication data (publisher, LC card number, month and year of publication [if known, in the form "10-59" for October 1959], pagination, price, stock number, with dates of reissues by the same publisher), plus cover artist and similar data for all known reprints. The list of secondary sources includes thirty-four items and more than a hundred book reviews. There is no general index. The book is shot from very clear word-processed copy and bound with staples in paper covers. Data are complete through 1989.

The addition of an index and magazine paginations to future editions would be useful. As the only current guide to this neglected writer's fiction, Stephensen-Payne and Benson's bibliography will be an essential starting point for all future scholarly investigations of Kornbluth.

Katherine Kurtz

407. Clarke, Boden, and Mary A. Burgess. **The Work of Katherine Kurtz: An Annotated Bibliography & Guide.** San Bernardino, CA, The Borgo Press, 1993. 128 p. index. (Bibliographies of Modern Authors, No. 7). LC 85-31401. ISBN 0-89370-386-9; ISBN 0-89370-486-5 (pbk.).

Kurtz is a popular American writer of historical fantasy novels, now living in Ireland.

Contents: "Introduction: 'Bridges: An Appreciation of Katherine Kurtz', by Andrew V. Phillips"; "A Katherine Kurtz Chronology"; "A. Books"; "B. Short Fiction"; "C. Short Nonfiction"; "D. Songs"; "E. Editorial Credits"; "F. Scripts"; "G. Other Media"; "H. Unpublished Works"; "I. Honors and Awards"; "J. Secondary Sources"; "K. Miscellanea"; "Quoth the Critics"; "Afterword: 'Talking with Katherine Kurtz,' by Jeffrey M. Elliot & Robert Reginald"; "Afterword: 'Imaginary History: A Genealogical Approach,' by Kurtz"; "Index"; "About the Authors."

In each section, the author's works are arranged chronologically and numbered consecutively chapter by chapter. A typical book entry includes: item number, title (in boldface), place of publication, publisher, year of publication, pagination, format (*e.g.,* "paper"), type of publication (*e.g.,* "novel"), with full bibliographical data for all reprint editions, translations, republications, etc. The books are fully annotated, with complete contents listings or plot summaries and other pertinent data; entries from other sections are selectively annotated as needed.

A typical short work entry includes: item number, title (bold quotes), magazine title, volume or issue number, date, pagination, with bibliographical data on all known reprints. The introduction provides background material on the author's life and works. The chronology provides a year-by-year account of the author's professional and personal life in block paragraph format. "Secondary Sources" includes all known secondary works. The "Miscellanea" section includes information on book dedications, memberships, Library of Congress cataloging data, career highlights, and other data.

"Quoth the Critics" includes selected excerpts of reviews and other comments by leading critics on the author's work. The afterword consists of a lengthy written interview with Kurtz conducted originally by Dr. Elliot, edited, updated, and expanded for this edition by Robert Reginald; this and the reprinted essay by the author provide much illumination of her personality and avocations. The index correlates titles and item numbers only. The book is nicely designed and typeset, and the hardcover version is bound to library standards. Coverage is complete through 1992, with some forthcoming entries projected to mid-1993.

Kurtz has a large and loyal following for whom this volume provides the first organized guide to her life and work. Much of the material was derived from Kurtz's own files and personal library, supplemented by follow-up questions and later correspondence.

Clearly presented, well designed, and comprehensive, but useful primarily for large research collections.

Henry Kuttner

408. Anderson, Karen. **Henry Kuttner: A Memorial Symposium.** Berkeley, CA, Seva-gram Enterprises, 1958. 34 p. (pbk.).

Kuttner died in 1958 in his forties, after a twenty-year career during which he produced hundreds of short stories and several dozen novels. Immediately after his death, a number of his California friends put together a memorial volume, which includes reminiscences by his colleagues, a Kuttner story, and a brief bibliography of his SF works compiled by the well-known Australian bibliographer, Donald H. Tuck. Although Tuck covers Kuttner's periodical and monographic fictions in the science-fiction field, none of his mystery novels or stories are mentioned, or his work in other genres, and the guide shows signs of hasty composition. Prefer Utter and Benson's more current bibliography (see #440).

Utter, Virgil, and Gordon Benson, Jr. & Phil Stephensen-Payne **Catherine Lucille Moore and Henry Kuttner: A Working Bibliography.** *See the entry for C. L. Moore* (see #440).

R. A. Lafferty

409. Drumm, Chris. **An R. A. Lafferty Checklist: A Bibliographical Chronology with Notes and Index.** Polk City, IA, Chris Drumm Books, 1983 (1984). [31] p. index. ISBN 0-936055-04-9 (pbk.).

Lafferty, an eccentric, iconoclastic engineer-turned-science fiction writer, is the focus of this brief 4.25" x 7" checklist. The author's works are arranged in one straight chronological sequence. Entries are grouped by year and under each year by month; items are numbered in sequence from 1-192. Books are underlined, short stories listed in quotation marks.

A typical short fiction entry includes: item number, title, category code (*e.g.*, "s" = short story), magazine, month of publication, paginations, and estimated wordage; or book title if the first appearance is in an anthology, plus editor, publisher, year of publication, paginations, and estimated wordage. Subsequent reprintings are grouped under the original edition, with similar data provided.

A typical book entry includes: item number, title, category code (*e.g.*, "c" = collection), publisher, stock number, month of publication (if known), pagination, price, format (*e.g.*, "pb" = paperback), contents of collections. "See" references, title index, and contents listings are keyed to item number. A few secondary materials are mentioned in passing in their appropriate years, but are not easily retrievable. Data are complete through early 1984. The book is shot from typed copy; the text runs too close to the right-hand margin to allow rebinding by libraries. A long, one-paragraph autobiographical essay by Lafferty on page (3) provides a brief introduction to the author and his work.

Drumm has published many of Lafferty's collections and novels since this bibliography first appeared; a second, more elaborate update of this booklet would clearly be justified.

Keith Laumer

410. Stephensen-Payne, Phil, and Gordon Benson Jr. **Keith Laumer, Ambassador to Space: A Working Bibliography.** 2nd rev. ed. Leeds, West Yorkshire, England, Galactic Central Publications, 1990. 9, 41 p. (Galactic Central Bibliographies for the Avid Reader, Vol. 30). ISBN 1-871133-04-1 (pbk.).

The late American diplomat and SF writer Laumer was best known for his tales of Retief, ambassador to the stars and rogue extraordinaire. This new checklist arranges the data by subject, then alphabetically by title.

Contents: Personal data on the author; "A. Stories"; "B. Fiction Books"; "C. Series"; "D. Poems & Songs" [blank section]; "E. Poem & Song Collections" [blank section]; "F. Articles"; "G. Miscellaneous" (introductions and interviews); "H. Non-Fiction Books"; "I. Edited Books"; "J. Media Presentations"; "K. Articles on Keith Laumer"; "L. Reviews" [of Laumer's books]; "M. Books About Keith Laumer" [blank section]; "N. Phantom and Forth-coming Titles"; "O. Related Books by Other Authors"; "P. Textual Variations" [blank section]; "Q. Chronological Index."

A typical book entry provides: item number, title (all caps), contents (where appro-priate, keyed to item number), publisher, format (*e.g.,* "hb" = hardback), stock number, month and year of publication ("8-76" = August 1976), pagination, price, cover artist, plus similar data for all known reprints and reissues.

A typical shorter work entry gives: item number, title, type (*e.g.,* "ss" = short story), magazine title and month and year of publication, or, for anthology appearances, book title (all caps), editor's last name, publisher, and year of publication, but no paginations; similar data are provided for all known reprints. Materials are numbered anew from the number one in each section, prefixed by the letter associated with that chapter (*e.g.,* A44, A45, A46, etc.). The eighteen secondary sources are listed alphabetically by critics' name, and reviews alphabetically by Laumer book title, then by magazine title. There is no overall index. The book is shot from very clear word-processed copy and bound through the side with staples.

Laumer has received little attention from the critics, even within the SF genre, despite his prolific output; this bibliography represents the first attempt to synthesize his literary career. SF scholars and major academic libraries should both include copies in their collec-tions.

J. Sheridan Le Fanu

411. Crawford, Gary William. **J. Sheridan Le Fanu: A Bio-Bibliography.** Westport, CT, Greenwood, 1995. ix, 155 p. index. (Bio-Bibliographies in World Literature, No. 3). LC 94-38419. ISBN 0-313-28515-2.

Contents: "Preface"; "Part I: Biography" ("1. Biography"; "2. Chronology)"; "Part II: Primary Bibliography" ("1. Magazines"; "2. Books"; "3. Anthologies"; "4. Manuscripts"); "Part III: Secondary Bibliography" ("1. Research Overview"; "2. Books"; "3. Essays"; "4. General Studies"; "5. Introductions"; "6. Articles"; "7. Reviews;" "8. Dissertations"); "Ap-pendix" ("Films and Plays Based on Le Fanu's Works"); "Index" ("Title Index to Primary Bibliography"; "Author Index to Secondary Bibliography").

This annotated bibliography of works by and about a well-known Victorian horror writer contains 473 main entries, of which 300 are secondary sources, covering sources published from 1838-1992, though some later information is included on a selective basis. Items are divided into separate sections based on the type of material, and numbered sequentially.

A typical monograph entry includes: reference number, title (underlined), year and place of publication, and publisher, but no paginations, plus similar information on reprint editions. Primary monographs may include (inconsistently) a summary of the book's contents (50-100 words). Crawford states in the preface that if he did not see the item, he did not annotate it. Secondary monographs follow the same pattern, but are almost always annotated.

Primary short story entries are arranged by name of magazine where they appeared, then chronologically by publication date. A typical shorter fiction entry includes: title (in quotation marks), volume number, month, year, pagination, an annotation that both summarizes and evaluates the story, followed by citations of reprints. Secondary short entries are arranged alphabetically by author, but otherwise follow the same basic bibliographical format.

The section called "Anthologies" is really a Le Fanu short story index, arranged alphabetically by title of the story, and listing the anthologies where each has appeared, with information on book title (underlined), editor, place of publication, publisher, and year of publication, but no paginations. Note that some of Le Fanu's novels are first listed in the "Magazines" chapter, with the information for their original serializations in magazine form; and it is here that one will find the descriptive annotations for those books, something not at all obvious to the casual user.

The two indices, a primary title index and a secondary author index, cross-reference data with item numbers. No foreign language editions of Le Fanu's works are mentioned.

In his 1996 review of this book, Jared Lobdell justly takes issue with a few of Crawford's facts, as well as with the author's sometimes awkward writing style. These issues, plus the occasional absence of complete bibliographical data for certain items, and the volume's somewhat cumbersome format, prevent this guide from being the last word on its subject, but it still contains much valuable information that can be found nowhere else. Durably constructed to library standards, it is recommended for purchase by larger research libraries.

Ursula K. Le Guin

412. Cogell, Elizabeth Cummins. **Ursula K. Le Guin: A Primary and Secondary Bibliography.** Boston, G. K. Hall & Co., 1983. xl, 244 p. index. (Masters of Science Fiction and Fantasy). LC 82-12071. ISBN 0-8161-8155-1.

Le Guin is generally regarded as one of the leading SF writers of the last three decades. Cogell's well-constructed bibliography contains: "Preface" (discussing the book's arrangement); "Introduction" (an excellent twenty-eight-page guide to the author's life and work); "Part A: Fiction"; "Part B: Miscellaneous Media": "Section One: Works by Le Guin," "Section Two: Adaptations of and Creative Responses to Le Guin's Work"; "Part C: Nonfiction"; "Part D: Critical and Bio-Bibliographical Studies"; "Indexes: I. Writings by Le Guin"; "II. Writings About Le Guin."

Each section is arranged chronologically, from the earliest published material to the latest, and numbered consecutively from one, section by section (*e.g.,* C1, C2, C3 for non-fiction). Books and shorter works are interfiled by year; reprints of books and stories are grouped as subsidiary entries under their first edition or appearance, chronologically by year of reprint; reprint editions of short stories include editor of anthology, title, place of publication, publisher, year, format (*e.g.,* "paper"), but no paginations.

Each book entry gives: item number, title (underlined), place of publication, publisher, format ("paper"), contents (for collections and anthologies, with years of original publication), but no paginations. Each shorter work entry includes: item number, title (in quotations), magazine, volume number, date, pagination, or, for those published originally in books, book title, book editor, place of publication, publisher, format, and pagination. Some entries, particularly in Sections B-C, include bibliographical or descriptive notes but no other annotations; all of the entries in Part D are extensively annotated.

"Part B: Miscellaneous Media" includes screenplays, teleplays, interviews, recordings, poetry, and other material that do not specifically fit the other three categories; for Le Guin, most of the 147 entries are poems or collections of verse. "Part C: Nonfiction" includes all the author's nonfiction publications, arranged chronologically.

"Part D" includes all known articles, reviews, and books about Le Guin, arranged chronologically by publication date, with author, title, bibliographical data (in the same format as the other sections, except that paginations are provided for books), and one- to five-paragraph annotations; most "Who's Who"-type publications are omitted. There are 761 secondary items noted, making this a substantial and extraordinarily valuable resource for the scholar. The indices correlate titles, names, and item numbers only. Coverage is complete through the first part of 1981. The book is reproduced from typed copy.

Cogell clearly is familiar with and sympathetic to Le Guin's work; thus, although her guide is now far out-of-date, this bibliography must still be regarded as the essential starting point for all scholarly examinations of the author's fiction. A newly updated edition is badly needed.

Tanith Lee

413. Soanes, Paul A., and Jim Pattison. **Daughter of the Night: A Tanith Lee Bibliography.** Toronto, Canada, The Gaffa Press, 1993. 44 p. index. (pbk.).

Contents: "Introduction"; "Separate Publications"; "Stories & Poems"; "Other Media"; "Sequels & Series"; "Chronology"; "Anthology & Magazine Checklist"; "Index"; "Secondary Bibliography"; "References."

A primary bibliography of all of the "English language publications in both England and North American" of popular British fantasy writer Tanith Lee, issued as an 8.5 x 11 stapled booklet, Soanes and Pattison's checklist is arranged by subject category, then chronologically in each section by publication date; materials are numbered consecutively from one in each chapter (for example, B1, B2, B3, etc., for stories and poems).

A typical monograph entry ("Separate Publications") includes: entry number, title (bold), type of material (children's book, young adult novel, novel, etc.), publisher, year and place of publication, pagination, ISBN, cover price, notes on illustrators, cover authors, etc., and a list of reprints with similar information. A typical shorter work entry gives: item number, title, type of material (short story, novelette, poem, etc.), magazine or book in which the item appeared (italics), month and year of publication, and a list of subsequent reprints with similar information. No paginations are included for short work entries. 226 entries are covered through June 1993, although reprint information makes the overall total greater.

The secondary bibliography is small, noting just twenty-six references on a single page, and does not include book reviews. Most of the items mentioned are interviews with Lee or entries about her in such standard reference works as *Twentieth-Century Science-Fiction Writers* (see #58) or Clute's *The Encyclopedia of Science Fiction* (see #12). The authors have also included a Tanith Lee chronology that includes material from all sections of the bibliography in one sequence, a series index, an anthology and magazine checklist, and a title index (labelled "Index") that cross-references items with entry numbers.

Soanes and Pattison issued this book in a limited edition of 100 copies, making it nearly impossible to find. However, after receiving positive feedback for their work, Pattison mounted the text on the web and has continued to update it ever since. The electronic edition employs much of the same structure as the print version, using the same headings in the table of contents, but has been enhanced to include scanned images of the covers of Lee's first editions, expanded indexing, and annotations of the book and short story entries.

While devoted collectors, fans, or archival libraries can choose to hunt for the few remaining print copies, most will prefer to use the free and improved electronic edition at (http://www3.sympatico.ca/jim.pattison/).

Fritz Leiber

414. Benson, Gordon, Jr., and Phil Stephensen-Payne. **Fritz Leiber, Sardonic Swordsman: A Working Bibliography.** 2nd rev. ed. Albuquerque, NM, and Leeds, West Yorkshire, England, Galactic Central Publications, 1990. 9, 90 p. (Galactic Central Bibliographies for the Avid Reader, Vol. 22). ISBN 0-912613-23-8 and 1-871133-24-6 (pbk.). Later reprintings of this book were issued in two volumes, labelled "Part 1: Fiction" and "Part 2: Non-Fiction," but continuing the same pagination throughout the books.

The late American author Fritz Leiber, a science fiction and fantasy writer of the classic period, is second only to Harlan Ellison as an overall winner of Hugo and Nebula Awards. This guide to Leiber's work is arranged by subject category, then alphabetically by title.

Contents: Author's full name, date and place of birth, pseudonyms, and awards and honors; "A. Stories"; "B. Fiction Books"; "C. Series"; "D. Poems, Songs & Plays"; "E. Poem, Song & Play Volumes"; "F. Articles"; "G. Miscellaneous"; "H. Non-Fiction Books"; "I. Books Edited by Fritz Leiber"; "J. Media Presentations"; "K. Articles on Fritz Leiber"; "L. Reviews" [of Leiber's books]; "M. Books About Fritz Leiber"; "N. Phantom & Forthcoming Titles"; "O. Related Items by Other Authors" [blank section]; "P. Textual Variations"; "Q. Chronological Index."

Materials are numbered consecutively from the number one in each section. For shorter works, the authors give: item number, title, category ("ss" = short story, "nt" =

novelette, etc.), magazine or book in which the item appeared, month and year of publication (for magazines in the form "6-57" for June 1957), or year of publication (for books), plus a list of all known reprints (for which title, publisher, year, and editor's last name are given), but no paginations.

Monographic entries provide: item number, title (in caps), contents (for collections and anthologies, keyed to item number), publication data (publisher, stock number, month and year of publication [if known, in the form "10-56" for October 1956], pagination, price, with dates of reissues by the same publisher), cover artist, plus similar data for all known reprint editions. Seventy-five secondary sources are listed and well over a hundred book reviews. There is no general index. The book is shot from clearly legible word-processed copy and bound with staples in paper covers. Data are complete through mid-1990.

The second edition of this bibliography represents a substantial improvement over the first, both quantitatively (increasing the page count from 35-90 pages) and qualitatively (adding substantial numbers of secondary sources and other works and improving physical appearance and organization). The addition of an index and magazine paginations in future editions would be helpful.

Compared to Morgan's guide (see #415), *Fritz Leiber, Sardonic Swordsman* includes considerably more information arranged in a superior format, and is a decade more current, clearly making it the better of the two.

415. Morgan, Chris. **Fritz Leiber: A Bibliography, 1934-1979.** Birmingham, England, Morgenstern, 1979. 36 p. index. (pbk.).

Morgan, a British fan with several other pamphlet-length bibliographies to his credit, here provides a brief chronological checklist of this well-known American fantasist and essayist.

Contents: "Brief Biography," by David Langford; "Notes"; "Books"; "Bibliography" (*i.e.,* sources consulted); "Special Magazine Issues"; "Awards"; "Articles"; "Key to Photographs"; "Stories"; two pages of jacket photographs; "Media"; "Index."

Each section is arranged by date of publication. Books are numbered in order from 1-37; a typical book entry includes: item number; title (underlined caps); subject and type (*e.g.,* "horror novel); contents (for collections); previous serialization of novels (if applicable); and a list of all known English-language editions in order of publication. Bibliographical entries are lettered in chronological order from "a," and include: country, format (*e.g.,* "hardcover"), publisher, month and year of publication, stock number, price, cover artist, other notes. No foreign-language versions or paginations are shown.

Materials in other sections are unnumbered, and are listed year-by-year, the year being centered at the head of each sub-section, and then by month of publication. A typical shorter work entry includes: title (in quotes); alternate titles (where applicable); magazine title (italics) and month of publication; or book title (for stories appearing originally in anthologies), and editor. Subsequent appearances of each piece in English, including stories or essays reprinted in Leiber's own books, are listed chronologically thereafter. No paginations and no bibliographical data for anthologies are provided.

The index is oddly arranged, cross-referencing titles and item numbers for books, but titles and years and months of publication for all other materials; essays are distinguished from short stories by having "ART" appended to each title. Materials are included through August 1979. The book is shot from fairly legible typed copy.

Although Morgan's guide includes illustrations not found in Benson/Stephensen-Payne's bibliography (see #414), the latter contains far more data in a much more usable format, and should be preferred by researchers and libraries.

Murray Leinster

416. Owings, Mark. **Murray Leinster (Will F. Jenkins): A Bibliography.** Washington, DC, Washington Science Fiction Association, 1970. [9] p. (pbk.).

Owings was a well-known bibliographer of science fiction during the early 1970s, producing several significant checklists with similar formats (see #308, #391, #423, #464, #470).

This booklet, the first of the series, is organized into one alphabetical sequence by title, with books being underlined. Each title is flush to the left-hand margin, the remainder of the entry being indented to set it off. There are no line breaks between entries, but several lines are skipped between letters of the alphabet.

A typical short fiction entry includes: title, magazine title, month and year of publication (in the form "6/58" for June 1958), and known reprint editions (with book title, editor, publisher, place of publication, stock number [for paperbacks], year of publication, format [e.g., "wpps" = paperback], total pagination of book, price, but no individual paginations).

A typical book entry gives: title, publisher, place of publication, year of publication, pagination, price, with similar data for known reprint editions. Some foreign-language editions are shown with translators and foreign-language title equivalents (such data are very difficult to locate elsewhere). The book is shot from sometimes faint typed copy that is now yellowing with age. Data are included through 1969, the year Leinster's last book was published.

Despite its poor production values, this brief bibliography remains an essentially complete record of the SF output of this very prolific pulp writer. Leinster now deserves a much fuller treatment, both of his life and of his many works for the pulps and book publishers of the 1920s-'60s.

H. P. Lovecraft

417. Bell, Joseph. **Howard Phillips Lovecraft: A Chronology** (title varies slightly from section to section). Toronto, Canada, Soft Books, 1984-87. 8 v. index. (Les Bibliotheques, Parts 1-8). (pbk.).

Bell has prepared an interesting chronological checklist of the publications of Howard Phillips Lovecraft, America's premier horror writer of the first half of the twentieth century.

Publications are arranged year by year (and in the earlier sections, month by month), then alphabetically under each year by title. Bell mentions *all* Lovecraft publications in his schematic, including reprints, reissues, and republications of stories and books previously issued elsewhere; thus, many of the popular collections (*e.g., At the Mountains of Madness and Other Novels*) or the frequently anthologized shorter works are repeated again and again, some of them dozens of times.

Short story entries are displayed in lower case boldface, and include numbers after the title indicating how many times this particular tale has been reprinted to the date of that particular entry. A typical shorter work entry includes: title, printing number, title of book or magazine (in italics), and (for anthologies) editor, publisher, place of publication, and the overall pagination of the book (but not of the story included within that volume), plus reissue data.

Book entries include: title (all caps), item number (correlated with Bell's checklist of Lovecraft's books, listed below), publisher, place of publication, pagination. An entry in all caps with boldface type indicates this is the first separate publication of this item. Part Six is an index to the preceding five sections; a title index to Parts Seven and Eight appears at the end of the latter volume, correlating: title, number of the section of the chronology in which it appears, page number, and type (*e.g.,* "essay").

Since many of the individual pieces of this long-running chronological bibliography are now out-of-print, a reprint in one volume with the indices merged into one alphabetical sequence would prove of great value to the collecting community.

418. Bell, Joseph. **Howard Philips Lovecraft: The Books (4), 1915-1986.** 2nd ed. Toronto, Canada, Soft Books, 1987. v, 63 p. index. (pbk.).

This latest edition of a collectors' guide to Lovecraft's monographs arranges (and numbers) his monographs in chronological order by year of publication, then alphabetically by title.

A typical entry includes: item number, title (large boldface letters), publisher, place of publication, pagination, binding style, price, year of first printing, other bibliographical notes, and complete contents listing. Similar details are provided about subsequent printings, with enough details included to specific identify edition states. Two separate indices, of book titles and individual story titles, are keyed both to item number and page number. The book is attractively printed in 8.5" x 11" format.

Bell's guide is designed primarily for collectors, providing sufficient edition points so that the experienced bookperson can find his or her way through the labyrinthine maze of Lovecraftiana. Libraries will prefer Joshi's more substantial literary bibliography (see #419).

419. Joshi, S. T. **H. P. Lovecraft and Lovecraft Criticism: An Annotated Bibliography.** Kent, OH, Kent State University Press, 1981. xxxiv, 473 p. index. (The Serif Series: Bibliographies and Checklists, No. 38). LC 80-84662. ISBN 0-87338-248-X. Joshi, S. T., and L. D. Blackmore. **H. P. Lovecraft and Lovecraft Criticism: An Annotated Bibliography Supplement, 1980-1984.** West Warwick, RI, Necronomicon Press, 1985. iv, 72 p. (pbk.).

Joshi's excellent bibliography covers the work of a particularly difficult writer, one who published his stories in a wide variety of amateur and semi-professional outlets.

Contents (original edition): "Introduction"; "Explanatory Notes"; "Abbreviations"; "I. Works by Lovecraft in English": "A. Books by Lovecraft"; "B. Contributions to Periodicals": "i. Fiction," "ii. Nonfiction," "iii. Poetry," "iv. Revisions and Collaborations," "v. Letters"; "C. Material Included in Books by Others"; "D. Works Edited by Lovecraft": "i.

Books," "ii. Periodicals"; "E. Apocrypha and Other Miscellany": "i. Apocrypha," "ii. Lost Works," "iii. Works Destroyed," "iv. Items Included Within Published Works by Lovecraft," "v. Award-Winning Stories by Lovecraft," "vi. Miscellany." "II. Works by Lovecraft in Translation": "A. Books by Lovecraft"; "B. Contributions to Periodicals": "i. Fiction," "ii. Nonfiction," "iii. Poetry," "iv. Revisions and Collaboration," "v. Letters"; "C. Material Included in Books by Others."

"III. Works about Lovecraft": "A. News Items and Encyclopedias"; "B. Bibliographies and Glossaries"; "C. Books and Pamphlets About Lovecraft"; "D. Criticism in Books or Periodicals"; "E. Academic Theses and Unpublished Papers": "i. Academic Theses," "ii. Unpublished Papers"; "F. Book Reviews": "i. Books in English," "ii. Books in Languages Other than English"; "G. Special Periodicals and Unclassifiable Data": "i. Periodicals Devoted Exclusively or Largely to Lovecraft," "ii. Single Issues of Periodicals Devoted to Lovecraft," "iii. Amateur Press Associations," "iv. Unclassifiable Data"; "Supplement." "IV. Indexes": "A. Works by Lovecraft"; "B. Works by Others"; "C. Names"; "D. Periodicals"; "E. Foreign Languages."

Monographs are listed in chronological order by date of publication, shorter works alphabetically by title. Entries are numbered consecutively from the number one in each section. A typical book entry includes: item number, title (in italics), year of publication, title page (occasionally cover page) copy, collation, binding, size (in centimeters), edition notes and points. Similar data are provided on all subsequent printings and editions, in chronological order by date of publication.

A typical shorter work entry includes: title (in quotes), magazine title (italics), volume and issue number, month and year of publication, pagination, and occasional notes. "Material Included in Books by Others" is arranged in alphabetical order by main entry (usually editor), giving item number, editor, book title (italics), place of publication, publisher, month and year of issue, total pagination of book, title of the Lovecraft work included, pagination of the Lovecraft work, and similar data on any subsequent reprintings (including any changes in paginations of the Lovecraft item within these volumes).

Translations are arranged chronologically for books and in alphabetical order by the original English-language title for shorter works; bibliographical data are arranged similarly to preceding sections, except that the shorter works chapters also include the title of the work in the foreign language and the translator (when known). Secondary sources are arranged by critic, except for book reviews, which are listed by title of the book being reviewed, then by critic's name. Complete bibliographical data are provided for all entries.

Joshi lists roughly 1,000 items in this section, making his book an immensely valuable resource for the student of Lovecraft's work (he even includes reviews of the critical monographs!). The indices are keyed to item number. Coverage is complete through 1979 (extended to 1984 with the supplement). The book is beautifully typeset and designed. The *Supplement* is arranged in exactly the same format as the original, except that it lacks an overall index, and is shot from legible typed copy, being bound with staples into stiff paper covers.

H. P. Lovecraft and Lovecraft Criticism is one of the finest single-author bibliographies ever produced on a writer of fantastic literature, on a par with Ashley's guide to Blackwood's works (see #319). It is comprehensive, knowledgeable, logically arranged, and beautifully executed. Everything that a researcher would ever want to know about Lovecraft's publications is here, carefully indexed and easily accessible to even the most obtuse user. Kudos to Joshi and his publisher for a first-class effort. Every university library should own a copy, and every would-be literary bibliographer should examine this book before embarking down that parlous road.

420. Joshi, S. T. **An Index to the Fiction & Poetry of H.P. Lovecraft.** West Warwick, RI, Necronomicon Press, 1992. 42 p. index. ISBN 0-940884-44-5 (pbk.). Cover art by Allen Koszowski.

Joshi's book is an index to proper names (including titles, characters, and place names) used by Lovecraft in his fiction and selected poetry, as based upon on the standard Arkham editions of these works, covering some 88 stories in approximately 2,800 entries.

A typical entry includes: proper name, an abbreviation of the story and volume title (the Abbreviations list is provided after the Explanatory Notes), and page citations for both the most recent standard Arkham House editions of the master's works, and for the now superseded first editions (in italics). Many entries have just one or two citations, but others, such as Salem (Massachusetts), may include several dozen. The booklet is shot from very clear typeset copy, but employs a rather small typeface, making it difficult to read for middle-aged eyes; the volume is stapled through the spine.

This pamphlet provides the beginnings of a potentially much larger index or concordance to all of Lovecraft's work. May Cthulhu forgive me, but this little guide will be primarily useful only for the diehard fans and intensive researchers of HPL.

421. Joshi, S. T. **An Index to the Selected Letters of H. P. Lovecraft.** West Warwick, RI, Necronomicon Press, 1980. 77 p. (pbk.).

Joshi's book indexes the five volumes of Lovecraft's *Selected Letters* (which were published by Arkham House between 1965-76) in one straight alphabetical sequence by author, title, and subject. Items are correlated to the volume and page number of the respective book (*e.g.,* "III.73" = Volume III, page 73). Five appendices provide: "I. A Brief Chronology of the Life of H. P. Lovecraft (1914-1937)"; "II. List of Lovecraft's Correspondents" (alphabetically by surname, keyed to letter number); "III. Index to Illustrations and Photographs" (alphabetically by artist's name, keyed to volume and page number); "IV. Prose and Poetry Excerpts in the *Selected Letters*" (alphabetically by writer's name, keyed to volume and page number); and "V. Errata in the *Selected Letters*" (by volume, page, and line number, listing the original error and the corrected text). The book is shot from legible typed copy and bound with staples in stiff paper covers.

Lovecraft was an enormously prolific (even obsessive) letter writer, covering a broad array of subjects in his many missives, now made accessible for the first time for scholars and fans alike. Researchers seriously interested in examining this author's writings will find this index a veritable literary gold mine.

422. Laney, Francis T., and William H. Evans. **Howard Phillips Lovecraft (1890-1937): A Tentative Bibliography.** Los Angeles, CA, An "Acolyte" Publication, FAPA, 1943. 12 p. (pbk.). Brennan, Joseph Payne. **A Select Bibliography of H. P. Lovecraft.** New Haven, CT, [Joseph Payne Brennan], 1952. 8 p. LC 52-24147. (pbk.). Brennan, Joseph Payne. **H. P. Lovecraft: A Bibliography.** [rev. ed.]. Washington, DC, Biblio Press, 1952. 13 p. LC 52-

32856 (pbk.). Wetzel, George T., ed. **Howard Phillips Lovecraft—Memoirs, Critiques, & Bibliographies.** North Tonawanda, NY, SSR Publications, 1955. 88 p. LC 55-9424 (pbk.). Chalker, Jack L., *et al.* **The New H. P. Lovecraft Bibliography.** Baltimore, MD, An Anthem Press Chapbook, 1962. 40 p. (pbk.). Owings, Mark, with Jack L. Chalker. **The Revised H. P. Lovecraft Bibliography.** Baltimore, MD, Mirage Press, 1973. viii, 43 p. LC 72-85408. ISBN 0-88358-010-1 (pbk.).

Each of these bibliographies was more or less pyramided upon its predecessor, with internal printed acknowledgments (page vi in Owings), and so they have been treated as one work here despite some differences in content and format (it should be noted in particular that Wetzel includes, in addition to separate bibliographies by Wetzel and Robert E. Briney, six essays on Lovecraft's life and work).

Contents (of Owings's guide): "Using This Bibliography"; "Preface"; "Essays"; "Verse"; "Fiction"; "Fiction Collaborations"; "Collections"; "Foreign-Language Collections"; "Revisions"; "Mythos Stories"; "Comic Book Adaptations"; "Material on Lovecraft."

Each chapter through the "Fiction" section is arranged in alphabetical order by title. A typical entry provides: title (small caps), magazine title (italics), month and year of original publication, with details of all known reprints, including those in Lovecraft's own collections, plus anthologies and foreign-language materials. No paginations are provided. Reprints in anthologies include: title (boldface), editor, publisher, place of publication, stock number (for paperbacks), format (*e.g.,* "wpps" = paperback), total pagination of the book, price, but no specific paginations of the Lovecraft story within the volume. Reprints in foreign-language collections and anthologies include the foreign-language title of the book, but not of the individual stories.

Collaborations and revisions are listed by collaborator name, then alphabetically by title, and include similar bibliographical data to the other sections. Collections are arranged in alphabetical order by book title, providing: title (small caps), publisher, place of publication, year of publication, exact pagination, price, reissues, contents. The foreign-language section includes book-length collections translated into other languages, arranged by language and then by title, with similar bibliographical data provided, *including* lists of the stories with their translated titles (because these are not given under the individual story listings, above, matching them with their correct English-language versions is not always easy). "Cthulhu Mythos" stories are also arranged by author. Comic book adaptations are arranged by comic book title. The secondary bibliography is very scanty, including only six items.

Owings's bibliography is attractively and professionally printed in 8.5" x 11" format; however, the format seems excessively jumbled, with no line breaks between entries, making the data crowd together on the page; the absence of any index does not help matters. All of these booklets have now been completely superseded by Joshi's definitive bibliography (see #419).

423. Owings, Mark, and Irving Binkin. **A Catalog of Lovecraftiana: The Grill/Binkin Collection.** Baltimore, MD, Mirage Press, 1975. 71 p. LC 73-93645. ISBN 0-88358-122-1; ISBN 0-88358-020-9 (pbk.).

This published catalog of the Lovecraft collection of Philip Jack Grill (1903-1970) serves as a kind of substitute bibliography of Lovecraft books, manuscripts, and other materials.

Contents: "Professional Periodicals"; "Amateur Press Works"; "Books by Lovecraft"; "Anthologies, Novels, and Author Collections with HPL Material"; "Books About Lovecraft"; "Letters"; "Photographs and Miscellaneous"; "Recent Additions" (subdivided into the same sections as above).

Materials are numbered consecutively from 1-668. The first two sections, comprising the majority of the text, are arranged by magazine title, then chronologically by date, providing: item number, magazine title, date, volume and issue number, title of Lovecraft story (in quotes), a list of the other authors featured in the same issue, cover artist, and condition of item.

The books section is arranged in alphabetical order by book title and includes: publisher, place of publication, year of publication, format (*e.g.,* "wpps" = paperback), pagination, and condition of item. Correspondence is arranged either by sender (to Grill) in the first section, or by recipient (from HPL) in the second; each of these entries includes: date, subject matter, and other notes. The book features twenty-four pages of photographic plates inserted in the middle of the volume, reproducing choice items from the collection (keyed to item number), plus a few rare photos of Lovecraft himself.

The absence of an index makes anything more than idle browsing impossible. Thus, while this volume is an intriguing guide to much peripheral Lovecraftiana, it basically will be of interest only to diehard collectors.

Brian Lumley

424. Blackmore, Leigh. **Brian Lumley: A New Bibliography.** Penrith, N.S.W., Australia, Dark Press Publication, 1984. 53 p. ISBN 0-9590367-0-9 (pbk.).

This illustrated checklist covers the works of a popular British horror writer.

Contents: "Explanatory Notes"; "Acknowledgments"; "I. Works by Lumley in English": "A. Books"; "B. Contributions to Periodicals": "i. Fiction," "ii. Nonfiction," "iii. Poetry," "iv. Letters"; "II. Works by Lumley in Translation": "A. Books"; "B. Contributions to Periodicals": "i. Fiction," "ii. Nonfiction"; "C. Material Included in Books by Others"; "A Portfolio of Early Fanzine Artwork by Lumley"; "III. Works about Lumley": "A. Reference Works"; "B. Bibliographies"; "C. Criticism in Books or Periodicals"; "D. Book Reviews": "i. Books in English," "ii. Books in Languages Other than English"; "E. Special Periodicals and Unclassifiable Data": "i. Single Issues of Periodicals Devoted to Lumley"; "Unclassifiable Data"; "Brian Lumley: A Chronology of His Fiction and Poetry"; "IV. Indexes": "A. Works by Lumley"; "B. Names"; "C. Periodicals."

Blackmore's format is very similar to that of Joshi's bibliography on Lovecraft (see #419; Blackmore co-authored the *Supplement* to that work). Materials are numbered anew from one in each section. Books are listed in chronological order by publication date. A typical book entry includes: item number, title (in italics), year of publication, exact title page transcription, collation, exact publication date, contents (where appropriate), paginations of each section, binding, size (in centimeters), cover artist, price, ISBN or stock number, plus other bibliographical or literary notes. Translated books are similarly listed in a separate section of their own.

Shorter works are filed alphabetically by title in each section, giving: item number, title (in quotes), magazine title (italics), volume and issue number, date, pagination, and other notes. Reprints in anthologies include: item number, main entry of anthology (usually editor), book title (in italics), place of publication, publisher, year of publication, total pagination of book, title of Lumley story included, and specific pagination of Lumley story in the book. Book reviews are arranged by work covered, then alphabetically by critic; full bibliographical data are provided.

The list of secondary sources is probably complete, although only nine items are included. Chronological lists of the fiction and poetry show Lumley's development as a writer. The indices are keyed to item number. The book is shot from legible typed copy and is illustrated throughout with reproductions of covers and a few of Lumley's own illustrations. Coverage is completed through part of 1984.

Although short, this is one of the better author checklists that we have seen: thorough, logically arranged, well-indexed, and very easy to use.

Arthur Machen

425. Danielson, Henry. **Arthur Machen: A Bibliography.** London, Henry Danielson, 1923. x, 59 p. LC 23-10829.

This interesting bibliography features an introduction by Henry Savage, "Arthur Machen: An Appreciation," and extensive commentaries by Machen himself. The bibliography proper lists Machen's books in chronological order by publication date.

A typical entry provides: book title (all caps) and year of publication (as part of the header), an exact transcription of the title page of the first edition, edition points, a detailed description of the binding and paper, contents listing (where appropriate), plus Machen's remarks on the volume. The latter range in size from one brief paragraph to seven pages, and provide much insight into each book's literary origins, and to Arthur Machen himself. Coverage is complete through 1922. The book is nicely designed and typeset, but lacks an index or table of contents.

The bibliographical data are largely duplicated in Goldstone and Sweetser's much more complete and current guide (see #426), but researchers will still find this little book of interest for the author's sidepieces.

426. Goldstone, Adrian, and Wesley Sweetser. **A Bibliography of Arthur Machen.** Austin, TX, University of Texas, 1965. 180 p. LC 65-63475.

Adapted from Sweetser's Ph.D. disssertation, this bibliography of the highly touted British horror and fantasy writer's works includes: "Introduction"; "Explanations & Acknowledgments"; "Books and Pamphlets"; "Translations"; "Contributions"; "Periodicals"; "Criticism and Commentary" (*i.e.,* secondary sources, divided into "Books & Pamphlets" and "Periodicals"); and "Index."

Most sections are arranged chronologically by publication date. A typical book entry includes: item number, title (all caps), year of publication, exact transcription of the title page copy, exact collation of the text, description of the binding and end papers, publication date, price, and similar data on all known reprint editions.

A typical shorter work entry in the "Contributions" section, which includes materials by Machen published in books by other authors, provides: item number, book title (italics), bibliographical description, specific pagination of the Machen contribution and a description of what it contains, with similar data for all known reprints.

The "Periodicals" chapter is organized alphabetically by magazine title, then chronologically by publication date. A typical entry includes: magazine title (small caps, as a running head for the section), Machen contribution (in italics), volume number, publication date, with specific pagination of the Machen item. Fiction and nonfiction materials are interfiled without any indication of subject matter, making it difficult for the user who is not already familiar with the author's work to separate out, for example, his short stories. Materials are numbered in the first three sections consecutively from 1-131; items listed in the fourth chapter are unnumbered, for no apparent reason.

The chapter on secondary sources ("Criticism and Commentary") includes: "Books & Pamphlets," arranged in alphabetical order by name, and giving: author or editor, title (italics), place of publication, publisher, year of publication, and an exact citation to and brief description of any references to Machen or his work; and "Periodicals," arranged alphabetically by periodical title, then chronologically by publication date, providing: magazine title (small caps), title of article (in italics), author's name, volume number, publication date, and specific pagination. The index coordinates the titles of Machen's works with page numbers; the secondary source section is not indexed, nor are the names of anthologies or their editors cross-referenced in any way. The book is nicely typeset and bound to library standards.

Goldstone and Sweetser have produced a sound if somewhat quirky guide to an equally odd writer. Their coverage of Machen's writings seems thorough, and the section on secondary materials is remarkably complete, including books that have even a passing reference to the author or his work. However, the organization of periodical contributions, both primary and secondary, is less than ideal, and will cause the casual user immediate problems. Specifically, the arrangement of articles about Machen by periodical title and date of publication, rather than by critic's name, without any additional indexing, makes this section almost unusable. A new edition correcting these flaws and updating the basic data base would certainly be warranted.

George R. R. Martin

427. Stephensen-Payne, Phil. **George R. R. Martin, the Ace from New Jersey: A Working Bibliography.** 2nd rev. ed. Leeds, West Yorkshire, England & Albuquerque, NM, Galactic Central Publications, 1989. 9, 23 p. (Galactic Central Bibliographies for the Avid Reader, Vol. 27). ISBN 0-871133-01-7 (pbk.).

George Martin is a well-regarded American SF writer, author of *Nightflyers* and an acclaimed fantasy series. This new bibliography is organized by subject category, then alphabetically by title.

Contents: Author's name, date and place of birth, and awards; "A. Stories"; "B. Fiction Books"; "C. Series" [blank section]; "D. Poems & Songs" [blank section]; "E. Poem

& Song Collections" [blank section]; "F. Articles"; "G. Miscellaneous"; "H. Non-Fiction Books" [blank section]; "I. Books Edited by George R. R. Martin"; "J. Media Presentations"; "K. Articles on George R. R. Martin"; "L. Reviews of Books by George R. R. Martin"; "M. Books About George R. R. Martin" [blank section]; "N. Phantom and Forthcoming Titles"; "O. Related Books by Other Authors" [blank section]; "P. Textual Variations" [blank section]; "Q. Chronological Index."

In each section materials are numbered anew from the number one. A typical shorter work entry includes: item number, title, category ("ss" = short story, "nt" = novelette, etc.), magazine or book in which the item appeared, month and year of publication (for magazines in the form "11-77" for November 1977) or year of publication (for books), a list of subsequent reprints (for which title, publisher, year, and editor's last name are given), but no paginations.

A typical book entry gives: item number, title (in caps), pseudonym, contents for collections keyed to item number, and publication data (publisher, stock number, month and year of publication [if known, in the form "10-59" for October 1959], pagination, price, with dates of reissues by the same publisher), plus cover artist and similar data for all known reprint editions. The list of secondary sources includes just ten items but is probably complete; there are roughly a hundred book reviews noted. The book lacks an overall index. The bibliography is shot from very clear word-processed copy and bound with staples into paper covers. Data are complete through the end of 1989, before Martin reached bestseller status.

One would hope for the addition of an index and magazine paginations to future editions. As the only current guide to this author's work, Stephensen-Payne's bibliography is a logical starting point for future scholarship on this writer. It should be updated as soon as possible.

Richard Matheson

428. Rathbun, Mark, and Graeme Flanagan. **Richard Matheson: He Is Legend: An Illustrated Bio-Bibliography.** Chico, CA, Mark Rathbun, 1984. 55 p. (pbk.).

This brief illustrated checklist focuses on a popular American SF, fantasy, and television writer.

Contents: "The Curious Child: A Preface" (by Rathbun); "Bon Homme Richard," by Robert Bloch; "Writing the Nightmare," by Rathbun; "SF Unlimited," by Matheson; "Comment," by Jack Finney; "Blood Son: Comments," by Richard Christian Matheson (the author's son, also a writer); Bibliography; "Comment," by William F. Nolan; "Filmography"; "Richard Matheson: The Early Years," by William Campbell Gault; "One for the Books: The Genesis of 'Duel'," by Jerry Sohl. The bibliography proper includes: "Novels," "Short Story Collections," "Short Stories," "Television Scripts" (published), "Interviews," "Foreign Translations," "Miscellanea," and "Adaptations."

Material in each of these sections is arranged alphabetically by title. A typical book entry includes: title (bold caps), publisher, stock number (for paperbacks), place of publication, year of publication, pagination, and price, with similar data for all subsequent reprints (listed in chronological order under the main entry). A typical short work entry includes: title (bold caps), magazine title, month and year of publication, but no paginations, plus all known reprint editions. Reprints in anthologies include: title (boldface), editor, and year of publication, but no other bibliographical data.

The "Filmography" includes: "Films," "Television," "Other Television Work," and "Unproduced Motion Picture and Television Scripts." In the first two sections, Matheson's screen- and teleplays are arranged in chronological order by date of production date, including the following data: title (bold caps), production company, year of production, script credits, one-sentence annotation, major stars, director's name; TV programs add the name of the series and the season number. The book is attractively illustrated with photos of the author, of his book and magazine covers, and with stills from selected Matheson movies.

While this checklist provides a beginning point for all future scholarship on this writer, the absence of both an index and any secondary sources (outside of nine interviews) is unfortunate. Matheson deserves a more extended treatment of his many works.

Julian May

429. Dikty, Thaddeus, and R. Reginald. **The Work of Julian May: An Annotated Bibliography & Guide.** San Bernardino, CA, The Borgo Press, 1985. 66 p. index. (Bibliographies of Modern Authors, No. 3). LC 84-21705. ISBN 0-89370-382-6; ISBN 0-89370-482-2 (pbk.).

May, an extraordinarily prolific children's book writer and SF novelist, with nearly 300 books to her credit in her fifty-year career, is here profiled by her late husband and agent, the well-known editor, Ted Dikty.

Contents: "Introduction," by Dikty; "A. Books"; "B. Articles"; "C. Short Fiction"; "D. Study Prints"; "E. Lesson Plans"; "F. Kits"; "G. Audio Cassettes"; "H. Audio Recordings"; "I. Music"; "J. Maps"; "K. Media Productions"; "L. About the Author"; "M. Unpublished Works"; "N. Miscellanea"; "Title Index."

In each section, the author's works are arranged chronologically and numbered anew from one, chapter by chapter. A typical book entry includes: item number, title (underlined), byline, place of publication, publisher, year of publication, pagination, format (paper or cloth), and type of publication (novel, nonfiction, etc.), with full bibliographical data on reprint editions, translations, republications, etc. The books are annotated with brief plot summaries and other pertinent data; entries from other sections are selectively annotated as needed.

A typical shorter work entry includes: item number, title (in quotes), magazine title, volume number, date, and pagination. Similar data are included for all reprint editions; a typical anthology listing includes: place of publication, publisher, year of publication, format ("cloth"), and pagination. Dikty's introduction provides a nostalgic look back at Julian May's life. "About the Author" includes all known secondary works. The "Miscellanea" section includes information on the author's pen names, memberships, Library of Congress cataloging data, career highlights, and other data. The index lists titles and item numbers only.

The format for this book, one of the first issued in the series, was somewhat cramped: the lack of line breaks between entries jumbles the data together despite the inclusion of hanging indents. The book is shot from eight- or nine-point size word-processed copy and is sometimes hard to read for middle-aged eyes. Coverage is complete through the end of

1984, before May attained her midlist status as a popular science fiction novelist. A second edition of this booklet would certainly be warranted.

Bruce McAllister

430. Bourquin, David Ray. **The Work of Bruce McAllister: An Annotated Bibliography & Guide.** San Bernardino, CA, The Borgo Press, 1985. 30 p. index. (Bibliographies of Modern Authors, No. 10). LC 85-22400. ISBN 0-89370-389-3; ISBN 0-89370-489-X (pbk.). **The Work of Bruce McAllister: An Annotated Bibliography & Guide.** [Rev. ed.]. San Bernardino, CA, The Borgo Press, 1986. 32 p. All other data the same as above.

McAllister, a well-known SF writer, poet, and American academic, sold his first story at the age of seventeen. This new bibliography is the first detailed guide to his work.

Contents (both versions): "Introduction," by Bourquin; "A. Books"; "B. Short Fiction"; "C. Nonfiction"; "D. Poetry"; "E. Graphic/Experimental Work"; "F. Papers"; "G. Editorial Posts"; "H. Media Appearances"; "I. Awards and Prizes"; "J. About the Author"; "Critical Comments"; "Title Index."

In each section, the author's works are arranged chronologically and numbered consecutively from the number one, chapter by chapter, prefixed by the appropriate letter code (*e.g.,* B1, B2, B3, etc.). A typical book entry includes: item number, title (in italics), place of publication, publisher, year of publication, pagination, format (*e.g.,* "paper"), type of publication (*e.g.,* "anthology"), with full bibliographical data on reprint editions, translations, republications, etc. The books are fully annotated, with complete contents listings or plot summaries and other pertinent data; entries from other sections are selectively annotated as needed.

A typical short fiction or verse entry includes: item number, title (in quotes), magazine title, volume number, date, pagination. Similar data are included for all reprint editions; a typical anthology listing gives: place of publication, publisher, year of publication, format ("cloth"), and pagination. Bourquin's introduction provides an informal look at the author's background. "Media Appearances" records the author's interviews on television and radio, participation in conferences, and speeches. "About the Author" includes all known secondary works (very few). "Critical Comments" includes selected excerpts of reviews and other comments by leading critics on the author's work. The index correlates titles and item numbers only.

Academic librarian Bourquin worked extensively with McAllister in the preparation of this brief guide. The original edition, shot from word-processed copy, was complete through mid-1985; the revised version was completely reworked and reset into a new, more legible (and more readable) format and style, and extended the data base by eight months.

Although McAllister has never been a prolific writer, the generally acknowledged literary quality of his stories and novels would certainly warrant an updating of this guide in the future.

Anne McCaffrey

Arbur, Rosemarie. **Leigh Brackett, Marion Zimmer Bradley, Anne McCaffrey: A Primary and Secondary Bibliography**. *See the entry for Leigh Brackett* (see #328).

431. Hargreaves, Mathew D. **Anne Inez McCaffrey: Forty Years of Publishing: An International Bibliography.** Seattle, WA, [Mathew D. Hargreaves], 1992. 338 p. Index. Limited to 500 copies signed by the author and McCaffrey. Illustrated with black-and-white photos and cover art.

Contents: "A Short Biography"; "Introduction"; "Section 1: Novels, Short Story Collections"; "Section 2: Edited Works"; "Section 3: Short Fiction"; "Section 4: Non-Fiction"; "Section 5: Unpublished Works"; "Section 6: Literary Criticisms"; "Section 7: Secondary Material & Related Merchandising"; "Section 8: Plays"; "Section 9: Published Interviews"; "Lists: Chronological Publishing Order and Related Series"; "Afterword," by Anne McCaffrey; "Index."

This bibliography attempts to cite all of the writings and related materials by popular SF writer Anne McCaffrey, author of the Dragonriders of Pern series, including English-language publications and as many foreign-language editions of her work that could be found. Items *not* covered include reviews of the author's writings, book review quotations, or published letters.

Each section is arranged alphabetically by title, employing the same basic format throughout. A typical entry includes: item number (numbered anew from the number one in each section), title of the work (bold caps underlined), word count (in parentheses), author's dedication (if applicable), and a plot summary averaging fifty words in length.

Editions are listed under each work in chronological order by publication date, numbered consecutively from the letter "A," and providing the following information: publisher, city of publication, book number (sometimes omitted), price, year of publication, format (hardcover, paperback, audio, etc.), the letter (P) if an illustration of the book's cover is included herein, and a detailed bibliographical and physical description of the item, providing binding details, printing information, cover illustrator, and specific pagination. Any awards the publication may have received are noted where appropriate. Every variant edition is meticulously described.

The specific paginations of the author's short stories are included for their first and subsequent appearances in magazines and book anthologies, *except* (for no apparent reason) in McCaffrey's own story collections, where the user is referred to the original book entry in the first section (see, for example, the main entry of McCaffrey's paperback compilation, *Get Off the Unicorn*).

215 main entries are included. Coverage is complete through 1992, with some tentative information added for 1993. The bibliography is attractively and sturdily bound in green cloth to library standards, with thick, copper-colored endpapers, and a tipped-in signature sheet up front. The reproductions of book and magazine covers are small and rather difficult to discern. The index cross-references McCaffrey's titles with the page numbers on which they appear, showing the main entries of each item in boldfaced type.

Hargreaves's book supersedes Arbur's now outdated bibliography (see #328), and can be supplemented by Stephensen-Payne/Benson's more recent work (see #432). A fine piece of work for the serious collector or scholar, or for the libraries serving them.

432. Stephensen-Payne, Phil, and Gordon Benson, Jr. **Anne McCaffrey, Dragonlady and More: A Working Bibliography.** 4th rev. ed. Leeds, West Yorkshire, England, & Albuquerque, NM, Galactic Central Publications, 1996. ix, 54 p. (Galactic Central Bibliographies for the Avid Reader, Vol. 13). ISBN 1-871133-47-5 (pbk.).

McCaffrey, author of the Dragonriders of Pern series, is a popular American fantasy writer who now resides in Ireland. This guide to her work is arranged by subject category, then alphabetically by title.

Contents: "Introduction"; Author's name, date and place of birth, list of awards won by the author; "A. Prose Fiction"; "B. Prose Fiction Books"; "C. Series"; "D. Poetry & Drama" [blank section]; "E. Poetry & Drama Books" [blank section]; "F. Articles"; "G. Miscellaneous" (including introductions and afterwords by Anne McCaffrey, letters, and interviews with the author); "H. Non-Fiction Books" [blank section]; "I. Publications Edited by Anne McCaffrey"; "J. Other Media"; "K. Articles about Anne McCaffrey"; "L. Reviews" (of McCaffrey's books, alphabetically by title of the book being reviewed, then by magazine title, giving date and reviewer); "M. Books About Anne McCaffrey"; "N. Phantom and Forthcoming Titles"; "O. Related Items by Other Authors"; "P. Textual Variations and Other Notes" [blank section]; "Q. Chronological Index of Prose Fiction" (by year and title).

In each section materials are arranged alphabetically by title, the author's works being numbered consecutively from one, and prefixed with the letter code appropriate to that part (*e.g.,* B1, B2, B3, etc.). A typical shorter work entry provides: item number, title, category ("ss" = short story, "nt" = novelette, etc.), magazine or book in which the item appeared, month and year of publication (for magazines in the form "12-73" for December 1973) or year of publication (for books), plus a list of subsequent reprints (for which title, publisher, year, and editor's last name are given), but no paginations.

Monograph entries include: item number, title (in caps), contents (for collections), publication data (publisher, stock number, month and year of publication [if known, in the form "10-59" for October 1959], pagination, price, with dates of reissues by the same publisher), cover artist, and similar data for all known reprints. There is no overall index. 391 entries are included, though reprint information makes the total greater; of these, some 149 represent secondary sources, 54 of which are book review categories, with hundreds of actual reviews being listed. The book is shot from legible word-processed copy and bound with staples into paper covers. Data are complete through part of 1996.

Arbur's guide (see #328) gives short fiction paginations (first appearances only), but lacks book paginations. Both her guide and Stephensen-Payne/Benson contain roughly the same number of secondary sources (Arbur shows 165 items, most of them book reviews). Arbur's data base continues through 1980; Stephensen-Payne and Benson's work adds a decade and a half of additional entries for this very prolific writer. However, Hargreaves's guide (see #431) is by far the best single bibliographical guide to McCaffrey's work, and is likely to remain so for some time to come.

Completists and scholars will find all three works useful, but many of McCaffrey's fans will find Stephensen-Payne more than adequate for their needs.

J. T. McIntosh

433. Covell, Ian. **J. T. McIntosh: Memoir & Bibliography.** Polk City, IA, Chris Drumm Books, 1987. 32 p. (plus one-page insert). index. ISBN 0-936055-28-6 (pbk.); ISBN 0-936055-29-4 (signed ed.).

Covell's book is organized differently from Drumm's usual format for this series. McIntosh, a well-known British SF writer, provides a fourteen-page memoir-*cum*-interview, giving much insight into his life and work, and detailing why he stopped writing in 1979.

The bibliography proper includes: "Abbreviations List"; "Pseudonyms Used"; "List A. Science Fiction"; "B. Contemporary Fiction"; "C. Non-Fiction"; plus a "Chronological List of Published Works," in turn broken into "Stories" and "Novels." Sections A-C are arranged in alphabetical order, interfiling book-length and shorter works. A typical book entry includes: title (underlined caps), publisher, nationality, stock number (for paperbacks), year of publication (*e.g.,* "54" = 1954), and similar data for all known reprints.

A typical short fiction entry includes: title, abbreviated magazine title, month and year of publication (in form "1.61" for January 1961). No paginations are included and there is no index. The book is reproduced from mostly clear typed copy.

McIntosh's memoir is utterly fascinating, but the bibliography section could use additional bibliographical details such as paginations, and a better organization. A one-page corrigenda sheet is included in most copies.

Judith Merril

434. Cummins, Elizabeth. **"Bibliography of Works by Judith Merril,"** in *Extrapolation,* Volume 42, Number 3 (Fall, 2001): 255-287.

The late Judith Merril was a well-known American-Canadian writer and editor. This is the first published guide to her work.

The bibliography proper is divided into five sections: "I. Fiction: Novels and Collections"; "II. Short Fiction: Novellas and Short Stories"; "III. Edited Anthologies: Books"; "IV. Nonfiction: Essays, Introductions, Reviews"; "V. Miscellanea: Dramatizations, Interviews, Letters, Poetry, Radio, Television, Translations."

Each part is arranged in chronological order by publication date, with interpolated, boldfaced headers (*e.g.,* "1950") to set off the works from each decade of Merril's career, beginning in the 1930s, and extending through the '90s. A typical shorter work entry includes: title (in quotation marks), pseudonym (when appropriate), magazine title (in italics), volume number, issue number, publication date, and pagination. A story's main entry is followed by a list of all known reprints, in chronological order by publication date, in all languages, including the author's own collections. Foreign-language reprints include the foreign-language title. Reprints in books give: book title (italics), editor (where appropriate), place of publication, publisher, year of publication, and the specific pagination for the Merril story in that volume. Not all entries display complete bibliographical data.

Book entries include: title (in italics), place of publication, publisher, and year of publication, but no paginations. A list of all known reprints follows the main entry, in chronological order by publication date, with similar data, plus the foreign-language title for overseas reprints. Merril's short story collections include complete contents listings. Cummins also provides a brief but helpful introduction, noting the highlights of the author's career, including the many awards and honors she received.

The bibliography appears to be both comprehensive and authoritative, lacking information (mainly publication years) only for several of the reprint editions. However, the absence of an overall title index, and the failure in some sections to offset the data clearly from the left-hand margin (see particularly p. 261) makes using this guide unnecessarily difficult for the average user.

A. Merritt

435. Wentz, W. Jas. **A. Merritt: A Bibliography of Fantastic Writings.** Roseville, CA, George A. Bibby, 1965. 33 p. (pbk.).

[not seen]

Walter M. Miller, Jr.

436. Roberson, William H., and Robert L. Battenfeld. **Walter M. Miller, Jr.: A Bio-Bibliography.** Westport, CT, Greenwood Press, 1992. xv, 149 p. index. (Bio-Bibliographies in American Literature, No. 3). LC 92-7335. ISBN 0-313-27651-X.

Contents: "Illustrations"; "Preface"; "Chronology"; "Walter M. Miller, Jr.: A Biographical and Critical Introduction"; "Part I: Writings by Walter M. Miller, Jr." ("A. Books"; "B. Short Fiction in Periodicals"; "C. Short Fiction in Anthologies"; "D. Nonfiction"; "E. Adaptations"; "F. Television Scripts"). "Part II: Writings About Walter M. Miller, Jr." ("G. Articles and Parts of Books"; "H. Book Reviews"; "I. Dissertations"); Glossaries ("Glossary of Characters and Terms in *A Canticle for Leibowitz*"; "Glossary of Allusions, References and Associations in *A Canticle for Leibowitz*"); "Time-Line for *A Canticle for Leibowitz*"; "Name/Title/Character Name Index to Part I"; "Name/Title/Subject Index to Part II."

This is primary and secondary annotated bibliography of Walter M. Miller, Jr., known primarily as the author of *A Canticle for Leibowitz* (cited herein as *ACFL*). The biographical introduction provides background material on the author's life and work, especially *Canticle* and its psychological roots in World War II. The chronology is brief, presented in block paragraph format.

Each section of the bibliography is arranged in chronological order by publication date. Parts A-F are the primary bibliography, while G-I comprise the secondary bibliography. There are 369 main entries, but because English-language editions are grouped together in the same entry, this number does not reflect the total information displayed.

A typical monograph entry includes: item number (alphanumeric by section), title (bold caps), imprint from the title page, collation, pagination, binding, contents, and original published price. The English-language annotations include detailed physical descriptions of the editions, but do not contain summaries or evaluations. Foreign-language publications include only item number (bold type), translated title (underlined), original title (brackets & underlined), translator, place of publication, publisher, pagination, and language.

A typical short fiction entry includes: item number (bold type), title (in quotation marks), periodical title (underlined), volume number, month of publication (in parentheses), pagination, a brief, non-evaluative summary (100 words), and a list of the main characters and their relationships. Entries in the secondary bibliography provide similar information and summaries, including occasional evaluations of the critiques. The index cross-references materials to item numbers only. The glossaries provide wonderful study aids to the author's best-known work, *A Canticle for Leibowitz.*

Well-presented and -researched, this is a particularly fine bibliography, nicely typeset and bound to library standards, lacking coverage only of Miller's final posthumous novel, *Saint Leibowitz and the Wild Horse Woman.* Recommended for interested scholars, collectors, fans, and research libraries.

Michael Moorcock

437. Bilyeu, Richard. **The Tanelorn Archives: A Primary and Secondary Bibliography of the Works of Michael Moorcock, 1949-1979.** Altona, Manitoba, Canada, Pandora's Books, 1981. 108 p. ISBN 0-919695-04-3; ISBN 0-919695-05-1 (pbk.).

Bilyeu's illustrated checklist of this popular British fantasy author's publications includes: "Introduction"; "Books"; "Stories"; "Non-Fiction"; "Reviews"; "Editorials"; "Self-Published"; "Letters"; "Blurbs for Others' Books"; "Comic Books and Strips"; "Music"; "Films"; "Manuscripts"; "Influenced Fiction"; "Influenced Non-Fiction"; "Posters, Portfolios, Art Books"; "War Games"; "Appendix 1—Avon and DAW"; "Appendix 2—Notes."

Most sections of this guide are arranged in alphabetical order by title. A typical book entry includes: title (in capital letters), series, publisher, stock number (for paperbacks), place of publication, year of publication, and similar data for all known reprintings.

Shorter work entries give: title, magazine title, volume and/or issue number, month and year of publication; or, for anthology listings, book title (all caps), editor, publisher, year of publication, and occasional notes. No paginations are included. A valuable, detailed inventory of the Moorcock manuscripts housed in the Texas A&M University Library is also provided. There is a three-page (very incomplete) list of secondary sources, including some book reviews. The book is shot from legible typed copy, and is illustrated throughout with reproductions of magazine and book covers and one photo of Moorcock; the cloth edition is bound to library standards.

Bilyeu's book is the most complete and best realized of the three Moorcock bibliographies published to date but it still is far from definitive, lacking both an index as well as many bibliographical details, and is now very much out-of-date. Moorcock deserves a complete, well-organized, current guide to his many works.

438. Callow, A. J. **The Chronicles of Moorcock.** Worcester, England, A. J. Callow, 1978. 43 p. (pbk.).

This amateurish hodgepodge is so badly organized that, short as it is, it must still be read through in its entirety in order to locate a specific item. Lacking both a contents page or index, *The Chronicles* arranges its data by series name and then in chronological *series* (not publication) order; non-series books are grouped after the series listings, in chronological order by publication date. No bibliographical details are provided other than publisher, year of publication, and format (*e.g.,* "paperback").

All of the books have one- to two-sentence annotations or contents listings (for collections). The rest of the book is a similar mass of miscellaneous, often uncorrelated data, jumbled onto pages with no sense of why anything is where it is. The booklet is photocopied from barely discernible typed copy. Abominable drivel. Prefer Bilyeu's much more thorough bibliography (see #437).

439. Harper, Andrew, and George McAulay. **Michael Moorcock: A Bibliography.** Baltimore, MD, T-K Graphics, 1976. 3-29 p. (pbk.).

Harper and McAulay's booklet is little better organized than Callow's. Covering only Moorcock's books, it provides not one iota more of additional bibliographical data than its competitors. Materials are arranged in chronological order by publication date. A typical entry includes: title (bold caps), one-line annotation or contents listing, publisher, date of publication, format (*e.g.,* "paperback"), and similar information on reprints. A few foreign editions are mentioned with their translated titles. Books by Moorcock published under pseudonyms are omitted, although the authors seem to indicate their awareness of these items (so why are they omitted?). A brief checklist of Moorcock's series concludes the book. There is no index, of course.

About all one can say of this wholly amateurish effort is that at least the typeset copy is legible. Prefer Bilyeu (see #437).

C. L. Moore

440. Utter, Virgil, Gordon Benson, Jr., and Phil Stephensen-Payne. **Catherine Lucille Moore & Henry Kuttner, a Marriage of Souls and Talent: A Working Bibliography.** 4th rev. ed. Leeds, West Yorkshire, England, Galactic Central Publications, 1996. x, 142 p. (Galactic Central Bibliographies for the Avid Reader, Vol. 21). ISBN 1-871133-44-0 (pbk.).

Like Brackett and Hamilton, Catherine Moore and Henry Kuttner were two science-fiction writers (both now deceased) who married after each had established a reputation separately; unlike the Hamiltons, however, the Kuttners almost immediately began to collaborate in their fiction on a scale never before seen in the genre, to the point where most of their work after 1940 is inseparable.

Contents: "Introduction"; "Part 1: C.L. Moore Solo": "Awards and Pseudonyms"; "A. Prose Fiction"; "B. Prose Fiction Books"; "C. Series"; "D. Poetry & Drama"; "E. Poetry & Drama Books"; "F. Articles"; "G. Miscellaneous"; "H. Non-Fiction Books"; "I. Publications Edited by C. L. Moore." "Part 2: Henry Kuttner Solo & with C. L. Moore": "Awards and Pseudonyms"; "A. Prose Fiction"; "B. Prose Fiction Books"; "C. Series"; "D. Poetry & Drama"; "E. Poetry & Drama Books"; "F. Articles"; "G. Miscellaneous"; "H. Non-Fiction Books"; "I. Publications Edited by Henry Kuttner." "Part 3: Secondary Material": "J. Other Media"; "K. Articles on Henry Kuttner & C. L. Moore"; "L. Reviews"; "M. Books about Henry Kuttner & C. L. Moore"; "N. Phantom and Forthcoming Titles"; "O. Related Items by Other Authors"; "P. Textual Variations and Other Notes"; "Q. Chronological Index of Prose Fiction."

The authors' basic checklist is arranged by subject category, then alphabetically by title; materials are numbered consecutively from one in each chapter (for example, B1, B2, B3, etc., for the author's books). Shorter work entries include: item number, title, category ("ss" = short story, "nt" = novelette, etc.), magazine or book in which the item appeared, month and year of publication (for magazines in the form "2-68" for February 1968) or year of publication (for books), a list of subsequent reprints (for which title, publisher, year, and editor's last name are given), but no paginations.

For monographs the authors provide: item number, title, contents (if a collection, by item number), publication data (publisher, stock number, month and year of publication [if known, in the form "10-59" for October 1959], pagination, price), cover artist, plus similar data for known reprints. There is no title index. 877 entries are counted for both authors, but reprint information makes the overall total much greater. Some 319 secondary sources are also noted, 39 of which are book review categories; hundreds of actual reviews are recorded in these sections. Some foreign language publications are listed. The addition of paginations for the short fiction sections would be helpful in future editions. Data are complete through 1995. The book is shot from very clear word-processed copy, and glued into paper covers.

Moore and Kuttner's guide is exceptionally complex, and the authors have done about as good a job bibliographically as anyone could do in piecing together their collaborations, absent access to some undiscovered cache of papers that might cast further light on these writers' pseudonymous and commingled work. An index is badly needed in future editions; the split of data between two authors makes the location of specific items unnecessarily difficult, despite the alphabetical arrangement of each section. In general, however, this volume is authoritative, thorough, and complete. No serious researcher of Kuttner and Moore's fiction could possibly begin his or her investigations without access to this book.

Kenneth Morris

Zahorski, Kenneth J., and Robert H. Boyer. **Lloyd Alexander, Evangeline Walton Ensley, Kenneth Morris: A Primary and Secondary Bibliography.** *See the entry for Lloyd Alexander* (see #305).

Talbot Mundy

441. Day, Bradford M. **Talbot Mundy Biblio: Materials Toward a Bibliography of the Works of Talbot Mundy.** New York, Science-Fiction & Fantasy Publications, 1955. 28 p. (pbk.).

Day's brief checklist of this classic fantasy adventure writer's fiction follows the format used in his other author bibliographies.

The book section is arranged alphabetically by title, a typical entry including: title (caps), publisher, place of publication, year of publication, pagination, brief cover copy quote, mention of magazine serialization, with magazine name and dates, plus binding color style. The short fiction section is arranged in chronological order by date of publication and gives: story title (caps), magazine title, year of publication, month of publication, and a record of that tale's reprints in Mundy's own books. Three series lists complete the guide. The book is mimeographed from typed copy. The basic bibliography was slightly (but not significantly) updated in Day's later bibliography, *Bibliography of Adventure* (see #234).

Grant's guide (see #442) is more current, but lacks some of the bibliographical details recorded by Day. Both books will thus be required by the serious researcher.

442. Grant, Donald M., ed. **Talbot Mundy: Messenger of Destiny.** West Kingston, RI, Donald M. Grant, 1983. 253 p. LC 83-243379. ISBN 0-937986-46-1.

This nicely illustrated bio-bibliography focuses on adventure and fantasy writer Talbot Mundy (1879-1940), whose real-life identity of William Lancaster Gribbon was only recently discovered by Peter Berresford Ellis (a major contributor to this volume).

Contents: "Introduction," by Grant; "Autobiography," by Mundy; "Willie—Rogue and Rebel," by Ellis; "Talbot Mundy," by Dawn Mundy Provost (Mundy's widow); "Ghosts Walk . . . ," by Darrel Crombie; "Talbot Mundy in *Adventure*" [the first of the bibliographic chapters]; "The Glory of Tros," by Fritz Leiber; "Books"; "Magazine Appearances"; "*The Jerusalem News*"; "*The Theosophical Path*"; "*The New York Times.*"

The bibliography occupies exactly half of the volume, the section on Mundy's contributions to *Adventure* magazine itself running fifty pages. This chapter is organized chronologically by publication date, a typical subsection including: year (as a running head), a list of the Mundy stories, novels, and essays published during that year, in descending order by issue date, plus extensive commentary, but no paginations.

The book section is arranged alphabetically by title, a typical entry providing: title (bold caps), place of publication, publisher, year of publication, pagination, format (*e.g.,* "paperback"), plus similar data on all known reprint editions, original title (if any), and notes of previous magazine publication and title(s).

The "Magazine Appearances" chapter includes fiction and nonfiction interfiled into one A-Z arrangement. A typical entry gives: title (bold caps), pseudonym (if any), magazine title (in italics; it should be noted that appearances in *Adventure* are also included in this section), month and year of publication, and mentions of subsequent book reprintings; no paginations are included.

The brief end chapters mention Mundy's contributions to three unusual periodicals. As usual with Donald M. Grant publications, the book is copiously illustrated with clear black-and-white reproductions of book and magazine covers, and bound to library standards.

Grant's bio-bibliography is more current than Day's checklist (see #441), although the latter does include more detailed information on binding states and other points of potential interest to collectors. The absence of an index in Grant is unfortunate, making it necessary for the reader to skim through large sections of text to locate one particular item.

Scholars will need access to both volumes; libraries will probably be satisfied with Grant.

Robert Nathan

443. Laurence, Dan H. **Robert Nathan: A Bibliography.** New Haven, CT, Yale University Library, 1960. xi, 97 p. index. LC 61-2221.

Nathan is best known for *Portrait of Jennie* and other works of haunting fantasy; this is the first bibliography of his works.

Contents: "Introduction"; "A. Books and Pamphlets"; "B. Contributions to Books"; "C. Periodical Publications"; "D. Works in Translation"; "E. Musical Contributions"; "Acknowledgment"; "Index of First Lines of Poetry"; "General Index."

In each section materials are listed chronologically by publication date and numbered anew from one, prefixed by the letter associated with that chapter (*e.g.,* C1, C2, C3, etc.). A typical book entry provides: item number, title (all caps), year of publication, an exact transcription of the title page copy, collation, size, price, description of binding, cover artist, number of copies published, exact publication date, similar data on the first British edition of each volume, a sketchy list of further reprints (giving place, publisher, and year of publication only), and notes, including complete contents listings of collections. Section B lists Nathan's contributions to books in chronological order by date, arranged similarly to the first chapter, but excluding collation and binding data, and including specific pagination and identification of the Nathan piece(s).

Chapter C, giving Nathan's contributions to periodicals (poetry, stories, and plays), is also organized chronologically by publication date. A typical entry records: item number (from C1-C207), title (prose contributions in all caps), magazine title (italics), volume number, month and year of publication, and specific pagination, with occasional bibliographical notes, including mentions of further reprintings in other sources.

The fourth section, "Works in Translation," is arranged alphabetically by language of translation, then separated by category (books, anthologies, periodicals) and listed chronologically by publication date, with complete bibliographical data and English-language titles. No paginations are given for monographs.

The final chapter, "Musical Contributions," is broken into three subsections: "Translations of Lyrics from the German or the Italian" (with musical settings by Richard Hageman); "Musical Settings of Lyrics by Robert Nathan"; and "Miscellaneous" (notes for the jacket liner of Beethoven's *Sixth Symphony*). Each of the twenty-two items in this section gives: item number, title, original title (where applicable) or first lines, the names of other artists associated with the project, place of publication, publisher, year of publication, and price.

Both indices correlate the data with item numbers only. The book is professionally typeset, and bound to library standards.

Laurence's guide is complete, well organized, and attractively presented. Nathan continued to write for another fifteen years after this volume was published (his last book was published in 1975), dying in 1985. A final bibliographical accounting of his many publications would certainly be welcome.

Larry Niven

444. Drumm, Chris. **A Larry Niven Checklist.** Polk City, IA, Chris Drumm Books, 1983. [24] p. index. ISBN 0-936055-07-3 (pbk.). Guptill, Paul, and Chris Drumm. **The Many Worlds of Larry Niven.** [2nd ed.]. Polk City, IA, Chris Drumm Books, 1989. ii, 63 p. index. ISBN 0-936055-44-8 (pbk.).

Niven is a well-known American "hard SF" author of the Ringworld series. In both editions of this 4.25" x 7" volume, the author's works are arranged in one chronological sequence. Entries are grouped by year and under each year by month; items are numbered in order from 1-198 (in the second edition). Books and short story titles are both listed in boldface, without distinction.

A typical short fiction entry includes: item number, title, category code (*e.g.,* "ss" = short story), magazine, month and year of publication, and pagination; or book title, if the first appearance is in an anthology, plus year and month of publication, pagination, and price. Subsequent reprintings are grouped under the original edition, with similar data provided.

A typical book entry includes: item number, title, series key, category code (*e.g.,* "coll" = collection), format (*e.g.,* "pb" = paperback), publisher, nationality (*e.g.,* American), month and year of publication, price, and complete contents of story collections. "See" references, title index, series index, and contents listings are keyed to item number. Foreign-language editions are arranged in order by the item numbers assigned to the English-language original versions; a typical entry provides: English-language title, category code, language of translation, foreign-language title, format, year, publisher, and cover artist. The awards section is similarly arranged in item number order.

Secondary materials (twenty-four items) are arranged in chronological order by publication year, as are the sixteen interviews. Data are complete through 1988. The book is produced from very clear word-processed copy, with good margins, and is generally a great improvement over the somewhat primitive first edition (and the other books in this series).

However, the lack of any clear differentiation between novels and stories (until one examines the specific bibliographical data), and the absence of specific data for book publications, limit the effectiveness of what could have been a first-class effort. Future editions should offset short story titles with quotation marks and provide exact paginations for monographs.

Recommended for all researchers of Niven's work.

William F. Nolan

445. Clarke, Boden, and James Hopkins. **The Work of William F. Nolan: An Annotated Bibliography & Guide.** San Bernardino, CA, The Borgo Press, 1988. 224 p. index. (Bibliographies of Modern Authors, No. 14). LC 87-6334. ISBN 0-89370-393-1; ISBN 0-89370-493-8 (pbk.). **The Work of William F. Nolan: An Annotated Bibliography & Literary Guide.** 2nd ed., rev. and expanded. San Bernardino, The Borgo Press, 1997. 256 p. index. (Bibliographies of Modern Authors, No. 14). LC 95-2762. ISBN 0-8095-0518-5 (cloth); ISBN 0-8095-1518-0 (pbk.).

This is a comprehensive guide to the many works of the prolific SF, mystery, and horror novelist, short story writer, bibliographer, and critic, who is best known for his Logan Trilogy.

Contents (First Edition): Introduction: "The Multi-Media Man," by Dr. Jeffrey M. Elliot; "William F. Nolan: A Chronology"; "A. Books"; "B. Short Fiction"; "C. Verse"; "D. Personality Profiles"; "E. Reviews"; "F. Other Nonfiction"; "G. Screenplays"; "H. Teleplays"; "I. Film and Television Outlines"; "J. Radio"; "K. Stage"; "L. Comics"; "M. Letters"; "N. Juvenilia"; "O. Interviews"; "P. Speeches and Public Appearances"; "Q. Television and Radio Appearances"; "R. Other Media"; "S. Artwork"; "T. Editorial Posts"; "U. Honors and Awards"; "V. About the Author"; "W. Unpublished Works"; "X. Miscellanea"; "Quoth the Critics"; "Index."

Contents (Second Edition): "Preface to the Second Edition"; "Introduction to the First Edition: The Multi-Media Man," by Jeffrey M. Elliot; "A William F. Nolan Chronology"; "Note"; "A. Books and Monographs"; "B. Short Fiction"; "C. Verse"; "D. Personality Profiles"; "E. Reviews"; "F. Other Nonfiction"; "G. Screenplays"; "H. Teleplays"; "I. Film and Television Outlines"; "J. Radio"; "K. Stage"; "L. Comics"; "M. Letters"; "N. Juvenilia"; "O. Interviews with William F. Nolan"; "P. Speeches and Public Appearances"; "Q. Television and Radio Appearances"; "R. Other Media"; "S. Artwork"; "T. Editorial Posts"; "U. Honors and Awards"; "V. Secondary Sources"; "W. Unpublished Works"; "X. Miscellanea"; "Quoth the Critics"; "'Preface: A Man Remembers,' by William F. Nolan"; "'A Year of Yesterdays: An Essay,' by William F. Nolan"; "'Preface: Simply a Beginning," by William F. Nolan; "Simply an Ending: A Short Story," by William F. Nolan; "Title Index."

In each section, the author's works are arranged chronologically and numbered consecutively from one, chapter by chapter, prefixed by the appropriate letter code (*e.g.,* P1, P2, P3, etc.). A typical book entry includes: item number, title (italics), place of publication, publisher, month and year of publication, pagination, format (*e.g.,* "cloth"), and type of publication (*e.g.,* "novel"), with complete data on reprint editions, translations, republications, etc., in all languages. The books are fully annotated, with contents listings, plot summaries, and other pertinent data; entries from other sections are selectively annotated as needed.

A typical shorter work entry includes: item number, title (in quotes), magazine title, volume number, pagination, plus detailed information on all known reprints in all languages; entries for stories reprinted or originally published in book anthologies include: book title, editor, place of publication, publisher, year of publication, format (cloth or paper), and specific pagination of the Nolan piece.

Elliot's entertaining introduction tells us something about Nolan the man as well as Nolan the writer. The chronology provides an extensive year-by-year account of the author's professional and personal life. "About the Author" includes all known secondary works, in chronological order by publication date. The "Miscellanea" section records information on pen names, book dedications, memberships, Library of Congress cataloging data, career highlights, and other data. "Quoth the Critics" includes selected excerpts of reviews and other comments by the leading critics. The index correlates titles and item numbers only. The first edition included eight pages of black-and-white plates reproducing Nolan book covers; these were dropped in the 1997 version.

The second edition supersedes the 1988 version, adding a new preface by Nolan. A few chapters, such as "N. Juvenilia," remain unchanged, but most sections include major new material, with some 300 additional main entries, for a total of 1,760.

"Quoth the Critics" has a clearer layout, and the typeface overall is much improved. Especially welcome are two previously unpublished pieces, a story and an autobiographical essay by Nolan. These additional writings by Nolan provide a perspective on the personality of the writer. Many "Who's Who"-type publication listings have been deliberately excluded from the "Secondary Sources" chapter, in both editions.

The amount of information included herein is simply enormous, being based on Nolan's own records. Data are complete through 1996. Recommended for all researchers of Nolan's work.

This was the last published volume in the Bibliographies of Modern Authors series.

Andre Norton

446. Schlobin, Roger C. **Andre Norton: A Primary and Secondary Bibliography.** Boston, G. K. Hall & Co., 1980. xxxii, 68 p. index. (Masters of Science Fiction and Fantasy). LC 79-18477. ISBN 0-8161-8044-X. Schlobin, Roger C., and Irene R. Harrison. **Andre**

Norton: A Primary and Secondary Bibliography. Rev. ed. Framingham, MA, NESFA Press, 1994. xxvii, 92 p. index. LC 94-69292. ISBN 0-915368-64-1 (pbk.).

Schlobin's bibliography covers the work of a librarian-turned-science fiction writer who began her career in the 1930s, attained great popularity in the 1960s and '70s, and was still actively producing books in the new millennium.

Contents (first edition): "Preface"; "Introduction"; "Part A: Fiction"; "Part B: Miscellaneous Media"; "Part C: Nonfiction"; "Part D: Criticism, Biography, and Selected Reviews"; "Appendix I: Genres"; "Appendix II: Series, Sequels, and Related Works"; "Primary Index"; "Secondary Index."

Contents (revised edition): "Preface," by Andre Norton; "Introduction to the Revised Edition," by Irene R. Harrison; "Introduction to the First Edition," by Roger C. Schlobin; "A. Fiction"; "B. Miscellaneous Media"; "C. Nonfiction"; "D. Criticism, Biography, and Selected Reviews"; "E. Phantoms and Pseudonyms"; "Appendix I: Genres"; "Appendix II: Series, Sequels, and Related Works"; "Primary Index (Alphabetical Listing)"; "Secondary Index."

Schlobin's twenty-page introduction provides a very sound critical and biographical introduction to Norton's work. The bibliography is arranged chronologically, section by section, from the earliest published material to the latest, and numbered consecutively (*e.g.,* A01, A02, for fiction). Books and shorter works are interfiled. No reprint editions or paginations are listed for monographs. Reprints of stories are listed under the main entry, chronologically by year of reprint, giving: anthology editor, book title, place of publication, publisher, year, format (*e.g.,* "paper"), but no paginations.

Each book entry provides: title, place of publication, and publisher. Entries of shorter works published originally in magazines provide: title (in quotations), magazine, volume number, date, pagination; those published originally in books give: title (in quotations), editor, book title, place of publication, publisher, format, but no paginations. Story collections include complete contents listings, plus the years in which the original stories were published. Some items include bibliographical notes, but no other annotations.

Part B includes screenplays, teleplays, interviews, recordings, poetry, and other material that does not specifically fit the other three categories. Part C includes all nonfiction works by the author, plus occasional annotations. Part D lists fifty-seven secondary works, including published book reviews, fan commentaries, critiques, and bibliographies, noting author, title, bibliographical data, and extensive subject annotations.

Appendix I categorizes Norton's works by genre, listing title and item number. Appendix II lists series and other works in sequence. The main index cites title and item number only, the second index (to critical studies) gives author, title, and item number. Unlike most other volumes in the Masters series (which were shot from typed copy), the first edition of this guide was nicely typeset and bound to library standards.

The revised edition contains 475 entries (adding about sixty entries in the book section), and is complete through November, 1994. The volume also includes a new preface by Andre Norton, a new introduction by collaborator Harrison, and the previous introduction by Schlobin. The data are arranged similarly as before. The new Section E is a two-page list of names and works improperly cited to Andre Norton in other bibliographies, plus information on her three known pseudonyms.

Inclusion of information on paginations remains uneven at best, with nonfiction articles sometimes having page citations, but often not, for no apparent reason. The citations to Norton's own works also lack paginations, making identification of book club reprints (for example) exceedingly difficult. The new introduction adds little material of interest, but the old introduction (by Schlobin) remains an informative and straightforward biography-*cum*-critique of Norton's work to that date (1980).

The lack of most reprint editions and the absence of book paginations are particularly noticeable for an author who owes much of her popularity to widely-circulated paperback versions of her books; thus, even though Norton has published well over a hundred books, the fiction section of the revised edition comprises just twenty-three pages of text.

A definitive bibliographical guide to Norton's work has yet to be published. See the comments under Stephensen-Payne's entry (see #447) for comparative details.

447. Stephensen-Payne, Phil. **Andre Norton, Grand Master of the Witch World: A Working Bibliography.** Leeds, West Yorkshire, England, Galactic Central, 1991. 9, 74 p. (Bibliographies for the Avid Reader, Vol. 41). ISBN 1-871133-30-0 (pbk.).

Andre Norton began her career as a writer of historical fiction, but soon had migrated to the young-adult SF market in the 1950s, and then to science fiction and fantasy in the 1960s and '70s.

Contents: Author's name, date and place of birth, and a list of awards won by the author (in chronological order, giving year, name of award, and title of work being honored), and her pseudonyms; "A. Stories"; "B. Fiction Books"; "C. Series"; "D. Poems"; "E. Poetry Collections" [blank section]; "F. Articles"; "G. Miscellaneous" (including introductions and afterwords by Norton, letters, and interviews with the author); "H. Non-Fiction Books"; "I. Books Edited by Andre Norton"; "J. Media Presentations"; "K. Articles on Andre Norton"; "L. Reviews" (of Norton's books, alphabetically by title of the book being reviewed, then by magazine title, giving date and reviewer); "M. Books About Andre Norton"; "N. Phantom & Forthcoming Titles"; "O. Related Items by Other Authors"; "P. Textual Variations"; "Q. Chronological Index" (by year and title).

The introduction clearly explains the many different sections of the bibliography. Stephensen-Payne's basic checklist is arranged by subject category, then alphabetically by title; materials are numbered consecutively from one in each chapter (for example, B1, B2, B3, etc., for the author's books).

Shorter work entries typically include: item number, title, category ("ss" = short story, "nt" = novelette, etc.), magazine or book in which the item appeared, month and year of publication (for magazines in the form "2-68" for February 1968) or year of publication (for books), a list of subsequent reprints (for which title, publisher, year, and editor's last name are given), but no paginations.

For book-length works, Stephensen-Payne provides: item number, title, contents (if a collection, by item number), publisher, stock number, month and year of publication (if known, in the form "10-59" for October 1959), pagination, price, cover artist, plus similar data for known reprints. There is no title index.

513 entries are covered in this bibliography, though reprint information makes the total much greater, of which 236 are secondary sources. 107 of the latter are book review categories, with many hundreds of actual reviews being listed. The author has made no

attempt to include foreign language publications, the introduction admits, due to lack of adequate reference sources.

An index would have been helpful, as would the addition of paginations for the short fiction sections. However, the data are sound, and the book is well organized, as with all of the volumes in this series.

In comparing Stephensen-Payne's work with Schlobin's (see #446), Schlobin includes paginations for original appearances of Norton's shorter works, but not for her novels, while Stephensen-Payne provides page counts for the novels, but not for the stories, and also gives details on numerous reprint editions of these publications. Schlobin annotates many of the secondary works, but Stephensen-Payne provides many more citations to such publications.

Serious researchers will therefore need to employ both of these guides to gain a comprehensive picture of Norton's enormous output.

448. Turner, David G. **The First Editions of Andre Norton.** Menlo Park, CA, David G. Turner, Bookman, 1974. 12 p. (Science Fiction Bibliographies, 1). (pbk.).

This very brief checklist to a popular SF writer's work includes: "Books," "Magazine Fiction," "Anthologies," "Articles," and "Series Listings."

Items are numbered anew from one in each part. In each section materials are arranged in chronological order by year of publication, and then alphabetically by title. A typical book entry includes: item number, title (caps), publisher, place of publication, year of publication (in parentheses), pagination, and brief categorization ("adventure novel"). Only first editions of Norton's works are listed.

The last three chapters are very brief, since Norton has done most of her work in book-length formats. A typical shorter work listing includes: item number, title (caps), pseudonym, magazine, volume and issue number, month and year of publication, but no paginations. The series listings are arranged by series title and proper series order. There is no index or list of secondary sources.

Now superseded by Schlobin's and Stephensen-Payne's bibliographies (see #446 and #447).

Chad Oliver

449. Hall, Hal W. **Chad Oliver: A Preliminary Bibliography.** Bryan, TX, Dellwood Press, 1985. vi, 86 p. (pbk.).

This preliminary version of *The Work of Chad Oliver* (see #450) includes: "Introduction," "Books," "Short Stories," "Letters," "Secondary Material," "News Releases," "Book Reviews," "Interview," "Second Thoughts."

Each section is arranged alphabetically by title. A typical book entry includes: title (boldface), place of publication, publisher, year of publication, pagination, format (*e.g.,* "pb" = paperback), Library of Congress Catalog Card Number, cover artist, stock number (for paperback editions), price, contents (for collections), some bibliographical notes, and similar information on all known reprints, including foreign-language editions.

A typical shorter work entry includes: title (in quotes), magazine, volume and issue number, pagination, month and year of publication, and all known reprints. Reprints in anthologies include: editor, book title, place of publication, publisher, year of publication, pagination. Oliver's numerous fan letters to professional SF magazines are arranged by magazine title, then chronologically by date, with full bibliographical data. Secondary sources are listed alphabetically by critic, with title of article or review, plus bibliographical data in the same formats as above. The text is shot from word-processed copy. There is no index.

Chad Oliver was produced in a 100-copy edition to commemorate the author's appearance as a guest of honor at a local science-fiction convention. Now superseded by the reorganized and updated version (see #450).

450. Hall, Hal W. **The Work of Chad Oliver: An Annotated Bibliography & Guide.** San Bernardino, CA, The Borgo Press, 1989. 88 p. index. (Bibliographies of Modern Authors, No. 12). LC 86-2288. ISBN 0-89370-391-5; ISBN 0-89370-491-1 (pbk.).

Hall, a well-known librarian and bibliographer, here contributes a comprehensive guide to the works of the late American SF and Western writer and anthropologist, Dr. Chad Oliver.

Contents: "Introduction: The Voice Out of the Whirlwind," by Howard Waldrop; "A Chad Oliver Chronology"; "A. Books"; "B. Short Fiction"; "C. Nonfiction"; "D. Letters"; "E. Other Media"; "F. Unpublished Works"; "G. About the Author"; "H. Honors and Awards"; "I. Miscellanea"; "An Interview with Chad Oliver," conducted by Hall and Richard D. Boldt; "Afterword: Second Thoughts," by Oliver; "Index."

In each section, the author's works are arranged chronologically by publication date and numbered anew from one, chapter by chapter, with the appropriate letter prefix (*e.g.,* H1, H2, H3, etc.). A typical book entry includes: item number, title (boldfaced), place of publication, publisher, year of publication, pagination, format (*e.g.,* "paper"), cover artist, stock number and price (for paperbacks), category (*e.g.,* "science fiction novel"), and full bibliographical data for all known reprint editions, translations, and republications. Monographs are annotated, with complete contents listings, plot summaries, and other pertinent data; entries from other sections are selectively annotated as needed.

A typical shorter work entry includes: item number, title (bold quotes), magazine title (in italics), volume number, month and year of publication, pagination, plus complete data on all subsequent reprints. Reprints in anthologies include: title, editor, place of publication, publisher, year of publication, format (*e.g.,* "cloth"), and specific pagination of the Oliver piece.

Waldrop's introduction provides a very personal look at Chad Oliver and his interesting life. The chronology gives a year-by-year account of the author's professional and personal life in block paragraph format. "About the Author" includes all known secondary works; a second subdivision of this section lists the University of Texas, Austin news releases relating to Oliver's professional career as an anthropology professor. The "Miscellanea" section includes information on Oliver's fanzine, education, professional career, and Library of Congress cataloging data. The lengthy interview with and afterword by Dr. Oliver provide much insight into his character and thoughts. The index correlates titles and item numbers only.

Hall worked closely with the author over a period of years, using Oliver's files and personal library to gather much of the data. Coverage is complete through mid-1989. This comprehensive, well-organized, and attractive professional effort by an experienced bibliographer will be welcomed by researchers of this writer's work.

Edgar Pangborn

451. Stephensen-Payne, Phil, and Gordon Benson, Jr. **Edgar Pangborn, the Persistent Wonderer: A Bibliography.** 4th rev. ed. Leeds, West Yorkshire, England, Galactic Central Publications, 1993. 9, 17 p. (Galactic Central Bibliographies for the Avid Reader, Vol. 5). ISBN 1-871133-36-X (pbk.).

The late American writer Edgar Pangborn wrote a number of poignant science-fiction novels and stories set in a post-holocaust America, especially *Davy,* his best-known work. This guide to his work is arranged by subject category, then alphabetically by title.

Contents: Author's name, date and place of birth and death, list of awards won by the author (in chronological order, giving year, name of award, and title of work being honored) and his pseudonyms; "A. Stories"; "B. Fiction Books"; "C. Series"; "D. Poems, Songs & Plays" [blank section]; "E. Poem, Song & Play Volumes" [blank section]; "F. Articles" [blank section]; "G. Miscellaneous" (including introductions and afterwords by Edgar Pangborn, letters, and interviews with the author); "H. Non-Fiction Books" [blank section]; "I. Books Edited by Edgar Pangborn" [blank section]; "J. Media Presentations" [blank section]; "K. Articles on Edgar Pangborn"; "L. Reviews" (of Pangborn's books, alphabetically by title of the book being reviewed, then by magazine title, giving date and reviewer); "M. Books About Edgar Pangborn" [blank section]; "N. Phantom & Forthcoming Titles"; "O. Related Items by Other Authors" [blank section]; "P. Textual Variations" [blank section]; "Q. Chronological Index" (by year and title).

The introduction is almost identical throughout the series, and clearly explains the many different sections of the bibliography. Stephensen-Payne and Benson's basic checklist is arranged by subject category, then alphabetically by title; materials are numbered consecutively from one in each chapter (for example, B1, B2, B3, etc., for the author's books). Shorter work entries include: item number, title, category ("ss" = short story, "nt" = novelette, etc.), magazine or book in which the item appeared, month and year of publication (for magazines in the form "2-68" for February 1968) or year of publication (for books), a list of subsequent reprints (for which title, publisher, year, and editor's last name are given), but no paginations.

For book-length works, Stephensen-Payne and Benson provide: item number, title, contents (if a collection, by item number), publication data (publisher, stock number, month and year of publication [if known, in the form "10-59" for October 1959], pagination, price), cover artist, plus similar data for known reprints. There is no title index.

This edition expands considerably on the four-page first edition, and supersedes all earlier versions. There are 79 entries, though reprint information makes the grand total much greater; of these, 29 are secondary sources, eight being book review categories, which are further subdivided to list the individual book reviews. Only a few foreign language publications are noted. The guide is shot from legible word-processed copy and stapled through the spine. An index would have been helpful, as would the addition of paginations for the short fiction sections.

Pangborn is not well-known today, but his work remains immensely literate and entertaining. Researchers and fans both will welcome this brief guide to his publications.

H. Beam Piper

452. Stephensen-Payne, Phil, and Gordon Benson. **Henry Beam Piper, Emperor of Paratime: A Working Bibliography.** 4th rev. ed. Leeds, West Yorkshire, England, Galactic Central Publications, 1994. 9, 22 p. (Galactic Central Bibliographies for the Avid Reader, Vol. 6). ISBN 1-871133-40-8 (pbk.).

H. Beam Piper, an avid gun collector, mystery novelist, and SF writer of the "Fuzzy" series, took his own life in 1964; ironically, his career rebounded in the 1980s with the republication of all his early work and the appearance of one previously unpublished novel. This checklist is arranged by subject category, then alphabetically by title.

Contents: Author's name, date, and place of birth and death; "A. Stories"; "B. Fiction Books"; "C. Series"; "D. Poems, Songs & Plays" [blank section]; "E. Poem & Song Volumes" [blank section]; "F. Articles"; "G. Miscellaneous" (including introductions and afterwords by H. Beam Piper, letters, and interviews with the author); "H. Non-Fiction Books"; "I. Books Edited by H. Beam Piper" [blank section]; "J. Media Presentations"; "K. Articles on H. Beam Piper"; "L. Reviews" (of Piper's books, alphabetically by title of the book being reviewed, then by magazine title, giving date and reviewer); "M. Books about H. Beam Piper"; "N. Phantom and Forthcoming Titles"; "O. Related Items by Other Authors"; "P. Textual Variations"; "Q. Chronological Index" (by year and title).

The introduction is almost identical throughout the series, and clearly explains the many different sections of the bibliography. Stephensen-Payne and Benson's basic checklist is arranged by subject category, then alphabetically by title; materials are numbered consecutively from one in each chapter (for example, B1, B2, B3, etc., for the author's books).

Shorter work entries include: item number, title, category ("ss" = short story, "nt" = novelette, etc.), magazine or book in which the item appeared, month and year of publication (for magazines in the form "2-68" for February 1968) or year of publication (for books), plus a list of subsequent reprints (for which title, publisher, year, and editor's last name are given), but no paginations.

For book-length works, the authors provide: item number, title, contents (if a collection, by item number), publication data (publisher, stock number, month and year of publication [if known, in the form "10-59" for October 1959], pagination, price), cover artist, plus similar data for known reprints. There is no title index.

Some 131 entries are covered, though reprint information makes the overall number somewhat greater. There are 73 secondary sources, 15 of which are book review categories; over 50 actual reviews are noted. Very few foreign language publications are recorded. The book is shot from very clear word-processed copy and stapled through the spine. An index would have been helpful, as would the addition of paginations for the short fiction sections.

A good bibliographical introduction to a popular writer, one that will be welcomed by fans and researchers alike.

Frederik Pohl

453. Stephensen-Payne, Phil, and Gordon Benson Jr. **Frederik Pohl, Merchant of Excellence: A Working Bibliography.** Leeds, West Yorkshire, England, Galactic Central Publications, 1989. 9, 109 p. (Galactic Central Bibliographies for the Avid Reader, Vol. 34). ISBN 1-871133-09-2 (pbk.). Later reprintings of the book were issued in two volumes, labelled "Part 1: Fiction" and "Part 2: Non-Fiction," with the same pagination being continued throughout.

Frederik Pohl has had a long and distinguished career as an award-winning SF editor, writer, and critic.

This new guide includes: Full name, date and place of birth, list of awards won (with dates and book or story titles), and pseudonyms; "A. Stories"; "B. Fiction Books"; "C. Series"; "D. Poems"; "E. Poem & Song Collections" [blank section]; "F. Articles"; "G. Miscellaneous" (including letters, interviews, afterwords, etc.); "H. Non-Fiction Books"; "I. Books Edited by Frederik Pohl"; "J. Media Presentations"; "K. Articles on Frederik Pohl"; "L. Reviews" [of Pohl's books]; "M. Books About Frederik Pohl"; "N. Phantom & Forthcoming Titles"; "O. Related Books by Other Authors" [blank section]; "P. Textual Variations" [blank section]; "Q. Chronological Index."

In each section materials are arranged alphabetically by title and numbered anew from the number one, chapter by chapter. A typical shorter work entry gives: item number, title, type ("NT" = novelette), magazine title, month and year of publication (in the form "11-41" for November 1941), pen name (where appropriate), and a list of all reprints, including the author's own collections. Reprints in anthologies provide: book title (all caps), editor's last name, publisher, and year of publication. No paginations are given for any short fiction entries.

A typical book entry records: item number, title (all caps), collaborator's name and/or pen name (where appropriate), contents (where appropriate, correlated to item numbers), publisher, format (*e.g.,* "hb" = hardback), stock number, month and year of publication (in the form "5-57" for May 1957), pagination, price, cover artist, and similar data for all known reprints. Sixty-six secondary sources are listed, and hundreds of book reviews, arranged alphabetically by title of the work being reviewed, then alphabetically by magazine title. There is no overall index. The book is shot from very clear word-processed copy and bound with staples into paper covers.

Although Stephensen-Payne and Benson's bibliography is extremely thorough and very professionally organized, the rigidity of the format forces the authors generally to gloss over Pohl's extensive career as a science-fiction magazine editor, summarizing dates and titles in the single entry, G17. This should be much expanded in any second edition. Nonetheless, this bibliography is an essential starting point for all future scholarship on this important author.

Tim Powers

454. Stephens, Christopher P., and Tom Joyce. **A Checklist of Tim Powers.** Hastings-on-Hudson, NY, Ultramarine Publishing Co., 1991. 15 p. index. ISBN 0-89366-198-8 (pbk.).

Powers is a well-known SF and fantasy writer, author of *The Drawing of the Dark.*

This checklist is organized into two sections ("Books" and "Short Stories"), then chronologically by publication date, with the books being numbered from A1-A11, and the stories from B1-3. A typical book entry provides: year (as a floating head), item number, title (underlined), pseudonym, publisher, stock or ISBN number, pagination, format (*e.g.,* "cloth with dust wrapper"), cover illustrator, price, and similar data for all known reprints (which are numbered, for example, A10a, A10b, A10c, etc., in descending order by publication date).

A typical short fiction entry gives: year (floating head), item number, story title (in quotes), magazine title (underlined), month and year of publication, but no paginations. The chapbook is shot from legible typed copy and bound with staples in stiff paper covers. The index correlates titles with years of publication only, not item numbers.

This is a good introductory checklist of Powers's works, one that now badly needs updating.

Robert Reginald

455. Burgess, Michael, and Jeffrey M. Elliot. **The Work of R. Reginald: An Annotated Bibliography & Guide.** San Bernardino, CA, The Borgo Press, 1985. 48 p. index. (Bibliographies of Modern Authors, No. 5). LC 84-21672. ISBN 0-89370-384-2; ISBN 0-89370-484-9 (pbk.). Burgess, Michael. **The Work of Robert Reginald: An Annotated Bibliography & Guide.** 2nd ed., rev. and expanded. San Bernardino, CA, The Borgo Press, 1992. 176 p. index. (Bibliographies of Modern Authors, No. 5). LC 87-6306. ISBN 0-8095-0505-3; ISBN 0-8095-1505-9 (pbk.).

This comprehensive guide to the works of a prolific librarian, SF publisher, bibliographer, editor, and critic includes: (First Edition): "I Fear the Greeks . . . : An Introduction," by Dr. Jeffrey M. Elliot; "A. Books"; "B. Articles and Reviews"; "C. Periodicals, Serials, and Publishing Companies"; "D. Juvenilia"; "E. Radio and Television Appearances"; "F. About the Author"; "G. Honors and Awards"; "H. Unpublished Works"; "J. Miscellanea"; "Index."

Contents (Second Edition): "Introduction: 'Comets Don't Slow Down'," by William F. Nolan; "Preface: 'It Was Twenty Years Ago Today . . . '," by Dr. Fran J. Polek; "A Robert Reginald Chronology"; "A. Books"; "B. Short Nonfiction"; "C. Short Fiction"; "D. Editorial Credits"; "E. Documents"; "F. Catalogs"; "G. Book Production and Design"; "H. Unpublished Works"; "I. Juvenilia"; "J. Public Appearances"; "K. Secondary Sources"; "L. Honors and Awards"; "M. Miscellanea"; "Quoth the Critics"; "Afterthoughts: 'Harvesting the Vineyards of Obscurity'," by Reginald; "Afterword: 'Robert Reginald: Force Majeure'," by Jack Dann; "Title Index."

In each section, the author's works are arranged chronologically and numbered consecutively from one, chapter by chapter. A typical book entry includes (second edition): item number, title (in bold type), byline, place of publication, publisher, month and year of publication, pagination, format (*e.g.,* "cloth"), type of publication (*e.g.,* "anthology"), and full bibliographical data on reprint editions and translations. The books are fully annotated with complete contents listings or plot summaries and other pertinent data; entries from other sections are selectively annotated as needed.

A typical shorter work entry includes (second edition): item number, title (bold quotes), magazine title (italics), volume number, month and year of publication, pagination. The introductions and afterwords provide background material (from different points of view) on Reginald's life and works. The chronology gives a year-by-year account of the author's professional and personal life, in block paragraph format.

There are eighty-seven books listed in the Second Edition, plus 134 short works, 542 editorial credits, fifty-six secondary works, and roughly 150 individual book reviews noted after the monographs in Chapter A. The "Miscellanea" section includes information on pen names, book dedications, memberships, Library of Congress cataloging data, career high-lights, and similar data. "Quoth the Critics" includes selected excerpts of reviews and other comments by leading critics on the author's works, arranged in chronological order by book title. Coverage is complete through 1991. The index cross-references titles and item numbers only.

For stupendously major research collections only.

Mack Reynolds

456. Drumm, Chris, and George Flynn. **A Mack Reynolds Checklist: Notes Toward a Bibliography.** Polk City, IA, Chris Drumm Books, 1983. 24 p. index. ISBN 0-936055-01-4 (pbk.).

Reynolds was a socialist SF writer who died in 1983 just before Drumm and Flynn's booklet was released. This 4.25" x 7" checklist arranges his works in one straight chrono-logical sequence.

Entries are grouped by year, and under each year by month; items are numbered in order from 1-242. Books are underlined, short stories listed in quotation marks. A typical short fiction entry includes: item number, title, category code (*e.g.,* "s" = short story), series note, magazine title, month of publication; or book title, if the first appearance is in an anthology, plus editor, publisher, and year of publication. There are no paginations listed for short stories. Subsequent reprintings are recorded chronologically under the original edition, with similar data provided.

A typical book entry includes: item number, title (underlined), category code (*e.g.,* "c" = collection), place of publication, publisher, stock number (for paperbacks), month of publication (if known), pagination, price, format (*e.g.,* "pb" = paperback), and contents of collections. "See" references, title index, and contents listings are keyed to item number. A few secondary materials are mentioned in passing in their appropriate years, but are not easily retrievable. Data are complete through mid-1983; a one-sheet corrigenda page is also included in some copies. The volume is shot from typed copy; the text runs too close to the margins to allow rebinding by libraries.

This booklet will provide a basic starting point for future research on the author, but a new, more elaborate edition would certainly be justified. Although Reynolds died the same year this checklist was published, he left over a dozen unpublished books, many of which were reworked or revised by other writers for subsequent publication.

Keith Roberts

457. Stephensen-Payne, Phil. **Keith Roberts, Master Craftsman: A Working Bibliography.** Leeds, West Yorkshire, England, Galactic Central Publications, 1993. 9, 33 p. (Bibliographies for the Avid Reader, Vol. 45). ISBN 1-871133-37-8 (pbk.).

The late British writer Keith Roberts is best known for his classic SF work, *Pavane.*

Contents: Author's name, date and place of birth, lists of awards won by the author (in chronological order, giving year, name of award, and title of work being honored) and his pseudonyms; "A. Stories"; "B. Fiction Books"; "C. Series"; "D. Poems, Songs & Plays"; "E. Poem, Song & Play Volumes"; "F. Articles"; "G. Miscellaneous" (including introductions and afterwords by Keith Roberts, letters, and interviews with the author); "H. Non-Fiction Books"; "I. Books Edited by Keith Roberts" [blank section]; "J. Media Presentations" [blank section]; "K. Articles on Keith Roberts"; "L. Reviews" (of Robert's books, alphabetically by title of the book being reviewed, then by magazine title, giving date and reviewer); "M. Books About Keith Roberts"; "N. Phantom & Forthcoming Titles"; "O. Related Items by Other Authors"; "P. Textual Variations" [blank section]; "Q. Chronological Index" (by year and title).

The introduction is almost identical throughout the series, and clearly explains the many different sections of the bibliography. Stephensen-Payne's basic checklist is arranged by subject category, then alphabetically by title; materials are numbered consecutively from one in each chapter (for example, B1, B2, B3, etc., for the author's books). Shorter work entries include: item number, title, category ("ss" = short story, "nt" = novelette, etc.), magazine or book in which the item appeared, month and year of publication (for magazines in the form "2-68" for February 1968) or year of publication (for books), a list of subsequent reprints (for which title, publisher, year, and editor's last name are given), but no paginations.

For book-length works, Stephensen-Payne provides: item number, title, contents (if a collection, by item number), publication data (publisher, stock number, month and year of publication [if known, in the form "10-59" for October 1959], pagination, price), cover artist, plus similar data for known reprints. There is no title index.

244 entries are included, although reprint information makes the overall total greater. Of these, 40 are secondary sources, 17 of which consist of book review categories, in turn further subdivided with lists of the actual reviews. There are very few foreign language publications mentioned. The book is shot from legible word-processed copy and stapled through the spine. An index would have been helpful, as would the addition of paginations for the short fiction sections.

Roberts became ill shortly after this guide was issued, and produced only one additional book in his life, *Lemady,* making this bibliography virtually complete as published save for recent reprints.

Kim Stanley Robinson

458. Joyce, Tom, and Christopher P. Stephens, **A Checklist of Kim Stanley Robinson.** Hastings-on-Hudson, NY, Ultramarine Publishing Co., 1991. 28 p. index. ISBN 0-89366-204-6 (pbk.).

Robinson achieved immediate fame and popularity with the publication of his first novel, *The Wild Shore,* in 1984; this is the first bibliography of his work.

Joyce and Stephens's checklist is arranged chronologically by publication date in two sections covering the author's books and short stories. A typical monograph entry provides: year (as a floating head), item number, title (underlined), pseudonym, publisher, stock or ISBN number, pagination, format (*e.g.,* "cloth with dust wrapper"), cover illustrator, price, and similar data for all known reprints (which are numbered, for example, A1a, A1b, A1c, etc., in descending order by publication date).

A typical short fiction entry gives: year (floating head), item number, title (in quotes), magazine title (underlined) and month and year of publication, or book title (for original anthology appearances; underlined), editor's name, publisher, and year of publication. No paginations are listed for short stories. Items are numbered consecutively from A1-A14 in the book section and from B1-B34 in the short fiction chapter. Robinson also provides an illuminating eight-page autobiographical introduction. The book is shot from legible typed copy and bound with staples in stiff paper covers. The index correlates titles with years of publication only.

This is a good beginning checklist of this popular writer's works, one that is intended primarily for the fan and collectors market. It badly needs updating.

Ross Rocklynne

459. Menville, Douglas. **The Work of Ross Rocklynne: An Annotated Bibliography & Guide.** San Bernardino, CA, The Borgo Press, 1989. 70 p. index. (Bibliographies of Modern Authors, No. 17). LC 88-34360. ISBN 0-8095-0511-8; ISBN 0-8095-1511-3 (pbk.).

Rocklynne, an American SF writer of the pulp era, died in 1988; this is the first guide ever published on his life and works.

Contents: "Introduction: A Man for All Magazines," by Arthur Jean Cox; "A Ross Rocklynne Chronology"; "A. Books"; "B. Short Fiction"; "C. Nonfiction"; "D. Fanzine Contributions"; "E. Radio"; "F. Juvenilia"; "G. About the Author"; "H. Unpublished Works"; "I. Miscellanea"; "Quoth the Critics"; "Index."

Rocklynne's works are arranged chronologically by publication date in each section and numbered anew from one, chapter by chapter; the numbers are prefixed by the appropriate chapter letter (*e.g.,* B1, B2, B3, etc.). A typical book entry includes: item number, title (bold type), place of publication, publisher, month and year of publication, pagination, format (*e.g.,* "paper"), type of publication (*e.g.,* "novel"), and full bibliographical data on reprint editions, including foreign. The books are fully annotated, with complete contents listings and plot summaries; entries from other sections are selectively annotated as needed. This chapter is very short, since Rocklynne worked primarily in the short fiction market.

A typical story entry includes: item number, title (bold quotes), magazine title (italics), volume number, month and year of publication, pagination, with complete bibliographical details on all known reprints (including those in Rocklynne's own books). Reprints in anthologies include: book title (italics), editor, place of publication, publisher, year of publication, format (*e.g.,* "paper"), pagination.

Cox's introduction provides a discussion of Rocklynne's life and works by one of the author's friends and colleagues. The chronology provides a year-by-year account of his professional and personal life. "About the Author" includes all known secondary works. The "Miscellanea" section includes information on pen names, book dedications, memberships, Library of Congress cataloging data, career highlights, and other data. "Quoth the Critics" includes selected excerpts of reviews and other comments by leading critics on the author's work. The "Index" lists titles and item numbers only.

Menville, a well-known film critic and editor, has produced a complete and sympathetic guide to the author's work, much of it deriving from Rocklynne's own files, gathered just before his untimely death. Complete data on this author's works are provided through mid-1989. Any researcher on the author's life or works must perforce begin here, with this attractive and thorough bibliographical rendition of his literary life.

Sax Rohmer

460. Day, Bradford M. **Sax Rohmer: A Bibliography.** Denver, NY, Science-Fiction & Fantasy Publications, 1963. 34 p. LC 63-4431 (pbk.).

This checklist of the classic British horror writer's work is presented in the same format as Day's previous bibliographies on Burroughs and Mundy (see #342, #441).

The book section is arranged alphabetically by title, a typical entry including: title (caps), publisher, place of publication, year of publication, pagination, mention of other editions (publisher and year only), brief cover copy quote, notes on previous magazine serialization (in parentheses), with magazine name and dates, plus binding color style.

The short fiction section is arranged in chronological order by date of publication, and lists: story title (all caps), magazine title, year of publication, month of publication, a list of reprints in Mundy's books, but no paginations. There is a brief biography and checklist of film adaptations, but no index. The book is mimeographed from typed copy and has begun to yellow.

The basic bibliography was slightly updated in Day's later book, *Bibliography of Adventure* (see #234). In the absence of a comprehensive bibliography of Rohmer's work, Day's hard-to-locate guide is the only one currently available to the scholar or researcher.

Eric Frank Russell

461. Stephensen-Payne, Phil, and Sean Wallace. **Eric Frank Russell, Our Sentinel in Space: A Working Bibliography.** 3rd rev. ed. Leeds, West Yorkshire, England, Galactic Central Publications, 1999. ix, 97 p. (Galactic Central Bibliographies for the Avid Reader, Vol. 24). ISBN 1-871133-55-6 (pbk.).

The late Englishman Eric Frank Russell was a "hard SF" writer who died in 1978. Stephensen-Payne and Wallace's guide to his work is arranged by subject category, then alphabetically by title.

Contents: "Introduction"; "Awards and Pseudonyms"; "A. Prose Fiction"; "B. Prose Fiction Books"; "C. Series" [blank section]; "D. Poetry & Drama"; "E. Poetry & Drama Books"; "F. Articles"; "G. Miscellaneous"; "H. Non-Fiction Books"; "I. Publications Edited by Eric Frank Russell" [blank section]; "J. Other Media"; "K. Articles on Eric Frank Russell"; "L. Reviews"; "M. Items Devoted to Eric Frank Russell"; "N. Phantom and Forthcoming Titles"; "O. Related Items by Other Authors"; "P. Textual Variations and Other Notes"; "Q. Chronological Index of Prose Fiction"; "R. Index by Magazine/Newspaper."

The introduction is almost identical throughout the series, and clearly explains the many different sections of the bibliography. Stephensen-Payne and Wallace's basic checklist is arranged by subject category, then alphabetically by title; materials are numbered consecutively from one in each chapter (for example, B1, B2, B3, etc., for the author's books).

Shorter work entries include: item number, title, category ("ss" = short story, "nt" = novelette, etc.), magazine or book in which the item appeared, month and year of publication (for magazines in the form "2-68" for February 1968), or year of publication (for books), a list of subsequent reprints (for which title, publisher, year, and editor's last name are given), but no paginations.

For book-length works, Stephensen-Payne and Wallace provide: item number, title, contents (if a collection, by item number), publication data (publisher, stock number, month and year of publication [if known, in the form "10-59" for October 1959], pagination, price), cover artist, plus similar data for known reprints. There is no title index, though there is a new section of articles listed by title of the periodical in which they were published.

Some 416 entries are recorded overall, although reprint information makes the total much greater. Of these, 136 constitute secondary sources, 18 of which are book review categories, with perhaps 50 actual reviews being listed. A general index would have been helpful, as would the addition of paginations for short fictions. The book is shot from very clear word-processed copy and perfect bound (*i.e.*, glued) in paper covers.

This bibliography should remain relatively current for some time to come; with the absence of any new material from Russell, the only future additions will be reprints of previously published works. Scholars will find this guide a necessary beginning point for any future research on Russell's fiction.

Fred Saberhagen

462. Stephensen-Payne, Phil. **Fred Saberhagen, Berserker Man: A Working Bibliography.** Leeds, West Yorkshire, England, Galactic Central Publications, 1991. 9, 28 p. (Galactic Central Bibliographies for the Avid Reader, Vol. 37). ISBN 1-871133-26-2 (pbk.).

Saberhagen, best known for his Berserker series and his modern adaptation of the Dracula mythos, is the target of this addition to the Galactic Central Series.

Contents: "A. Stories"; "B. Fiction Books"; "C. Series"; "D. Poems & Songs"; "E. Poem & Song Collections" [blank section]"; "F. Articles"; "G. Miscellaneous"; "H. Non-Fiction Books" [blank section]; "I. Books Edited by Fred Saberhagen"; "J. Media Presentations"; "K. Articles on Fred Saberhagen"; "L. Reviews" [of Saberhagen's books]; "M. Books About Fred Saberhagen" [blank section]; "N. Phantom & Forthcoming Titles"; "O. Related Items by Other Authors"; "P. Textual Variations"; "Q. Chronological Index."

Materials are arranged in each section alphabetically by title. A typical shorter work entry provides: item number, title, type ("ss" = short story), magazine title and month and year of publication, or (for an original anthology appearance) book title (all caps), editor's surname, publisher, and year of publication, but no paginations. Similar data are provided for all known reprints.

A typical monograph entry gives: item number, title (all caps), contents (correlated by item number), publisher, format (*e.g.,* "pb" = paperback), stock number, month and year of publication (in the form "10-81" for October 1981), pagination, price, and cover artist, with similar data on all known reprints. Items are numbered from the number one in each section, prefixed by the letter code assigned to that chapter (for example, B1, B2, B3, etc., for the Books section).

Some 195 entries are noted overall, though reprint information makes the grand total somewhat greater. Of these, some seventy secondary sources are listed and about a hundred book reviews in thirty-five review categories. Stephensen-Payne attempts to include all known foreign language publications, but the information here is very scanty. The book is shot from legible word-processed copy and bound with staples through the spine into paper covers. There is no index.

This is a good introductory guide to Saberhagen's writings. Future editions should add short fiction paginations and a comprehensive index.

Pamela Sargent

463. Elliot, Jeffrey M. **The Work of Pamela Sargent: An Annotated Bibliography & Guide.** San Bernardino, CA, The Borgo Press, 1990. 80 p. index. (Bibliographies of Modern Authors, No. 13). LC 88-34361. ISBN 0-89370-394-X; ISBN 0-89370-494-6 (pbk.). **The Work of Pamela Sargent: An Annotated Bibliography & Literary Guide.** 2nd ed., rev. and expanded. San Bernardino, CA, Borgo Press, 1996. 144 p. index. (Bibliographies of Modern Authors, No. 13). LC 96-15693. ISBN 0-89370-396-6 (cloth); ISBN 0-89370-496-2 (pbk.).

Sargent is a well-known writer in the SF field, with many award-winning credits as novelist, short-story writer, children's writer, and editor. She is closely associated with two other upstate New York writers, George Zebrowski and Jack Dann, on whom Elliot also prepared bibliographies (see #363 and #518).

Contents (first edition): "Introduction: Let the Rest Take Care of Itself," by Elliot; "A Pamela Sargent Chronology"; "A. Books"; "B. Short Fiction"; "C. Nonfiction"; "D. Unpublished Works"; "E. Editorial Credits"; "F. Other Media"; "G. Juvenilia"; "H. Public Appearances"; "I. Honors and Awards"; "J. About the Author"; "K. Miscellanea"; "Quoth the Critics"; "Afterword: 'Though the Looking Glass,'" by Sargent; "Index."

Contents (second edition): "Introduction: 'What Doesn't Kill You Makes You Stronger,'" by Jeffrey M. Elliot; "A Pamela Sargent Chronology"; "A. Books and Monographs"; "B. Short Fiction"; "C. Short Nonfiction"; "D. Unpublished Works"; "E. Editorial Credits"; "F. Other Media"; "G. Juvenilia"; "H. Public Appearances"; "I. Honors and Awards"; "J. Secondary Sources"; "K. Miscellanea"; "Quoth the Critics"; "Three Essays by Pamela Sargent: 'Nicotine Fits'; 'Writing, Science Fiction, and Family Values'; 'Afterword: Through the Looking Glass'"; "Notes"; "Index"; "About Jeffrey M. Elliot."

In each section, the author's works are arranged chronologically and numbered consecutively from one, chapter by chapter, prefixed by the appropriate letter code. A typical monograph entry includes: item number, title (boldface), place of publication, publisher, month and year of publication, pagination, format (*e.g.,* "cloth"), cover artist, series designation, type of publication (*e.g.,* "novel"), and full bibliographical data on all known reprint editions and translations. The books are fully annotated with complete contents listings or plot summaries, and other pertinent data; entries from other sections are selectively annotated as needed.

A typical shorter work entry gives: item number, title (bold quotes), magazine (italics), volume number, month and year of publication, pagination, and similar data on all known reprints. Reprints in anthologies include: book title (italics), editor, place of publication, publisher, year of publication, format (*e.g.,* "cloth"), pagination. Elliot's introduction provides a personal look at the author's life. The chronology provides a year-by-year account of the author's professional and personal life, in block paragraph format.

"About the Author" includes all known secondary works. The "Miscellanea" section includes information on pen names, book dedications, memberships, Library of Congress cataloging data, career highlights, and other data. "Quoth the Critics" includes selected excerpts of reviews and other comments by leading critics on the author's work. Sargent's short original afterword tells why and how she became a writer and how her nearsightedness led her into the world of literature. The index correlates titles and item numbers only. Coverage is complete through 1989.

The second edition closely follows the same as the first. Some headings have been relabeled (*e.g.,* "J. About the Author" has become "J. Secondary Sources"), but much of the text remains the same. The renamed introduction by Elliot preserves almost all of the previous essay, but concludes with a few new pages. The Afterword by Sargent remains the same, and sections D and G are almost wholly unchanged. Coverage has been extended through 1995, with some information from 1996. The number of main entries has increased to 300 from 182, which does not, however, reflect some additional citations for reprints and collected reviews.

A welcome addition in the new version are the two humorous and personal essays by Sargent, "Nicotine Fits" (from *Astromancer Quarterly,* 1992) and "Writing, Science Fiction, and Family Values" (*Amazing Stories,* 1994). The index refers only to titles and item numbers. The new typeface has considerably improved the readability of the text.

The second edition completely supersedes the first edition, and remains a good base for future scholarship on this writer. Recommended for scholarly collections devoted to the study of science fiction and/or women writers.

James H. Schmitz

464. Owings, Mark. **James H. Schmitz: A Bibliography.** Baltimore, MD, Croatan House, 1973. [33] p. (Croatan House Bibliographies). ISBN 0-88358-902-8 (pbk.).

Owings's brief checklist of the late American science fiction writer's works includes a nineteen-page critical introduction, "The Natural Heroine of James H. Schmitz," by novelist Janet Kagan. The bibliography proper, which consists of just six pages of copy, is arranged by title in one alphabetical sequence, book titles being underlined. A typical short fiction work entry gives: title, abbreviated magazine title (an abbreviations list appears on page [3]), month and year of publication (in the form 7/49 for July 1949), but no paginations, plus known reprint editions. Reprints in anthologies include: book title (underlined), editor, publisher, place of publication, year of publication, total book pagination, price, but no individual story paginations.

A typical book entry includes: title (underlined), publisher, place of publication, year of publication, pagination, price, and similar data on all known reprint editions. A complete contents listing is provided for collections. The book is shot from very legible typed copy. Two appendices provide an alphabetical list of the author's books and a chronological check-list of all his publications by year and month.

Schmitz published relatively little between 1973-81 (the year of his death), so this concise guide to his work still remains fairly current. A larger, more elaborate bibliographical synthesis of Schmitz's work would now be warranted.

Bob Shaw

465. Stephensen-Payne, Phil, and Gordon Benson, Jr. **Bob Shaw, Artist at Ground Zero: A Working Bibliography.** 5th rev. ed. Leeds, West Yorkshire, England, Galactic Central Publications, 1993. 9, 42 p. (Galactic Central Bibliographies for the Avid Reader, Vol. 14). ISBN 1-871133-38-6 (pbk.).

The late Bob Shaw, a native of Northern Ireland, is best known for his "hard SF" stories and novels. This new checklist, earlier versions of which were co-authored with Chris Nelson and Benson, arranges materials by subject category, then alphabetically by title.

Contents: Author's name, date and place of birth, list of awards won by the author (in chronological order, giving year, name of award, and title of work being honored); "A. Stories"; "B. Fiction Books"; "C. Series"; "D. Poems & Songs" [blank section]; "E. Poem & Song Collections" [blank section]; "F. Articles"; "G. Miscellaneous" (including introductions and afterwords by Bob Shaw, letters, and interviews with the author); "H. Non-Fiction Books"; "I. Edited Books" [blank section]; "J. Media Presentations"; "K. Articles on Bob Shaw"; "L. Reviews" (of Shaw's books, alphabetically by title of the book being reviewed, then by magazine title, giving date and reviewer); "M. Books About Bob Shaw"; "N. Phantom Titles"; "O. Related Items by Other Authors"; "P. Textual Variations"; "Q. Chronological Index" (by year and title).

Each section arranges the material alphabetically by title, the author's works being numbered anew from one in each section and prefixed by the appropriate letter code. For shorter works, the authors give: item number, title, category ("ss" = short story, "nt" = novelette, etc.), magazine or book in which the item appeared, month and year of publication (for magazines in the form "4-82" for April 1982) or year of publication (for books), plus a list of subsequent reprints (for which title, editor's last name, publisher, and year are given), but no paginations.

A typical book entry provides: item number, title (in caps), publication data (publisher, stock number, month and year of publication [if known, in the form "10-59" for October 1959], pagination, price, with dates of reissues by the same publisher), cover artist. There is no general index. There are 299 entries included, although reprint information makes the total number somewhat greater. 67 of these are secondary sources, 27 of which consist of book review categories; the actual number of reviews mentioned approach 100. Coverage is complete through 1993. The book is shot from clear word-processed copy and bound with staples in paper covers.

The inclusion of an index and short fiction paginations would be desirable additions to future editions of this useful bibliography. Even with its limitations, this guide provides a wealth of hard-to-locate data organized into an easily accessible format. Research libraries should acquire a copy.

Lucius Shepard

466. Joyce, Tom, and Christopher P. Stephens. **A Checklist of Lucius Shepard.** Hastings-on-Hudson, NY, Ultramarine Publishing Co., 1991. 18 p. index. ISBN 0-89366-203-8 (pbk.).

Shepard began publishing poetry in the 1960s, but first achieved popularity in the SF field with *Green Eyes,* a novel published in 1984.

Joyce and Stephens's checklist arranges the data into two sections covering his books and short stories, then chronologically by publication date. Items are numbered consecutively, books from A1-A9, short fiction from B1-B41. A typical book entry provides: year (as a floating head), item number, title (underlined), publisher, stock or ISBN number, pagination, format (*e.g.,* "cloth with dust wrapper"), cover illustrator, price, and similar data for all known reprints (which are numbered, for example, A8a, A8b, A8c, etc., in descending order by publication date).

Shorter work entries include: item number, title (in quotes), magazine title (underlined) and month and year of publication, or (for original anthology appearances) book title (underlined), editor's name, publisher, and year of publication, with similar data for all known reprints. There are no paginations for the short stories. The booklet is shot from legible typed copy and bound with staples in stiff paper covers. The index correlates titles with years of publication only.

Shepard's fiction and verse has found a solid following who will appreciate this carefully compiled checklist. Now badly in need of updating.

M. P. Shiel

467. Morse, A. Reynolds. **The Works of M. P. Shiel: A Study in Bibliography.** Los Angeles, CA, Fantasy Publishing Co. Inc., 1948. xvii, 170 p. index. LC 49-1086. Originally published in cloth, but some unbound sheets were later issued in paper covers. **The Works of M. P. Shiel Updated: A Study in Bibliography, Including "About Myself," by M. P. Shiel, 1865-1947 (New Revised Version), with a New Appendix on Louis Tracy (1863-1928).** 2nd and updated ed. Dayton, OH, Reynolds Morse Foundation in Association with JDS Books, 1980. 858 p. in 2 v. index. (The Works of M. P. Shiel, Vols. 2-3). LC 79-88144. ISBN 0-934236-01-1.

Morse's comprehensive guide to this somewhat obscure British fantasy writer is obviously a labor of love.

Contents (Second Edition): "1. A Checklist of the Various Editions of the Novels and Short Stories of M. P. Shiel"; "2. The Collations": "a) "Notes on Collations," "b) 1895-1901," "c) 1901-1914," "d) 1923-1937"; "3. The Short Stories of M. P. Shiel"; "4. Miscellaneous Works by M. P. Shiel": a) and b) in Books, Anthologies, etc.," "c) in Periodicals and Newspapers," "d) M. P. Shiel and Arthur Machen"; "5. Known Manuscripts, Corrected

Texts, Proofs, Typescripts, Published and Unpublished, of M. P. Shiel"; "6. Bibliography" [*i.e.,* Secondary Sources]: "M. P. Shiel a) in Books," "b) in Periodicals, etc." (arranged chronologically); "7. a) 'About Myself,' by M. P. Shiel," "b) Biographical Notes," "c) The Personal Library of M. P. Shiel," "d) An Epilogue: The Address of Edward Shanks at the Funeral of Matthew Phipps Shield," "e) Bohemia in London," "f) Introduction to the Original Edition of 1948"; "8. The Shielography Update" (an essay on the years 1948-1979); "9. The Conquest of M. P. Shiel's Redonda"; "10. New Appendix on Louis Tracy (Including the Novels of "Gordon Holmes" and the Lamb-Morse Bibliography on the Works of Tracy)"; "11. Acknowledgments"; "12. Index."

Shiel worked mainly in book-length form, and the basic bibliography of monographs is arranged in chronological order by publication date. Each book entry includes: title (caps), lengthy annotation (from one-to-two pages covering both the plot or contents of the book and other items of interest), bibliographical data for each known edition of the work, including publisher, place of publication, month and year of publication, exact title page transcription, collation, physical size, binding (all known variations, with edition states and priorities).

Similar data are provided for Shiel's short stories, articles, translations, and poems, without annotations, as they appeared in magazines, newspapers, and known book reprints (with paginations). Morse also includes a list of the books in Shiel's personal library, a guide to the known manuscripts, proofs, and typescripts, and a complete bibliographical guide to the eight mystery novels of "Gordon Holmes," a house pseudonym that included several Shiel collaborations.

The autobiographical "About Myself" and several similar pieces provide much background information on the author's life. Morse's secondary list is exhaustive, including many sources that are difficult to locate, with complete bibliographical data and brief annotations summarizing the Shiel material. A title index (correlated to page number) completes a very well organized and presented bibliography.

The second edition subsumes, expands upon, and corrects the earlier work, but is otherwise arranged very similarly.

Both books are nicely typeset and illustrated, and the second edition is bound to library standards. Clearly, no scholar could even begin to think of researching Shiel without consulting Morse's extraordinarily complete guide.

Robert Silverberg

468. Clareson, Thomas D. **Robert Silverberg: A Primary and Secondary Bibliography.** Boston, G. K. Hall & Co., 1983. xxx, 321 p. index. (Masters of Science Fiction and Fantasy). LC 83-154. ISBN 0-8161-8118-7.

Robert Silverberg is one of the most prolific writers of modern fantastic literature, having authored (as writer or editor) over a hundred SF books and over a hundred additional monographs in other categories, some under pseudonyms, plus several hundred short stories. The late Tom Clareson was an acknowledged expert on Silverberg's work, having previously published a critique of his work.

Contents: "Preface"; "Acknowledgments"; "Introduction"; "Comprehensive Short-Title List of Silverberg's Books"; "A. Science Fiction and Fantasy"; "B. Miscellaneous

Fiction"; "C. Edited Anthologies"; "D. Nonfiction"; "E. Silverberg on Science Fiction"; "F. Other Media"; "G. Reviews and Critical Studies of Silverberg's Works"; "Appendix 1: Silverberg's Articles in the *Bulletin of the Science Fiction Writers of America*"; "Appendix 2: Silverberg's Pseudonymous Works Listed by Pen Name"; "Appendix 3: Awards and Nominations"; "Indexes: The Works of Robert Silverberg"; "Reviews and Critical Studies."

Clareson's brief introduction provides a cursory critical and biographical introduction to Silverberg's work. The bibliography is arranged chronologically from the earliest published material to the latest and numbered consecutively (*e.g.,* A1, A2, A3, for his science fiction). Books and shorter works are interfiled.

Each book entry gives: title, place of publication, publisher, and contents (for collections), with years of publication of the individual stories and their entry numbers. Reprints of monographs are arranged in chronological order by year of publication under the primary entry, and include: place of publication, publisher, year of publication, and an indication of whether the book was issued in paperback format.

Shorter works published originally in magazines provide: title (in quotes), magazine, volume number, month of publication (in parentheses), and pagination; those published originally in books give: title (in quotes), editor, book title, place of publication, publisher, format (*e.g.,* "paper"), and paginations. Reprints of stories are listed under the main entry, chronologically by year of reprint, with the editor of the anthology, title, place of publication, publisher, year, format (*e.g.,* "paper"), but no paginations. Story collections include complete contents listings, plus the years in which the original stories were published. Some entries contain bibliographical notes, but no other annotations.

In Part B Clareson summarizes Silverberg's many soft-porn titles of the 1950s and '60s, reportedly numbering in the hundreds, providing a skeletal listing without complete bibliographical details; also mentioned in this chapter are ten titles Silverberg wrote in other genres, arranged in the same format as Part A.

Part C lists sixty-seven anthologies edited by Silverberg in chronological order by publication date, with title, place of publication, publisher, and year of publication, but no contents listings.

Part D includes ninety-one nonfiction pieces by Silverberg, most of them juvenile or young adult books on science, biography, and history. Part E lists all of Silverberg's nonfiction essays on fantastic literature, plus his fanzine contributions, with lengthy annotations. Part F, "Other Media," includes four records and filmstrips.

The secondary bibliography is extensive, covering almost 800 items, including published book reviews, fan commentaries, critiques, biographies, and bibliographies, giving: author, title, bibliographical data, and subject annotations, many of them lengthy and analytical.

Appendix 1 lists Silverberg's essays in the *SFWA Bulletin*; Appendix 2 provides a checklist of his pseudonymous work, alphabetically by pen name and then by title, with references to the main-entry item numbers of each; Appendix 3 is a useful list of the author's awards and award nominations in descending, chronological order by year. The main index cites title and item number only, the second index (to critical studies) author and title (separately), plus item number. The book is shot from generally clear typed copy and bound to library standards.

The lack of book paginations in this volume is very noticeable, as is the absence of anthology contents; Silverberg was one of the leading editors of original and reprint anthologies in the field for the ten-year period from 1970-80, and inclusion of such data (with appropriate indices) would have provided scholars with a much better sense of his contributions to this area. Coverage is complete through 1981, making this book now lamentably outdated. This guide can provide only an early introduction to this complex and prolific writer's many publications.

Clifford D. Simak

469. Becker, Muriel R. **Clifford D. Simak: A Primary and Secondary Bibliography.** Boston, G. K. Hall & Co., 1980. xliii, 149 p. index. (Masters of Science Fiction and Fantasy). LC 79-18124. ISBN 0-8161-8063-6.

The late Clifford D. Simak was a well-regarded writer of pastoral science fiction stories that combined his love of nature and the Wisconsin countryside with a sense of wry nostalgia. Becker's bibliography provides a good basic guide to this American author's works.

Contents: "Preface"; "Acknowledgments"; "Introduction"; "Clifford D. Simak Interviewed"; "Documents Consulted"; "Brief Chronology"; "Awards and Honors"; "Part A: Science Fiction"; "Part B: Miscellaneous: Westerns, Air War Stories, and Media"; "Part C: Nonfiction"; "Part D: Critical and Bio-Bibliographical Studies"; "Appendix A: Periodical Reviews Excluded"; "Appendix B: Overview of MSS44, the Clifford D. Simak Papers"; "Appendix C: Title Changes"; "Appendix D: Anthologies in Which Simak's Stories Appear"; "Appendix E: Works in U.S. Science Fiction Book Club Editions"; "Index I: The Writings of Clifford D. Simak: Parts A, B., C"; "Index II: About Clifford D. Simak: Part D."

The introduction provides a broad critical and biographical introduction to Simak's work. The bibliography is arranged chronologically, from the earliest published material to the latest, and numbered consecutively (*e.g.,* D1, D2, D3, etc.). Books and shorter works are interfiled.

Each book entry gives: title, place of publication, publisher, but no paginations. Reprints of books are listed chronologically under the main entry, with place of publication, publisher, year of publication, and format (*e.g.,* "paper"). Story collections include: complete contents listings, plus the years in which the original stories were published.

Shorter works published originally in magazines give: title (in quotations), magazine, volume and issue number, month of publication (in parentheses), and pagination; those published originally in books include: title (in quotations), editor, book title, place of publication, publisher, format, and pagination. Reprints of stories are listed under the main entry, chronologically by year of reprint, with the editor of the anthology, title, place of publication, publisher, year, format (*e.g.,* "paper"), and paginations. Some entries include bibliographical notes, but no other annotations.

Part B includes fiction in other genres, most of it published during the pulp era, plus a few interviews and speeches. Part C lists all nonfiction works by the author, including fanzine contributions, with occasional annotations. Part D lists roughly 200 secondary works, including published book reviews, fan commentaries, critiques, and bibliographies, with author, title, bibliographical data, and extensive subject annotations.

Appendix A indexes otherwise unrecorded reviews of individual Simak works alphabetically by book title, then chronologically by review, with abbreviated magazine title, volume, pagination, date of publication, and reviewer. Appendix B is a detailed itemization of the seventeen boxes of the Clifford D. Simak papers at the University of Minnesota Libraries. Appendix C correlates title changes in Simak's fiction. Appendix D indexes the anthologies in which Simak's stories have appeared, alphabetically by editor and book title, with the item number (but not the title) of the Simak story; the lack of story titles makes this section somewhat difficult to use. Appendix E is a chronological checklist of Simak's books selected by the American version of the Science Fiction Book Club.

The main index cites title and item number only, the second index (to critical studies) author, title, and item number. Unlike most books in this series, Becker's volume is attractively typeset and bound to library standards.

Data are complete through 1978; however, Simak's 1988 death means that this book will remain relatively current indefinitely, lacking only the author's last few books and a handful of short stories, plus subsequent reprintings. The absence of monograph paginations, a standard feature of this series, is unfortunate, but could easily be restored in a revised and updated "definitive" edition. Until then, this book and Stephensen-Payne's bibliography (see #471) must remain the essential starting points for all future scholarship on Simak's writings.

470. Owings, Mark. **Clifford D. Simak.** Baltimore, MD, Alice & Jay Haldeman, 1971. [11] p. (The Electric Bibliograph, Part 1). (pbk.).

This brief 8.5" x 11" checklist of Simak's science fiction stories, novels, and collections is arranged in the standard Owings format, alphabetically by title in one master sequence.

A typical short fiction entry includes: title, abbreviated magazine title, month and year of publication (in the form "3/51" for March 1951), and bibliographical data on all known reprints in other collections and anthologies, with title, editor, publisher, place of publication, year of publication, total pagination of book (but not of the individual story), price, format (*e.g.,* "wpps" = paperback).

A typical book entry includes: title (in italics), original magazine serialization information (where appropriate), publisher, place of publication, year of publication, pagination, price, and similar data on all known reprint editions, including some foreign-language versions (with foreign-language titles and translators). A brief afterword mentions the lone story collaboration and three nonfiction books written or edited by Simak. The booklet was reproduced on sometimes faint mimeographed sheets that are now yellowing.

Although largely superseded by Becker's more current and complete work (see #469), Owings's bibliography does provide paginations and prices for the author's early books, and can thus be used as a supplement to the former. This was the first volume of a series that sputtered along for a few volumes before finally dying.

471. Stephensen-Payne, Phil. **Clifford D. Simak, Pastoral Spacefarer: A Working Bibliography.** Leeds, West Yorkshire, England, Galactic Central Publications, 1991. 9, 64 p. (Bibliographies for the Avid Reader, Vol. 39). ISBN 1-871133-28-9 (pbk.).

The late SF writer Clifford D. Simak is best known today for such books as *City* and *Way Station.*

Contents: Author's name, date and place of birth and death, and a list of awards won by the author (in chronological order, giving year, name of award, and title of work being honored); "A. Stories"; "B. Fiction Books"; "C. Series"; "D. Poems, Songs & Plays" [blank section]; "E. Poem, Song, & Play Volumes" [blank section]; "F. Articles"; "G. Miscellaneous" (including introductions and afterwords by Clifford D. Simak, letters, and interviews with the author); "H. Non-Fiction Books"; "I. Edited Books"; "J. Media Presentations"; "K. Articles on Clifford D. Simak"; "L. Reviews" (of Simak's books, alphabetically by title of the book being reviewed, then by magazine title, giving date and reviewer); "M. Books About Clifford D. Simak"; "N. Phantom & Forthcoming Titles"; "O. Related Items by Other Authors" [blank section]; "P. Textual Variations"; "Q. Chronological Index" (by year and title).

The basic introduction is almost identical throughout the series, and clearly explains the many different sections of the bibliography. Stephensen-Payne's basic checklist is arranged by subject category, then alphabetically by title; materials are numbered consecutively from one in each chapter (for example, B1, B2, B3, etc., for the author's books). Shorter work entries include: item number, title, category ("ss" = short story, "nt" = novelette, etc.), magazine or book in which the item appeared, month and year of publication (for magazines in the form "2-68" for February 1968) or year of publication (for books), a list of subsequent reprints (for which title, publisher, year, and editor's last name are given), but no paginations.

For book-length works, Stephensen-Payne provides: item number, title, contents (if a collection, by item number), publication data (publisher, stock number, month and year of publication [if known, in the form "10-59" for October 1959], pagination, price), cover artist, plus similar data for known reprints. There is no title index. 391 entries are recorded, though reprint information makes the overall total greater. 142 of these are secondary sources, 46 of them being book review categories (the reviews themselves number in the hundreds). There are a few foreign language publications included. An index would have been helpful, as would the addition of paginations for the short fiction sections.

Stephensen-Payne's bibliography is much more current than Becker's (see #469), but the latter includes paginations for shorter works that this guide lacks; however, Becker lacks the paginations for monographs that Stephensen-Payne includes. Both should prove useful to the scholarly researcher, but Stephensen-Payne will prove quite sufficient for the average reader.

John Sladek

472. Drumm, Chris. **A John Sladek Checklist: Pre-Publication Version.** Polk City, IA, Chris Drumm Books, 1984. [26] p. index. (pbk.).

The late John Sladek's experimental and sometimes controversial SF is aptly chronicled in this new 4.25" x 7" checklist. The author's works are arranged in one chronological sequence. Entries are grouped by year and under each year by month; items are numbered in order from 1-114. Books are listed in bold italics, short stories in quotation marks.

A typical short fiction entry includes: item number, title, category code (*e.g.,* "s" = short story), series note, magazine title (in italics), month of publication; or book title (in italics) if the first appearance is in an anthology, plus editor, publisher, and year of publication. There are no paginations listed for short stories. Subsequent reprintings are listed chronologically under the original edition, with similar data provided.

A typical book entry includes: item number, title (bold italics), type (*e.g.,* "story collection"), place of publication, publisher, stock or ISBN number, pagination, price, format (*e.g.,* "pb" = paperback), and contents of collections. Similar data are provided on all reprint editions, including a few foreign monographs, with foreign-language titles and translators. Contents listings of collections include original year of publication with each story title. The index correlates titles and years of publication only. A few secondary materials are mentioned in passing in their appropriate years, but are not easily retrievable. Data are complete through part of 1984. The book is shot from very legible word-processed copy; margins are much wider than in earlier books from this publisher.

Drumm's book was updated by Phil Stephensen-Payne in 1998 (see #473).

473. Stephensen-Payne, Phil, and Chris Drumm. **John T. Sladek, Steam-Driven Satirist: A Working Bibliography.** Leeds, West Yorkshire, England, Galactic Central Publications, 1998. ix, 54 p. (Bibliographies for the Avid Reader, Vol. 49). ISBN 1-871133-50-5 (pbk.).

The late British writer Sladek wrote a number of very interesting novels (*Tik-Tok,* for example) satirizing modern society.

Contents: Author's name, date and place of birth, a list of awards won by the author (in chronological order, giving year, name of award, and title of work being honored), and his pseudonyms; "A. Prose Fiction"; "B. Prose Fiction Books"; "C. Series"; "D. Poetry & Drama"; "E. Poetry & Drama Books" [blank section]; "F. Articles"; "G. Miscellaneous" (including introductions and afterwords by John T. Sladek, letters, and interviews with the author); "H. Non-Fiction Books"; "I. Publications Edited by John T. Sladek"; "J. Other Media"; "K. Articles on John T. Sladek"; "L. Reviews" (of Sladek's books, alphabetically by title of the book being reviewed, then by magazine title, giving date and reviewer); "M. Books About John T. Sladek"; "N. Phantom and Forthcoming Titles"; "O. Related Items by Other Authors"; "P. Textual Variations and Other Notes"; "Q. Chronological Index of Prose Fiction" (by year and title).

The introduction is almost identical throughout the series, and clearly explains the many different sections of the bibliography. Stephensen-Payne's and Drumm's basic checklist is arranged by subject category, then alphabetically by title; materials are numbered consecutively from one in each chapter (for example, B1, B2, B3, etc., for the author's books). Shorter work entries include: item number, title, category ("ss" = short story, "nt" = novelette, etc.), magazine or book in which the item appeared, month and year of publication (for magazines in the form "2-68" for February 1968) or year of publication (for books), a list of subsequent reprints (for which title, publisher, year, and editor's last name are given), but no paginations.

For book-length works, Stephensen-Payne and Drumm provide: item number, title, contents (if a collection, by item number), publication data (publisher, stock number, month and year of publication [if known, in the form "10-59" for October 1959], pagination, price), cover artist, plus similar data for known reprints. There is no title index. The book records some 305 entries, although reprint information makes the overall total somewhat greater. There are 75 secondary sources, 19 of which are book review categories; perhaps 50 actual reviews are noted. Coverage of foreign language publications is incomplete. The table of contents, not previously found in the series, is a welcome and helpful addition. The volume is reproduced from legible word-processed copy, and is stapled through the spine. An index would have been helpful, as would the addition of paginations for the short fiction sections.

This book was partially adapted from and completely supersedes Drumm's earlier separately published checklist (see #472), and will be welcomed by fans and scholars alike. A very workmanlike publication.

Clark Ashton Smith

474. Bell, Joseph, and Roy A. Squires. **The Books of Clark Ashton Smith.** Toronto, Canada, Soft Books, 1987. 28 p. index. ("Old Masters" Series, Number Two). (pbk.).

Bell's bibliographies of Lovecraft and other weird fiction writers are essentially collectors' guides to the authors' books.

Contents: "Index of Book Titles" (with title, publisher, year of publication, and page number of entry); "Information Is Given as Follows" (Bell's description of the basic entry format); "The Books of Clark Ashton Smith"; "Alphabetical Index of Fiction" (an index to the short stories, correlated to Smith collections in which they are included with year of book publication); and "A Chronological Listing of Book Titles" (essentially the first section rearranged by year).

The bibliography proper is arranged chronologically by year of publication. A typical entry includes (for all known editions): title (bold underlined caps), publisher, place of publication, pagination, number of copies printed, cover artist, printer's name, binding and paper states (arranged in priority order), original price, month of publication, and contents (for collections).

For a writer like Smith who has had many of his works issued in small press chapbook editions, this kind of guide is useful to establish first-edition points, but as a bibliography it can only be considered a brief supplement to Sidney-Fryer's much more complete and detailed work (see #476).

475. Cockcroft, T. G. L. **The Tales of Clark Ashton Smith: A Bibliography.** Lower Hutt, New Zealand, Thomas G. L. Cockcroft, 1951. vi p. (pbk.). **The Tales of Clark Ashton Smith: A Bibliography.** Rev. ed. Lower Hutt, New Zealand, Thomas G. L. Cockcroft, 1959. vii p. (pbk.).

This brief checklist of Smith's works was professionally printed and produced by an early bibliographer of the field, and is typical of the best of fan scholarship.

Contents: "Collections"; "In Preparation"; "Anthology Representations"; "Stories; "Addenda" (1959; pages [vi-vii]).

Smith's story collections are listed chronologically by year of publication; a typical entry includes: title (italics), publisher, place of publication, year of publication, pagination, format (*e.g.,* "wraps"), with physical dimensions measured in inches. "Anthology Representations" is also arranged chronologically, and includes: book title (italics), editor, publisher, place of publication, year of publication, and the title of the Smith story included (in italics).

The story section is arranged alphabetically by story title, a typical entry giving: title (italics), magazine of publication, the Smith collection in which the story is included (keyed to three-letter codes; *e.g.,* "TDS" = *The Double Shadow*), and month and year of publication. The addendum includes materials published through the 1950s, and additional stories not previously mentioned.

Now wholly superseded by Sidney-Fryer (see #476).

476. Sidney-Fryer, Donald. **Emperor of Dreams: A Clark Ashton Smith Bibliography.** West Kingston, RI, Donald M. Grant, 1978. 303 p. LC 79-103877.

Sidney-Fryer's immense bibliography includes practically anything any scholar might want to know about this well-regarded American poet and fantasy writer, but its size, complexity, and lack of an index make it unnecessarily difficult to use.

Contents: "Introduction"; "Acknowledgements"; "Principal Facts of Biography"; "Collections"; "Clark Ashton Smith: In Memory of a Great Friendship," by Eric Barker; "Poems"; "Poems in French"; "Poems in Spanish"; "Translations of Poems: From the French, from the Spanish"; "Prose Translations of Verse"; "Contents of Poetry Collections"; "Uncollected Poems"; "Appearances of Poems in Anthologies," etc.; "Poems in Prose"; "Collections of Poems in Prose"; "Tales"; "Addendum"; "Contents of Prose Collections"; "Uncollected Tales"; "Appearances of Tales in Anthologies"; "Epigrams and Pensées"; "Miscellaneous Prose"; "Juvenilia"; "Periodicals"; "Published Letters"; "*The Auburn Journal* and *Weird Tales*"; "About Clark Ashton Smith"; "Library Holdings of Smith Mss."; "Pseudonyms"; "Five Approaches to the Achievements of Clark Ashton Smith, Cosmic Master Artist," by Marvin R. Hiemstra; "Index to First Lines of Poems"; "The Sorcerer Departs," by Clark Ashton Smith. Also included are fourteen tribute or biographical letters from well-known writers and/or friends of Smith, and eight pages of photographs.

Shorter works are arranged alphabetically by title, chapter by chapter; monographs are organized in chronological order by date of publication. A typical shorter work entry includes: title (bold caps), date of composition, magazine title, month and year of publication, plus a list of books in which the story or poem has been collected or anthologized (giving book title [all caps] and year only). No paginations are included for magazine publication of shorter works.

A typical book entry includes: title (bold caps), publisher, place of publication, year, pagination, cover artist, price, format (*e.g.,* "paperbacked"), number of copies printed, and an exact collation of the contents. Reprints are interfiled by publication year; "See" references refer the reader back to the original edition, but not forward *from* the original. Some foreign-language materials are included. The list of secondary sources is excellent as far as it goes; these materials are arranged chronologically by year of publication. The volume is beautifully designed and printed, as is usual with Don Grant's books, and bound to library standards.

However, although Sidney-Fryer clearly knows his material well and includes an enormous amount of carefully gathered data, the absence of an index is fatal to what could have been *the* standard book on Smith. The complicated format makes immediate access to any particular title almost impossible without extensive reading of the text. A reorganized and updated version would clearly be desirable.

Cordwainer Smith

477. Bennett, Mike. **A Cordwainer Smith Checklist.** Polk City, IA, Chris Drumm Books, 1991. [28] p. index. (Drumm Booklet #37). ISBN 0-936055-49-9 (pbk.).

Under his real name, Paul M. A. Linebarger, Smith was a well-known intelligence officer and political scientist; his science-fiction works have long been praised for their insights into war, politics, and sociology. This checklist organizes the author's works into two sections, the first covering his SF output as Cordwainer Smith, the second his real-life career as political scientist and mainstream novelist under the names Paul Linebarger, "Felix C. Forrest," and "Carmichael Smith."

In each section materials are arranged chronologically by publication date. A typical monograph entry includes: item number, title (in quotes, underlined), type (*e.g.,* "n" = novel), contents (referring to the other item numbers for Smith's short works), publisher, stock number, month and year of publication, pagination, price, and similar data for all known reprints.

A typical shorter work entry gives: item number, title (in quotes), magazine title (underlined), month and year of publication, specific pagination, and similar data for all known reprints, including the author's own collections. Reprints in anthologies note: anthology title (underlined), editor's name, publisher, year of publication, and specific pagination. Books and stories are interfiled in their respective sections; materials in the first section are numbered from 1-43, and in the section half from 1-24. There are separate indices for each section, correlating titles and item numbers. The booklet is shot from legible typed copy, and bound with staples into limp paper covers. A one-page addenda runs on the last page of text.

This guide will provide a good starting point for all future scholarship on this intriguing writer. Future editions should attempt to include secondary sources, and should combine the indices into one straightforward list.

Margaret St. Clair

478. Stephensen-Payne, Phil, and Gordon Benson, Jr. **Margaret St. Clair, Space Frontierswoman: A Working Bibliography.** 3rd rev. ed. Leeds, West Yorkshire, England, Galactic Central Publications, 1997. ix, 30 p. (Galactic Central Bibliographies for the Avid Reader, Vol. 15). ISBN 1-871133-48-3 (pbk.).

The late American writer Margaret St. Clair wrote numerous science fiction stories and novels during the 1940s-'60s. Stephensen-Payne and Benson's checklist arranges her work by subject category, then alphabetically by title.

Contents: Author's name, date and place of birth and death, list of awards won by the author [blank section] and her pseudonyms; "A. Prose Fiction"; "B. Prose Fiction Books"; "C. Series"; "D. Poetry & Drama" [blank section]; "E. Poetry & Drama Books" [blank section]; "F. Articles"; "G. Miscellaneous" (including introductions and afterwords by Margaret St. Clair, letters, and interviews with the author); "H. Non-Fiction Books" [blank section]; "I. Edited Books" [blank section]; "J. Media Presentations" [blank section]; "K. Articles on Margaret St. Clair"; "L. Reviews" (of St. Clair's books, alphabetically by title of the book being reviewed, then by magazine title, giving date and reviewer); "M.

Books About Margaret St. Clair"; "N. Phantom and Forthcoming Titles"; "O. Related Items by Other Authors" [blank section]; "P. Textual Variations" [blank section]; "Q. Chronological Index of Prose Fiction" (by year and title).

The introduction is almost identical throughout the series, and clearly explains the many different sections of the bibliography. Stephensen-Payne's and Benson's basic checklist is arranged by subject category, then alphabetically by title; materials are numbered consecutively from one in each chapter (for example, B1, B2, B3, etc., for the author's books). Shorter work entries include: item number, title, category ("ss" = short story, "nt" = novelette, etc.), magazine or book in which the item appeared, month and year of publication (for magazines in the form "2-68" for February 1968) or year of publication (for books), a list of subsequent reprints (for which title, publisher, year, and editor's last name are given), but no paginations.

For book-length works, Stephensen-Payne and Benson provide: item number, title, contents (if a collection, by item number), publication data (publisher, stock number, month and year of publication [if known, in the form "10-59" for October 1959], pagination, price), cover artist, plus similar data for known reprints. There is no title index. 176 entries are covered, although reprint information makes the overall total somewhat greater; of these, 26 consist of secondary sources, six of which are book review categories; perhaps 30 actual reviews are mentioned. Very few foreign language publications are included.

The table of contents, not previously found in this series, is a welcome and helpful addition. However, the quality of the type in this book is not as clear as in the other recent volumes of the Galactic Central Bibliographies, and there is a section of faint copy running vertically across almost all the pages. The book is stapled through the spine. An index would have been helpful, as would the addition of paginations for the short fictions.

This is the only guide to this little-known author's work, and should be consulted by anyone seriously interested in investigating her work.

Brian Stableford

479. Stephensen-Payne, Phil. **Brian Stableford, Genetic Revolutionary: A Working Bibliography.** Leeds, West Yorkshire, England, Galactic Central, 1997 x, 133 p. in 2 v. (Bibliographies for the Avid Reader, Vol. 48). ISBN 1-871133-49-1 (pbk.). Published in two volumes, labelled "Part 1: Major Items" and "Part 2: Minor Items," but paginated consecutively throughout.

The well-known British SF writer and critic had sold a million words of fiction by the time he was in his early twenties, and has since produced hundreds of essays, short stories, and novels, becoming not only a well-known fiction writer, but one of the leading modern critics of fantastic literature.

Contents: Author's name, date and place of birth, a list of awards won by the author (in chronological order, giving year, name of award, and title of work being honored), and his pseudonyms; "A. Prose Fiction"; "B. Prose Fiction Books"; "C. Series"; "D. Poetry & Drama"; "E. Poetry & Drama Books" [blank section]; "F. Articles"; "G. Miscellaneous" (including introductions and afterwords by Brian Stableford, letters, and interviews with the author); "H. Non-Fiction Books"; "I. Publications Edited by Brian M. Stableford"; "J. Other Media"; "K. Articles on Brian M. Stableford"; "L. Reviews" (of Stableford's books, alphabetically by title of the book being reviewed, then by magazine title, giving date and reviewer); "M. Books About Brian M. Stableford" [blank section]; "N. Phantom & Forthcoming Titles"; "O. Related Items by Other Authors" [blank section]; "P. Textual Variations"; "Q. Chronological Index" (by year and title); "R. Reference Book Entries and Reviews" (contributed by Stableford himself).

The introduction is almost identical throughout the series, and clearly explains the many different sections of the bibliography. Stephensen-Payne's basic checklist is arranged by subject category, then alphabetically by title; materials are numbered consecutively from one in each chapter (for example, B1, B2, B3, etc., for the author's books). Shorter work entries include: item number, title, category ("ss" = short story, "nt" = novelette, etc.), magazine or book in which the item appeared, month and year of publication (for magazines in the form "2-68" for February 1968) or year of publication (for books), a list of subsequent reprints (for which title, publisher, year, and editor's last name are given), but no paginations.

For monographs, Stephensen-Payne provides: item number, title, contents (if a collection, by item number), publisher, stock number, month and year of publication (if known, in the form "10-59" for October 1959), pagination, price, cover artist, plus similar data for known reprints. There is no title index. 697 major item entries are covered, although reprint information makes the total much greater. Of these, 125 constitute secondary sources, 59 of them being book review categories; well over a hundred actual reviews are mentioned.

The so-called "minor items" in the second volume ("Section R") provide a listing of unnumbered, unpaginated citations to Stableford's hundreds of essay contributions to 27 major reference volumes and 24 science fiction periodicals. These total approximately 850 entries, divided into three main sections: "1. Author-Specific Entries & Reviews"; "2. Magazine Entries & Reviews"; and "3. General Entries." In each section materials are arranged in alphabetical order by title, entries being keyed to the magazine and book abbreviations listed at the end of the volume.

The table of contents, not previously found in the series, is a welcome and helpful addition. The volumes are shot from clear, word-processed copy, and are stapled through the spine. An index would have been helpful, as would the addition of paginations for the short works sections.

Stableford is almost more important as a critic than as a fiction writer (his essays have filled most of the major collaborative reference volumes in the field), and it is helpful to have this guide to his voluminous (and very perceptive) critical output. This volume should be purchased by all major research libraries.

Olaf Stapledon

480. Satty, Harvey J., and Curtis C. Smith. **Olaf Stapledon: A Bibliography.** Westport, CT, London, Greenwood Press, 1984. xxxviii, 167 p. index. (Bibliographies and Indexes in World Literature, No. 2). LC 84-6549. ISBN 0-313-24099-X.

This very well-organized and comprehensive bibliography of the English SF writer and philosopher's work is a major contribution to the scholarship of the genre.

Contents: "Preface"; "Acknowledgments"; "Abbreviations"; "Location Symbols"; "Introduction"; "The Peak and the Town," by Olaf Stapledon; "A. Books and Pamphlets"; "AA. Omnibus Collections and Complete Novel Reprints"; "B. Contributions to Books and

Pamphlets"; "BB. Reprinted Contributions to Books"; "C. Contributions to Periodicals and Newspapers"; "CC. Reprinted Contributions to Periodicals"; "D. Contributions to Periodicals, Newspapers, and Pamphlets in Collaboration with Others"; "E. Manuscripts of Published Writings in Public Archives"; "EE. Manuscripts of Unpublished Writings in Public Archives"; "F. Translations"; "G. Bibliographies"; "Selected Secondary Bibliography"; "Addenda"; "Index."

Each section is arranged chronologically by date of publication, Stapledon's works being numbered consecutively from one in each chapter (*e.g.,* A1, A2, A3, etc., for books). A typical book entry includes: item number, title (all caps), exact transcription of title page, copyright page, and cover or jacket copy, collation, contents collation, typography, paper and binding details, month of publication, price, number of copies printed, exact physical proportions of the book and jacket in millimeters, plus a list of libraries known to have copies (vastly incomplete, of course), as taken from the *National Union Catalog,* plus other notes. Similar data are provided for all known issues and binding states.

A typical shorter work contribution to periodicals includes: title (in quotes), magazine title (italics), volume and issue number, year and month of publication, pagination, plus some subject annotations. Contributions to books include data similar to the books section. Reprints appear in separate sections, with "See" references back to the original listings. The guide to Stapledon's manuscripts will prove most useful to scholars, and the list of secondary sources, although noted as selective, seems very complete. All of the internal references and the index correlate the data with item numbers only. The book is shot from very clear word-processed copy and bound to library standards. Data are complete through early 1984.

Satty and Smith have provided an immeasurable resource for the scholar, one that will benefit students of Stapledon's work for generations to come. The data are well presented, easily accessible, and very complete. Kudos to both authors for this excellent bibliographic guide.

Bram Stoker

481. Dalby, Richard. **Bram Stoker: A Bibliography of First Editions.** London, Dracula Press, 1983. [xii], 81 p. index. LC 84-242632. ISBN 0-7212-0643-4 (pbk.).

Dalby's brief but valuable guide to this English horror writer's work contains: "Quest for Stoker" (Dalby's informative introduction); [The Books]; "Articles, Short Stories, and Serials"; "Biographies of Bram Stoker"; "Index."

Each section is arranged chronologically by date of publication. A typical book entry includes: item number (numbered consecutively from the beginning of this section), title (all caps), place of publication, publisher, year of publication, collation, binding details, and notes, including price, month of publication, and contents (for collections) or brief description (for novels). Similar data are provided for notable reprint editions. Many reproductions of the original title pages of the books are also included, together with several drawings of Stoker from contemporary sources.

Brief checklists are also included of Stoker's magazine publications (fiction and non-fiction in one chronological list), and of major biographies and miscellanea relating to Stoker and his best-known creation, Count Dracula, from the novel *Dracula.* The index correlates titles and page numbers.

Dalby's bibliography will provide a very good beginning point for students of this popular author's works; a revised edition should add a more comprehensive list of secondary sources and pastiches.

Theodore Sturgeon

482. Benson, Gordon Jr., and Phil Stephensen-Payne. **Theodore Sturgeon, Sculptor of Love and Hate: A Working Bibliography.** Leeds, West Yorkshire, England, Galactic Central Publications, 1989. 9, 75 p. (Galactic Central Bibliographies for the Avid Reader, Vol. 32). ISBN 1-871133-07-6 (pbk.). Later reprintings divide the book into two volumes, labelled "Part 1: Fiction" and "Part 2: Non-Fiction," with the same pagination being continuing throughout.

Benson and Stephensen-Payne's bibliography covers works by and about the late American SF writer Sturgeon, known chiefly for his short stories.

Contents: Author's full name, dates of birth and death, awards, and pseudonyms; "A. Stories"; "B. Fiction Books"; "C. Series"; "D. Poems and Songs"; "E. Poem and Song Collections" [blank section]; "F. Articles"; "G. Miscellaneous" (including reviews, editorships, forewords, interviews, introductions, etc.); "H. Non-Fiction Books" [blank section]; "I. Books Edited by Theodore Sturgeon" [blank section]; "J. Media Presentations"; "K. Articles on Theodore Sturgeon"; "L. Reviews [of Sturgeon's books]"; "M. Books About Theodore Sturgeon"; "N. Phantom Titles and Editions"; "O. Related Items by Other Authors" [blank section]; "Textual Variations" [blank section]; "Chronological Index."

Materials in each section are arranged alphabetically by title and numbered anew from one, prefixed by the appropriate letter code for that chapter. A typical book entry gives: item number, title (all caps), contents (keyed to item number), publisher, format (*e.g.,* "pb" = paperback), stock number, month and year of publication (in the form "12-66" for December 1966), pagination, price, cover artist, and similar data for all known reprints.

A typical shorter work entry includes: item number, title, type (*e.g.,* "NA" = novella), magazine title, month and year of publication (in the form "1-58" for January 1958), pseudonym (where applicable), and similar data for all known reprints, including the author's own books. Stories appearing in anthologies give: book title (all caps), editor's surname, publisher, and year of publication. No paginations are listed for short fictions.

Ninety-seven secondary sources are listed and about a hundred book reviews, arranged alphabetically by title of the book being reviewed, then alphabetically by magazine title. The book is shot from very clear word-processed copy and bound with staples into paper covers. Data are complete through the end of 1988.

In comparing this bibliography with Diskin's (see #483), Benson and Stephensen-Payne's volume is a decade more current and includes book paginations that Diskin's work lacks, but lacks the story paginations that Diskin's work includes; it also lists more secondary works. Researchers and libraries will want access to both volumes; fans will find Benson and Stephensen-Payne's guide more than adequate.

483. Diskin, Lahna F. **Theodore Sturgeon: A Primary and Secondary Bibliography.** Boston, G. K. Hall, 1980. xxvii, 105 p. index. (Masters of Science Fiction and Fantasy). LC 79-18120. ISBN 0-8161-8046-6.

This early volume in the Masters series by the author of a critical monograph on Sturgeon covers the works of the late American SF and fantasy writer.

Contents: "Preface"; "Primary and Secondary Source Documents"; "Abbreviations"; "Theodore Sturgeon: Toward a Chronology"; "Introduction"; "Part A: Science Fiction"; "Part B: Miscellaneous Media"; "Part C: Nonfiction"; "Part D: Critical Studies"; and six separate indices.

Diskin's introduction provides a brief critical introduction to Sturgeon's work. The bibliography is arranged chronologically, from the earliest published material to the latest, and numbered consecutively (*e.g.,* A1, A2, A3, etc., for fictional works). Books and shorter works are interfiled. Each book entry gives: title, place of publication, publisher, but no paginations. Reprints of books are listed chronologically under the main entry, with place of publication, publisher, year of publication, and format (*e.g.,* "paper"). Story collections include complete contents listings, plus the years in which the first stories were published.

Shorter works published originally in magazines give: title (in quotations), magazine code (full title is given in the abbreviations list at the front of the book; some codes are not obvious), month of publication (in parentheses), and pagination; those published originally in books give: title (in quotations), editor, book title, place of publication, publisher, format, and pagination. Reprints of stories are listed under the main entry, chronologically by year of reprint, with the editor of the anthology, title, place of publication, publisher, year, format (*e.g.,* "paper"), and pagination. Some entries include bibliographical notes, but no other annotations.

Part B includes radio, television, and stage plays, and some comic book adaptations and audio recordings. Section C lists all of the nonfiction works by the author, with occasional annotations.

Part D records some 116 secondary works about Sturgeon, including published book reviews, critiques, and bibliographies, with author, title, bibliographical data, and extensive subject annotations. The six indices correlate the data by item number only; they include a general index to Sturgeon's works, separate indices for each of the four sections, and a rearrangement of the book reviews covered in Section D by the title of the Sturgeon book being reviewed. Unlike most later books in this series, this volume is attractively typeset and is bound to library standards.

Data are complete through 1978; since Sturgeon had largely stopped writing fiction by 1975 and has now died, Diskin's book remains relatively current, lacking only a handful of the author's last essays, reprints, and additional critical works. A definitive revision and updating would certainly be justified, but until then, this bibliography will provide students and scholars with plenty of access points to Sturgeon's writings. Benson and Stephensen-Payne's guide (see #482) may serve as a supplement.

Thomas Burnett Swann

484. Collins, Robert A. **Thomas Burnett Swann: A Brief Critical Biography and Annotated Bibliography.** Boca Raton, FL, Thomas Burnett Swann Fund, College of Humanities, Florida Atlantic University, 1979. [ii], 29 p. (pbk.).

American academic and novelist Thomas Burnett Swann died at the age of forty-seven in 1976; this booklet was intended as a memorial to the man and his work.

Collins's eighteen-page introduction provides an excellent biographical and critical background on Swann the writer and teacher. The bibliography proper is arranged in one chronological sequence, year by year, and then by month of publication. A typical book entry includes: title (in italics), category (*e.g.,* "novel," in parentheses), place of publication, publisher, pagination, contents (for collections), a one-paragraph plot summary (averaging four sentences), and a list of reviews (giving reviewer name, magazine title, issue number, date, and pagination).

A typical shorter work entry provides: title (in quotes), category (*e.g.,* "novelette," in parentheses), magazine title (italics), volume and issue number, month and year of publication, pagination, and plot summary (two or three sentences). Some translations are also included, with foreign-language titles and translators' names, in addition to other data. A chronological table of Swann's fictional worlds is provided by Bob Roehm.

The absence of an index in this brief bibliography is unnoticeable. The book is beautifully typeset and produced and serves generally as an excellent introductory guide to Swann's writings. Collins acknowledges Roehm's contributions (see #485).

485. Roehm, Bob. **A Thomas Burnett Swann Bibliography.** Rev. ed. Clarksville, IN, Bob Roehm, 1978 (originally 1976). [4] p., plus one-page supplement. (pbk.).

This brief checklist of the late American fantasy writer's works is arranged by category ("Short Fiction," "Novels & Collections," "Poetry," "Non-Fiction," "Anthology Appearances," "and "Foreign Publications"), then chronologically by publication date.

Shorter work entries include: title (in quotes), magazine title (underlined), and month and year of publication (British magazines include issue numbers). Book entries include: title (underlined), references to magazine serializations and original titles (if any), contents, publisher, year of publication, and cover artist. No paginations are mentioned. An unnumbered, one-page insert supplements the original volume, with data complete through the end of 1977. The booklet is shot from clear typed copy.

Now wholly subsumed into Collins's more substantial bibliography (see #484), to which Roehm contributed.

William F. Temple

486. Ashley, Mike. **The Work of William F. Temple: An Annotated Bibliography & Guide.** San Bernardino, CA, Borgo, 1994. 112 p. index. (Bibliographies of Modern Authors, No. 28). LC 93-334. ISBN 0-8095-0507-X (cloth); ISBN 0-8095-1507-5 (pbk.).

Contents: "Preface"; "About Mike Ashley"; "Reminiscences," by Arthur C. Clarke; "William F. Temple: A Short Biography"; "A William F. Temple Chronology"; "William F. Temple: An Introduction to His Works"; "About the Format"; "A. Books"; "B. Short Fiction"; "C. Short Nonfiction"; "D. Editorial Credits"; "E. Fan Writings"; "F. Unpublished Works"; "G. Other Media"; "H. Honors and Awards"; "I. Public Appearances"; "J. About the Author"; "K. Miscellanea"; "Quoth the Critics"; "Afterword," by Forrest J Ackerman; Selected Early Writings by William F. Temple: "The Hunting of the Flat" and "Chingford Chiaroscuro"; "The British Fan: William F. Temple," by Arthur C. Clarke; "The Final Word," by Joan Temple; "Index."

Intended as a comprehensive bibliographical guide and tribute to the late British "hard SF" writer, William F. Temple, Ashley's tribute provides a good biographical introduction and background material on the author's life and works. The chronology gives a year-by-year account of the author's professional and personal life in block paragraph format. "Quoth the Critics" includes selected excerpts of reviews and other comments by leading critics on the author's work. The afterword by agent Forrest J Ackerman and widow Joan Temple provide a glimpse into the cantankerous and highly sensitive nature of Temple, and well-known SF writer Arthur C. Clarke contributes a reminiscence of the two men's early careers in pre-World War II Britain, when they shared an apartment.

Each section of the bibliography is arranged in chronological order by publication date. There are 267 main entries, but reprints and secondary sources run the total number of editions much higher. The typical monograph entry includes: item number, title (bold italics), place of publication, publisher, date of publication, pagination, binding, book or ISBN number (in parentheses), series information (where applicable), cover illustrator (where known), type of book (in brackets; *e.g.,* [science-fiction novel]), notes, plot summary or contents (50-100 words), a list of subsequent reprints in all languages with similar bibliographical data, in descending order by publication date, and a list of secondary sources and reviews in alphabetical order by critic or magazine.

A typical short work entry includes: item number, title (boldfaced in quotation marks), magazine title, volume or issue number, date, pagination, illustrator (where known), type of story (in brackets), plot summary or contents (25-75 words), and bibliographic data on all known reprints. The index correlates titles, editors, and periodical titles with item numbers. The book is nicely designed and typeset, and the cloth edition bound to library standards.

A very thorough volume on a relatively obscure author, Ashley's bibliography is recommended for very large academic library collections, and for any scholars interested in the development of British science fiction.

William Tenn

487. Stephensen-Payne, Phil, and Gordon Benson, Jr. **William Tenn, High Klass Talent: A Working Bibliography.** 4th ed. Leeds, West Yorkshire, England, Galactic Central Publications, 1993. 9, 22 p. (Galactic Central Bibliographies for the Avid Reader, Vol. 7). ISBN 1-871133-39-4 (pbk.).

American writer William Tenn, the pseudonym of academic Philip Klass, wrote a number of significant books and stories in the science fiction field during the 1950s and '60s.

Contents: Author's name, date and place of birth, and his pseudonyms; "A. Stories"; "B. Fiction Books"; "C. Series"; "D. Poems, Songs & Plays" [blank section]; "E. Poem, Song, and Play Volumes" [blank section]; "F. Articles"; "G. Miscellaneous" (including introductions and afterwords by William Tenn, letters, and interviews with the author); "H. Non-Fiction Books" [blank section]; "I. Books Edited by William Tenn"; "J. Media Presentations"; "K. Articles on William Tenn"; "L. Reviews" (of Tenn's books, alphabetically by title of the book being reviewed, then by magazine title, giving date and reviewer); "M. Books About William Tenn"; "N. Phantom & Forthcoming Titles"; "O. Related Items by

Other Authors" [blank section]; "P. Textual Variations"; "Q. Chronological Index" (by year and title).

The introduction is almost identical throughout the series, and clearly explains the many different sections of the bibliography. Stephensen-Payne and Benson's basic checklist is arranged by subject category, then alphabetically by title; materials are numbered consecutively from one in each chapter (for example, B1, B2, B3, etc., for the author's books). Shorter work entries include: item number, title, category ("ss" = short story, "nt" = novelette, etc.), magazine or book in which the item appeared, month and year of publication (for magazines in the form "2-68" for February 1968) or year of publication (for books), a list of subsequent reprints (for which title, publisher, year, and editor's last name are given), but no paginations.

For book-length works, Stephensen-Payne and Benson provide: item number, title, contents (if a collection, by item number), publication data (publisher, stock number, month and year of publication [if known, in the form "10-59" for October 1959], pagination, price), cover artist, plus similar data for known reprints. There is no title index. 118 entries are covered, although reprint information makes the actual total somewhat larger. Of these, 29 are secondary works, 9 of which consist of book review categories; perhaps 30 actual reviews are mentioned. The book is shot from very clear word-processed copy and stapled through the spine. An index would have been helpful, as would the addition of paginations for the short fiction sections.

Although Tenn is not well-known outside the SF field, his work deserves reprinting, and this guide will provide a solid entrée into his fiction.

James Tiptree, Jr.

488. Stephensen-Payne, Phil, and Gordon Benson, Jr. **James Tiptree, Jr., a Lady of Letters: A Working Bibliography.** Leeds, West Yorkshire, England, Galactic Central Publications, 1988. 9, 26 p. (Galactic Central Bibliographies for the Avid Reader, Vol. 31). ISBN 1-871133-05-X (pbk.).

Tiptree, the professional name of the late American author Alice Sheldon, was one of the best regarded SF writers during her relatively brief career.

Contents: Full name and dates of birth and death, awards, and pen names; "A. Stories"; "B. Fiction Books"; "C. Series" [blank section]; "D. Poems & Songs" [blank section]; "E. Poem & Song Collections" [blank section]; "F. Articles"; "G. Miscellaneous"; "H. Non-Fiction Books" [blank section]; "I. Edited Books" [blank section]; "J. Media Presentations"; "K. Articles on James Tiptree, Jr."; "L. Reviews" [of Tiptree's books]; "M. Books About James Tiptree, Jr."; "N. Phantom Titles"; "O. Related Books by Other Authors" [blank section]; "P. Textual Variations" [blank section]; "Q. Chronological Index."

In each section, materials are arranged alphabetically by title and numbered from one, chapter by chapter, with the appropriate letter prefix. A typical story entry includes: item number, title, type (*e.g.,* "NT" = novelette), magazine title and month and year of publication (in the form "12-85" for December 1985), or (for stories appearing in anthologies) book title (all caps), editor's last name, publisher, and year of publication, plus similar data for all known reprints. No paginations are listed for shorter works.

A typical monograph entry records: item number, title (all caps), contents (where applicable, with materials listed by item number), publisher, format ("hb" = hardback), stock number, month and year of publication (in the form "4-86" for April 1986), pagination, price, and cover artist, plus similar information for all known reprint editions. Thirty-four secondary sources are noted and about thirty reviews of Tiptree's works. The book is shot from word-processed copy and bound with staples through the spine into paper covers. Data are included through 1988.

Tiptree died in 1987, so this guide will likely remain current for quite some time. Future editions should add short fiction paginations and a comprehensive index.

J. R. R. Tolkien

489. Johnson, Judith A. **J. R. R. Tolkien: Six Decades of Criticism.** Westport, CT & London, Greenwood Press, 1986. viii, 266 p. index. (Bibliographies and Indexes in World Literature, No. 6). LC 85-27248. ISBN 0-313-25005-7.

This annotated checklist of Tolkien's work and Tolkien criticism is a good example of valuable research buried beneath a terrible format.

Contents: "Preface"; "Introduction"; "Chapter I: The First Three Decades, 1922-1953"; "II: The Fourth Decade, 1954-1963"; "III. The Fifth Decade, 1964-1973"; "IV. The Sixth Decade, 1974-1984"; "V. The Future"; "Appendix: Tolkien-Related Organizations, Societies, and Publications"; "Index of Critics"; "Index of Tolkien's Works and Critical Response to Them." Each of the four main chapters is further subdivided into two sections: "A. Works by Tolkien"; "B. Critical Response" (by far the larger portion of the book). Works by Tolkien are arranged in each chapter alphabetically by title.

A typical book entry includes: item number, title (underlined), place of publication, publisher, and year of publication. Shorter works (interfiled with books) record: item number, title (in quotes), magazine (underlined), volume and issue number, month and year of publication, and pagination; shorter works published in books include: item number, title (quotes), book title (underlined), editor, place of publication, publisher, year of publication, and pagination.

The 1,649 secondary works are listed chronologically by publication date, year by year, then alphabetically by main entry (usually critic), and provide similar information. Tolkien's works are numbered consecutively from A1; secondary sources consecutively from B1. The indices correlate critics and item numbers; and also Tolkien's works, critics, and item numbers (the latter index provides a very useful guide to what the critics have said about specific Tolkien novels or stories). The book is shot from typed copy and bound to library standards.

Astonishingly, however, there is no general index to secondary source titles, making it extraordinarily difficult to locate a specific work if the critic in question has been at all prolific; for example, under Richard West, author of the book listed below (see #490), one finds some fifteen items, none distinguishable from each other without separate examination. Even worse is the division of data into annual components, a particularly bad choice for the arrangement of secondary sources. Instead of having one (or even four) places to search for materials about Tolkien, we are left with dozens of mini-bibliographies crammed into one book.

Thus, despite Johnson's plethora of material, her book is virtually impossible to access without hours to dig out the data. An English Department chairperson really should know better. Compare with West's guide (see #490).

490. West, Richard C. **Tolkien Criticism: An Annotated Checklist.** Kent, OH, Kent State University Press, 1970. xv, 73 p. index. (The Serif Series: Bibliographies and Checklists, No. 11). LC 71-626235. ISBN 0-87338-052-5. **Tolkien Criticism: An Annotated Checklist.** Rev. ed. Kent, OH, Kent State University Press, 1981. xiv, 177 p. index. (The Serif Series: Bibliographies and Checklists, No. 39). LC 81-8135. ISBN 0-87338-256-0.

West's checklist of publications by and about this popular British fantasy writer and academic includes (Revised Edition): "Introduction"; "List of Abbreviations"; "I. Tolkien's Writings, Arranged Chronologically"; "II. Critical Works on Tolkien"; "III. Book Reviews": "A. Reviews of Tolkien's Writings, Arranged by Title"; "B. Reviews of Critical Works on Tolkien"; "IV. Indexes": "A. Tolkien's Writings, Arranged by Title"; "B. Anthologies, Books, Monographs on Tolkien, Arranged by Author"; "C. Critical Works on Tolkien, Arranged by Title"; "D. Doctoral Dissertations and Master's Theses"; "E. Tolkien-Related Groups and Publications."

Materials in Part I are arranged in chronological order by year of publication; those in Part II are arranged in alphabetical order by name of critic; "Book Reviews" in Part III are arranged in alphabetical order by title of the book being reviewed, then alphabetically by critic (with "See" references to the more complete entries in section II). Items in each section are consecutively numbered anew from one (*e.g.,* II-1, II-2, II-3, etc., for Part II); the indexes coordinate titles and item numbers only.

Section I covers all of Tolkien's known writings, fiction and nonfiction, monographs and short pieces, through 1980. A typical book entry includes: item number, title (in italics), place of publication, publisher, year of publication, but no paginations, and a short annotation.

A typical shorter work entry provides: item number, title (in quotes), magazine (italics), volume and issue number, month and year of publication, pagination, and a short annotation; shorter works appearing in books include: item number, title (in quotes), book title (italics), editor, place of publication, publisher, year of publication, pagination, and short annotation. Similar data are included for the 755 secondary sources, except that the annotations tend to be longer and more analytical. The book is nicely designed and typeset and bound to library standards.

Johnson's guide (see #489) includes more entries but fewer annotations, and is more current; however, Johnson's peculiar format makes finding material in her book considerably more difficult than in West. Thus, neither book now has a decided advantage over the other, but any new edition of West would probably be preferable.

It is astonishing to note, however, that two such major Tolkien bibliographies by self-acknowledged experts cannot supply such basic bibliographical details such as the paginations for Tolkien's famous *Lord of the Rings Trilogy,* or a complete listing of all of the English-language printings of that masterpiece (though West does mention several paperback editions), not to mention foreign-language materials.

O bibliographia, O mores!

E. C. Tubb

491. Wallace, Sean, and Philip Harbottle. **The Tall Adventurer: The Works of E. C. Tubb.** Harold Wood, Essex, England, Beccon Publications, 1998. 200 p. index. ISBN 1-870824-32-6 (pbk.).

Contents: "Dedications and Acknowledgements"; "Introduction," by Wallace; "Profile," by Harbottle; "Background Information"; "Interview," by Vincent Clarke; "SF Magazine Listing"; "SF Magazine Story Listing"; "SF Novels and Books"; "SF Series" (*Dumarest of Terra, Cap Kennedy,* and *Space: 1999*); "Non-SF Novels" (Westerns, Detective Thriller, Historical Adventure); "Miscellaneous Items"; "Fanzines"; "Book Reviews"; "SF Magazine Short Story Title Index"; "Book and Novel Title Index."

This is an illustrated bibliographic guide to every book, story, comic, and piece of non-fiction published by British science fiction and historical fiction writer, E. C. Tubb, including translations and reprints. The profile and background essays provide information into the career of the writer, and the interview lends insight into his childhood and the author's philosophy of science fiction writing.

The bulk of the book is divided into five sections: science fiction magazines, science fiction stories, science fiction novels and books, science fiction series, and non-science fiction novels. The SF Magazine Listing is arranged in tabular form, alphabetically by periodical title (bold caps), and includes: country of publication (in parentheses), month of publication, year, issue number, story title, and pseudonym (where appropriate), but no paginations. Materials are arranged chronologically by date within a single periodical.

The SF Magazine Story Listing section includes 237 numbered entries in alphabetical order by story title. The typical entry includes: title (bold type), pseudonym (in parentheses, where appropriate), a predefined code identifying the type of story (*e.g.,* short story = s, short short story = ss, novelette = n, novella = na, novel = N, serialized novel = SN), the country of publication (usually UK), periodical title, issue number, month or season, year, illustrator, and a brief, evaluative summary (averaging fifty words), plus all known reprint editions, including those in the author's own collections.

SF Novels and Books notes sixty-four unnumbered entries arranged in alphabetical order by title, first under the author's real name, and then by pseudonym. A typical entry includes: title (bold caps), place of publication, publisher, format (hardcover = hb and paperback = pb), pagination, month and year of publication, cover artist, critique, ISBN (if any), and an evaluative summary (averaging 200 words). A list of all reprint editions and translations is attached to the main entry, including as much data as is known, although foreign-language editions sometimes lack basic bibliographical elements (most often pagination or cover artist). Revised and expanded versions of books appear under their own separate entries. Black-and-white reproductions of the cover art featured on the books are scattered throughout this chapter.

The Series section lists the thirty-four entries from the *Dumarest of Terra* series, eighteen from the *Cap Kennedy* series, and five entries from the *Space: 1999* novelization series. Listed last, in their own section, are the sixteen non-SF novels, presented in similar fashion to the others. The book concludes with skeletal citations to reviews, interviews, critical analyses, and bibliographies about the writer, letters to the editor (by Tubb), television scripts, photographs of Tubb, and other miscellanea.

This volume has all of the making of an excellent bibliography, the annotations having been based on an actual viewing of and re-reading of the items described. However, the ardent fannish enthusiasm of the compilers is all too evident in the introduction, making their overwhelmingly positive evaluations of Tubb's work somewhat suspect. On those rare occasions when an artistic failing of the writer is noted, it is excused by saying that Tubb was rushed to complete the work, was forced to cut the original story length, etc.

Also, there is a certain lack of consistency in the presentation of data. Tubb's short stories are numbered, his novels are not. Pseudonyms in the story section are listed in parentheses to one side of title, but in the book section they are displayed in small caps at the head of each subsection. The absence of running headers makes navigation throughout the volume unnecessarily difficult for the average reader. The useful story index cross-references story numbers, while the novel index notes just page numbers.

A new edition that resolves these problems could make this bibliography the definitive guide to Tubb's work. Recommended for larger libraries collecting science fiction.

Wilson Tucker

492. Stephensen-Payne, Phil, and Gordon Benson, Jr. **Wilson "Bob" Tucker, Wild Talent: A Working Bibliography.** 4th rev. ed. Leeds, West Yorkshire, England, Galactic Central Publications, 1994. 9, 29 p. (Galactic Central Bibliographies for the Avid Reader, Vol. 8). ISBN 1-871133-41-6 (pbk.).

Wilson Tucker wrote a number of interesting SF and mystery stories and novels during a thirty-five-year period beginning in the 1940s. This new checklist of his work is arranged by subject category, then alphabetically by title.

Contents: Author's name, date and place of birth, list of awards won by the author (in chronological order, giving year, name of award, and title of work being honored) and his pseudonyms; "A. Stories"; "B. Fiction Books"; "C. Series"; "D. Poems, Songs & Plays" [blank section]; "E. Poem, Song & Play Volumes" [blank section]; "F. Articles"; "G. Miscellaneous" (including introductions and afterwords by Bob Tucker, letters, and interviews with the author); "H. Non-Fiction Books"; "I. Fanzines Edited by Bob Tucker"; "J. Media Presentations" [blank section]; "K. Articles on Wilson/Bob Tucker"; "L. Reviews" (of Tucker's books, alphabetically by title of the book being reviewed, then by magazine title, giving date and reviewer); "M. Books About Wilson/Bob Tucker"; "N. Phantom & Forthcoming Titles"; "O. Related Items by Other Authors" [blank section]; "P. Textual Variations"; "Q. Chronological Index" (by year and title).

The introduction is almost identical throughout the series, and clearly explains the many different sections of the bibliography. Stephensen-Payne and Benson's basic checklist is arranged by subject category, then alphabetically by title; materials are numbered consecutively from one in each chapter (for example, B1, B2, B3, etc., for the author's books). Shorter work entries include: item number, title, category ("ss" = short story, "nt" = novelette, etc.), magazine or book in which the item appeared, month and year of publication (for magazines in the form "2-68" for February 1968) or year of publication (for books), a list of subsequent reprints (for which title, publisher, year, and editor's last name are given), but no paginations.

For book-length works, Stephensen-Payne and Benson provide: item number, title, contents (if a collection, by item number), publication data (publisher, stock number, month and year of publication [if known, in the form "10-59" for October 1959], pagination, price), cover artist, plus similar data for known reprints. There is no title index. Some 197 entries are included, though reprint information makes the total greater. 68 of these comprise secondary sources, 15 of which are book review categories; perhaps 50 actual reviews are noted. A few foreign language publications are mentioned. The book is shot from clear word-processed copy and stapled through the spine. An index would have been helpful, as would the addition of paginations for the short fiction sections.

Although Tucker's work has faded from the book shelves in recent years, he remains a writer of significance in both the mystery and SF genres, and this updated bibliography will be useful both to scholars and fans alike.

493. Stephens, Christopher P. **A Checklist of Wilson Tucker.** Hastings-on-Hudson, NY, Ultramarine Publishing Co., 1991. 13 p. index. ISBN 0-89366-211-9 (pbk.).

Tucker is best known for his time-travel novels. Stephens's checklist records Tucker's monographs in chronological order by publication date, books being numbered consecutively from one.

A typical entry provides: year (as a floating head), item number, title (underlined), pseudonym, publisher, stock or ISBN number, pagination, format (*e.g.,* "cloth with dust wrapper"), cover illustrator, price, and similar data for all known reprints (which are numbered, for example, A2a, A2b, A2c, etc., in descending order by publication date). The chapbook is shot from legible typed copy and bound with staples in stiff paper covers. The index correlates titles with years of publication only.

Now superseded by Stephensen-Payne and Benson's more current and complete work (see #492).

A. E. van Vogt

494. Stephensen-Payne, Phil, and Ian Covell. **A. E. van Vogt, Master of Null-A: A Working Bibliography.** Leeds, West Yorkshire, England, Galactic Central, 1997. viii, 106 p. (Bibliographies for the Avid Reader, Vol. 47). ISBN 1-871133-45-9 (pbk.).

The late Canadian-American SF writer, A. E. van Vogt, is best known for his Null-A and Weapon Shop novels and stories.

Contents: "Introduction"; "Awards and Pseudonyms"; "A. Prose Fiction"; "B. Prose Fiction Books"; "C. Series"; "D. Poetry & Drama"; "E. Poetry & Drama Books" [blank section]; "F. Articles"; "G. Miscellaneous"; "H. Non-Fiction Books"; "I. Publications Edited by A. E. van Vogt" [blank section]; "J. Other Media"; "K. Articles on A. E. van Vogt"; "L. Reviews"; "M. Books about A. E. van Vogt"; "N. Phantom and Forthcoming Titles"; "O. Related Items by Other Authors"; "P. Textual Variations and Other Notes"; "Q. Chronological Index of Prose Fiction."

The introduction is almost identical throughout the series, and clearly explains the many different sections of the bibliography. Stephensen-Payne and Covell's basic checklist is arranged by subject category, then alphabetically by title; materials are numbered consecutively from one in each chapter (for example, B1, B2, B3, etc., for the author's books).

Shorter work entries include: item number, title, category ("ss" = short story, "nt" = novelette, etc.), magazine or book in which the item appeared, month and year of publication (for magazines in the form "2-68" for February 1968) or year of publication (for books), a list of subsequent reprints (for which title, publisher, year, and editor's last name are given), but no paginations.

For book-length works, Stephensen-Payne and Covell provide: item number, title, contents (if a collection, by item number), publication data (publisher, stock number, month and year of publication [if known, in the form "10-59" for October 1959], pagination, price), cover artist, plus similar data for known reprints. There is no title index. The bibliography records some 556 entries, although reprint information makes the grand total somewhat greater. 250 secondary sources are noted, 56 of which are book review categories; over a hundred actual reviews are noted. An index would have been helpful, as would the addition of paginations for the short fiction sections.

This book was produced in the newest format for this series, including title and contents pages, and an attractive, glued paperback binding. Van Vogt retains a strong fan following, and this new bibliography should be acquired by all major research institutions.

Jack Vance

495. Hewett, Jerry, and Daryl F. Mallett. **The Work of Jack Vance: An Annotated Bibliography & Guide.** San Bernardino, CA, The Borgo Press; Penn Valley, Calif. & Lancaster, Penn., Underwood-Miller, 1994. xxii, 293 p. index. (Bibliographies of Modern Authors, No. 29). LC 92-28056. ISBN 0-8095-0509-6 (library cloth); ISBN 0-8095-1509-1 (pbk.); ISBN 0-88733-165-3 (trade cloth); ISBN 0-88733-166-1 (signed, slipcased edition).

The Work of Jack Vance is intended as a primary and secondary bibliography of well-known American SF and mystery novelist Jack Vance's works.

Contents: "Foreword: Two Years and Two Hundred Hours," by Hewett and Mallett; "Introduction: The World of Jack Vance," by Robert Silverberg; "A Jack Vance Chronology"; "A. Books"; "B. Short Fiction"; "C. Verse and Poetry"; "D. Nonfiction"; "E. Other Media"; "F. Interviews"; "G. Maps and Drawings"; "H. Phantom Editions and Works"; "I. Unpublished Manuscripts"; "J. Honors and Awards"; "K. Guest of Honor Appearances"; "L. Interviews with Jack Vance"; "M. Secondary Sources"; "N. Miscellanea"; "The Genesee Slough Murders: Outline for a Novel," by Jack Vance; "Afterword: Jack Vance: The Man and the Myth," by Tim Underwood; "Index."

The chronology provides a year-by-year account of the author's professional and personal life in block paragraph format. Each section of the bibliography is arranged in chronological order by publication date. There are 480 main entries, but detailed reprint information, as well as secondary sources, easily triple that figure.

The typical monograph entry includes: item number (section letter plus cardinal number; *e.g.,* A3, A4, etc.), title (bold italics), place of publication, publisher, date of publication, pagination, binding, series information (where applicable), type of book (in brackets; *e.g.,* [novel] or [collection]), plot summary or contents (50-100 words), collation, binding, notes (cover artist, issue price, translator, etc.), a list of subsequent reprints in all languages, with all bibliographical data in descending order by publication date, and a list of secondary sources and reviews in alphabetical order by critic or magazine.

A typical short work entry includes: item number, title (bold, quotation marks), magazine title, volume or issue number, date, pagination, and bibliographic data of all known reprints. The index includes item numbers only, and is broken into eight sections, covering Jack Vance's Works, Artists, Editors, Translators, Fiction Magazines and Anthologies, Publishers, Secondary Sources, and Critics and Reviewers. An integrated index would have been far easier to use for the average reader. The book is nicely designed and typeset, and the cloth edition bound to library standards.

This is a remarkably thorough bibliographical guide to a well-known genre figure, including far more information on the writer's publications than any other available source. Recommended for serious fans, academics, and large academic libraries, or any library collecting science fiction.

Compare with Levack, Cockrum, and Underwood (see #496).

496. Levack, Daniel J. H., and Tim Underwood. **Fantasms: A Bibliography of the Literature of Jack Vance.** San Francisco, CA and Columbia, PA, Underwood/Miller, 1978. 91 p. cloth and pbk. Cockrum, Kurt, Daniel J. H. Levack, and Tim Underwood. **Fantasms II: A Bibliography of the Literature of Jack Vance.** [Rev. ed.]. Riverside, CA, Kurt Cockrum, 1979. vi, 99 p. (paper printout).

Levack has produced a series of similary formatted bibliographies on de Camp, Dick, Herbert, and Zelazny (see #364, #369, #393, #519).

Contents: "Introduction"; "Books"; "Notes on Books"; "Stories"; "Series and Connected Stories"; "Pseudonyms"; "Chronological Order of Publications of Vance's Work"; "Television Appearances"; "Acknowledgments."

Materials are listed alphabetically by title and numbered consecutively from one in each section, with some 150 total items included. A typical book entry includes: item number, title (bold caps), series (when appropriate) or category (*e.g.,* "Mystery"), manuscript title (if different), byline (if under some other name than Jack Vance), contents (if a collection), publisher, stock number (for paperback editions), place of publication (not included for paperbacks), year of publication, format (*e.g.,* "paper"). Reprints are listed in chronological order by publication date; some foreign editions are included, with foreign-language titles, but no translators.

A typical shorter work entry includes: item number, title (in quotes), estimated wordage, series note, magazine or book title, month and year of publication; stories in anthologies include: title, editor, publisher, place of publication, year of publication, but no paginations. All subsequent reprint editions (including Vance's own collection) are listed in chronological order underneath the first printing of each story, with similar data. The series index and chronological checklist of Vance's writings are both useful guides to the writer's work. Materials are included through early 1978.

The book is beautifully typeset and designed and is illustrated throughout with reproductions of book and magazine covers featuring Vance's novels and stories. Unfortunately, despite its attractive appearance, this volume lacks such basic features as an index, story and book paginations, and secondary sources, making it much less the standard source it should have become.

Prefer Hewett and Mallett (see #495), which does not, however, include the cover illustrations; and Stephensen-Payne and Benson (see #497). Both of these are more current.

497. Stephensen-Payne, Phil, and Gordon Benson, Jr. **Jack Vance, a Fantasmic Imagination: A Working Bibliography.** 2nd rev. ed. Leeds, West Yorkshire, England, Galactic Central Publications, 1990. 9, 61 p. (Galactic Central Bibliographies for the Avid Reader, Vol. 28). ISBN 1-871133-02-5 (pbk.).

Vance is a well-regarded American SF and mystery writer whose exotic characters and worlds have long been regarded with affection by aficionados.

Contents: Author's full name, date and place of birth, awards won, and pseudonyms; "A. Stories"; "B. Fiction Books"; "C. Series"; "D. Poems & Songs"; "E. Poem & Song Collections" [blank section]; "F. Articles"; "G. Miscellaneous"; "H. Non-Fiction Books" [blank section]; "I. Books Edited by Jack Vance" [blank section]; "J. Media Presentations"; "K. Articles on Jack Vance"; "L. Reviews" [of Vance's works]; "M. Books About Jack Vance"; "N. Phantom and Forthcoming Titles"; "O. Textual Variations" [blank section]; "P. Related Items by Other Authors"; "Q. Chronological Index."

In each part the author's works are arranged alphabetically by title and numbered anew from one, with the appropriate letter prefix. A typical short fiction entry includes: item number, title, category ("ss" = short story, "nt" = novelette, etc.), magazine or book in which the item appeared, month and year of publication (for magazines in the form "12-50" for December 1950) or year of publication (for books), plus a list of subsequent reprints (for which title, editor's last name, publisher, and year are given), but no paginations.

A typical book entry provides: item number, title (all caps), publication data (publisher, stock number, month and year of publication [if known, in the form "10-59" for October 1959], pagination, price, with dates of reissues by the same publisher), cover artist, and similar data for all known reprint editions. Collections include lists of the author's stories, cross-referenced to the item numbers in the first section. The secondary sources chapter records 82 fan and professional books and articles and roughly 250 book reviews. Coverage is complete through early 1990. The text is shot from very legible word-processed copy and bound with staples into paper covers.

Levack *et al.*'s guide (see #496) is more attractively designed, with numerous cover reproductions, and it also includes some data (chiefly foreign-language reprints and estimated word counts) not found in the Stephensen-Payne and Benson; while Hewitt and Mallett (see #495) is more current and has more complete bibliographical details, making it more suitable for library collections and researchers. However, *Jack Vance, a Fantasmic Imagination* will likely be preferred by SF fans as an inexpensive, authoritative alternative.

Jules Verne

498. Gallagher, Edward J., Judith A. Mistichelli, and John A. Van Eerde. **Jules Verne: A Primary and Secondary Bibliography.** Boston, G. K. Hall, 1980. xxi, 387 p. index. (Masters of Science Fiction and Fantasy). LC 80-20206. ISBN 0-8161-8106-3.

Verne has always been a particularly difficult writer to track, because so many of his works were either reworked, cut, divided, or retitled for their English-language editions, the same novel going through many different incarnations from various American and British publishers. This carefully researched bibliography of both the author's French and English editions is the first real guide to his work ever published in English, and as such, it will be heartily welcomed both by scholars and students of this seminal French SF writer.

Contents: "Preface"; "Introduction"; "Abbreviations"; "Part A: Fiction"; "Part B: Miscellaneous Media"; "Part C: Nonfiction"; "Part D: Critical Studies in English"; "Part E: Critical Studies in French"; "Index to Verne's Work"; "Index to Critical Studies."

The introduction provides a brief biographical and critical evaluation of Verne. The bibliography proper is arranged chronologically, from the earliest published material to the latest, items being numbered consecutively in each section from one (*e.g.,* A1, A2, A3, etc., for Verne's fiction). Books and shorter works are interfiled; reprint editions of books are listed under the first edition in chronological order by publication date; both French- and English-language printings are included, with appropriate titles, but many paperback editions are omitted. A typical monograph entry gives: item number, title (underlined), place of publication, publisher, but no paginations.

Shorter works published originally in magazines include: item number, title (in quotes), magazine (underlined), volume number, date, but no paginations. Reprints of stories are listed under the main entry, chronologically by year of reprint, with the editor of the anthology, title, place of publication, publisher, year, format (*e.g.,* "paper"), but no paginations. Story collections include complete contents listings plus the item numbers of the original stories (if published previously).

Part B includes the author's plays and songs (twenty-one items). Part C includes all known nonfiction works by Verne, with occasional annotations (thirty-two items).

Parts D and E, covering secondary works about the author, make up the greater part of the book, providing an immense resource for the scholar, listing some 450 sources in English and almost 900 in French, with complete bibliographical data and extensive subject annotations. The indices cross-reference titles, authors (of critical works), and item numbers only, ensuring quick access to the material. Coverage is complete through 1979. The book is shot from legible typed copy and bound to library standards.

This is perhaps the most bibliographically significant book in the entire fourteen-volume Masters series, a long-overdue guide to Verne's many works: well-conceived and -executed, and generally a first-rate piece of work. One laments, however, the lack of paginations for books, particularly when they are so hard to find for many of Verne's novels, both originals and translations. A future edition should restore these missing data.

Other than this minor *caveat, Jules Verne* is nearly flawless, and should be on the shelves of every academic library in the country. Highly recommended.

499. Margot, Jean-Michel. **Bibliographie Documentaire sur Jules Verne: Catalogue par Mots-Clés et par Auteurs.** Paris, Société Jules Verne, 1978. 142 p. (pbk.). Ostermundigen, Chez l'Auteur [*i.e.,* published by the author], 1978. 4, 35, 21, 109, 8, 64 p. LC 79-365008 (pbk.).

This peculiarly arranged bibliography to secondary sources on or about French author Jules Verne quickly stumbles headlong over its own data.

Contents: "Introduction"; "Nombre de Documents Publiés par Année"; "Catalogue par Mot-Clés"; "Catalogue par Auteurs"; "Catalogue par Cote"; "Oeuvres de Jules Verne"; "Thesaurus."

The first section, "Nombre de Documents," records 1,300 items in a statistical table, year by year, with a series of asterisks representing each item. The "Catalogue par Mot-Clés" indexes the documents section alphabetically by key word (*e.g.,* "albatros"), correlating them with item numbers, and, at the end of this chapter, by year and item number. The "Catalogue par Auteurs" rearranges the data alphabetically by author surname and item number.

The "Catalogue par Cote" records items in chronological order by publication name, numbering the materials consecutively from the number one. A typical entry in this section includes: item number, author's name (inverted), title, magazine title, month and year of publication, pagination, volume number, type (*e.g.,* "article"), key words, and a series of two-letter codes referring to the specific Verne works mentioned in the book or essay. Monographic entries give: item number, author (name inverted), title, place of publication, publisher, year of publication, pagination, type, key words, and letter codes. One thousand three hundred items are recorded in this largest (109-page) chapter of the volume.

The section "Oeuvres de Jules Verne" correlates the two-letter codes referencing the master's own publications, providing title and type (*e.g.,* "roman"). The "Thesaurus" correlates key words with other related, broader, or narrower terms, with other "See" references. Data are complete through 1978. The book is shot from primitive computer-generated copy, photoreduced from the original; parts of the documents section are often difficult to read or discern.

This problem with readability, combined with the overwrought design of the volume, should send the reader forthwith to the better-organized and much more reader-friendly bibliography by Gallagher *et al.* (see #498).

500. Myers, Edward, and Judith Myers. **A Bibliography of the First Printings of the Writings of Jules Verne in the English Language, Together with Information on Numerous Reprints, and a Key to Title Interpretation.** New Hartford, CT, Country Lane Books, 1989. 68, [5] p., [6] p. of plates, plus [5]-page addendum. (pbk.).

This guide to Verne's English-language editions is organized alphabetically by title (using the earliest known English-language title as a key). A typical entry gives: item number, title (all caps, underlined), place of publication, publisher, year of publication, pagination, description of binding and dust jacket, series name and number (where appropriate), and other notes providing information necessary for discovering specific printings. Similar data are provided for all other early significant printings in the U.S. and U.K. The main entries of Verne's monographs are numbered consecutively from 1-60; subsidiary editions are unnumbered. A final entry records the "Collected Works of Jules Verne" (five different sets).

End matter includes a brief bibliography of "Works about Jules Verne," and an "Index of Titles," correlated with item and page numbers. Five pages of addenda sheets are inserted loose into the rear of the book. The plates and frontispiece display thirty-nine book covers in clear black-and-white reproductions, plus several illustrated title pages of early Verne editions. The bibliography itself is shot from sometimes faint typed copy, and rather poorly bound in paper covers (sheets were coming loose from the binding on the specimen examined).

Myers's guide will be useful primarily to collectors and book dealers; scholars and libraries will prefer Gallagher's more complete and more usable literary bibliography of Verne (see #498).

Karl Edward Wagner

501. Marek, Joe. **"Death Angel: A Bibliography of Karl Edward Wagner,"** in *One More Barbarian* 2 (Sept. 1979): 1-32.

This checklist of the late American fantasy writer's work appeared as an entire single issue of a fan magazine.

Contents: "Foreword"; "Books"; "Fiction"; "Poetry"; "Non-Fiction"; "Series Index"; "Index to Periodicals"; "About the Author"; "One Letter" (from Wagner); "Afterword."

Wagner's books are listed chronologically by year of publication. A typical entry includes: title (all caps), publisher, place of publication, month and year of publication, pagination, price, format (*e.g.,* "paperbound"), stock number and/or ISBN, printing size, and cover artist, with similar data on all known reprint editions, including some foreign, with foreign-language titles and translators.

The rest of the primary bibliography is arranged section by section in alphabetical order by title. A typical shorter work entry includes: title, magazine title (italics), volume and issue number, month and year of publication, but no paginations; shorter works appearing in books include: title, book title (italicized), publisher, editor, year of publication, but no paginations. All known reprint editions (including some foreign) are listed in chronological order under the original publication data.

Secondary sources in the "About the Author" section are arranged by main entry (usually critic), and include mostly book reviews and fan commentary, with similar bibliographical data as before. The two indices to series and to works appearing in periodicals, arranged by periodical name, are useful, but do not substitute for a full title index. There are a dozen reproductions of Wagner covers and other fan illustrations, but the 8.5" x 11" booklet is so badly mimeographed that many of the covers are faint (as is part of the text). A one-sheet insertion includes supplementary material through early 1980.

An updated, more professionally produced version of this bibliography would definitely be warranted.

Evangeline Walton

Zahorski, Kenneth J., and Robert H. Boyer. **Lloyd Alexander, Evangeline Walton Ensley, Kenneth Morris: A Primary and Secondary Bibliography.** *See the entry for Lloyd Alexander* (see #305).

Ian Watson

502. Mackey, Douglas A. **The Work of Ian Watson: An Annotated Bibliography & Guide.** San Bernardino, CA, The Borgo Press, 1989. 148 p. index. (Bibliographies of Modern Authors, No. 18). LC 88-36646. ISBN 0-8095-0512-6; ISBN 0-8095-1512-1 (pbk.).

British writer Watson has produced a number of interesting philosophical SF novels; this is the first published bibliography on his work.

Contents: "Introduction: Elementary Watson," by Mackey; "An Ian Watson Chronology"; "A. Books"; "B. Short Fiction"; "C. Nonfiction"; "D. Letters"; "E. Poetry"; "F. Campaign Literature"; "G. Other Media"; "H. Unpublished Manuscripts"; "I. Awards"; "J.

Editorial Posts"; "K. Public Appearances"; "L. Interviews"; "M. About the Author"; "N. Miscellanea"; "Quoth the Critics"; "Afterword: Dancing on a Tightrope," by Watson; "Index."

In each section, the author's works are arranged chronologically and numbered consecutively from one, chapter by chapter, with the appropriate letter prefix. A typical monographic entry includes: item number, title (boldface), place of publication, publisher, month and year of publication, pagination, format (*e.g.,* "paper"), type of publication (*e.g.,* "collection"), and full bibliographical data on all known reprint editions and translations, including foreign, with foreign-language titles and translators. The books are fully annotated, with complete contents listings and/or plot summaries and other pertinent data; entries from other sections are selectively annotated as needed. Each book entry also includes all known secondary sources and reviews, arranged in alphabetical order by critic, with complete bibliographical data.

A typical shorter work entry includes: item number, title (bold quotes), magazine title (in italics), volume number, month and year of publication, pagination, and similar data on all known reprints. Reprints in anthologies include: title (italics), editor, place of publication, publisher, year of publication, format (*e.g.,* "cloth"), pagination. Mackey's short introduction provides an excellent critical introduction to the author's work, one that is certain to be cited by all future critics.

The chronology provides a year-by-year account of the author's professional and personal life, in block paragraph format. "About the Author" includes all known secondary works except individual reviews of specific titles, which are listed in Section A under those works. The "Miscellanea" section provides: "Books Dedicated to Ian Watson," with complete bibliographical data and verbatim transcriptions of the dedications; "Library Holdings of Ian Watson's Papers"; "Memberships"; and Library of Congress cataloging data.

"Quoth the Critics" includes selected excerpts of reviews and other comments by leading critics on the author's work. Watson's concluding essay, original to this book, provides a fascinating autobiographical glimpse into the author's life and politics (Watson has been a Labour Party candidate for local council offices). The index correlates titles and item numbers only. Coverage is complete through mid-1989. The book is nicely typeset and the cloth edition bound to library standards.

This is an excellently conceived and compiled bibliography by a well-known critic who clearly sympathizes with his subject. However, Watson is little-known in the United States, and only the largest research libraries will need this guide.

Manly Wade Wellman

503. Stephensen-Payne, Phil, and Gordon Benson, Jr. **Manly Wade Wellman, the Gentleman from Chapel Hill: A Memorial Working Bibliography.** 3rd rev. ed. Leeds, West Yorkshire, England, Galactic Central Publications, 1998. ix, 76 p. (Galactic Central Bibliographies for the Avid Reader, Vol. 17). ISBN 1-871133-51-3 (pbk.).

Manly Wade Wellman (1903-1986), brother of well-known historical novelist Paul I. Wellman, was a science-fiction and fantasy writer who began writing during the pulp era. This checklist arranges his writings by subject category, then alphabetically by title.

Contents: "Introduction"; "Awards and Pseudonyms," "A. Prose Fiction"; "B. Prose Fiction Books"; "C. Series"; "D. Poetry & Drama"; "E. Poetry & Drama Books"; "F. Articles"; "G. Miscellaneous" (including introductions and afterwords by Wellman, letters, and interviews with the author); "H. Non-Fiction Books"; "I. Publications Edited by Manly Wade Wellman"; "J. Other Media"; "K. Articles on Manly Wade Wellman"; "L. Reviews" (of Wellman's books, alphabetically by title of the book being reviewed, then by magazine title, giving date and reviewer); "M. Books About Manly Wade Wellman"; "N. Phantom and Forthcoming Titles"; "O. Related Items by Other Authors"; "P. Textual Variations"; "Q. Chronological Index of Prose Fiction."

The introduction is almost identical throughout the series, and clearly explains the many different sections of the bibliography. Awards and Pseudonyms provides date and place of birth and death, list of awards won by the author (in chronological order, giving year, name of award, and title of work being honored) and his pseudonyms. Stephensen-Payne and Benson's basic checklist is arranged by subject category, then alphabetically by title; materials are numbered consecutively from one in each chapter (for example, B1, B2, B3, etc., for the author's books).

Shorter work entries include: item number, title, category ("ss" = short story, "nt" = novelette, etc.), magazine or book in which the item appeared, month and year of publication (for magazines in the form "2-68" for February 1968) or year of publication (for books), a list of subsequent reprints (for which title, publisher, year, and editor's last name are given), but no paginations.

For book-length works, the authors provide: item number, title (caps), contents (if a collection, by item number), publication data (publisher, format (pb or hb), stock number, month and year of publication [if known, in the form "10-59" for October 1959], pagination, price), cover artist, plus similar data for known reprints. There is no title index.

This edition expands on Benson's previous solo efforts and completely supersedes them. There are some 534 entries covered, although reprint information makes the grand total much greater. 105 of these consist of secondary sources, 27 of which are book review categories; more than 50 individual reviews are mentioned. A few foreign language publications are noted. The table of contents, not previously found in the series, is a welcome and helpful addition. The book was shot from clear word-processed copy and stapled through the spine. An index would have been helpful, as would the addition of paginations for the short fiction sections.

Wellman's work seems likely to survive the test of time, possessing, as it does, a strong regional flavor reflective of his roots in North Carolina. Recommended for major research collections.

H. G. Wells

504. H. G. Wells Society. **H. G. Wells: A Comprehensive Bibliography.** Edgware, England, H. G. Wells Society, 1966. viii, 61 p. LC 67-87305 (pbk.). **H. G. Wells: A Comprehensive Bibliography.** 2nd ed. London, H. G. Wells Society, 1968. vi, 69 p. LC 68-114049 (pbk.). **H. G. Wells: A Comprehensive Bibliography.** 3rd ed. London, H. G. Wells Society, 1972. vi, 74 p. LC 73-156022. ISBN 0-902291-65-3 (pbk.). **H. G. Wells: A Comprehensive Bibliography.** 4th ed. London, H. G. Wells Society, 1986. 58 p. ISBN 0-

903592-08-8 (pbk.). The foreword to the fourth edition mentions that "this edition has been prepared by Patrick Parrinder, A. H. Watkins, and J. R. Hammond."

This brief but very handy guide to Wells's works is organized by broad subject chapters. In the fourth edition the first section, devoted to the author's monographs, is arranged chronologically by publication date. A typical book entry includes: item number, year of publication (as a centered head), title (italicized), notes on illustrations, introductory material, etc., pagination, publisher, place of publication, binding height in centimeters, and a one-paragraph descriptive annotation, with notes referencing other significant tie-in editions. First editions only are described, and only partial contents are given for story collections.

Section II covers posthumous works, also organized chronologically by publication date, and similar data. Part III lists Wells's short stories in the same order in which they appear in *The Complete Short Stories of H. G. Wells* (1927). A typical shorter work entry provides: item number, title (in italics), magazine title (in single quotes), and month and year of original publication, but no paginations and no list of subsequent reprintings. Nineteen additional stories from the posthumous collection, *The Man with a Nose and Other Uncollected Stories of H. G. Wells,* are listed at the end of this section.

Part IV records the materials published in The Atlantic Edition of the Works of H. G. Wells (1924) in volume-number order. Section V, "Miscellaneous Writings of H. G. Wells" (mostly essays), is presented in chronological order by publication date, with similar data to Part III and no paginations; the second half of this section records prefaces by H. G. Wells in the works of other writers chronologically by publication date, giving item number, year of publication, author (in inverted order, surname in all caps), title, place of publication, publisher, but no paginations.

Section VI covers biographies of Wells in book form, arranged alphabetically by main entry (usually author), giving: item number, author, title (in italics), publisher, and year of publication, but no paginations. Chapter VII lists "Bibliographies and Dictionaries," organized similarly to the previous section. Part VIII records "Other Writings on H. G. Wells" (critical monographs, but no articles), arranged similarly to the previous section, but adding (for no apparent reason) pagination and volume size (measured in centimeters); if these were regarded by the authors as worth noting for *some* secondary sources, why were they not included for all?

The final chapter gives "Films, Radio, and Stage Productions During Wells's Lifetime," arranged chronologically by production date, and listing: item number, year of production, title (in italics), production company, producer's name, director's name, and principal actors; a brief note comments generally on Wellsian film productions since 1946, but does not provide credits (another anomaly). A brief subsection mentions radio adaptations through 1946.

Materials are numbered consecutively throughout the book (Fourth Edition) from 1-472. The index correlates titles and authors with item numbers, but uses such small type (about a six-point level) that it is virtually unusable by anyone over the age of forty. The volume is professionally typeset and bound in paper covers.

This bibliography will provide a useful introductory guide to Wells's works; although it does record three posthumous collections not mentioned in Hammond's more complete work (see #505), plus early media adaptations, the latter will still be preferred by most libraries and scholars.

505. Hammond, J. R. **Herbert George Wells: An Annotated Bibliography of His Works.** New York & London, Garland Publishing, 1977. xvi, 257 p. index. (Garland Reference Library of the Humanities, Vol. 84). LC 76-52667. ISBN 0-8240-9889-7.

John Hammond founded the H. G. Wells Society in 1960 and co-authored the check-list mentioned above (see #504).

This comprehensive bibliography includes: "Preface"; "Part One, Fiction": "A. Novels," "B. Romances," "C. Short Stories," "D. Essays"; "Part Two, Non-Fiction": "E. Books," "F. Pamphlets"; "Part Three, Collected Editions": "G. The Atlantic Edition," "H. Other Editions"; Part Four: "I. Posthumously Published Works"; Part Five: "J. Letters"; Part Six: "K. Books by Other Writers Containing Prefaces by Wells"; Part Seven: "L. Books by Other Writers Containing Contributions by Wells"; Part Eight: "M. Illustrations"; Appendices: "I. The Works of H. G. Wells, Chronologically Arranged"; "II. Note on Unreprinted Writings"; "III. Critical, Biographical, and Bibliographical Studies"; "IV. Principal Collections of H. G. Wells Material"; "V. The H. G. Wells Society"; "Index."

In each section materials are arranged chronologically by publication date and numbered anew from one, the numbers being prefixed by the appropriate letter code associated with that chapter. A typical book entry includes: item number, title, and year of publication as centered headings; exact title-page transcription; printing description, physical height of the volume (in centimeters), pagination, and detailed itemization of the contents; detailed description of the binding; mention of previous appearances and significant bibliographical variants in later publications; and other notes as needed.

Unusually, the "Short Stories" section is organized around Wells's book collections, each entry providing complete contents listings in addition to the bibliographical data recorded in earlier chapters; but only item #C8, *The Short Stories of H. G. Wells* (1927), which collects together most of his short fiction into one volume, provides details of previous publications of these works, giving magazine title and month and year of publication for each, but no specific paginations and certainly no coordinated list of the collections or anthologies into which each of these pieces has been gathered. Thirteen additional uncollected tales are mentioned at the end of C8, with previous publication data. This seems a very odd and awkward arrangement indeed.

The chapters recording Wells's contributions to other books provide: item number and year of publication (centered heads), book title, author, publisher, place of publication, category (*e.g.,* "introduction"), and specific pagination of the Wells's piece. The final chapter lists Wells's drawings as they appear in his books, showing specific page numbers on which they are reproduced. The end matter includes a chronology of Wells's works (but only the books), with years of publication and item numbers.

There are also sections on the unreprinted writings of Wells, a list of "Critical, Biographical, and Bibliographical Studies" (monographs only, also arranged by publication date, a particularly bad format choice for this kind of material), and a very useful guide to the "Principal Collections of H. G. Wells Material" in library archives around the world. A description of the aims of the H. G. Wells Society founded by Hammond represents the last section of the text. The index correlates titles with item numbers.

No attempt has been made to record Wells's dozens (or even hundreds) of unreprinted journalistic essays, or to give a comprehensive listing of the hundreds (or even thousands) of short critical pieces that have been penned about this influential author and his work. The text is shot from sometimes faint typed copy and bound to library standards.

There is no doubt that Hammond knows his material, and also no doubt that his volume represents the best Wells bibliography currently available. However, the book's format is unnecessarily cumbersome, coming between the text and the user, and making any overall assessment of Wells's development as a writer extraordinarily difficult. Also, Garland's decision to produce a major bibliography on a major author without typesetting the text must certainly be questioned by any scholar and librarian: some of the material is very dense and difficult to distinguish. A revised and expanded second edition is now needed.

506. Watkins, A. H., ed. **Catalogue of the H. G. Wells Collection in the Bromley Public Libraries.** Bromley, England, London Borough of Bromley Public Libraries, 1974. xi, 196 p., [4] p. of plates. LC 75-316320. ISBN 0-901002-02-X.

Wells was born at Bromley in 1866, so it is not surprising that the public library there began collecting Wellsiana beginning in 1952, using a large 1958 purchase as the core of its collection.

Materials in this catalog are ordered into broad subject categories: "Introduction"; "Acknowledgements"; "I. The Works of H. G. Wells": "(a) Collected Works," "(b) Individual Books and Articles," "(c) Books Containing Writings by Wells," "(d) Introductions and Prefaces by Wells"; "II. Bibliographies, Catalogues, Dictionaries"; "III. Biography": "(a) H. G. Wells and Family," "(b) Obituaries, Tributes, The Will," "(c) 13 Hanover Terrace," "(d) Wells As a Character in Fiction," "(e) People Who Knew Wells"; "IV. Books and Articles Relating to Wells, Other Than Biography"; "V. Reviews": "(a) Of Books by Wells," "(b) Of Books About Wells"; "VI. Periodicals"; "VII. Letters": "(a) Wells's Letters," "(b) Letters Written by Mrs. Wells on Behalf of Her Husband," "(c) Letters by Other Hands," "(d) Correspondence with Dr. Henry Hick and Family," "(e) Fabian Society, Correspondence and Papers"; "VIII. Pictorial Material": "(a) Portraits and Photographs of Wells," "(b) Cartoons," "(c) Picshuas," "(d) Places," "(e) H. G. Wells Centenary, 21 September 1966"; "IX. Miscellany"; "Index of Wells's Writings"; "General Index."

Materials in most sections are listed in alphabetical order by title. A typical monograph entry provides: item number (boldfaced), title, place of publication, publisher, year of publication, pagination, height of book (in centimeters), and notes of interest. A typical shorter work entry (in the "Periodicals" chapter) gives: item number (boldfaced), magazine title, volume and/or issue number, month and year of publication, pagination, and notes.

Secondary sources are arranged alphabetically by main entry (usually author's surname); a typical entry records: item number, author (inverted name, surname in all caps), title, and bibliographical data (for books: place of publication, publisher, year of publication, pagination, and notes; for articles: magazine title [in italics], month and year of publication, specific pagination, and notes). Two indices, to Wells's own works and to all other references, are keyed to item numbers. The materials in the book are numbered consecutively throughout the bibliography from 1-1,290. The catalog is professionally typeset and bound to library standards.

This guide will be most useful to those scholars of Wells's life and work who are interested in travelling to Bromley. However, there is also much of interest here for other researchers, since the catalog records many peripheral items not mentioned in Hammond's more complete bibliography (see #505). Recommended for major research collections.

507. Wells, Geoffrey H. **The Works of H. G. Wells, 1887-1925: A Bibliography, Dictionary, and Subject-Index.** London, George Routledge & Sons, 1926. xxv, 274 p. index. LC 26-14925. New York, Burt Franklin, 1970. xxv, 274 p. index. LC 77-20335.

Geoffrey Wells, who apparently was unrelated to H. G. or to his paramour, Rebecca West, also used the name Geoffrey West in later life.

Contents: "Introduction"; "Addenda"; "Part One: Books and Pamphlets"; "Part Two: Books and Pamphlets Containing Miscellaneous Publications"; "Part Three: Books by Other Writers with Prefaces"; "Appendix i: Chronological List of Unreprinted Writings"; "Appendix ii. Letters to the Press"; "Appendix iii. Translation into Foreign Languages"; "Appendix iv. Parodies by Various Writers"; "Appendix v. Critical Studies of H. G. Wells"; "A Dictionary of the Works of H. G. Wells"; "A Subject-Index to the Works of H. G. Wells."

In each section materials are listed chronologically by publication date. A typical monograph entry provides: item number, title (all caps italics), and year of publication as centered headings; exact title page transcription; an exact description of the interior of the book, including pagination, number of advertisements, etc.; a careful description of the binding, including mention of variations in later issues; and other bibliographical notes (usually one long paragraph) giving details of previous publication, contents (for collections), and a plot description. Materials are numbered consecutively from 1-89, the last item being "The Atlantic Edition of the Works of H. G. Wells."

Part II gives books incorporating Wellsiana, a typical entry providing: year of publication (centered head), title, author or editor, publisher, place of publication, year of publication, specific pagination of the Wells's piece, and a brief descriptive note. Part III is similarly arranged and presented.

The first appendix provides a chronological list of the author's unreprinted essays and stories, with no bibliographical data beyond year of publication (as a centered heading). Appendix ii includes a selection of Wells's letters to newspapers and magazines, giving: title (actually subject theme, in italics), magazine title, and month and year of publication, but no paginations. Appendices iii-iv are both slight and sketchy.

The last appendix is subdivided into three parts: "(a) Books"; "(b) Essays in Books"; "(c) Essays in Periodicals." Each section is arranged chronologically by publication date. A typical book entry gives: title (italics), author, publisher, place of publication, year of publication, and series name (where appropriate). Section (b) lists: book title (italics), author or editor, publisher, place of publication, year of publication, essay title (in italics), and specific pagination of the piece. Section (c) gives: essay title (italicized), author, magazine title, and month and year of publication, but no paginations.

The dictionary section actually comprises the bulk of the book (163 pages). It provides an A-Z record of the author's works, fictional and nonfictional, plus mentions of all the major and significant minor characters. A typical character entry gives: name (small caps), occupation, physical description, the work in which he or she appears, and a description of his or her fate. The remaining entries (about half) concern Wells's essays, stories, novels, pamphlets, etc., typically giving: item number, title (small caps), a reference (where appropriate) to the item number in the bibliography section where the item occurs, or bibliographical data (usually for short pieces, providing magazine title and month and year of publication, but no paginations), and detailed description or plot summary. Only those entries describing Wells's individual works are numbered (from 1-753).

The subject index correlates names, titles, and subjects with the item numbers in the dictionary chapter (not those from the bibliography section). The book is beautifully typeset and designed, and bound to library standards.

Although much of these data are subsumed into Hammond's more current and comprehensive bibliography (see #505), the serious researcher will also want access to this earlier guide, which provides much first-hand background information on Wells's books (obviously derived from the author himself), plus detailed descriptions of so many of the minor works in the dictionary section; indeed, much of the latter data cannot be located in any other single source. Hammond's volume (see #505) should be acquired by all four-year academic and all large public libraries; research collections should have all four works herein described (see #504-#507). Also compare the dictionary chapter with Ash's and Connes's dictionaries of Wells's characters (see #576, #577).

James White

508. Benson, Gordon, Jr., and Phil Stephensen-Payne. **James White, Doctor to Aliens: A Working Bibliography.** 2nd ed. Leeds, West Yorkshire, England, Galactic Central Publications, 1989. 9, 23 p. (Galactic Central Bibliographies for the Avid Reader, Vol. 12). ISBN 1-871133-14-9 (pbk.).

The late SF writer James White, a native of Northern Ireland, penned a number of science fiction tales of future medics and doctors interfacing with alien patients. This checklist is arranged by subject category, then alphabetically by title.

Contents: Author's name, date and place of birth, list of awards won by the author (in chronological order, giving year, name of award, and title of work being honored); "A. Stories"; "B. Fiction Books"; "C. Series"; "D. Poems & Songs" [blank section]; "E. Poem & Song Collections" [blank section]; "F. Articles"; "G. Miscellaneous" (including introductions and afterwords by James White, letters, and interviews with the author); "H. Non-Fiction Books" [blank section]; "I. Edited Books" [blank section]; "J. Media Presentations" [blank section]; "K. Articles on James White"; "L. Reviews" (of White's books, alphabetically by title of the book being reviewed, then by magazine title, giving date and reviewer); "M. Books About James White"; "N. Phantom Titles"; "O. Related Items by Other Authors"; "P. Textual Variations"; "Q. Chronological Index" (by year and title).

In each part materials are arranged by title, White's works being numbered anew from one. A typical short fiction entry includes: item number, title, category ("ss" = short story, "nt" = novelette, etc.), magazine or book in which the item appeared, month and year of publication (for magazines in the form "11-55" for November 1955) or year of publication (for books), plus a list of subsequent reprints (for which title, editor's last name, publisher, and year are given), but no paginations.

A typical book entry provides: item number, title (in underlined caps), publication data (publisher, stock number, month and year of publication [if known, in the form "10-

59" for October 1959], pagination, price, with dates of reissues by the same publisher), cover artist, and similar data for known reprints. Collections include lists of the author's stories referenced to the item numbers in the first section.

There are 137 entries included, though reprint information makes the actual total of bibliographical records somewhat greater. Some 31 secondary sources noted, 16 of which are book review categories (the actual book reviews cited number over a hundred). Only a few foreign language publications are mentioned. The book is shot from very clear word-processed copy and stapled through the spine. An index would have been helpful, as would the addition of paginations for the short fiction sections. Coverage is complete through part of 1989.

White is not well known outside the SF field, but scholars mining the back veins of fantastic literature and fans of White will welcome this checklist.

Charles Williams

509. Glenn, Lois. **Charles W. S. Williams: A Checklist.** Kent, OH, Kent State University Press, 1975. viii, 128 p. index. (The Serif Series: Bibliographies and Checklists, No. 33). LC 75-17277. ISBN 0-87338-179-3.

Charles Williams (1886-1945) was a friend and colleague of both J. R. R. Tolkien and C. S. Lewis, and a well-known British fantasy writer in his own right.

Contents: "Introduction"; "I. Williams's Works": "A. Books" (subdivided into "Poetry," "Novels," "Plays," "Criticism," "Theology," "Biographies"); "B. Poems and Stories"; "C. Articles and Letters"; "D. Reviews"; "E. Edited Works"; "II. Works About Williams": "A. Books"; "B. Articles, Chapters, and Dissertations"; "C. Reviews" (subdivided into Williams's individual books, which are arranged in chronological order by publication date); "D. Dissertations"; "III. Indexes": "A. Index of Names"; "B. Index of Titles of Williams's Works"; "C. Index of Titles of Works About Williams."

The arrangement in Section I is chronologically by date of each of Williams's works, but Section II, secondary sources, is arranged alphabetically by main entry (usually critic's name); in both sections, materials are further divided into many different subdivisions, as indicated by the chapter titles, and are numbered anew from one in each *sub*-section.

A typical book entry includes: item number, title (in italics), place of publication, publisher, year of publication, and pagination, with similar data on all known reprint editions, plus a short (one- to two-sentence) annotation.

A typical shorter work entry includes: item number, title (in quotes), magazine title (italics), volume number, month and year of publication, pagination; or, for works appearing originally in anthologies, book title (italics), editor, place of publication, publisher, year of publication, pagination within the book, and a brief, one-sentence (or several-word) annotation. Similar data are included for all known reprints.

Secondary works are similarly recorded, with one- to two-sentence annotations. Section II, Chapter D, on dissertations, essentially excerpts those entries from their original appearances in II-B. The three indices are keyed to item numbers (in the form "I-A-iv-6" or "II-B-178," for example). The book is nicely designed and typeset and bound to library standards.

The author appears familiar with her material, and the data appear complete. However, one must question the wisdom of breaking a relatively small book into so many subdivisions. For example, separating Williams's books into six sections in just eleven pages of text, each chronologically arranged, makes overall comprehension of his monographic work extraordinarily difficult to any but the most intensive user. However, in partial compensation, the material *is* easily accessed through the indices, and Glenn's volume will provide a sound beginning point for both the scholar and student. It should also be on the shelves of every research library.

Jack Williamson

510. Benson, Gordon, Jr. **Jack (John Stewart) Williamson, Child and Father of Wonder: A Working Bibliography.** Leeds, West Yorkshire, England, Galactic Central Publications, 1989?. v, 14 p. (Galactic Central Bibliographies for the Avid Reader, Vol. 10). ISBN 0-912613-22-X (pbk.).

Dr. Jack Williamson, who began writing SF in the 1920s, later became one of the first academics to teach classes in fantastic literature at the university level. Benson's checklist supplements Myers (see #512), arranging the author's work by subject category, then alphabetically by title.

Contents: Author's full name, date and place of birth, pseudonyms, and awards; "A. The Stories"; "B. The Books"; "C. Books: Non-Fiction"; "D. Articles, Editorials, Introductions, etc."; "E. Miscellaneous."

In each part the material is arranged alphabetically by title. A typical shorter work entry includes: item number, title, category ("ss" = short story, "nt" = novelette, etc.), magazine or book in which the item appeared, month and year of publication (for magazines in the form "2-39" for February 1939), or year of publication (for books), plus a list of subsequent reprints (for which title, editor's last name, publisher, and year are given), but no paginations.

A typical book entry provides: item number, title (in underlined caps), publication data (publisher, stock number, LC card number, month and year of publication [if known, in the form "10-59" for October 1959], pagination, price, with dates of reissues by the same publisher), cover artist. There are no indices; several pages of general secondary sources are included in Section E. Coverage is complete through 1986, although some of the non-specific reference sources have dates as late as 1989. This bibliography has yet to be updated into the new series format. The volume is shot from typed copy, with some of the text running occasionally into the right margin, and is stapled through the spine into paper covers.

Benson's guide is more current than Myers's (see #512) and includes the book paginations the latter omits, but lacks the magazine paginations Myers includes. Hauptmann (#511) is by far the most comprehensive bibliography, but fans may prefer this less sophisticated checklist.

511. Hauptmann, Richard A. **The Work of Jack Williamson: An Annotated Bibliography and Guide.** Framingham, MA, NESFA Press, 1998. xvii, 185 p. index. ISBN 1-886778-12-4.

Contents: "Acknowledgments"; "A Note on Presentation"; "Jack Williamson: The Legionnaire of Space," by Frederik Pohl; "A Jack Williamson Chronology"; "A. His Books"; "B. His Short Fiction"; "C. His Nonfiction"; "D. Other Media"; "E. Miscellanea"; "Secondary Sources"; "Quoth the Critics"; "References and Bibliography"; "Afterword," by Jack Williamson; "Title Index"; "General Index".

Hauptmann has compiled a bibliography using the Borgo Press standard that includes not only the fiction and non-fiction of Williamson, but citations to reviews of the books, foreign language publications, pseudonyms, a personal chronology cross-referenced with book publications, degrees and honors, appearances at science fiction conventions, and more. It also includes an afterword commenting on the bibliography by Williamson himself.

In each section, the author's works are arranged chronologically and numbered consecutively (*e.g.*, B1., B2., etc.). A typical book entry includes: item number, title (bold italics), place of publication, publisher, year of publication, pagination, format (*e.g.*, "paper"), type of publication (*e.g.*, "novel"), with full bibliographical data for all reprint contents listings or plot summaries and other pertinent data; entries from other sections are selectively annotated as needed.

Citations to reprints and foreign publications and translations of the main work are listed beneath the major entry, in chronological order by publication date, including the same basic information, as available, plus language and occasional notes indicating the reasons for missing information. This is followed by a summary annotation averaging 100 words in Part A, and half that size for the short fiction annotations in Part B. Parts C and D contain few such summaries. Following each annotation is a list of secondary sources and reviews, giving: periodical title and date, reviewer's or critic's name, plus an occasional excerpt, some of them lengthy quotations.

Parts A-D include 411 main entries; however, since the entries are often further subdivided to include additional data, especially in Parts A and B, the amount of detailed bibliographical information provided is extensive. Part E: Miscellanea includes several lists of quantitative data, most notably a tabular breakdown of Williamson's publications by decade. The volume also contains a title index, a general index, as well as a bibliography of cited sources and a bibliography of sources used but uncited. The book is attractively and sturdily bound to library standards.

A thoroughly good source for collectors, scholars, serious fans, and those libraries serving them, Hauptmann's book now completely supersedes the guides previously compiled by Benson and Myers (see #510, #512).

512. Myers, Robert E. **Jack Williamson: A Primary and Secondary Bibliography.** Boston, G. K. Hall & Co., 1980. xiii, 93 p. index. (Masters of Science Fiction and Fantasy). LC 79-18471. ISBN 0-8161-8158-6.

Myers here covers the work of a respected American science fiction writer of the pulp era who later earned his Ph.D. in English Literature with a dissertation on the works of H. G. Wells.

Contents: "Preface"; "Introduction"; "Part A: Fiction"; "Part B: Miscellaneous Media"; "Part C: Nonfiction"; "Part D: Criticism and Reviews"; "Part E: A Selection of Non-English Editions and Publications of Williamson's Works"; "Appendix: A Selected List of

Additional Reviews and Criticism"; "Index I: Subject-Author Index, Listing Titles in Parts A, B, C and English Titles in Part E"; "Index II: Listing of Criticism-Reviews in Part D."

The introduction provides a very brief biographical and critical introduction to Williamson's work. The bibliography proper is arranged chronologically, from the earliest published material to the latest, and numbered consecutively in each chapter from one (*e.g.,* A1, A2, A3, etc., for Williamson's fiction). Books and shorter works are interfiled; reprint editions are listed under the first edition in chronological order.

Each book entry gives: item number, title (in italics), place of publication, publisher, but no paginations. Shorter works published originally in magazines list: item number, title (in quotations), magazine, volume number, date, and paginations; those published originally in books give: title (in quotes), book title (italics), editor, place of publication, publisher, format, but no paginations. Story collections include complete contents listings, plus the years in which the original stories were published.

Part B includes a handful of teleplay adaptations and audio tapes. Part C includes all nonfiction works by the author, with occasional annotations. Part D lists all known secondary works (ninety-nine items), including some published book reviews, profiles, critiques, and bibliographies, giving: author, title, bibliographical data, and extensive subject annotations.

Part E includes all known foreign editions of Williamson's works (particularly books), listed alphabetically by English-language title, then in chronological order by date of publication of the foreign edition, with all known bibliographical data, including foreign-language titles and translators. The main index cites title or subject and item number only; the second index (to critical studies) records author, title, and item number. The book is nicely typeset and bound to library standards.

Myers's data are complete only through 1978 (with one entry from 1979), making the book somewhat out-of-date for a writer who remains moderately active, and his guide lacks the book paginations that Benson's more current bibliography (see #510) supplies. Now superseded by Hauptmann (see #511).

Colin Wilson

513. Stanley, Colin. **The Work of Colin Wilson: An Annotated Bibliography & Guide.** San Bernardino, CA, The Borgo Press, 1989. 312 p. index. (Bibliographies of Modern Authors, No. 1). LC 84-11181. ISBN 0-89370-817-8; ISBN 0-89370-917-4 (pbk.).

This massive, extremely comprehensive guide to the works of the well-known British novelist and philosopher was the flagship volume of the Bibliographies of Modern Authors series.

Contents: "Acknowledgments and Note"; "Introduction: The Quest for Colin Wilson," by Stanley; "A Colin Wilson Chronology"; "A. Books"; "B. Short Fiction"; "C. Nonfiction"; "D. Introductions and Afterwords"; "E. Book Reviews"; "F. Other Media"; "G. Editorial Credits"; "H. About the Author: Monographs"; "I. About the Author: Critiques, Profiles, Interviews"; "J. About the Author: Short Bio-Bibliographies"; "K. About the Author: Other Materials"; "L. Miscellanea"; "Quoth the Critics"; "Afterword: Inside Outside: Reflections on Being Bibliographed," by Colin Wilson; "Title Index to Colin Wilson's Works"; "Subject Index with Author/Title Index."

In each section, the author's works are arranged chronologically and numbered consecutively, chapter by chapter, with the appropriate letter prefix. A typical book entry includes: item number, title (boldface), place of publication, publisher, year of publication, pagination, format (*e.g.,* "paper" = paperback), type of publication (*e.g.,* "novel"), and similar data on reprint editions, translations, republications, anthologizations, etc., which are listed chronologically under the main entry. The books are fully annotated, with completely analyzed and very detailed contents and subject listings and/or plot summaries, lists of book reviews and other secondary sources (in alphabetical order by critic), and other pertinent data (for example, verbatim transcriptions of the dedications at the front of each Wilson title); entries from other sections are selectively annotated as needed.

A typical shorter work entry includes: item number, title (in boldfaced quotes), magazine title (italics), volume or issue number, month and year of publication, and paginations; shorter works appearing originally in books include: item number, title (boldface quotes), book title (italics), editor, place of publication, publisher, format (*e.g.,* "cloth"), and paginations. Similar data are provided for all known reprints, including foreign editions, with foreign-language titles and translators.

Stanley's introduction provides an excellent introductory guide to the author's life and works. The chronology gives a year-by-year account of the author's professional and personal life, in block paragraph format. "About the Author" includes all known secondary works, which are so numerous in this volume that they have been further subdivided into four chapters by type; reviews of individual Wilson books are included, however, under their respective entries in Section A.

The "Miscellanea" section includes information on library holdings of Wilson manuscripts, spurious titles, screenplays adapted from Wilson novels, books dedicated to Wilson (with verbatim transcriptions of the dedications and full bibliographical data), Wilson's plays and unpublished works, and Library of Congress cataloging data. "Quoth the Critics" includes selected excerpts of reviews and other comments by leading critics on the author's work, arranged chronologically by Wilson book title. The very comprehensive indices correlate Wilson's titles with their item numbers and, in the second index, with all other references to authors, titles, and subjects, again by item number. Wilson's original, twenty-page afterword sums up the philosophical basis for his entire career.

This is a major literary reference work. Particularly important are Stanley's extensive annotations and descriptive contents listings, which not only delineate Wilson's development as a writer and philosopher, but also provide much background information for future researchers through numerous quotations from specific Wilson titles, as well as contemporary critical reactions *to them.* Much of the material derives directly from Wilson's own files and personal library of his works, with coverage complete through the end of 1988. Even though this book is now somewhat outdated (Wilson has continued to produce enormous numbers of books and essays through the 1990s), it is difficult to see how any serious student of Colin Wilson could possibly ignore this superb condensation of his life and career. Recommended for all academic collections.

Richard Wilson

514. Drumm, Chris. **A Richard Wilson Checklist.** Polk City, IA, Chris Drumm Books, 1986. 13, 20 p. Index. Bound upside down with *Adventures in the Space Trade: A Memoir,* by Richard Wilson. LC 90-108879. ISBN 0-936055-24-3 (pbk.); ISBN 0-936055-25-1 (ltd. ed.).

The late Richard Wilson, who died just before this 4.25" x 7" booklet was published, was a well-regarded American SF writer and academic. Drumm's checklist arranges the author's works in one straight chronological sequence.

Entries are grouped by year and under each year by month; items are numbered consecutively in order from 1 to 100. Books are underlined, short stories listed in quotation marks. A typical shorter work entry includes: item number, title, category code (*e.g.,* "s" = short story), magazine (underlined), month of publication, but no paginations; or book title, if the first appearance is in an anthology, plus editor, publisher, and year of publication. Subsequent reprintings are grouped chronologically under the original edition, with similar data provided.

A typical book entry includes: item number, title (all caps), category code (*e.g.,* "c" = collection), publisher, stock number, month of publication (if known), pagination, price, format (*e.g.,* "pb" = paperback), contents of collections. "See" references, title index, and contents listings are keyed to item number. A few secondary materials are mentioned in passing in their appropriate years, but are not easily retrievable. Data are complete through 1986. The book is shot from typed copy; the text runs too close to the right-hand margin to allow rebinding by libraries.

The original autobiographical memoir by Wilson provides a poignant look back at the author's life and career. An expanded edition with further primary and secondary resources would certainly be justified.

Gene Wolfe

515. Stephens, Christopher P. **A Checklist of Gene Wolfe.** Hastings-on-Hudson, NY, Ultramarine Publishing Co., 1990. 37 p. index. ISBN 0-89366-181-3 (pbk.).

Wolfe is best known for his tetralogy, *The Book of the New Sun.* This checklist to his works is organized into two sections, "Books" and "Stories," then chronologically by publication date. Books are numbered consecutively from A1-A29, and short stories from B1-B125.

A typical monograph entry provides: year (as a floating head), item number, title (underlined), pseudonym, publisher, stock or ISBN number, pagination, format (*e.g.,* "cloth with dust wrapper"), cover illustrator, price, and similar data for all known reprints (which are numbered, for example, A12a, A12b, A12c, etc., in descending order by publication date).

A typical short fiction entry gives: item number, title (in quotes), pagination, magazine title, month and year of publication, volume and issue number; or, for materials appearing in anthologies, book title (underlined), editor's name, publisher, and year of publication, but no paginations. Similar data are provided for all known reprints. The book is shot from legible typed copy and bound with staples in stiff paper covers. The two indices (to books and stories) correlate titles with years of publication only; these would have been more useful amalgamated into one alphabetical list and correlated with specific item number.

Compare with Stephensen-Payne and Benson (see #516).

516. Stephensen-Payne, Phil, and Gordon Benson, Jr. **Gene Wolfe, Urth-Man Extraordinary: A Working Bibliography.** Leeds, West Yorkshire, England, Galactic Central Publications, 1991. 9, 53 p. (Bibliographies for the Avid Reader, Vol. 19). ISBN 1-871133-31-9 (pbk.).

American writer Gene Wolfe is generally considered to be one of the most significant SF writers of the latter decades of the twentieth century.

Contents: Author's name, date and place of birth, list of awards won by the author (in chronological order, giving year, name of award, and title of work being honored) and his pseudonyms [blank section]; "A. Stories"; "B. Fiction Books"; "C. Series"; "D. Poems"; "E. Poetry Volumes"; "F. Articles"; "G. Miscellaneous" (including introductions and afterwords by Gene Wolfe, letters, and interviews with the author); "H. Non-Fiction Books"; "I. Books Edited by Gene Wolfe" [blank section]; "J. Media Presentations" [blank section]; "K. Articles on Gene Wolfe"; "L. Reviews" (of Wolfe's books, alphabetically by title of the book being reviewed, then by magazine title, giving date and reviewer); "M. Books About Gene Wolfe"; "N. Phantom & Forthcoming Titles"; "O. Related Items by Other Authors" [blank section]; "P. Textual Variations"; "Q. Chronological Index" (by year and title).

The introduction is almost identical throughout the series, and clearly explains the many different sections of the bibliography. Stephensen-Payne and Benson's basic checklist is arranged by subject category, then alphabetically by title; materials are numbered consecutively from one in each chapter (for example, B1, B2, B3, etc., for the author's books). Shorter work entries include: item number, title, category ("ss" = short story, "nt" = novelette, etc.), magazine or book in which the item appeared, month and year of publication (for magazines in the form "2-68" for February 1968) or year of publication (for books), a list of subsequent reprints (for which title, publisher, year, and editor's last name are given), but no paginations.

For book-length works, Stephensen-Payne and Benson provide: item number, title, contents (if a collection, by item number), publication data (publisher, stock number, month and year of publication [if known, in the form "10-59" for October 1959], pagination, price), cover artist, plus similar data for known reprints. There is no title index. 381 entries are covered, although reprint information inflates the total. Of these, 88 are secondary sources, 21 of which constitute book review categories; dozens of actual reviews are noted. Foreign language publications are mentioned when known, but few are included. The book is shot from very clear word-processed copy and stapled through the spine. An index would have been helpful, as would the addition of paginations for the short fiction sections.

In comparing Stephens's guide (see #515) with Stephensen-Payne/Benson's, the former has paginations for shorter works that the latter lacks, but the latter volume includes a great deal of supplemental data missing from Stephens, including secondary sources. Both bibliographies will be needed by the researcher.

John Wyndham

517. Stephensen-Payne, Phil. **John Wyndham, Creator of the Cosy Catastrophe: A Working Bibliography.** 2nd rev. ed. Leeds, West Yorkshire, England, Galactic Central Publications, 1989. 9, 39 p. (Bibliographies for the Avid Reader, Vol. 16). ISBN 1-871133-16-5 (pbk.). The first edition appeared under the title, *John Wyndham Parkes Lucas Beynon Harris: A Bibliography.*

The late John Wyndham, the pseudonym of John Beynon Harris (1903-1969), was the premier British exponent of the near-future disaster novel.

Contents: Author's name, date and place of birth and death, his pseudonyms; "A. Stories"; "B. Fiction Books"; "C. Series"; "D. Poems and Songs" [blank section]; "E. Poem and Song Collections" [blank section]; "F. Articles"; "G. Miscellaneous" (including introductions and afterwords by John Wyndham, letters, and interviews with the author); "H. Non-Fiction Books" [blank section]; "I. Books Edited by John Wyndham" [blank section]; "J. Media Presentations"; "K. Articles on John Wyndham"; "L. Reviews" (of Wyndham's books, alphabetically by title of the book being reviewed, then by magazine title, giving date and reviewer); "M. Books About John Wyndham"; "N. Phantom Titles and Editions"; "O. Related Items by Other Authors"; "P. Textual Variations"; "Q. Chronological Index" (by year and title).

The introduction is almost identical throughout the series, and clearly explains the many different sections of the bibliography. Stephensen-Payne's basic checklist is arranged by subject category, then alphabetically by title; materials are numbered consecutively from one in each chapter (for example, B1, B2, B3, etc., for the author's books). Shorter work entries typically include: item number, title, category ("ss" = short story, "nt" = novelette, etc.), magazine or book in which the item appeared, month and year of publication (for magazines in the form "2-68" for February 1968) or year of publication (for books), a list of subsequent reprints (for which title, publisher, year, and editor's last name are given), but no paginations.

For monographs, Stephensen-Payne provides: item number, title, contents (if a collection, by item number), publication data (publisher, stock number, month and year of publication [if known, in the form "10-59" for October 1959], pagination, price), cover artist, plus similar data for known reprints. There is no title index. 196 entries are mentioned, although reprint information makes the total even greater. 70 of these are secondary sources, 19 of them being book review categories; over 50 actual reviews are recorded. The book is shot from word-processed copy and is stapled through the spine. An index would have been helpful, as would the addition of paginations for short fiction.

This volume is one of the better Galactic Central bibliographies, one that will become *the* essential reference tool for any student of Wyndham's writings. For larger research collections.

George Zebrowski

518. Elliot, Jeffrey M., and R. Reginald. **The Work of George Zebrowski: An Annotated Bibliography & Guide.** San Bernardino, CA, The Borgo Press, 1986. 54 p. index. (Bibliographies of Modern Authors, No. 4). LC 84-24239. ISBN 0-89370-383-4; ISBN 0-89370-

483-0 (pbk.). **The Work of George Zebrowski: An Annotated Bibliography & Guide.** 2nd ed., rev. and expanded. San Bernardino, CA, The Borgo Press, 1990. 118 p. index. (Bibliographies of Modern Authors, No. 4). LC 89-7093. ISBN 0-8095-0514-2; ISBN 0-8095-1514-8 (pbk.). **The Work of George Zebrowski: An Annotated Bibliography & Literary Guide.** 3rd ed., rev. and expanded. San Bernardino, Borgo Press, 1996. 144 p. index. (Bibliographies of Modern Authors, No. 4). LC 96-15694. ISBN 0-89370-392-3; ISBN 0-89370-492-X (pbk.).

Zebrowski is the acclaimed writer of *Macrolife,* in addition to being a highly regarded SF editor.

Contents (first edition): "Introduction," by Elliot; "A. Books"; "B. Short Fiction"; "C. Translations"; "D. Articles and Reviews"; "E. Journals and Publishing Series"; "F. Juvenilia"; "G. About the Author"; "H. Honors and Awards"; "I. Public Appearances"; "J. Unpublished Works"; "K. Miscellanea"; "Quoth the Critics"; "Title Index."

Contents (second edition): "Introduction: Between Sensitivity and Concern," by Elliot; "A George Zebrowski Chronology"; "A. Books"; "B. Short Fiction"; "C. Nonfiction"; "D. Translations"; "E. Juvenilia"; "F. Editorial Credits"; "G. Unpublished Works"; "H. Other Media"; "I. Honors and Awards"; "J. Public Appearances"; "K. About the Author"; "L. Miscellanea"; "Quoth the Critics"; "Afterword: 6,250 Bits of Immortality," by Zebrowski; "Index"; "About the Authors."

Contents (third edition): "Introduction," by Elliot; "A George Zebrowski Chronology"; "A. Books and Monographs"; "B. Short Fiction"; "C. Short Nonfiction"; "D. Short Translations"; "E. Editorial Credits"; "F. Juvenilia"; "G. Unpublished Works"; "H. Other Media"; "I. Honors and Awards"; "J. Public Appearances"; "K. Secondary Sources"; "L. Miscellanea"; "Quoth the Critics"; "Afterword: 6,250 Bits of Immortality," by Zebrowski; "Index"; "About Jeffrey M. Elliot & Robert Reginald."

In each section, the author's works are arranged chronologically and numbered consecutively, chapter by chapter, with the appropriate letter prefix. A typical entry includes: item number, title (bold type), place of publication, publisher, month and year of publication, pagination, format (*e.g.,* "cloth"), type of publication (*e.g.,* "anthology"), similar bibliographical details on known reprint editions, including foreign versions, with foreign-language titles and translators, and a list of secondary sources and reviews, arranged alphabetically by main entry (usually critic). The books are fully annotated, with complete contents listings and/or plot summaries and other pertinent data; entries from other sections are selectively annotated as needed.

A typical shorter work entry includes: item number, title (bold quotes), magazine title (italics), volume number, month and year of publication, and paginations; a shorter work appearing in an anthology lists item number, title (bold quotes), book title (italics), editor, place of publication, publisher, and paginations, with similar data on all known reprintings.

Elliot's introduction provides an interesting and entertaining introduction to the author's life and works. The chronology provides a year-by-year account of the author's professional and personal life, in block paragraph format. "About the Author" includes all known secondary works, arranged chronologically by publication date, with full bibliographical data. The "Miscellanea" section includes information on pen names, book dedications, memberships, Library of Congress cataloging data, career highlights, and other data.

"Quoth the Critics" includes selected excerpts of reviews and other comments by leading critics on the author's work, arranged in chronological order by book title. Zebrowski's original afterword comments perceptively on the function of bibliography and the state of the author at mid-life. The index correlates titles and item numbers only.

The third edition follows the same format as the second, although some headings have been relabeled in the new version (*e.g.*, "K. About the Author" has become "K. Secondary Sources"). The introduction by Elliot, though lacking the identifying sub-title of the previous version, is also identical, as is the concluding essay by Zebrowski, and several minor chapters of the bibliography (D, F, and L). The update extends the coverage through 1995, with some information from 1996. The number of main entries increased from 320 in the second edition to 388 in the third, but this does not reflect some additional citations for reprints and collected reviews that are unnumbered and buried internally within the text. The index correlates titles and item numbers only.

The new typeface in this version has considerably improved readability. The third edition supersedes both previous editions, and remains a good research guide to the work of a well-known SF writer. For larger research libraries.

Roger Zelazny

519. Levack, Daniel J. H., with annotations by Darrell Schweitzer. **Amber Dreams: A Roger Zelazny Bibliography.** San Francisco, CA & Columbia, PA, Underwood/Miller, 1983. 151 p. ISBN 0-934438-40-4; ISBN 0-934438-39-0 (pbk.). Westport, CT, Meckler Publishing, 1986. 151 p. ISBN 0-88736-098-X.

Levack, who compiled similarly formatted bibliographies on de Camp, Dick, Herbert, and Vance (see #364, #369, #393, #496), has produced another attractive but bibliographically insipid volume on the late American SF and fantasy writer.

Contents: "Introduction"; "Books"; "Edited Books"; "Stories"; "Magazine Checklist"; "Works About Roger Zelazny"; "Miscellaneous"; "Connected Stories and Continuing Characters"; "Pseudonyms"; "Collaborations"; "Verse Index"; "Non-Fiction Index"; "Chronological Order of Publication of Roger Zelazny's Work"; "Acknowledgments."

Works are listed alphabetically by title and numbered consecutively from one, section by section, 251 items being covered. A typical book entry includes: item number, title (bold caps), series note (when appropriate), previous magazine serialization data (title, magazine title, parts, dates of publication), awards won, award nominations, contents (if a collection) or one-paragraph annotation (if a novel), both in boldface type, publisher, stock number (for paperback editions), place of publication (inconsistently for paperbacks), price (in parentheses), year of publication, edition points, but no paginations. Reprints are listed in chronological order by publication date; many foreign editions are included, with foreign-language titles. An asterisk after a specific edition indicates it has been viewed by Levack.

A typical shorter work entry includes: item number, title (in bold quotes), estimated wordage, type or other notes (*e.g.*, "verse"), one- to two-sentence annotation (in bold type), magazine or book title, date, volume number, issue number, but no paginations. All subsequent reprint editions (including some foreign-language materials, with foreign-language titles) are listed with similar data. Anthology appearances include: title, editor, publisher, stock number, price, year of publication, format (*e.g.,* "paper"), but no paginations.

The magazine checklist records those publications in which Zelazny stories have appeared, alphabetically by title, keyed to issue date and to item number in the short fiction section. There is also a master chronological checklist of Zelazny's work, year by year, with all publications interfiled, and a brief list of twenty-five secondary sources in alphabetical order by title, but no overall title index.

As usual with this series, the book is beautifully typeset and designed, and is illustrated throughout with reproductions of book and magazine covers featuring Zelazny's fiction. The Meckler cloth edition is bound to library standards, but is otherwise a facsimile reprint, with no additional data.

Levack's guide includes three more years of data than Sanders's bibliography (see #520) plus illustrations and edition points, but lacks an overall index (which Sanders includes) and story or book paginations. Stephens (see #521) includes these data, but does not list shorter works. Levack's bibliography records only twenty-five secondary sources, as compared with over 300 in Sanders, 120 in Stephensen-Payne (see #522), and none in Stephens. The latter two volumes also contain seven and eight years' more data, respectively. However, Levack includes illustrations of cover art missing in all of his competitors' guides.

For the serious scholar and the academic librarian, all four titles will be necessary complements, but Sanders is far the superior bibliographically.

520. Sanders, Joseph L. **Roger Zelazny: A Primary and Secondary Bibliography.** Boston, G. K. Hall, 1980. xxx, 154 p. index. (Masters of Science Fiction and Fantasy). LC 80-20253. ISBN 0-8161-8081-4.

Zelazny was the well-known American author of the Amber Series and other major SF and fantasy novels and stories.

Contents: "Preface"; "Introduction"; "Acknowledgments"; "A: Fiction"; "B: Poetry"; "C: Nonfiction"; "D: Critical Studies"; "Appendixes": "A. Nominations, Awards, and Honors"; "B. Foreign Language Editions"; "C. Manuscripts and Papers"; "Index to Primary Works"; "Index to Secondary Sources."

Sanders's introduction provides a brief biography to and broad critical evaluation of Zelazny's life and work. The bibliography itself is arranged chronologically, from the earliest published material to the latest, and numbered consecutively (*e.g.,* A1, A2, A3, etc., for Zelazny's fiction). Books and shorter works are interfiled; reprint editions of books are listed under the first edition, in chronological order.

A typical book entry gives: item number, title (underlined), place of publication, publisher, but no paginations. Shorter works published originally in magazines list: item number, title (in quotations), magazine, volume number, date, paginations; those published originally in books give: item number, title (in quotations), book title (underlined), book editor, place of publication, publisher, format (*e.g.,* "paper"), and paginations. Reprints of stories are listed under the main entry, chronologically by year of reprint, with the editor of the anthology, title, place of publication, publisher, year, format (*e.g.,* "paper"), but no paginations. Story collections include complete contents listings, plus the years in which the original stories were published. A few entries include bibliographical notes, but no other annotations.

Part B records Zelazny's many published poems. Part C includes all nonfiction works by the author, with occasional annotations. Part D lists some 300 secondary works, including published book reviews, fan commentaries, critiques, and bibliographies, with author, title, bibliographical data, and extensive subject annotations. The appendices list Zelazny's awards (chronologically); selected foreign editions (by language, then chronologically, with foreign-language title, English-language title, place of publication, publisher, year of publication, and format); and a complete description of the Roger Zelazny manuscripts and papers held by two library collections, a potentially major resource for future scholarship. The primary index cites title and item number only, the secondary index (to critical studies) correlates author, title, and item number. Coverage is complete through 1979. The book is shot from sometimes faint typed copy and bound to library standards.

This is an excellent bibliographical guide to Zelazny's works, but given the fact that the author remained very active for another decade and a half after this book was published, it has aged more rapidly than most volumes in this series, and badly needs an expanded and updated edition. Nonetheless, it remains the best available introduction to the writer's many works, superior in every respect to three more recent bibliographies of Zelazny's writings (see #519, #521, and #522). Stephens's and Stephensen-Payne's checklists (see #521 and #522) can be used as supplements.

521. Stephens, Christopher P. **A Checklist of Roger Zelazny.** Hastings-on-Hudson, NY, Ultramarine Publishing Co., 1990. 20 p. index. ISBN 0-89366-166-X (pbk.).

Stephens's checklist is organized into two sections covering books written by Zelazny and anthologies edited by him, then chronologically by publication date. Materials are numbered consecutively from A1-A47 (first section), and B1 (the single entry in part two). A typical entry provides: year (as a floating head), item number, title (underlined), pseudonym, publisher, stock or ISBN number, pagination, format (*e.g.,* "cloth with dust wrapper"), cover illustrator, price, and similar data for all known reprints (which are numbered, for example, A46a, A46b, A46c, etc., in descending order by publication date). The chapbook is shot from legible typed copy and bound with staples in stiff paper covers. The index correlates titles with years of publication only.

Although Stephens's guide is a decade more current than Sanders's (see #520) and includes monograph paginations the latter omits, it will be useful primarily as a supplement to Sanders's more scholarly work and as a brief checklist of Zelazny's very collectible books for fans and collectors. Fans will prefer Levack's illustrated guide (see #519) or Stephensen-Payne's more complete bibliography (see #522).

522. Stephensen-Payne, Phil. **Roger Zelazny, Master of Amber: A Working Bibliography.** Leeds, West Yorkshire, England, Galactic Central Publications, 1991. 9, 65 p. (Bibliographies for the Avid Reader, Vol. 38). ISBN 1-871133-29-7 (pbk.).

This primary and secondary bibliography covers the works of the late fantasy and SF writer, Roger Zelazny.

Contents: Author's name, date and place of birth, a list of awards won by the author (in chronological order, giving year, name of award, and title of work being honored), and his pseudonyms; "A. Stories"; "B. Fiction Books"; "C. Series"; "D. Poems"; "E. Poem and Song Collections"; "F. Articles"; "G. Miscellaneous" (including introductions and afterwords by Roger Zelazny, letters, and interviews with the author); "H. Non-Fiction Books"; "I. Books Edited by Roger Zelazny"; "J. Media Presentations"; "K. Articles on Roger Zelazny"; "L. Reviews" (of Zelazny's books, alphabetically by title of the book being reviewed, then by magazine title, giving date and reviewer); "M. Books About Roger Zelazny"; "N. Phantom and Forthcoming Titles"; "O. Related Items by Other Authors"; "P. Textual Variations" [blank section]; "Q. Chronological Index" (by year and title).

The introduction is almost identical throughout the series, and clearly explains the many different sections of the bibliography. Stephensen-Payne's basic checklist is arranged by subject category, then alphabetically by title; materials are numbered consecutively from one in each chapter (for example, B1, B2, B3, etc., for the author's books).

Shorter work entries include: item number, title, category ("ss" = short story, "nt" = novelette, etc.), magazine or book in which the item appeared, month and year of publication (for magazines in the form "2-68" for February 1968) or year of publication (for books), a list of subsequent reprints (for which title, publisher, year, and editor's last name are given), but no paginations.

For book-length works, Stephensen-Payne provides: item number, title, contents (if a collection, by item number), publication data (publisher, stock number, month and year of publication [if known, in the form "10-59" for October 1959], pagination, price), cover artist, plus similar data for known reprints. There is no title index.

The book includes some 449 entries, though reprint information makes the grand total somewhat larger. Of these, there are 120 secondary sources, 58 of which are book review categories covering Zelazny books (the actually number of reviews mentioned number in the hundreds). Some foreign language publications are listed, but this coverage is acknowledged to be incomplete.

An index would have been helpful here, as would the addition of paginations for short fiction. Stephensen-Payne's guide is more current than those of his competitors noted above, and will be used by scholars in the field to complement and update the more detailed data provided by Sanders (see #520). Fans, however, may well prefer this less expensive, more current alternative.

ARTIST BIBLIOGRAPHIES

SCOPE NOTE: This chapter includes guides to art work produced by individual artists (in alphabetical order by name of the artist) and general works indexing SF art by many artists. Biographies of some of these artists can be found in general encyclopedias (see the first section of this book) or in Weinberg's *A Biographical Dictionary of Science Fiction and Fantasy Artists* (see #59).

GENERAL WORKS

523. Page, Bill. **Index to SF Cover Art.** Bryan, TX, Dellwood Press, 1979-80. 3 v. index. (pbk.).

Page attempts to index artwork used on the covers of science-fiction and fantasy paperbacks; a fourth volume indexing the dustjacket art on hardcover books and Science Fiction Book Club editions was also announced, but has not been seen.

The arrangement is similar in each volume: works are indexed alphabetically by artist surname, then alphabetically by surname of the author of the work on which the art has appeared. A typical entry includes: artist name (surname first), item number (materials are numbered consecutively from the number one in the first volume through number 1,502 in the third volume), author's name (surname first), book title (underlined), publisher, stock number, month and year of publication.

Most of the books covered were published in the 1960s and '70s; however, each volume includes a random selection of paperbacks from this time period, with no obvious criteria for selection; major artists such as Jack Gaughan appear in all three volumes. The books are shot from occasionally faint typed copy, but are generally readable, line breaks and hanging indents serving to set the entries off from each other quite clearly and legibly.

Page's idea is sound, but the absence of an overall artist index, or of author and title indices for the works mentioned, limits the usefulness of what could have been a major resource guide for future study. A comprehensive reference guide to SF paperback art is badly needed.

BIBLIOGRAPHIES OF INDIVIDUAL ARTISTS

Vaughn Bodé

524. Beahm, George W., and Vaughn Bodé. **Vaughn Bodé Index.** Newport News, VA, Distributed by C. W. Brooks, Jr., 1976. 64 p. LC 76-371310 (pbk.).

This bibliography of Bodé's works was already underway before the artist's tragic death in 1975, and was then converted into a tribute to his life and art.

Contents: "Dedication"; "Genesis of an Index," by Beahm; "Chronology of Important Events"; "Bodé Consciousness," by Bodé; "Daydream" (a cartoon by Bodé); "Bodé's Cartoon Concert" (unsigned critique); "Bodé's Milestone Cartoons" (reproductions of artwork); "Vaughn Bodé Index"; "Two Portraits" (photographs of the artist).

The bibliography proper is organized into eleven sections: "I. Books"; "II. Periodicals"; "III. Newspapers"; "IV. Convention Material"; "V. Comic Books"; "VI. Bodé Oriented Projects"; "VII. Posters"; "VIII. Stationary"; "IX. Flyers"; "X. Miscellaneous Publications"; "XI. Bodé's Cartoon Concert."

The material is arranged roughly chronologically, but each of the major sections (particularly I-II) is so broken up into subdivisions that discovering any real order to this mass of data can only be serendipitous. Complete bibliographical details are provided, including paginations, and many of the entries include illuminating comments by Bodé himself. The book is attractively typeset and designed, featuring numerous reproductions of Bodé drawings and photos of the artist and his family.

However, the absence of an index plus the difficult structure of the book make access to the material virtually impossible without reading through entire sections. A better-organized version would definitely be desirable.

Hannes Bok

525. Brooks, C. W., Jr. **Interim Hannes Bok Illustration Index.** Newport News, VA, Purple Mouth Press, 1967. [16 leaves]. (pbk.). Brooks, Ned [*i.e.,* C. W., Jr.], and Don Martin. **Hannes Bok Illustration Index.** Newport News, VA, National Fantasy Fan Federation, 1970. 22 p. (pbk.). Brooks, C. W., Jr. **The Revised Hannes Bok Checklist.** Baltimore, T-K Graphics, 1974. [45] p. (with one-page addendum). (pbk.).

American writer and artist Hannes Bok (1904-1964) is justly regarded as one of the finest SF illustrators of the 1940s and '50s. These are three successive versions of the same index to his published artwork.

Contents: "I. Magazines"; "II. Books"; "III. Artfolios"; "IV. Fanzines"; "V. Miscellaneous Items"; "VI. Collaborations with Dolgov"; "VII. Non-SF Sources"; "Addendum."

Materials are arranged alphabetically by publication title, chapter by chapter, then chronologically by date. In Section I, Bok's work for the professional SF magazines is organized by magazine title, then chronologically by issue number. A typical entry includes: magazine title (all caps), month and year of publication, paginations of Bok drawings or paintings (with the story title and author for the illustrated work).

The books section lists monographs illustrated by Bok in alphabetical order by title, giving: title (underlined), author, publisher, place of publication, year of publication, and the page numbers on which the Bok illustrations appear. Other chapters are similarly organized. Some of the entries include explanatory annotations by Brooks.

An index would have been useful here, but its absence is not fatal to this strongly organized artist's guide. A definitive version covering all known Bok artwork, including the unpublished pieces, as well as his fantasy fiction, is long overdue and badly needed.

Virgil Finlay

526. Bell, Ian. **Virgil Finlay Indexed: The Eighth Book of Virgil Finlay.** Chalgrove, Oxfordshire, England, Ian Bell, 1986. 40 p. (pbk.).

[Not seen.]

Tim Kirk

527. Beahm, George, and Tim Kirk. **Kirk's Works.** Newport News, VA, Heresy Press, 1980. 121 p. LC 81-116969. ISBN 0-9603276-2-2; ISBN 0-9603276-1-4 (pbk.).

This lavishly illustrated guide to this American artist's work was published in an oversized 9" x 12" format.

Contents: "Introduction"; "Foreword," by William Rotsler; "Tim Kirk: An Appreciation," by George Barr; "Tim Kirk: Wizard of Whimsey," by Mike Glicksohn; "The Making of Monsters," by Kirk (autobiographical); "A Conversation with Tim Kirk," conducted by George Beahm; "Kirk's Works: An Annotated Index": "Index of Books"; "Professional Periodicals"; "Fanzines"; "Semi-Professional Periodicals"; "Convention Material"; "APA Material"; "Portfolios"; "Calendars"; "Greeting Cards"; "Flyers"; "Games"; "Miscellaneous Items."

Most sections are organized alphabetically by title of the work illustrated, although a few (the books chapter, for example) vary from this slightly, dumping miscellaneous titles or publishers at the beginning of the chapter without apparent reason. Complete bibliographical data are provided, including specific page numbers on which Kirk artwork appears. The book is beautifully typeset and designed, and is filled with dozens of black-and-white illustrations of Kirk paintings and drawings, plus photos of the artist himself. The introductory materials, particularly the Kirk interview, provide much background material on the artist and his life. An overall title index would have been very helpful in locating specific works.

Unlike the other artists covered in this section (all of whom died before their indexes were published), Tim Kirk remains quite active as an artist, and so this guide to his work is now very much out-of-date; an updated version should be contemplated.

CHARACTER DICTIONARIES & AUTHOR CYCLOPEDIAS

SCOPE NOTE: This section includes general dictionaries or directories of one or more authors' works, the primary focus being on the author's created world and/or characters, arranged alphabetically by name or place. Books whose primary intent is to provide a guide to the created place names in the author's fictional world are included in the "Atlases and Gazetteers" section.

GENERAL WORKS

528. Hamilton, Frank, and Link Hullar. **Amazing Pulp Heroes.** Brooklyn, NY, Gryphon Publications, 1988. 59 p. ISBN 0-936071-09-5 (pbk.).

This poorly organized, badly written, and wretchedly presented publication features biographies of created fictional heroes and villains from the pulp magazine era. Descriptions range in size from one short paragraph to several pages, and typically include: background, attributes, lists of companions (and the villains who regularly oppose him), and brief mentions of the magazine(s) that featured his adventures (but with no bibliographical details). There is no discernible arrangement in the book, entries appearing haphazardly; without an overall index, access to the material is difficult. Hamilton's full-page drawings of each hero accompany the text by Hullar.

The idea behind this booklet is laudable, but Rovin has done it much better (see #533).

529. Jones, Diana Wynne. **The Tough Guide to Fantasyland.** London, Vista, 1996. 223 p. ISBN 1-57560-106-X (pbk.). New York, DAW Books, 1998. 302 p. LC 99-168702 ISBN 0-88677-832-8 (pbk.).

Part travel guide and part dictionary, this well-written volume imitates both in recording fictitious places taken from major works in the fantasy genre. The approximately 550 entries are arranged alphabetically, with the typical entry including the term (boldfaced type) and a definition, with each entry averaging 150 words. "See Also" references are included in small caps within the entry. Decorating the margins is a collection of small icons similar to those found in travel guides (tents, rivers, first aid crosses). They are not meant to be taken seriously, of course, but do add to the volume's overall ambience.

This is an amusing book for dipping, but the parody will be more entertaining for the experienced reader who will understand better the tongue-in-cheek humor of the definitions. Although not entirely suitable for reference, in spite of its format, *The Tough Guide* does work as a humorous addition to a fantasy fan's library.

530. Melton, J. Gordon. **The Vampire Gallery: A Who's Who of the Undead.** Detroit, London, Visible Ink, 1998. xiv, 500 p. index. LC 99-160747. ISBN 1-57859-053-1 (pbk.).

Contents: "Introduction," by Melton; "Count Dracula: King of the Vampires"; "The Who's Who"; "Vampire Groups and Clans"; "Vampire Hunters and Associates"; "Photo and Illustration Credits"; "Index."

With nearly 350 character names included, *The Gallery* provides an A-Z guide to vampires featured in nineteenth- and twentieth-century fiction, comic books, drama, poetry, and films, with smaller, separate sections covering Count Dracula, vampire associations, and the hunters of the undead, the latter providing alphabetical coverage of the groups and hunters within each section.

The entries average several hundred words in length, but vary considerably in size; most feature a list of sources at the end of each article. The mini-essays note the initial appearance of each vampire, providing known details about his or her life, general attributes, physical aspects, plot details from the motion pictures or novels in which the vampire is featured, and any significant variations from the usual vampire credo. *The Gallery* is illustrated with black-and-white stills from movies and television, and with cover art from comics and novels.

Although enjoyable and well-written, the book does display a few problems. The index includes the names of vampires, authors, directors, actors, and movie and book titles, but its coverage is incomplete. Some actors are mentioned, while others who are discussed in the entries (such as Sarah Michelle Geller or Kristy Swanson) are not included, for no apparent reason. The text also contains some organizational or word choice errors, using, for example, the word "episode" in place of "season," or placing the entry for the Southern Coalition Against Vampires in the vampire groups section of the book rather than in the vampire hunters section. Cross references buried in the entries are noted in bold type, but seem rather skimpy for a volume of this size.

This book has far fewer entries than Bunson's *Vampire Encyclopedia* (see #2), but the descriptions of the characters are somewhat fuller and better cited. Combined with Melton's *Vampire Book* (see #10), which focuses on actors, organizations, and themes, *The Vampire Gallery* provides a thorough coverage of vampirism. However, the ultimate reference guide to vampires in fiction and on screen has yet to be written.

531. Pringle, David. **Imaginary People: A Who's Who of Modern Fictional Characters.** London & Glasgow, Grafton Books, 1987. x, 515 p. ISBN 0-246-12968-9. New York, World Almanac, 1988. x, 518 p. LC 88-60375. ISBN 0-88687-364-9. London, Paladin, Grafton Books, 1989. x, 518 p. ISBN 0-586-08744-3 (pbk.).

Pringle, former editor of the British publication *Foundation* and current editor of the magazine *Interzone,* has assembled an annotated alphabetical directory of 1,300 well-known literary, motion picture, television, and comic book heroes and other characters dating from the dawn of the modern novel, from the early 1700s through the 1980s.

A typical entry includes character name (boldfaced, all caps) and a description of the fictional person, ranging from one sentence to four pages in length, focusing on the character's life, attributes, career, and real name, with details of the publication(s) and/or films and television productions featuring the person, their authors, and the years of publication or release. Internal cross-references in the entries (names mentioned in all caps) lead the reader to other names of interest.

Many of the fictional personages derive from genre literature, and perhaps one-fourth relate directly or indirectly to fantastic fiction, making this book a valuable guide to major characters in the field, including such worthies as The Prisoner, Mad Max, Dracula, Han Solo, Titus Groan, Lemuel Gulliver, Jules de Grandin, James Bond, Bomba, Sumuru, "Carrie" White, The Wolf Man, Zorro, Indiana Jones, Fafhrd and the Gray Mouser, and many others. The volume is attractively illustrated throughout with movie and TV stills and black-and-white reproductions of book and magazine covers and previously published drawings. A six-page bibliography of works consulted completes the book.

The volume displays a slight British bias, as might be expected, but Pringle's coverage seems complete, objective, and highly literate, and includes many American heroes little known in Britain.

532. Rovin, Jeff. **The Encyclopedia of Monsters.** New York, Oxford, Facts on File, 1989. ix, 390 p. index. LC 89-30417. ISBN 0-8160-1824-3; ISBN 0-8160-2303-4 (pbk.).

Rovin's guide to the monsters of film, comic books, and literature shares the faults and high points of its two predecessors (see #533 and #534).

The basic arrangement is alphabetical by creature name (some of the appellations are well-known or self-evident, but others have been created by Rovin himself). A typical entry includes: name (bold caps), medium (*e.g.*, "C" = comic books), first appearance, species, gender, size, features and powers, biography, and general comment. An Appendix covers "Monstrous Lands," listed in alphabetical order by country or regional name, with appearance, location, history, and flora and fauna. The book is illustrated throughout with black-and-white movie stills and reproductions of comic book and magazine covers. The index includes references to every name and title, with boldface references to main entry essays.

As usual in this series, Rovin's guide draws heavily from motion pictures and comics while including relatively few entries from science fiction or fantasy literature. This particular volume restricts its coverage to mutated humans, beasts, and other critters with horrible aspects; villains as such are covered in the companion volume (see #534). Thorough but lightweight.

533. Rovin, Jeff. **The Encyclopedia of Superheroes.** New York & Oxford, Facts on File Publications, 1985. xi, 443 p., 32 p. of plates. index. LC 85-10329. ISBN 0-8160-1168-0.

This alphabetical guide to superheroes, their careers and attributes, focuses primarily on comic book characters with superhuman powers.

Contents: "Introduction"; "Entries A-Z"; Appendices: "A. Superhero Teams"; "B. Obscure or Borderline Golden Age Comic Book Superheroes," "C. Foreign Superheroes"; "D. Minor Superheroes"; "E. Superheroes Featured in "Dial 'H' for Hero""; "Late Arrivals" (*i.e.,* addenda); "Index."

A typical entry includes: superhero name (all caps), medium in which the hero has appeared (*e.g.,* "C" = comics), alter ego (the real-life identity of the hero), first appearance, occupation, costume, tools and weapons, biography, quote ("profound or characteristic declarations from the lips of the superhero"), and comment (additional miscellaneous information). Although some characters from the pulp magazines of the 1920s and '30s are included, plus other fictional and motion picture superheroes, the vast majority of the more than 1,000 entries derive ultimately from comic book sources.

The appendices include heroes who don't quite fit the parameters in the main section: superhero teams, foreign heroes, and borderline cases; although all of these characters can be located through the index, it might have been wiser to interfile them with their other crime-fighting brothers and sisters rather than separate them into seventy extra pages with five separate alphabetical sequences. The index correlates all names and publishers with page numbers. The book is beautifully typeset and designed, and includes black-and-white cover reproductions and movie stills throughout, as well as thirty-two four-color plates illustrating classic comic book and pulp magazine covers.

Rovin clearly knows his subject well: his book is complete and detailed, with all the information an aficionado might want to know. There is, however, an occasional problem with locating particular individuals, since Rovin regards appellations (Captain, Doc, Mr., etc.) as part of each hero's name and files them accordingly; with no "See" references and no reverse entries in the index, one can easily get lost.

See also the companion volumes, *The Encyclopedia of Super Villains* (see #534) and *The Encyclopedia of Monsters* (see #532).

534. Rovin, Jeff. **The Encyclopedia of Super Villains.** New York & Oxford, Facts on File Publications, 1987. ix, 416 p. 32 p. of plates. index. LC 87-8831. ISBN 0-8160-1356-X; ISBN 0-8160-1899-5 (pbk.).

Rovin's companion volume to *The Encyclopedia of Superheroes* (see #533) and *The Encyclopedia of Monsters* (see #532) is organized much the same way, alphabetically by name of super-character.

Contents: "Introduction"; "Entries A-Z"; Appendix: "Super Villain Teams"; "Index."

A typical entry includes: name (all caps), source (*e.g.,* "TV" = television), real name, first appearance, costume, weapons, chief henchman, biography, quote, and comment. As with the book on superheroes, the majority of entries here derive from comic book sources, but the percentage in this volume is much less than in the earlier work. The volume is nicely designed and typeset, and includes numerous black-and-white cover illustrations and movie stills and thirty-two pages of color plates, mostly reproducing comic book and pulp covers. The index references individuals and publishers to title pages.

Super Villains appears less focused than Rovin's earlier work, perhaps because it covers a wider range of sources; for example, Rovin includes Freddy Krueger from *The Nightmare on Elm Street* movie series but not Jason from the *Friday the 13th* series. Why? Similarly, the book lists "The Wolf" from "Little Red Riding Hood," and The Wolf Man from the serial *The Lightning Warrior,* but not the Wolf Man of motion picture fame. Various vampire villains are included, but not all.

The problem of locating specific individuals is also more pronounced in this new volume: Freddy appears in the alphabetical sequence under his *first name,* and is indexed under both first and last name, making it possible to find him either way; but Superman's perennial foe, Lex Luthor (similarly alphabetized by his first name), is *not.* Captain Nemo appears in the "C" section, and is so indexed, but "Nemo" is not. Dr. Gregory Gruesome is listed in the "D" part of the alphabet, for "Doctor," but is not indexed under either of his names.

The absence of cross references either in the text or in the index makes searching these villains unnecessarily difficult, unless one checks entries several different ways, and is an inexcusable lapse in a book published by a major publisher with major production values. Pretty as this volume is, it is less than it could be.

INDIVIDUAL AUTHOR AND CHARACTER DICTIONARIES

Lloyd Alexander

535. Tunnell, Michael O. **The Prydain Companion: A Reference Guide to Lloyd Alexander's Prydain Chronicles.** New York, Westport, CT, & London, Greenwood Press, 1989. xvii, 257 p. LC 88-7705. ISBN 0-313-26585-2.

Alexander's Prydain Chronicles, a five-novel fantasy series written for the young adult market, received much acclaim when it was published in the 1960s.

Contents: "Foreword," by Alexander; "Lloyd Alexander: A Biographical Sketch"; "How to Use the Companion"; "The Prydain Companion"; "Appendix: Category of Entry Headings"; [Bibliographical] "References."

The companion proper is an A-Z guide to the people, places, and things in Alexander's created universe, which is loosely adapted from the Welsh epic, *The Mabinogion.* Major entries are preceded by double asterisks ("**"); single asterisks are used throughout the text to refer the reader to other names or terms that have separate entries (there are also numerous "See" references scattered throughout the text).

Entries range in size from one sentence to fifteen pages (for the chief character of the saga, Taran Wanderer), and tend to be descriptive, utilizing excerpts from the stories themselves to illustrate plot developments and physical descriptions of characters or places. References are keyed to an abbreviations list on page xvi, citing the five main books of the Prydain Chronicles, plus three peripheral books, and two other sources: Charlotte Guest's translation of the *Mabinogion,* and Robert Graves's classic guide to mythology, *The White Goddess;* the citations use a one- to three-letter code plus page number (*e.g.,* "HK 162 + " = *The High King,* page 162 and following).

Tunnell also includes some additional references that cite authors and works listed in the three-page bibliography by surname, year of publication, and pagination (*e.g.,* "Jacobs, 1978:281-282," referencing pages 281-82 of James S. Jacobs's "Lloyd Alexander: A Critical Biography," an unpublished 1978 doctoral dissertation). Also included are numerous quotations from Alexander himself, taken from letters, published interviews or essays, and from personal communications with the author; these add a great deal of insight into the author's work and into the origins of Prydain and its characters. Many entries also feature a pronunciation guide to help those readers unfamiliar with Alexander's orthography.

The final section, "Categories of Entry Headings," is a very useful subject guide to the entries by general topic, covering, for example, "common folk," "characters," "potters," "female characters," "realms," etc. The book is beautifully typeset and arranged, illustrated with very clear black-and-white reproductions of the covers of the eight Prydain books and a Prydain map, and is bound to library standards.

Tunnell's work is authoritative, well written, well referenced, and very well organized. All collections with an interest in modern children's and/or recent fantasy literature should own a copy, as should all research collections. A current bibliography of Alexander's work is also badly needed.

Piers Anthony

536. Anthony, Piers, and Jody Lynn Nye. **Piers Anthony's Visual Guide to Xanth.** New York, Avon Books, 1989. 236 p. LC 89-91277. ISBN 0-380-75749-4 (pbk.).

This beautifully designed and copiously illustrated potpourri includes descriptive chapters on various aspects of Piers Anthony's created world, together with numerous alphabetical lists of characters, places, things, flora, and fauna relating to Xanth.

Contents: "Introduction to Xanth: Great Events in the History of Xanth"; "Xanth, The Demon X(A/N)[th] and the Balance of Existence"; "People of Xanth: Magic and Customs of the People of Xanth, Magicians and Kings, Harpies and Goblins, Demons, Centaurs, Other Races of Equine Descent, Fairies, Imps, Elves, and Gnomes, Ogres, Voles, Zombies, Nymphs and Fauns, Other Human and Humanlike Folk, Other Individuals"; "Places in Xanth: North of the Gap, North Village, The Gap, South of the Gap, Good Magician Humfrey's Castle, Castle Roogna, Centaur Isle, The Gourd"; "Hazards of Xanth"; "The Bestiary of Xanth"; "The Best Things in Xanth Are Free: Flowers, Plants, Trees; Magical Things of Xanth"; "Calendar of Xanth"; "Afterword"; "Appendix: *Crewel Lye,* Chapter I."

The short alphabetical listings of characters, place names, things, flora and fauna, of the Xanth universe that follow many of the narrative sub-sections typically include: the term (in boldfaced or italic type), plus a one-sentence to three-paragraph description. These are illustrated with maps and illustrations by Todd Cameron Hamilton and James Clouse, which are both appropriate and illuminating.

The book's main fault is its relative inaccessibility: an index would have made it useful both as a browser's guide to the author's work and as a reference source for future literary scholarship. Similarly, a brief bibliography of the Xanth books, with a listing of their various editions, would have added another dimension to the volume. Without them, all we have here is a superficially attractive guide that's as lightweight as the fiction it covers. The book is nicely typeset and perfect bound in paper covers.

Now badly outdated.

(Note: *The Xanth Encyclopedia,* mentioned internally as one of Nye's other book credits, is *not* a reference volume, but one of a series of fictional interactive game pastiches of the Xanth universe created with Anthony's approval.)

Arthurian Romances

537. Karr, Phyllis Ann. **The Arthurian Companion: The Legendary World of Camelot and the Round Table.** Oakland, CA, Chaosium, 1997. 570 p. ISBN 1-56882-096-8 (pbk.). A shorter version of this book appeared previously under the title of *The King Arthur Companion.*

Contents: "Foreword to the New Edition"; "Foreword"; "About the Entries"; "About the Text"; "About the Heraldry"; "The Arthurian Companion" (including: Chief Incidents in *Le Morte d'Arthur* [chart]; Arthur and the Orkney Kin [chart]; Lancelot's Kin [chart];

The Fisher Kings and the Kin of Pellinore [chart]); "Arthurian Britain" [map]; "Appendices"; "Bibliographical Note."

Karr's guide is whimsically described in a false subtitle as "a personal guide to the people, places, and things of legendary Camelot and the world beyond, as revealed by the tales themselves, discussed and related by the authoress with warm concern. Herein are the greatest and the humblest in the realm, interpreted in hundred of entries arranged alphabetically for convenient reference and secure pleasure."

Thomas Malory's *Morte d'Arthur* provides the foundation for this guide, along with the French prose authors that Malory used as primary sources, including Chrétien de Troyes. Karr is interested in the literature, not the history or archeology, of King Arthur. The text covers characters, weapons, artifacts, and geographical locations from Arthurian literature. The over 1000 entries are arranged alphabetically by the first distinctive word (*e.g.,* "Queen of the Out Isles" is found under "O" for "Out"), except when the author disregards her rule for reasons not always stated.

A typical entry includes the term itself (boldfaced caps), plus a definition averaging 150 words in length (although some entries on major figures run much longer than this), summarizing the generally accepted version of that person's or place's history in the Arthurian chronicles. Often a citation is provided (in brackets at the end of the entry) to Malory or some other source. Copious "See" references scattered throughout the text help the user move about the book. The appendices include a tentative chronology of Arthur's Reign, which seems somewhat out of place given the author's stated lack of interest in the reality of a King Arthur, plus eighteen general entries on topics such as "Blood Feuds" and "Prophecies," and a list and discussion of the sources used to compile to book.

The author might consider using a strict alphabetical order in a new edition, to facilitate access by inexperienced users, or a detailed index with all the variant spellings of the personal and place names. Still, this is a very well-written and thorough guide to the classic Arthurian mythos, certainly suitable for any large public or academic library.

538. Lacy, Norris J., ed. **The Arthurian Encyclopedia.** New York, Garland Publishing, 1986. xxxvii, 649 p. index. LC 84-48864. ISBN 0-8240-8745-3. New York, Peter Bedrick Books, 1987. xxxvi, 649 p. index. LC 87-47756. ISBN 0-87226-164-6 (pbk.). **The New Arthurian Encyclopedia.** [Rev. ed.]. New York, Garland Publishing, 1991. xxxviii, 577 p. index. LC 90-23700. ISBN 0-8240-4377-4. London, St. James Press, 1991. xxxviii, 577 p. index. LC 91-171258. ISBN 1-55862-125-3. **The New Arthurian Encyclopedia.** Updated pbk. ed. New York, Garland Publishing, 1996. xxxviii, 615 p. index. (Garland Reference Library of the Humanities, Vol. 931). LC 95-36107. ISBN 0-8153-2303-4 (pbk.). Associate Editors: Geoffrey Ashe, Ness Ihle, Marianne E. Kalinke, and Raymond H. Thompson.

Contents (Updated Edition): "Preface," "The Contributors," "List of Entries Arranged by Category," "List of Illustrations," "Selected Bibliography," "Chronology," "The Encyclopedia," "Map," "Index," "Supplement, 1990-1995."

The revised and expanded 1996 edition completely supersedes all previous versions of this work. "Like its predecessor, it deals with Arthuriana of all periods, from the earliest legends and texts to the present." The guide includes 1,200 entries contributed by some 130 scholars from 94 countries. Over 100 of original entries from the 1986 original have been significantly expanded, revised, or replaced, while many others have received minor revision. Discussion of characters has expanded to almost ninety entries from the original thirty. A general index has been added, covering authors, artists, title, places, and subjects, with the pages of the primary discussion shown in bold type.

Entries are organized alphabetically, and typically include the main entry (boldfaced caps) and a general description, averaging 100 words in length. Contributions are signed by the contributors, and most include citations for further reading or for the original material (as in the entry "Godfrey of Viterbo," which notes his 1559 Italian publication). Some entries are much longer than the norm, with a number providing extended analyses and critical evaluations on the major texts or authors.

Much of this book covers King Arthur as a legendary figure of English mythology, tracing his impact on world culture and literature in all media throughout the past thousand years, and is, thus, of only peripheral interest here. However, enough recent works and authors of neo-Arthurian fantasies are covered, particularly in the supplement, to provide some material relevant to the student of modern fantastic literature, although it is sometimes difficult to filter these from the overwhelming mass of text.

This excellent resource includes a collection of black-and-white illustrations and photographs of ruins, manuscripts, movies, and other art forms representing the Arthurian mystique. *The New Arthurian Encyclopedia* is an attractive addition to any academic library, or to large public libraries serving fans or scholars of Arthurian literature.

539. Lerond, Dennis. **An Arthurian Concordance.** [Baltimore, T-K Graphics], 1974. [51] p. (pbk.).

This alphabetical guide to Arthurian characters, places, implements, and events provides a good general introduction to this legendary character and his associated mythological world. A typical entry includes name (all caps) and brief description (in italics, ranging in size from several words to five sentences). No sources are cited (Malory's *Le Morte d'Arthur*, for example), making it difficult to identify the level of Lerond's research. The book is shot from legible typed copy and bound with staples through the spine into stiff paper covers.

Marion Zimmer Bradley

540. Breen, Walter. **The Darkover Concordance: A Reader's Guide.** Berkeley, CA, Pennyfarthing Press, 1979. ix, 163 p. LC 79-84472. ISBN 0-930800-10-9; ISBN 0-930800-07-9 (pbk.).

Bradley's former husband here contributes, with the cooperation of the author and the fan organization, "Friends of Darkover," an excellent alphabetical guide to the Darkover universe.

Contents: "Foreword," by Bradley; "To the Reader," by Breen; "Chronological Sequence of the Darkover Novels"; "Guide to Pronunciation of Darkover Words"; "Concordance" [141 pages]; Appendices: "The Ballad of Hastur and Cassilda"; "The Ballad Commonly Called 'The Outlaw'"; "The Oath of the Comhi-Letzii"; "Darkovan Proverbs and Proverbial Expressions"; "Some Notes on the New Hebrides Communal Songs"; "The Darkover Novels: Publishing Histories and Story Summaries"; "Darkovan Genealogies."

A typical entry includes: character name (boldfaced; italics signify words of Darkover origin, while those in all caps are characters who actually appear in the story in question);

a description ranging in length from a few words to a double-columned page; and citation (boldfaced, in the form **"WW 97"** for page 97 of *The World Wreckers*). Excellently rendered line drawings by Melisa Michaels are scattered throughout the text.

The guide is exceptionally detailed, referencing even typographical errors and misspellings of names in the original texts and noting various inconsistencies in the saga; and the appendices provide very useful supplemental materials, including a complete bibliography of the Darkover books, with all known English-language and foreign-language reprint editions and complete bibliographical data.

A new edition including the Darkover novels of the last decade would certainly be justified, particularly in the wake of Marion Zimmer Bradley's death; even without coverage of the numerous recent books in the series, Breen's volume will be an essential starting point for any student of this well-known author's work.

Edgar Rice Burroughs

541. Brady, Clark A. **The Burroughs Cyclopaedia: Characters, Places, Fauna, Flora, Technologies, Languages, Ideas and Terminologies Found in the Works of Edgar Rice Burroughs.** Jefferson, NC, McFarland & Co., 1996. 402 p. index. LC 96-32787. ISBN 0-89950-896-0.

Contents: "Preface"; "Abbreviations Used"; "The Cyclopaedia"; Appendices ("A. Chronology of Events in Burroughs' Fiction"; "B. Selected Words from Featured Languages"; "C. Story Map for Burroughs' Fiction Works"); "Bibliography"; "Index."

Brady has compiled an inclusive list of characters, places, terms, and ideas found in the fiction of Edgar Rice Burroughs, as well as terms related to that fiction (for example, *Argosy* is the magazine in which of the author's several publications first appeared), including unfamiliar or made-up words, older words or allusions not necessarily recognized by the modern reader, and foreign-language words or phrases. Abbreviations refer to the 87 books covered in the text, but the "Abbreviations Used" section is clearly organized and makes a nice guide to the author's many fantasy series. Materials are organized alphabetically for the approximately 4,000 entries, including copious "See" references.

A typical entry includes: term or place or character name (bold type), definition (averaging 50 words), and an abbreviated reference to the book(s) in which the term appears, sometimes including specific series, section, and chapter numbers. Cross-references are listed in bold type. Though easy to use, the index gathers together repeated entries and often gives the multiple page numbers where they are discussed, without distinction. The appendices are full of useful information for Burroughs fans. The volume is nicely typeset and bound to library standards.

In comparing Brady's guide to McWhorter's book (see #544), both volumes contain terms or names that the other misses, and each sometimes includes more information about a particular character than the other. Brady's comprehensive index gives his tome a slight edge, but scholars of ERB's writings will want access to both works.

542. Harwood, John, and Allan Howard. **Tarzan Encyclopedia,** in *Burroughs Bulletin* no. 45/46 (January/February, 1975): [1-41]. (pbk.).

This alphabetical guide to the persons, places, and things of the Tarzan mythos was issued as a special double issue of this well-known Burroughs fanzine, with both the magazine and book title appearing on the front cover.

A typical entry includes: term (all caps), brief description (one to ten sentences, but occasionally extending to several paragraphs for major entries), and book reference (in the form "(LION)" for *Tarzan and the Lion Man*). Included in the main alphabetical sequence are the Tarzan books, under the second element of the title (for example, *Tarzan at the Earth's Core* is referenced as EARTH'S CORE, TARZAN AT THE).

A typical book entry includes: title (all caps), brief bibliographical data (first magazine serialization, with magazine title and date, and first book publication, with publisher and year), and extensive plot summary (ranging in size from one to two full columns of text). An interesting and very useful feature of this guide is a series of brief dictionaries of the main languages used in the Tarzan saga, gathered together under the generic term "LANGUAGE," and subarranged by language and then alphabetically by word, each with its English-language equivalent. The volume is shot from legible typed copy arranged in double 8.5" x 11" columns and stapled through the spine.

In comparing Harwood and Howard's dictionary with McWhorter's (see #544) and Brady's (see #541), all three volumes contain about the same level of description; however, the former's inclusion of mini-dictionaries of Burroughs's invented languages, as well as extensive separate plot summaries of the Tarzan books, and a guide to the Clayton (*i.e.,* Tarzan's) family, makes the *Tarzan Encyclopedia* valuable in its own right.

A more elaborate and updated version, with better production values, should be contemplated; the original is now virtually impossible to locate.

543. Kudlay, Robert R., and Joan Leiby. **Burroughs' Science Fiction, with an Analytical Subject and Name Index.** Geneseo, NY, School of Library and Information Science, State University College of Arts and Science, 1973. 236 p. index. (Geneseo Studies in Library and Information Science, No. 5). LC 74-172705 (pbk.).

This curious set of indices was evidently produced as a library science school project.

Contents: "Preface"; "Introduction," by Kudlay; "Introduction to the Indexes"; "I. Pellucidar"; "Symmes' Hole"; "Synopsis of the Pellucidarian Saga"; "Animal Kingdom of Pellucidar"; "Tribes of Pellucidar"; "People of Pellucidar"; "A Note on Aging and Ages"; "Burroughs' Social Thought"; "How to Use the Index"; "Index to Pellucidar"; "II. Other Science-Fiction Romance"; "Synopsis"; "Indexes: Caspak, Cave Girl, Lost Continent, Moon, Poloda"; "III. Bibliographies": "Burroughs in the Literature"; "Bibliography"; "Symmes' Bibliography"; "IV. Illustrations."

The section on Pellucidar, the underworld kingdom created by Burroughs in a seven-book series, comprises about half of the text (110 pages). This chapter is broken into various sub-sections, each dealing with a specific theme (*e.g.,* "Tribes of Pellucidar"), under which terms or names are listed in alphabetical order, in chart format, with related terms such as "Description" and "Ruler(s)" (in the tribes section), or individual "Names," "Title(s)," "Native Land," and "Relatives" (in the people section), sorted into their respective columns. Each world (Pellucidar, Caspak, etc.) is then cross-referenced separately at the end of its respective section or chapter to an abbreviation representing the book title and page and/or chapter number of the Burroughs's work from which it derives (*e.g.,* "P(15)" = *Pellucidar,* page 15). The volume is decorated with several amateurishly drawn maps and fannish illustrations, and includes a much outdated bibliography of secondary sources on Burroughs. The book is shot from typed copy, printed on yellowing paper, and poorly bound in paper covers.

A one-alphabet dictionary format would have been much more useful here, together with a single index, but the volume still provides some hard-to-find data for the diehard Burroughs fan. Prefer McWhorter's and Brady's guides (see #544 and #541).

544. McWhorter, George T. **Burroughs Dictionary: An Alphabetical List of Proper Names, Words, Phrases, and Concepts Contained in the Published Works of Edgar Rice Burroughs.** Lanham, MD & New York, University Press of America, 1987. xiii, 446 p. LC 87-14266. ISBN 0-8191-6512-3.

This long overdue guide to a master fantasy writer's many works organizes into one alphabetical sequence every place, person, and term appearing in Burroughs's seventy-seven published works, omitting only those general geographical locations (such as "Africa") for which no explanation is necessary.

A typical entry includes: name (boldface), description, and citation (keyed to a one- to three-letter code, in the form [TC] for *Tarzan and the Castaways*). The descriptions often include brief illuminating quotations from Burroughs's original text. The citations lack page or chapter numbers; short stories included in larger collections are separately cited.

In addition to the alphabetical directory, which comprises the vast majority of the work, McWhorter includes an introductory section of explanatory notes, and a two-page Edgar Rice Burroughs chronology at the end. The author also cites many other reference works throughout the text, both as explanation to terms and personages no longer part of the current American consciousness and to demonstrate Burroughs's antecedants. Roughly 6,500 entries are included, a number far exceeding the combined total of all other available sources. The book is shot from very legible word-processed copy and bound to library standards.

McWhorter's descriptions are not as detailed as some of those appearing in Roy's more limited work on the eleven Martian books (see #545), or in Harwood and Howard's comprehensive guide to the Tarzan series (see #542), and Brady's work (see #541) includes some terms that McWhorter misses (and vice versa). Still, scholars of Burroughs's fiction and libraries with a popular culture focus will both need access to this book.

545. Roy, John Flint. **A Guide to Barsoom: Eleven Sections of References in One Volume, Dealing with the Martian Stories Written by Edgar Rice Burroughs.** New York, A Del Rey Book, Ballantine Books, 1976. [viii], 200 p. LC 76-11849. ISBN 0-345-28595-6 (pbk.).

Roy, a long-time Burroughs fan, compiled this mass-market guide to the Martian tales as a tribute to the author and his work.

Contents: "Introduction"; "I. A Brief History of Pre-Carter Barsoom"; "II. A Geography of Barsoom, Including a Gazetteer-Index and Hemispheric and Polar Maps of Its Surface"; "III. A Biography of Barsoom, Including a Dictionary of People, Past and Present, Whose Names Appear in the Barsoomian Sagas"; "IV. The Flora and Fauna of Barsoom, Including a Dictionary of Barsoomian Plants and Animals"; "V. Measurements on Barsoom—Linear, Time, Monetary—and a List of Barsoomian Numbers"; "VI. The Language, Religions, and Customs of Barsoom"; "VII. A General Barsoomian Glossary: Terms, Titles, Organizations, Games, Weapons, Buildings, Streets, Etc."; "VIII. Quotations, Proverbs, and Expletives—From the Rich Heritage of Barsoom and the Pen of John Carter"; "IX. Barsoomian Science and Invention"; "X. Through Space to Barsoom?"; "XI. Edgar Rice Burroughs: A Brief Biographical Sketch"; "Acknowledgments and Sources"; "From the Author."

Each chapter includes three to five pages of narrative background materials on the topic in question, followed by alphabetically arranged guides at the end of most chapters providing details about specific places, characters, things, concepts, and flora and fauna of Burroughs's imagined Mars. A typical entry includes: name (boldface), citation (with two- to three-letter keys to the eleven book titles, plus chapter number, in the form "*PM*/18,19" for *A Princess of Mars,* Chapters 18-19), and an annotation ranging in size from a few words to several pages.

For individuals, Roy generally gives their complete history and background as described in the books, including parentage, associates, family members, noble titles, and an exact account of what they accomplished during the saga. It is obvious that Roy has contributed some of the "history" to this volume, particularly in the narrative sections; this is perhaps inevitable given the inconsistencies in the original novels.

The descriptions herein are generally better wrought and more fully fleshed than those in McWhorter's dictionary (see #544). However, the lack of an overall index, and the fractured organization of Roy's guides (four separate alphabetical lists as opposed to one A-Z sequence in McWhorter's volume), makes the latter much more accessible. *A Guide to Barsoom* is nicely illustrated throughout with line drawings by Neal MacDonald.

David Eddings and Leigh Eddings

546. Eddings, David, and Leigh Eddings. **The Rivan Codex: Ancient Texts of the Belgariad and the Malloreon.** New York, A Del Rey Book, Ballantine Books, 1998. 394 p. LC 98-29234. ISBN 0-345-42402-6. London, HarperCollins, 394 p. 1998. ISBN 0-00-224677-5; ISBN 0-00-224702-X (deluxe ed.). New York, A Del Rey Book, Ballantine Books, 1999. 600 p. LC 99-90778. ISBN 0-345-43586-9 (pbk.). London, Voyager, 1999. 600 p. ISBN 0-00-648349-6 (pbk.).

Contents: "Introduction"; "Preface: The Personal History of Belgarath the Sorcerer"; "Part I: The Holy Books"; "Part II: The Histories"; "Part III: The Battle of Vo Mimbre"; "Part IV: Preliminary Studies to the Malloreon"; "Part V: The Mallorean Gospels"; "Part VI: A Summary of Current Events"; "Afterward" [sic].

First written to help guide the development of a fantasy novel in the Eddings' Mallorean Sequence, *The Rivan Codex* is a sociological textbook to the world of the epic, twelve-book fantasy series. The lengthy introduction and shorter afterword provide first-person presentations that move briskly through the literary history of the fantastic romance, describe its basic elements, and give advice on what to read and how to write to succeed in the genre.

"Part II: The Histories," which comprises the greater part of the text, looks at each of the kingdoms mentioned in the series (Alorn, Sendaria, Arendia, Ulgoland, Nyissa, and Angarak), and systematically describes the elements of each, such as geography (with maps), people, history, coinage, costume, address, rank, population, holidays, commerce, and manners. Other sections provide the texts to the holy books of the kingdoms in a Biblical style of writing that supplements the existing fiction. Footnotes explain how the authors changed their material as they developed the series.

Although not really a reference guide, *The Rivan Codex* provides an enjoyable and informative adjunct to this popular fantasy series. Suitable for public libraries.

Alan Dean Foster

547. Teague, Robert. **A Guide to the Commonwealth: The Official Guide to Alan Dean Foster's Humanx Commonwealth Universe.** Roy, UT, Galagraphics, 1985. 70 p. (pbk.). Illustrated by Michael Goodwin.

This interesting and well-illustrated reference book focuses on the fictional future universe created by American SF writer Foster in a series of a dozen novels and several short stories.

After an Introduction by Foster and Forewords by Teague and Goodwin, the first section, "Galographics," provides a guide to place names in the "known universe," with separate alphabetical listings of worlds in the AAnn Empire, The Blight, and the Humanx Commonwealth (including physical descriptions, brief histories, and lists of races, etc.). This section also includes maps of the three empires, and of the known universe as explored by mankind. Part Two, "Natural History," gives two alphabetical lists of flora and fauna in the universe, with the worlds on which they occur, and chief attributes.

Section Three, "Intelligence," lists all known alien races (alphabetically by name), extinct races, a rendition of the Thranx alphabet, diagrams (drawings) of aliens, and the Commonwealth T-Standard Calendar. Part Four, "Technology," includes drawings and lists of the spacecraft and weaponry employed by the intelligent races known to man. A final section, "General," provides "Commonwealth Chronology"; "Classification of Planets"; "Measurement Standards"; "Chemicals, Drugs, Medicines, and Poisons"; and "Mineralogy." The book is attractively designed and typeset in 8.5" x 11" format and bound with staples into paper covers.

Although an index would have been desirable, plus a brief bibliography of Foster's works (the authors only include a barebones list of the books consulted, without further data), Teague and Goodwin's excellent guide provides virtually everything that the fan and scholar would want to know about Foster's fictional world.

A new edition would be welcome.

Diana Gabaldon

548. Gabaldon, Diana. **The Outlandish Companion: In Which Much Is Revealed Regarding Claire and Jamie Fraser, Their Lives and Times, Antecedents, Adventures, Companions, and Progeny, with Learned Commentary (and Many Footnotes) by Their Humble Creator.** New York, Delacorte Press, 1999. xxix, 577 p. LC 99-22969. ISBN 0-385-32413-8. Toronto, Doubleday Canada, 1999. ISBN 0-385-25739-2. As: **Through the Stones: The Diana Gabaldon Companion.** London, Century, 1999. xxix, 577 p. ISBN 0-712-68099-3; ISBN 0-712-67978-2 (pbk.).

Contents: "Acknowledgments"; "Prologue"; "Part One: Synopses" (*Outlander, Dragonfly in Amber, Voyager, Drums of Autumn*); "Part Two: Characters" ("Where Characters Come From: Mushrooms, Onions, and Hard Nuts"; "Cast of Characters"; "I Get Letters . . ."; "Magic, Medicine, and White Ladies"); "Part Three: Family Trees" ("A Genealogical Note"); "Part Four: Comprehensive Glossary and Pronunciation Guide" ("A Very Brief Guide to Gaelic Grammar"; "Comprehensive Glossary of Foreign Terms [Including British Slang]"); "Part Five: Outlandish Web Sites and Online Venues" ("The Web Sites"; "The Diana Gabaldon Home Page"; "LOL—The Ladies (and Lads) of Lallybroch"; "Through the Stones"; "The Outlandish Timeline"; "Clan Outlandish on AOL"; "The Free Gallery of Authors' Voices"; "CompuServe Readers and Writers Ink Group"); "Part Six: Research" ("Researching Historical Fiction: Hot Dogs and Beans"; "Botanical Medicine: Don't Try This at Home"; "Penicillin Online: A Writer's Thread");

"Part Seven: Where Titles Come from (and Other Matters of General Interest)" ("*Outlander* vs. *Cross Stitch*"; "The Gabaldon Theory of Time Travel"); "Part Eight: The View from Lallybrock: Objects of Vertue, Objects of Use" ("Lallybroch"; "Arma Virumque Cano"); "Part Nine: Frequently Asked Questions" ("Answers"); "Part Ten: Controversy" ("Communication"); "Part Eleven: Work in Progress: Excerpts of Future Books" ("*The Fiery Cross*"; "*King, Farewell*"; "*The Cannibal's Art*"); "Annotated Bibliography" ("Eighteenth Century"; "Scotland"; "Medicine"; "African Cultures"; "Ghosts and Ghost Stories"; "Literature"; "Language Resources"; "Magic"; "Medicine [Including all Herbals]"; "Natural History Guides and Resources"; "North Carolina"; "Foods and Cookery"; "Native American Cultures and History, Etc."; "Rather Odd Books"; "Miscellaneous"); "Appendixes": "I: Errata"; "II: Gaelic (Gaidhlig) Resources"; "III: Poems and Quotations"; "IV: Roots: A Brief Primer on Genealogical Research"; "V: A Brief Discography of Celtic Music"; "VI: Foreign Editions, Audiotapes, and Strange, Strange Covers"; "VII: The Methadone List."

This incredibly varied guide to the Outlander Series, a set of time-travel romances by Diana Gabaldon, provides everything one might want to know about this popular series of time-traveling fantasies. The prologue alone makes a good introduction to the author, whose remarkable narrative voice humorously relates how she became an author of fiction while researching bird gizzards.

Part One is made up of lengthy plot summaries (each a minimum of five pages) of four of the novels; Part Two is a character dictionary, introduced by an essay on how the characters come to life for Gabaldon, plus a small narrative essay on the real-life historical figures in her books. This is followed by an alphabetical list of the fictional characters in the novels. A typical entry includes: character name (in boldfaced type), brief description (5-25 words), and the novel or novels in which the character appears (in brackets).

Part Three contains genealogical charts, family crests, and a dictionary of foreign terms, plus a pronunciation guide. Part Five provides a list and description of a dozen Web sites devoted to the series, including Gabaldon's own. Part Six is a research guide, including details on how to use any library's electronic catalog (Gabaldon clearly knows her way around an OPAC). Part Seven explains the differences in the British and American editions of her works, and where the titles of the books originated.

Part Eight is a collection of excerpts describing places and things mentioned in the books, accompanied by illustrations from some of them. Part Nine contains a FAQ of some sixty questions from the author's fans, together with Gabaldon's responses. In Part Ten, the writer discusses some of the difficulties that certain fans have voiced about her books, such as depictions of sex, profanity, homosexuality, abortion, and wife-beating. The last part of the book features excerpts from future books in the series.

The author's bibliography will be helpful to fans who want to do more research into material found in her books, whether it be historical or medical. Any fan of the Outlander books will be enthralled with this inside look at a very popular series. The text is informative and entertaining, and the illustrations (mostly black-and-white photographs and sketches) quietly and attractively supplement the text without supplanting it. Those who have not read the series will find this guide a wonderful instruction manual for writing and research, and an inspiration to pick up the author's first novel.

Although not really suitable for reference collections because of the highly varied material and the absence of an index, *The Outlandish Companion* is still highly recommended, both for the many fans of this series and the many libraries serving them.

Frank Herbert

549. McNelly, Willis E., ed. **The Dune Encyclopedia.** New York, G. P. Putnam's Sons, 1984. ix, 526 p. LC 84-4824. ISBN 0-399-12950-2. New York, Berkley Books, 1984. ix, 526 p. ISBN 0-425-06813-7 (pbk.). London, Corgi Books, 1984. ix, 526 p. ISBN 0-552-99131-7 (pbk.).

McNelly's book differs from the other guides included in this section in two respects: it includes contributions from forty-three fans and scholars, arranged in an alphabetical, encyclopedic format; and much of the material is invented, though based upon the future world created by Frank Herbert in his six Dune sagas. Thus, not all the characters or places mentioned by Herbert in the Dune books may be listed; and those that do may have entries featuring a combination of "factual" (*i.e.,* based upon Herbert's story lines) and supplemental material created by the contributors.

Thus, the list of "Emperors of the Known Universe," by Robert Reginald, although it incorporates the few emperors actually mentioned by Herbert, and was used by McNelly to coordinate the "history" of the Dune mythos in this *Encyclopedia,* is largely invented out of whole cloth and relatively useless to the student of Herbert. Even the bibliographical citations at the end of each article, and the bibliography proper at the end of the book, both feature nonexistent titles and authors, as well as legitimate cross references to other articles of interest. The result, while amusing, is more an exercise in literary pastiche than a real guide to the author's work.

Robert E. Howard

550. Weinberg, Robert. **The Annotated Guide to Robert E. Howard's Sword & Sorcery.** West Linn, OR, Starmont House, 1976. vii, 152 p. LC 76-16708. ISBN 0-916732-20-7 (produced in 1980); ISBN 0-916732-00-2 (pbk.).

Although the reference value of this guide is minimal, it is mentioned here because it complements *A Gazeteer of the Hyborian World of Conan,* by Lee N. Falconer (*i.e.,* Julian May; see #21).

Contents: "Introduction"; "Solomon Kane"; "King Kull"; "Bran Mak Morn and the Picts"; "James Allison"; "Turlogh Dubh"; "Non-Series Stories"; "Conan"; "The Chronological Conan"; "The Conan Saga" (as written by Robert E. Howard).

Each chapter covers a specific Howard fantasy hero. Several pages of narrative text at the beginning of each section give background information on the character, a physical description of his attributes, a brief account of his life as described in Howard's stories, a chronological listing of those fictions, and other material of interest.

The remainder of each chapter lists the stories chronologically by publication date, or occasionally in reading order, a typical entry providing: title (all caps), magazine title (in italics) and month and year of publication, or book title (in all caps), publisher, and year of publication, for those stories that appeared first in anthologies or collections; a list of the principal characters featured in that tale; several paragraphs of plot summary; and a one-to-three-paragraph commentary. The book is nicely typeset and the cloth edition is bound to library standards.

The absence of an index makes access to the material in this volume unnecessarily difficult, requiring the reader to peruse whole sections to find specific character references. Although May's book (see #21) does include an excellent A-Z guide to the geographical names and principal tribes and states of Hyboria (the Conan fictional universe), but not to the rest of Howard's creations, a concise, one-volume alphabetical guide to the proper names in Howard's entire canon has yet to be written.

Robert Jordan

551. Jordan, Robert, and Teresa Patterson. **The World of Robert Jordan's** *The Wheel of Time.* New York, Tor, 1997. 304 p. index. LC 97-13271. ISBN 0-312-86219-9 (acid free paper).

Contents: "Section 1: The Wheel and the Power": Chapter 1: "The Wheel and the Pattern"; Chapter 2: "The One Power and the True Source." "Section 2: The Age of Legends": Chapter 3: "The Age of Legends"; Chapter 4: "The Fall into Shadow"; Chapter 5: "The Dark One and the Male Forsaken"; Chapter 6: "The Female Forsaken and the Dark-friends"; Chapter 7: "Shadowspawn"; Chapter 8: "The Breaking of the World." "Section 3: The World Since the Breaking": Chapter 9: "Formation of the White Tower"; Chapter 10: "Rise and Fall of the Ten Nations"; Chapter 11: "The Second Dragon and the Rise of Artur Hawkwing"; Chapter 12: "The Reign of the High King"; Chapter 13: "The War of the Hundred Years"; Chapter 14: "The New Era." "Section 4: Some Narrative Paintings of Questionable Authenticity." "Section 5: The World of the Wheel": Chapter 15: "The World After the Breaking"; Chapter 16: "Shara"; Chapter 17: "Seanchan"; Chapter 18: "The Exotic Animals of Seanchan"; Chapter 19: "The Sea Folk Islands"; Chapter 20: "The Aiel"; Chapter 21: "The Ogier"; Chapter 22: "The Ways"; Chapter 23: *"Tel'aran'rhiod."* "Section 6: Within the Land": Chapter 24: "The White Tower"; Chapter 25: "The Children of the Light"; Chapter 26: "The Military of the Land"; Chapter 27: "Andor"; Chapter 28: "The Borderlands: Shienar, Arafel, Kandor, and Saldaea"; Chapter 29: "Cairhien"; Chapter 30: "The Other Nations"; Chapter 31: "Holidays and the Calendar"; Chapter 32: "The Prophecies of the Dragon." "Index."

Not an A-Z encyclopedia as such, Jordan and Patterson's guide is a companion to the multi-book fantasy series *The Wheel of Time* by Robert Jordan, covering through Book Seven of the epic. The preface invites the reader to include this work canonically with the series, and the material here is inserted into the author's fictional universe with the tone and style of a history/sociology text. While fans will have no difficulty with the style and structure of the volume, it is virtually impenetrable for someone unfamiliar with Jordan's world, providing neither ready reference for the fan nor giving a general overview of the series. Indeed, the text uses the specialized language of the novels without even trying to explain itself to the novice.

The index does some help in locating some specific information on characters, places, and objects in the series, and where they are actually mentioned. Primary page references are listed in boldfaced type, while illustrations are noted in italics. There is no doubt as to the beauty of the book's overall production: it includes 70 new, full-color paintings of world maps, character portraits, objects, flags, landscapes, and the seven dustjackets created by artist Darrell Sweet for the novels, as well as previously published maps of the world and the Seanchan Empires, some of them reproduced in black-and-white.

This guide would perhaps be more suitable setting next to a shelf full of Jordan's epic fictions rather than on the library reference shelf, but it remains an excellent addition for any public library circulating the series. Fans of Jordan's work will treasure this occasionally interesting sideshow to the novels.

Stephen King

552. Beahm, George. **Stephen King from A to Z: An Encyclopedia of His Life and Work.** Kansas City, MO, Andrews McMeel Publishing, 1998. xiv, 251 p. LC 98-22006. ISBN 0-8362-6914-4 (pbk.).

Contents: "Stephen King, Beowulf and the Necessary Landscapes of Darkness," by Michael R. Collings; "Introduction: 'Stephen's Kingdom'," by Beahm; the Encyclopedia proper, which includes the following contributed essays: "*Bag of Bones:* A Review," by Michael R. Collings, "Stephen King's Face on Barn?" by Annie Lynn Steffard, and "Literary Posterity," by Anne Rice, plus eleven pieces by Beahm.

This fan encyclopedia covers the master's books and stories, and the television and motion picture adaptations of King's works, plus anything else that is directly or peripherally related to King, including the author's opinion on, say, astrology (he doesn't believe in it). Entries typically average eighty words, though there are fourteen mini-essays blended into text.

The sections covering King's books include: citation, dedication, table of contents, a summary, and, fairly often, quotations from published reviews and from King himself. Some of the quotes, which are also featured in the film entries, are intended to be humorous, coming from somewhat less prestigious sources (see, for example, Joe-Bob Briggs's coverage of the motion picture, *Children of the Corn*); others derive from *Library Journal, Kirkus Reviews,* and *The New York Times Book Reviews,* to name but a few.

The interpolated mini-essays are printed with a gray backdrop to make them stand out in the text. While occasionally interesting, too often these articles focus on George Beahm the commentator and personage rather than on Stephen King the author, as in the

"B is for Bachman" piece, giving the entire book a "faanish" aura that is quite unfortunate. The foreword by well-known scholar Michael R. Collings is both informative and entertaining, as usual with this critic. The volume is illustrated throughout with clear, black-and-white cover illustrations, photographs of King and his associates, and a few line drawings.

While *Stephen King from A to Z* is a fun, knowledgeable browse for King fans, there's very little here that isn't available somewhere else.

553. Spignesi, Stephen J. **The Lost Work of Stephen King: A Guide to Unpublished Manuscripts, Story Fragments, Alternative Versions, and Oddities.** Secaucus, NJ, Birch Lane Press, 1998. xxii, 361 p. index. LC 98-24116. ISBN 1-555972-469-2 (alk. paper).

Contents: "Acknowledgments"; "Preface: The Hidden World of the Lost King"; "Introduction: Welcome to Our Nightmare!", "Stephen King: A Life in the Dread Zone, 1947-2000"; "The Lost Work, 1956-the Present"; "The Final Word"; "Appendixes": "A. How to Become a Stephen King Collector"; "B. The Royal Library: A Reader's Guide to the Work of Stephen King, from *Carrie* to *Bag of Bones,* 1974-1998"; "The King of Hollywood: Stephen King Movies, from 1976's *Carrie* to 1998's *Storm of the Century*"; "D. Books About Stephen King"; "E. Sources and Resources."

Spignesi discusses and summarizes 75 works or fragments by King that even the most ardent fan of the author may not have seen. The entries are arranged chronologically by publication or writing date, with a typical entry including: title, quotation from the piece, brief description (labelled "What It is," averaging 20-100 words), "Chances of Finding a Copy" (50-100 words), commentary and description (20-200 words), plot summary (250-300), citation (giving year, title, publisher, and place of publication), and publishing history (if any). The summary section is highlighted for the reader with a skull and crossbones icon.

Over fifty of the items included are short pieces of fiction and nonfiction, including introductions to the books of others, interviews, etc. Plot summaries, especially for the books, can be longer than average, summarizing the work chapter by chapter whenever possible. (The author did not personally examine every item.) An insert provides black-and-white pictures of King, his home, reproductions of parts of some items listed in the book, and a year-by-year chronology of the author, "A Life is the Dread Zone," in block format from 1947-2000.

Appendix A offers advice on how to collect King's work. Appendix B provides summaries and light commentaries for all of the author's published works, including his short stories. Appendix C reviews the movie adaptations (television or feature film) of King's works. Appendix D describes five books about King. Appendix E gives the phone numbers, addresses, and Web sites for beginning a collection of Stephen King's works. The index notes all mentions of a piece throughout the guide, cross-referenced to page numbers.

Though most of the commentary herein lacks any critical focus, with even the earliest pieces cited as indicating King's burgeoning genius, Spignesi does document some items that even diehard King fans might have missed. Recommended for the library of any serious fan, all libraries serving fans, and academic libraries collecting Stephen King.

554. Spignesi, Stephen J. **The Shape Under the Sheet: The Complete Stephen King Encyclopedia.** Ann Arbor, MI, Popular Culture, Ink., 1991. xx, 780 p. LC 91-61010. ISBN 1-56075-018-9. As: **The Complete Stephen King Encyclopedia: The Definitive Guide to**

the Works of America's Master of Horror. Chicago, Contemporary Books, 1991? xx, 780 p. ISBN 0-8092-3911-6; ISBN 0-8092-3818-7 (pbk.).

Contents: "Contents Classifieds"; "Foreword by the Publisher"; "Introduction"; "Part I: The Shape Takes Form: An Introduction to Stephen King & His Work"; "Part II: 'I Write Fearsomes': Inside Stephen King"; "Part III: 'Yerrrnnn Unber Whunnnn Fayunnnn': Stephen King Fans, Conventions & Collectors"; "Part IV: A Visit to *Castle Rock:* A Look at the Stephen King Newsletter"; "Part V: Horrors Small and Large: Stephen King's 'Strange and Wonderful World'" ("Published Works, 1974-1990"; "Unpublished & Uncollected Works"; "Motion Picture Adaptations"; "Miscellaneous Formats: Spoken Word Recordings & Poetry"; "A Stroll Among the Headstones: A Guided Tour"); "Part VI: Beneath the Sheet: Commentary on King's 'Marketable Obsessions'"; "Part VII: In a Region with No Proper Name: The Hidden Horrors of Stephen King"; "Illustrations."

This rather overwhelming collection of articles and essays, fiction, bibliographies, a biography, concordances, indices, interviews, material on motion pictures, published works, references, unpublished and uncollected works, and miscellanea contains 82 discrete sections divided into seven major chapters.

Part I introduces us to King's background, and discusses the meaning of his metaphor, The Shape Under the Sheet. Part II offers interviews with friends and relatives, articles, and other features that attempt to bring us still closer the "King the man." Part III concentrates on the world of King fandom. Part IV offers full details on the history and content of *Castle Rock: The Stephen King Newsletter.* Part V includes concordances and features designed to facilitate the exploration of King's work: a first line index, a section on his film adaptations (including many related sidebars), a discussion of his poetry, an annotated guide to the audiotape versions of his stories, plus several features and character indexes. Part VI offers perspective and commentary through an annotated bibliography and interview with King's literary contemporaries on King's place in American fiction. Part VII examines stories unfinished or as yet unwritten by King.

Throughout this large mass of data, there are several features meant to guide the reader. The end pages reference King's works by title and page numbers. The left running headers identify each section of the book. The concordance (p. 152-456), which is really a who's who and what's what of all of King's published novels and collected short stories issued through 1990, is arranged in chronological order by publication date. A typical entry provides: story or novel title, dedication, table of contents (if any), and an alphabetically-arranged dictionary to each work, each subdivided into three sections: People, Places, Things. The explanations for each character or term are very brief and simplistic, usually expressed in phrases rather than whole sentences, and the choice of entries itself is highly questionable in some cases (referenced under the novel *Carrie,* for example, is "Stephen King's First Use of Double-Margin Exclamation Points"; is this *really* something anyone needs to know?). This overtly amateurish arrangement is both unnecessarily cumbersome and difficult to use, even for dedicated Stephen King fans.

The character index (p. 650-659) cross-references character surnames to the code numbers assigned each work in the concordance section; one can only determine these numbers, however, by checking a separate "Page Number Key to Master Codes Cited in the Character Indexes," a very awkward way indeed of accessing this information. The character index itself is typeset in very small, boldfaced, all-caps characters arranged in a five-column format that is almost illegible to middle-aged eyes.

The concordance to 39 unpublished and uncollected works on p. 460-542 became the seed for the guide later published as *The Lost Work of Stephen King*. The section on motion picture adaptations is arranged chronogically by release date, a typical entry including: distributor, running time, rating, director, screenplay, producer, associate producer, editor, directory of photography, music, art directors, budget, gross box-office receipts, cast (with character names), commentary, and brief quotations from reviews of the movie, with author and publication cited, but no dates or paginations. Entries are broken up with interviews and other odd information.

Though the overall tone of the book is fan-to-fan, some sections seem almost too casual, with occasional sexist comments from the author that are intended to be humorous but fall way short of the mark.

The Encyclopedia contains an incredible collection of Stephen King minutiae for readers and trivia buffs, but while it does include some useful reference material buried amidst all the verbiage, the volume's organization is so sloppy and convoluted that accessing the data becomes a real chore at times. Also, of course, Stephen King has produced a large number of new works in the years since this guide was originally published, making it increasingly out-of-date and overwrought. For diehard fans only.

Katherine Kurtz

555. Kurtz, Katherine, and Robert Reginald. **Codex Derynianus: Being a Comprehensive Guide to the Peoples, Places, & Things of the Derynye & the Human Worlds of the XI Kingdoms: Including Historyes of the Major & Minor States & the Occurrences Which Have Been of Most Importance to Them: With Compleat Biographyes of the Prominent Personages & Holy Saints of Gwynedd, Torenth, Meara, Bremagne, Mooryn, Howicce, Llannedd, The Connait, R'Kassi, Orsal & Tralia, Fallon, Byzantyun, The Forcinn Buffer States, & the Other Countryes of This Region from the Birth of Our Lord Jesus Christ unto Anno Domini MCXXVI: Together with a Detail'd Chronological Historye of the Great Sovereign Kingdom of Gwynedd and All Her Neighbours: Also Including a Liturgical Calendar of the Saints of Gwynedd: With Many Lists of the Patriarchs, Primates, Kings, Princes, Dukes, Earls, Counts, & Other Nobles & Notables of These States: With Much True Opinions & Observations Regarding Same.** San Bernardino, CA, Borgo Press; Grass Valley, CA, Underwood Books. 1998. 329 p. [6 maps, 3 genealogical charts]. LC 96-44355. signed, ltd., slipcased cloth edition of 500 copies. ISBN 0-89370-011-8 (Borgo Press); ISBN 1-887424-33-4 (Underwood Books). Cover art by Hannah M. G. Shapero. Maps by Charles Morehead.

Contents: "Dedicatio/Dedication"; "Introductio/Introduction": "Uncovering the Codex"; "Codex Derynianus"; "Praefatio/Preface: Gaudeamus!"; "Ordo Temporum: A Chronology of the XI Kingdoms"; "Calendarium Liturgicum XI Regnorum: A Liturgical Calendar of the XI Kingdoms"; "Genealogiae Familiarum Regiarum XI Regnorum: Genealogies of the Royal Families of the XI Kingdoms"; "Tabulae XI Regnorum: Maps of the XI Kingdoms," by Charles Morehead; "De Auctoribus et Bibliographia Librorum/About the Authors and a Bibliography of Books."

A guide to the world of the Deryni books of Katherine Kurtz, couched as an ancient lost manuscript from that time and place, this volume is presented as an A-Z encyclopedia of organizations, places, and characters relating to the Deryni universe, plus their significance. The materials are partially taken from fifteen novels and one collection of short stories (*The Deryni Archives*), from 1970's *Deryni Rising* to 1994's *The Bastard Prince,* although the title page assures the reader that some of the material here has "not been previously related in volume form." The book includes approximately 1,400 entries, plus frequent "See" references, intersprinkled with numerous stories and anecdotes, some of them humorous.

A typical entry includes: main entry (boldfaced type), description and commentary (averaging 50-150 words, though a few entries run much larger), and the title of the story or novel in which the events are mentioned or related (in brackets). The last quarter of the book consists of a detailed chronology of the XI Kingdoms from 9 B.C. to 1126 A.D. A much smaller section provides a Deryni liturgical calendar, followed by several genealogies of the major royal families of the XI Kingdoms, and six maps of the world. Much newly invented history and details on the Deryni world and its characters have been created here to flesh out Kurtz's created universe, all of them officially sanctioned by the author, with the actual writing being done by Robert Reginald.

Physically, this is a very attractive book, signed and numbered by the authors in a red cloth binding housed in a decorated gift box. The material is clearly presented while maintaining the entertaining fiction of an ancient, translated text. The volume sold out within three months of publication in 1998 and is now virtually unobtainable (several copies have sold for $800 apiece on an Internet auction site).

C. S. Lewis

556. Ford, Paul F. **Companion to Narnia.** New York, Harper & Row, 1980. xxxii, 313 p. LC 80-7734. ISBN 0-06-250340-5 (pbk.). **Companion to Narnia.** 2nd ed. San Francisco, Harper & Row, 1983. xxxix, 448 p. LC 82-21172. ISBN 0-06-250341-3 (pbk.). **Companion to Narnia.** 3rd ed. New York, Collier Books, Macmillan Publishing Co., 1986. xli, 450 p. LC 86-5352. ISBN 0-02-084940-0 (pbk.).

Ford has continued to expand this very detailed guide to Lewis's fantasy septology through several separate editions.

Contents (Third Edition): "List of Illustrations and Maps"; "Foreword," by Madeleine L'Engle; "Preface to the Third Edition"; "Acknowledgements"; "Introduction"; "Using the Companion"; "The Companion from A to Z"; "Appendix One: Chronology of the Composition and Publication of *The Chronicles*"; "Appendix Two: List of Comparative Ages"; "Appendix Three: A Comparison of Narnian and Earth Time"; "About the Author."

The main section of the book (450 pages) is an A-Z rendering of the people, places, and things in Lewis's fictional universe. Entries range in size from one sentence to thirty pages (for Aslan, the Lion King of Narnia), and typically include: term (all caps, boldfaced), single-sentence description (*e.g.,* "one of the Seven Noble Lords"), physical attributes, a detailed accounting of the events that have affected the person or place, a list of references (keyed to the abbreviations recorded on pages xl-xli, in the form "PC 16, *15"* for *Prince Caspian,* page 16 of the Collier mass-market edition, and page 15 of the trade paperback edition), and footnotes. There are numerous "See" references scattered throughout the text; "See Also" references to other terms of interest are noted by an asterisk following the term. The book is very nicely typeset, illustrated with maps of Narnia and black-and-white reproductions of full-page drawings from Lewis's original volumes, and perfect bound in paperback.

Ford knows his material, and his work is far more complete and detailed than Sammons's guide (see #558). However, the absence of running heads sometimes results in unnecessary difficulty in finding one's way through the alphabet; for example, the intrusion of thirty pages of unlabelled text into the "A" section for the entry on Aslan makes searching entries in this area extraordinarily difficult. Also, the latter entry includes twelve pages of very intrusive footnotes in small type; if this material was worth including, it should have been integrated into the text, or, at the very least, gathered together at the end of the volume into a footnotes section. Fortunately, most sections of the book do not suffer unduly from these design problems, and the *Companion* can be recommended to all research libraries and to any scholar studying Lewis's fiction.

557. Sammons, Martha C. **A Guide Through C. S. Lewis' Space Trilogy.** Westchester, IL, Cornerstone Books, 1980. 189 p. LC 80-68329. ISBN 0-89107-185-7 (pbk.).

Sammons, author of a companion volume to Narnia (see #558), covers Lewis's Perelandra Trilogy in both narrative and dictionary formats.

Contents: "Introduction"; "Chapter 1: Maker of Myths: C. S. Lewis and Science Fiction"; "Chapter 2: The Myth of Deep Heaven"; "Chapter 3: Medieval Perspectives and the Trilogy"; "Chapter 4: Mythology, Arthurian Legend, and the Trilogy"; "Chapter 5: Myth Became Fact: Science and Spirit in the Trilogy"; "Chapter 6: Man and His World in the Trilogy"; "Chapter 7: Maleldil and His Reign: Biblical Background and Themes"; "Appendix: A Summary of the Trilogy"; "The Languages in the Trilogy"; "A Dictionary of Deep Heaven"; "Notes."

The narrative sections (140 pages) cover the Perelandra Trilogy's major topics, themes, and characters in their respective chapters, in one or two pages of descriptive and evaluative text. The chapter on languages (four pages) gives brief summaries of Malacandrian, Hrossan, Pfifiltriggian, and Surnibur, with short lists of words and their English-language equivalents. The "Dictionary of Deep Heaven" (thirty-seven pages) is an A-Z listing of the people, places, and things in the Perelandra mythos. A typical entry provides: term (boldfaced), citation ("OSP" = *Out of the Silent Planet*, "P" = *Perelandra*, "THS" = *That Hideous Strength*), and a brief (one sentence to one paragraph) description of the person or item, plus its significance to the stories, with internal "See Also" references to other terms of interest (indicated with an asterisk before the term). Roughly 300 items are listed. The book is professionally typeset and designed, but will not withstand library use without rebinding.

Sammons has provided enough material here to guide any beginning student into the world of Lewis's fictional universe, but her work is no substitute for the kind of full-length alphabetical guide Ford has produced on The Narnia Chronicles (see #556). Future editions should include a general index, without which access to anything but the dictionary itself is unnecessarily difficult.

558. Sammons, Martha C. **A Guide Through Narnia.** Wheaton, IL, Harold Shaw Publishers, 1979. 164 p. LC 78-26476. ISBN 0-87788-325-4 (pbk.). London, Hodder & Stoughton, 1979. 164 p. (pbk.).

Sammons's guide, like her companion volume on the Perelandran tales (see #557) consists of broad narrative chapters, plus a character and place dictionary at the end of the volume.

Contents: "Introduction"; "Chapter 1: The Creator of the Narnia Chronicles"; "Chapter 2: The Creation of the Narnia Tales"; "Chapter 3: The Chronicles of Narnia"; "Chapter 4: The Country of Narnia"; "Chapter 5: The Creator of Narnia—Aslan"; "Chapter 6: Characters of Narnia"; "Chapter 7: Creations of Evil"; "Chapter 8: Christian Concepts in the Narnia Tales—A Summary"; "Index of Names and Places"; "A Note on Names and Creatures"; "Notes."

The narrative chapters are further subdivided into one- to three-page sections covering specific characters, places, and concepts, in no apparent order. Without an index, these mini-essays, while interesting in themselves, remain basically inaccessible to the average reader.

The "Index of Names and Places" is a twenty-six-page, A-Z guide to the major persons and sites in the Narnia Saga. A typical entry gives: term (boldfaced, all caps), citation (in the form "HHB" for *The Horse and His Boy*), and a brief, one-paragraph description. The "Note on Names and Creatures" describes the different kinds of men and creatures found in Narnia, and the given names with which C. S. Lewis honored them. The book is nicely designed and typeset, but the paperback binding will not withstand library usage.

Sammons appears to know her material well, but her brief introductory guide to the Narnia series is clearly outshown by Ford's much more comprehensive and copiously referenced dictionary (see #556).

559. Schultz, Jeffrey D., and John G. West, Jr., eds. **The C. S. Lewis Readers' Encyclopedia.** Grand Rapids, MI, Zondervan Publishing House, 1998. 464 p. index. LC 98-5459. ISBN 0-310-21538-2.

Contents: "Foreword," by Christopher Mitchell; "Clive Staples Lewis, 1898-1963: A Brief Biography," by John Bremer; "The C. S. Lewis Readers' Encyclopedia"; "Appendices" ("A. C. S. Lewis Resources"; "B.C. S. Lewis Timeline"); "Entry Guides" ("Biographical Essay"; "The Works of C. S. Lewis"; "Concepts, Places, People, and Themes"; "Uncollected Published Letters"; "Individual Poems"); "List of Contributors."

This A-Z encyclopedia of Lewis's life and work begins with a very full biography by Bremer (p. 9-65), and includes excerpts from letters and the author's introductions from his books to clarify his opinions on the personal and professional events in his life.

The bulk of the book, the encyclopedia proper, includes over 800 entries covering articles, poems, letters, and books by Lewis, his associates (friends, colleague, critics, historical figures), and philosophical or political terms important to the author's work. The foreword notes especially that "there are entries describing the sixty-three letters to editors Lewis wrote during his lifetime, the vast majority of which have never been collected and published elsewhere. Likewise, there are entries for many of the poems Lewis wrote that are not available in any of the collections yet printed."

The typical entry averages 150 words, but may vary considerably in length. Most include anecdotes or quotations to illustrate Lewis's character or opinions, and all entries are signed by the forty-three contributors; some also have mini-bibliographies attached. Entries focusing on essays by Lewis provide a complete bibliographical citation, including paginations in the original publication sources, while book entries note place of publication, publisher, and year of first edition, but no paginations. There are abundant cross-references in boldfaced type to other entries and works.

The book is illustrated throughout with black-and-white photographs of Lewis taken from life and from his book covers. The appendices offer a wealth of information. Appendix A is a directory of places holding manuscripts or selling Lewis's books, organizations devoted to Lewis, and a small collection of World Wide Web addresses. Appendix B provides a timeline to events important to Lewis's life, in descending block paragraph format by date, giving month and year and event.

The entry guides are actually separate indices to different periods of Lewis's life (from the biography); the author's works; concepts, places, people, and themes; uncollected published letters; and individual poems, all cross-referenced to appropriate page numbers. The foreword indicates that the brief biography is not as complete as it could be, given the fact that some of the material is covered in the *Encyclopedia* proper.

Any future editions should better coordinate the material in Bremer's biographical essay with the entries themselves, including the cross-references in the biography proper, so that users can more easily jump from one section to the other. Overall, however, this guide more than accomplishes its stated objective to help the reader "to gain a deeper and richer understanding of Lewis's own work and thinking." While the entries are occasionally uneven, for the most part the contributors seem well informed, and their essays are fascinating to read. Nicely designed and typeset, illustrated with cover reproductions, and bound to library standards, the *Encyclopedia* is highly recommended for academic libraries, scholars, mature fans, and all libraries with any interest in the life or works of C. S. Lewis.

H. P. Lovecraft

560. Harms, Daniel. **Encyclopedia Cthulhiana.** Oakland, CA, Chaosium, 1994. viii, 274 p. ISBN 1-56882-039-9 (pbk.). Harms, Daniel, with timeline by Shannon Appel. **The Encyclopedia Cthulhiana.** 2nd ed. Oakland, CA, A Chaosium Book, 1998. xix, 423 p. (Call of Cthulhu Fiction). ISBN 1-56882-119-0 (pbk.).

Contents (Second Edition): "How to Use This Book"; "Foreword"; "Suggestions for Further Reading"; "Encyclopedia, A-Z"; "Appendix A: History of *The Necronomicon*"; "Appendix B: Locations of *The Necronomicon*"; "Appendix C: Contents of *The Necronomicon*"; "Appendix D: Timeline of the Mythos"; "Bibliography."

The well-known American horror writer H. P. Lovecraft used in his fiction a collection of veiled and recurring imagery, characters, and ideas that gradually became known by his followers as the Cthulhu Mythos. After HPL's death in 1937, his friends began freely borrowing from his notions and employing the same characters and extrapolated situations in their work, without any real rules or consistency.

This guide is a dictionary of Cthulhu Mythos terms, characters, entities, fictional texts, and places, taken both from Lovecraft's own writings and from those of his followers.

The approximately 750 entries are organized alphabetically, with a typical entry including: the term (bold caps), a definition, appropriate "See Also" references, and the titles and authors of stories focused on that character or theme. "See" references point readers from variant spellings to a single entry, a necessity for the Mythos.

Entries vary considerably in size, from about fifteen words to over 500. Though the foreword indicates that the book is for beginners, rather than experts or scholars of Lovecraft and related fiction, the bibliography does not provide the kind of assistance to new readers that one might expect. The citations include only the authors' name, the title of the piece, and the year in which it was originally published.

Appendix A provides a timeline of the imaginary book, *The Necronomicon,* with notes on disputes or contradictions between various writers on this topic. Appendix B shows the supposed locations of *The Necronomicon* throughout time. Appendix C annotates some of the contents of *The Necronomicon* (formulas, poetry, spells, etc.). *The Encyclopedia* does not claim to be a comprehensive compendium of all Mythos-related fiction, but only to include major stories; some of the contents derives from game scenarios generated by Chaosium itself, which fans may dispute as authoritative.

The second edition is similar to the first in layout and contents, adding more than 150 entries overall to the original, but dropping others, and occasionally rewriting some of the entries that are carried over from one edition to the next. Some sources in the second edition have a letter code following them to indicate that the source material is originally from Lovecraft or his circle ("O"), or from role-playing materials ("G"). As usual with this kind of book, it is sometimes difficult to tell the "real" information from the invented, but Harms helps considerably by placing personal, real world comments in brackets at the end of some definitions.

The second edition cut a great many entries that had been mentioned in only one work, in favor of more frequently used elements of the mythology, generally to the benefit of the text. Also new is the excellent essay in the foreword entitled, "A Brief History of the Cthulhu Mythos," which examines the growth of the mythology from the 1920s to modern times, plus illustrations of important symbols, a collection of materials about the fictional volume, *The Necronomicon* (Appendices A, B, and C), and a timeline of the mythos from 4.5 billion years ago to the present. Most of the Appendices cite their sources.

The Encyclopedia Cthulhiana is a good guide to the complicated mythos that grew out of Lovecraft's fiction, but the bibliography featured in both editions continues to be a disappointment, lacking any of the specific data needed actually to identify the original publications. Diehard Cthulhu fans will want both versions.

561. Weinberg, Robert E. **A Reader's Guide to the Cthulhu Mythos.** Hillside, NJ, Robert Weinberg, 1969. [unknown] p. (pbk.). Weinberg, R[obert] E., and E. P. Berglund. **Reader's Guide to the Cthulhu Mythos.** 2nd rev. ed. Albuquerque, NM, The Silver Scarab Press, 1973. 88 p. index. (pbk.).

American writer Howard Phillips Lovecraft (1890-1937) based many of his horror tales around a common background that he invited many of his young correspondents to share. This shared milieu gradually became known as the "Cthulhu Mythos" after the name of one of the Elder Gods featured as a background "character" in the stories.

This brief checklist of Cthulhu Mythos stories includes (second edition): a two-page "Introduction" by the authors, a "Chronological Listing by Publication Dates"; "Alphabetical Listing by Title"; "Alphabetical Listing by Author"; "Series Listing"; "Alphabetical Listing by Author of Non-Fiction"; "Alphabetical Listing by Author of Parodies"; "Alphabetical Listing by Author of Poetry" [including many by Lovecraft himself]; "Alphabetical Listing by Title of Books, Pamphlets, Brochures, etc."; "Non-English Publications"; "Errata"; "Addenda."

The chronological checklist includes an abbreviations guide at the beginning of the listing, then arranges the data by publication date. A typical entry gives: year of publication, month of publication, title, author, and an abbreviation signifying the magazine name or book publisher. Items considered an integral part of the Cthulhu Mythos are so indicated with an asterisk following the entry. The title listing correlates titles and authors only. The author index lists: author's name, title, magazine title (in italics), month and year of publication, or (for monograph appearances) book title (all caps), publisher, and year of publication (in the form "45" for 1945), plus similar data for all known reprints. No paginations for books or periodical listings are given anywhere in the volume.

The alphabetical listings give: book title (all caps), author or editor, publisher, year of publication, and complete contents for anthologies and single-author collections (many of the entries), with each edition of the book being listed separately. The foreign-language section is arranged alphabetically by translated title, giving: title (all caps), author or editor, translator, publisher, place of publication, year of publication, and complete contents for anthologies and collections, with original, English-language titles in parentheses. The book is attractively designed, but the binding tends to disintegrate with usage.

Now decades out-of-date, *A Reader's Guide* has been largely supplanted by Harms's more current and comprehensive guide (see #560).

Julian May

562. May, Julian. **A Pliocene Companion: Being a Reader's Guide to** *The Many-Colored Land, The Golden Torc, The Nonborn King, The Adversary.* Boston, Houghton Mifflin Co., 1984. xiii, 219 p. LC 84-9124. ISBN 0-395-36516-3. New York, A Del Rey Book, Ballantine Books, 1985. xiii, 219 p. ISBN 0-345-32290-8 (pbk.). London, Collins, 1985. xiii, 219 p. ISBN 0-00-222970-6. London & Sydney, Pan Books, 1985. xiii, 220 p. ISBN 0-330-28986-1 (pbk.).

Although most character dictionaries are compiled by fans of a writer's work, May comes well qualified to produce this dictionary of her own created world of Pliocene Exile, having previously authored (under the pen name Lee N. Falconer) a similar book on Robert E. Howard (see #21).

The main section of the book (118 pages) is an alphabetical guide to the persons, places, and implements of the quatrology, a typical entry including: name (boldfaced), pronunciation guide, description (ranging in size from a few words to an entire page), and "See" references (all caps). This is followed by "A Chronology of the Saga"; "The Remillard Family Tree" (a genealogical chart); "The Ocala Rebels and Their Offspring" (table); "Author's Three Original Maps of Pliocene Europe"; "Two Maps of Ocala Island and Vicinity"; "The Good Ship Killikki" (description and diagram); "The Double Ourobouros" (description and drawing); "Music in My Head—Science Fiction As Opera" (an article by May on the musical background of the Saga); "Certain Poems Quoted in the Saga"; "The Pliocene Wildcat Lives!" (on cats); "Three Interviews with Julian May"; and "A Selective Bibliography" (of materials used by May to research the saga). Several black-and-white photographs of May are included near the end of the book. The book is well designed and typeset, and bound to library standards.

A Pliocene Companion provides an excellent introduction to May's popular fictional creation. Indeed, this attractive and comprehensive guide is a paradigm of what a character dictionary should be, and is recommended as a model to prospective compilers of such volumes.

Anne McCaffrey

563. Nye, Jody Lynn, with Anne McCaffrey. **The Dragonlover's Guide to Pern.** New York, A Del Rey Book, Ballantine Books, 1989. xi, 178 p. LC 89-6715. ISBN 0-345-35424-9. **The Dragonlover's Guide to Pern.** 2nd ed. New York, A Del Rey Book, Ballantine Books, 1997. xi, 260 p. index. LC 97-92989. ISBN 0-345-41274-5 (pbk.). Illustrated by Todd Cameron Hamilton; maps and additional illustrations by James Clouse.

This beautifully designed volume is intended for fans of McCaffrey's popular Pern Cycle.

Contents: "Introduction"; "I. Overview"; "II. Fit for Human Habitation"; "III. The Red Star"; "IV. From Dragonets to Dragons"; "V. Weyrlings"; "VI. Training and Fighting Dragons," by Todd Johnson; "VII. Threadfall Charts"; "VIII. Fort, the First Hold"; "IX. Benden, the Second Weyr"; "X. Holds, Crafthalls, and Weyrs"; "XI. Pronunciation Guide to Names on Pern"; "Sources" (*i.e.,* bibliography).

Contents (Second Edition): "Introduction"; "I. Overview"; "II. Fit for Human Habitation"; "III. The Red Star"; "IV. From Dragonets to Dragons"; "V. Weyrlings"; "VI. Training and Fighting Dragons," by Todd Johnson; "VII. Threadfall Charts"; "VIII. Fort, the First Hold"; "IX. Bendon, the Second Weyr"; "X. Holds, Crafthalls, and Weyrs"; "XI. The End of Thread"; "XII. Life After Thread"; "XIII. Dolphineers"; "XIV. New Life for the Dragons"; "XV. Pronunciation Guide to Names on Pern"; "XVI. Dragons and Their Riders"; "Sources"; "Index."

Each narrative chapter is organized around a specific topic, then broken into subdivisions covering specific subjects. For example, Chapter IX, on "Benden Weyr," includes sections on "The Queen's Weyr," "The Support Structure of the Weyr," "Duties," "Benden Hold," "Benden Wine," plus scattered interpolated sections giving recipes, oaths, and other material. Other chapters are similarly broken into their component pieces. Some of the material is taken directly from McCaffrey's fiction, but Nye has also clearly added text of her own, with or without the author's connivance. The distinction between the two is deliberately blurred, so that one is never sure whether or not the customs or places described are actually derived from the tales themselves. The pronunciation guide, while useful, does not cover every character from the Pern books. The absence of an index in the First Edition makes the material virtually inaccessible without extensive reading. The original book is bound to library standards.

Although the Second Edition is revised and expanded from the 1989 version, it actually contains exactly the same material up to the tenth chapter. The pronunciation guide has been moved here from Chapter Eleven (First Edition) to Chapter Fifteen (Second Edition). All subsequent information and illustrations are new to this version. The new chapters incorporate material from McCaffrey's *The Renegades of Pern, All the Weyrs of Pern, The Chronicles of Pern: First Fall, The Dolphins of Pern,* and *Dragonseye,* and cover the post-thread development of the planet and its technology, and the advent of the Dolphineers. There is an extensive list (thirty-eight pages) of dragons and their riders in Chapter Sixteen that includes: character, dragon, rank, novel where they appear, and group affiliation. The index is a welcome addition that makes finding specific information much easier; however, there is no cross-referencing within the text itself.

Like the First Edition, this version was written in consultation with McCaffrey, and was designed primarily for the fan who would take the time to read the book from cover to cover. The tone of the volume takes the reality of Pern very seriously, almost contributing another volume to the series. Thus, it is not really a reference volume, but it still makes a good addition to public or school libraries serving McCaffrey readers.

However, a comprehensive A-Z guide to the persons, places, and things in Mc-Caffrey's fictional universe has yet to be produced. Compare with Fonstad's *Atlas of Pern* (see #23), which shares similar problems.

John Myers Myers

564. Lerner, Fred, ed. **A *Silverlock* Companion: The Life and Works of John Myers Myers.** Center Harbor, NH, Niekas Publications, 1988. 52 p. ISBN 0-910619-02-6 (pbk.).

Myers wrote many works of Western Americana, but is best known in fantastic literature for his rousing fantasy adventure *Silverlock.*

Contents: "Preface"; "John Myers Myers: A Brief Biography," by James M. Crane; "John Myers Myers: A Tribute," by Lerner; "Recollections," by Edmund R. Meskys; "*Silverlock* and *The Moon's Fire-Eating Daughter:* An Appreciation," by Charlotte Moslander; "A Reader's Guide to the Commonwealth: A Glossary of Literary, Mythological, and Geographical Allusions in *Silverlock,*" by Lerner and Anne J. Braude; "The *Silverlock* Library," by Lerner; "The Western Writings," by James M. Crane; "The Inside Scoop on John Myers Myers," by Myers; "A Bibliography," by Crane; "The Makers' Muse," by Myers.

The reader's guide, which occupies twenty-eight pages of text, is an A-Z listing of the people, places, and things that fill the allusion-strewn pages of *Silverlock.* A typical entry gives: term (boldfaced, all caps), page number (referenced to the 1949 E. P. Dutton cloth edition of the book), identification of the reference (with one paragraph of description), its role in the narrative, and (in parentheses) the original author and title (both in English and in the original language, if the work was first published overseas), nationality and genre, and original date of publication.

Crane's "Bibliography" is broken into "Part I: The Books"; "Part II: Essays and Articles"; "Part III: The Poems"; "Part IV: Unpublished Writings." In each section materials are arranged chronologically by publication date, each printing of a title being listed separately. A typical book entry provides: year of publication (boldfaced), book title (boldfaced), place of publication, publisher, year of publication, pagination, first edition points, height of the book in centimeters, and a list of all printings, with months and years noted, and other notes. Crane also includes translations into other languages when known.

The shorter works sections give: year of publication (boldfaced), title (boldfaced, in quotes), magazine title (in italics), month and year of publication, specific pagination, and bibliographical notes. The list of unpublished writings gives date and manuscript page count. The guide is very attractively typeset and designed, filled with illustrations, and bound with staples into paper covers.

Myers died shortly after this book was produced, and it is unlikely much will be added to his bibliography in the future. Students of this important regional writer will use this guide as an essential starting point for their research.

Mervyn Peake

565. Metzger, Arthur. **A Guide to The Gormenghast Trilogy.** [Baltimore, T-K Graphics], 1976. 35 p. (pbk.).

This brief guide to Peake's best-known fictional creation includes a poignant introduction by Michael Moorcock adapted from his 1969 obituary of Peake in *New Worlds.* The dictionary section is arranged alphabetically by main entry (persons, places, or things), a typical entry including name (bold caps), citation (to book and chapter number), and description. Entries range in size from one sentence to several pages (for Titus Groan, the key figure in the Trilogy). Many items feature illustrative quotations from Peake's original text, as, for example, the entry for Mr. Gumshaw: "His polished pate reflects a brace of candles."

Nicely typeset, this very readable but exceedingly brief guide deserves wider circulation than it originally received.

Anne Rice

566. Ramsland, Katherine. **The Vampire Companion: The Official Guide to Anne Rice's The Vampire Chronicles.** New York, Ballantine Books, 1993. xvii, 507 p. LC 93-2378. ISBN 0-345-37922-5. London, Little, Brown, 1993. xvii, 508 p. ISBN 0-316-90901-7. **The Vampire Companion: The Official Guide to Anne Rice's The Vampire Chronicles.** 2nd rev. ed. New York, Ballantine Books, 1995. xvii, 581 p. LC 95-10620. ISBN 0-345-39739-8. London, Little, Brown, 1995. xvii, 577 p. ISBN 0-316-87781-6.

Contents: "Acknowledgments"; "Introduction"; "Abbreviations"; "Entries A to Z"; "Time Line"; "Vampire Atlas" (Ancient World, Modern World, San Francisco, New Orleans and the French Quarter, France Paris, The Gathering of Immortals, Voyage of the *QE II*); "Bibliography."

Contents (second edition): "Acknowledgments"; "Introduction"; "Abbreviations"; "Entries A to Z"; "Time Line"; "Vampire Atlas" (Ancient World, Modern World, San Francisco, New Orleans and the French Quarter, France Paris, The Gathering of Immortals, Voyage of the *QE II*); "'Interview with the Vampire': The Short Story, August 1973 (Approx.)," by Rice; "Bibliography."

Similar to *The Witches' Companion* (see #567), *The Vampire Companion* is a handbook to Rice's series *The Vampire Chronicles,* covering (in the 1993 edition) the novels

Interview with the Vampire, The Vampire Lestat, The Queen of the Damned, and *The Tale of the Body Thief,* providing an A-Z encyclopedia of "characters, places, themes, literary allusions and devices, symbols, famous quotes, and vampire-related terminology," along with plot summaries, and over 100 drawings and photographs. The roughly 1,000 entries (including "See" references) average about 100 words in length, though individual entries may vary considerably in size. The definitions are well-written and intelligent, and feature various historical details or brief scientific facts providing background information on the books, in addition to each entry's relevance to the novels.

This is a more textually-centered book than *The Witches' Companion,* so the absence of citations to sources is not as great a problem as in the other guide, although it still hinders the book's usefulness as a reference tool. There are page references to the Ballantine mass market paperback editions of the novels for the first or primary reference, but these are not exhaustive. Entries often have one or more "See Also" references, and include frequent quotations from Rice providing insight into the writing of her books. Ramsland has also seen earlier drafts of the author's novels, and sometimes makes tantalizing references to these variora in order to address particular points. A timeline and maps of significant locations mentioned in the books are very helpful.

The revised 1995 edition is similarly organized, but also includes material on the novel *Memnoch the Devil,* plus the previously unpublished short story that later became *Interview with the Vampire,* and coverage of the motion picture adaptation of the latter novel.

Written in close consultation with Rice, *The Vampire Companion* will be sucked up by the many fans of this popular series, and wholly ignored by everyone else.

567. Ramsland, Katherine. **The Witches' Companion: The Official Guide to Anne Rice's Lives of the Mayfair Witches.** New York, Ballantine Books, 1994. xvii, 522 p. LC 94-9747. ISBN 0-345-38947-6.

Similar to *The Vampire Companion* (see #566), *The Witches' Companion* is a handbook to Rice's complex trilogy, comprised of *The Witching Hour, Lasher,* and *Taltos.* There are also mentions to *The Queen of the Damned* and *The Tale of the Body Thief,* but only as they relate to the Mayfair Witches.

The guide proper is an A-Z encyclopedia of "characters, places, literary and historical references, symbols, terminology, plot summaries, page references, cross-references, drawings, and photographs" in the novels. Approximately 1,500 entries are covered (including "See" references), averaging 125 words each, though the size of the entries varies considerably. The definitions are well-written and intelligent, and sometimes include various real-life historical details or facts, as necessary to explain the entries in question. However, the sources of such extraneous materials are never cited, so the various interesting pieces of data can neither be confirmed nor readily followed up by the reader, limiting the book's usefulness as a reference tool.

The Companion contains page references from the major entries to the Ballantine mass market paperback editions of the books. Entries frequently have one or more "See Also" references pointing to related topics. A family tree of the three centuries of Mayfair witches begins the book, while a chronology of events and a series of maps showing significant locations in the novels conclude it.

The book is illustrated with black-and-white photographs and reproductions of art-work. Written in consultation with Anne Rice, this guide will prove popular among the fans of the Mayfair Witches series, or for the public library that serves them. For anyone else, "hex" marks the spot!

Cordwainer Smith

568. Lewis, Anthony R. **Concordance to Cordwainer Smith.** Boston, New England Science Fiction Association, 1984. [iv], 90 p. LC 84-236060. ISBN 0-915368-24-2 (pbk.).

Intended as a preliminary version of a larger dictionary index to Smith's work (which has never appeared), the *Concordance* provides a guide to the people, places, and things of the author's fictional future history, but excludes his early mainstream and spy novels, *Ria, Carola,* and *Atomsk.*

Following a brief preface and a key to the works cited, Lewis arranges the material in alphabetical order by name. A typical entry includes: term, line break, description, and title code (in the form "UP" for *The Underpeople*). The entries tend to be short (from a few words to two brief paragraphs) and straightforward; however, Lewis does include references to known or extrapolated sources for Smith's often punning or deliberately derivative names (*e.g.,* "Englok, Lord. Built the Brown and Yellow Corridor as a thoughtproof shelter during the ancient wars. [DL] eng + loch (German) = narrow gate, opening. 'Enter by the Narrow Gate'—Gospels.").

Interfiled with the descriptive entries are the titles of Smith's books and stories; a typical book entry includes: title (underlined), contents (if a collection), publisher, place of publication, pagination, year of publication, cover artist, and price (if a paperback). A typical short story entry includes: title (all title entries are followed by the word "story"), category, magazine title, month and year of publication, and brief description (*i.e.,* time, setting, broad story line). There are numerous "See" references from similar names or terms to other entries scattered throughout the text. The book is shot from very legible double-columned word-processed copy, and is bound with staples into paper covers.

Lewis's book is a good beginning guide to this well-known author's stories; however, the descriptions are sometimes so terse as to be incomprehensible to someone unfamiliar with Cordwainer Smith's work. A more elaborate version, perhaps including the missing books, with the bibliographical data separated into their own section, would certainly be appropriate.

J. R. R. Tolkien

569. Blackwelder, Richard E. **A Tolkien Thesaurus.** New York & London, Garland Publishing, 1990. 277 p. (Garland Reference Library of the Humanities, Vol. 1326). LC 90-31755. ISBN 0-8240-5296-X.

More of a concordance than a thesaurus, this index allows users "to locate occurrences of all major words, including names, from Prologue through Appendices," of the three volumes of *The Lord of the Rings* trilogy by J. R. R. Tolkien, using the most common American, as well as several British, editions. Some 40,000 entries are referenced under

15,000 word headings arranged in two columns per page, with cross-references for synon-ymous names of people, places, and things.

The typical entry includes: the term (all caps), with any alternative word forms (*e.g.*, share, shared), the part of the sentence where the word appears, and a reference to the page(s) where it will be found in the text (for example, "R.115/140" means *The Return of the King*, p. 115 and 140). The volume is bound to library standards, but employs a rather small typeface that is somewhat difficult for middle-aged eyes to discern.

This book is a wonderful aid to scholars and students of Tolkien's trilogy, although this reader would also prefer to see *The Hobbit* added to any subsequent editions of this thesaurus. Recommended for Tolkien scholars, all academic libraries, and larger public libraries.

570. Day, David. **A Tolkien Bestiary.** New York, Ballantine Books, 1979. 287 p. index. LC 79-9961. ISBN 0-345-28283-3. London, Mitchell Beazley, 1979. 287 p. index. ISBN 0-85533-188-7. London, Emblem, 1982. 287 p. index. ISBN 0-85533-414-2 (pbk.). New York, Crescent Books, 1983. 287 p. index. ISBN 0-517-47325-9; ISBN 0-517-12077-1. Madeira Park, B.C., Harbour Publishing, 1984. 287 p. index. ISBN 0-920080-47-2. New York, Gramercy Books, 1998. 287 p. index. ISBN 0-517-12077-1. Illustrated by Ian Miller, Michael Foreman, Allan Curless, Lidia Postma, John Blanche, Pauline Martin, Sue Porter, Linda Garland, Jaroslav Bradac, Victor Ambrus, and John Davis.

Contents: "Author's Preface"; "List of Illustrations"; "A Map of Middle-earth and the Undying Lands"; "A Chronology of Middle-earth and the Undying Lands"; "A Chronology of the Kingdoms on Middle-earth in the Ages of the Sun"; "A Bestiary of the Beasts, Monsters, Races, Deities, and Flora"; "Genealogies of the Races and Kingdoms of Elves and Men"; "Index of Principal Sources"; "General Index."

Written in the tradition of the medieval bestiary, this playful A-Z encyclopedia de-scribes the appearance, habitation, habits, and weaknesses of the races, animals, monsters, and plants in Tolkien's Middle-earth, covering *The Lord of the Rings, The Hobbit, The Adventures of Tom Bombadil,* and *The Silmarillion.* The over 200 entries average 100 words each, but important entries, such as "Hobbit," can reach well over 1,000 words. The book is copiously illustrated with black-and-white and color illustrations, with the two-page color spreads being particularly appealing.

The Index of Principal Sources uses two-letter abbreviations to guide the reader to the book and chapter where Tolkien's explanations can be found. The general index cross-references multiple mentions of the term, primary entry pages being shown in bold; this can be useful, since the entries themselves do not employ "See" or "See Also" references.

Primarily a fan publication, rather than a complete guide to the world of Middle-earth, this book has been almost entirely superseded by Day's later publication, *Tolkien: The Illustrated Encyclopedia* (see #571).

571. Day, David. **Tolkien: The Illustrated Encyclopædia.** New York, Macmillan; To-ronto, Maxwell Macmillan Canada; New York, Maxwell Macmillan International, 1991. 279 p. index. LC 91-12921. ISBN 0-02-031275-X. London, Mitchell Beazley, 1991. 279 p. index. ISBN 0-85533-924-1; ISBN 1-85732-346-7 (pbk.). New York, Collier Books; Toronto, Maxwell Macmillan Canada; New York, Maxwell Macmillan International, 1992. 279 p. index. LC 92-10865. ISBN 0-02031-275-X.

Contents: "Introduction"; "The Life and Literary Works of J. R. R. Tolkien"; "Chapter One: History"; "Chapter Two: Geography"; "Chapter Three: Sociology"; "Chapter Four: Natural History"; "Chapter Five: Natural History"; "Index to Principal Sources"; "General Index."

This illustrated guide to Middle-earth is arranged in five major sections: history, geography, sociology, natural history, and biography. "History" is divided into the Ages of Lamps, Trees, Darkness, Stars, and the three Ages of the Sun, with the events of each age explained as if this were a textbook of real history. There are two chronological charts showing the development of events in Tolkien's invented universe.

"Geography" includes a collection of twelve color maps of Middle-earth as it evolved through the ages, from a flat world to the beginnings of the current world. This is followed by an "A to Z of the cities, countries, forests, rivers, lakes and seas of Middle-earth and the Undying Lands." The approximately 150 entries describe the location of each place and its significance to the races.

"Sociology" is "a complete guide to all the people of Middle-earth and the Undying Lands. It includes the racial, national and tribal categories of Men, Elves, Dwarves, Hobbits, Ents, Maiar, and Valar with which Tolkien populated his world." The length of the approximately 120 entries varies considerably.

"Natural History" is a "naturalist's dictionary of all the flora and fauna of Middle-earth and the Undying Lands." It provides the description, characteristics, and history of "every species and subspecies ever named in Tolkien's word, including birds, beasts, and insects, ghosts, demons, and monsters." Over 100 entries are included.

"Biography" is a "who's who" of Tolkien's fictional universe. Each of the roughly 100 entries explains "the lineage, physical appearance, personal attributes, dates of birth and death, and major events" of these characters.

Fans will find much that is familiar in *Tolkien: The Illustrated Encyclopedia*. Many of the entries, particularly the sections on natural history and sociology, have been pulled wholesale from Day's earlier publication, *A Tolkien Bestiary* (see #570), although other entries from that earlier work have been deleted, or have had minor changes made to their content. The chronological tables that begin the "History" section of the original book are also duplicated, as are many of the illustrations. But there is also substantial new material here, especially in the "Geography" chapter.

The descriptive paragraph defining each new chapter is a useful feature. The book contains two indices: the Index of Principal Sources lists all of the entries covered and cites appropriate cross-references in Tolkien's works, using abbreviations and chapter numbers for *The Silmarillion, The Hobbit, The Lord of the Rings, The Adventures of Tom Bombadil, Unfinished Tales, The Book of Lost Tales I, The Book of Lost Tales II, The Lays of Beleriand, The Shaping of Middle-earth,* and *The Lost Road.*

The General Index is useful in this classified scheme for finding all of the multiple references to a term (with the primary entry in bold type), but the cross-references could be better (*e.g.,* Pippin has no cross reference, but is only listed in the text and the index as Peregrin Took). The illustrations fail to dazzle: some of the more impressive two-page color illustrations from *A Tolkien Bestiary* (see #570) have been shrunk to a fraction of their size, thus reducing their impact significantly.

Overall, this will be an attractive purchase for a new fan to Tolkien who wants a good overview of Middle-earth, but for the serious Middle-earth scholar, or for academic libraries, it does not supplant either *The Tolkien Companion* (see #573) or *The Complete Guide to Middle-earth* (see #572).

572. Foster, Robert. **A Guide to Middle-earth.** Baltimore, Mirage Press, 1971. xiii, 283, [8] p. LC 72-94777. Cloth and pbk. New York, Ballantine Books, 1974. 283 p. ISBN 0-345-24138-X (pbk.). **The Complete Guide to Middle-earth, from the Hobbit to the Silmarillion.** Rev. and enlarged ed. New York, A Del Rey Book, Ballantine Books, 1978. xvi, 575 p. LC 77-26825. ISBN 0-345-27320-9; ISBN 0-345-30974-X (trade pbk.); ISBN 0-345-27975-1 (mass market pbk.). London, George Allen & Unwin, 1978. xii, 441 p. ISBN 0-04-803002-3; ISBN 0-04-803001-5 (pbk.).

Foster's comprehensive guide to Tolkien's works was expanded in 1978 to encompass the then-recent publication of *The Silmarillion.*

Contents (Revised Edition): "Introduction"; "Sources and Abbreviations"; "Complete Guide"; "Appendix A: A Chronology of the First Age"; "Appendix B: Genealogical Tables"; "Appendix C: Conversion of Page References to Houghton Mifflin Editions."

The main section (555 pages in the Revised Edition) is an A-Z guide to the persons, places, and things in Tolkien's *Lord of the Rings* Trilogy, *The Hobbit,* and *The Silmarillion.* A typical entry gives: term (bold all caps); language abbreviation (*e.g.,* "S" = Sinhardin), and English-language meaning of the word, where appropriate; brief description; significance; and citation (*e.g.,* "I 206" = *The Fellowship of the Ring,* revised Ballantine edition, p. 206). The descriptions range in size from one sentence to several pages, averaging one paragraph. Roughly 2,500 terms are covered. There are numerous "See" and "See Also" references scattered throughout the text. The book is shot from nicely designed typeset copy, and the cloth versions are bound to library standards.

Although both Foster and Tyler (see #573) cover essentially the same territory at comparable lengths, Foster's copious use of citations makes his work more useful for scholars and researchers, and is generally to be preferred. Curiously, neither of these works has been updated to include the collections of previously unpublished Tolkien material released during the 1980s-'90s.

573. Tyler, J. E. A. **The Tolkien Companion.** London, Macmillan, 1976. 531 p. ISBN 0-333-19633-3. New York, St. Martin's Press, 1976. 10, 531 p. LC 76-5203. (pbk.). New York, Avon, 1977. 10, 530 p. ISBN 0-380-00901-3 (pbk.). New York, Bell Publishing Co., 1979. 10, 530 p. ISBN 0-517-27914-2. **The New Tolkien Companion.** [2nd ed.]. New York, St. Martin's Press, 1979. xiii, 649 p. LC 79-22773. ISBN 0-312-57066-X. London, Macmillan, 1979. xiii, 649 p. ISBN 0-333-27532-2. London & Sydney, Pan Books, 1979. xiii, 651 p. LC 79-32311. ISBN 0-330-25801-X (pbk.). New York, Avon, 1980. xiii, 649 p. LC 79-89235. ISBN 0-380-46904-9 (pbk.).

As with Foster's guide (see #572), Tyler updated his work when Tolkien's last major work, *The Silmarillion,* was published in 1978, but has not revised it since, despite the publication of numerous posthumous collections.

Contents: "Acknowledgements"; "Preface"; "Compiler's Note"; "The Companion."

Materials are arranged alphabetically by term. A typical entry includes: term (bold-faced), dates (if the term describes an individual whose dates of reign or birth and death are known), description, and significance. Items range in length from a few words to four pages, averaging one paragraph; about 2,500 terms are covered. A few citations appear in the notes sections following the last term for each letter of the alphabet, but verification of sources is much more difficult in this work than in Foster's very carefully compiled guide. The book is nicely typeset, and the cloth editions are bound to library standards.

Both Foster's *Complete Guide* (see #572) and this volume contain specific entries that cover their topics in greater depth than in the competing volume, and both have about the same number of entries and describe the same Tolkien works. Completists or intensive researchers will undoubtedly want access to both books, but libraries can be satisfied with Foster's work (see #572), which cites all references, and is the more scholarly of the two volumes.

Jules Verne

574. Taves, Brian, and Stephen Michaluk, Jr. **The Jules Verne Encyclopedia.** Lanham, MD, Scarecrow Press, 1996. xvii, 257 p. index. LC 95-4060. ISBN 0-8108-2961-4 (cloth). Contributors: Edward Baxter, Ray Cartier, Evelyn Copeland, Olivier Dumas, James Iraldi.

Contents: "Contributors"; "Greetings from France," translated by Evelyn Copeland; "Preface," by Brian Taves, translated by Evelyn Copeland; "1. Jules Verne: An Interpretation," by Brian Taves; "2. The American Jules Verne Society," by Stephen Michaluk, Jr.; "3. A Day in Amiens," by James Iraldi; "4. Jules Verne's Autobiography: A Collage of Interviews," edited by Brian Taves; "5. The Tribulations of a Translator of Jules Verne," by Edward Baxter; "6. The Uncensored Jules Verne: Completing Yesterday and Tomorrow"; "7. Jules Verne: A Bibliographic and Collecting Guide," by Stephen Michaluk, Jr.; "8. Philatelic Tributes to Jules Verne," by Ray Cartier; "9. Hollywood's Jules Verne," by Brian Taves; "Index."

The purpose of this volume is to "document [Verne's] influence and popularity, especially in the English-speaking world." It attempts to create "an authoritative publishing history of the English-language books, articles, and stories by Verne."

Thus, this is not an A-Z encyclopedia, but a collection of essays and miscellaneous pieces on the author. Chapters 1-6 and chapter 9 contain essays studying Verne (*par example,* Chapter One provides an interpretive overview of Verne; Chapter Four is a compilation of twenty sources pasted together to create a *faux* autobiography; Chapter Six is a translation of Verne's "The Humbug" by Edward Baxter, while Chapter Eight is a checklist of postage stamps dedicated to Jules Verne.

Chapter Seven, the bibliographical meat of the volume, begins with a Title Cross Reference table alphabetically listing title variants, the standard title for the work, and a reference number ("V" for Verne plus a cardinal number). Following the table, this section includes an annotated bibliography of American and British editions of Verne. The typical entry includes: reference number, standard title, year of publication (all bold caps), French-language title (small bold caps), illustrator and number of illustrations (bold), and an annotation. The annotations range from 3,000-10,000 words in length, averaging 5,000, and include comments on changes from previous editions, plus characteristics and the history of the translation. The book is decorated with pictures of earlier editions of English translations of Verne's work, as well as images of stamps containing Verne images.

Suitable for academic libraries and possibly useful for scholars of Jules Verne, but a bit too full of itself for anyone else. Prefer Gallagher *et al.*

Kurt Vonnegut

575. Leeds, Marc. **The Vonnegut Encyclopedia: An Authorized Compendium.** Westport, CT, Greenwood Press, 1995. xvi, 693 p. index. LC 94-16122. ISBN 0-313-29230-2 (alk. paper).

Contents: "Foreword," by Kurt Vonnegut; "Preface"; "A Note About the Text"; "The Encyclopedia"; "Index."

This book is something of a hybrid, part concordance and part cyclopedia integrated into an A-Z text. Leeds attempts "to organize and identify a good portion of Vonnegut's most frequently reappearing images and all his characters,..[to] quickly find the passages" in one of the eighteen novels, short stories, plays, or essays covered in the book (from 1952's *Player Piano* to 1991's *Fates Worse Than Death*).

The cyclopedic entries are usually brief and descriptive, covering character names, locations, and institutions. Entries on Vonnegut's novels generally run much longer than the others, but often do not provide plot summaries, focusing instead on themes and imagery, and often employing Vonnegut quotations cited to book title (using two-letter abbreviations) and appropriate page and line numbers. Concordance entries usually consist of themes or imagery, and also include lengthy discussions, quotations, and citations.

Approximately 1,800 entries are included, varying in length from 40 words for a small character to over 2,000 for the key novel, *Cat's Cradle.* The detailed index is essential for guiding the reader through multiple mentions of terms scattered throughout the volume, though some "See" and "See Also" references are also embedded in the text. Bold numbers in the index represent primary discussions of the term.

Alas, however, Leeds's book resembles an alphabetized list of researcher's notes attached to page references, being neither true concordance nor real cyclopedia, with a strong element of inconsistency in the way entries are written and presented. Sometimes a character entry will provide a citation to that individual's appearance in a novel, but on other occasions Leeds includes only a very brief description of the person, just tied to the overall novel. The frequent font changes from italic to plain text, intended to set off the author's discussion from the numerous quotations of Vonnegut's texts, all too often distracts and confuses the average reader. Citations will sometimes appear prior to a quotation, sometimes after, for no apparent reason. The discussions of the novels often consist of stream-of-consciousness blatherings, apparently intended to resemble Vonnegut's prose, but without the master's sparkle to light the way.

A researcher or fan of Vonnegut may find the entries occasionally useful and/or intriguing, but those less familiar with the author's work will struggle to be enlightened rather than baffled. As the only book of its kind, *The Vonnegut Encyclopedia* is certainly suitable for larger academic libraries, but it's not quite the breakfast of champions that "leeds" us to an appropriate digestion of a great literary chef's scrumptious orts.

H. G. Wells

576. Ash, Brian. **Who's Who in H. G. Wells.** London, Elm Tree Books, Hamish Hamilton, 1979. xvii, 299 p. LC 79-311512. ISBN 0-241-89597-9.

Ash's work is an A-Z guide to the significant peoples and characters in Wells's fiction. A typical entry includes: term (all caps), description, significance, a record of the events affecting the person or place, and a citation (giving the title of the Wells story or novel and original year of publication, but no paginations). Most entries run to one or two middle-sized paragraphs.

Ash also includes two appendices: the "Bibliography of Novels" records Wells's book-length fictions (including *The Time Machine,* which is sometimes listed among his shorter works) in chronological order by publication date, giving: year of publication, title (in italics), publisher, place of publication, author's dedication, and the name of the chief character covered in the dictionary part of the book.

The "Bibliography of Short Stories," Appendix Two, lists the author's short stories in the same order in which they appear in *The Complete Short Stories of H. G. Wells* (1927), a typical entry providing: title (in quotes), magazine in which the story first appeared (in italics), month and year of original publication, and the name of the principal character from the story who is mentioned in the main section of Ash's book. A "Select Bibliography of Studies of Wells's Life and Fiction" completes the volume. The book is nicely typeset and bound to library standards.

Curiously and unfortunately, Ash's book has never found an American publisher, which makes the location of copies difficult for the average researcher. Ash's dictionary includes a wider range of characters than Wells's guide (see #507), and provides more detailed descriptions than Connes's (see #577). All three works include some entries not found in the others, and Ash covers a number of the relatively minor fictions published in the last two decades of H. G. Wells's life.

Serious researchers of Wells's characters and characterizations will require all three works; most libraries will find Ash's volume sufficient as a character dictionary, although academic collections should also retain Geoffrey Wells's guide for its bibliographical data (see #507).

577. Connes, G. A. **A Dictionary of the Characters and Scenes in the Novels, Romances, and Short Stories of H. G. Wells.** Dijon, France, M. Darantière, 1926. 489 p. LC 27-21949. New York, Haskell House Publishers, 1971. 489 p. LC 73-174698. ISBN 0-8383-1353-1.

Georges Connes covers fictions published by H. G. Wells through 1924. The first section of his book annotates the author's novels and stories in chronological order by publication date. A typical short story entry provides: title (small caps), abbreviation code, magazine title (in italics), month and year of publication (but no paginations), and a one-paragraph annotation.

A typical book entry gives: abbreviation code, item number, title (all caps), publisher, place of publication, month and year of publication, book dedication, and a plot summary that averages one page in length. The annotations are descriptive rather than evaluative.

The main text of the volume consists of an A-Z dictionary of the people and things mentioned in Wells's stories and novels through the mid-1920s. A typical entry includes: term (in italics), citation (in the form "WW" for *The War of the Worlds*), and a one-sentence to one-paragraph descriptive annotation. Connes is compulsively complete: there are six short separate entries, for example, for the generic character "Agent," including the man who "Procured Trafford and Marjorie their house" in *Marriage*. The majority of entries run no more than twenty words.

Thus, while Connes's dictionary covers more "persons" (including many individuals who consist only of such labels as "agent") than Ash's guide (see #576), Ash describes characters from an additional two decades of Wells's works, and provides more detailed annotations for the persons he does cover. Serious students of Wells's fiction will want both works for comparison; most libraries can "make do" with Ash's dictionary (#576).

Roger Zelazny

578. Krulik, Theodore. **The Complete Amber Sourcebook.** New York, AvoNova, 1996. xv, 494 p. LC 95-35076. ISBN 0-380-75409-6 (pbk.).

Contents: "The Amber Novels: Guide to Abbreviations"; "Scribe's Preface"; "Introduction"; [The Sourcebook Proper]; "Appendix A: Shadow Worlds"; "Table of Correspondence Between Amber-Time and Time on the Shadow Earth"; "Appendix B: Explanation of Amber's System of Chronological Dating"; "Works Consulted."

Krulik, a well-known critic of the field, here provides an A-Z guide of the places, characters, and events featured in Roger Zelazny's ten-novel Amber series, presented as if it were being written by a scribe of the Amber world.

The guide contains some 213 entries, all listed in the table of contents, averaging at least 1,000 words per entry, with some, such as the piece on the character "Benedict," running 30,000 words. Quotations from the novels are frequently employed to illustrate a point, each quote being cited from the novel in question using a two-letter book abbreviation and appropriate page numbers. Ten novels are covered: *Nine Princes of Amber, The Guns of Avalon, Sign of the Unicorn, The Hand of Oberon, The Courts of Chaos, Trumps of Doom, Blood of Amber, Sign of Chaos, Knight of Shadows,* and *Prince of Chaos.* Some entries include "See Also" references in capital letters.

Appendix A provides a chronology correlating Amber-time with the time on our own Shadow Earth, while Appendix B explains Amber-time using various tables.

The Amber novels are justly regarded by readers and critics alike as classics of fantasy fiction. Alas, Zelazny's 1995 death means that this book is probably as complete as it will ever be. Fans of the series will love this guide.

579. Zelazny, Roger, and Neil Randall. **Roger Zelazny's Visual Guide to Castle Amber.** New York, Avon Books, 1988. 218 p. LC 88-18860. ISBN 0-380-75566-1 (pbk.).

Randall adapted this guide from Zelazny's (then nine-volume) Amber sequence, and from four days of intensive interviews with the author. The first hundred pages provide detailed descriptions of the fictional Castle Amber itself, its environs, rooms, apartments, library, etc., including floor plans. Pages 119-169 cover The Greater Trumps (*i.e.,* the chief characters of the Amber saga), with brief biographies of each of the Princes of Amber, plus their portraits on facing pages.

The rest of the book includes chapters on such topics as "The Pattern of Amber," "The Arts," "Religion and Mythology," "Flora and Fauna," etc. The appendix provides a detailed genealogical chart of the liaisons and descendants of Oberon, first King of Amber. The book is beautifully typeset and designed, and is illustrated throughout with black-and-white drawings by Todd Cameron Hamilton and maps by James Clouse. There is no index.

Designed for fans of this popular fantasy series, this lightweight volume contains minimal reference value, but will nonetheless be read and enjoyed by public library patrons.

FILM AND TELEVISION CATALOGS

SCOPE NOTE: This chapter includes general film and TV catalogs and guides, as well as handbooks on individual programs or motion pictures, alphabetically by film or series title. Additional information on some SF pictures and television programs can be found in the encyclopedias covered in the first chapter of this book.

GENERAL WORKS

580. Anderson, Craig W. **Science Fiction Films of the Seventies.** Jefferson, NC & London, McFarland & Co., 1985. ix, 261 p., [32] p. of plates. index. LC 83-42898. ISBN 0-89950-086-2 (pbk.).

Anderson provides a chronological look at the good, the bad, and the ugly of SF films released during a seminal decade for motion pictures. Materials are arranged in chapters corresponding to the decade from 1970-79, being organized by release date. A typical entry provides: film name (boldfaced head), production company, running time, color process, other technical information (for example, whether the film used 70mm cameras and Dolby sound), month and year of release; "Synopsis"; "Commentary"; and "Cast and Credits." The "Synopsis" section for each film summarizes the major plot elements of the motion picture in about a page of text. Anderson's perceptive "Commentary" adds another two-to-four pages of evaluative remarks. The "Cast and Credits" section includes lists of all major characters and technical crew who worked the film.

Two questions must be asked of this kind of book: 1) does it indeed cover all the noteworthy films of the decade? 2) are the author's comments fair and balanced? The answers to both of these queries are positive. Anderson tries to walk a middle line between the pretentious and folksy, keeping a colloquial style suited for the average reader while providing serious comments on why these films worked or did not work. Most importantly, he very conscientiously attempts to sprinkle comments of other reviewers (taken from periodical articles and film books) throughout his own material, showing different sides of each question, and, with controversial movies such as *Zardoz,* displaying a variety of opinions at opposite ends of the critical spectrum. The reader is thus able to gain a perspective beyond the author's own, very clearly stated position. It should also be noted that Anderson's commentaries average 1,500 words each, generally running much longer (and providing more details) than those in competing works.

Unlike many film books, this guide contains a very thorough index to every name and film mentioned in the volume, keyed to page number. The book is nicely typeset; unfortunately, the publisher chose not to issue it in cloth form. The forty-three black-and-white illustrations, although relatively common, are very clearly reproduced on good quality stock.

On the whole, this is an excellent introductory guide to this key decade in the genre's film development. For many of these pictures, Anderson's comments are the longest and most thorough evaluations available in book form.

581. Benson, Michael. **Vintage Science Fiction Films, 1896-1949.** Jefferson, NC & London, McFarland & Co., 1985. ix, 219 p. index. LC 83-42889. ISBN 0-89950-085-4.

This guide from McFarland covers in narrative style the development of the fantastic film through its early decades.

Contents: "Acknowledgements"; "Silents"; "Sound"; "Serials"; "Filmography"; "Bibliography"; "Index."

"Science fiction" is here interpreted in the broadest possible terms, including such monster films as *Mighty Joe Young* and *King Kong,* the horror flick *The Hands of Orlac,* and other borderline pictures. Coverage is more or less chronological by release date, a typical entry providing: title (in italics), production year, a detailed plot summary, and analysis. The longest entry runs three pages (about 1,500 words), and tends to be descriptive, although some attempt at evaluation is included, particularly for the better films.

A separate filmography occupies fifty-two pages of text, arranged alphabetically by film title. A typical entry includes: title (boldfaced italics), production year, color or black-and-white, running time, production company, principal staff (director, producer, screenwriter, cinematographer, special effects technicians, art director, editor, make-up artist, and composer), and main actors with their assigned roles.

A three-page bibliography of other major film books, organized alphabetically by author, gives: author, title (in italics), place of publication, publisher, year of publication, pagination, notation of index, and one- to two-sentence annotation; this listing lacks some significant critiques of the field. The very detailed index correlates all references in the volume to page numbers. The book is nicely typeset, illustrated throughout with black-and-white stills, and bound to library standards.

In reality, there were not very many good SF films made during this period, unless one stretches the definition, as Benson (and many other historians) have been forced to do. One can count on the fingers of one hand the serious, significant attempts to depict a future civilization in motion pictures produced prior to 1950. Benson does about as good a job as any of his fellow critics given the limitations of the genre, covering roughly the same number of films as *Things to Come* (see #599) at greater length, although with fewer and less significant stills. Recommended for research collections.

582. Everman, Welch. **Cult Horror Films: From Attack of the 50 Foot Woman to Zombies Mora Tau.** Secaucus, NJ, A Citadel Press Book, Carol Publishing Group, 1993. 227 p. LC 93-11664. ISBN 0-8065-1425-6 (pbk.).

Contents: "Introduction"; "The Films."

Well-known film and literary critic Everman provides summaries and commentary on eighty-three cult horror films, the entries being arranged alphabetically by title. A typical entry includes: title, year of release, alternate title (if any), director, producer, screenwriter, leading cast, production company, and video distributor, following the same format as the author's *Cult Science Fiction Films* (see #583). The entries average 1,000 words each.

The films covered include classics made from the thirties through the seventies, with such infamously bad titles as *Blood Orgy of the She-Devils* and *The Undying Brain;* a few actually featured well-known actors and directors, including *Audrey Rose* and *The Fury.* There is strong international influence evident here. Everman intentionally omitted blockbuster films.

At times, the author's attempts at levity outweigh any measure of analysis in the entries, which thus often degenerate into *faannish*-style reviews rather than real critiques. However, Everman's detailed plot summaries and brief analytical conclusions are still longer than the treatment most of these flicks have received in similar books, and the 350 rare black-and-white stills are priceless.

The book is weakened by the author's somewhat arbitrary selection criteria. Everman insists that the entries must be horror cult films, and all must be currently available (in 1993) on videocassette. Beyond that, outright trash associates cheek to jowl with real pearls of cinematic horror, without discrimination. Another problem is that, unlike Everman's companion guide to SF movies, this volume has no index, the lack of which makes finding actors, directors, and other film personnel nigh onto impossible. A future edition might also consider a chronology of the films, so that the historical context of the films can be more easily compared.

Cult Horror Films is an enjoyable browse for movie fans, but not an essential purchase for reference collections. For larger public and academic libraries.

583. Everman, Welch. **Cult Science Fiction Films: From The Amazing Colossal Man to Yog—Monster from Space.** New York, A Citadel Press Book, Carroll Publishing Group, 1995. 255 p. index. LC 94-46557. ISBN 0-8065-1602-X (pbk.).

Contents: "Introduction"; "The Films."

Everman provides summaries and commentary on seventy-five cult science fiction films. The entries are arranged alphabetically by title, and include: film title, year of release, alternate title (if any), director, producer, writer, leading cast, production company, and video distributor, following the same format as his *Cult Horror Films* (see #582). The summary/critiques average 1,000 words each. Most of the entries are movies made in the 1950s with such famously bad titles as *Cat-Women of the Moon,* but a few feature major actors and directors, including *The Boys from Brazil, Demon Seed,* and *Medusa Touch.* Blockbuster films have intentionally been omitted.

At times, the author's levity outweighs critical analysis in these evaluations, which often read like fan reviews. But the detailed summaries of the often rather obscure productions are longer than in most similar books. As with Everman's companion guide, *Cult Science Fiction Films* is somewhat weakened by the author's rather arbitrary selection criteria. Entries must be science fiction cult films, as defined in the introduction, and they must all be currently available on videocassette (in 1995). But Everman states that he included "those movies about which [he] felt [he] had something to say," and that he left out many that could have been included. Approximately 375 black-and-white photographs are included from the movies under discussion, at least one per page.

The index is useful for finding actors, directors, and titles of movies, but does not reference any other information mentioned in the entries, such as producers and writers. A

454 / Film and Television Catalogs

future edition might also consider adding a chronology of the movies, so their context in film history and with each other can be more easily compared.

Lightweight and enjoyable, but not an essential reference guide. For large public and academic library collections.

584. Frank, Alan. The Horror Film Handbook. Totowa, NJ, Barnes & Noble Books, 1982. 194 p. index. LC 81-22882. ISBN 0-389-20260-6. London, B. T. Batsford, 1982. 194 p. index. ISBN 0-7134-2724-8.

Frank's catalog is divided into three main sections: "Films," "People," and "Themes." The major part of the book (138 pages) is an A-Z description of all the major (and many minor) horror films from the age of the silents through 1980.

A typical entry records: title (boldfaced caps), country and year of production, production company, principal credits (producer, director, screenwriter, etc.), cast, a one-paragraph plot synopsis, and up to a half dozen brief quotations from other critical sources. Roughly 350 films are covered.

The second section is an alphabetical biographical directory of the major actors and film makers, giving: name (boldfaced), occupation (*e.g.*, "make-up artist"), date and place of birth, highpoints of the individual's career, and a genre filmography (listing film title and production date only).

The final chapter lists basic themes of the horror film (*e.g.*, "Baron Frankenstein"), with a one-paragraph history of the development of that theme, and a detailed chronological filmography that gives: film title, alternate titles, chief star, nationality of film, and year of production. There is a separate checklist of alternative titles and a personal name index keyed to page number. The book is well designed and typeset, illustrated with 232 postage stamp-sized stills, and bound to library standards.

This is a handy one-volume guide to this ever-popular genre, although Hardy (see #588), Stanley (see #605), and Willis (see #609) all cover many more films, sometimes in greater depth. Libraries can safely pass this one by.

585. Frank, Alan. The Science Fiction and Fantasy Film Handbook. Totowa, NJ, Barnes & Noble Books, 1982. 187 p. index. LC 82-8802. ISBN 0-389-20319-X. London, B. T. Batsford, 1982. 187 p. index. ISBN 0-7134-2726-4.

Like his companion volume on horror films (see #584), Frank's guide is divided into three sections covering "Films," "People," and "Themes."

In the "Films" chapter materials are listed alphabetically by title, a typical entry providing: title (boldfaced caps), nationality (abbreviated), release year, production company, producer, director, screenwriter(s), and other major production credits, cast (actors and the characters they play), a one-paragraph plot summary, and a synthesis of critical reactions from other previously published sources. Roughly 400 films are covered, including some foreign-language flicks. The longer entries, dealing with several of the major SF motion pictures from the late 1970s, run two pages.

The twenty-five-page section on "People" is an A-Z guide to the major stars, directors, writers, and other principals who have made significant contributions to SF cinematography. A typical entry gives: name (boldfaced caps), place and date of birth, one-paragraph biographical summary, and principal SF film credits, listed chronologically by title.

The final chapter groups the films by major theme (*e.g.,* "Apocalypse and After," "Time Travel," etc.), then chronologically by year of release. Seven unnumbered pages at the end of the book provide a list of alternative movie titles and an index to persons mentioned in the book, arranged by profession (*e.g.,* "Producers," "Art Directors," etc.), then alphabetically by surname. The book is nicely designed and illustrated throughout with small-sized stills, and bound to library standards.

The liberal inclusion of critical quotes gives the reader an immediate choice of sometimes diverse opinions on every film, but the small number of motion pictures covered severely limits this book's usefulness. Also, the quirky arrangement of the index impedes access for the average user. Prefer Hardy's much more comprehensive work (see #589) as a reference guide, and Stanley's book (see #605) as a filmgoer's guide.

586. Fulton, Roger. **The Encyclopedia of TV Science Fiction.** Bungay, Suffolk, England, Boxtree, 1990. 596 p. (pbk.). **The Encyclopedia of TV Science Fiction.** 2nd ed. Bungay, Suffolk, England, Boxtree, 1995. 727 p. ISBN 1-8528-3953-8 (pbk.). **The Encyclopedia of TV Science Fiction.** 3rd ed. London, Boxtree, 1997. 697 p. ISBN 0-7522-1150-1 (pbk.). Fulton, Roger, & John Betancourt. **The Sci-Fi Channel Encyclopedia of TV Science Fiction.** New York, Aspect, Warner Books, 1998. 668 p. LC 98-33572. ISBN 0-446-67478-8 (pbk.).

Contents (1998 edition): "Preface"; "Entry Format"; "A-Z Listing of Shows"; "Series Databank"; "41 Obscure Shows You'll Probably Never Hear of Again."

The Boxtree editions of Fulton's guide provide a massive, illustrated index to every SF series, serial, one-off play, and animated work shown on British television from 1951 to date, with each new edition updating and subsuming the previous. The American revision by John Betancourt completely incorporates Fulton's work, using the same format as before, but adds new material on U.S. productions not covered in the originals.

The Sci-Fi Channel Encyclopedia covers programs airing from the 1949 debut of *Captain Video* "through roughly the first half of 1998," including some 239 television programs produced for American, British, or Australian television, all of them science fiction, fantasy, and horror, plus several related comedies (*e.g., Third Rock from the Sun*). The shows are arranged alphabetically by series title. Included in each entry is an evaluative overview averaging about 500 words, with much greater coverage of such significant programs as *Star Trek: The Next Generation* and *Doctor Who.* The basic introduction to each series describes its premise, development, and demise, plus lists of the regular cast and character names, production credits, the production company, the number and duration of episodes, the number of episodes produced in black-and-white and color, and premiere dates.

Some (but not all) of the series listings also feature an annotated episode guide in transmission order, with a summary of each episode, plus a record of the writer of that program, the director, guest stars, and character names used in each episode. This lack of consistency in presentation is never explained by the authors. Many popular shows, such as *Xena, Bewitched,* and *Profiler,* only include barebones episode listings without any additional information, while some relatively minor single-season runs (*Logan's Run, Nowhere Man*) have detailed plot summaries. Why?

With most of the American book's information on British programs pulled word-for-word from the Fulton's *The Encyclopedia of TV Science Fiction,* one would have expected these kinds of problems to have been sorted out years ago. The haphazard nature of the authors' information-gathering is never explained, however, particularly since the data are often readily available in other reference sources. Future editions should include annotated episodes for all programs and entries. On the other hand, the detailed chronology that appears in the British editions of this book is omitted in the American version, again for no apparent reason. An index would also have been helpful.

While *The Sci-Fi Encyclopedia* provides an enjoyable guide for fans to skip through, those readers interested in an excellent reference volume on SF television shows should consult instead the *Science Fiction, Horror & Fantasy Film and Television Credits* (see #592) and its several supplements. Not recommended for libraries.

587. Gerani, Gary, with Paul H. Schulman. **Fantastic Television.** New York, Harmony Books, 1977. 192 p. index. LC 76-56821. ISBN 0-517-52646-8; ISBN 0-517-52645-X (pbk.).

Amidst a cornucopia of guides to fantastic films of all kinds, this was the first cyclopedia of fantastic television programs, now long out-of-print and out-of-date, but still a worthy acquisition for any library.

The main section is arranged by series name, in chronological order by initial production date from *The Adventures of Superman* (1953-57) through *Space: 1999* (1975-77). A typical entry gives: two- to eight-page history of the series; summary of continuing credits (seasons produced, total number of episodes, production company, network on which it was aired, usual running time, medium [color or black-and-white], regular cast, and continuing production credits); and an index of episodes, listed season by season, chronologically by production date, giving episode title (bold caps), writer, director, guest cast, and a one- to two-sentence plot summary.

The second section of the volume (thirty-seven pages) includes chapters on "American Telefantasy," an A-Z guide to minor programs with fantastic content, listing: series title (bold caps), seasons, network name, continuing cast, brief series premise and history; "British Telefantasy," organized similarly to the preceding chapter, but covering series that were produced in the U.K.; "Kid Stuff," listing children's live and animated series, with the same data as before; and "Made-for-TV Movies," an alphabetical checklist of all known fantastic films produced for television through 1977. The index coordinates titles and personal names with page numbers. The book is attractively designed, copiously illustrated with many rare stills, and the cloth edition is bound to library standards.

Gerani and Schulman cover thirteen series in depth and many others peripherally, and although their book lacks original air dates (mentioned in Lentz's checklist [see #592]), their coverage of the series in question is more extensive than that in Fulton and Betancourt's more complete and current guide (see #586). The latter does, however, include many more series produced in recent decades, and is thus to be preferred by scholars and fans alike. An updated version would be welcome.

588. Hardy, Phil, ed. **Horror.** London, Aurum, 1986. 408 p. Index. (The Aurum Film Encyclopedia, Volume 3). As: **The Encyclopedia of Horror Movies.** New York, Harper & Row, 1987. 408 p. index. LC 86-45718. ISBN 0-06-055050-3; ISBN 0-06-096146-5 (pbk.). London, Octopus Books, 1986. 408 p. index. LC 88-161097. ISBN 0-7064-2771-8.

Horror. 2nd ed. Woodstock, NY, Overlook Press, 1994. xiii, 496 p. index. LC 93-23387. (The Overlook Film Encyclopedia). ISBN 0-87951-518-X. Contributions by Tom Milne, Kim Newman, Paul Willemen, Julian Petley, Tim Pulleine.

Contents (Second Edition): "Preface to the First Edition"; "Preface to the Second Edition"; "The Horror Film in Perspective"; "The Early Days: Tales of Terror"; "The Twenties: European Nightmares and American Daydreams"; "The Thirties: The Sons and Daughters of Universal"; "The Forties: Horror in Limbo"; "The Fifties: Dracula, Frankenstein and Horror Triumphant"; "The Sixties: The Horror Film Goes International"; "The Seventies: Big and Small Budgets, Horror Goes Up and Down Market"; "The Eighties: Tales of Violence"; "The Nineties: Into the Mainstream"; "All-Time Horror Rental Champs"; "Most-Filmed Horror Writers"; "Index."

This chronological guide to major and minor horror films released between 1896-1992 is organized by year of release date, then alphabetically by title. A typical entry gives: title (boldfaced), English-language title (for foreign films, also boldfaced), production company, nationality, color or black-and-white, running time, a one- to two-paragraph annotation, and major production and casting credits ("d" = director, "p" = producer, "s" = screenwriter, "c" = cinematographer, "lp" = leading players). The annotations are descriptive rather than evaluative, although the final sentence usually provides a summation of a sort (*e.g.,* "sluggishly directed and very wordy").

The second Appendix is an interesting table showing major horror writers (past and present) and their specific works (stories or novels) that have been adapted to the screen; it's no surprise that Edgar Allan Poe dominates the list. The index coordinates film titles and production years. The book is illustrated throughout with small but clearly reproduced black-and-white stills, and is attractively typeset and designed; the cloth version is bound to library standards. Of particular note is the strong introductory essay describing the development of the horror film. The contributors are all British, and there is a noticeable pro-European, anti-American bias evident in selected entries.

Hardy has produced one of the most comprehensive guides to the horror film yet published, detailing some 2,000 motion pictures dating from the very beginnings of the film era through 1992. In particular, the authors' coverage of foreign-language titles is unsurpassed in any other source, and provides sufficient justification in itself for all research libraries to include this volume and its companion works in their collections. Compare with John Stanley's guide (see #605).

589. Hardy, Phil, ed. **Science Fiction.** London, Aurum Press, 1984, 400 p. index. LC 85-145954. (The Aurum Film Encyclopedia, Volume 2). ISBN 0-906053-82-X (pbk.). New York, William Morrow, 1984. 400 p. index. LC 84-60579. ISBN 0-688-00842-9. As: **The Encyclopedia of Science Fiction Movies.** 2nd ed. Minneapolis, MN, Woodbury Press, 1986. 408 p. index. ISBN 0-8300-0436-X. London, Octopus Books, 1986. 408 p. index. ISBN 0-7064-2557-X. **Science Fiction.** 3rd ed. Woodstock, NY, The Overlook Press, 1995, 512 p. index. LC 93-24440. (The Overlook Film Encyclopedia). ISBN 0-87951-626-7 (pbk.). Contributions by Denis Gifford, Anthony Masters, Kim Newman, Paul Taylor, and Paul Willemen.

Contents (Third Edition): "Notes on the Entries"; "Abbreviations and Explanation of Terms"; "Preface to the First Edition"; "Preface to the Second Edition"; "Preface to the Third

Edition"; "The Science Fiction Film in Perspective"; "The Early Years: Innocent Beginnings"; "The Twenties: Dark Visions and Brash Adventure"; "The Thirties: Mad Scientists and Comic Book Heroes"; "The Forties: Science Fiction Eclipsed"; "The Fifties: Science Fiction Reborn"; "The Sixties: Science Fiction Becomes Respectable"; "The Seventies: Big Budgets and Big Bucks"; "The Eighties: Science Fiction Triumphant"; "The Nineties and Beyond: Back to the Future"; "All-Time Science Fiction Rental Champs"; "Critics' Top Tens"; "Science Fiction Oscars"; "Select Bibliography"; "Index" (which only gives the year under which each film is to be found).

This companion volume to Hardy's *Horror* (see #588) is similarly arranged and organized. Films are listed chronologically by year of release, then alphabetically by title. A typical entry provides: movie title (boldfaced), production company, film stock (*e.g.,* "b/w" = black-and-white), running time, one- to three-paragraph annotation, and major production and casting credits (using the same abbreviations as in the volume on horror films [see #588]). The annotations average 150-200 words in length, and are both descriptive and evaluative, with a one- to two-sentence critical summation. Coverage is complete through 1994, with each new edition completely subsuming all previous versions.

The Critics' Top Ten Appendix features top ten SF movie lists from seventeen SF writers and critics, with a paragraph each of discussion. The title index is keyed to production year only, not page numbers, and is reproduced in faint, difficult-to-read six-point type. The volume is illustrated throughout with hundreds of small-sized black-and-white stills (averaging three inches square). *Science Fiction* is nicely designed and printed, and the cloth edition is bound to library standards.

Hardy's coverage of foreign films is excellent, providing plot details on many hard-to-locate SF motion pictures from Europe and Asia. The contributors are all British, and there is a noticeable pro-European, anti-American bias evident in selected entries. Roughly 1,550 movies are delineated in this volume, less than in Stanley's guide (see #605) or in Willis's three-volume set (see #609), but more than in the average pictorial history.

A good acquisition for those medium-sized public libraries or smaller academic collections that can afford just one volume on the subject.

590. Javna, John. **The Best of Science Fiction TV: The Critics' Choice from *Captain Video* to *Star Trek,* from *The Jetsons* to *Robotech*.** New York, Harmony Books, 1987. 144 p. LC 87-21120. ISBN 0-517-56650-8 (pbk.).

Javna's book is fun to read but has very little reference value. The first section of the volume lists the top fifteen SF television series of all time, as voted upon by a group of over a hundred critics, science-fiction writers, fans, and other experts. "Science fiction" is here defined very loosely, with anthology programs such as *Night Gallery* (which usually featured horror and fantasy stories) being included.

A typical entry provides: title, history and development of the series, flashback (well-known quotes taken from various episodes), "Vital Stats" (background setting, brief biographies of the continuing characters, and other basic data), and "Critics' Comments," original mini-critiques by the voting experts on why the series worked or failed. The section part of the book covers "The Worst Ten" SF programs of all time.

Additional chapters cover: "The Classics," "Cult Favorites" (subdivided into "It Came from Japan," "British Science Fiction," "Super-Marionation," "Anthologies," "Cartoons" [in two sections, "The Best and The Worst" and "Golden Age Science Fiction TV"]). A final chapter on sources lists "Recommended Reading," "Photos & Collectibles," and "Fan Clubs." The book is nicely illustrated and designed, but the paperbound version will disintegrate rapidly on library shelves.

Javna's guide covers many more series in far less depth, while *Fantastic Television* (see #587) provides far more detailed technical information and episode guides. The absence of an index in Javna's book is unfortunate, although the very detailed table of contents on pages 4-5 does provide some access. Prefer Fulton and Betancourt's more complete and current guide (see #586).

591. Lee, Walt, and Bill Warren. **Reference Guide to Fantastic Films: Science Fiction, Fantasy, & Horror.** Los Angeles, Chelsea-Lee Books, 1972-74. xli, xviii, xxii, 559, 80, 38, 14 p. in 3 v. LC 72-88775. ISBN 0-913974-04-8 (set); ISBN 0-913974-01-3 (v.1); ISBN 0-913974-02-1 (v.2); ISBN 0-913974-03-X (v.3) (pbk.).

This immense compilation is divided into three sections in each volume: the reference guide proper, "Problems" (printed on blue sheets), and "Exclusions" (printed on yellow sheets), plus front and end matter. Materials are arranged alphabetically by title, the first book covering the letters A-F, the second G-O, and the third P-Z.

A typical entry includes: title (underlined), original title (if first released in a foreign country), year of release, production company, color or black-and-white, running time, production credits (director, producer, screenwriter, art director, cinematographer, editor, score), cast (but not the roles each played), subject categorization (*e.g.,* "SF" = science fiction: "white man's brain transplanted into black man's body"), and references to reviews in the film and SF media and to critical coverage in books (*e.g.,* "MPW 12:150" = *Motion Picture World,* Vol. 12, p. 150), plus "See" references to sequels or other related pictures.

The second (blue-colored) section in each book lists "problems," including motion pictures that may or may not have fantastic content and may not even exist. The third (yellow-colored) part of each volume lists titles that have been listed in other sources as fantastic or whose titles make them sound fantastic, but which have been verified as having no fantasy or SF content. The introductory sections of each volume provide detailed instructions on how to use the book, with duplicate abbreviations' lists. Volume Three contains an original afterword by Forrest J Ackerman at the end of the work, plus a detailed bibliography of sources consulted. There are numerous "See Also" references from one title to another scattered throughout the text, and each book includes a number of clearly reproduced black-and-white stills.

The books are shot from typed copy that is generally legible, but has been reduced to such an extent (to about a six-point level, in four columns per page) that it is difficult for the middle-aged user to read. The paper binding will not withstand heavy use.

This is one of the most detailed A-Z guides to fantastic films yet published, covering in excess of 2,000 titles. Hardy's two catalogs (see #588, #589) are more current, better produced physically, and include plot details not listed in Lee and Warren's work, but lack the latter's subject categories, review sources (very valuable for further study), and lists of peripheral and unverified titles. Libraries and serious researchers into the SF film should own both sets; libraries are advised to rebind the *Reference Guide* immediately into cloth before its heavy weight damages it beyond repair.

592. Lentz, Harris M., III. **Science Fiction, Horror, & Fantasy Film and Television Credits: Over 10,000 Actors, Actresses, Directors, Producers, Screenwriters, Cinematographers, Art Directors, and Make-Up, Special Effects, Costume, and Other People; Plus Full Cross-References from All Films and TV Shows.** Jefferson, NC, McFarland & Co., 1983. xx, 1,374 p. in 2 v. index. LC 82-23956. ISBN 0-89950-071-4 (set); ISBN 0-89950-069-2 (v.1); ISBN 0-89950-070-6 (v.2). **Science Fiction, Horror, & Fantasy Film and Television Credits Supplement 1987.** Jefferson, NC, McFarland & Co., 1989. xii, 924 p. index. LC 88-42646. ISBN 0-89950-364-0. **Science Fiction, Horror, & Fantasy Film and Television Credits Supplement 2: Through 1993.** Jefferson, NC and London, McFarland & Co., 1994. x, 854 p. index. LC 93-33878. ISBN 0-89950-927-4. **Science Fiction, Horror & Fantasy Film and Television Credits.** 2nd ed. Jefferson, NC., McFarland, 2001. xxi, 2227 p. in 3 v. index. LC 00-38656. ISBN 0-7864-0942-8 (set); ISBN 0-7864-0950-9 (v. 1); ISBN 0-7864-0951-7 (v. 2); ISBN 0-7864-0952-5 (v. 3).

Contents (Second Edition): "Acknowledgments"; "Introduction"; "Volume 1: Actor and Actress Credits; Director, Producer, Screenwriter, Cinematographer, Special Effects Technician, Make-Up Artist, Art Director, and Other Credits"; "Volume 2: Filmography"; "Volume 3: Television Shows."

This detailed guide is very simply arranged. Volume 1 is broken into two sections, providing alphabetical listings of "Actor and Actress Credits" and of "Director, Producer, Screenwriter, Cinematographer, Special Effects Technician, Make-Up Artist, Art Director, and Other Credits."

A typical actor entry includes: name (boldfaced), exact dates of birth and death (if known), film credits, and television credits. Only roles in SF, fantasy, or horror motion pictures, television films, or TV shows are included, giving (for films): title (in quotes), year of production (which may also be coupled with the initials "TVM" for a "made for TV movie" or with an abbreviation indicating nationality for overseas flicks), and name of character portrayed; and/or (for television roles) series name (italicized), episode name (in quotes), air date, and character name. Credits are listed in both subsections in descending order by release date. It should be noted that this volume is selective; not all of the individuals listed in the other two volumes are covered here.

Volume 2 comprises the "Filmography." This is arranged alphabetically by film title, typically including: title (boldfaced), year of production, nationality (if other than American), alternate title(s), director, producer, screenwriter (and author of the story credit, if necessary), art director, cinematographer, special effects technician, make-up artist, editor, composer ("Music"), plus a list of all known acting credits, including the name of the character being portrayed by each actor (in parentheses). Television movies include the exact original air date (when known). Alternate titles are cross-referenced to the original or primary title of the film.

Volume 3, covering television series, is organized alphabetically by series name, then chronologically by episode air date, typically providing: series title (boldfaced), production years, continuing series regulars and the characters portrayed by each (with seasons, if they did not serve the entire span); plus a record of each episode aired, listed chronologically by air date, and giving: teleplay title (in quotes), first air date, and the actors and actresses (other than series regulars) who appeared in that episode, with the characters played by each. The books are nicely typeset and bound to library standards.

There are several minor problems with this set. The layout of the "Television Shows" volume often results in multi-seasonal series being listed in long columns of text that tend to blend together for the average user: the use of boldfaced heads, added in the second edition, does help delineate the beginning of each series, particular for short-lived programs, but try, for example, easily to distinguish the various *Star Trek* series listed on pages 2098-2115. It can't be done. The running heads (in this case simply displaying the word "Star" throughout) are no help whatever.

Still, these are relatively minor quibbles, for the two main indices in Volume 1, by actor and by production personnel, provide detailed information generally not available in any other printed source, and give the user quick and invaluable access to this useful material. The Second Edition supersedes all previously-published volumes in these series.

This thoroughly-researched and enormously valuable set should be owned by all academic libraries and every major public library system.

593. Lofficier, Jean-Marc, and Randy Lofficier. **French Science Fiction, Fantasy, Horror and Pulp Fiction: A Guide to Cinema, Television, Radio, Animation, Comic Books and Literature from the Middle Ages to the Present.** Jefferson, NC, McFarland & Co., 2000. xi, 787 p. index. LC 00-39420. ISBN 0-7864-0596-1 (pbk.).

Contents: "Book 1: Science Fiction, Fantasy, Horror and Pulp Fiction in Cinema, Television, Radio, Animation, and Comic Books": "Preamble"; "I. Cinema"; "II. Television;" "III. Radio"; "IV. Animation"; "V. Comic Books and Graphic Novels"; "VI. Selected Biographies."

"Book 2: Science Fiction, Fantasy, Horror and Pulp Fiction in Literature": "Preamble"; "I. The Middle Ages (1100-1500)"; "II. The Renaissance (1500-1650)"; "III. The Enlightenment (1650-1800)"; "IV. 19th Century Fantastique (1800-1914)"; "V. 19th Century Science Fiction (1800-1914)"; "VI. The Fantastique Entre-Deux Guerres (Between the Wars) (1918-1945)"; "VII. Science Fiction Entre-Deux Guerres (Between the Wars) (1918-1950)"; "VIII. Modern Fantastique (After World War II)"; "IX. Modern Science Fiction (After 1950)"; "X. French-Canadian Science Fiction and Fantastique"; "XI. Dictionary of Authors"; "XII. Major Awards"; "Bibliography"; "Index."

The Lofficiers have produced a survey of French fantasy/science fiction/horror across many media up to 1997, with "French" being defined broadly to include Belgian, Swiss, and sometimes French-Canadian works or authors. The text prefers the French word *fantastique* instead of fantasy, because it incorporates fantasy, horror, fairy tales, gothic tales, surrealism, and much more into the definition. Thematically, though not physically, the book is divided into two sections, the first dealing with cinema (feature films and selected short features), television, radio, animation, and comic books/graphic novels, while the second addresses literature.

In Book 1 each chapter begins with a historical overview, a brief essay introducing the art form and its history within *fantastique,* and a list of titles in that medium in alphabetical order by title. There are approximately 350 cinema entries, with the typical entry including: title (bold italics), a translation of the title into English, the title as it actually was distributed in English (if different), a note indicating color or black-and-white, running time, year of first French release, director, main cast (with character names sometimes appearing after the actors' names in parentheses), plot summary (averaging one sentence), and occasionally a note indicating remakes, origin of the story, and other points of interest.

The approximately 150 television entries follow the same format, though some are expanded to include episode entries within the series, again using roughly the same format. Many of the 95 radio serial and play entries are less detailed than other entries, sometimes lacking information on voice actors or plot summaries. The section on animation is as small as the comic book/graphic novel section is large. The 58 entries for animation combine feature films, television, and selected short features, again using the same general format.

The typical entries for the approximately 700 comic books and graphic novel entries show: title (bold italics), translated title (in brackets), and the names of writers and artists. Sometimes a general story arc or genre description note is also included in the "Story" field, and other miscellaneous notes may add additional information, where appropriate. Since many graphic novels are serialized, the series title will often be followed by the issue title (italics), the translated title (in brackets), the publisher, and the year of first release. Occasionally, reprint information will be added as well. Because of information on the specific issue titles, the amount of information provided in this section is much larger than the number of entries might indicate.

The final chapter of Book 1 is a series of brief biographies of the principals in the first half of the book, divided into sections covering filmmakers, comic book writers, and artists. Each of these subsections is organized alphabetically by surname. The typical filmmaker entry includes: name (bold type), years of birth and death (as available), genre films with translated title and year of release, and a brief, professional biography averaging 125 words. The writer and artist section is similarly organized, although there is no clear list of genre publications (they are mentioned throughout the text), with the professional bio usually running less than 100 words. Also included in Book 1 are three interviews with Luc Besson, Rene Laloux, and Moebius.

Book 2 surveys French SF and fantasy literature, much of it reading like a literary history of *fantastique,* with each chapter exploring a specific time and genre, discussing both the literary movements, the significant authors, and their works (p. 293-459).

Chapter XI: Dictionary of Authors provides a title checklist organized by author's last name. The typical entry includes: author's name (bold type), birth and death years (as known), and a list of the writer's book publications in chronological order by publication date, with title (italics), translated title in English (italics), book publisher or periodical name (the latter employing abbreviations from a list of publishers provided at the beginning of the chapter), and year of publication. Many entries lack dates of birth and death, and there are no author biographies similar to those listed in Book 1. Approximately 3,000 author entries are included in this section.

Throughout the text of both books, some names have been highlighted in boldfaced type, indicating that these authors have entries in either the biographical section of Book 1 or in Book 2. Titles highlighted by bold italics are the subject of separate entries in their respective categories. With so many subdivisions, the index becomes an essential finding tool for the names of actors, directors, authors, and artists, both for their biographical entries as well as entries covering their their works; and it does a credible job of gathering the information together and pointing the reader to the pertinent pages.

However, while film titles and series titles appear in the index, the publication titles from Chapter XI in Book 2 are *not* included covered therein, making these impossible to locate unless one already knows the name of the author. The numerous "See" and "See Also" references do help somewhat to move the reader back and forth through different sections of the volume. The book is nicely illustrated throughout with some 500 black-and-white reproductions of posters, people, and cover art.

In spite of a few gaps in coverage and the absence of biographical data for some of the individuals covered (which probably could not be found elsewhere), this is an incredible compilation, highly useful for its reference value and for its chapters of fascinating, clear literary and film history.

No scholar of French cinema or French popular fiction should be without this guide. Highly recommended for all research libraries.

594. Lucas, Tim. **Your Movie Guide to Horror Video Tapes and Discs.** New York, Signet Books, New American Library, 1985. 128 p. ISBN 0-451-13929-1 (pbk.).

One of six such guides prepared by Lucas for *Video Times Magazine,* this book is arranged alphabetically by film title. A typical entry gives: title (bold caps), release year (boldfaced), C[olor] or B[lack and]/W[hite], director, stars, running time (boldfaced), motion picture industry rating (PG, R, etc.), format availability (Beta, VHS, etc.), price, vendor, Lucas's quality rating (one to four asterisks, four being best), and a one-paragraph plot summary.

The annotations are descriptive rather than evaluative, although a tag line at the end of each entry makes some effort at summation. There are scattered "See" references throughout the text to alternative titles. The book is typeset with ragged-right paragraphs, and illustrated throughout with postage stamp-sized stills that reproduce wretchedly on the poor-quality paper. A brief, now obsolete list of video vendors and their addresses complete the text.

All of these data are, of course, laughably out-of-date, and this guide is now not even marginally useful.

595. Lucas, Tim. **Your Movie Guide to Science Fiction/Fantasy Video Tapes and Discs.** New York, Signet Books, New American Library, 1985. 128 p. ISBN 0-451-13930-5 (pbk.).

Lucas prepared six of these slight video guides, two of them on fantastic films and the others on other genres. Data are arranged alphabetically by film title. A typical entry gives: title (bold caps), release year (boldfaced), C[olor] or B[lack and]/W[hite], director, stars, running time (boldfaced), motion picture industry rating (PG, R, etc.), format availability (Beta, VHS, etc.), price, vendor, Lucas's quality rating (one to four asterisks, four being best), and a one-paragraph plot summary.

The annotations are descriptive rather than evaluative, although a tag line at the end of each entry makes some effort at summation. There are scattered "See" references throughout the text to alternative titles. The book is typeset with ragged-right paragraphs and illustrated throughout with postage stamp-sized stills that are barely discernible on the poor-quality paper. A brief, now useless list of video vendors and their addresses completes the text.

Completely outdated.

597. McCarty, John. **Video Screams 1983: The Official Source Book to Horror, Science Fiction, Fantasy, and Related Films on Videocassette and Disc.** Albany, NY, FantaCo Enterprises, 1983. xxxix, 253 p. ISBN 0-938782-02-9 (pbk.).

This basic guide to horror and SF flicks available on videocassette and videodisc arranges its data in alphabetical order by film title. A typical entry gives: motion picture title (boldfaced), rating (one to four screaming head logos, four being best), production year, color or b&w, running time, director, major casting credits, one-paragraph plot summary (ten to one hundred words), and a list of video vendors and availability codes (*e.g.,* "VC" = videocassette).

The appendices include "1. Additional Titles"; "2. Video Sources" (addresses and phone numbers of the vendors); "3. Directors and Their Films" (arranged alphabetically by director's name). The book is illustrated throughout with poorly reproduced black-and-white stills, and cheaply printed on yellowing paper. Now completely outdated and not much good for anything else.

598. Menville, Douglas, and R. Reginald, with Mary A. Burgess. **Futurevisions: The New Golden Age of the Science Fiction Film.** North Hollywood, CA, A Greenbriar Book, Newcastle Publishing Co.; San Bernardino, CA, The Borgo Press, 1985. 192 p. index. LC 85-20098. ISBN 0-89370-681-7 (Borgo); ISBN 0-87877-081-X (pbk.).

This sequel to *Things to Come* (see #599) is organized very similarly.

Contents: "Introduction," by William F. Nolan; "Foreword," by Reginald; "Chapter 1: Futures Past (1897-1976)" [a summary of the material covered in *Things to Come*]; "Chapter 2: Starships and Superheroes (1977-1979)"; "Chapter 3: Telepaths and Time Travelers (1980-1981)"; "Chapter 4: Horrors and Holocausts (1982-1983)"; "Chapter 5: Dreams and Dimensions (1984-1985)"; "Selected Bibliography"; "Title Index."

In each section films are listed chronologically by release date. A typical entry gives: title (boldfaced italics), production year, director, production, production company, and principal actors, embedded within the narrative text. The entries are both descriptive and evaluative, ranging in size from 150-1,500 words (averaging 250), and focusing around each motion picture's integrity to its story and fictive world. The index coordinates titles and page numbers only, principal entries being indicated with boldfaced numbers. The 8.5" x 11" book is nicely illustrated with black-and-white stills that are clearly reproduced in sizes sufficiently large that the connoisseur can distinguish even the smallest details; the cloth edition is bound to library standards.

This is not a major book, but with its predecessor does provide a good introductory guide to the genre during a period of time when some of the best-known flicks in SF film history were released on an unsuspecting public.

599. Menville, Douglas, and R. Reginald. **Things to Come: An Illustrated History of the Science Fiction Film.** New York, Times Books, 1977. [xii], 212 p. index. LC 77-79033. ISBN 0-8129-0710-8; ISBN 0-8129-6287-7 (pbk.).

This basic film guide includes: "Introduction," by Ray Bradbury; "Foreword"; "1. Moon Voyages and Metal Maidens (1895-1929)"; "2. Serials and Scientists (1930-1949)"; "3. Monsters and Menaces (1950-1959)"; "4. Monoliths and Monkeys (1960-1969)"; "5. Wars and Wizards (1970-1977)"; "Selected Bibliography"; "Index of Titles."

In each section materials are arranged chronologically by release date. A typical entry includes: title (boldfaced), production company, release year, and principal actors, embedded in a continuous narrative style. The annotations are both descriptive and evaluative, ranging in size from 50-1,500 words, averaging 150, with entries in the earlier sections being shorter than those in the latter three chapters (the modern period). The 8.5" x 11" book is beautifully illustrated with many rare black-and-white stills, including some running half a page or more in size, with every detail obvious to the devotee. The index coordinates page numbers and titles, principal entries being indicated with italicized numbers. The cloth edition is bound to library standards.

Although not deep, this volume (and its companion book) provide a good basic introduction to the history and chronology of SF film making. The sequel, *Futurevisions* (see #598), continues the narrative through 1985.

600. Newman, Kim, ed. **The BFI Companion to Horror.** London, Cassell, 1996. 352 p. LC 97-131165. ISBN 0-304-33213-5; ISBN 0-304-33216-X (pbk.).

Contents: "Foreword," by Ramsey Campbell; "Contributors"; "Introduction"; [the guide proper].

The BFI Companion to Horror includes more than 1,300 signed entries on "actors, creative personnel, authors, historical figures, major themes, television series, radio shows, cliches, recurrent characters, sub-genres, properties, ephemera, and much else" relating to the horror and dark fantasy genres, arranged alphabetically by main entry, with individual names making up the majority of entries. Crossover entries from science fiction, crime, and comedy are included, so long as they "are depicted in a manner explicitly designed to provoke horror."

A typical entry for individuals includes: entry header (boldfaced type), birth and death years plus nationality (*e.g.,* "American director", "German-born cinematographer"), and a summary of each person's career, usually consisting of a brief general description followed by a list of films (in italics) in which the individual appeared. Entries are usually short, although a few occasionally run much longer (1,757 words for the general topic, "Jack the Ripper"). Although some horror writers are covered, most of the text focuses on personages prominent in film and television production, including actors. "See Also" references buried within an entry are indicated with the use of boldfaced type.

Although most of the black-and-white illustrations derive from motion pictures, there are actually very few entries in this guide covering specific movies, unless the film produced sequels, such as *Alien, The Amityville Horror,* and *Hellraiser,* or has been remade repeatedly, such as *Dracula* or *Gaslight.* Horror television series that aired either in the United Kingdom or in the United States are also included. In addition, topical entries on "Mutation," "Mummies," "Ecohorror," "China," "Hammer Films," "Expressionism," and "Universities," to name but a few, provide much supplemental coverage on related topics.

The thirty-five contributors are mostly well-known British critics, whose middle-of-the-road judgments seem based on considerable knowledge of the field. The volume is attractively typeset in a three-column format, bound to library standards, and illustrated with one-to-three stills per page, plus a four-page color insert in the introduction. The frequent "See Also" references and the alphabetical arrangement mitigate somewhat against the absence of a general index.

Hovering somewhere between an international "who's who" of horror and a coffee table-style guide to the genre, *The BFI Companion* is a good cinematic café for film fans to visit, and a convenient starting point for researchers of the genre. For medium-sized libraries.

601. Parish, James Robert, and Michael R. Pitts. **The Great Science Fiction Pictures.** Metuchen, NJ, Scarecrow Press, 1977. viii, 382 p. LC 77-5426. ISBN 0-8108-1029-8. **The Great Science Fiction Pictures II.** Metuchen, NJ & London, Scarecrow Press, 1990. x, 489 p. LC 89-24058. ISBN 0-8108-2247-4.

Both of these volumes are similarly organized. The unnumbered Volume 1 includes: "Authors' Note and Acknowledgments"; "The Great Science Fiction Pictures"; "Science Fiction Shows on Radio and Television," by Vincent Terrace; "A Select Bibliography of Science Fiction Bibliographies, Indexes and Checklists," by Stephen Calvert; "About the Authors and Staff." Volume 2: "Acknowledgments"; "Introduction"; "Great Science Fiction Pictures II"; "Science Fiction on Radio and TV"; "About the Authors."

In each volume, the main section is arranged alphabetically by film title. A typical entry provides: title (all caps), production company, year of release, running time, all major (and many minor) production credits, all major (and many minor) casting credits, with the names of characters each actor portrays, a one-to-two-paragraph plot summary (running 100 to 250 words), and one-to-two paragraphs of analysis and critique, including excerpts from previously published reviews of the film. The critical bibliography at the end of Volume 1 is now wholly outdated and utterly useless.

The brief checklists of fantastic radio and TV series at the rear of both volumes (in alphabetical order by series title) provide a skeletal and incomplete guide that lists: series title (all caps), production network, first and last air dates, and series cast regulars (but without the names of the characters they portray); this information can be found in much greater detail in Fulton and Betancourt (see #586). The first volume is shot from clear typed copy; the second volume is nicely typeset, and both are bound to library standards. Both books are illustrated throughout with clearly reproduced but rather small film stills.

Roughly 350 films are covered in Volume 1, and 450 in Volume 2. Although the second work generally focuses on motion pictures produced from 1977-86, approximately one-fourth of the entries consist of older flicks not covered in the first guide, spanning the entire history of fantastic films; and since the second book fails to include a list of the titles covered in Volume 1, one must constantly flip back and forth between the two to determine if a particular work has been analyzed by the authors. This is just bad design, and the problem will only get worse when future volumes appear.

So far as content is concerned, Parish and Pitts make an effort in their guides to provide both critical analyses as well as descriptions, sprinkling their own opinions with numerous quotations from other critics, some excerpted from published reviews, some from other film histories and catalogs. The result provides the reader with a good mixture of favorable and unfavorable views of particular films from a wide variety of sources.

This set should be acquired by most academic and all large public libraries. Future volumes should include a master checklist of all the films covered in the set, referencing the appropriate volume number.

602. Phillips, Mark, and Frank Garcia. **Science Fiction Television Series: Episode Guides, Histories, and Casts and Credits for 62 Prime Time Shows, 1959 through 1989.** Jefferson, NC, and London, McFarland & Co., 1996. xii, 691 p., index. LC 95-47667. ISBN 0-7864-0041-2.

Contents: "Acknowledgments"; "Foreword," by Kenneth Johnson; "Introduction"; "A-Z List of Series"; "Appendix A: Honorable Mentions"; "Appendix B: Unsold Science Fiction Television Pilots"; "Appendix C: Emmy Award Nominees and Winners in Science Fiction Television"; "Bibliography"; "Index."

With one exception (*Science Fiction Theater*), this book covers shows that began their runs between 1959-89. Excluded are horror programs, mentioned in Appendix A, associated programs such as *The Wild, Wild West* and *The Man from U.N.C.L.E.,* science fiction/situation comedies such as *Mork and Mindy,* and children's live-action and cartoon presentations. Of the 62 entries featured, most are American productions, but four British series are included: *UFO, The Prisoner, The Champions,* and *Space: 1999.*

Entries are arranged alphabetically by title. A typical entry header includes: program title and general air dates (bold type; specific air dates of individual programs are not provided), and the premise of the show (centered italics). This is followed in the body of each entry by a list of the continuing cast (actors and their character names), production crew (producers, music score, theme), studio, and typical episode running time. The next part of the entry includes a description of the development and demise of each show (averaging 2000-6000 words), using quotations from "over 250 writers, directors, actors, stuntmen and craftsmen, plus the shows' creators." The final section of each entry is "Cast Notes," in which each regular cast member is either briefly profiled, and/or sometimes quoted with their opinions on the show.

The episode guide portion of the entry typically includes: episode title, plot synopsis (averaging 25 words), writer, director, and guest actors' names and characters (in parentheses). Oddly, Phillips and Garcia include air times figured *with* commercials. The general index covers all of the individuals mentioned, which is very useful for finding directors and actors who worked across several shows, as well as establishing connections to other programs not given main entries in the book.

The extensive quotations from cast and crew, which are not cited to any bibliographical source, provide much supplemental material of interest to both fans and students of genre television alike. For those who want just episode summaries and general production information on SF TV programs, books such as *The Sci-Fi Channel Encyclopedia of TV Science Fiction* (see #586) will more than suffice. For everyone else, this is a good, solid, one-volume guide to genre programming information.

603. Pickard, Roy. **Science Fiction in the Movies: An A-Z.** London, Frederick Muller, 1978. 139 p., [16] p. of plates. index. ISBN 0-584-10442-1.

This curious little volume covers actors, directors, characters, terms, and films in one alphabetical sequence. A typical film entry gives: title (boldfaced type), year of production (italics), one-paragraph plot summary, production company, major credits, nationality, and running time. A typical personal entry provides: name (boldfaced type), years of birth and death (where available, when appropriate), nationality, occupation, and a one-paragraph summary of his or her career in SF films.

Other entries feature places ("Sorgo, a space-age Gomorrah . . . "), things ("The Space Gun, a vertical gun of vast dimensions . . . "), and a hodgepodge of other irrelevancies. Sixteen pages of plates grouped between pages 68-69 clearly reproduce rather common black-and-white movie stills. There is also a brief bibliography of eight items, and a three-page index listing names and film titles with page numbers.

Obviously issued to capitalize on the *Star Wars* phenomenon, this wholly forgettable guide has absolutely nothing unique to offer either the researcher, fan, or librarian, and may thus be safely consigned to the black hole of SF film criticism.

604. Senn, Bryan, and John Johnson. **Fantastic Cinema Subject Guide: A Topical Index to 2500 Horror, Science Fiction, and Fantasy Films.** Jefferson, NC, and London, McFarland & Co., Inc., 1992. xv, 682 p. LC 91-51230. ISBN 0-89950-681-X.

Contents: "Acknowledgments"; "Introduction (or, How to Use This Book)"; "Index to Subjects Covered"; [the guide itself]; "Appendix A: Blaxploitation"; "Appendix B: 3-D"; "Appendix C: Westerns"; "Title Index (Including the Authors' Rating, from 1-10, of 1,908 of the Films)."

Senn and Johnson's book was created to serve as a movie advisory subject guide for fans and researchers. Roughly 2,500 entries covering international science fiction, horror and fantasy films released before May 1991 are organized alphabetically, first under 29 major subject headings (plus additional sub-headings and "See" references), and then alphabetically by title.

Each subject area includes a brief general introduction "defining the subject and its various particulars: origins, highlights, 'lowlights,' and the trends." A typical film entry includes: title (bold type), year of release, "See" reference(s) (where appropriate), distributor, country of origin (if not U.S.), alternate title(s), director, producer, screenwriter, cinematographer, cast, and a plot synopsis averaging 100 words. Often the authors add a quotation from the movie itself, and sometimes a bullet will set off an interesting sidenote. Three small appendices, covering associated blaxploitation, 3-D, and western films, each provide a list of 10-22 films that fall into those categories. The book is illustrated throughout with black-and-white stills from the movies.

The title index includes all of the films covered in the guide, in alphabetical order by title, giving production year, rating, and page number(s) where featured; a boldfaced number cross-references the inclusion of a still from that movie. Some (but not all) of the motion pictures listed in the title index show a rating code following the production year, from 1-10 (in brackets), the number 10 being best, but these are not at all obvious, and may be lost to all but the savviest users.

While the classified organization of the movies is certainly a useful datum not readily obtainable elsewhere, the actual scheme of the book may be too fragmented for the average movie fan to use well. For example, there are separate sections for movies about "Zombie Flesh Eaters" and just plain "Zombies," and while the authors provide a "See Also" reference to help users find both, is this really something the world needs to know? The material is set in very small type, and all of the paragraphs and bulleted commentary in one entry are run together. Particularly in the longer entries, the text is very difficult to distinguish with middle-aged eyes. Finally, no indexing is provided for casts and crew.

Fan audiences may prefer the glitzier, more pungent publications such as the Overlook encyclopedias (see #588 and #589), but *Fantastic Cinema Subject Guide* remains much more comprehensive than many similar stand-alone volumes, covering large numbers of "B" films of the 1950s and '60s, and providing subject access that cannot be found elsewhere. Recommended for academic libraries.

605. Stanley, John. **The Creature Features Movie Guide; or, An A to Z Encyclopedia to the Cinema of the Fantastic; or, Is There a Mad Doctor in the House?** Pacifica, CA, Creatures at Large, 1981. 208 p. LC 81-67664. ISBN 0-940064-00-6 (pbk.). **The Creature Features Movie Guide; or, An A to Z Encyclopedia to the Cinema of the Fantastic; or, Is There a Mad Doctor in the House?** [2nd] rev. ed. New York, Warner Books, 1984. xv, 304 p. LC 83-23574. ISBN 0-446-38006-7 (pbk.); ISBN 0-446-38008-3 (pbk.; Canada). **Revenge of the Creature Features Movie Guide; or, An A to Z Encyclopedia to the Cinema of the Fantastic; or, Is There a Mad Doctor in the House?** 3rd rev. ed. Pacifica, CA, Creatures at Large Press, 1988. xxiv, 420 p. LC 87-91426. ISBN 0-940064-05-7; ISBN 0-940064-04-9 (pbk.). **John Stanley's Creature Features Movie Guide Strikes Again: An A to Z Encyclopedia to the Cinema of the Fantastic; or, Is There a Mad Doctor/ Dentist in the House?** 4th rev. ed. Pacifica, CA, Creatures at Large Press, 1994. 454 p. LC 93-74251; ISBN 0-940064-10-3; ISBN 0-940064-09-X (pbk.); ISBN 0-940064-08-1 (Creature Features Series). **Creature Features: The Science Fiction, Fantasy, and Horror Movie Guide.** New [5th] ed. New York, Boulevard Books, 1997. x, 582 p. LC 97-116578. ISBN 1-57297-225-4 (pbk.). **Creature Features: The Science Fiction, Fantasy, and Horror Movie Guide.** Updated [6th] ed. New York, Berkley Bouvelard Books; London, Turnaround, 2000. xii, 596 p. LC 00-709627. ISBN 0-425-17517-0 (pbk.).

Contents (Fourth Edition): "Introduction: Day of the Terminating Dinosaur: Are Humans Becoming Extinct?," by John Stanley; "The Age of Morphing"; "Electronic Home Delivery"; "Fourth Edition—Read All About It"; "Video/Laserblast"; "Important Video/ Laser Companies"; "Thanks for the . . . " (acknowledgments); "Loving Horror"; "The Guide" (an A-Z list of films).

This continuing reference guide had expanded to 5,614 mini-reviews of fantastic films by the fourth edition (1994), making it the largest single-volume catalog of science-fiction, fantasy, and horror films yet published. Materials are arranged alphabetically by film title.

A typical entry includes: title (boldfaced caps), year of release (parentheses), and a one-paragraph annotation. Made-for-TV flicks are included with the rest and so indicated in the body of the text. The descriptions include both plot summaries and evaluations, with witty comments occasionally added to enliven the material, plus mention of the leading players; the director is usually listed at the end of the entry, and occasionally the screenwriter, as is the production company.

Following the entry (in the third edition only) is a code ("VC") indicating whether the film is available on videocassette; in the fourth edition this is indicated by the words "Laser" or "Video" in parentheses. All fourth editions are illustrated with different black-and-white stills, well reproduced (if small in size) from the original motion pictures. The books are nicely typeset and designed, and the cloth version of the third edition is bound to library standards.

Stanley's guides are intended to provide quick reference sources for the TV and VCR viewer and SF film fan, and in no way supplant the more detailed volumes covered herein, particularly Hardy's two books (see #588 and #589), or Willis's catalog (see #609). The author obviously intends to keep his work current and to continue expanding and developing earlier entries (for example, the entry for *The Bamboo Saucer,* a very forgetable 1967 flick, has been wholly recast in the third edition, expanding its size to three times the original version and providing many more details). A useful addition to a future edition would be a rating system.

The fifth edition "cut down on the number of entries, eliminating many older titles, obscure and/or lost movies," but also includes 500 new feature films and TV and straight-to-video movies. There are still over 5,000 entries covered, including abundant "See" references for name changes. This version does not refer to the earlier editions, so there is no way to know what titles have been removed or where to find a review. All pictures and illustrations have been eliminated. However, the fifth edition does include a welcome rating system (one star through five stars, with half-star increments) for fans who want to target the best flicks in the genre.

The sixth edition includes "all the major releases, and some minor ones, since 1997," including some 4,000 main entries with over 1,500 "See" references. The introduction provides a nice review of the trends and pitfalls of current genre movie-making. Older entries remain unchanged in this edition, and few stills have been included here.

Only days before the fourth edition went to press, horror film guru Joe-Bob Briggs mentioned that he keeps a copy of *The Creature Features Movie Guide* by his bed, stating that, in his opinion, "Never has so much worthless information been gathered together in one place." We couldn't agree more, but what Joe-Bob fails to mention is just how much fun this book is, for fans and film buffs alike.

Stanley's handy guides should be purchased by all large public library systems. Prefer the definitive (and better printed) fourth edition, using the fifth and sixth editions primarily as supplements.

606. Strickland, A. W., and Forrest J Ackerman. **A Reference Guide to American Science Fiction Films, Volume 1.** Bloomington, IN, T.I.S. Publications Division, 1981. xvii, 397 p. index. LC 81-158697. ISBN 0-89917-268-7.

Projected as a four-volume set (of which only the first was ever published), *A Reference Guide to American Science Fiction Films* organizes its data chronologically by publication date, year by year, then alphabetically by title within each year.

Contents: "Foreword"; "Preface"; "List of Illustrations"; "Explanation Key and Abbreviations"; "Acknowledgements"; "Films: 1897-1909"; "1910-1919"; "1920-1929"; "Filmography"; "Summary Classification of Films"; "Summary Releasing Companies"; "References"; "Bibliography"; "Index."

A typical entry provides: title (boldfaced caps, centered), release date, production company, description (*e.g.,* "silent" or "sound"), number of feet of film, classification (*e.g.,* "SF" = science fiction), references (keyed to a list of numbered secondary sources on pages 385-87, and giving item number, volume number, and page number), production credits, casting credits, and an annotation ranging in size from fifty words (for some early silent shorts) to over 2,000 words for several of the major pictures of the 1920s. The descriptions include detailed plot summaries, historical notes, evaluations, and extensive excerpts from contemporaneous critical reviews (with exact citations of sources). The entries are illustrated with very rare, full-page stills carefully reproduced in black-and-white; few of these are available in any other source.

Each chapter includes at the end of that decade's films a classification list, arranging films by subject and production year, plus an index to production companies and the SF films they released, year by year. End matter includes a detailed filmography arranged in chronological order, giving film titles and production years, an overall classification of SF movies from 1897-1929 (arranged similarly to the chapter classifications), an overall index to production companies and their films (arranged as above), a list of references and the reference numbers assigned to each by the authors, a detailed bibliography of periodical sources, and a title index coordinating films with page numbers for their entries.

The amount of data here on early SF motion pictures is unsurpassed in any other source. The combination of Ackerman's knowledge of the origins of the fantastic film and his immense collection of early film memorabilia and stills, and the academic documentation brought to the project by Dr. Albert Strickland, make this work *the* standard resource volume on SF pictures of the silent era. All research libraries should own copies of this outstanding guide.

607. Warren, Bill; research associate, Bill Thomas. **Keep Watching the Skies! American Science Fiction Movies of the Fifties.** Jefferson, NC & London, McFarland & Co., 1982-86. xvi, 467, xx, 839 p. in 2 v. index. LC 81-19324. ISBN 0-89950-191-5 (set); ISBN 0-89950-032-3 (v.1); ISBN 0-89950-170-2 (v.2).

Warren attempts to annotate every science-fiction film released in America between 1950-62 inclusive, Volume 1 covering 1950-57, and Volume 2 the years 1958-62.

Contents (v.1): "Acknowledgments"; "The Chapter Illustrations"; "1950"; "1951"; "1952"; "1953"; "1954"; "1955"; "1956"; "1957"; "Appendix I: Cast and Credits"; "Appendix II: Films in Order of Release"; "Appendix III: Announced (But Not Produced) Films"; "Appendix IV: SF Serials of the 1950s"; "Index."

Contents (v.2): "Acknowledgments"; "The Illustrations"; "A Note on Quotations in the Text"; "Preface"; "1958"; "1959"; "1960"; "1961"; "1962"; "Addenda" (to Volume 1); "Selected Bibliography" (for Volumes I and II); "Appendix I: Credits and Cast"; "Appendix II: Films in Order of Release"; "Appendix III: Announced (But Not Produced) Titles"; "Index"; "A Final Word."

The motion pictures covered herein are organized in chronological order by release date, year by year, then alphabetically by title. Main entries include no credits, which are provided separately in an alphabetically arranged appendix at the end of each book. A typical credits entry gives: title (boldfaced type), production credits, casting credits (characters' names in italics), production company, color or black-and-white, running time, alternate titles, and other details of interest.

The annotations in the main section of each volume are quite lengthy, running from 400-6,000 words (averaging 1,500), and are simultaneously descriptive, analytic, and historical, providing extensive information on how each film was made, how well it was received (both contemporaneously and by present-day critics, with selected quotations), and Warren's own reactions to it.

The books are illustrated throughout with clearly reproduced, full- and half-page black-and-white stills from the pictures. At the end of each volume, in addition to the extensive lists of credits, Warren includes appendices providing chronological checklists of the exact release dates of each motion picture (so far as they are known), and lists of movie projects that were announced but never completed. Serials are not covered in these guides, but a brief checklist of serial productions appears at the end of Volume 1. Both books contain comprehensive indices correlating all personal names and film titles with page numbers, photo pages being indicated with boldfaced type. The set is nicely typeset and bound to library standards.

These are immense productions, filled with data and background details that are just not available in any other single source. Warren's mini-essays represent in most cases the lengthiest critical analyses generally available on each of these motion pictures. This set should be purchased by every research library worthy of the name, and by any film critic seriously interested in the development of the SF film.

608. Widner, James F., and Meade Frierson III. **Science Fiction . . . on Radio: A Revised Look at 1950-1975.** Birmingham, AL, A.F.A.B., 1996. 194 p. LC 96-83951. ISBN 0-9639544-4-X (pbk.; spiral-bound).

Contents: "Dedications"; "Acknowledgements"; "Sources and Resources"; "Radio's Appeal and the Focus of This Book"; "Science Fiction and Its Role on Radio before 1950"; "Science Fiction on Radio in the Period 1950-1959"; "Science Fiction on Radio in the Period 1960-1975"; "Index"; "Backword."

Previous versions of this history and checklist of radio SF programs in the United States and Great Britain were issued in limited circulation editions between 1972-76.

Materials are arranged in chronological order by the earliest known production date of the radio program series, the series titles being listed on the contents page at the front of the book. A typical series entry provides: series title (boldfaced type, centered), brief history of the program, number of episodes, producer, director, host, announcer, series broadcast schedule, list of the individual episodes with SF content, in chronological order by air date, and title index for that series. Individual SF episodes are assigned a chronological item number (*e.g.*, "T-1" is the first episode of the series, *2000 Plus*), and usually include the following information: item number (boldfaced), episode title (boldfaced), original air date, story and adaptation writing credits, cast with the names of the characters each played, plot summary (when known, in italics), and "Publishing Notes" providing publication data on the original story or novel on which the adaptation is based, with brief bibliographical data.

The title index correlates personal names, episode and series titles, and production companies with episode numbers (boldfaced type) and page numbers (listed in bracketed regular type after the episode numbers). Birth and death years of individuals are included within parentheses (when known) after each person's name in the index. The book is nicely typeset and spiral-bound in stiff paper covers, allowing the pages to lie completely flat.

Widner and Frierson's history seems complete and thorough, but the chronological arrangement of the radio series titles may become irritating to the casual user; an alphabetical listing would perhaps have better served the researcher. Still, there's nothing else available that includes even a tenth of this information.

For larger research libraries, and collections specializing in communication.

609. Willis, Donald C. **Horror and Science Fiction Films: A Checklist.** Metuchen, NJ, Scarecrow Press, 1972. xi, 612 p. LC 72-3682. ISBN 0-8108-0508-1. **Horror and Science Fiction Films II.** Metuchen, NJ & London, Scarecrow Press, 1982. xiv, 474 p. LC 81-23295. ISBN 0-8108-1517-6. **Horror and Science Fiction Films III.** Metuchen, NJ & London, Scarecrow Press, 1984. xiii, 335 p. LC 84-13885. ISBN 0-8108-1723-3.

Willis's guides cumulatively provide one of the most comprehensive reference work yet published on the fantastic film, although they suffer somewhat from being broken into three separate alphabetical sequences.

Contents (Volume I): "Introductory Notes and Acknowledgments"; "Explanatory Notes"; 'Abbreviations"; "Horror and Science-Fiction Films: A Checklist"; "Titles Announced for Release in 1971-1972"; "Shorts (1930-1971), and Animated and Puppet Films"; "Out List" (*i.e.,* borderline or misleading titles, those with only slight SF elements, or items that cannot be verified); "References."

Contents (Volume II): "Introduction"; "Explanatory Notes"; "Abbreviations"; "Horror and Science Fiction Films II: Main List"; "Peripheral and Problem Films"; "Principal References"; "Addenda."

Contents (Volume III): "Introduction"; "Explanatory Notes"; "Abbreviations"; "Horror and Science Fiction Films III: 1982-1983: Main List"; "Peripheral and Problem Films"; "Alternate Titles" (Volumes I & II); "Principal References"; "Addenda."

The bulk of each book consists of an alphabetical list of film titles. A typical entry provides: title (all caps), production company, year of release, color or black-and-white, running time, alternate title(s), director, screenwriter, and other production credits, references to the publication (listed in the bibliography at the end of the volume) from which verification was cited, casting credits, and annotation. The annotations in Volume I are either nonexistent (for many early silent shorts) or very brief (for later films), usually consisting of no more than one or two sentences (*e.g.,* "Men on Mars and the moon in the year 2021").

Volume II expands the annotations into a full paragraph, although comments on lesser films remain brief. In Volume III Willis has increased his annotations up to several pages of text for better films, the average being two paragraphs, although some entries remain very short. End matter for each book includes: unverified titles (listed alphabetically by title, with the source of reference indicated), bibliography, and (for Volumes II and III) brief addenda sections. The books are shot from sometimes faint typed copy, and bound to library standards. There are no illustratations.

Willis includes an enormous amount of data in these books, covering 4,400 titles in Volume I, 2,350 in II, and 760 in III, for a total of roughly 7,500 foreign and domestic motion pictures with some fantastic content. Many of the films are peripheral by anyone's standards, and few are important to the development of the field; yet it is still necessary that they be recorded.

The major problem with these volumes, other than the fact that an important library publishing company has once again issued a set of major reference sources "on the cheap," without bothering to have them professionally typeset, lies in their organization. The user must run through five alphabetical sequences (the three main sections, plus two addenda; titles from the first addenda have not been incorporated into the text of Volume III) potentially to locate a particular title. This is because the second and third volumes include, in addition to many new titles, numerous "fill-ins" missing from the original guide. Without a coordinating index, there is simply no easy way for the reader to determine where a title may be found, or indeed *if* it will be located, in any of the three books. Perhaps this problem is insurmountable given the nature of this type of guide, but it should be addressed in any fourth volume.

In the meantime, these books will provide the scholar with an immense amount of research material, and should be included in every large academic collection.

610. Willis, Donald C., ed. *Variety's* **Complete Science Fiction Reviews.** New York & London, Garland Publishing Co., 1985. xiv, 479 p. index. LC 85-25257. ISBN 0-8240-6263-9; ISBN 0-8240-8712-7 (pbk.).

Willis has compiled contemporaneous reviews of fantastic films reproduced facsimile from the weekly movie industry journal, *Variety.* The first essay, taken from the November 23, 1907 issue of the magazine, discusses *Liquid Electricity,* and the last, dated December 26, 1984, evaluates the Mexican film, *Historias Violentas.* Approximately 1,200 motion pictures are covered, in essays ranging in size from 100-1,000 words, averaging 300. The annotations are both descriptive and evaluative, and typically include: casting and production credits, running time, MPAA rating, and other particulars of interest. For those who have not previously seen *Variety,* the emphasis here is on the marketability of the films being reviewed, and not necessarily on their art or literacy, although such factors are often mentioned in passing.

The essays are shot facsimile from the original publications and pasted onto a three-column format, with some type (particularly from the early years) being very small (around a six-point level) and/or faint and difficult to read. A dozen full-page illustrations are sprinkled throughout the text; the cloth edition is bound to library standards. The index coordinates film titles and page numbers only.

Variety's reviews tend towards the dyspeptic, but this is a refreshing change from the often adulatory critiques featured in many other film guides. All research libraries should acquire copies, whether or not they own a complete run of the magazine.

611. Wingrove, David, ed. **The Science Fiction Film Source Book.** Harlow, England, Longman, 1985. vi, 312 p. LC 86-215261. ISBN 0-582-89239-2; ISBN 0-582-89310-0 (pbk.).

Wingrove, the author of an earlier volume on SF authors and their works, *The Science Fiction Source Book* (see #106), here provides a similarly designed rating guide to SF films. Materials are arranged alphabetically by film title.

A typical entry includes: title (boldfaced), production year, description, ratings, director, writer, major cast credits, and an abbreviation indicating which of the entries were contributed by the editor's panel of five judges (a majority of entries were penned by Wingrove himself). The annotations are both descriptive and evaluative, typically running 150 words and including a one-sentence critical summation; selected entries on major films range up to 500 words in length.

A unique feature of this guide is a series of four ratings for each motion picture, evaluating Plot (P), Technical Merit (T), Enjoyment (E), and Artistic Merit (A), using a five-star system, five being best. Roughly 1,350 films are covered, from earliest times through 1984. There are a few postage stamp-sized, black-and-white stills scattered throughout the text.

Other matter includes: "Foreword" by Brian W. Aldiss; a one-page "Chronology of Important Films" (through 1984); "The SF Serials, 1913-1956"; "Creators of SF on Screen" (brief biographies and filmographies of the major directors, actors, and others, arranged in alphabetical order by name); "The Literary Sources: Books into Film" (a very useful guide, arranged alphabetically by surname, to the authors and their stories or novels of material that has been adapted into SF films); "Special Effects in Science Fiction Cinema" (a ten-page essay by well-known critic John Brosnan); "All-Time Rental Figures for SF Films" (now vastly outdated); and "Select Bibliography." There is no index. The book is attractively designed and typeset, and the cloth edition is bound to library standards.

Unfortunately, Wingrove's guide never achieved U.S. publication, making it one of the least known works covered in this section. It deserved better. The judgments here are sound and balanced, and the ratings fairly apportioned; the section delineating SF "Books into Film" provides a unique perspective unavailable in any other source. A new edition would definitely be warranted.

612. Wright, Gene. **The Science Fiction Image: The Illustrated Encyclopedia of Science Fiction in Film, Television, Radio, and the Theater.** New York, Facts on File Publications, 1983. 336 p., [16] p. of plates. LC 82-2348. ISBN 0-87196-527-5. As: **Who's Who & What's What in Science Fiction Film, Television, Radio, & Theater.** New York, Bonanza Books, 1985. ix, 336 p. LC 85-14680. ISBN 0-517-48886-8. The latter includes a new introduction, "The S.F. Success," by Isaac Asimov, but is otherwise identical internally.

Like Pickard's guide (see #603), Wright's encyclopedia tries to be all things to all people and suffers from similar problems. *The Science Fiction Image* mixes entries on SF films, television programs, radio series, writers, directors, actors, and other terms in one alphabetical sequence.

A typical film entry gives: title (boldfaced caps), type (*e.g.,* "TV film"), release year, nationality, running time, color or black-and-white, annotation, production credits, and casting credits. A typical personal entry provides: name (boldfaced caps), years of birth and death (if known), a description of the individual's career, and a brief filmography of the person, listing motion pictures (in italics) with release years of productions in which the person has been active. The annotations range in size from 50-1,000 words (averaging 200), and are both descriptive and evaluative. "See Also" references are noted by highlighting text within an entry in boldfaced type; Wright also includes some "See" references from alternate titles to main entries. The book is illustrated throughout with 200 clearly reproduced black-and-white stills, plus sixteen pages of color stills, and is bound to library standards.

There are several problems with this book. The volume shows signs of having been thrown together with great haste. For example, an entry header is missing on page 111, the entries on pages 237-38 are way out of alphabetical sequence, the *Millennium Falcon* entry is misspelled, at least one photo on the color plates is completely miscredited, etc. There is simply no excuse for these kinds of lapses appearing in a reference work from a major publisher.

One must also question the selection criteria employed by Wright. On what basis were some films or filmmakers included, and others not? The choices seem haphazard at best: *Star Trek* (both television series and motion pictures) is covered in great detail, with separate entries on Mr. Spock (under "M"), Ensign Pavel Chekhov (under "E" in the alphabet, with no "See" references), Leonard Nimoy, the Klingons, the Romulans, the *Enterprise,* Gene Roddenberry, Transporter Room, Tricorder, Phaser, etc., but *not* on William Shatner, Capt. James T. Kirk, Leonard McCoy (or DeForest Kelley), or any of the other characters or principals. Why?

One can get a better idea of the problem by noting that the halfway point in the text (pages 168-69) features entries covering the early "G" part of the alphabet, when we would expect it to find terms from the "L"'s or "M"'s. In fact, the last one hundred pages of text, less than a third of the entire book, feature entries from Ma-Z, more than half of the alphabet. One has the clear impression that the author was forced at the last minute to cull a significant amount of wordage from this section to make the book fit into a preconceived size.

The result is a hodgepodge, occasionally entertaining or enlightening (Wright's comments are usually sound), but more often than not simply frustrating to the potential user. If extensively reworked and expanded, this volume has the potential to become a true SF film encyclopedia, but in its present form, it lacks authority.

SPECIFIC MOVIES, TV PROGRAMS, OR SUBJECTS

Babylon 5

613. Bassom, David. **The A-Z Guide to *Babylon 5*.** New York, Dell, 1997. 309 p. index. ISBN 0-440-22385-7 (pbk.).

Contents: "Introduction"; "A Key to the Abbreviations"; "The A-Z Guide to *Babylon 5*"; "Appendix I: Timeline of Important Events"; "Appendix II: Story Guide"; "Appendix III: Indexes by Group"; "Appendix IV: Index of Sources"; "Appendix V: Alphabetical Index of Sources"; "Appendix VI: The *Babylon 5* Jokebook."

Bassom provides an A-Z dictionary of *Babylon 5*'s people, places, and things appearing in the program's first fifty-one episodes (or, in other words, through the first four episodes of season three), plus the eleven comic books issues and four *B5* novels that had appeared by the time of publication. Approximately 550 entries are included, the typical entry including: topic (boldfaced), definition (about 50 words), and an abbreviation of the episode title (all caps in parentheses). Entries for important figures (Delenn or Sheridan, for example), can run much larger. The abbreviations key is located at the front of the book.

Appendix I includes a brief time line of major events. Appendix II summarizes the episodes, comics, and books covered in the dictionary, a typical entry including: title (boldfaced), abbreviation used in the book, writer(s), and synopsis (averaging 125 words) of events. The headings "Story Arc" and/or "Points of Interest" may also appear in these entries, noting a significant event to the overall plotline or an interesting bit of trivia. Appendix III lists most of the entries by type (characters/people, places/worlds, vessels/vehicles, institutions/organizations/projects/corporations, battles/wars/historical events/treaties, devices/technology, foods/drinks/medicines/chemicals, alien races/creatures, weapons, titles/terms). Appendix IV includes the sources summarized in Appendix II, with abbreviations in order of appearance. Appendix V arranges the same sources in alphabetical order. Appendix VI provides three jokes that have appeared on the program, with the abbreviated title of the original episode in which they appeared.

Because of its scope, and through no fault of the author, the book includes some incorrect information, primarily because the *B5* story arc was largely incomplete at the time of the book's publication. Generally, however, the entries are fairly sound as far as they go, but often inconsistent in their coverage of particular episodes. For example, a guest actor's name is sometimes included in the character definition, and other times absent, for no apparent reason. More "See Also" references would have been helpful. Eight unnumbered pages of black-and-white publicity photos add very little to the volume.

While ardent fans of the series may want a copy of Bassom's guide, Killick's and Lane's guides (see #614 and #615) are a far better source of information.

614. Killick, Jane. **Signs and Portents.** London, Boxtree, 1997; New York, A Del Rey Book, Ballantine Books, 1998. 176 p. (*Babylon 5:* Season by Season Series, v. 1). LC 97-97204. ISBN 0-345-42447-6 (pbk.). **The Coming of Shadows.** London, Boxtree, 1997; New York, A Del Rey Book, Ballantine Books, 1998. 178 p. (*Babylon 5:* Season by Season Series, v. 2). LC 98-96029. ISBN 0-345-42448-4 (pbk.). **Point of No Return.** London, Boxtree, 1998; New York, A Del Rey Book, Ballantine Books, 1998. 176 p. (*Babylon 5:* Season by Season Series, v.3). LC 98-92945. ISBN 0-345-42449-2 (pbk.) **No Surrender, No Retreat.** London, Boxtree, 1998; New York, A Del Rey Book, Ballantine Books, 1998. 178 p. (*Babylon 5:* Season by Season Series, v.4). LC 98-96414. ISBN 0-345-42450-6 (pbk.). **The Wheel of Fire.** London, Boxtree, 1998; New York, A Del Rey Book, Ballantine Books, 1999. 180 p. (*Babylon 5:* Season by Season Series, v.5). LC 98-96859. ISBN 0-345-42451-4 (pbk.).

Contents (Volume 1): "Acknowledgments"; "Foreword," by Michael O'Hare; "Getting *Babylon 5* into Orbit"; "*Babylon 5*'s First Season"; "Signs and Portents: Episode Guide." (Volume 2): "Acknowledgments"; "By Any Means Necessary: Making *Babylon 5* on a Budget"; "*Babylon 5*'s Second Season"; "The Coming of Shadows: Episode Guide." (Volume 3): "Special Effects"; "*Babylon 5*'s Third Season"; "Point of No Return: Episode Guide." (Volume 4): "Acknowledgments"; "Script to Screen"; "*Babylon 5*'s Fourth Season"; "No Surrender, No Retreat: Episode Guide." (Volume 5): "Acknowledgments"; "Looking Back Over Five Years"; "*Babylon 5*'s Fifth Season"; "'The Deconstruction of Falling Stars'"; "The Wheel of Fire: Episode Guide."

Each book in this series of five provides a record of one full season (twenty-two episodes) of J. Michael Straczynski's five-season television space epic, *Babylon 5,* including a lengthy introduction to the season in question, followed by individual epidode guides. Each entry includes: the title of the episode, a list of regular cast members and guest stars with appropriate character names, an episode summary (in italics), and a commentary consisting of quotations from articles and interviews from crew and cast, as well as insight from Killick on the episode's effect on the story arc and the characters. Also included in each book is a color insert of eight publicity photographs. There is no index.

Volume 1 also features a brief but complimentary Foreword by actor Michael O'Hare (who played Commander Sinclair on the show), plus two essays, one on the development of the series, and the second on the triumphs and disappointments of the first season. Volume 2 contains two essays, one on the cost of producing science fiction for television, and the second on developments in the story during the second season. Volume 3 includes two essays, one discussing *Babylon 5*'s special effects, and the second examining the story arc in season three. Volume 4 includes essays on the script production process, and on the advancement of the overall story in season four. Volume 5 has a retrospective on the five-year story arc, and a second essay focusing on particular plot developments in the final season of the series. The half dozen *Babylon 5* television movies are not covered.

As an officially-sanctioned publication of the series, these volumes tend to be un-critical of the show, and take no interest in examining varying levels of writing quality, plot inconsistencies, etc. Thus, while they may be enjoyable if light reading, the books' total absence of such vital details as the names of directors, writers, and other associated person-nel, and the absence of episode production order numbers, make these guides a secondary choice for reference purposes. Prefer Lane's *The Babylon File* (#615).

615. Lane, Andy. **The Babylon File: The Definitive Unauthorised Guide to J. Michael Straczynski's TV Series,** *Babylon 5.* London, Virgin Publishing, 1997. 428 p. index. ISBN 0-7535-0049-3 (pbk.). **The Babylon File, Volume 2: The Definitive Unauthorised Guide to J. Michael Straczynski's TV Series,** *Babylon 5.* London, Virgin Publishing, 1999. xii, 286 p. ISBN 0-7535-0233-X (pbk.).

Contents (Volume 1): "Introduction"; "Sources"; The Background: "Approaching Babylon," by J. Michael Straczynski, "Between the Essence and the Descent," "Choices, Consequences and Responsibilities"; The Episodes: "Key to Episode Guide Entries," "The-matic Episode Lists," "Recurring Characters," "The Rep Company," "Military Ranks in Earthforce," "The Pilot: 'The Gathering'," "Season 1: 'Signs and Portents'," "Season 2: 'The Coming of Shadows'," "Season 3: 'Point of No Return'," "Season 4: 'No Retreat, No Sur-render'," "The Future"; Books and Comics: "The Books," "The Comics," "Afterword."

Contents (Volume 2): "Foreword"; "Introduction"; The Lists: "Directors," "Thematic Episodes," "Recurring Characters," "Culture Shock," "Other Worlds"; "Key to Episode Guide Entries"; The TV Episodes: "Seasons 1 to 3: Addenda and Corrigenda," "Season 4: 'No Surrender, No Retreat'," "Season 5: Wheel of Fire"; The TV Movies: "*In the Beginning,*" "*Thirdspace,*" "*The River of Souls,*" "*A Call to Arms*"; "The Books"; "The Comics"; "The Games"; Essays: "Cast . . . in a Bad Light," "There's Always a 'Boom' Tomorrow," "Beyond the Rim to the Sea," "More Questions Than Answers"; "What Was, and What Will Be: *Crusade*"; "Afterword"; "Bibliography (Volumes 1 and 2)."

This episode guide to and critique of J. Michael Straczynski's 5-year television space epic, *Babylon 5,* opens with a series of essays discussing various aspects of the show. "Approaching Babylon" by Straczynski, a reprint of an article in *Foundation* (Summer, 1995), tells about the difficulties of putting science fiction on television, and the almost impossible task of getting *Babylon 5* on the air. "Between the Essence and the Descent" is a Jungian analysis of the program, while "Choice, Consequences and Responsibilities" talks about how the characters in the series grow to appreciate the consequences of their actions and original choices. The essays provide exceptionally literate and literary commentary in their analyses.

The Thematic Episodes list includes useful data on Telepathy and Psi Corps, Minbari and Human Souls, President Clark and Nightwatch, The Narn/Centauri War, and The Shadow War, with episodes being noted by transmission number and title. The Recurring

Characters list arranges characters alphabetically by name, with the names of the actors and the episode transmission number. The Rep Company list itemizes actors who were used repeatedly for alien characters, but who may not be recognizable under their make-up, listed by actor's name, and including the alien race, transmission number, and title of the episode.

The bulk of the first volume (which is not, however, internally noted as "Volume 1") consists of a detailed episode guide examining sixty-six episodes produced through the beginning of the fourth season of *Babylon 5*. Each season includes a brief introduction that features a transcription of that season's opening voice-over, the regular and semi-regular cast with character names, and a brief look at changes in cast occurring during that season.

A typical episode entry provides: transmission number (plus airing order); production number, writer(s); director; guest cast and character names; date within the story arc; plot (broken down into plot A, plot B, and plot C, as necessary); the (Story) Arc; Observations; and any of a collection of recurring headings, such as Dialogue to Rewind/Fast Forward; Literary, Mythological and Historical References; I've Seen That Face Before; Accidents Will Happen; Questions Raised (a section for inconsistencies, plot holes, and other problems), and others.

Volume 1 concludes with a look at the six novels and four comic books featuring the *Babylon 5* universe, which are endorsed and considered part of the story line by Straczynski. The headings used in this section are the same as those employed in the episode guide.

The second volume wraps up his episode guide, covering seasons four and five of the show, and including other material on the TV movies, comics, books, games, etc., related to the program. The foreword by Jeffrey Willerth (background artist, stand-in, Producer's Associate, actor as Kosh, and husband of fellow *Babylon 5*-er, Patricia Tallman) gives us a fascinating inside look at the rumors, benefits disputes, and the brief crew strike in the third season. Willerth writes with honest criticism and simultaneous affection for the show.

Lane contributes a melancholy introduction, mourning the show's decline in quality (in his opinion) during season four, and its plummet during season five. He also includes points he missed in Volume 1, plus a large list (with page numbers) of errata in that book. The section of lists has been expanded to include directors, correlated with the transmission numbers and titles of episodes they directed. "Thematic Episodes" indexes the threads Telepathy and Psi Corps, President Clark and Nightwatch, The Narn/Centauri War, and The Shadow War and its Legacy for seasons four and five. "Culture Shock" is an alphabetical list of the alien races encountered in the show, with a description of each. "Other Worlds" lists the planets of the known universe alphabetically, noting the political alignment of each (Centauri colony, Earth colony, etc.), and whether it appears in a game or novel.

However, the bulk of the book still consists of the episode guide, which focuses particularly on the forty-four episodes from the fourth and fifth seasons. Each chapter has a brief introduction that includes that season's opening voice-over, the regular and semi-regular cast with character names, and a brief look at changes in cast during the season. The episode entries follow the structure established in the first volume. The one comic book, one game, and four books not mentioned in the other volume are also discussed, as are four made-for-TV *Babylon 5* motion pictures.

The last section is a collection of essays by Lane. "Cast . . . in a Bad Light" discusses changes in the arc forced due to the loss of a cast member, and discusses Straczynski's hidden "trap doors," designed to eliminate a character from the story line if and when it ever became necessary. This is Lane's weakest essay, structuring a great deal of personal conjecture upon a relatively small number of facts. "There's Always a 'Boom' Tomorrow" covers the departure of series regular Claudia Christian after season four. The nature of death and the afterlife as portrayed in *Babylon 5* is the subject of "Beyond the Rim to the Sea." The final piece, "More Questions Than Answers," examines a few of the unanswered questions left at the end of the series.

Lane closes Volume 2 with speculation on the *Babylon 5* spin-off series, *Crusade.* An afterword by Pat Tallman (who played the telepathic character, Lyta Alexander) provides a sad but fond view of the program.

The tone of Volume 2 varies dramatically from Volume 1. The essay selections are more morose, the analyses not nearly as strong. Lane would aver (as he does in his introduction to this volume) that there was simply much less to analyze in these two weaker seasons of the program. The episode guide remains strong, except for those occasions when Lane moves too far from his reasoned approach to a more emotional one ("Who are these aliens," he asks, "and why do they wear such crappy costumes?" [page 134]). In addition, the excellent index that was so useful in Volume 1 has been scrapped in the sequel.

Together, these two books serve as an excellent critical analysis of *Babylon 5,* and indeed, could well provide a paradigm for what such guides should contain. Lane points out the laudable scenes, lines, and character development in *B5,* but never fails to note plot inconsistencies and poor writing when they occur. Running heads indicating the season under discussion would have improved the reader's navigation. The index in Volume 1 is excellent, noting the page numbers for episode, book, and comic titles; actors', characters', and planets' names; other film or television titles (*e.g., The Addams Family, The African Queen*); historical figures; and directors' and writers' names. The volumes are well written and thoughtfully considered, and make for good reading cover-to-cover as well as for spot reference.

Highly recommended for the fans, the public libraries serving them, and any collection of science fiction or popular culture.

Battlestar Galactica

616. Kraus, Bruce. **Encyclopedia Galactica: From the Fleet Library Aboard the *Battlestar Galactica.*** New York, Windmill Books and E.P. Dutton, 1979. [57] p. LC 79-4649. ISBN 0-525-61039-1.

This illustrated A-Z guide to the persons, places, and things in the *Battlestar Galactica* universe was designed for the adolescent market.

Entries cover the principal characters (Adama, Starbuck, Imperious Leader, etc.), worlds visited by the *Galactica* (Kobol, Borallus), and other terms (Viper, Warrior, etc.). A final page provides "A Chronology of Major Events in Human [*i.e.,* Twelve Colonies] History." The book is nicely illustrated throughout with color stills from the television series and bound to library standards. Some of the entries include fictional elaborations that may or may not be based on the series "Bible" or on events that were mentioned during the course of the program's short run.

For diehard *Galactica* fans only.

Dark Shadows

617. Gross, Edward, and James Van Hise. *Dark Shadows* **Tribute.** Las Vegas, NV, Pioneer Books, 1990. 144 p. ISBN 1-55698-234-8 (pbk.).

Dark Shadows was a popular television gothic soap opera from 1966-71, which also spun off two separately produced motion pictures and a reworked night-time television series during the 1990/91 season.

Contents: "Introduction"; "Origins: Dan Curtis, Art Wallace, Robert Costello"; "What It Is . . . "; "Jonathan Frid"; "The Reluctant Vampire"; "Barnabas Collins"; "Collinwood Memories: Louis Edmonds, Grayson Hall, Jerry Lacy, Alexandra Moltke"; "Star Panel: John Sedwick, Ron Sprout"; "Appendix: The Episodes"; "A Gallery of *Dark Shadows.*"

The narrative sections have little reference value, but the episode guide, occupying pages 68-131, provides one-paragraph plot summaries of the 600 episodes beginning with the introduction of Barnabas Collins (Jonathan Frid) as a continuing vampire character (the sequence actually begins with the 210th program of the series, the previous segments having occupied themselves with more-or-less standard gothic fare). The book is illustrated throughout with black-and-white full- and partial-page illustrations of the characters and sets.

Gross and Van Hise's plot descriptions are a little fuller than Scott's (see #618), but their book provides summaries for less than half of the episodes actually televised. Prefer Scott's more comprehensive guide.

618. Scott, Kathryn Leigh. **The *Dark Shadows* Companion: 25th Anniversary Collection.** Los Angeles & London, Pomegranate Press, 1990. 208 p. LC 90-62402. ISBN 0-938817-26-4; ISBN 0-938817-25-6 (pbk.).

Scott was one of the principal actresses on the *Dark Shadows* television series from 1966-71 and previously published *My Scrapbook Memories of Dark Shadows.*

Contents: "Acknowledgements"; "Dedication"; "Introduction," by Scott; "Foreword," by Jonathan Frid; "Out of Angélique's Shadow," by Lara Parker; "*Dark Shadows* and Me," by Matthew Hall; "A Word from Me," by Sam Hall; "The *Dark Shadows* History," by Melody Clark, Kathleen Resch, and Marcy Robin: "Picture Gallery," "The Journey Continues," "The Cousin from England," "When Every Day Was Opening Night," "That Year of Insanity," "A Werewolf with a PhD," "Rain, Snow, and a Drafty Old House," "The Last Days at Collinwood"; "Episode Guide," by Jim Pierson; "Update: Where Are They Now?"; "Collectibles"; "In Memoriam."

The narrative sections are both interesting and informative, and copiously illustrated with full-page, black-and-white and color stills and personal photographs of the series and the stars. The very detailed episode guide provides one-sentence plot summaries of each of the 1,225 programs; the plot developments are so complicated and convoluted, involving travels back and forth in time and into parallel dimensions, that the reader is advised to use the guide in conjuction with the detailed history of the series by Clark, Resch, and Robin, who show exactly how each plot segment segued into the next.

The update section gives brief biographies of each of the principals involved in the series (including actors, directors, writers, and others), listing other credits and the names of the character(s) each of the cast portrayed (again, because of the complex array of plot lines, most of the actors played more than one character in the Collins family). The "Collectibles" chapter lists the thirty-two *Dark Shadows* novels, plus other monographs, recordings, videos, periodicals, merchandise, and the addresses of two fan clubs. The book is beautifully designed, printed on high-quality glossy paper, and the cloth edition bound to library standards.

This is a superior tribute to a TV program that remains popular in syndication. Future editions should include original air dates in the episode directory and an overall index to the book.

Doctor Who

619. Haining, Peter. *Doctor Who:* **The Time-Travelers' Guide.** London, W. H. Allen, 1989. 272 p. ISBN 0-86379-188-3 (pbk.).

Haining's guide is one of several publications he has produced on this long-running popular British SF series.

Contents: "Introduction"; "1. The Science that Inspired *Doctor Who*"; "2. Back in the Mists of Time Travel"; "3. Time and the Lords of Gallifrey"; "4. Regeneration—The Mystery of Ages"; "5. A Who's Who of Enemies"; "6. A Tourist's Guide to Alien Worlds"; "7. Space Craft Checklist"; "8. Time Travel Update."

The main sections of reference value are Chapters 5-8. "A Who's Who of Enemies" is further subdivided into three sections: "I. Villainous Humanoids"; "II. Dangerous Robots"; "III. Evil Monsters." In each section villains are arranged alphabetically by name or type. A typical entry gives: name (bold caps), episode(s) in which it appeared, telewriter, year of production, actor(s), and a one-paragraph description.

Chapter 6 is an A-Z listing of the worlds and places visited by Doctor Who in his travels through time and space. A typical entry provides: place name (bold caps), location, and the role it played in the saga. The guide to spacecraft (Chapter 7) is arranged chronologically by appearance date, giving: type of craft (bold caps), first sighting date, and the part each played in the plot. The final chapter includes a detailed programme log by Jeremy Bentham covering the period from 1983-86, with over a thousand words of plot summary for each episode.

The book is beautifully illustrated with full- and partial-page black-and-white and color stills and photographs. All fans of *Doctor Who* will want a copy of this guide; libraries will probably prefer Haining's 25th anniversary tribute (see #620), which includes a complete episode log from 1963-87.

620. Haining, Peter. *Doctor Who:* **25 Glorious Years: XXV.** London, Virgin, 1988. 224 p., [12] p. of plates. ISBN 0-86369-324-5 (pbk.).

Doctor Who is the longest-running science-fiction television series in history, the first episodes having been shown in 1963. Well-known horror anthologist and critic Peter Haining has here produced a marvelously detailed tribute to the program and its stars.

Contents: "The Legend Begins"; "Introduction"; "The Great Whovian Mystery"; "The Silver Decade"; "Inside the World of *Doctor Who*"; "The Seven Faces of *Doctor Who*"; "Who Are These Doctors!"; "The Doctor We Presume?"; "Stories of Intergalactic Guest Stars"; "*Doctor Who* and the Merchandisers"; "The Doctor in the Comics"; "The Lost Stories of *Doctor Who*"; "Time Travels: The Seven Doctors' 150 Adventures in 25 Years."

The narrative sections that comprise the bulk of the book delineate the history of the program, the careers of the seven fictional Doctor Whos and the lives of the seven actors who have played him, and other material of interest. "The Doctor, We Presume?" records in chronological order the characters (and actresses) who have portrayed the Doctor's female companions, giving details of their fictional and factual lives.

The "Time Travels" section provides a chronological checklist of the 150 *Doctor Who* mini-series, giving producer, episode number, title, telewriter, director, guest stars, and original air dates, season by season. The metamorphosis of each Doctor Who into his re-generated new body (*i.e.,* portrayal by a new actor) is also noted, in large bold letters. The book is beautifully illustrated with reproductions of black-and-white and color stills from the original series, and is nicely typeset and designed.

Doctor Who has seen a resurgence of critical interest in recent decades; this carefully compiled tribute will provide a useful starting point for all future scholarship.

621. Howe, David J., Mark Stammers, and Stephen James Walker. *Doctor Who:* **The Handbook: The First Doctor.** London, Doctor Who Books, 1994. 347 p. ISBN 0-426-20430-1 (pbk.). Howe, David J., Mark Stammers, and Stephen James Walker. *Doctor Who:* **The Handbook: The Second Doctor.** London, Doctor Who, 1997. 304 p. ISBN 0-426-20516-2 (pbk.). Howe, David J., and Stephen James Walker. *Doctor Who:* **The Handbook: The Third Doctor.** London, Doctor Who, 1996. 256 p. ISBN 0-426-20486-7 (pbk.). Howe, David J., Mark Stammers, and Stephen James Walker. *Doctor Who:* **The Handbook: The Fourth Doctor.** London, Doctor Who, 1992. [256] p. ISBN 0-426-20369-0 (pbk.). Howe, David J., and Stephen James Walker. *Doctor Who:* **The Handbook: The Fifth Doctor.** London, Doctor Who, 1995. 292 p. ISBN 0-426-20458-1 (pbk.). Howe, David J., Mark Stammers, and Stephen James Walker. *Doctor Who:* **The Handbook: The Sixth Doctor.** London, Doctor Who, 1993. [256] p. ISBN 0-426-20400-X (pbk.). Howe, David J., and Stephen James Walker. *Doctor Who:* **The Handbook: The Seventh Doctor.** London, Doctor Who Books, 1998. x, 310 p. index. ISBN 0-426-20527-8 (pbk.).

This series of guides provides "both a broad overview and a detailed analysis" of the *Doctor Who* television series, focused around each of the seven actors who have portrayed the title character: William Hartnell, Patrick Troughton, Jon Pertwee, Tom Baker, Peter Davison, Colin Baker, and Sylvester McCoy, in that order. All of the handbooks follow the same basic structure very closely, with some minor variations in style.

Each volume includes biographical information and interviews with the particular actor in question and the technical crews associated with him, plus an episode guide, with all of the story arcs employing this actor. The typical story arc entry includes: title (boldfaced caps), individual episode titles, a small table with episode numbers, original air dates, starting times, running times, numbers of viewers, and chart position (out of the top 200). Another chart displays subsequent repeats of the programs in Great Britain with similar information. Production Details include filming dates, studio recording dates and locations, and plot summaries (averaging 300 words) of each arc.

Other material featured in these books includes "*Who* Fax, Quotes, and Comment," giving interesting miscellanea (novelization of the stories, video release dates, and other trivia), quotations from the cast and crew of each arc, and an evaluation. The Comment section employs a rating system of 0-10 to rate each story. The volumes may also contain essays on various parts of *Doctor Who,* production diaries, and information on how the program was advertised and sold to the public. The books conclude with a table of production credits for each arc, listing: title, author, director, costumes, make-up, music, designer, producer, associate producer, and story editor.

The *Handbook* provides an amazingly detailed look at *Doctor Who,* and sets a standard for guides to popular TV programming. The writing is well done, speaking equally well to fans, students, or scholars of television. The first six volumes lack an index, but the seventh volume in the series includes an errata section covering the six earlier guides, plus a detailed index to all of the books in the series, making access to the entire set much easier. Recommended for all *Doctor Who* fans.

Dracula Films

622. Glut, Donald F. **The Dracula Book.** Metuchen, NJ, Scarecrow Press, 1975. xx, 388 p. index. LC 75-4917. ISBN 0-8108-0804-8.

Although Glut also covers Dracula books, comic books, and other media in passing, the primary emphasis here is on film adaptations of the caped count.

Contents: "Acknowledgments"; "Preface"; introductions by Christopher Lee and William Marshall; "1. Vlad Dracula, the Impaler"; "2. The Vampire Image"; "3. The Ancestors of Dracula"; "4. Bram Stoker's Classic"; "5. Dracula Dramatized"; "6. Dracula on the Silent Screen"; "7. Dracula Haunts Universal"; "8. The Hammer Horrors of Dracula"; "9. Dracula Flies Again"; "10. Stay Tuned for Dracula"; "11. Other Dracula Books"; "12. Dracula Meets the Comics"; "13. Dracula Eternal"; "Afterword"; "Index."

The narrative chapters having reference value include 5-12, which delineate in chronological order the various stage adaptations, motion pictures, television and radio appearances, novels and short stories featuring Dracula and other Dracula-like vampires (but also those books having the word "Dracula" in the title, even when no vampire is actually present), comic book adaptataions, and other media. Some foreign-language books and films are covered (with the original titles followed by their English-language translations). The annotations range in size from 50-500 words, averaging 250, and tend to be descriptive, with some evaluation at the end of each summary.

Motion picture production and casting credits (generally the producer, director, screenwriter, and major stars) are buried in the narrative text, each film's title being highlighted in all-capital letters (book titles are underlined). Materials are covered through 1974. The comprehensive index correlates all names and titles with page numbers. The book is shot from legible typed copy, illustrated throughout with clearly reproduced black-and-white stills and cover illustrations, and bound to library standards.

Glut clearly knows his material, and his judgments seem sound. Any scholar doing research on the vampire myth in film and literature will want a copy of this book. A new edition with better production values (and possibly reorganized along the lines of Glut's *Frankenstein Catalog* [see #623]) would definitely be warranted.

Frankenstein Films

623. Glut, Donald F. **The Frankenstein Catalog: Being a Comprehensive Listing of Novels, Translations, Adaptations, Stories, Critical Works, Popular Articles, Series, Fumetti, Verse, Stage Plays, Films, Cartoons, Puppetry, Radio & Television Programs, Comics, Satire & Humor, Spoken & Musical Recordings, Tapes, and Sheet Music Featuring Frankenstein's Monster and/or Descended from Mary Shelley's Novel.** Jefferson, NC & London, McFarland & Co., 1984. xiii, 525 p. index. LC 81-6026. ISBN 0-89950-029-3.

In this companion volume to *The Dracula Book* (see #622), Glut again covers all media in his exploration of the Frankenstein theme, although the dramatic presentations occupy half the book.

Contents: "Acknowledgments"; "Preface"; "Chapter One: Mary Shelley's *Frankenstein*"; "Chapter Two: The Frankenstein Chronicles"; "Chapter Three: Frankenstein on Stage"; "Chapter Four: Frankenstein on Film"; "Chapter Five: Frankenstein on Radio and Television"; "Chapter Six: Frankenstein in the Comics"; "Chapter Seven: Frankenstein Recordings, Music, and Lyrics"; "Name Index"; "Title Index."

Most publications sections are arranged alphabetically by main entry; most film sections are arranged chronologically by release date. Chapters are subdivided into as many as nine sections, covering such topics as "Frankenstein Fiction"; "Film Series"; "Writings About *Frankenstein*" [the novel]; "Television Movies"; "Newspaper Strips"; etc. Both primary and secondary sources are included; particularly in Chapters One and Two, there are extensive lists of articles and books about Mary Shelley's work and on the Frankenstein theme in general. Foreign-language materials are interfiled with the rest, with English-language translations in brackets.

A typical film entry gives: item number, title (italicized), production company, year of release, running time, color or black-and-white, alternate (or English-language) title, production and casting credits, and a one-paragraph plot summary, with occasional additional notes and/or "See" references to other items of interest.

A typical book entry provides: item number, author, title (italicized), place of publication, publisher, year of publication, pagination, similar data for all known reprint or variant editions, and a one-paragraph plot summary. A typical short prose work entry gives: item number, author, title (in quotes), magazine title (italicized), month and year of publication, and pagination. Materials are numbered consecutively throughout the book from 1-2,666. The book is nicely typeset and designed, illustrated throughout with clearly reproduced black-and-white stills and cover shots, and bound to library standards. The indices correlate names and titles to specific item numbers.

It is difficult to imagine how any researcher even remotely interested in the Frankenstein theme in literature or film could bypass this work. Every datum that might possibly be desired is present, well-organized, and easily accessible through the indices. Kudos to Glut on a job well done. All four-year college libraries and all research institutions should own a copy.

The Outer Limits

624. Schow, David J., and Jeffrey Frentzen. *The Outer Limits:* **The Official Companion.** New York, Ace Science Fiction Books, 1986. 406 p. index. LC 87-400050. ISBN 0-441-37081-0 (pbk.).

The Outer Limits was one of the most imaginative of the SF anthology series to run on television during the 1960s, exceeded, perhaps, only by individual episodes of *The Twilight Zone.*

Contents: "Introduction"; "Part One: The Awe and Mystery of the Universe"; "Part Two: We Are Controlling Transmission"; "Part Three: Fear of the Unknown"; "Part Four: The Devil's Puppeteer"; "Part Five: Man's Endless Thirst for Knowledge"; "Part Six: Beyond *The Outer Limits*"; "Appendixes"; "Index."

The annotations for each of the episodes are interspersed throughout the narrative part of the text, arranged in chronological order by production (not broadcast) date. A typical entry includes: episode title (bold caps), broadcast date, writer, director, assistant director, director of photography, cast (characters and players), voiceover introduction from that episode, one- to two-paragraph plot summary, and several pages of background material, including excerpts from selected dialogue, interviews with the principals, and other material of interest.

The appendices include: "The Canons of *Please Stand By*" (the original title for the series), "*The Outer Limits* That Never Were: Unfilmed Episodes," "Production & Broadcast Schedules" (showing exact dates of filming for each episode, and air dates), "End Credits" (a list of the executive staff at Daystar Productions, producers of the series). The detailed index correlates all names and titles with page numbers. The book is illustrated throughout with sometimes fuzzy stills from the programs, printed on poor-quality paper that is already beginning to yellow, and rather cheaply bound.

. This limited production values of this volume are unfortunate, because *The Outer Limits* deserves permanent preservation as a homage to a program that stretched the limits of both the imagination and of special-effects technology. Everything the fan or scholar would want to know about the series is here, easily accessible through the index. Any library collection with an interest in the history of television should acquire this book, and immediately have it rebound in cloth and deacidified.

Prehistorical Creatures in Films

625. Kinnard, Roy. **Beasts and Behemoths: Prehistoric Creatures in the Movies.** Metuchen, NJ & London, Scarecrow Press, 1988. xi, 179 p. index. LC 87-23424. ISBN 0-8108-2062-5.

Librarian Kinnard annotates thirty-seven motion pictures featuring primitive beasties, from the early silents to *Baby* (1985). Materials are arranged in chronological order by production date.

A typical entry provides: item number, title (all caps), production company, release year, principal production credits, cast, and critique. The annotations range in size from 200-4,000 words (the longest entry covers *King Kong*), averaging 400, and are both descriptive, historical, and evaluative, including much background information on the making of each film. The book is nicely illustrated with little-seen stills from the motion pictures, and shot from word-processed copy.

The appendices add a "Feature Film Checklist," listing all known prehistoric creature pictures in chronological order by release date, with asterisks following those titles that are *not* annotated in this guide; and a "Japanese Feature Film Checklist," including the Godzilla series and related titles. Two indices, to names and titles, coordinate these data with page numbers; underlined page numbers indicate illustrations.

Kinnard certainly knows his material, and his coverage is both knowledgeable and thorough, but his guide can only be regarded as a rather peripheral acquisition for most personal and institutional collections.

The Prisoner

626. Rogers, Dave, edited by Charlotte Mortensson. *The Prisoner.* New York, Barnes & Noble Books, 1993. v, 123 p. ISBN 1-56619-163-7. Excerpted from the book, *The Prisoner & Danger Man,* a much larger volume published by Boxtree in England in 1989.

This episode guide to the 1960s British cult series, *The Prisoner,* covers all seventeen episodes of the program. The lengthy preface describes the development of the series by the show's star/executive producer/sometime writer and director, Patrick McGoohan. A typical episode entry includes: episode title, writer(s), director, guest stars with character name, and plot summary (ranging from 3,500-5,500 words). Half a dozen black-and-white stills are featured per entry.

Unfortunately, some information that readers might find useful is absent here, including the original air dates of the programs, and vital production data. The absence of an index is also unfortunate.

Thus, while Rogers has penned a guide that will not only help readers relive the series, but also engage those who have never seen it, his book lacks the material that even a dedicated fan website contains. Prefer White and Ali's much more detailed volume (see #627).

627. White, Matthew, and Jaffer Ali. **The Official *Prisoner* Companion.** New York, Warner Books, 1988. ix, 244 p. LC 88-5606. ISBN 0-446-38744-4 (pbk.); ISBN 0-446-38745-2 (pbk.; Canada). London, Sidgwick & Jackson, 1988. ix, 244 p. ISBN 0-283-99598-X (pbk.).

When *The Prisoner* first aired on television in 1968, it created a great deal of puzzlement among viewers, but later developed a cult following. Many critics now regard it as one of the finest TV series ever broadcast.

Contents: "Acknowledgments"; "Introduction"; "Chapter One: *Prisoner* Episode Guide"; "Chapter Two: Notes, Anecdotes, and Nonsense"; "Chapter Three: The Great Debates"; "Chapter Four: What Does It All Mean?"; "Chapter Five: Talking with McGoohan"; "Patrick McGoohan Films"; "Appendix A: Sources of Information"; "Appendix B: The Shooting Scripts."

The first half of the book consists of a detailed guide to the individual programs in the official order established by the production company. A typical entry provides: title (boldfaced caps), writer, script editor, producer, director, executive director, cast (players and characters), crew, synopsis, and observations. The synopsis usually runs 800-1,000 words, the observations averaging 500-600 words.

Other material of reference value includes the Patrick McGoohan filmography, listing his motion picture roles in chronological order by production date, and giving title (bold-faced), nationality, release year, and one-paragraph synopsis. The "Sources of Information" section features a now outdated list of *Prisoner* fan clubs and addresses, books about *The Prisoner* series, conventions, videotapes, and sources of memorabilia. There are some very valuable excerpts from the program's shooting scripts, highlighting key moments from the series. The book is nicely illustrated throughout with black-and-white stills and typeset; the binding will not withstand library use.

Both the scholar and fan will welcome this very complete handbook on a TV series that seems likely to endure the test of time. Recommended for all collections with an interest in the history of television.

Red Dwarf

628. Howarth, Chris, and Steve Lyons. *Red Dwarf:* **Programme Guide.** London, Virgin, 1993, 228 p. ISBN 0-86369-682-1 (pbk.). *Red Dwarf:* **Programme Guide.** Rev. ed. London, Virgin, 1995. 286 p. ISBN 0-86369-682-1 (pbk.). *Red Dwarf:* **Programme Guide.** 2nd ed. London, Virgin, 1997. vii, 337 p. ISBN 0-86369-682-1 (pbk.). *Red Dwarf:* **Programme Guide.** 3rd ed. London, Virgin, 2000. 359 p. ISBN 0-7535-0402-2 (pbk.).

Contents (Second Edition): "Acknowledgement"; "Section 1: Mission Brief"; "Section 2: Crew Roster"; "Section 3: Ship's Log"; "Section 4: Database"; "Section 5: Supplemental Log"; "Section 6: Cargo Inventory."

With an irreverent tone suitable to the series it covers, Howarth and Lyons's book provides an episode guide/dictionary for the comic British science fiction television show, *Red Dwarf* (1988-98). Section 1 provides a basic introduction to the show. Section 2 looks at each character's background (averaging 1,800 words) and the actor who portrays him/her (150-200 words).

The program consisted of eight separate series, here called *Red Dwarf* I, II, III, etc., usually comprising six episodes each. Section 3 includes an episode guide though Series VII. The typical entry includes: order number and episode title (bold caps), the original air date, guest cast with character names in parentheses, plot summary (200-300 words), and four or five bulleted, behind-the-scenes comments.

Section 4 is an A-Z dictionary (about 1,000 entries) covering the books, names, jokes and funny lines, planets, and trivia mentioned in the series. Section 5 covers stories from other sources set in the *Red Dwarf* universe, including the several novels based on the series, plus the failed American television pilot. Section 6 is a brief and general catalog of *Red Dwarf* merchandise, including books, magazines, music, and videos (other types of merchandise were covered in the first edition of this guide).

The book is set in small but legible type, and bound in typical mass-market paperback format, with rather poor binding that will not hold up to library use.

Howarth and Lyons have provided an enjoyable guide for the many fans of this long-running British TV series, including some tongue-in-cheek humor of their own, interspersed with a narrative voice that speaks directly to the regular viewers of the program.

The Third (2000) Edition has not been examined.

Star Trek

629. Altman, Mark, and Edward Gross. ***Deep Space* Log Book: A First Season Companion.** London, Boxtree, 1994. 110 p. ISBN 1-85283-388-2 (pbk.).

Contents: "Introduction"; "Chapter One: The Golden Child"; "Chapter Two: Rick Berman"; "Chapter Three: Michael Pillar"; "Chapter Four: Welcome to Bajor"; "Chapter Five: Singing the Sound Stage Blues"; "Chapter Six: As the Space Station Turns"; "Chapter Seven: Get Thee to the Gamma Quadrant"; "Season One Episode Guide"; "Appendix A; The Comic"; "Appendix B: The Next Generation on Deep Space"; "Appendix C: A Day in the Life"; "Appendix D: Question & Answer Session."

Altman and Gross describe in several introductory chapters (p. 7-47) the development of this darkly-hued *Star Trek* spin-off, using ample, uncited quotations from producers Rick Berman and Michael Piller, as well as from directors, cast, and other staff of the series. The bulk of the book consists of an episode guide for the nineteen stories that made up the twenty shows of the first season.

A typical entry includes: episode number (it isn't clear here whether these are production numbers or airing order numbers), title (boldfaced), original air date, writer(s), director, guest casts and character names (parentheses), a plot summary and commentary (separated by an icon), and ratings by the authors. The summaries average 100 words, and are, for the most part, clear and concise. The commentaries can run triple the length of the summaries, often including additional quotations from those involved in the production of that episode. All of the text is fannishly oriented. The authors add their own rating system to each episode, from 1-4 stars in half-star increments.

Especially enjoyable for the fan is Appendix D, a now-dated transcript of a question-and-answer panel session including Berman, Piller, and the cast. Without an index, finding an individual director or guest actor is difficult, but the small number of entries eases the problem somewhat. The book is illustrated with black-and-white photographs of the actors, in and out of costume, plus magazine covers from fan publications.

Overall, a solid little episode guide designed primarily for fans, but including more hard information than most.

630. Asherman, Allan. **The *Star Trek* Compendium.** New York, A Wallaby Book, Simon & Schuster, 1981. 187 p. LC 81-140016. ISBN 0-671-79145-1 (pbk.). **The *Star Trek* Compendium.** [Rev. ed.]. London, A Star Book, W. H. Allen & Co., 1983. 194 p. ISBN 0-352-31355-2 (pbk.). **The *Star Trek* Compendium.** [Rev. ed.]. New York, Pocket Books, 1986. 184 p. index. LC 87-400763. ISBN 0-671-62726-0 (pbk.). **The *Star Trek* Compendium.** [Rev. ed.]. New York, Pocket Books, 1989. 182 p. index. LC 89-199904. ISBN 0-671-68440-X (pbk.).

Each of these books has been updated from the previous version, usually by adding coverage of an additional *Star Trek* movie (the 1989 edition covers through *Star Trek V, The Final Frontier*), but are otherwise similarly organized.

Contents (1989 edition): "Introduction"; "The Beginnings"; "The Episodes"; "The Long Road Back"; "Indices."

The first chapter discusses the origins of the series, including credits and plot summaries for the first pilot, "The Cage" and the recut two-part version, "The Menagerie." More than half of the volume is concerned with "The Episodes," arranged chronologically by production date (not air date). A typical entry provides: episode title (boldfaced caps), episode number, writer(s), director, characters, a one- to two-paragraph plot summary, and roughly 500-600 words of commentary giving background information on how technical problems were solved, sidelights on guest stars and the principal actors, changes made in the story line from the original script, etc.

The episodes are organized into three chapters corresponding to the three seasons that the first *ST* television series was in production; Asherman provides a general introduction at the beginning of each chapter. "The Long Road Back" includes coverage of the animated episodes of *Star Trek,* the five *Star Trek* movies, and the abortive television series, *Star Trek II,* but nothing on *Star Trek: The Next Generation.* Two indices, to the series episodes (giving production number and original air date in addition to title), and to character names, correlated with episode number and actor's name, provide access to the text; there is no separate index to the actors' real names. The book is nicely typeset and illustrated throughout with black-and-white stills from the television programs and motion pictures.

Asherman's continuing work is the most current guide to the original *Star Trek* universe, and is generally recommended over all other competing volumes listed below, although Jones and Trimble's *Concordance* (see #635) does provide more detailed coverage of the *ST* series.

631. Farrand, Phil. **The Nitpicker's Guide for Classic Trekkers.** New York, Dell, 1994. xiv, 393 p. index. LC 94-18374. ISBN 0-440-50683-2 (pbk.). London, Titan, 1994. xiv, 393 p. index. ISBN 1-85286-587-3 (pbk.). New York, Science Fiction Book Club, 1994. xiv, 393 p. index. (hardcover edition).

Contents: "First Season," "Second Season," "Third Season," "First Pilot," "The Movies."

Farrand has made a career producing critical guides on cult television series, and a sharp-eyed job he does here. Farrand points out bloopers, poor writing, inconsistencies, contrivances, and much more in the 79 original series *Star Trek* episodes (plus the pilot), in addition to the all of the *ST* movies through *Star Trek VI: The Undiscovered Country.*

The book is divided into seasons, one through three, and looks at each episode in order of airing. The pilot and movies are covered in separate chapters. A typical entry includes: episode title (bold caps), star date(s) for the episode in question, trivia notes, plot summary, and sections dealing with such things as "Ruminations," "Syndication Cuts," "Plot Oversights," "Changed Premises," "Equipment Oddities;" "Continuity Problems," "Production Problems," and "Trivia Answers."

The chapter on "Syndication Cuts" is particularly interesting to fans, but does not appear in Farrand's *Next Generation* guides. It describes scenes or reaction shots cut from trimmed-down syndication reruns that have created subsequent problems to viewers in plot and continuity. Each entry runs about 600 words. The index is very useful for finding references by page number to episode names, concepts, characters, and places.

Not really a reference book, *The Nitpicker's Guide* is still a fun book for both fans and the libraries that serve them.

632. Farrand, Phil. **The Nitpicker's Guide for *Deep Space Nine* Trekkers.** New York, Dell, 1996. xvi, 399 p. index. LC 96-22816. ISBN 0-440-50762-2 (pbk.). London, Titan, 1996. xvi, 399 p. index. ISBN 1-85286-736-1 (pbk.).

Contents: "Acknowledgments"; "Introduction"; "First Season"; "Second Season"; "Third Season"; "Fourth Season."

In his series of entertaining guides, Farrand points out bloopers, poor writing, inconsistency, contrivances, continuity errors, and more in the various *Star Trek* television series. This new book is divided into seasons, from one to four, and examines each *DS9* episode in order of airing.

A typical episode entry includes: title (boldfaced caps), star dates, trivia questions, plot summary, and headings such as "Ruminations," "Plot Oversights," "Changed Premises," "Equipment Oddities;" "Continuity Problems," "Production Problems," and "Trivia Answers." The average entry runs about 1,300 words. Farrand's insights are noteworthy, and his detailed analyses should be read by anyone interested in becoming a television writer, or who wishes to understand better the collaborative process involved in producing a modern television series.

The index is very useful for finding references by page number to episode names, concepts, characters, and places. Farrand writes a fun guide for fans and the libraries that serve them. Recommended.

633. Farrand, Phil. **The Nitpicker's Guide for *Next Generation* Trekkers.** New York, Dell, 1993. xiv, 433 p. index. LC 93-3543. ISBN 0-440-50571-2 (pbk.). London, Titan, 1994. xiv, 433 p. index. ISBN 1-85286-513-X (pbk.). **The Nitpicker's Guide for *Next Generation* Trekkers, Volume II.** New York, Dell, 1995. xxiv, 407 p. index. LC 93-3543. ISBN 0-440-50716-2 (pbk.).

Contents (unnumbered first volume): "First Season," "Second Season," "Third Season," "Fourth Season," "Fifth Season," "Sixth Season."

Contents (Volume II): "Seventh Season"; "The Movie (*Generations*)"; "Guild Submissions (Seasons One Through Six)."

Farrand continues his series of nitpicking guides to cult television series with *Star Trek: The Next Generation,* pointing out bloopers, poor writing, inconsistency, continuity errors, contrivances, and more. The first book is divided into seasons one through six, and examines each episode in order of airing. A typical episode entry includes: title (boldfaced caps), star dates, trivia questions, summary of the plot, and such recurring topics as "Ruminations," "Plot Oversights," "Changed Premises," "Equipment Oddities;" "Continuity Problems," "Production Problems," and "Trivia Answers." The typical entry averages about 500 words in length. The index is very useful for finding page references to episode names, concepts, characters, and places.

Volume II adds coverage for the seventh and final season of *Next Generation,* and provides commentary on the first motion picture featuring the *NG* actors, plus additional material on episodes from Seasons 1-6 (including some responses from the fans to criticisms levied by Farrand in Volume I). The Guild comments are often debatable, and not as clearly thought out as Farrand's original and more discerning remarks.

As with the guide to *Classic Trek,* Farrand's volume is of questionable reference value, but of great interest to prospective television writers and students of TV production techniques, as well as, of course, to diehard *Star Trek* fans everywhere. This is sure a lot more fun than mowing the lawn.

634. Gross, Edward, and Mark A. Altman. **Captains' Logs: The Unauthorized Complete *Trek* Voyages.** Boston, Little, Brown, 1995. 361 p. index. LC 96-18892. ISBN 0-316-32957-6 (pbk.). Gross, Edward, and Mark A. Altman. **Captains' Logs Supplemental: The Unauthorized Guide to the New *Trek* Voyages.** Boston, Little, Brown, 1996. 185 p. index. LC 96-18892. ISBN 0-316-32920-7 (pbk.).

Contents (1995 volume): "Introduction"; "Chapter One: The Trek Begins"; "Chapter Two: Season One Episode Guide"; "Chapter Three: Trekking to Season Two"; "Chapter Four: Season Two Episode Guide"; "Chapter Five: Voyages Interruptus"; "Chapter Six: Season Three Episode Guide"; "Chapter Seven: The Remaking of *Star Trek,* 1970-1978"; "Chapter Eight: 1970's Episode Guide"; "Chapter Nine: *Star Trek:* The Movies"; "Chapter Ten: *Star Trek II: The Wrath of Khan*"; "Chapter Eleven: *Star Trek III: The Search for Spock*"; "Chapter Twelve: *Star Trek IV: The Voyage Home*"; "Chapter Thirteen: *Star Trek V: The Final Frontier*"; "Chapter Fourteen: *Star Trek VI: The Academy Years*"; "Chapter Fifteen: *Star Trek VI: The Undiscovered Country*"; "Chapter Sixteen: There Are the New Voyages"; "Chapter Seventeen: Season One Episode Guide"; "Chapter Eighteen: Season Two"; "Chapter Nineteen: Season Two Episode Guide"; "Chapter Twenty: Season Three"; "Chapter Twenty-One: Season Three Episode Guide"; "Chapter Twenty-Two: Season Four"; "Chapter Twenty-Three: Season Four Episode Guide"; "Chapter Twenty-Four: Season Five"; "Chapter Twenty-Five: Season Five Episode Guide"; "Chapter Twenty-Six: Season Six"; "Chapter Twenty-Seven: Season Six Episode Guide"; "Chapter Twenty-Eight: Season Seven"; "Chapter Twenty-Nine: Season Seven Episode Guide"; "Chapter Thirty: *Star Trek: Generations*"; "Chapter Thirty-One: *Star Trek: Deep Space Nine*"; "Chapter Thirty-Two: *Star Trek: Voyager.*"

Contents (1996 volume): "Introduction"; "Chapter One: *Deep Space Nine:* In the Beginning"; "Chapter Two: *Deep Space Nine:* Season One"; "Chapter Three: *Deep Space Nine:* Season One Episode Guide"; "Chapter Four: *Deep Space Nine:* Season Two"; "Chapter Five: *Deep Space Nine:* Season Two Episode Guide"; "Chapter Six: *Deep Space Nine:* Season Three"; "Chapter Seven: *Deep Space Nine:* Season Three Episode Guide"; "Chapter Eight: *Deep Space Nine:* Season Four"; "Chapter Nine: *Deep Space Nine:* Season Four Episode Guide"; "Chapter Ten: *Voyager:* Season One"; "Chapter Eleven: *Voyager:* Season One Episode Guide"; "Chapter Twelve: *Voyager:* Season Two"; "Chapter Thirteen: *Voyager:* Season Two Episode Guide"; "Chapter Fourteen: Making Contact: Behind the Scenes of *Star Trek VIII*"; "Index."

This is probably the best and most thoughtful *Trek* episode guide ever published, and a serious *Trek* fan's dream. Alternating between essays and episode guides, Gross and

Altman discuss thoroughly each season of the original *Star Trek* series and *Star Trek: The Next Generation*. The essays are so complete, full of quotations from interviews and speeches from actors and members of the production crew, that you almost expect them to be cited in a bibliography (alas, they're not).

A typical entry in the episode guide gives: episode number, title (in quotation marks), original air date, writer(s), director, guest star(s) and their character name (in parentheses), plot summary, and commentary. The plot summaries run 50-100 words, the commentaries about 500-1000 words. The commentaries are similar to the essays in including numerous quotations from many different sources, rather than just relying on the authors' own opinions, as in many episode guides.

The *ST* motion pictures are covered through *Star Trek: Generations*. Technical information for the films (director, screenwriter, etc.) is not included, for no apparent reason, and should be added to any new edition. There is no detailed episode information on *Star Trek: Deep Space Nine* or *Star Trek: Voyager,* which rather gives the lie to the subtitle, "the complete *Trek* voyages," since *DS9* began production in 1993. The volume is illustrated throughout with numerous black-and-white photographs and stills, plus a color insert in the center of the book. The index is useful in finding actors' and character names and episode titles.

The supplement focuses on *Star Trek: Deep Space Nine* (through its fourth season) and *Star Trek: Voyager* (through its second season). The essays and episode guide follow the same model as in the first volume. The *ST* movies are not covered, though *Star Trek: First Contact* is anticipated and discussed under the title, *Star Trek VIII*.

Of all the *Star Trek* episode guides, these are the ones to purchase for any library collecting popular culture and science fiction. Trekkers will love 'em.

635. Jones, Dorothy; edited by Bjo Trimble. **Star Trek Concordance of People, Places, & Things.** Berkeley, CA, Mathom House Publications, 1969. 84 p. (pbk.). Trimble, Bjo, and Dorothy Jones. **The Third Season Supplement to the Star Trek Concordance.** Los Angeles, Mathom House Publications, 1973. [70] p. (pbk.). Trimble, Bjo, with Dorothy Jones. **The Star Trek Concordance.** [Rev. ed.]. New York, Ballantine Books, 1976. 256 p. index. LC 76-9778. ISBN 0-345-25137-7 (pbk.). Trimble, Bjo. **Star Trek Concordance: The A to Z Guide to the Classic Original Television Series and Films.** Rev. and updated ed. Secaucus, NJ: Carol Publishing Group, 1995. ix, 322 p. index. LC 94-46369. ISBN 0-8065-1610-0 (pbk.).

Contents (1995 Edition): "Introduction"; "Alphabetical List of Episodes/Movies with Lexicon Code"; "Episodes by Air Date"; "Episodes"; "Introduction to the *Star Trek* Animated Series"; "Animated Episodes"; "Feature Films"; "*Star Trek: The Next Generation*"; "*Star Trek: Deep Space Nine*"; "Lexicon"; "*Star Trek* Vessels"; "Parts and Sections of *Star Trek* Vessels"; "Cosmos: *Star Trek* Astronomical References"; "Actor Cross-Reference"; "Production Cross-Reference"; "Production Cross-Reference"; "Research Sources."

The first version of this guide to the *Star Trek* universe, together with its *Supplement,* were both produced in rather amateurish fashion, offset from typed copy and bound through the spine with metal clasps. The much more professional revised version of 1976 is broken into two major sections.

The first half of the book discusses the individual episodes from both the original and animated series in chronological order by air date. A typical entry provides: title (bold caps), writer(s), stardate, air date, plot summary (400-600 words), characters and players, and "Lexicon" references. The second half of the work, the "Lexicon," provides an A-Z guide to the people, places, and things mentioned in the television series. The entries range in size from one sentence to 650 words, and cross-reference the specific episode in which the item appears (in the form TSP for "This Side of Paradise"), keyed to "An Index of Episode Abbreviations" on page 256. The latter is not quite as useful as it might be, citing page numbers only and not listing the actual episode titles. Trimble also provided a *Star Trek* time line (listing each episode in chronological order by "stardate"), and an index to episode titles on pages 14-15. A portfolio of amateurish "Fan Art" fills pages 17-31; other black-and-white line drawings are sprinkled throughout the text.

The 1995 edition was heavily revised from the 1976 version to include the six motion pictures (but only those featuring the original cast), and those few episodes of *Star Trek: The Next Generation* and *Star Trek: Deep Space Nine* that include members of the original *Star Trek* series. As in the earlier edition, the text is divided into an episode guide and lexicon.

A typical entry in the episode guide includes: episode title, abbreviation, writer(s), director, production number, story number, air date, the title reference (explanation of the title), a translation of the title into a handful of other languages (usually Afrikaans, Catalan, German, Italian, Japanese, Portuguese, Spanish, Zulu), a non-evaluative summary (200-300 words), a cast list correlating character and actor, and a list of terms in the lexicon where the episode is discussed. The lexicon entries are usually quite brief, ranging from a phrase to several sentences, and citing other episodes where the character, theme, or object has appeared, using an episode abbreviation called the Lexicon code. This system is not as useful as it might be since the volume lacks any abbreviation index.

The "Alphabetical List of Episode/Movies" and the "Episodes by Air Date" include the abbreviations, but do not index them, making it difficult for the user to match the information to a particular episode (one must scan the alphabetical list visually to find specific abbreviations). Including page number references in this section would have been more useful for the reader. "See Also" references are noted in bold type throughout the lexicon.

This episode guide offers the most detailed trivia for the serious fan than any other non-evaluative guide, including such data as the translated titles in foreign countries, and the identity of stunt doubles and non-speaking characters. The lexicon contains explanations both of commonly known Trekker trivia ("Sarek" or "dilithium," for example) and the truly obscure ("Akharin" or "alien in bar"). The text is supplemented with abundant, black-and-white fan illustrations of very uneven quality.

Diehard Trekkers and fans of the original *Star Trek* series will appreciate the level of detail here. A quirky book with much useful material, the *Concordance* should be beamed up to all large library systems.

636. Nemecek, Larry. **The *Star Trek: The Next Generation* Companion.** New York, Pocket Books, 1992. ix, 213 p. index. LC 93-120337. ISBN 0-671-79460-4 (pbk.). **The**

***Star Trek: The Next Generation* Companion.** Rev. and updated ed. New York, Pocket Books, 1995. xi, 337 p. index. LC 95-220262. ISBN 0-671-88340-2 (pbk.).

Contents (First Edition): "Introduction"; "Rebirth" ("Creation in Flux"; "Assembling the Team"; "Of Stars and Starships"; "Drafting a Crew"; "Faces for the Names"; "Countdown and Launch"); "First Season"; "Second Season"; "Third Season"; "Fourth Season"; "Fifth Season"; "Beyond the Future"; "Indices."

Contents (Revised Edition): "Introduction"; "Rebirth" ("Creation in Flux"; "Assembling the Team"; "Of Stars and Starships"; "Drafting a Crew"; "Faces for the Names"; "Countdown and Launch"); "First Season"; "Second Season"; "Third Season"; "Fourth Season"; "Fifth Season"; "Sixth Season"; "Seventh Season"; "*Star Trek: Generations*"; "Indices."

Pocket Books and Nemecek have produced what is probably the best-known and most heavily-used episode guide for *Star Trek: The Next Generation.*

The volume is divided into chapters covering each season, with each section featuring an introduction describing the changes and developments that occurred that year. A typical entry includes: episode title, production number, air date, stardate(s), episode code, director, writer(s), guest cast with character names, plot summary (averaging 200 words), and commentary with behind-the-scenes insight (averaging 300 words). The latter is clearly separated in the text from the plot summary by a small bar graphic, plus a distinctive change in font style.

The episode index lists all the titles in tabular form in order of production, providing brief information similar to that included in the more detailed record in the main section of the book (production number, air number, title, code, star date, first air date, and the page number on which that episode is covered in the *Companion*), but there is no overall title index, making the location of a specific episode harder than it should be. There are separate indices to writers and directors, but nothing for guest actors. The book is illustrated with numerous, large black-and-white stills (about one per page), but they are sometimes grainier than one would expect from such a high-quality production.

The Revised Edition completely supersedes the original, adding coverage for seasons six and seven of the series, as well as the motion picture, *Star Trek: Generations.* The format and content are exactly the same, although a new index for guest stars has now been included. Although *Captain's Logs* (see #634) is the most thoughtfully presented of the *Star Trek* episode guides, Nemecek's book might be preferred by those who want a less verbose, more simply organized volume with more plot summaries and less commentaries. A good choice for fans.

637. Okuda, Michael, and Denise Okuda. ***Star Trek* Chronology: The History of the Future.** New York, Pocket Books, 1993. viii, 184 p. index. LC 93-186826. ISBN 0-671-79611-9 (pbk.). ***Star Trek* Chronology: The History of the Future.** Rev. and updated ed. New York, Pocket Books, 1996. x, 342 p. LC 97-120510. ISBN 0-671-53610-9 (pbk.).

Contents (First Edition): "Introduction"; "Acknowledgments"; "Chapter 1.0: The Distant Past"; "Chapter 2.0: The Twentieth Century"; "Chapter 3.0: The Twenty-first Century"; "Chapter 4.0: The Twenty-second Century"; "Chapter 5.0: The Twenty-third Century" ("5.1: *Star Trek*: Original Series, Year 1 (2266-7)"; "5.2: *Star Trek*: Original Series, Year 2 (2267-8)"; "5.3: *Star Trek*: Original Series, Year 3 (2268-9)"; "5.4: *Star Trek*: Motion Pictures I-VI (2271-93))"; "Chapter 6.0: The Twenty-fourth Century" ("6.1: *Star Trek: The Next Gen-*

eration, Year 1 (2364)"; "6.2: *Star Trek: The Next Generation,* Year 2 (2365)"; "6.3: *Star Trek: The Next Generation,* Year 3 (2366)"; "6.4: *Star Trek: The Next Generation,* Year 4 (2367)"; "6.5: *Star Trek: The Next Generation,* Year 5 (2368))"; "Chapter 7.0: The Far Future"; "Appendix A: Undatable Events and Other Uncertainties"; "Appendix B: Alternate Timelines"; "Appendix C: Timeline Chart"; "Appendix D: Regarding Stardates"; "Appendix E: Writing Credits"; "Index"; "About the Authors."

Contents (Revised Edition): "Introduction"; "Acknowledgments"; "Chapter 1.0: The Distant Past"; "Chapter 2.0: The Twentieth Century"; "Chapter 3.0: The Twenty-first Century"; "Chapter 4.0: The Twenty-second Century"; "Chapter 5.0: The Twenty-third Century" ("5.1: *Star Trek:* Original Series, Year 1 (2266-7)"; "5.2: *Star Trek:* Original Series, Year 2 (2267-8)"; "5.3: *Star Trek:* Original Series, Year 3 (2268-9)"; "5.4: *Star Trek:* Motion Pictures (2271-93))"; "Chapter 6.0: The Twenty-fourth Century" ("6.1: *Star Trek: The Next Generation,* Year 1 (2364)"; "6.2: *Star Trek: The Next Generation,* Year 2 (2365)"; "6.3: *Star Trek: The Next Generation,* Year 3 (2366)"; "6.4: *Star Trek: The Next Generation,* Year 4 (2367)"; "6.5: *Star Trek: The Next Generation,* Year 5 (2368)"; "6.6: *Star Trek: The Next Generation,* Year 6 (2369)"; "*Star Trek: Deep Space Nine,* Year 1"; "*Star Trek: Generations*"; "6.7: *Star Trek: The Next Generation,* Year 7 (2370)"; "*Star Trek: Deep Space Nine,* Year 2"; "6.8: *Star Trek: Deep Space Nine,* Year 3 (2371)"; "*Star Trek: Voyager,* Year 1"; "6.9: *Star Trek: Deep Space Nine,* Year 4 (2372)"; "*Star Trek: Voyager,* Year 2"); "Chapter 7.0: The Far Future"; "Appendix A: Notes on *Star Trek:* The Original Series Characters"; "Appendix B: Notes on *Star Trek: The Next Generation* Characters"; "Appendix C: Notes on *Star Trek: Deep Space Nine* Characters"; "Appendix D: Notes on *Star Trek: Voyager* Characters"; "Appendix E: Notes on Starfleet and the Starships *Enterprise*"; "Appendix F: Notes on Science and Technology"; "Appendix G: Notes on Planets and Societies"; "Appendix H: Alternate Timelines"; "Appendix I: Regarding Stardates"; "Appendix J: Writing Credits"; "Index"; "Bibliography"; "About the Authors."

Created at the suggestion of Gene Roddenberry in order to maintain a consistency to the history of the *Star Trek* universe, the *Chronology* was organized by *ST* designer Michael Okuda and his wife, and has been extensively employed by the staff writers of the various *ST* programs. The information was derived from the actual episodes of the original *Star Trek* series, *Star Trek: The Next Generation,* and the (then) new *Star Trek: Deep Space Nine* series, plus the first six *ST* films, excluding material that is external to the official *Trek* programs (such exceptions are noted in the text). The animated series was almost entirely discarded for reasons discussed in the introduction.

The chronology begins 15 billion years ago, at the Big Bang, and continues into the thirty-third century, with the last *Star Trek: The Next Generation* episode represented being from the show's fifth season. Each entry includes either a general period designation or an exact year of occurrence, with a description of the event running 50-100 words in length, including the official stardate(s) whenever possible. This is followed by an informal citation, including the title of the episode whence the information derived, and (often) exactly what was said therein. Integrated with the *Star Trek* universe are dates of significance to Earth history to give the timeline context, such as "500-600 B.C. Birth of Confucianism and Buddhism."

The original version includes approximately 750 entries. The book is illustrated throughout with numerous small, black-and-white pictures of characters from the events in the timeline. The appendices offer snapshot information about characters, ships, and some events that remain undated. Appendix A includes several small timelines comparing the lives of characters, grouped by specific show. The index is very thorough, correlating the names of actors, characters, ships, planets, and other significant locations, episodes, and events, with page numbers (a boldfaced number indicates the main coverage for a particular episode). Curiously, the episode titles are not integrated with the main index, but combined under the overall heading "episodes," and then listed alphabetically thereunder.

The headers on odd-numbered pages, which show the primary year under discussion on that page, are exceptionally helpful in guiding the reader through the book. There are some basic assumptions and guesswork used to create dates, when no exact date was given in the original episode, but these are well explained in the introduction as well as being noted in the text.

The Revised Edition supersedes the first book, being considerably expanded to include approximately 1,800 entries, with this edition now covering all seven years of *Star Trek: The Next Generation,* four years of *Star Trek: Deep Space Nine,* two years of *Star Trek: Voyager,* and all the movies to up *Star Trek: First Contact,* plus the original *ST* series. The motion picture information is highlighted more clearly in the table of contents than in the earlier book, and the appendices have been greatly expanded, in some cases being renamed to reflect their contents better than before.

The indexing is also stronger than in the first edition, with the episode titles being integrated into the rest of the index entries. Also included are new sets of stills, and the welcome addition of color to all of the snapshot photographs. Many of the entries from the first edition remain the same in this superseding version, though overall they seem fuller, now averaging about 75-100 words each.

The Okudas have improved on something that was already a very good reference guide. Highly recommended for amateur and professional writers interested in television writing and the *Star Trek* universe, for all avid Trekkers, and also for large public and research libraries.

638. Okuda, Michael, Denise Okuda, and Debbie Mirek. **The *Star Trek* Encyclopedia: A Reference Guide to the Future.** New York, Pocket Books, 1994. iv, 396 p. index. LC 94-198834. ISBN 0-671-88684-3; ISBN 0-671-86905-1 (pbk.). **The *Star Trek* Encyclopedia: A Reference Guide to the Future.** Updated and expanded ed. New York, Pocket Books, 1997. vi, 630 p. LC 98-184562. ISBN 0-671-53607-9. **The *Star Trek* Encyclopedia: A Reference Guide to the Future.** Updated and expanded 3rd ed. New York, London, Pocket Books, 1999. vi, 745 p. LC 00-708781. ISBN 0-671-03475-8; ISBN 0-671-53609-5 (pbk.).

Written by *Star Trek* insider and designer, Michael Okuda, and his wife, promoter Denise Okuda, the *Encyclopedia* is an A-Z guide to the *Trek* universe, providing entries for main and supporting characters, alien races, planets and stars, weapons and tools, scientific terms, equipment, and much more. The first edition includes approximately 6,500 entries, while the third almost doubles that figure, to roughly 12,000 items.

The third edition completely supersedes its predecessors, with material covering the original *ST* series up through part of *Star Trek: Deep Space 9*'s seventh and final season, and *Star Trek: Voyager*'s fifth season, and the motion pictures through *Star Trek: Insurrec-*

tion. New material in this version appears as a 100-page supplement to the text from the Second Edition, added between pages 577-684.

A typical entry includes: term (boldfaced type), definition, title of the episode in which the item is featured or which supports the definition (in quotation marks), and an abbreviation for the specific program reference (*TOS* for the original *Star Trek* series, *TNG* for *Star Trek: The Next Generation, DS9* for *Star Trek: Deep Space Nine, VGR* for *Star Trek: Voyager*; names of the motion pictures are written in full). Copious "See" and "See Also" references (in bold type) assist the user in navigating the text. The average entry size runs 25-75 words, though significant entries (Kirk, Spock, Picard, etc.) can extend much longer.

The narrative voice of the text pretends that both the authors and the readers are living in the late 24th century, long past the action of the events described, except for interpolations in italic type, which provide certain behind-the-scenes production or other information by the "editors." This tone is neither obvious nor intrusive. The third edition is illustrated with numerous small, color or black-and-white illustrations per page, plus occasional special drawings and charts (*e.g.,* Starship Chart).

Appendix A lists Federation Starships & Ships of Earth Registry; Appendix B displays the Ships of the Galaxy; Appendix C lists Historical Events in the *Star Trek* Universe; Appendix D is a Timeline of *Star Trek* Production; Appendix E provides Writer and Director Credits; Appendix F lists the Cast credits; Appendix G displays Production Personnel; and Appendix H is a Bibliography of books used by the authors to help compile their book.

This is an outstanding source for fans, writers of all levels, or for reference libraries serving fans. The text is well-written and -presented, the material authoritative, and the extrapolations reasonable and based on in-house materials inaccessible to anyone else. Without question, this is the premier A-Z guide to the *Star Trek* universe, and will remain so for as long as it is kept updated and available. Highly recommended.

639. Peel, John; edited by Hal Schuster. **The *Trek* Encyclopedia.** Las Vegas, NV, Pioneer Books, 1988. 365 p. ISBN 1-55698-205-4 (pbk.). Peel, John, with additional material by Hal Schuster and Scott Nance. **The *Trek* Encyclopedia.** 2nd ed. Las Vegas, NV, Pioneer Books, 1992. 211 p. ISBN 1-55698-350-6 (pbk.).

Contents (both editions): "The Characters"; "The People"; "The Planets"; "Appendix: Ships & Devices."

Peel has written dozens of nonfiction works on SF television programs and motion pictures, and also a number of *Star Trek* novels. The first chapter is an A-Z listing of the characters, peoples, and things filling the *Star Trek* universe.

A typical character entry provides: name, actor's name, title of episode(s) in which the character appeared (in chronological order), and description, ranging in size from one sentence to several paragraphs. The other entries feature creatures or national groups; the entry for the "Klingons," for example, lists each of the Klingon characters featured in the series, episode by episode, with the actors who portrayed them, "See" references to specific character names covered elsewhere in the *Encyclopedia,* plus a two-page narrative description of the Klingon Empire, Klingon attributes, and interactions with Federation personnel.

The second section indexes actors and actresses, directors, and writers featured in the *Star Trek* television series and the first four *Star Trek* motion pictures, alphabetically by surname. A typical entry provides: person's name, episode title(s), role, and biography, including a brief filmography of each. The third chapter is an alphabetical guide to the planets mentioned (or visited) in the *Star Trek* saga, a typical entry giving: planet name (bold caps), story title, and one-to-two-paragraph description. The appendix provides a narrative description of *The Enterprise* itself, and a separate section detailing (in no particular order) some of the devices used in the series. The book is rather poorly designed and printed on cheap paper that will oxidize within a few years, and the entry heads are sometimes difficult to read. The text is also filled with misprints and poorly proofread copy.

The second edition does not enhance the book at all. Sampling reveals that not a word of the original text (not even the introduction) has been altered to improve the material or its style, making the insufficiencies of the text all that much worse. The frequent typographical errors and missing capital letters at the beginning of sentences are faithfully reproduced. Bah!

Prefer Okuda (see #638).

640. Schuster, Hal, and Wendy Rathbone, edited by Mira Schwirtz. *Trek:* **The Encyclopedia.** Las Vegas, NV, Pioneer Books, 1994. 229 p. ISBN 1-55698-331-X (pbk.).

Covering all the *Star Trek* programs and films to 1994 (*Star Trek, Star Trek: The Next Generation* through the sixth season, the animated *Star Trek,* twelve episodes of the first season of *Star Trek: Deep Space 9,* and the movies through *Star Trek VI: The Undiscovered Country*), this is an A-Z encyclopedia of trivia and definitions, including songs, significant *ST* phrases, poetry, planets, episode titles, characters, actors and production personnel, ships' names, and more.

A typical entry includes: the word or phrase described (in bold type, though names of episodes and people, both real and fictional, appear in capital letters as well), and the definition, which averages 35 words. There are over 4,000 entries, illustrated with thirty-two unnumbered pages of full-page color photographs of the principal actors taken at *ST* conventions.

Appendix One lists all of the *ST* episodes (to 1994) of each series in viewing order, while Appendix Two lists *Star Trek* novels by publisher (title and author only). While the book titles do not appear as entries in the encyclopedia, the authors' names do, and the book titles are given in the body of the entry.

This is actually a fairly good quick-and-easy reference guide, filled with all kinds of fun trivia, being relatively clear and easy to navigate, and one of the better Pioneer Books publications. However, Okuda (see #638) is still to book the beat in this category, being far and away the best single reference volume ever published on *Star Trek,* and also the most current.

641. Schuster, Hal. **The Trekker's Guide to** *Voyager:* **Complete, Unauthorized, and Uncensored.** Rocklin, CA, Prima Publishing, 1996, v, 202 p. LC 96-8195. index. ISBN 0-7615-0572-5 (pbk.).

Contents: "Preface"; "Acknowledgments"; "Chapter 1: Launching *Star Trek: Voyager*"; "Chapter 2: Creating the Continuing Saga"; "Chapter 3: Casting the Crew"; "Chapter 4: Placing *Voyager* in the *Star Trek* Universe"; "Chapter 5: Meeting the Women of *Star Trek*"; "Chapter 6: Speaking *Trek* Tech"; "Chapter 7: Examining the Prime Directive";

"Chapter 8: Understanding the Maquis"; "Chapter 9: Navigating the Delta Quadrant"; "Chapter 10: Nitpicking the Episodes"; "Appendix A: Trekker's Guide to the Internet"; "Appendix B: Episode Credits"; "Bibliography"; "Index."

Schuster's guide is a straightforward look at what was then the latest entry in the *Star Trek* franchise, *Star Trek: Voyager.* About half of the book covers background information on both this series and the *ST* universe in general. Of particular interest from a reference point of view are the guides to the characters and the actors playing them, occupying 56 pages of text, and the detailed analyses of the 42 episodes broadcast during the first two season of *Voyager.*

A typical entry from the latter includes: Episode Number, Episode Title, Production Number, Stardate, Air Date, Writer, Director, Guest Stars, Spoiler-Free Opinion Service Rating, Nielsen Rating (for the original broadcast), plot summary (averaging about 50 words), Plot Misfires, Equipment Malfunctions, Memory Failures. These latter three categories provide detailed analyses on logical lapses in the *Trek* scripts.

The book is well-organized and typeset, and the index provides access to all of the persons, characters, subjects, and episodes mentioned. Some of this material can be found in the Okuda *Encyclopedia* (see #638), but Schuster's guide still contains unique observations that remain valid.

642. Turnbull, Gerry, ed. **A *Star Trek* Catalog.** New York, Grosset & Dunlap Publishers, 1979. 160 p. LC 77-71296. ISBN 0-448-14053-5 (pbk.).

This catalog tried to provide the *Star Trek* fan with a basic guide to the series and its spin-offs.

Contents: "Introduction"; "An Interview with Gene Roddenberry"; "The Cons"; "The Clubs and Organizations"; "The Crew"; "The Episodes"; "The Animated *Star Trek*"; "The Marketspace"; "The Bookcase"; "The Future Voyages."

The "Clubs and Organizations" chapter lists fan groups alphabetically by state, then by city of location, giving group name, address, meeting schedule, and other data. The "Crew" section provides biographies of the principal continuing actors of *Star Trek,* with brief filmographies. The "Episodes" and animated chapters give a chronological checklist (by air date) of the programs from the main and animated series, a typical entry providing: title (boldfaced), episode number, telewriter, one-paragraph plot summary, and air date. The "Marketspace" section is an A-Z rendering of the business firms selling *Star Trek* memorabilia. The "Bookcase" provides an annotated guide to the *Star Trek* books published through 1977. The book is illustrated throughout with stills and photos; there is no index.

All of this is, of course, wholly outdated and now only of peripheral interest to the diehard fan. Prefer Gibson-Downs and Gentry's more current and complete catalog (see #667), and Van Hise's *Fan's Handbook* (see #647).

643. Van Hise, James. **The Classic *Trek* Crew Book.** Las Vegas, NV, Pioneer Books, 1993. 220 p. ISBN 1-55698-368-9 (pbk.).

Contents: "Forewords: Classic *Trek*—Foundations of the Future"; "The Captain"; "The Science Officer"; "The Doctor"; "The Communicator"; "The Engineer"; "The Helmsman"; "The Navigator"; "The Nurse"; "Afterwords: *Star Trek, Star Trek*—Everyone Had an Opinion."

This guide to the characters and cast of the original *Star Trek* series includes eight main entries, one for each recurring character, each section being subdivided into three chapters. The first provides a character history, the second the biography of the actor who played the character, and the third commentary derived from interviews with the actors.

The character histories are organized much like biographies of real-life indivdiuals, but much of the information might be unfamiliar even to fans, and there are no sources indicated to authenticate any of the material; thus, some of the text may well be fictitious or derived from the *Trek* novels, which are considered nonstandard by Paramount Productions, the owners of *Star Trek.* The actor biographies have little to say about the individual's pre-series life, but detail their lives during the production of the series. Quotations from the actor are used to illustrate their feelings for the show and for their characters. The "interviews" do not include citations for their origins, and their dates can only be loosely inferred from the quotations.

The afterword features a hodge-podge of critiques from books and magazines reviewing *Star Trek,* with the author's commentary on those reviews. The abundant use of quotations makes this book a somewhat meatier read than previous efforts by Van Hise, but not by much. The book includes black-and-white illustrations of characters, and black-and-white photos of the actors. Only for diehard fans.

644. Van Hise, James. *Deep Space* **Crew Book.** Las Vegas, NV, Pioneer Books, 1994. 193 p. ISBN 1-55698-335-2 (pbk.).

Contents: "Meet the Cast of *Deep Space Nine*"; "Character Profile: Commander Ben Sisko"; "Actor Profile: Avery Brooks"; "Character Profile: Jake Sisko"; "Actor Profile: Cirroc Lofton"; "Character Profile: Major Kira Nerys"; "Actor Profile: Nana Visitor"; "Character Profile: Miles O'Brien"; "Actor Profile: Colm Meany"; "Character Profile: Keiko O'Brien"; "Actor Profile: Rosalind Chao"; "Character Profile: Doctor Julian Bashir"; "Actor Profile: Siddig el Fadil"; "Character Profile: Lt. Jadzia Dax"; "Actor Profile: Terry Farrell"; "Character Profile: Odo"; "Actor Profile: Rene Auberjonois"; "Character Profile: Quark"; "Actor Profile: Armin Shimerman"; "Character Profile: Rom"; "Character Profile: Nog"; "Character Profile: Zek, The Grand Nagus"; "Character Profile: Li Nalas"; "Character Profile: Gul Dukat"; "A Look at the Deep Space Nine."

Van Hise's Crew books typically offer alternating actor and character biographies. True to form, this smaller version also includes character bios on irregular characters Rom, Nog, Zek, Li Nalas, and Gul Dukat, not found in the larger, cross-*Trek* book, *Trek Crew Companion* (see #645). However, like all of the other Crew books, the entries here are extremely inconsistent, ranging in length from 150-4,000 words.

Dates and concrete personal data are often rare, with most information entirely revolving around the actors' experiences as a Trek player. For example, there is an embarrassing lack of hard data on actress Rosalind Chao, missing her date and place of birth, professional training, or how she became involved with *Star Trek: Deep Space 9*. She is represented primarily with a collegial and unenlightening quote of friendship contributed by actor Colm Meany.

Character biographies frequently do not cite the episodes that are the source of the information, making all of the material vague and possibly untrustworthy. The style and tone is of one Trekker speaking to another. Black-and-white photographs of the actors in and out of costume illustrate the book.

As light as cotton candy, and about as meaningful.

645. Van Hise, James, and Hal Schuster. *Trek* **Crew Companion.** Las Vegas, NV, Pioneer Books, 1994. 377 p. ISBN 1-55698-345-X (pbk.).

Contents: "Intro: The Crews"; "Meet the Cast of *DS 9*"; "The Classic Crew" (Captain Kirk, William Shatner, Mr. Spock, Leonard Nimoy, Dr. McCoy, De Forest Kelley, Montgomery Scott, James Doohan, Mr. Sulu, George Takei, Uhua, Nichelle Nichols); "The Next Generation" (Capt. Picard, Patrick Stewart, William T. Riker, Jonathan Frakes, Data, Brent Spiner, Deanna Troi, Marina Sirtis, Geordi La Forge, LeVar Burton, Worf, Michael Dorn, Dr. Beverly Crusher, Gates McFadden, Guinan, Whoopi Goldberg); "The Deep Space Nine" (Ben Sisko, Avery Brooks, Kira Nerys, Nan Visitor, Miles O'Brien, Colm Meaney, Keiko O'Brien, Rosalind Chao, Dr. Bashir, Siddig El Fadil, Jadzia Dax, Terry Farrell, Odo, Rene Auberjonois, Quark, Armin Shimerman).

This appears to be an amalgamation of several separately published guides to the characters and casts for three of the *Star Trek* television series: Classic *Trek, Next Generation,* and *Deep Space Nine.* There are forty-four main entries, divided into three groups corresponding to the three programs, that alternate between recurring characters and the cast members who played them.

The text is very similar, even identical, to that in Van Hise's other Crew Books, and the deficits of those publications have changed not a whit. The poor writing and uncited, unsubstantiated, and inconsistent information do not commend the book. Many of the photographs, too, are taken directly from earlier crew books. In fact, the previously published individual guides actually include entries for less frequently seen characters that are excluded from this volume.

Poorly proofread, poorly presented, and poorly compiled, the *Trek Crew Companion* can qualify for no more than the poor man's alternative to something of quality. Try watching the programs instead.

646. Van Hise, James, and Hal Schuster. *Trek: Deep Space Nine:* **The Unauthorized Story.** Las Vegas, NV, Pioneer Books, 1993, [160] p. (pbk.). **The Unauthorized *Trek: Deep Space:* The Voyage Continues.** Las Vegas, NV, Pioneer Books, 1995. 198 p. ISBN 1-55698-340-9 (pbk.).

Contents (Second Season): "Intro"; "Background" (including Creation, Behind-the-Scenes, Season Two, The Books, *The Larry King Show*); "Characters" (Dax, Bashir, Kira, O'Brien, Odo, Quark, Sisko, The Aliens, The Dominion, The Maquis); "Stories: Season Two."

The second volume in this series is divided into four sections, but also covers background material, characters, and some episodes from season two of *Star Trek: Deep Space Nine,* continuing the coverage of the first book.

The introduction provides a history of the development of this TV series. There are ten character entries, which vary in size from 1,300-3,000 words, including: character biography, the character's development, and the character's relationships with other continuing characters on the show. The fourteen episode entries, covering #32-45, include: episode number (it is unclear whether this reflects the production number or actual airing order), title (bold caps), writer(s), regular cast and characters, guest cast and characters, and a combined summary and commentary averaging 650 words.

The text is uncritical and fannish in orientation. Also featured are 32 pages of color photos of the actors appearing at *ST* conventions. The production values are shoddy, as is typical with this publisher's books, being both badly proofread and poorly arranged. There's absolutely nothing here that can't be found somewhere else.

647. Van Hise, James. **The *Trek* Fan's Handbook.** Las Vegas, NV, Pioneer Books, 1990. 109 p. ISBN 1-55698-271-2 (pbk.).

One of a series of rather trashy guides to films and television mass produced by this Las Vegas firm, the *Handbook* contains: "Introduction"; "Brief History of *Star Trek* Fandom"; "The *Star Trek* Welcommittee"; "Guide to *Star Trek* Fan Clubs"; "Books About *Star Trek*"; "*Star Trek* Fan Fiction"; "Guide to *Star Trek* Fan Publications"; "*Star Trek* Conventions"; "A Guide to *Star Trek* Merchandise"; "*Star Trek* on Home Video."

The most useful sections of this guide include Chapter Three, which provides a comprehensive list of fan clubs, arranged alphabetically by state and city; Chapter Four (by Wendy Rathbone), an alphabetical index of nonfiction works about *Star Trek* and its characters, including fanzine and magazine publications in addition to monographs, with partial bibliographical data; Chapter Six, the bibliography of *Star Trek* fan fiction, in alphabetical order by title, including both fanzines and self-published novels, with names and addresses of authors and/or proprietors; and Chapter Eight, "A Guide to *Star Trek* Merchandise," which lists materials in alphabetical order by type (*e.g.,* "Audio Cassette," "Belt Buckle," etc.), but provides no vendor names. The book is printed on better-quality paper than is usual from this publisher.

Trekkers will welcome this guide, but most libraries and researchers can safely pass. Now largely outdated, of course.

648. Van Hise, James. **Trek: The Next Generation.** Las Vegas, NV, Pioneer Books, 1991, [160] p. (pbk.). **Trek: The Next Generation.** 2nd ed. Las Vegas, NV, Pioneer Books, 1992. 186 p. ISBN 1-55698-353-0 (pbk.). **Trek: The Next Generation.** 3rd rev. ed. Las Vegas, NV, Pioneer Books, 1994. 268 p. ISBN 1-55698-353-0 [sic] (pbk.). Van Hise, James, and Hal Schuster. **The Unauthorized *Trek:* The Complete *Next Generation*.** Las Vegas, NV, Pioneer Books, 1995. 171 p. ISBN 1-55698-377-8 (pbk.).

Another series of winners (*not!*) from Pioneer's Schlock Central USA, now mercifully defunct. These two-bit guides, building one upon another, are organized into unlabelled sections representing the different seasons of *Star Trek: The Next Generation,* finally reaching a full seven parts in the last book in the sequence. Each chapter provides synopses of the episodes for that season, beginning with an evaluative introduction (averaging 250 words) that reviews the general quality and development of the show throughout that season. A typical entry includes: episode number, title, writer(s), director, guest cast, and a non-evaluative plot synopsis averaging 300 words.

Additional material featured in the earlier books includes profiles of the actors (lacking, however, any real biographical data), and some relatively unintense discussion of the production of the series. While fans might find some parts of the episode guides enjoyable, the books have significant production, textual, and quality problems. Separate sections are not specifically identified by season (save in the final volume), making casual navigation exceedingly difficult. It is unclear whether the episode numbers are production numbers or airing numbers. Air dates are completely absent. Character names are not included with the guest cast. The lack of an index makes locating specific episodes or data almost impossible. The proofreading leaves much to be desired. The layout and production values are abysmal. The only significant addition to the final book in the set, other than distinct chapter breaks, is a 32-page inset of color photographs of the *Star Trek: The Next Generation* actors as they appeared at fan conventions (but not in stills taken from the program).

The Star Trek: The Next Generation Companion (see #636), and especially *Captains' Logs* (see #634) are much to be preferred. Beam them away, Scotty!

649. Van Hise, James. *Trek: The Next Generation* **Crew Book.** Las Vegas, NV, Pioneer Books, 1993. 155 p. ISBN 1-55698-363-8 (pbk.).

Contents: "Introduction: When Lighting [sic] Struck the Same Place Twice"; "Chapter 1: Captain Jean-Luc Picard"; "Chapter 2: Patrick Stewart"; "Chapter 3: Commander William T. Riker"; "Chapter 4: Jonathan Frakes"; "Chapter 5: Lieutenant Commander Data"; "Chapter 6: Brent Spiner"; "Chapter 7: Lt. Commander Deanna Troi Ship's Counselor"; "Chapter 8: Marina Sirtis"; "Chapter 9: Lt. J.G. Geordi La Forge"; "Chapter 10: Levar [sic] Burton"; "Chapter 11: Lieutenant Worf"; "Chapter 12: Michael Dorn"; "Chapter 13: Dr. Beverly Crusher"; "Chapter 14: Gates McFadden"; "Chapter 15: Guinan"; "Chapter 16: Whoopi Goldberg"; "Chapter 17: Transporter Chief Miles O'Brien"; "Chapter 18: Colm Meaney"; "Chapter 19: Security Chief Tasha Yar"; "Chapter 20: Denise Crosby"; "Chapter 21: Ro Laren"; "Chapter 22: Michelle Forbes"; "Chapter 23: Wesley Crusher"; "Chapter 24: Will Weaton [sic]"; "Chapter 25: Dr. Katherine Pulaski/The Actress Diana Muldaur"; "Chapter 26: *Enterprise* 1701-D"; "Chapter 27: The Starship: Standing Sets."

One of a host of interminably boring crew books on the several *Star Trek* television series, Van Hise's guide alternates between character and cast biographies, providing entries that are both inconsistent in the type of information provided and unreliable even for the data included. The lengths of the entries vary considerably, from 400-7,000 words. Character biographies have been expanded considerably from the television series and motion pictures; the author may have pulled basic background information on the characters from *ST* tie-in novels (which are not regarded by Paramount Studios as authoritative), or may have invented some of the details himself, but since no sources are cited, there is no way for the reader to discern this. Thus, much of the material is of questionable value.

The actor biographies focus on *Trek*-related trivia, and dates and incidences from the actors' personal lives prior to their involvement with the series are extraordinarily brief or even lacking. Unlike the *Trek Crew Companion* (see #645), this smaller version includes biographies of the characters Ro Laren and Dr. Pulaski (and actors Michele Forbes and Diana Muldaur). Black-and-white photographs of the actors and sketches of the characters by artist Allen K. illustrate the volume.

How many trees had to be slaughtered to publish this mess?

650. Van Hise, James. *Trek:* **The Printed Adventures.** Las Vegas, NV, Pioneer Books, 1993. 152 p. ISBN 1-55698-356-5 (pbk.).

Contents: "Introduction: 20th Century Odyssey"; "Chapter 1: *Star Trek* Novels"; "Chapter 2: The Bantam *Star Trek*"; "Profile: Greg Bear" ;"Chapter 3: The Pocket Books"; "Profile: Laurell K. Hamilton"; "Chapter 4: Pocket Specials"; "Chapter 5: Next Gen & Deep Space"; "Chapter 6: Next Gen Specials"; "Profile: Ann Crispin"; "Chapter 7: A Brief History"; "Chapter 8: *Star Trek* Fanfict"; "Chapter 9: Legendary Fan Writer"; "Chapter 10: Is Fan Fiction Legal?"; "Special Section: Directory of Fanzines."

This book discusses the television series *Star Trek* as a print phenomenon, from professional publishing to fan productions. The focus is on classic *Trek* novels, though some reviews are included on *Star Trek: The Next Generation* fiction, plus a very small amount on *Star Trek: Deep Space Nine*.

A typical entry includes the book title (bold caps), and a review (averaging 250 words), which provides both plot summaries and critical evaluations, but from a fannish perspective (*Yesterday's Son* and *Stranger from the Sky* are each called here "a masterwork"). Few bibliographical details are mentioned save for a sidebar buried in the first chapter called "A Handy List of *Star Trek* Fiction Between Hard Covers." This list of 56 books does include title (all caps), author, year, pagination, physical dimensions, a description of the binding, and an indication whether the book has a dust jacket. Two other lists provide title, author, and series number for the paperbacks, but these too are difficult to locate in the rather dense text of Chapter One, being formatted as bulk paragraphs rather than an easier-to-read, title-by-title bibliography, and including no other data but author, title, and series number.

The profiles focusing on amateur and professional *Trek* writers range from 2,000-6,000 words, and explain how each writer came to produce a *Star Trek* novel. Other sections discuss the legality of fan fiction, and provide a now outdated directory of *Star Trek* fanzines. The absence of an index is sorely felt, and navigation through this small book is extremely difficult, since the chapters heads break down discussion by the different publishers who have released *Trek* fiction.

The volume is illustrated with black-and-white sketches and cartoons of *Trek* characters. Not recommended save for *Star Trek* completists.

651. Van Hise, James, and Hal Schuster. *Trek:* **The Unauthorized Story of the Movies.** Las Vegas, NV, Pioneer Books, 1995. 208 p. ISBN 1-556-98375-1 (pbk.).

Contents: "Introduction"; "*The Motion Picture*"; "*The Wrath of Khan*"; "*The Search for Spock*"; "*The Voyage Home*"; "*The Final Frontier*"; "*The Undiscovered Country*"; "*Generations*"; "The End of an Era."

This is a companion volume to *The Unauthorized Trek: The Complete Next Generation* (see #648). Each section in the book contains a loose series of anecdotes on behind-the-scenes incidences in sparsely-worded prose typeset in a large font size. Sometimes the source of the quotation or paraphrase is given (although never cited), but usually the actors' feelings and actions are related with no concern for how the information was obtained or for its ultimate accuracy. The book's only positive contribution may be the large, color photographs (taken by a fans at *ST* movie premieres or conventions), arranged in two sections of inserts. There's no index, of course, and the production values are lamentable. Stash for the trash generation.

Star Wars

652. Mangels, Andy. *Star Wars:* **The Essential Guide to Characters.** New York, A Del Rey Book, Ballantine Books, 1995. xi, 199 p. LC 95-35242. ISBN 0-345-39535-2 (pbk.). London, Boxtree Books, 1996. xi, 199 p. ISBN 0-7522-0109-3 (pbk.).

Contents: "Acknowledgments"; "Introduction"; [alphabetical listing of characters]; "Bibliography."

Laid out like a role-playing character guide, this book includes 101 characters from all media (including spin-off novels, the motion pictures, comic books, etc.) mentioned as living in the *Star Wars* universe through September 1995, organized alphabetically by character name.

A typical entry includes: a full-body, pen-and-ink drawing (or black-and-white movie stills) of the character, labels indicating its species, gender, hair color, eye color, height, home world, political affiliation, weapon(s) of choice, vehicle of choice, first appearance, and manner of death (if necessary). A profile of the character follows (averaging 650 words), describing his or her or its origin, nature, and history.

It is unclear whether the material included from extraneous sources such as the novel spin-offs is considered canonical by George Lucas and his company, Lucasfilm, but most of the text focuses on these outsider characters. Written in a gushy, fannish style, and illustrated with cartoonish drawings, this guide will be of interest only to diehard *Star Wars* aficionados.

653. Velasco, Raymond L. **A Guide to the *Star Wars* Universe.** New York, A Del Rey Book, Ballantine Books, 1984. xlvii, 215 p. index. LC 84-90943. ISBN 0-345-31920-6 (pbk.). Slavicsek, William. **A Guide to the *Star Wars* Universe.** 2nd ed., rev. and exp. New York, A Del Rey Book, Ballantine Books, 1994. xlviii, 495 p. LC 93-46930. ISBN 0-345-38625-6 (pbk.). London, Boxtree, 1995. xlviii, 495 p. 0-7522-0859-4 (pbk.). Slavicsek, William. **A Guide to the Star Wars Universe.** 3rd ed., rev. and exp. New York, A Del Rey Book, Ballantine Books, 2000. 596 p. LC 00-104015. ISBN 0-345-42066-7 (pbk.).

The major part of the first edition of this book is an A-Z guide to the people, places, and things in the *Star Wars* universe. A typical character entry provides: name (listed under given name, not surname), brief description, a more detailed account of his or her life and career as derived from the canon, and a set of letter codes referencing original sources (*e.g.,* "SW" = *Star Wars*). Other entries focus on places, creatures, devices, weapons, etc.

The front matter includes indices to "Alien Creatures and Species," "Characters and Character Names," "Devices and Things," "Droid Names and Types of Droids/Automata," "Historical Events," "Slang/Colloquialisms," "Social Customs and Institutions," "Technical Concepts and Other Abstractions," "Vehicles/Vessels," "Weaponry," and "Worlds and Places," all of them used as entries in the main dictionary. A list of abbreviation codes on pages lxv-lxvii references 27 published *Star Wars* books and associated items (including map and art portfolios).

Velasco's definitions are based upon these printed sources and not directly on the three motion pictures themselves; there are a number of discrepancies between the movies and their novelized adaptations, and some of the other printed spin-off items include fictional elaborations not mentioned elsewhere. The book is nicely typeset, illustrated with postage stamp-sized black-and-white drawings, but printed on poor-quality paper.

The second edition of the *Guide* was completely rewritten and updated from the first, although the intent is the same: an A-Z guide to the people, places, and things in the Star Wars universe. Unlike the earlier version, however, it now includes information from "original Lucasfilm source[s]—the films, the radio dramas, or the original novelizations," in addition to role-playing games, sourcebooks, storybooks, sketchbooks, etc., that "may or may not agree with George Lucas's vision of the Star Wars galaxy." As before, there is a list of abbreviations for these sixty-eight sources at the beginning of the text.

The categories of information are only slightly altered and expanded upon: "Alien Creatures, Species, Families"; "Battles, Wars, Historical Events"; "Characters and Characters' Names"; "Devices and Things"; "Droid Names and Types"; "Food, Medicines, Chemicals"; "Geology, Plant Life"; "Places, Worlds, Customs, Institutions"; "Terminology, Slang, Colloquialisms, and Other Abstractions"; "Vehicles and Vessels"; and "Weaponry." The black-and-white illustrations remain sparse, and add little to the text, although they are somewhat larger in size.

With 147 sources, the "third edition has been expanded to include all the novels and comics and other new material produced from 1994 through 1999. It features some material pertaining to *Episode I: The Phantom Menace* and the New Jedi Order [book] series." Some readers may miss the categories section from the second edition that helped them sort through the types of information available. The illustrations here are somewhat finer in detail and accretion has naturally enlarged some entries, especially for the significant characters in the series, but this is perhaps the best edition of this volume yet.

Highly recommended for *Star Wars* fans.

The Twilight Zone

654. Prouty, Howard H. **TZX: The *Twilight Zone* Index.** North Hollywood, CA, [Howard H. Prouty], 1985. 40 p. index. (pbk.).

Designed as a supplemental index to Zicree's work (see #655), this guide is broken into four sections: "Directors," "Writers/Authors," "Selected Performers," and "Episode Titles." In each part materials are arranged alphabetically by person or title.

A typical Directors entry gives: director (all caps), episode title, network, original air date, and format (*e.g.,* "FB/30" = film, black-and-white, thirty-minute running time). A typical entry from the writers' section includes: name (all caps), episode, network, original air date, credit (*e.g.,* "ot" = original teleplay), story source (where applicable; "ps" = published story), and format (*e.g.,* "TB/30" = videotape, black-and-white, thirty-minute running time). A typical performers' entry gives: name (all caps), episode title, network, original air date.

The guide to episode titles provides: title, network, original air date, format, and the page number in Zicree's book (see #655), which annotates that episode (however, episode titles *are* indexed in the latter volume). The booklet is shot from clearly reproduced typed copy and bound with staples into paper covers.

Students of this ever-popular television series will want copies of this index; all others may safely pass.

655. Zicree, Marc Scott. **The *Twilight Zone* Companion.** Toronto & New York, Bantam Books, 1982. 447 p. index. LC 82-90326. ISBN 0-553-01416-1 (pbk.). **The *Twilight Zone* Companion.** 2nd ed. New York & Toronto, Bantam Books, 1989. 466 p. index. LC 89-6754. ISBN 0-553-34744-6 (pbk.).

Zicree's book pays homage to this long-running and critically acclaimed television series in a marvelously well-wrought guide to the programs and to the writers and other principals who contributed to its success. Individual episodes are arranged in chronological order by production date.

A typical entry gives: title (bold caps), air date, writer, producer, director, director of photography, music, cast (characters and actors), a transcription of Serling's introduction (in italics), one-paragraph plot summary, Serling's coda, and background details on the development of the story and on the characters, including occasional excerpts from the script.

Interspersed throughout the text are separate sections on the major writers, actors, directors, and other principals involved in the making of *The Twilight Zone,* usually associated with their first appearance on the program, and including snippets of interviews, either with the individuals themselves or with those who knew them, and much other associational information of importance. The book is very well designed and typeset, and illustrated with rare black-and-white stills from the television program. Unfortunately, the quality of paper used by Bantam means that the text will oxidize within a short period of time. The index correlates all names and titles with page numbers.

This is one of the best TV series guides yet published: Zicree is knowledgeable and informative, but never intrusive. Fans and scholars alike will welcome this volume; research libraries should immediately rebind and deacidify their copies.

The X-Files

656. Edwards, Ted. *X-Files* **Confidential: The Unauthorized X-Philes Compendium.** Boston, Little, Brown, 1996. xv, 277 p. LC 96-28561. ISBN 0-316-21252-0 (pbk.). *X-Files* **Confidential: The Unauthorized X-Philes Compendium.** Revised and updated ed. Boston, Little, Brown, 1997. xv, 320 p. LC 99-199792. ISBN 0-316-21808-1 (pbk.).

Contents: "Foreword" by Jeff Rice; "Acknowledgments"; "An Introduction"; Part I: "1. Mulder and Scully Meet *The Night Stalker*"; "2. It's Alive! Creating *The X-Files*"; "3. Two of a Kind: David Duchovny and Gillian Anderson"; Part II: "4. The Beginning: A Season in Hell; Season One Episode Guide"; "5. Year Two: The Cult Goes Mainstream; Season Two Episode Guide"; "6. Year Three: The Mythology; Season Three Episode Guide"; Part III: "The X-Phile Encyclopedia."

Contents (Revised Edition): "Foreword" by Jeff Rice; "Acknowledgments"; "An Introduction"; Part I: "1. Mulder and Scully Meet *The Night Stalker*"; "2. It's Alive! Creating *The X-Files*"; "3. Two of a Kind: David Duchovny and Gillian Anderson"; Part II: "4. The Beginning: A Season in Hell; Season One Episode Guide"; "5. Year Two: The Cult Goes Mainstream; Season Two Episode Guide"; "6. Year Three: The Mythology; Season Three Episode Guide"; "7. Year Four: The Creative Challenge; Season Four Episode Guide"; Part III: "The X-Phile Encyclopedia."

An episode guide and A-Z dictionary, *X-Files Confidential* also includes essays on the development of the *outré* television series, *The X-Files.* Much of the introductory material and Chapter One emphasize *The Night Stalker* connection to the series, from the introduction by Jeff Rice (author of *The Kolchak Papers,* the novel that later became *The Night Stalker*), through most of Chapter One (though Chris Carter has stated that the connection "is overstated"). Chapter Two features numerous quotations by Carter on the development of the show, while Chapter Three looks at lead actors Duchovny and Anderson's perceptions of the program.

The episode guide begins in Chapter Four, covering the 73 episodes from seasons 1-3. Each of these sections includes an introduction describing overall developments in that season. A typical episode entry gives: air number, title, original air date, writer(s), director, guest stars with character names in parentheses, a plot summary averaging 100 words in length (in italics), commentary made up of quotations from writers, directors, etc. (100-1,000 words), and the rating/audience share.

The "Encyclopedia" section contains over 1,000 entries, arranged alphabetically by main entry, consisting primarily of characters' names, but also including prop identification and story locations. A typical entry includes: name or item (all caps), description, and episode title (in brackets and quotation marks). There are frequent "See Also" references in bold-faced type, often distracting the eye from the main entry itself, which does not stand out quite as clearly. A few black-and-white photographs of Carter, Duchovny, and Anderson are scattered throughout the text.

The absence of an index makes finding a particular episode harder than it might be, but the "Encyclopedia" helps by pointing the reader to episodes through access to other information. The strength of the book lies in the collected commentaries for each episode from the writers and directors, but the fact that they remain wholly uncited is unfortunate.

The Revised Edition adds coverage for the episodes from the fourth season, plus entries in the "Encyclopedia" section for characters' names, props, and locations deriving from that season. The commentary and quotations for the fourth season, however, represent an improvement over the previous edition, with more opinions dealing with such difficult matters as the departure and return of producer/writers Morgan and Wong.

Edwards's comments, even on the worst episodes, are soft and uncritical, and his writing is permeated with a "*faanish*" aura that complements his avid, overt enthusiasm for the series, but tells us very little that we do not already know.

Trust no one! Prefer the better-organized and more authoritative *Official Guide* series (see #660).

657. Farrand, Phil. **The Nitpicker's Guide for X-Philes.** New York, Dell, 1997. xiv, 385 p. index. LC 97-14878. ISBN 0-440-50808-8 (pbk.).

Contents: "Acknowledgments"; "Guild Acknowledgments"; "Introduction"; "First Season"; "Second Season"; "Third Season"; "Fourth Season"; "Onscreen Locations Index"; "Index."

Farrand has made a writing career producing nitpicking guides to cult television series, especially *Star Trek.* Now he turns his sharp-eyes to *The X-Files.* He points out bloopers, poor writing, inconsistencies, and contrivances in the first 97 episodes of the series (Seasons 1-4).

The book examines each episode in order of its airing, with a typical entry (averaging 4500 words) including: episode title (boldfaced type), the dates of the action, onscreen locations, a summary of the episode, and headings such as "Unanswered Questions," "Geographical Inconsistencies," "Ruminations," "Plot Oversights," "Changed Premises," "Equipment Oddities," "Continuity Problems," and "Production Problems." Farrand includes trivia quizzes in the margins of the book, and sub-sections devoted to *X-Files* humor, such as "You Might be an X-Phile . . . "

The OnScreen Locations Index is a unique contribution to the literature, giving all onscreen locations used in seasons 1-4, plus the titles of each episode and the page numbers where each is nitpicked. The general index is very useful for finding references by page to episode names, concepts, and characters.

As always, Farrand provides a fun guide for fans and for the public libraries that serve them.

658. French, Michael. **The Mixtake Files: A Nit-Picker's Guide to *The X-Files*.** Chichester, England, Summersdale, 1997. 191 p. ISBN 1-84024-008-3 (pbk.).

French locates continuity and plot problems throughout the first seventy-three episodes of *The X-Files* (seasons 1-3). The entries are arranged in episode order, arranged by original air date. The typical entry includes: episode production number and title ("3x22" is the twenty-second episode of the third season), brief summary (averaging 50 words), three to four nitpicks per episode (averaging 75 words each), recurring actors, best line and scenes in the episode, and title explanations (not all entries have all this information). Nitpicks are also labelled by type, such as plot discrepancy, continuity problem, or subject matter; but the tagging is inconsistent and generally unhelpful in classifying various consistency errors.

The section on recurring actors creates another small problem, because the names are listed without any context, such as references to the appropriate character names. The reader must examine the Recurring Actor List at the rear of the book to locate additional information. French also includes other fanworthy information, providing lists of episodes that include the numbers "1121" (Chris Carter's wife's birthday) or "1013" (Carter's own birthday), and episodes with sinister events occurring in a bathroom. He also notes the overall death toll by episode and by season. The editing and punctuation is sometimes sloppy, as is the research; see, for example, the discussion of the episode "Ghost in the Machine," which mentions only Arthur Koestler's 1967 novel of the same name, rather than the original source of the phrase, René Descartes.

French does provide occasional moments that serious fans might enjoy, but those with limited budgets will choose the better-organized and more comprehensive work by Phil Farrand (see #657).

659. Joseph, Michael, ed. by David Richter. ***The X-Files* X-Posed.** London, Arrowhead Books, 1997. 81 p. ISBN 1-901674-43-6 (pbk.). Edited by David Richter.

Contents: One: "X Marks the Spot"; Two: "The Fox File"; Three: "X Appeal"; Four: "The X-Men"; Five: "The Complete Guide to *The X-Files,* Season 1-4"; Six: "X Out."

At least half of this brief guide consists of chapter-length essays about Carter's, Duchovny's, and Anderson's personal and professional lives, and the development of the television show, *The X-Files*. Chapter One covers creator Chris Carter and his TV program; Chapter Two looks at David Duchovny and his alter-ego, Fox Mulder; Chapter Three discusses Gillian Anderson and her character, Dana Scully; Chapter Four sorts out such supporting actors and characters as Mitch Pileggi's Walter Skinner, William B. Davis's Ciga-rette-Smoking Man, and others.

Chapter Five begins the reference portion of the book, taking up about half its length (p. 40-73), and covering 96 *X-Files* episodes (through season four), in order by air date. A typical entry includes: airing number (cardinal numbering), date of the first U.S. showing, writer(s), director, cast, plot summary (averaging 100 words in length), and comments (also averaging 100 words).

While Joseph's information is often to the point, it's also somewhat uneven. The comments sections vary from mentions of nitpicking errors to more solid reviews of various program themes. The section covering guest actors does not include their character names, an unfortunate omission. The episode guide proper often uses page-sized, black-and-white illustrations as the background for the text, sometimes dominating the page so completely that the words themselves are unnecessarily difficult to read. There is no index and no division by seasons, making navigation harder than necessary for most users.

The truth is out there! There's nothing here that can't be found in more (and better) detail in Lowry and Meisler's *Official Guides* to *The X-Files* (see #660).

660. Lowry, Brian, with Sarah Stegall. **The Truth Is Out There: The Official Guide to** *The X-Files.* New York, HarperPrism, 1995. 277 p. LC 95-45337. ISBN 0-06-105330-9 (pbk.). Lowry, Brian, with Sarah Stegall. **Trust No One: The Official Third Season Guide to** *The X-Files.* New York, HarperPrism, 1996. xxi, 262 p. LC 96-42078. ISBN 0-06-105353-8 (pbk.). Meisler, Andy, with Sarah Stegall. **I Want to Believe: The Official Guide to** *The X-Files.* New York, HarperPrism; London, Voyager, 1998. 302 p. LC 98-156050. ISBN 0-06-105386-4 (pbk.). Meisler, Andy. **Resist or Serve: The Official Guide to** *The X-Files.* New York, HarperEntertainment; London, HarperCollins, 1999. 288 p. LC 99-181152. ISBN 0-06-107309-1 (pbk.); ISBN 0-00-257133-1 (British edition; pbk.). Meisler, Andy. **The End and the Beginning: The Official Guide to** *The X-Files.* New York, HarperEntertainment, 2000. 299 p. LC 00-698908. ISBN 0-06-107595-7 (pbk.).

Contents (*The Truth Is Out There*): "Introduction"; "Conception and Evolution"; "Behind the Scenes"; "Making *The X-Files*"; "Pro-Files"; "The Episodes" (Season 1, Season 2, Season 3); "X-Philes"; "Ratings"; "Reviews"; "Awards and Honors"; "Character Dossiers."

Contents (*Trust No One*): "Acknowledgments"; "Introduction"; "1. The Making of 'Talitha Cumi'" ("Part I: Boarding & Writing"; "Part II: Preproduction"; "Part III: Production"; "Part IV: Postproduction"; "Part V: Epilogue: To Millennium . . . and Beyond"); "2. The Third Season: The Episodes"; "3. Writing *The X-Files*"; "4. Frequently Asked Questions About *The X-Files*"; "5. Ratings: Season 3"; "6. Awards and Honors"; "Appendix."

Contents (*I Want to Believe*): "Introduction"; "The Fourth Season"; "The Fifth Season: 'Redux' and 'Redux II'"; "Awards and Honors"; "Worldwide Broadcast Outlets"; "Ratings"; "Appendix: Season One, Season Two, Season Three."

Contents (*Resist or Serve*): "Introduction"; "Unusual Suspects"; "Redux"; "Redux II"; "Detour"; "Christmas Carol"; "The Post-Modern Prometheus"; "Emily"; "Kitsunegari"; "Schizogeny"; "Chinga"; "Kill Switch"; "Bad Blood"; "Patient X"; "The Red and the Black"; "Travelers"; "Mind's Eye"; "All Souls"; "The Pine Bluff Variant"; "Folie à Deux"; "The

End"; "1997-98 Awards and Honors"; "Worldwide Broadcast Outlets"; "Ratings: Season 5"; "Appendix" (Season One, Season Two, Season Three, Season Four).

Contents (*The End and the Beginning*): "Introduction"; "The Beginning"; "Drive"; "Triangle"; "Dreamland"; "Dreamland II"; "Terms of Endearment"; "The Rain King"; "How the Ghosts Stole Christmas"; "Tithonus"; "S.R. 819"; "Two Fathers"; "One Son"; "Arcadia"; "Agua Mala"; "Monday"; "Alpha"; "Trevor"; "Milagro"; "Three of a Kind"; "The Unnatural"; "Field Trip"; "Biogenesis"; "1998-99 Awards and Honors"; "Worldwide Broadcast Outlets"; "Ratings: Season 6"; "Appendix" (Season One, Season Two, Season Three, Season Four, Season Five).

More than just an episode guide, these books cover many different aspects of the award-winning television series, *The X Files*. The text in Volume One is divided into three sections. The first looks at the history and development of the show, and provides a "day-on-the-set" glimpse of the filming, plus brief actor biographies (300-2800 words). The second section covers forty-nine episodes from *The X-Files,* in chronological order by air date, primarily from the first and second season, with two shows from the third. A typical episode entry includes: episode title, original air date, writer(s), director, guest stars (with character names in parentheses), "log line" (the premise of the episode summarized in twenty words), principal setting, a synopsis (400 words), "back story" (behind the scenes information in 50-100 words), and several black-and-white stills from that episode.

Seasons one and two begin with a numbered map of the United States, and a corresponding numbered list of the episodes, so the reader can visualize how the action from the series travels across the nation and around the world. The final section of the book gives a few phrase excerpts from initial reviews of the show, a list of awards (or nominations for awards) received by the program during 1993-94, and character profiles, including details from the program up to that time in their development (including badge number, height, weight, hair, eye color, address, phone number, family, weapon, significant dates in their life/career, and the general perspective of the character). Less regular characters are listed with the episode titles where that character appears. Finally, a chart lists original air dates, episode titles, millions of viewers for that episode, and the rating/share according to Nielsen Media Research.

Throughout the book, the margins often contain notes, insights, and other trivia. There is no overall index, so finding particular data is more difficult than it should be.

In Volume Two, *Trust No One,* the episode guide covers only the twenty-four episodes of the third season. As in the first book, there is a great deal of supplementary material provided. The introduction contains some of the same history and development as in the first volume, with a quick evaluation of the third season and how it differed from one and two. A new section describes the making of an episode from pre-production through post-production. The episode guide is organized similarly to the first volume, save that the synopses and back-story sections are larger, with more quotations in the synopses from the script, highlighting humorous or classic lines and/or exchanges.

The third section of Volume Two includes a section on writing for *The X-Files,* which is not a how-to guide, but a look at the telewriters' own perspectives to this unusual program. An FAQ answers the twelve most frequently asked questions from fans. As in the first book, there is a ratings chart (showing original air date, episode name, rating/share, and viewers in the millions) and awards and honors (either nominated or won) from 1993-96.

The book concludes with an appendix that lists all of the episodes from seasons 1-2, with the title, air order number, and a twenty-word summary. Unlike the first volume, this book includes eight unnumbered pages of color pictures in the center of the book.

I Want to Believe features a new author, who brings to this volume a slightly different focus, with less supplemental material. The introduction covers the development of the show, but the tone and slant are new, correlating world events with developments in the program. The episode guide portion of the book includes only the twenty-four episodes of the fourth season, plus two from the fifth. This section features the same type of information as before. However, the synopses here are significantly longer than those in the previous two volumes, with numerous quotations cited from the scripts. The "back story" information, however, has suffered somewhat, being much sparser than before. Unlike the previous volume, the awards section in this book covers only the season in question (1996-97). A new section lists all the countries where *The X-Files* is televised. The ratings chart still shows original air date, episode title, rating/share according to Nielsen Media Research, and the viewers in the millions. The book concludes with an appendix that lists all of the episodes from seasons 1-3 with the title, air order number, and a twenty-word summary. A four-color, pull-out poster "detailing *The X-Files* mythology as revealed over the past four seasons" is folded into the back of the volume.

Resist or Serve, the fourth in the Official Guide series, includes only the twenty episodes from the fifth season, with the same kind of information included as in the previous volume. The synopses here are still quite long, with many quotations from scripts. The awards section covers only the season in question (1997-98). There is still a section that lists all the countries where *The X-Files* is televised. The ratings chart shows original air date, episode title, rating/share according to Nielsen Media Research, and the viewers in the millions. The book concludes with an appendix itemizing the episodes from seasons 1-4, with title, air order number, and a twenty-word summary. There is no index, but the table of contents, unlike the other volumes, actually lists all the episode titles for Season 5, so that the user can easily find a specific episode. An eight-page color insert with illustrated photographs from the series supplements the black-and-white pictures sometimes used as a backdrop to the text.

Volume Five, *The End and the Beginning,* features an introduction that is somewhat weaker than those we've seen before, being more promotional cheerleading than substance. The episode guide portion of the book includes only the twenty-two episodes of the sixth season, with the same kind of information as in Volumes Three and Four. The synopses remain lengthy, incorporating many quotations from the shows. The awards section covers only the season in question (1998-99). The end matter is similar to that included in Volumes 3-4. The book concludes with an appendix that lists the episodes from seasons 1-5, with the title, air order number, and a twenty-word summary. There is no index. As in Volume Four, the table of contents provides detailed listings of titles so that the user can easily locate a specific episode. There is an eight-page color insert in the center of the book illustrated with stills from the series. Pictures are sometimes used as a backdrop to the text, making it difficult to read.

This is a particularly fine series of guides to *The X-Files,* with almost all of the information that a reader could want or need. Lack of an index aside, there is much here of interest to *The X-Files* fan, as well as for the public libraries serving those patrons.

661. Schuster, Hal. **The Unauthorized Guide to** *The X-Files*. Rocklin, CA, Prima Publishing, 1997. xii, 228 p. index. LC 97-8798. ISBN 0-7615-0845-7 (pbk.).

Contents: "Acknowledgments"; "Preface"; Part I: The Making of *The X-Files:* "1. The Man Behind *The X-Files:* Creator Chris Carter"; "2. Opening the *Files:* Creating and Producing the Series"; "3. Year One"; "4. Year Two"; "5. Year Three"; "6. Year Four"; "7. Children of *The X-Files*"; "8. Precursors to *The X-Files*"; Part II: The Cast of *The X-Files*. "9. Gillian Anderson"; "10. Special Agent Dana Katherine Scully"; "11. David Duchovny"; "12. Special Agent Fox William Mulder"; "13. The Other Players"; Part III: Episode Guide. "14. Season One"; "15. Season Two"; "16. Season Three"; "17. Season Four; "18. Conspiracy"; Part IV: The World of *The X-Files*. "19. The X-Philes"; "20. Novels, Comics, and More"; "21. *The X-Files* Jokebook"; Part V: Appendixes. "A. The Federal Bureau of Investigation"; "B. Real-Life *X-Files* and the Organizations That Investigate Them"; "C. For Further Sleuthing"; "D. Addresses"; "Bibliography"; "Index."

This companion to *The X-Files* television show consists of a series of essays about the show's development, stars, and character profiles, plus an episode guide, and other miscellanea that fans of the show will enjoy. The episode guide covers shows from the first season through the seventeenth episode (out of twenty-four) of the fourth season. A typical entry includes: airing number ("4.5" is the fifth show aired in the fourth season), writer, director, date of original broadcast, guest cast with character name in parentheses, and a brief summary (25-50 words). The episode guide section makes up such a small portion of the book (p. 85-122), and is now so far out of date, that its reference value is questionable.

However, *The Unauthorized Guide* is a good fan book for cover-to-cover reading, with copious insights and honest analyses of the show. Schuster is not blindly complimentary, criticizing weak writing and the occasional overall lack of direction in the show. Many of the essays use quotations from those involved in the production of the series, and include more citations than many similar books do, often mentioning the title of the periodical where the quotation appeared, if not the actual date and pages. There is also a guide to *The X-Files* comic books (twenty-five issues), giving issue number, title, date, writer, artist, cover artist, and plot summary (10-24 words).

The bibliography in Appendix C is an interesting addition, with citations to mainstream books about the CIA, FBI, and unusual scientific phenomenon. The index includes not only episode titles and characters, but also mentions of real events in the text, such as Chernobyl, the Emmy awards, and FBI current hiring activity.

Fans and those libraries circulating to fans will enjoy Schuster's lowbrow guide.

PRINTED GUIDES TO THE INTERNET

SCOPE NOTE: This section covers guides to Internet access for materials relating to science fiction and fantasy.

662. Wolff, Michael. **Your Personal Net Sci-Fi: Your Guide to the Best SF on the Internet.** New York, Wolff New Media, 1996. xvi, 410 p. index. ISBN 0-679-77322-3 (pbk.). As: **Net Sci-Fi: A Compendium of the Best Science Fiction on the Internet.** New York, Dell, 1996. viii, 319 p. index. ISBN 0-440-22423-3 (pbk.).

Contents: "YPN Supersites"; "FAQ"; "Part 1: Center of the Universe"; "Part 2: Sci-Fi Screen"; "Part 3: *Star Trek*"; "Part 4: Sci-Fi Literature"; "Part 5: Cyberpunk"; "Part 6: It Came from Comics"; "Part 7: Sci-Fringe"; "Part 8: Sci-Fi Games"; "Part 9: New Worlds"; "Appendix" (includes index).

Divided into nine sections, this directory lists Internet web pages, mailing lists, and newsgroups relating to science fiction and fantasy. The FAQ, explaining the contents and uses of the book, also makes a fair introduction to the Internet for the novice. Each chapter of the guide covers a large subgenre of science fiction on the Internet, and is further broken down into subsections such as "Sci-Fi Screen," which covers movies and television (*e.g, 2001: A Space Odyssey* and *Babylon 5*), plus SF film personalities such as James Cameron and Steven Spielberg. The focus is always on the popular, rather than the esoteric. Even those not active in science fiction will recognize the films, programs, and authors included in this book.

Each chapter opens with a highlighted "YPN Supersite" for its comprehensive coverage of the topic, then continues with a list of sites covered inconsistently under such headings as "cyberzines," "archives," "fan fiction," "newsgroups," "mailing lists," "humor," and many more. Not every chapter includes representative sites from every heading employed.

A typical entry includes: title of the site (boldfaced type), a brief description (25-100 words), and the address (or AOL keyword). The web addresses are shown in a small typeface, but are easy to pick out because of the red, bold letters "WEB" printed next to each one. Many of the pages include black-and-white illustrations or quotations from the sites in question.

Not a great deal was revised in the Dell edition, and some of the changes that were made are unwelcome. The structure and contents are largely unchanged, but the print size here is significantly smaller and the URLs are not highlighted as they were in the Wolff Media publication. Readability will definitely be a problem for some users.

Naturally, any directory that tries to pin down the Internet is going to have a short shelf life, but this is especially true of a book that looks at so many personal fan pages. A sample of the contents indicates that a good percentage of these sites have now disappeared, changed servers, or altered the contents so to make them something completely different.

Both editions are now badly outdated. Put them in your virtual trashcan!

CALENDARS AND CHRONOLOGIES

SCOPE NOTE: This section includes chronologies of fantastic literature arranged by year and month in descending order, and historical calendars in book form arranged by month and day and year.

663. Post, Joyce. **Let's Drink to That: Being a Compendium of Events, Real & Imaginary, of Interest to the Reader of Science, Fiction, & Science Fiction.** Philadelphia, The Terminus, Owlswick, & Ft. Mudge Electrick Street Railway Gazette, 1970. 58 p. (pbk.).

Post, wife of map compiler J. B. Post, has here assembled a literary calendar of science fiction and related topics. The basic arrangement is by month, then by date. Under each day events that occurred on that date in history are listed in descending order by year, from the earliest to the latest.

January 1st, for example, includes entries for 1879, 1889, 1921, 1923, 1928, and 1948, noting the births of E. M. Forster and Seabury Quinn, the release of the serial version of *Around the World in 18 Days,* the opening of the first air-conditioned office building, and the formation of The Spectator Club. Entries average from one-to-two lines each, and there are two to fifteen entries per date. Post mentions the dates of birth and death of all major SF authors and editors through 1970, scientific advances of all kinds, space exploration, the production or release of major fantastic films, etc. The booklet is shot from legible typed copy, illustrated throughout by Roy Krenkel, and bound with staples into paper covers.

Although entertaining at times, this calendar is now decades out-of-date. An updated version with better production values would certainly be warranted.

QUOTATIONS DICTIONARIES

SCOPE NOTE: This section includes reference books that feature quotations from works of fantastic literature.

664. Gaiman, Neil, and Kim Newman. **Ghastly Beyond Belief.** London, Arrow Books, 1985. 343 p. ISBN 0-09-936830-7 (pbk.).

Gaiman and Newman have compiled a collection of unintentionally humorous SF quotations taken from mostly bad science-fiction and fantasy novels and films, and including enough passages from even the top-name writers in the field to make one wonder how the field ever survived to this day.

Contents: "Foreword and Acknowledgements"; "Introduction," by Harry Harrison; "Part One: The Books": "Attention Please"; "Characters, Human and Otherwise"; "Language!"; "Preoccupations"; "Special Effects"; "Writers and Rules"; "Part Two: The Movies": "For Starters"; "Expectations"; "The Nasties"; "SF Styles"; "The Cast"; "Science"; "Funny Bits"; "Countdown"; "Just Testing."

Each of these chapters is further subdivided into specific subjects ("Love and Marriage," for example), with quotations listed randomly thereunder. A typical entry includes: quotation, book author (all caps) and title (italics), or film title (italics) and year of release. The quotations range in size from one line to several paragraphs, and were chosen for their out-of-context amusement value, with appropriate side remarks by the editors (in boldfaced type preceding the quote). The book is nicely typeset and the text can be quite amusing.

However, the absence of an index makes the volume almost completely unusable as a reference work.

665. Rotsler, William, ed. **Science Fictionisms.** Salt Lake City, UT, Gibbs-Smith Publisher, 1995. 144 p. LC 95-9428. ISBN 0-87905-693-2 (pbk.).

Contents: "Witticisms"; "Futurisms"; "Politicisms"; "Educationisms"; "Lifeisms"; "Artisms"; "Militaryisms"; "Writingisms"; "Environmentalisms"; "Physicsisms"; "Truisms."

The late SF cartoonist and writer William Rotsler collected together as his final book these 334 very brief, mostly humorous, and, alas, entirely uncited quotations from such well-known science fiction writers as Arthur C. Clarke, Ray Bradbury, Frank Herbert, Anne McCaffrey, and others. The volume is divided thematically into broad, subject-oriented sections, but has no other obvious organization.

An index and/or a citations' list would have been helpful to those who might want to track down the original sources of these neat and pithy sayings. A pleasant enough browse for those who enjoy reading quotations from their favorite authors, but not very high on any library's need-to-buy list.

666. Sherwin, Jill. **Quotable** *Star Trek.* New York, Pocket Books, 1999. x, 374 p. index. LC 00-710559. ISBN 0-671-02457-4 (pbk.).

Contents: "Introduction"; "1. The Human Condition"; "2. The Quality of Life"; "3. Simple Pleasures"; "4. Human Nature"; "5. Making Sense of the Universe"; "6. The Search for Knowledge"; "7. Life and Death"; "8. Good and Evil"; "9. Theology and Faith"; "10. Parents, Children, and Family"; "11. Love"; "12. The Sexes"; "13. Friendship and Loyalty"; "14. Honesty and Trust"; "15. Courtesy and Respect"; "16. Communication and Diplomacy"; "17. Justice and Law"; "18. Peace and War"; "19. Politics"; "20. Freedom"; "21. Leadership"; "22. Duty and Honor"; "23. Humor"; "24. Challenge and Risk"; "25. Fear and Prejudice"; "26. Logic and Emotion"; "27. Business"; "28. Technology"; "29. Medicine"; "30. Dramatis Personae"; "31. For the Fans"; "32. Personal Favorites"; "Acknowledgments"; "Index."

Organized thematically, the entries in each section of this collection of quotations from the TV series *Star Trek* include: quotation (in quotes), name of the character speaking, individual(s) to whom the character is speaking, abbreviation representing the series title, and episode title (in quotes).

The text features quotations from the original *Star Trek* ("*TOS*"), *Star Trek: The Next Generation* ("*TNG*"), *Star Trek: Deep Space Nine* ("*DS9*"), and *Star Trek: Voyager* ("*VGR*"), plus the first eight *Star Trek* movies (cross-referenced to the subsidiary movie title; *e.g.*, *The Undiscovered Country*), illustrated with occasional full-page, black-and-white stills from the various series.

The index cross-references page numbers of the quotations included in the book with specific character names and episode titles (the latter found under the generic heading of the each series [*e.g.*, *Star Trek: Deep Space Nine*]).

Quotable Star Trek is an enjoyable romp for fans of the Star Trek universe, who will want to memorize the sayings and quiz their friends. Libraries, however, can safely pass.

COLLECTORS' AND PRICE GUIDES

SCOPE NOTE: Included in this section are price and collectors' guides to science-fiction and fantasy books, films, and memorabilia. Catalogs of one author's works are included in the Author Bibliographies chapter. Also covered herein are lists of SF bookstores and dealers.

667. Gibson-Downs, Sally, and Christine Gentry. **Encyclopedia of Trekkie Memorabilia: Identification and Value Guide.** Florence, AL, Books Americana, 1988. iii, 269 p., [8] p. of plates. LC 88-208326. ISBN 0-89689-066-X (pbk.).

This very detailed guide to *Star Trek* collectibles is arranged in alphabetical order by subject category, then alphabetically by title or description.

Categories include: "Artwork and Cels," "Blueprints," "Clothing and Accessories," "Film and Photography," "Games," "Hobby Kits," "Housewares," "ID's," "Printed Wall-hangings," "Jewelry," "Literature," "Music," "Posters and Posterbooks," "Props," "School and Office Supplies," "Scripts," "Toys," "Trading Cards," "Promoting *Star Trek*" (in two sections, covering special promotions, contents, display/exhibits, offers and specials, premiums, publicity releases, souvenirs; and conventions and live performances), and "Bibliography." Introductory chapters cover "What's It All About," "Your *Star Trek* Collection," and "Storing Your Collection."

A typical entry gives: item or title (boldfaced), publisher or production company, description, original issue price (in dollars), current price range (in dollars). The volume includes numerous black-and-white illustrations of the products and books described, and eight pages of color reproductions.

Serious Trekkers will welcome this guide, although the price listings are far out-of-date; libraries will probably find the book too limited in scope to add to their collections; researchers may discover that "Literature" chapter of interest, since it provides, in essence, a complete bibliography of all *Star Trek* fiction and nonfiction published through 1987. Compare with Cornwell and Kott's price list (see #670).

668. Halpern, Frank M. **International Classified Directory of Dealers in Science Fiction and Fantasy Books and Related Materials.** Haddonfield, NJ, Haddonfield House, 1975. x, 90 p. index. LC 74-22449. ISBN 0-88366-003-2.

The main section of this directory is arranged alphabetically by dealer name. A typical entry gives: business name, proprietor (if different), address, phone number, hours, specializations. Two indices reference the dealers' names by subject and geographically, by country or state and city. There are also brief lists of dealers who accept want lists, dealer appraisers, and search services. The book is shot from very clear typed copy and bound to library standards.

Lamentably, this guide is so far out-of-date as to render it almost useless.

669. Howlett-West, Stephanie. **The Inter-Galactic Price Guide to Science Fiction, Fantasy & Horror 1996.** Modesto, CA, Stephanie Howlett-West, 1997. 408 p. (laminated pbk.; spiral-bound). **The Inter-Galactic Price Guide to Science Fiction, Fantasy & Horror 1997.** Modesto, CA, Stephanie Howlett-West, 1997. 373 p. (laminated pbk.; spiral-bound). **The Inter-Galactic Price Guide to Science Fiction, Fantasy & Horror 1999.** Modesto, CA, Stephanie Howlett-West, 1999. 242 p. (laminated pbk.; spiral-bound). The 1999 version is also available on CD-ROM under the same title.

Contents: "Participating Dealers"; "Alphabetical Listing of Dealer Abbreviations"; "Abbreviations for Publishers"; "Abbreviations for Terms"; "How to Use This Guide: A Sample Entry"; "Inter-Galactic Guide (A-Z listing by author)."

This continuing price guide has been compiled from sixty-five catalogs of about twenty-five specialty book dealers, to help in locating current pricing data "from all types of science fiction/fantasy & horror, from the early days to current listings." The author states that an effort is being made to update the guide annually by the end of the first quarter of the year, with prices taken from catalogues and on-line listings, but a number of cycles have now been skipped.

Each volume records an estimated 20,000 entries (the third edition, published in 1999, contains fewer pages than the previous guides, but uses a smaller typeface, and thus includes almost the same number of entries). Because the author's focus is on collectibles, the minimal price levels for a volume to be listed herein is $20 for a hardback book and $10 for a paperback. Materials are organized alphabetically by the author's last name, then alphabetically by title.

A typical entry includes: author (bold type), title, publication year, publisher, condition, edition/notation, price, and dealer and catalog abbreviation. Abbreviations are also used to indicate whether the book has been signed, inscribed, published in a limited edition, etc. The books are attractively and legibly typeset, and the spiral binding is suitable for a personal library.

None of these data are readily available elsewhere, despite the advent of the Internet, and these volumes will prove very useful to science fiction and fantasy book collectors, particularly since they reflect actual sales data, and not the speculative estimates posted in the most other price guides.

670. The Official Price Guide to *Star Trek* and *Star Wars* Collectibles. 2nd ed. Orlando, FL, House of Collectibles, 1984. 236 p. LC 82-84639. ISBN 0-87637-437-2 (pbk.). **The Official Price Guide to *Star Trek* and *Star Wars* Collectibles.** 3rd ed. Orlando, FL, House of Collectibles, 1985. 257 p. LC 82-84639. ISBN 0-87637-494-1 (pbk.). Cornwell, Sue, and Mike Kott. **The Official Price Guide to *Star Trek* and *Star Wars* Collectibles.** 1st ed. New York, House of Collectibles, Ballantine Books, 1986. 377 p. Cornwell, Sue, and Mike Kott. **The Official Price Guide to *Star Trek* and *Star Wars* Collectibles.** 2nd ed. New York, House of Collectibles, Ballantine Books, 1987. 415 p. Cornwell, Sue, and Mike Kott. **The Official Price Guide to *Star Trek* and *Star Wars* Collectibles.** 3rd ed. New York, House of Collectibles, Ballantine Books, 1991. 277 p. LC 84-644977 (pbk.). ISSN 0748-1128.

The early versions of this price guide were unattributed, although Cornwell and Kott are acknowledged in the 1985 edition as having been contributors. Ballantine Books purchased and reworked the House of Collectibles list in 1986, established Cornwell and Kott as editors of this series, and called the heavily reworked volume a "1st edition."

Contents (1987 edition): "Market Review"; "*Star Trek*: From the Beginning"; "The *Star Trek* Movies"; "The Creation of *Star Wars*"; "*Revenge (Return) of the Jedi*"; "Building a Collection"; "Condition and Care"; "Conventions"; "Dealer Directory"; "Publications"; "About the Prices in This Book"; "How to Use This Book"; *Star Trek*: "Action Figures," "Artwork," "Blueprints," "Books," "Bumper Stickers," "Buttons," "Calendars," "Cels and Storyboards," "Ceramics," "Certificates and Diplomas," "Clothing and Accessories," "Comic Books," "Convention Program Books," "Costumes and Uniforms," "Decals and Stickers," "Fan Clubs," "Fanzines," "Games and Accessories," "Greeting Cards," "Household Wares," "Jewelry," "Magazines," "Medallions," "Model Kits," "Patches," "Postcards," "Poster Books," "Posters," "Promotional Items," "Puzzles," "Scripts," "School and Office Supplies," "Sheet Music," "Stills, Slides and Photographs," "Toys, Trading Cards," and "Video Cassettes." *Star Wars*: "Action Figures and Accessories," "Artwork," "Badges," "Buttons and Bumper Stickers," "Blueprints," "Books," "Cards," "Clothing and Accessories," "Collector Plates," "Comic Books," "Cosmetics," "Costumes," "Fan Clubs," "Fanzines," "Figurines," "Films and Video Cassettes," "Games," "Greeting Cards," "Household Wares," "Jewelry," "Magazines," "Models," "Party Goods," "Patches," "Posters," "Promotional Items" (Studio), "Puzzles" (Jigsaw), "Records and Tapes," "Scripts," "Sheet Music," "Stationery and School Supplies," "Toys," "Toys" (Action-Figure Related), and "Video Games."

In each section materials are listed alphabetically by description or title. A typical entry gives: item (boldfaced), description, and price range. The book is illustrated throughout with a small number of black-and-white reproductions of the items described and printed on poor-quality paper. Gibson-Downs and Gentry's guide (see #667) is generally much more helpful for *Star Trek* items; for example, both catalogs list Blish's early fictionalizations of *Star Trek* episodes (*Star Trek 1-Star Trek 12*), but the *Encyclopedia* gives contents listings, pagination, and a complete rundown of changes in ISBN numbers and original prices, alterations of cover art, etc. However, Cornwell and Kott's guide will be helpful to *Star Wars* collectors, and collectors will no doubt want to compare prices in any case.

Now largely outdated.

671. Resnick, Michael D. **Official Guide to the Fantastics.** Florence, AL, House of Collectibles, 1976. 212 p. (pbk.). **Official Guide to Comic Books and Big Little Books.** [2nd ed.]. Florence, AL, House of Collectibles, 1977. ii, 264 p. **Official Price Guide to Comic and Science Fiction Books.** [3rd ed.]. Orlando, FL, House of Collectibles, 1979. 422 p. (pbk.). Hudgeons, Thomas E., III. **The Official 1981 Price Guide to Comic and Science Fiction Books.** [4th ed.]. Orlando, FL, House of Collectibles, 1981. 437 p. (pbk.). Hudgeons, Thomas E., III, and William Roger. **The Official 1982 Price Guide to Comic and Science Fiction Books.** [5th ed.]. Orlando, FL, House of Collectibles, 1982. 501 p. (pbk.). **The Official Price Guide to Science Fiction and Fantasy Collectibles.** [6th ed.] Orlando FL, House of Collectibles, 1983. 526 p. Hudgeons, Thomas E., III. **The Official Price Guide to Science Fiction and Fantasy Collectibles.** [7th ed.]. Orlando, FL, House of Collectibles, 1985. 537 p. (pbk.). Thompson, Don, and Maggie Thompson. **The Official Price Guide to Science Fiction and Fantasy Collectibles.** 3rd ed. [*sic*]. New York, House of Collectibles,

Ballantine Books, 1989. viii, 482 p., [8] p. of plates. index. LC 84-647218. ISBN 0-87637-754-1 (pbk.). ISSN 8755-2787.

This guide has gone through a variety of styles and formats in its history, but was reworked extensively when Ballantine Books bought out House of Collectibles in the late 1980s; Ballantine has chosen to call the first version of its revised publication the "Third Edition."

Contents (1989 edition): "Acknowledgments"; "Introduction"; "Getting to Know Science Fiction and Fantasy"; "Collecting Science Fiction and Fantasy"; "Evaluating Science-Fiction and Fantasy Collectibles"; "History of the Field"; "The Market"; "Science-Fiction and Fantasy Names"; "American Fiction Magazines"; "British Fiction Magazines"; "Science Fiction and Fantasy in Comic Books"; "Science-Fiction and Fantasy Drama"; "Filksongs and Other Recordings"; "Collecting the Best"; "You Can't Have It All"; "Science-Fiction and Fantasy Glossary"; "Non-Fiction/Reference Material"; "Afterword"; "Index."

The main section of the book, "Names," is an A-Z bibliography of major science fiction authors. A typical entry gives: author's name (bold caps), real name (if a pseudonym, in parentheses), years of birth and death (when known), brief one-paragraph biography, a list of the awards the author has received (with years and titles of the fiction being honored), and a checklist of the writer's major book publications, in ascending, chronological order by publication date, giving year of publication, and title (in italics, plus any alternate titles in parentheses), and some prices (but many items are unpriced). No bibliographical data are recorded, making identification of first editions virtually impossible.

The two chapters on magazines are each arranged in alphabetical order by magazine title, a typical entry providing: title (bold caps), alternate titles, years of publication, brief history (one to two paragraphs), and a checklist of issues and prices, year by year and month by month. The drama chapter includes brief sections on *Doctor Who, Star Trek, Star Wars, The Man from U.N.C.L.E.,* and other TV programs and motion pictures, but again provides little in the way of identification beyond title. The book is illustrated with a handful of black-and-white reproductions of some of the items described, plus eight pages of seemingly randomly chosen color plates, and is printed on poor-quality paper.

It is difficult to see how the neofan or beginning collector could ever make sense of this catalog, which provides no edition points, very little in the way of descriptions, and a paucity of pricing data in the book section. In fact, this is one collectible that need not be collected by anyone (including the earlier editions, which, if anything, are even worse).

672. Rovin, Jeff. **The Science Fiction Collector's Catalog.** San Diego, A.S. Barnes & Co., 1982. 181 p., [8] p. of plates. LC 81-3593. ISBN 0-498-02562-4 (pbk.). London, The Tantivy Press, 1982. 181 p., [8] p. of plates. (pbk.).

Contents: "Foreword," by Adam West; "Preface"; "1. Where to Collect"; "2. Pulp Magazines"; "3. Big Little Books"; "4. Comic Books"; "5. Comic Strips"; "6. Books"; "7. Motion Pictures"; "8. Film Stills and Posters"; "9. Movie Props"; "10. Record Albums"; "11. Science Fiction Magazines"; "12. Picture Cards"; "13. Edgar Rice Burroughs"; "14. *Star Trek*"; "15. Toys"; "16. SF Wargames"; "Bibliography."

Each chapter provides a very basic introduction to its subject, with a list of major dealers, and mentions of a handful of major collectibles, with tentative prices (now decades out-of-date). The chapter on books, for example, gives two pages of introductory material, lists twenty-seven major authors and roughly a hundred hardcover titles, notes years of publication and suggested prices, but no other bibliographical data; a separate subsection lists roughly a hundred paperbacks grouped by price category and then alphabetically by title (the previous section was arranged by author).

None of the other sections are any better organized. The book is illustrated throughout with well-reproduced black-and-white covers and stills, plus eight pages of color illustrations, and attractively typeset.

Of no use whatsoever.

673. Snyder, Jeffrey B. **A Trekker's Guide to Collectibles with Values.** Atglen, PA, Schiffer Publishing Co., 1996. 159 p. LC 95-25792. ISBN 0-88740-965-2 (pbk.).

Contents: "Introduction"; "Chapter I: Science Fiction, Science and the Road to the Twenty-Third Century"; "Chapter II: Details, Details: Life in the Twenty-Third Century and Beyond"; "Chapter III: *Star Trek*: The Collectibles"; "Bibliography."

Snyder describes an array of collectibles (action figures, books, calendars, comics, ceramics, costumes, decals, film and video, games, jewelry, magazines and fanzines, figurines, plates, postcards, posters, toys, trading cards, and more) for the several *Star Trek* programs (*Star Trek, Star Trek: The Next Generation, Star Trek: Deep Space Nine,* and *Star Trek: Voyager,* plus the associated motion pictures), and provides estimated values for all the items listed, using the dollar-range system (*e.g.,* $25-30 for the 1980 paperback novelization of *Star Trek: The Motion Picture*). The movie products featuring the original cast are included with the first *Star Trek* section, while *TNG* movie items are grouped with that show.

The first two chapters outline the development and history of the *ST* TV shows and movies, and the *Star Trek* phenomenon in general. Chapter Three, the main portion of the book, is divided into sections by *Star Trek* television series, then alphabetically by type of collectible or manufacturer. Each sub-section has a paragraph introducing the product, its history, and producer. The entries are arranged like a checklist, including a small box to the left of each item for personal record-keeping. Snyder gives a brief description of each item, and then the price range.

Approximately 3,000 products are described and valued, with 2-3 color pictures per page illustrating the products. The emphasis is on English-language collectibles. Although the book has no index, the detailed contents list basically serves the same purpose.

Collectors and fans will enjoy browsing and using the book. The text is very well written, even providing footnotes in the first two introductory chapters, plus a bibliography at the end of the book. Snyder includes some practical advice on maintaining the best value for these materials, as well as describing known flaws in each item. The author provides no explanation of how he arrived at the price levels in question, although he does acknowledge being a lifelong collector of *Star Trek* memorabilia.

An enjoyable and useful book for collectors and fans alike, completely superseding Cornwell and Kott (see #670) and Gibson-Downs and Gentry (see #667).

674. Wells, Stuart W. III. **Science Fiction Collectibles: Identification & Price Guide.** Iola, WI, Krause Publications, 1999. v, 249 p., [16] p. of color plates. LC 98-87371. ISBN 0-87341-684-8 (pbk.).

Contents: "Acknowledgments"; "Introduction"; "Action Figures"; "Books (Collecting Hardcover Publishers; Collecting Paperback Publishers; Collecting Authors)"; "Media Books (Pulp Magazines; Science Fiction Magazines)"; "Comics"; "Models and Statues"; "Toys"; "Trading Cards"; "Index."

Items in this guide have been categorized into what the author calls "The Book World" and "The Media World." Readers, he says, collect books (including magazines and cover art), and "fans" collect memorabilia, toys, comics and trading cards. The present volume has been designed to cover "the whole range of science fiction collectibles from both worlds." Because of space considerations, the selection criteria include only those items to be judged as "science fiction," with fantasy, horror, and superheroes categories being excluded. The proposed prices are for items in "near mint" condition.

Each chapter is subdivided by type of collectible, and includes an introduction on collecting that type of product, followed by alphabetical sub-sections broken down either by the manufacturer, publisher, product type, subject, media tie-in, or some other primary identification point. The "Books" chapter, for example, includes a general introduction, followed by a sub-section arranged by collectible publisher (beginning with "Arkham House"), and thence chronologically by year of publication; the second sub-section lists collectible authors, arranged alphabetically by surname, and then by publication year; a third section arranges materials by anthology editor, and thence by date. The typical entry in the "Books" chapter includes: title (italics), publisher, year of publication, and other information of interest.

Other chapters include varying data sufficient to identify the product in question. The book is illustrated with black-and-white photographs of popular items, plus a color insert in the center of the volume displaying a number of vintage science fiction collectibles.

It's difficult to evaluate the accuracy of the price estimates provided in this type of book. One can say, for example, that Roger Zelazny's *Nine Princes in Amber* (Doubleday, 1970), is grossly undervalued, at least in comparison with the other volumes in the Amber series listed herein, but do the other prices for Zelazny books mirror the actual market for his pubications? Perhaps.

Diehard book collectors will probably prefer the Howlett-West guides (see #669), which at least feature specific, accurate market data for the years in question, and which cover a great many more publications than Wells can ever hope to evaluate. Collectors of comics may find the Overstreet and other comic book price guides more current and far-reaching in their coverage. But some of the data listed in Wells are simply not available anywhere else, and for this reason alone, specialists in certain collecting fields may well find this guide useful.

Most suitable for large public library collections.

PROFESSIONAL WRITERS' GUIDES

SCOPE NOTE: Included in this section are guides intended to be used by professional and apprentice writers in developing their skills, contacts, market data, and other sources of information.

675. Tompkins, David G., ed. **Science Fiction Writer's Market Place and Sourcebook.** Cincinnati, OH, Writer's Digest Books, 1994. 486 p. index. LC 94-646955. ISBN 0-89879-692-X. Borcherding, David H., ed. **Science Fiction and Fantasy Writer's Sourcebook.** 2nd ed. Cincinnati, OH, Writer's Digest Books, 1996. 502 p. index. LC 97-640050. ISBN 0-89879-762-4.

Contents (First Edition): Section I: Science Fiction Trends. "Trends and Genres in Science Fiction: From Space Opera to Steampunk," by Peter Heck; Section II: Craft and Technique. "Writing: The Basics," by Algis Budrys; "Characters in Science Fiction," by Orson Scott Card; "Style: Knock Out Weak Verbs!" by Darrell Schweitzer; "Plot: Using Coincidence in Your Fiction," by Nancy Kress; Section III: Markets for Short Fiction. "Marketing Your Short Story," by Robin Gee; "Primary Short Fiction Markets"; "Secondary Short Fiction Markets"; "Overseas Short Fiction Markets"; "The Science Fiction Anthology Market";

Section IV: Markets for Novels. "Marketing Your Science Fiction Novel," by Robin Gee; "Primary Novel Markets"; "Secondary Novel Markets"; "Overseas Novel Markets"; "The Gaming Market: Writing Role-Playing Games"; Section V: Finding an Agent. "Finding and Getting the Most Out of a Science Fiction Agent"; "SF/Fantasy Agent Listings"; Section VI: Editors at Work. "Anatomy of a Sale: 'Due Process' to *Aboriginal Science Fiction*"; "Anatomy of a Sale: 'From the Corner of the Eye' to *Analog Science Fiction and Fact*"; "Anatomy of a Sale: 'Mom's Little Friends' to the *Magazine of Fantasy & Science Fiction*"; "Anatomy of a Sale: *Sleipnir* to Baen Books"; Section VII: Resources. "Online Services"; "Organizations"; "Conventions"; "Workshops; Nonfiction Magazines/Publications of Interest"; "Bookstores"; "The Science Fiction Book Club"; "Must-Read Lists"; "Nebula and Hugo Award Winners"; "Contests"; "Glossary"; "Contributors to the Instructional Articles"; "Contributors to the Market Listings"; "General Index/Market Categories Index."

Contents (Second Edition): "From the Editor"; Section I: Science Fiction & Fantasy Trends. "Doors to Other Worlds: Trends in Science Fiction and Fantasy," by Peter Heck; Section II: Craft & Technique. "Creating and Using Near Future Settings," by Maureen F. McHugh; "The Fantasy Series: Tips, Pitfalls . . . and Joys," by Joel Rosenberg; "Take My Wizard . . . Please! The Serious Business of Writing Funny Fantasy and Science Fiction," by Esther M. Friesner; "Finding Your Short Story's True Beginning," by Darrell Schweitzer; Section III: Markets for Short Fiction. "Marketing Your Short Fiction"; "Primary Short Fiction Markets"; "Other Short Fiction Markets"; "Overseas Short Fiction Markets";

Section IV: Novel Markets. "Marketing Your Novel"; "Primary Novel Markets"; "Other Novel Markets"; "Overseas Novel Markets"; "Opportunities for Writers in the Comic

Book Market," by Mark Clark; Section V: Finding an Agent. "Finding and Getting the Most Out of an Agent," by Russell Galen; "SF/Fantasy Agent Listings"; Section VI: Success Stories. "Anatomy of a Sale: 'Pacifica' to *Realms of Fantasy*," by Shawna McCarthy; "Anatomy of a Sale: *The Fortunate Fall* to Tor Books," by Patrick & Teresa Nielsen Hayden; "Anatomy of a Sale: *An Exchange of Hostages* to AvoNova," by Eluki bes Shahar; "The Road to a First Novel," by J. V. Jones and Betsy Mitchell; "First Sales," by Kathleen Ann Goonan, Jonathan Lethem, Jeff Noon, and Ron Sarti; Section VII: Resources. "Online Resources"; "Organizations"; "Conventions," by Patrick Souhan; "Workshops"; "Contests"; "Nonfiction Magazines/Publications of Interest"; "Glossary of Science Fiction and Fantasy Terms"; "About the Contributors"; "Editor Index"; "Category Index/Markets"; "Category Index/Agents"; "General Index."

Part directory and part how-to guide, the first edition of this book was intended for people trying to improve the quality of their writing and enter professional writing in the sf/fantasy/horror genres. The writing style is instructional and informal. The text includes an article on characters by well-known SF author Orson Scott Card, and two chapters of a published first novel, *Sleipnir,* with an analysis by editor Toni Weisskopf explaining why she accepted the piece. There are also two examples of accepted stories following much the same format.

The directory lists over 100 markets for science fiction/fantasy fiction. Primary market entries include a large periodical/publisher title/agent, address, contact name, genre specialization (cyberpunk, space opera, military, etc.), discussion of expectations and needs (500-1,000 words), payment, and brief instructions for submission. The secondary market and agent listings provide the same information, but the discussion in these sections is much shorter (averaging 125 words).

The second edition was retitled and extensively revised and updated. Sections I and II contain new, signed articles offering sound authorial advice and encouragement to help new writers develop their writing skills, as well as strategies for selling their material. Later chapters feature profiles of approximately 300 magazines, book publishers, and agents who are friendly to genre fiction (100 more listings than the previous edition).

Each profiled entry includes: publication title (if a periodical), publisher, founding year, frequency of publication, categories of writing accepted (hard science fiction, cyberpunk, etc.), profile of the publisher or periodical (averaging 1,000 words in length), contact instructions, payment terms, addresses, and URLs. Quotations from the editors are used to describe exactly what they are seeking in new material. Secondary markets are not heavily profiled, but those covered follow much the same format. The three indices make navigating through this information an easy process.

Dropped from the second edition are lists of science fiction book clubs, a "must read" bibliography, and Hugo and Nebula Award winners; these deletions actually help to focus the book, and the loss is not greatly felt. The article in Tompkins on role-playing games has been replaced by a piece on "Opportunities for Writers in the Comic Book Market."

While the second edition certainly supersedes the 1994 version in its directory information, the essays by the pros on writing and selling prose have not aged in the slightest, so the first edition should not be casually discarded.

Recommended for all potential SF and fantasy writers, with the *caveat,* however, that the marketing information is now mostly outdated.

FAN GUIDES

SCOPE NOTE: Among the items featured in this chapter are fan guides, convention guides, and other reference books relating to fandom, except directories, which are included in the Directories section of this book.

676. Speer, Jack Bristol. **Fancyclopedia.** Los Angeles, Los Angeles Science Fiction Society, 1944. 97 p. (pbk.). Eney, Dick, ed., based on the work of Jack Speer. **Fancyclopedia II.** Alexandria, VA, Operation Crifanac, 1959. 186 p. (pbk.).

These rare guides were mimeographed from typed copy and bound into paper covers. Both books are arranged alphabetically by term.

A typical entry includes term (all caps) and description, from one sentence to one page. Items include fan groups, "*faanish*" names, club name abbreviations, and much else that defies description (*e.g.,* "Kehli. Lee Hoffman's horse, which sparked her first retirement from fandom"; "KTP. Kaj tiel plu; Esperanto and so forth, equivalent to Latin etc. and Deutsch usw").

None of this is particularly important, of course, but libraries with collections of fantastic literature will want to have these volumes for their historical value as SF memorabilia. Some of the original pages are faint and yellowed, as might be expected, and both books were produced in runs of less than 500 copies; existing copies are fragile and now very hard to find.

677. Strauss, Erwin S. **The Complete Guide to Science Fiction Conventions.** Port Townsend, WA, Loompanics Unlimited, 1983. 56 p. (pbk.).

Erwin "Filthy Pierre" Strauss, compiler of MIT's *Index to the S-F Magazines, 1951-1965* (see #168), here provides a brief guide to attendance at and production of SF conventions (cons).

Contents: "What Goes on at a Science Fiction Convention, Anyway?"; "Filthy Pierre Steps Out to a Con"; "A Bestiary of Conventions"; "Here's What Goes On at an SF Con"; "So You Want to Run a Con"; "Access" [*i.e.,* bibliography and directory].

Most of the sections provide very general but sound advice on various aspects of con functions, fan language, and what the neofan might expect to see at his or her first con. The "Access" chapter, now outdated, includes addresses of basic publications and convention registration services or groups (the *Star Trek* Welcommittee, for example). The book is nicely typeset, but not designed for library usage. The narrative parts of this guide remain valid; the reference section badly needs updating. Libraries can pass.

678. Tucker, Bob. **Neo-Fan's Guide to Science Fiction Fandom.** Hartford City, IN, Robert & Juanita Coulson, 1966. 16 p. (pbk.).

[Not seen.]

MAJOR ON-LINE RESOURCES

SCOPE NOTE: This chapter includes very selective coverage of on-line sites devoted to science fiction, fantasy, or horror, covering both major reference sources and several subject-focused web pages. Users should be aware that even the larger web pages tend to be fluid, changing URLs often, or even disappearing in their entirety on occasion. Inevitably, many sites of interest to some SF researchers or readers will have been either missed or deliberately omitted here.

679. Adherents.com. **Religions in Literature.** http://www.adherents.com/lit/.

Contents: "Top 50 Most Famous Science Fiction/Fantasy Writers"; "SF/F Writers of Various Faiths"; "Quaker Science Fiction"; "Amish Science Fiction"; "Latter-day Saints in Science Fiction"; "Baha'i Science Fiction"; "Zoroastrian Science Fiction"; "Sikhs in Science Fiction"; "Tibetan Buddhism in Science Fiction"; "Unitarian-Universalists in Science Fiction."

Part of the Adherents.com site (www.adherents.com), this site uses the Hugo, Nebula, Sidewise, and Locus award-winning science fiction novels, plus other major books in the genre (*e.g.*, Piers Anthony's "Tarot" series or Octavia Butler's *EarthSeed*), as sources to determine within these works the stated religious affiliations of characters or groups. Adherents.com also provides lists of the major authors in the field with their known religious affiliations, derived from biographies, profiles, dustjacket copy, and other sources, as cited.

The 735 lists included on the site are arranged in alphabetical order by subject, asterisks indicating references to literary groups (most of these do *not* cover SF material). Links are provided to the tables of data incorporating some 14,500 references from science fiction and fantasy literature. Different arrangements are employed for specific charts or tables, but the intent is always to demonstrate a religious connection to the authors and/or their fictional creations—or lack thereof, in the case of agnostics and atheists.

This site is well organized, easy to navigate, and includes good internal documentation. The narrowness of the subject restricts the usage somewhat, but this is a good place to begin an investigation into the representation of religion in science fiction.

680. Brian, Paul. **Science Fiction Research Bibliography: A Bibliography of Science Fiction Secondary Materials in Holland Library, Washington State University.** http://www.wsu.edu/~brians/science_fiction/sfresearch.html.

Contents: "Encyclopedias and General Checklists"; "Indexes to Short Stories"; "Indexes to Criticism and Reviews"; "Film, Illustrations, Sound Recordings, Miscellaneous"; "Histories and Criticism"; "Studies of Individual Authors"; "Periodicals."

This is an introductory bibliography of secondary materials for science fiction compiled by a professor at Washington State University. The list is not comprehensive, but only reflects the holdings of that institution's library. Scholars will be familiar with much of material on this biblio, which is made up of many standard reference sources, but students or beginning researchers will discover a list of almost 600 items that will give them a solid grounding in science fiction/fantasy secondary sources. Entries are divided into general subject sections, with each section arranged alphabetically by author surname. A typical entry includes: author, title, and LC call number at the Washington State University Library.

This site could be developed at some future point into a more thorough guide to SF secondary sources.

681. Chronological Bibliography of Science Fiction Criticism. http://www.depauw.edu/sfs/.

This chronological bibliography gathers together "a large number of critical materials on SF that the editors of *SFS* [*Science Fiction Studies*] deem to be important, influential, or historically noteworthy," from 1634-2000, with over 500 entries of articles or books. The typical monographic entry includes: author, title, place and date of publication, and publisher. The typical shorter entry includes: author, article title, periodical or book source, date, and pagination. A few items are linked to either the full text of the piece or an abstract.

This is a good resource for scholars, students, or fans interested in the history of science fiction scholarship.

682. Day, Linda. **Science Fiction and Fantasy for Children: An Annotated Bibliography for Educators.** http://libnt1.lib.uoguelph.ca/SFBib/index.htm.

Contents: "About the Database"; "Help"; "Search the Database"; "Comments."

Compiled by a librarian at the University of Guelph Library, this database/bibliography is intended to provided information about science fiction and fantasy works suitable for elementary school students, plus some materials suitable for older children. Two types of stories are excluded: traditional fairy tales in picture book form (a novelization that significantly expands a traditional story, or a modern story in fairy-tale style, will be included); and animal stories other than those involving animal-human interaction or magic/science fiction elements.

The site allows for a simple keyword search for author, title, series title, and annotated text. A more complicated search allows searching by type, grade or age level, recommendation, and nationality of the author. The advanced search feature is quite good, allowing the user to employ specific parameters in the search. Although the site has a well documented "Help" section, some of the codes and instructions are difficult to find on the search screens. A few examples to help prompt the user would be useful.

The results of a search can be displayed either in a table or in citation form, but the site only displays the author and title in either format, with the title linked to an annotation. Clicking the latter link takes the user to a complete record screen, typically including: author, title (boldfaced type), series title (if any), plot summary (averaging 250 words), age level(s), grade level(s), children's choice rating, type of book, and nationality of the author. The annotations could be written more clearly.

Coverage is very spotty, and this does not appear to be due to the age of the material (the site is noted as last being updated in 1997). For example, searching the house name "Victor Appleton" only produces one entry, the twelfth (and last) title in the modern, mass market paperback (fourth) series of the "Tom Swift" juveniles. What happened to the other eleven? Clicking on "Ursula K. Le Guin" produces four titles in the Earthsea series—*The Farthest Shore, Tehanu, The Tombs of Atuan,* and *A Wizard of Earthsea*—but misses several other books that would qualify for inclusion herein, including the two additional books in this series published after 1997. And so on.

Although the navigation of the site is sound, the author provides no indication of why certain books were included and others omitted, other than that's what was readily available to her. A sometimes useful tool that could (and should) have been even more useful.

683. Gunn, Alastair G. **Cyclopaedia of Ghost Story Writers.** http://www.jb.man.ac.uk/ ~agg/ghosts/ghocyc.html.

"The Cyclopaedia of Ghost Story Writers is an ever-expanding database of information (bibliographic and biographic) of authors who have written at least one published short story (generally less than 30,000 words) with the theme of haunting or another related aspect of the supernatural during the Georgian, Victorian or Edwardian period. The current definition of whether an author belongs within this period is vague but as a general rule no author born after about 1920 is included. For each author is given, if possible, some basic biographic information, followed by a list of known short stories by the author, most but not all of which are supernatural or specifically ghostly in nature, followed by known publications (and dates thereof) containing one or more of the named short stories. This information is in no way comprehensive or complete."

Most of the writers covered herein are classic authors of supernatural fiction, including many nineteenth-century and early twentieth-century figures. The organization of the database makes it difficult for the average user to distinguish between short story and book titles, both of which are italicized. No bibliographical data are provided. All of the listings are vastly underreported, making this site of little use to any but the most unsophisticated of fans.

684. Hall, Hal W. **Science Fiction and Fantasy Research Database.** http://library.tamu.edu/cushing/sffrd/.

"*The Science Fiction and Fantasy Research Database* provides access to articles, books, news reports, obituaries, motion picture reviews, and other material about science fiction and fantasy. Some coverage of horror, gothic, and utopian literature is included. Fiction, such as novels or short stories, is not indexed here. Book reviews are not indexed."

This is an online, searchable version of the standard reference volumes, *Science Fiction and Fantasy Reference Index, 1878-1985, Science Fiction and Fantasy Reference Index, 1985-1991,* and *Science Fiction and Fantasy Reference Index, 1992-1995* (see #117), plus new material located since the publication of the last printed volume.

Hall's guide is an incredible resource to have available free on the Web, being an essential starting place for anyone who studies or enjoys science fiction or fantasy. The resource takes itself seriously, explaining the scope and methodology of the compilation, and providing good explanations for searching, as well as a thesaurus for more precise searches. The simple search allows for field level searches using a default "OR", while the advanced search employs a pull-down menu for "AND", "OR", and "AND NOT."

A typical entry includes: author, title, imprint (for either articles or books), and subject. Book chapters and article citations include specific paginations. Navigation and documentation are very clear and professionally organized.

This should be in everyone's browser bookmarks, and will be the first starting point for all SF researchers. Five stars for this extraordinarily useful site.

685. Husted, Ted, and Kevin Rhodes. **A Hitchhiker's Guide to Science Fiction: Travelogue and Phrasebook.** http://husted.com/hgsf/.

Contents: "Preface"; "FAQ"; "Notify"; "See Also"; "Entries"; "Titles"; "Authors"; "Awards"; "Themes"; "Bookstore"; "Search"; "Home."

This encyclopedic hypertext index to science fiction literature focuses only on stories that have won a Hugo or Nebula award. Entries "deal mostly with background events," and do not reveal plot or endings. The data are viewable by entry, title, author, or award, as well as through a theme index (15 themes are cited). Each access point uses an alphabetical list to show entries, source titles, etc.

This very selective site covers some 200 entries from 37 sources. Entries vary in size from 100-500 + words. Source entries, which are viewable from the title list, include the list of entries and links, the Hugo or Nebula awards each has won, crosslinks of interest, and other notes (as necessary).

However, *A Hitchhiker's Guide* does not appear to have been updated since 1997, with the award listings and the source list stopping at the end of 1996, thus limiting the usefulness of what might have been a very interesting series of web pages. Hitch a ride somewhere else.

686. Kelly, Mark R. *Locus* **Index to Science Fiction Awards.** http://www.locusmag.com/ SFAwards/index.html.

This is a subsection of the enormous—and enormously useful—*Locus* site (www.locusmag.com), displaying some sixty active and defunct genre awards, with still others noted on the master index as under development.

Awards are arranged on the main page under general categories (*e.g.*, "Major Awards," "Career Honors," etc.). Clicking on the award name brings up either a complete list of the award winners (where the information can be accomodated on one page), or a master index page for that award. As an example, the first page of "The Hugo Awards" gives an overview of the award, plus its full name, first year given, short history, sponsoring organization, physical shape of the trophy, when and where it is presented, scope, award categories, eligibility period, dating convention (*e.g.*, "year of award"), multiple winners, "Losers Club," "Never Won," "Never Even Nominated," how the award is selected, other miscellaneous comments, and website (where applicable).

Trailing down the lefthand column of this primary page is a descending list of years the award was presented. Clicking on one of these years will display a comprehensive list of nominees and winners for that year, arranged in descending order from the most prestigious to the least prestigious award categories (in general, the "novel" category is always listed first, where appropriate, following by the lesser fiction categories of novella, novelette, and short story, and then all of the remaining categories). Each category entry provides: category name, title and author of the award (title in red type, author in bold blue), and the remaining award nominees (title in black type, authors in lighter blue), with original publication data for all (first edition publisher for books, magazine title and issue date for stories first published in such publications, or book title for those shorter works originally issued as part of an anthology or collection.

In addition, the Hugo Awards page includes indices for: "Novel Winners" (a bare-bones record of just of the winners of the Hugo Award novel category, in descending order by award date); "All Winners" (similar data for every Hugo Award winner, in descending order by award date); and "Tallies," statistical lists of major overall winners and losers of this particular award. Similar data are available for each of the sixty awards covered on the site, where applicable.

The site's main page also provides links (in the upper righthand corner of the page) to six general indices: "Winners & Nominees," "Titles," "Magazine Categories," "Publisher Categories," "Dramatic Categories," and "Judges and Jurors" (master lists of panels of the judges of those awards selected in this fashion). The same section of the page also includes links to two parts of the "Tallies & Statistics" area, providing a "Chart of Majors" and "Cumulative Tallies," both giving detailed statistic charts of all of the major award winners (and losers).

The site is remarkably well organized and easy to navigate. As soon as the remaining overseas and minor SF awards have been added (probably in 2002), this website will supplant all printed sources for science fiction, fantasy, and horror awards, both in comprehensiveness and currency.

Access to the site is free to the public, although plans are afoot to produce annual CD-ROM versions of the site through Locus Press. Highly recommended.

687. Literatura Genérica en Español = Genre Fiction in Spanish. http://spin.com.mx/~mschwarz/mexgenre.html.

Contents: "Science Fiction"; "Crime Fiction"; "Publications" (new books, magazines and e-zines, with a new e-zine from Argentina); "Mexican and Latin American Authors Currently Writing Genre Fiction"; "Awards with Puebla Award Information, Kalpa Science Fiction Award and the International Hammett Award for Spanish Language Crime Fiction."

This small site is organized as two pages (one in English and a mirror in Spanish), with the content links being internal, directing the reader lower in the page rather than to another address. The site is a good introduction to its topic, rather like a short entry in an encyclopedia, with an overview of the development of genre fiction in Latin America, plus recommendations for the major authors and/or works embedded in the text. Some of the information, such as lists of award winners, is incomplete and outdated (the last update was in 2000). The site touches on crime fiction as well, but only peripherally.

With further development, this site could be a real asset in introducing Anglo fans to genre activity in the southern hemisphere.

688. *Locus* Online. http://www.locusmag.com/.

Locus: The Newspaper of the Science Fiction Field is the standard monthly periodical providing news relating to science fiction and allied literatures and its practitioners. This web page is a palimpsest of the magazine.

The main page displays covers from the last two issues of *Locus,* and includes several features from each, but does not generally reproduce the contents of the individual issues (which may run 70+ printed pages). Links are provided to the *Locus* bestseller lists, to

"New & Notable Books" lists, to new reviews of significant SF books, to "Newslog" (snippets of awards announcements, obituaries, and other items of interest), to "Web Logs" (links to science fiction, fantasy, and horror reviews in general publications), to "Reviews & Commentaries," to major forthcoming books, to the *Locus* archives, to other SF news sites of interest, to author events (signings, for example), to the *Locus* proprietary online indices (*The Locus Index to Science Fiction,* in four different sections by years), and to the *Locus Index to Science Fiction Awards.*

All of this material is both timely and very useful to SF professionals and fans. The sight is user-friendly, easy to navigate and access, and visually attractive. Highly recommended.

689. Magic Dragon Multimedia. **The Ultimate Science Fiction Web Guide.** http://www.magicdragon.com/UltimateSF/SF-Index.html.

Contents: "Aliens"; "Author"; "Books"; "Genres"; "Movies"; "TV"; "Time Travel"; "Timeline"; "Games"; "General"; "News."

This site is a collection of several large lists of often unreliable, rarely updated information. It is arranged into 11 main sections. "Aliens" is an alphabetical list of 337 movies about aliens, typically giving: title, year, a code indicating a made-for-TV film ("TV"), and alternative title (if appropriate). A few titles are hyperlinked to the *Internet Movie Database,* but not nearly as many as could be.

The "Authors" section provides hotlinks for 3,284 writers out of the 9,392 listed. Writers are listed alphabetically by surname and/or pseudonym. This area is poorly and unattractively organized, mixing authors' names with general entries such as "Abatos: one of the horses of Pluto." Some author entries contain no data whatever, while others display birth and death dates and bibliographies. The latter typically include a list of the writer's books, with publishers, place of publication, year of publication, ISBN, and (sometimes) cover price.

The section called "Books" actually covers book reviews, but is extremely underdeveloped. Two reviewers have links to sites where they review science fiction books, and three larger sites are also listed. A handful of book titles are linked to full-text reviews, but most of the links are inactive.

The "Genres" section provides links to 37 science fiction genres, each leading to a definition and brief discussion of the topic, and a list of well-known books of fiction (and sometimes non-fiction) that are considered to fall into that genre. The book entries usually display author, date of publication (sometimes missing), and occasionally other data. Some titles may include a brief plot summary.

"Movies" leads to several chronological lists of science fiction, fantasy, and horror movies and reviews. Each film in the 1997, 1998, 1999 lists have entries that usually include: plot summary, production personnel (director, cinematographer, producer, writer, music, special effects), principal cast, and more. Information is often spotty, freely using a series of question marks ("????") when the name of the person or character is unknown. The site does include such interesting data as a log of a film's box office receipts from week to week for those few pictures that were rated among the top ten movies nationwide, plus lists of reviews, giving: author, periodical, article title, but without dates or citations.

There are ten other chronological lists in this section, each covering a decade from the 1890s-1990s. Each of these lists includes the linked title of the movies featured and their release date. Other information, such as director, stars, or a one-sentence plot summary may be added irregularly. Titles are linked to the *Internet Movie Database* for further information. Each decade also includes a separate list of "Other Key Dates," and a chronological checklist of years of birth of significant figures from science fiction.

The "TV" section lists in alphabetical order 142 linked television shows broadcast in the United States, plus 161 shows with no links. Each linked show goes to a program entry, normally including: running dates, premise, cast, production crew, and some further web links. Much of the material has not been updated for two years, and some data are even further out of date. In addition, all of the information fields except the title can be incomplete to one degree or another.

"Time Travel: Movies and TV Movies About Time Travel or TimeLoops" is an alphabetical list of 105 motion pictures. Entries typically include: title and year of release, and may also feature a plot summary and/or provide various production information (director, screenplay, cast). Much of the commentary and summaries are freely pulled from *Steven's Time Travel Page* (http://users.metro2000.net/~stabbott/timetravel.htm).

"Timeline" is the best section of the site, probably because its sources are *The Timetables of Science,* by Alexander Hellemans and Bryan Bunch (New York: Simon & Schuster, 1988) and other reference works. It provides links to sections of history, usually divided by century. Each century contains a summary of the period, an overview of significant people, and a chronology of events decade by decade.

"Games" is a completely out-of-date alphabetical listing of 21 science fiction games (for PlayStation or Sega) dating from 1997—an eternity in the gaming community. Also included is a list of 219 Software Game Companies, also outdated by four years. Many links in this section are marked "to be done."

"General" is the true directory area, with some 80 alphabetical links to other resources. A few entries contain one-sentence annotations, others have only the linked title. Though it claims to have been updated in 2001, many of the links have now moved or no longer exist, indicating that links are not checked frequently for accuracy.

"News," the last section, is fairly sparse (a few paragraphs long), with the latest news dated June 1997.

This hodge-podge site has clearly grown way beyond the control of its manager. Its lack of focus, loose organization, absence of updating, and incomplete or even erroneous data makes the entire site untrustworthy. Even pages that claim to have been updated recently often contain misinformation and/or incorrect or dead links. Some pages are too big to load into computers with small amounts of memory.

Not really a directory, not really a reliable source of information, *The Ultimate Science Fiction Web Guide* is ultimately worthless.

690. Martinez, Michael L. **Science Fiction and Fantasy: Xenite.Org: Worlds of Imagination on the Web.** http://www.xenite.org/.

Contents: "Xenite.Org"; "About Us"; "Autoresponders"; "Awards, Fantasy Sites"; "Hercules/Xena Sites"; "Mailing Lists"; "Forums"; "Movie Sites"; "News & Comics"; "Other Sites"; "Posting Policy"; "Privacy Policy"; "Reciprocal Links"; "News Group Info."

Xenite.org seeks to bring together "fans of science fiction and fantasy from all over the Internet through our mailing lists, message boards, link directories, and other resources," with a primary focus on fans of *Xena: Warrior Princess* and *Hercules: The Legendary Journeys*. Related interests are included haphazardly, such as Andromeda, Middle-earth, and (mostly) other science fiction or fantasy television programs.

The list of information sources here is rather small, perhaps representing Martinez's conception of the best on the Web. The fan will not find pictures, audio, or other electronic collectibles, but can secure active opportunities to communicate with others. Unfortunately, the site seems to be mounted on a personal, perhaps home-based, server. Thus, the response time, even on the best system, is very slow, temporarily freezing up the browser while the page is being loaded. There is a great deal of advertising on the site, and sometimes the links to these alternate sites can be confused with Xenite.org's original content.

Fans who don't know how to enter the electronic conversation of their favorite SF/F television program will be glad to find the lists, but more experienced Internet denizens won't be surprised (or pleased) by the contents.

691. Parkin, Marny K. **Bibliography of Mormon Speculative Fiction.** http://home.airswitch.net/MormonBib/.

Contents: "Novels"; "Short Stories"; "Poetry"; "Nonfiction"; "Forthcoming Works"; "Author Index"; "Addition/Correction"; "Recommended Reading List"; "Authors' and Related Links"; "Reviews"; "Authors' Awards."

"This bibliography contains works published by or about LDS authors, including novels, short stories, poetry, and theses/dissertations, articles, and interviews [about them]. My definition of 'speculative fiction' has broadened as I've gone along. Some of the entries may not be what you think qualifies, but I have included more than I've excluded (if I've found it) in an effort to be comprehensive."

A typical book entry includes: author's name, title of the work, place and year of publication, and publisher. Shorter work entries add specific pagination of the work in the magazine or anthology in which it first appeared. Of particular interest to the librarian and researcher are the large number of critical works recorded, a resource that can be found nowhere else in this concentrated form.

The major SF writer covered herein is, of course, Orson Scott Card, but a number of other well-known figures also appear, including Elizabeth Boyer, Tracy Hickman, Raymond F. Jones, and Dave Wolverton.

The navigation of the site is straightforward and the pages are plainly displayed and organized, but print out very well. This site is also regularly maintained and updated, and will be a welcome addition for those fans and readers focusing on this particular topic.

692. Science Fiction and Fantasy Writers of America, Inc. http://www.sfwa.org/

Contents: "About Science Fiction and Fantasy Writers of America, Inc."; "Nebula Awards"; "Ergonomics For Writers and Editors"; "Reading"; "FAQs"; "Writing: The Craft"; "Writing: The Business"; "Writer Beware"; "Links."

This site is the homepage of SFWA (see #704), a respected group of professional genre writers that also sponsors and presents annually the highly-regarded Nebula Awards for the best science fiction and fantasy of the year.

Two parts of this web page contain items of interest to the reference librarian. The Obituaries Archive section includes one-page memorials for prominent (and some minor) writers and editors who have died (for the most part) since 1998, and the list of Nebula Awards provides the official record of those accolades, arranged in descending order by year of publication of the work being honored (this means that a Nebula and Hugo won for the exact same work will display different award years; *e.g.*, see Frank Herbert's classic novel, *Dune,* winner of the 1965 Nebula Award and 1966 Hugo Award for Best Novel). It should be noted that two other sites, *Locus Online* and *Internet Speculative Fiction Database* (see #688 and #696), also include the nominees, but the SFWA is definitive.

The rest of the website covers material of interest to the professional SF writer, including some areas that are password protected. Overall, the design of these pages is not as consistently attractive or easy to navigate as one might expect from such a notable association, but fans and pros alike will find much of interest here.

693. Sheriff, Espana N. **Alpha Ralpha Boulevard: Science Fiction & Fantasy Bibliographies.** http://www.Catch22.COM/~espana/SFAuthors/.

Contents: "Authors"; "Artists"; "Local Info"; "Outside Links."

This fan-created collection of bibliographies of 400 genre writers and 35 genre artists attempts to provide basic publication data and short biographies of SF and fantasy writers and artists. The sections for authors and artists are completely separate, each being organized into a series of alphabetical surname lists broken into sections. Clicking on the surname span produces a list of specific authors (or artists) for that section. Clicking on the author or artist name brings one to the main entry for that individual.

A typical entry includes: name of the author or artist, years of birth and death (where known), brief biography (one sentence), and bibliography, usually giving: book title (bold-faced type, listing alphabetically by title), publisher, publication date (month and year), and ISBN. Similar data are provided for the author's short fiction, in a separate, alphabetically-arranged section beneath the bibliography of monographs. A great many records, however, lack anything more than just a barebones title. Some reprint information is occasionally and irregularly included, and a few titles contain links to Amazon.com, but inconsistently. Authors' web pages or other official websites may also be linked. The search feature provides every-word access to the site.

In checking several entries at random, we found that the bibliographical listing for fantasy writer Katherine Kurtz failed to include her year of birth (a well known datum), and only noted ten of her more than thirty published books, most of them from early in her career, in the 1970s and '80s; just two of these works indicated publisher's name.

Completely unreliable, out-of-date, and generally not to be trusted.

694. The SF Site: The Home Page for Science Fiction and Fantasy. http://sfsite.com/

Though it doesn't actively bill itself as one, *The SF Site* is basically an e-zine devoted to science fiction and fantasy, featuring a "mixture of book reviews, opinion pieces, author interviews, fiction excerpts, author and publisher reading lists and a variety of other features. At the same time, [there is] a comprehensive list of links to author and fan tribute sites, SF conventions, SF TV and movies, magazines and e-zines, writer resources, publishers and small press sites, and many other SF resources."

This professionally-designed website uses direct links to move through its myriad of book reviews, interviews, media reviews, and other features. The commentaries are quite well written and usually feature a cover image; they include a brief bio giving the reviewer's credentials. *The SF Site* also covers films and television programs, but these reviews seem shorter, less analytical, and more casual in tone.

All of the material can be accessed very easily through *The SF Site* homepage, which includes a number of review excerpts of current SF releases; by clicking on the title one can immediately go to the full review, which averages one page in length. One can also do a boolean search on the entire site, or jump to the index page to find coverage of previously reviewed books.

To find reviews on the recent works of Katherine Kurtz, for example, one need only click on the "index" link at the bottom of the main page, locate the "Past Feature Reviews" logo, an image of a keyboard at the center of the index page, and click on the letter "K." Excerpts from two pages of works by authors whose last names begin with the letter "K" are displayed in alphabetical order by surname, and thence alphabetically by book title. Click on the title to read the full review. Most of the titles covered have been published since the mid-1990s, although a few older titles have been included as they are reprinted.

Other indices link to *The SF Site*-supported authors' pages, to back issues of the on-line magazine (beginning in mid-1997), to the site's cumulated feature columns, to previously-recorded interviews, to "link sites," to awards, to lists of small presses, magazines, and publishers, and to much other information of interest to the SF fan and professional.

The "Author & Fan Tribute Sites" is a large and well-maintained collection of links that includes both official authors' sites and fan sites about SF authors, with access provided through the same alphabetical keys as that employed in the review section. "Conventions" provides a chronological list of forthcoming SF conventions, including name of the con, type (gaming, comics, etc.), and date and place of occurrence.

Other links are provided on the main homepage to several major sites supported by *The SF Site,* including the *Internet Speculative Fiction Database* (see #696) and *Gary Westfahl's Biographical Encyclopedia of Science Fiction Film* (see #697).

Everything this site offers is slickly and professionally done, and very easy to navigate. The reviews are readable, informative, and sometimes analytical. The number of links *The SF Site* provides to other web pages is enormous; inevitably, some of these will prove to be inactive at any one time, but most are fairly current.

This is certainly one of the best, most-informative, and current websites for any SF and fantasy fan.

695. Steampunk. http://www.steampunk.com/.

Contents: "Archives"; "Authors"; "Awards"; "Bibliographies"; "Bookstores"; "Communities"; "Fiction"; "Organizations"; "Publishers"; "Reviews"; "Television"; "Writing"; "Zines."

This directory of genre information appears to be undergoing a renovation. Some contents links have "[old]" after their headers to indicate the material is from the previous incarnation of the site and may contain out-of-date information. Thus, "Archives [old]" is a small collection of outdated links to archives of fan fiction across the Web.

While the "Authors" area includes an impressive list of authors to choose from, many of the links here are also dead. The fine layout of bibliographies, interviews, excerpts, and reviews of authors and their works does little good when the sites they are linked to have vanished.

The awards section is years outdated, also being "[old]." The author bibliographies, in "Bibliographies," rely entirely on John Wenn's *Authorlists,* a site that has also changed its web address, making the entire list useless. However, the subject bibliographies in this section could be useful, incorporating links to bibliographies on cyberpunk, ecofeminism, post-apocalyptic books, and more.

"Bookstores" is useless, with no valid links. "Communities" lists a collection of MUDs that are outdated, plus a paltry list of newsgroups of interest to genre fans. "Fiction" is one of the best sections on the site, with many of the links to short stories (often by well-known writers), excerpts, and novels (public domain) still active. "Organizations" and "Publishers" are both marked "[old]."

"Organizations" is a small, out-of-date collection of mostly non-functioning links to genre organizations, while "Publishers" admits to being an "outdated sampling" of six links, with none of the six still functioning. "Reviews," "Television," "Writing," and "Zines" are all equally filled with bad links, making them practically useless.

It's a shame that this site has been allowed to deteriorate to the point of almost total uselessness. Good organization and ease of use have been obviated by lack of maintenance. Avoid this one.

696. von Ruff, Al, ed. **Internet Speculative Fiction DataBase: ISFDB.** http://sfsite.com/ISFDB.

"The ISFDB is an effort to catalog works of Science Fiction, Fantasy, and Horror. It links together various types of bibliographic data: author bibliographies, publication bibliographies, award listings, magazine content listings, anthology and collection content listings, yearly fiction indexes, and forthcoming books."

Whew! That's a great deal to promise. The question, of course, is how well the site actually attains these lofty goals, something that is particularly difficult to ascertain on a website as expansive as this one.

The main homepage of the website, which is supported as an adjunct database of *The SF Site* (see #694), clearly displays the major directories available: "Authors," "Magazines," "Forthcoming [Titles]," "Lists," "Submissions," and "Publishers." The upper righthand corner of the page displays a box labelled "Information and Statistics About the Database," which provides links to "What's New," "List of FAQs," "Numerical Statistics, Displaying the Total Number of Novels . . . ," and "Graphed Statistics, with Totals Graphed by Category and Year." The lower righthand box features "Other SF Bibliographic Sites of Interest," providing clickable links to other major web pages, including the *Locus* site (see #688) and Hal Hall's *Science Fiction and Fantasy Research Database* (see #684). Running down the lefthand side of the main page are two additional boxes, allowing the user to conduct a "Fiction Database Search" or an "Awards Database Search."

Fantasy author Katherine Kurtz was used as a sample term for the Fiction Database Search. The result was a two-page display called "Katherine Kurtz—Bibliography Summary." It lists, in rough descending, chronological order by publication date, the author's

Awards, [Book] Series, Novels, Anthology Series, Anthologies, Non-Fiction Series, Short Fiction, and Essays/Articles.

One award is listed: the 1982 Balrog Award for best novel, listed as "Balrog Award: [*1982*]." Clicking on the date results in a list of all Balrog winners for that year.

Two book series are noted for Kurtz: "The Adept" and "Chronicles of the Deryni." Six items are listed under the heading "The Adept": five novels and a short story. Four of these books are labelled from number 1-4, but the fifth novel in the series, *Death of an Adept,* carries no series number. Clicking on one of the underlined book titles takes one to a separate screen giving the various editions of that particular volume (where appropriate). One must click on the appropriate edition to find the bibliographical data, a typical presentation providing: author (underlined), year of publication, ISBN, publisher, publication price, pagination, and type (*e.g.*, "hc" = hardcover, "pb" = paperback). Anthologies or collections will also provide a list of the stories included in the volume, as they appear in the book, giving type (*e.g.*, "sf" = science fiction), title, and author. The author portion of each line is underlined, meaning that one can click on the name to get a bibliography of the writer's other works, at least as provided by the database.

So far, so good. However, as one begins exploring these listings in more depth, problems immediately begin to emerge. Under Chronicles of the Deryni, for example, four subseries are noted: "The Histories of King Kelson," "The Legends of Camber of Culdi," "Chronicles of the Deryni," "The Heirs of Saint Camber," and "Deryni," with various books titles being listed under each header. *King Kelson's Bride,* the most recently published novel in the sequence, is incorrectly recorded as the fourth book in The Histories sequence, when it is, in fact, a standalone book in the series. *Bride*'s publication date (1997) is also wrong. Clicking on this title produces a list of four editions, two published by Ballantine Del Rey, and two by Ace Books. But the Ballantine editions never appeared, as was widely noted in the SF media, and the correct first edition of this book is the 2000 Ace hardcover, item 3 on the list.

There are similar problems elsewhere on this site. *Deryni Magic,* a nonfiction work, is listed first as part of the Kurtz's generic novels, and again under the category "Non-Fiction Series," both being linked to the same bibliographical record. "*Codex Deryniux*" manages to attach an incorrect title (the correct one is *Codex Derynianus*) to another ghost entry, a Ballantine paperback edition that was announced but never actually appeared. In fact, the first edition of this work, published in hardcover by Underwood Books and Borgo Press in 1998, is not recorded anywhere in the database.

And so it goes. Part of the problem with this site is that it posts expansive lists of forthcoming SF titles, but fails to purge them systematically when the inevitable happens, and a few of the books are cancelled or postponed. Kurtz is fairly well known, and her works are relatively easy to track; one would expect her bibliography to be current and complete. What a shame it isn't.

Lesser-known writers receive much less attention. Douglas Menville, for example, is listed under that name with just one book, the anthology *Ancestral Voices,* plus nine "Essays/Articles," editorials and book reviews that appeared in the professional magazine, *Forgotten Fantasy.* However, a further examination reveals two other books under a separate heading, "Doug Menville," which the author has never actually used as a byline, and is not cross-referenced in either direction with "Douglas Menville." These include the anthologies,

King Solomon's Children and *They;* both lack the subtitles that appeared on the original volumes. These two books are linked with the co-editor, "R. Reginald." A check of "R. Reginald"'s entry only gives the three anthologies co-edited with Menville. However, under the header "Robert Reginald" we find eleven more non-fiction works, including the previously noted mistitled and misidentified *"Codex Deryniux,"* which he co-authored with Kurtz (but *not* until 1998), plus a lone fantasy short story (one of seventeen he has published).

None of the four listings for Menville and Reginald, taken together or apart, are in any way definitive or comprehensive. Menville actually co-edited nine anthologies with Reginald for Arno Press during the 1970s, and co-authored with him two books on SF films that were widely distributed; only one of these (listed as *"Future Visions"*; the correct title is actually *FutureVisions,* written as one word) is displayed under the "Robert Reginald" entry, and it fails to indicate Menville (and a third writer) as co-authors. Menville also published another book on SF films under his own name during this period, but you would never know it by searching the *ISFBD.* Reginald's 2001 collection of fantasy stories, *Katydid & Other Critters,* is completely missing; in fact, of the 40 books by Reginald that might conceivably fall within the subject parameters of the *ISFBD,* only fourteen are noted, several with incorrect and/or incomplete data. Tsk tsk tsk. All of these materials can be found in the *Locus* database (see #688).

The awards section of this site is somewhat better constituted than the bibliographical parts, and very easy to search, but it duplicates the information found on the *Locus* site, and the latter covers more awards overall. Since the *Locus* web page also includes much more complete, substantiated bibliographical data, the fan or researcher should prefer it in every case, unless, of course, one only wishes to deal with "virtual" information.

697. Westfahl, Gary. **Gary Westfahl's Biographical Encyclopedia of Science Fiction Film.** http://www.sfsite.com/interzone/gary/intro.htm.

Written by a professor at the University of California, Riverside, this site offers professional biographies and critical analysis of the work of actors and film makers prominent in SF entertainment.

Containing only about 100 entries (although growing steadily), this site provides a very personal view of some of the major science fiction actors, directors, screen- and telewriters, and personalities, both living and deceased, in genre television and film. A typical entry includes: name, birth and death dates (as appropriate), brief identifier ("Mexican Actor," "French Director," etc.), a mini-essay discussing the individual's career (averaging 500 words), plus a list of each person's science fiction, fantasy, and horror film and television credits. Most of the persons covered are actors, but a few directors such as Chris Marker and Steven Spielberg are featured, as well as two "personalities" (Elvira and Robby the Robot).

Main entries can be accessed using a stable alphabet bar across the top of each page or through an "All Entries" link. The essays are thoughtful and informed, but highly opinionated; in his coverage of Harlan Ellison, for example, Westfahl spends most of his wordage lamenting the writer's supposed lack of activity in the SF media, when in fact Ellison has penned several of the most remarkable and memorable hours in the history of genre television. These credits are acknowledged by the critic in the course of his commentary, but one is still left with an overall negative impression of the telewriter.

The navigation for this site is simple and straightforward, and the clean layout makes the material easy to read and easy to print. However, this is far from a definitive examination of its subject, and one might hope for a larger expansion of the author's theme in the future. For now, the *Biographical Encyclopedia* can only serve as a minor way station on the yellow brick road to Hollywoodland.

698. Willick, George. **Spacelight: The Library of Science Fiction & Fantasy Vital Statistics and Personal Data.** http://members.tripod.com/~gwillick/sffobit.html.

"This site is designed primarily for the literary researcher to quickly locate vital statistics and personal data on deceased members of the F&SF community," including science fiction and fantasy writers, artists, and editors.

A typical entry includes: author's photograph; full name; age at death; date and place of birth and death; Social Security number; place interred (or an indication that the body was cremated); spouse name(s) and marriage date(s); awards or honors received; a roughly 200-word biography and brief critical comment; pen name(s); link to Willick's bibliography of the author's works, plus links to other appropriate bibliographical data; citations to further biographies; literary agent for the estate, and address; citations to one or more obituaries, often from the *New York Times,* plus links (where appropriate).

The biographies often include one or more brief quotations from the writer's work, giving his or her philosophy or critical posture, or providing an autobiographical comment. For example, writer H. Beam Piper's suicide note is given in its entirety. The comments by Willick are generally approbatory and middle-of-the-road, providing an honest appraisal of both major and minor writers and other figures (artists, for example) associated with science fiction and fantasy.

This site is well-designed and easy to navigate, and is frequently updated within days of each new major death in the genre. Kudos to George Willick for providing an excellent way station for surfers of the Internet.

699. World Science Fiction Society. http://www.wsfs.org/.

The World Science Fiction Society is the loosely-organized group that sponsors the annual World Science Fiction Convention. Their site is important for providing the official list of World Science Fiction Conventions, from 1939 to date, and the official list of the major and minor awards presented annually at the con: the Hugos, Campbells, and special accolades that are the oldest and most generally accepted reader-voted honors given in the SF field.

The main homepage lists the three forthcoming worldcons for the present year, the next year, and the year after that, providing website links and a summary of dates and places. Further down the first page, under the heading "Purposes," are clickable links to "The List of World Science Fiction Conventions (Worldcons)" and "Hugo Awards (Science Fiction Achievement Awards."

The worldcons are arranged in descending order by year of occurrence, and include, in tabular form, the following data: con number (from 1-62), year when the con took place, official name, city where the con took place, actual site of the con within the city, official guest(s), con chair(s), and official attendance. This information is unavailable elsewhere in such complete yet compact form.

The presentation of Hugo and affiliated awards is complete and authoritative. The main list is organized in reverse descending order by presentation year, the most current awards being listed first, and then by major award categories to lesser, beginning with "Novel." Books and magazines are displayed in italics, shorter fiction in regular type offset by quotation marks. A separate file arranges the data by category (*e.g.*, "Novel"), and thence alphabetically by title of the work or person being honored. These data are available at several other sites (for example, *Locus Online* and *Internet Speculative Fiction Database* [see #688 and #696]), which also include nominees, but the World Science Fiction Society material is definitive.

Well-organized and -presented, this site is a joy to use, and exceptionally easy to navigate. Fans will love it.

CORE PERIODICALS

SCOPE NOTE: Relatively few SF periodicals, fanzines, or newsletters have had any consistent reference value. Those listed herein are grouped into appropriate categories:

700. Newsletters and Newspapers.

The principal newszines of the SF field have included *Fantasy Times/SF Times* (1941-69), *Luna Monthly* (1969-77), *Locus* (1968-DATE), and *(Science Fiction) Chronicle* (1979-DATE). Each of these publications has featured contemporaneous news items, obituaries of authors and other figures important to the field, film columns, convention reports, and much other material of interest. *Locus* also includes (since the early 1980s) a monthly register of the books published in the field, arranged alphabetically by author with complete bibliographical data, and (in more recent years) a similar listing of SF monographs published in Great Britain. Some of this information was cumulated between 1984-91 into the annual volumes of *Science Fiction, Fantasy, & Horror* (see #33), and later made available on the Internet (www.locuspress.com).

701. Review Magazines.

Professionally produced nonfiction magazines having significant numbers of reviews of science-fiction and fantasy works have included: *Delap's F & SF Review** (1975-77), *Fantasy Newsletter/Fantasy Review** (1978-87), *Luna Monthly* (1969-77), *Locus* (1968-DATE), *Science Fiction & Fantasy Book Review** (1979-80, 1982-83), *Science Fiction Chronicle* (1979-DATE), *SF Booklog** (1975-77), *SFRA Newsletter* (1971-DATE).

Those titles with asterisks were primarily review journals (all now defunct). The *SFRA Newsletter* became primarily a review publication in the 1990s. *Locus* and *(Science Fiction) Chronicle* run twenty-five or more reviews of new books per issue, although their primary focus remains the reporting of news events. All of these reviews are indexed in Hal W. Hall's *Science Fiction Book Review Index* (see #116).

702. Scholarly Magazines.

Scholarly journals devoted specifically to science fiction and fantasy have included: *Extrapolation* (1959-DATE), *Foundation* (1972-DATE), *Journal of the International Association for the Fantastic in the Arts* (1985?-DATE), *Science-Fiction Studies* (1973-DATE).

Very few articles with reference value have been published in these journals. *Extrapolation* did run in its first issue a bibliography of early American science fiction by Founding Editor Thomas D. Clareson, an article that later became the basis of his book, *Science Fiction in America* (see #231). In addition, Tymn's annual guide to nonfiction works about SF, *The Year's Scholarship in Science Fiction and Fantasy* (see #130) was first published each year in *Extrapolation,* and later in *Journal of the International Association for the Fantastic in the Arts.* Since none of the annuals after 1982 has yet been issued in book form, researchers and librarians should have access to the magazine issues containing the supplements.

703. Other Publications of Interest.

Science-Fiction Collector (1976-81) occupies a unique position among semi-professional fanzines, being filled with a cornucopia of bibliographies, checklists, and bibliographical articles on a wide variety of subjects. Often published on poor-quality paper, the issues include single-author bibliographies, subject bibliographies, publisher checklists, and much else of interest to the SF collector and bibliographer. 150 three-volume sets were bound into cloth in 1980-81 by Editor-Publisher Grant Thiessen; however, the issues in Volume One badly need deacidification (later issues were published on better stock).

One issue of *Fantasy Research & Bibliography* (dated December, 1980-February, 1981/March, 1981-May, 1981) was produced by Editor-Publisher Leslie Kay Swigart in 1981, including two articles: "Starguide," by Larry Roeder, an attempt at defining the genre through very detailed subject headings; and Swigart's Second Edition of *Harlan Ellison: A Bibliographical Checklist,* covered elsewhere in this volume (see #379). Lamentably, the journal ceased after its maiden outing.

PROFESSIONAL ORGANIZATIONS

704. Professional Writers' Groups.

Two organizations for writers serve the field of fantastic literature: Horror Writers Association (HWA) and Science Fiction and Fantasy Writers of America, Inc. (SFWA). Both are open to active membership only by professionals working in their respective genres, although both do provide separate rates for institutional and affiliate memberships. Each organization publishes a variety of public and private newletters, journals, and directories (the latter are covered elsewhere in this book; see #38 and #41). Neither specifically sponsors publications outside of these directories that contain anything of reference value.

705. Scholarly Groups.

Two groups service scholars in the science-fiction and fantasy fields: International Association for the Fantastic in the Arts (IAFA; founded by Dr. Marshall B. Tymn) and The Science Fiction Research Association (SFRA; founded by the late Dr. Thomas D. Clareson). Both produce a journal, a newsletter, and a directory (the latter are covered in #39 and #40). Several of these publications have produced articles or features having reference value, but the bulk of these organizations' efforts have been directed toward the publication or dissemination of criticism, not bibliographies or indices. Both groups also sponsor a series of annual awards honoring scholarship in the field; a handful of the honorees have been bibliographers (for example, SFRA's Pilgrim Award for 1991 was presented to the late Pierre Versins).

CORE COLLECTIONS

SCOPE NOTE: Excluded from these lists are books limited to very specific topics (for example, single-author bibliographies, guides to particular television series, etc.), since selection of these materials will depend much more heavily on individual collection orientation. Very large research libraries may wish to gather as many of these materials as possible, particularly those produced to higher bibliographical standards and/or by major reference publishing houses. This section is divided into three levels covering academic libraries, public libraries, and individual research collections; entries are keyed to item number and title.

ACADEMIC LIBRARIES

Research University Collections

3. *Science Fiction: The Illustrated Encyclopedia.*
4. *The Encyclopedia of Fantasy.*
5. *The MUP Encyclopaedia of Australian Science Fiction & Fantasy.*
8. *The New Encyclopedia of Science Fiction.*
10. *The Vampire Book.*
12. *The Encyclopedia of Science Fiction/The Science Fiction Encyclopedia.*
13. *The Ultimate Encyclopedia of Fantasy.*
14. *The Ultimate Encyclopedia of Science Fiction.*
17. *The Penguin Encyclopedia of Horror and the Supernatural.*
18. *The Encyclopedia of Science Fiction and Fantasy Through 1968.*
19. *Encyclopédie de l'Utopie, des Voyages Extraordinaires, et de la Science Fiction.*
20. *Critical Terms for Science Fiction and Fantasy.*
26. *The Dictionary of Imaginary Places.*
27. *An Atlas of Fantasy.*
28. *The Dictionary of Science Fiction Places.*
30. *A Guide to Science Fiction & Fantasy in the Library of Congress Classification Scheme.*
33. *The Locus Index to Science Fiction.*
34. *Science Fiction & Fantasy Book Review Annual.*
39. *International Association for the Fantastic in the Arts Membership Directory.*
40. *Science Fiction Research Association Annual Directory.*
42. *Illustrated Book of Science Fiction Lists.*
43. *The Complete Book of Science Fiction and Fantasy Lists/The SF Book of Lists.*
45. *The Hugo, Nebula, and World Fantasy Awards.*
47. *Reginald's Science Fiction and Fantasy Awards.*
48. *The PENDEX.*
49. *Science Fiction and Fantasy Pseudonyms.*

50. *Who's Hugh?*
52. *Who's Who in Horror and Fantasy Fiction.*
53. *Twentieth-Century American Science-Fiction Writers.*
54. *Contemporary Science Fiction, Fantasy, and Horror Poetry.*
55. *St. James Guide to Fantasy Writers.*
56. *St. James Guide to Horror, Ghost & Gothic Writers.*
57. *Stella Nova/Contemporary Science Fiction Authors, First Edition.*
58. *St. James Guide to Science Fiction Writers.*
59. *A Biographical Dictionary of Science Fiction and Fantasy Artists.*
60. *More Than 100: Women Science Fiction Writers.*
62. *Anatomy of Wonder.*
63. *Fantasy and Horror.*
64. *Fantasy Literature.*
65. *Horror Literature.*
66. *What Fantastic Fiction Do I Read Next?*
67. *The Guide to Supernatural Fiction.*
68. *Science Fiction, the Early Years.*
69. *Science Fiction Writers.*
70. *Supernatural Fiction Writers, Fantasy and Horror.*
78. *Benchmarks.*
79. *Fantasy: The 100 Best Books.*
81. *Reader's Guide to Twentieth-Century Science Fiction.*
83. *British Fantasy and Science-Fiction Writers Before World War I.*
85. *Horror: 100 Best Books.*
87. *Women of the Future.*
89. *Fantasy for Children/Fantasy Literature for Children and Young Adults.*
91. *Survey of Modern Fantasy Literature.*
92. *Survey of Science Fiction Literature.*
94. *A Reference Guide to Modern Fantasy for Children.*
95. *Modern Fantasy: The Hundred Best Novels.*
96. *Science Fiction: The 100 Best Novels.*
97. *The Ultimate Guide to Science Fiction.*
98. *A Reader's Guide to Fantasy.*
99. *A Reader's Guide to Science Fiction.*
100. *Magill's Guide to Science Fiction and Fantasy Literature.*
101. *Fantasy Literature: A Core Collection and Reference Guide.*
102. *Horror Literature: A Core Collection and Reference Guide.*
103. *The Science Fiction Reference Book.*
104. *The Hills of Faraway.*
105. *Images in a Crystal Ball.*
106. *The Science Fiction Source Book.*
108. *Horror.*
110. *SF Bibliographies.*
111. *Science Fiction Criticism.*
113. *The Gothic's Gothic.*

114. *Gothic Fiction.*
115. *Guide to the Gothic.*
116. *Science Fiction Book Review Index.*
117. *Science Fiction and Fantasy Reference Index/Science Fiction and Fantasy Research Index.*
118. *Utopian/Dystopian Literature.*
119. *Science Fiction, Fantasy, and Horror Reference.*
120. *Science Fiction Master Index of Names.*
123. *The Eighteenth-Century Gothic Novel.*
125. *The English Gothic.*
128. *A Research Guide to Science Fiction Studies.*
129. *Survey of Science Fiction Literature: Bibliographical Supplement.*
130. *The Year's Scholarship in Science Fiction, Fantasy, and Horror.*
131. *Science/Fiction Collections.*
134. *Dictionary Catalog of the J. Lloyd Eaton Collection of Science Fiction and Fantasy Literature.*
136. *Science-Fiction: The Gernsback Years.*
137. *Science Fiction, Fantasy, and Weird Fiction Magazines.*
138. *The Supernatural Index.*
140. *Index to the Science Fiction Magazines.*
143. *Index to the Weird Fiction Magazines.*
144. *A Checklist of Science-Fiction Anthologies.*
145. *Index to Science Fiction Anthologies and Collections.*
149. *Index to the Science-Fiction Magazines, 1926-1950.*
153. *The Science Fiction Magazines.*
156. *The Index of Science Fiction Magazines, 1951-1965.*
157. *Science Fiction, Fantasy, & Weird Fiction Magazine Index.*
159. *Index to the Science Fiction Magazines (and Original Anthologies).*
160. *Monthly Terrors.*
163. *The Pulp Magazine Index.*
164. *Science Fiction and Fantasy Magazines, 1923-1980.*
168. *The MIT Science Fiction Society's Index to the S-F Magazines, 1951-1965.*
170. *Index to Stories in Thematic Anthologies of Science Fiction.*
207. *Paralittératures.*
208. *The Checklist of Fantastic Literature.*
209. *The Supplemental Checklist of Fantastic Literature.*
211. *A Spectrum of Fantasy.*
212. *Science Fiction and Fantasy Literature.*
214. *The Science Fiction and Heroic Fantasy Author Index.*
216. *CDN SF & F.*
228. *Russian Science Fiction.*
231. *Science Fiction in America, 1870s-1930s.*
234. *Bibliography of Adventure.*
237. *Arthurian Fiction.*
241. *Dystopian Literature.*

242. *The Literature of Fantasy.*
244. *Science Fiction and Fantasy Authors.*
246. *The Tale of the Future.*
247. *Voices Prophesying War, 1763-3749.*
248. *Future War Novels.*
249. *The First Gothics.*
250. *Gothic Novels of the Twentieth Century.*
251. *A Gothic Bibliography.*
252. *The Gothic Novel, 1790-1830.*
253. *The Imaginary Voyage in Prose Fiction.*
254. *Clockworks.*
255. *Nuclear Holocausts.*
256. *The Checklist of Fantastic Literature in Paperbound Books.*
258. *Who Goes There?*
260. *Science Fiction and Fantasy Series and Sequels.*
261. *Uranian Worlds.*
262. *Voyages in Space.*
266. *Utopian Literature.*
267. *British and American Utopian Literature.*
269. *The Vampire in Literature.*
270. *The Transylvanian Library.*
271. *Vampires Unearthed.*
272. *Urania's Daughters.*
273. *The Science Fantasy Publishers.*
297. *Bibliographies of Modern Authors.*
299. *Galactic Central Bibliographies for the Avid Reader.*
300. *Masters of Science Fiction and Fantasy.*
530. *The Vampire Gallery.*
531. *Imaginary People.*
580. *Science Fiction Films of the Seventies.*
581. *Vintage Science Fiction Films, 1896-1949.*
584. *The Horror Film Handbook.*
585. *The Science Fiction and Fantasy Film Handbook.*
587. *Fantastic Television.*
588. *Horror/The Encyclopedia of Horror Movies.*
589. *Science Fiction/The Encyclopedia of Science Fiction Movies.*
591. *Reference Guide to Fantastic Films.*
592. *Science Fiction, Horror, & Fantasy Film and Television Credits.*
593. *French Science Fiction, Fantasy, Horror and Pulp Fiction.*
598. *Futurevisions.*
599. *Things to Come.*
600. *The BFI Companion to Horror.*
601. *The Great Science Fiction Pictures.*
602. *Science Fiction Television Series.*
604. *Fantastic Cinema Subject Guide.*

605. *Creature Features.*
606. *A Reference Guide to American Science Fiction Films.*
607. *Keep Watching the Skies!*
609. *Horror and Science Fiction Films.*
610. *Variety's Complete Science Fiction Reviews.*
612. *The Science Fiction Image.*
681. *Chronological Bibliography of Science Fiction Criticism.*
684. *Science Fiction and Fantasy Research Database.*
686. *Locus Index to Science Fiction Awards.*
688. *Locus Online.*
694. *The SF Site.*
696. *Internet Speculative Fiction Database.*

State University Collections

3. *Science Fiction: The Illustrated Encyclopedia.*
4. *The Encyclopedia of Fantasy.*
8. *The New Encyclopedia of Science Fiction.*
10. *The Vampire Book.*
12. *The Encyclopedia of Science Fiction/The Science Fiction Encyclopedia.*
17. *The Penguin Encyclopedia of Horror and the Supernatural.*
18. *The Encyclopedia of Science Fiction and Fantasy Through 1968.*
20. *Critical Terms for Science Fiction and Fantasy.*
26. *The Dictionary of Imaginary Places.*
27. *An Atlas of Fantasy.*
30. *A Guide to Science Fiction & Fantasy in the Library of Congress Classification Scheme.*
33. *The Locus Index to Science Fiction.*
42. *Illustrated Book of Science Fiction Lists.*
45. *The Hugo, Nebula, and World Fantasy Awards.*
47. *Reginald's Science Fiction and Fantasy Awards.*
50. *Who's Hugh?*
52. *Who's Who in Horror and Fantasy Fiction.*
53. *Twentieth-Century American Science-Fiction Writers.*
54. *Contemporary Science Fiction, Fantasy, and Horror Poetry.*
53. *Twentieth-Century Science-Fiction Writers.*
55. *St. James Guide to Fantasy Writers.*
56. *St. James Guide to Horror, Ghost & Gothic Writers.*
58. *St. James Guide to Science Fiction Writers.*
59. *A Biographical Dictionary of Science Fiction and Fantasy Artists.*
62. *Anatomy of Wonder.*
63. *Fantasy and Horror.*
66. *What Fantastic Fiction Do I Read Next?*
67. *The Guide to Supernatural Fiction.*
68. *Science Fiction, the Early Years.*
69. *Science Fiction Writers.*

247. *Voices Prophesying War, 1763-3749.*
248. *Future War Novels.*
249. *The First Gothics.*
250. *Gothic Novels of the Twentieth Century.*
251. *A Gothic Bibliography.*
253. *The Imaginary Voyage in Prose Fiction.*
255. *Nuclear Holocausts.*
260. *Science Fiction and Fantasy Series and Sequels.*
261. *Uranian Worlds.*
262. *Voyages in Space.*
266. *Utopian Literature.*
267. *British and American Utopian Literature.*
269. *The Vampire in Literature.*
270. *The Transylvanian Library.*
272. *Urania's Daughters.*
297. *Bibliographies of Modern Authors.*
299. *Galactic Central Bibliographies for the Avid Reader.*
300. *Masters of Science Fiction and Fantasy.*
531. *Imaginary People.*
580. *Science Fiction Films of the Seventies.*
581. *Vintage Science Fiction Films, 1896-1949.*
587. *Fantastic Television.*
588. *Horror/The Encyclopedia of Horror Movies.*
589. *Science Fiction/The Encyclopedia of Science Fiction Movies.*
591. *Reference Guide to Fantastic Films.*
592. *Science Fiction, Horror, & Fantasy Film and Television Credits.*
601. *The Great Science Fiction Pictures.*
602. *Science Fiction Television Series.*
604. *Fantastic Cinema Subject Guide.*
605. *Creature Features.*
606. *A Reference Guide to American Science Fiction Films.*
607. *Keep Watching the Skies!*
609. *Horror and Science Fiction Films.*
610. *Variety's Complete Science Fiction Reviews.*
684. *Science Fiction and Fantasy Research Database.*
686. *Locus Index to Science Fiction Awards.*
688. *Locus Online.*
694. *The SF Site.*

Small Private and Community College Collections

3. *Science Fiction: The Illustrated Encyclopedia.*
4. *The Encyclopedia of Fantasy.*
10. *The Vampire Book.*
12. *The Encyclopedia of Science Fiction/The Science Fiction Encyclopedia.*

17. *The Penguin Encyclopedia of Horror and the Supernatural.*
26. *The Dictionary of Imaginary Places.*
33. *The Locus Index to Science Fiction.*
42. *Illustrated Book of Science Fiction Lists.*
45. *The Hugo, Nebula, and World Fantasy Awards.*
47. *Reginald's Science Fiction and Fantasy Awards.*
50. *Who's Hugh?*
58. *Twentieth-Century Science-Fiction Writers.*
62. *Anatomy of Wonder.*
63. *Fantasy and Horror.*
66. *What Fantastic Fiction Do I Read Next?*
69. *Science Fiction Writers.*
70. *Supernatural Fiction Writers, Fantasy and Horror.*
85. *Horror: 100 Best Books.*
87. *Women of the Future.*
95. *Modern Fantasy: The Hundred Best Novels.*
96. *Science Fiction: The 100 Best Novels.*
97. *The Ultimate Guide to Science Fiction.*
100. *Magill's Guide to Science Fiction and Fantasy Literature.*
111. *Science Fiction Criticism.*
114. *Gothic Fiction.*
116. *Science Fiction Book Review Index.*
117. *Science Fiction and Fantasy Reference Index/Science Fiction and Fantasy Research Index.*
130. *The Year's Scholarship in Science Fiction, Fantasy, and Horror.*
137. *Science Fiction, Fantasy, and Weird Fiction Magazines.*
145. *Index to Science Fiction Anthologies and Collections.*
149. *Index to the Science-Fiction Magazines, 1926-1950.*
153. *The Science Fiction Magazines.*
156. *The Index of Science Fiction Magazines, 1951-1965.*
157. *Science Fiction, Fantasy, & Weird Fiction Magazine Index.*
212. *Science Fiction and Fantasy Literature.*
231. *Science Fiction in America, 1870s-1930s.*
242. *The Literature of Fantasy.*
244. *Science Fiction and Fantasy Authors.*
246. *The Tale of the Future.*
247. *Voices Prophesying War, 1763-3749.*
250. *Gothic Novels of the Twentieth Century.*
251. *A Gothic Bibliography.*
253. *The Imaginary Voyage in Prose Fiction.*
255. *Nuclear Holocausts.*
260. *Science Fiction and Fantasy Series and Sequels.*
261. *Uranian Worlds.*
262. *Voyages in Space.*
267. *British and American Utopian Literature.*

270. *The Transylvanian Library.*
297. *Bibliographies of Modern Authors.*
531. *Imaginary People.*
587. *Fantastic Television.*
588. *Horror/The Encyclopedia of Horror Movies.*
589. *Science Fiction/The Encyclopedia of Science Fiction Movies.*
592. *Science Fiction, Horror, & Fantasy Film and Television Credits.*
605. *Creature Features.*
609. *Horror and Science Fiction Films.*
684. *Science Fiction and Fantasy Research Database.*
688. *Locus Online.*

PUBLIC LIBRARIES

Large City Systems

1. *The Visual Encyclopedia of Science Fiction.*
2. *The Vampire Encyclopedia.*
3. *Science Fiction: The Illustrated Encyclopedia.*
4. *The Encyclopedia of Fantasy.*
6. *The Encyclopedia of Horror.*
8. *The New Encyclopedia of Science Fiction.*
9. *Encyclopedia of Science Fiction.*
10. *The Vampire Book.*
12. *The Encyclopedia of Science Fiction/The Science Fiction Encyclopedia.*
13. *The Ultimate Encyclopedia of Fantasy.*
14. *The Ultimate Encyclopedia of Science Fiction.*
17. *The Penguin Encyclopedia of Horror and the Supernatural.*
18. *The Encyclopedia of Science Fiction and Fantasy Through 1968.*
20. *Critical Terms for Science Fiction and Fantasy.*
26. *The Dictionary of Imaginary Places.*
27. *An Atlas of Fantasy.*
28. *The Dictionary of Science Fiction Places.*
33. *The Locus Index to Science Fiction.*
37. *Fandom Directory.*
42. *Illustrated Book of Science Fiction Lists.*
43. *The Complete Book of Science Fiction and Fantasy Lists/The SF Book of Lists.*
45. *The Hugo, Nebula, and World Fantasy Awards.*
47. *Reginald's Science Fiction and Fantasy Awards.*
48. *The PENDEX.*
49. *Science Fiction and Fantasy Pseudonyms.*
50. *Who's Hugh?*
52. *Who's Who in Horror and Fantasy Fiction.*
53. *Twentieth-Century American Science-Fiction Writers.*
54. *Contemporary Science Fiction, Fantasy, and Horror Poetry.*

55. *St. James Guide to Fantasy Writers.*
56. *St. James Guide to Horror, Ghost & Gothic Writers.*
57. *Stella Nova/Contemporary Science Fiction Authors, First Edition.*
58. *St. James Guide to Science Fiction Writers.*
59. *A Biographical Dictionary of Science Fiction and Fantasy Artists.*
60. *More Than 100: Women Science Fiction Writers.*
62. *Anatomy of Wonder.*
63. *Fantasy and Horror.*
64. *Fantasy Literature.*
65. *Horror Literature.*
66. *What Fantastic Fiction Do I Read Next?*
67. *The Guide to Supernatural Fiction.*
68. *Science Fiction, the Early Years.*
69. *Science Fiction Writers.*
70. *Supernatural Fiction Writers, Fantasy and Horror.*
78. *Benchmarks.*
79. *Fantasy: The 100 Best Books.*
81. *Reader's Guide to Twentieth-Century Science Fiction.*
82. *Hooked on Horror.*
85. *Horror: 100 Best Books.*
86. *Supernatural Fiction for Teens.*
87. *Women of the Future.*
89. *Fantasy for Children/Fantasy Literature for Children and Young Adults.*
90. *Science Fiction, Fantasy, and Horror Writers.*
91. *Survey of Modern Fantasy Literature.*
92. *Survey of Science Fiction Literature.*
94. *A Reference Guide to Modern Fantasy for Children.*
95. *Modern Fantasy: The Hundred Best Novels.*
96. *Science Fiction: The 100 Best Novels.*
97. *The Ultimate Guide to Science Fiction.*
98. *A Reader's Guide to Fantasy.*
99. *A Reader's Guide to Science Fiction.*
100. *Magill's Guide to Science Fiction and Fantasy Literature.*
101. *Fantasy Literature: A Core Collection and Reference Guide.*
102. *Horror Literature: A Core Collection and Reference Guide.*
103. *The Science Fiction Reference Book.*
104. *The Hills of Faraway.*
105. *Images in a Crystal Ball.*
106. *The Science Fiction Source Book.*
108. *Horror.*
111. *Science Fiction Criticism.*
113. *The Gothic's Gothic.*
114. *Gothic Fiction.*
115. *Guide to the Gothic.*
116. *Science Fiction Book Review Index.*

256. *The Checklist of Fantastic Literature in Paperbound Books.*
258. *Who Goes There?*
260. *Science Fiction and Fantasy Series and Sequels.*
261. *Uranian Worlds.*
262. *Voyages in Space.*
266. *Utopian Literature.*
267. *British and American Utopian Literature.*
269. *The Vampire in Literature.*
270. *The Transylvanian Library.*
271. *Vampires Unearthed.*
272. *Urania's Daughters.*
273. *The Science Fantasy Publishers.*
297. *Bibliographies of Modern Authors.*
299. *Galactic Central Bibliographies for the Avid Reader.*
300. *Masters of Science Fiction and Fantasy.*
530. *The Vampire Gallery.*
531. *Imaginary People.*
580. *Science Fiction Films of the Seventies.*
581. *Vintage Science Fiction Films, 1896-1949.*
582. *Cult Horror Films.*
583. *Cult Science Fiction Films.*
584. *The Horror Film Handbook.*
585. *The Science Fiction and Fantasy Film Handbook.*
587. *Fantastic Television.*
588. *Horror/The Encyclopedia of Horror Movies.*
589. *Science Fiction/The Encyclopedia of Science Fiction Movies.*
591. *Reference Guide to Fantastic Films.*
592. *Science Fiction, Horror, & Fantasy Film and Television Credits.*
598. *Futurevisions.*
599. *Things to Come.*
600. *The BFI Companion to Horror.*
601. *The Great Science Fiction Pictures.*
602. *Science Fiction Television Series.*
604. *Fantastic Cinema Subject Guide.*
605. *Creature Features.*
606. *A Reference Guide to American Science Fiction Films.*
607. *Keep Watching the Skies!*
609. *Horror and Science Fiction Films.*
610. *Variety's Complete Science Fiction Reviews.*
612. *The Science Fiction Image.*
666. *Quotable Star Trek.*
675. *Science Fiction and Fantasy Writer's Sourcebook.*
684. *Science Fiction and Fantasy Research Database.*
686. *Locus Index to Science Fiction Awards.*
688. *Locus Online.*

694. *The SF Site.*
698. *Spacelight.*

Medium County and City Libraries

2. *The Vampire Encyclopedia.*
3. *Science Fiction: The Illustrated Encyclopedia.*
4. *The Encyclopedia of Fantasy.*
10. *The Vampire Book.*
12. *The Encyclopedia of Science Fiction/The Science Fiction Encyclopedia.*
13. *The Ultimate Encyclopedia of Fantasy.*
14. *The Ultimate Encyclopedia of Science Fiction.*
17. *The Penguin Encyclopedia of Horror and the Supernatural.*
26. *The Dictionary of Imaginary Places.*
27. *An Atlas of Fantasy.*
37. *Fandom Directory.*
42. *Illustrated Book of Science Fiction Lists.*
45. *The Hugo, Nebula, and World Fantasy Awards.*
47. *Reginald's Science Fiction and Fantasy Awards.*
50. *Who's Hugh?*
52. *Who's Who in Horror and Fantasy Fiction.*
55. *St. James Guide to Fantasy Writers.*
56. *St. James Guide to Horror, Ghost & Gothic Writers.*
58. *St. James Guide to Science Fiction Writers.*
62. *Anatomy of Wonder.*
63. *Fantasy and Horror.*
66. *What Fantastic Fiction Do I Read Next?*
69. *Science Fiction Writers.*
70. *Supernatural Fiction Writers, Fantasy and Horror.*
82. *Hooked on Horror.*
85. *Horror: 100 Best Books.*
86. *Supernatural Fiction for Teens.*
87. *Women of the Future.*
89. *Fantasy for Children/Fantasy Literature for Children and Young Adults.*
90. *Science Fiction, Fantasy, and Horror Writers.*
95. *Modern Fantasy: The Hundred Best Novels.*
96. *Science Fiction: The 100 Best Novels.*
97. *The Ultimate Guide to Science Fiction.*
98. *A Reader's Guide to Fantasy.*
99. *A Reader's Guide to Science Fiction.*
111. *Science Fiction Criticism.*
114. *Gothic Fiction.*
116. *Science Fiction Book Review Index.*
117. *Science Fiction and Fantasy Reference Index/Science Fiction and Fantasy Research Index.*

128. *A Research Guide to Science Fiction Studies.*
130. *The Year's Scholarship in Science Fiction, Fantasy, and Horror.*
145. *Index to Science Fiction Anthologies and Collections.*
149. *Index to the Science-Fiction Magazines, 1926-1950.*
153. *The Science Fiction Magazines.*
156. *The Index of Science Fiction Magazines, 1951-1965.*
212. *Science Fiction and Fantasy Literature.*
242. *The Literature of Fantasy.*
244. *Science Fiction and Fantasy Authors.*
248. *Future War Novels.*
250. *Gothic Novels of the Twentieth Century.*
251. *A Gothic Bibliography.*
253. *The Imaginary Voyage in Prose Fiction.*
255. *Nuclear Holocausts.*
260. *Science Fiction and Fantasy Series and Sequels.*
261. *Uranian Worlds.*
267. *British and American Utopian Literature.*
270. *The Transylvanian Library.*
531. *Imaginary People.*
587. *Fantastic Television.*
588. *Horror/The Encyclopedia of Horror Movies.*
589. *Science Fiction/The Encyclopedia of Science Fiction Movies.*
592. *Science Fiction, Horror, & Fantasy Film and Television Credits.*
601. *The Great Science Fiction Pictures.*
602. *Science Fiction Television Series.*
605. *Creature Features.*
609. *Horror and Science Fiction Films.*
688. *Locus Online.*
694. *The SF Site.*

Small Public and County Libraries

3. *Science Fiction: The Illustrated Encyclopedia.*
4. *The Encyclopedia of Fantasy.*
12. *The Encyclopedia of Science Fiction/The Science Fiction Encyclopedia.*
13. *The Ultimate Encyclopedia of Fantasy.*
14. *The Ultimate Encyclopedia of Science Fiction.*
17. *The Penguin Encyclopedia of Horror and the Supernatural.*
26. *The Dictionary of Imaginary Places.*
27. *An Atlas of Fantasy.*
42. *Illustrated Book of Science Fiction Lists.*
52. *Who's Who in Horror and Fantasy Fiction.*
55. *St. James Guide to Fantasy Writers.*
56. *St. James Guide to Horror, Ghost & Gothic Writers.*
58. *St. James Guide to Science Fiction Writers.*

62. *Anatomy of Wonder.*
63. *Fantasy and Horror.*
66. *What Fantastic Fiction Do I Read Next?*
82. *Hooked on Horror.*
85. *Horror: 100 Best Books.*
89. *Fantasy for Children/Fantasy Literature for Children and Young Adults.*
95. *Modern Fantasy: The Hundred Best Novels.*
96. *Science Fiction: The 100 Best Novels.*
97. *The Ultimate Guide to Science Fiction.*
128. *A Research Guide to Science Fiction Studies.*
145. *Index to Science Fiction Anthologies and Collections.*
212. *Science Fiction and Fantasy Literature.*
244. *Science Fiction and Fantasy Authors.*
531. *Imaginary People.*
587. *Fantastic Television.*
588. *Horror/The Encyclopedia of Horror Movies.*
589. *Science Fiction/The Encyclopedia of Science Fiction Movies.*
605. *Creature Features.*
688. *Locus Online.*

PERSONAL RESEARCH LIBRARIES

3. *Science Fiction: The Illustrated Encyclopedia.*
4. *The Encyclopedia of Fantasy.*
10. *The Vampire Book.*
12. *The Encyclopedia of Science Fiction/The Science Fiction Encyclopedia.*
13. *The Ultimate Encyclopedia of Fantasy.*
14. *The Ultimate Encyclopedia of Science Fiction.*
17. *The Penguin Encyclopedia of Horror and the Supernatural.*
18. *The Encyclopedia of Science Fiction and Fantasy Through 1968.*
26. *The Dictionary of Imaginary Places.*
33. *The Locus Index to Science Fiction.*
39. *International Association for the Fantastic in the Arts Membership Directory.*
40. *Science Fiction Research Association Annual Directory.*
42. *Illustrated Book of Science Fiction Lists.*
45. *The Hugo, Nebula, and World Fantasy Awards.*
47. *Reginald's Science Fiction and Fantasy Awards.*
50. *Who's Hugh?*
52. *Who's Who in Horror and Fantasy Fiction.*
54. *Contemporary Science Fiction, Fantasy, and Horror Poetry.*
55. *St. James Guide to Fantasy Writers.*
56. *St. James Guide to Horror, Ghost & Gothic Writers.*
58. *St. James Guide to Science Fiction Writers.*
59. *A Biographical Dictionary of Science Fiction and Fantasy Artists.*
62. *Anatomy of Wonder.*

63. *Fantasy and Horror.*

66. *What Fantastic Fiction Do I Read Next?*

67. *The Guide to Supernatural Fiction.*

68. *Science Fiction, the Early Years.*

79. *Fantasy: The 100 Best Books.*

85. *Horror: 100 Best Books.*

87. *Women of the Future.*

94. *A Reference Guide to Modern Fantasy for Children.*

95. *Modern Fantasy: The Hundred Best Novels.*

96. *Science Fiction: The 100 Best Novels.*

97. *The Ultimate Guide to Science Fiction.*

98. *A Reader's Guide to Fantasy.*

99. *A Reader's Guide to Science Fiction.*

111. *Science Fiction Criticism.*

114. *Gothic Fiction.*

116. *Science Fiction Book Review Index.*

117. *Science Fiction and Fantasy Reference Index/Science Fiction and Fantasy Research Index.*

120. *Science Fiction Master Index of Names.*

130. *The Year's Scholarship in Science Fiction, Fantasy, and Horror.*

137. *Science Fiction, Fantasy, and Weird Fiction Magazines.*

138. *The Supernatural Index.*

145. *Index to Science Fiction Anthologies and Collections.*

149. *Index to the Science-Fiction Magazines, 1926-1950.*

153. *The Science Fiction Magazines.*

156. *The Index of Science Fiction Magazines, 1951-1965.*

157. *Science Fiction, Fantasy, & Weird Fiction Magazine Index.*

159. *Index to the Science Fiction Magazines (and Original Anthologies).*

160. *Monthly Terrors.*

163. *The Pulp Magazine Index.*

208. *The Checklist of Fantastic Literature.*

212. *Science Fiction and Fantasy Literature.*

231. *Science Fiction in America, 1870s-1930s.*

242. *The Literature of Fantasy.*

244. *Science Fiction and Fantasy Authors.*

246. *The Tale of the Future.*

247. *Voices Prophesying War, 1763-3749.*

248. *Future War Novels.*

250. *Gothic Novels of the Twentieth Century.*

251. *A Gothic Bibliography.*

253. *The Imaginary Voyage in Prose Fiction.*

260. *Science Fiction and Fantasy Series and Sequels.*

261. *Uranian Worlds.*

267. *British and American Utopian Literature.*

269. *The Vampire in Literature.*

270. *The Transylvanian Library.*
272. *Urania's Daughters.*
273. *The Science Fantasy Publishers.*
297. *Bibliographies of Modern Authors.*
299. *Galactic Central Bibliographies for the Avid Reader.*
300. *Masters of Science Fiction and Fantasy.*
531. *Imaginary People.*
581. *Vintage Science Fiction Films, 1896-1949.*
587. *Fantastic Television.*
588. *Horror/The Encyclopedia of Horror Movies.*
589. *Science Fiction/The Encyclopedia of Science Fiction Movies.*
591. *Reference Guide to Fantastic Films.*
592. *Science Fiction, Horror, & Fantasy Film and Television Credits.*
601. *The Great Science Fiction Pictures.*
602. *Science Fiction Television Series.*
605. *Creature Features.*
609. *Horror and Science Fiction Films.*
684. *Science Fiction and Fantasy Research Database.*
686. *Locus Index to Science Fiction Awards.*
688. *Locus Online.*
694. *The SF Site.*
696. *Internet Speculative Fiction Database.*
698. *Spacelight.*

AUTHOR INDEX

References are to item numbers.

TITLE INDEX

References are to item numbers.

& *Analog: January 1930-December
1979* (Ashley & Jeeves), 176

*The Complete Robert Bloch: An Illustrated
International Bibliography* (Larson),
326

*The Complete Stephen King Encyclopedia:
The Definitive Guide to the Works
of America's Master of Horror*
(Spignesi), 554

Concordance to Cordwainer Smith
(Anthony Lewis), 568

*Contemporary Science Fiction Authors,
First Edition* (Reginald), 57

Contemporary Science Fiction Authors II
(Reginald), 212

*Contemporary Science Fiction, Fantasy,
and Horror Poetry: A Resource
Guide and Biographical Directory*
(Green), 54

A Cordwainer Smith Checklist (Bennett),
477

*The Creature Features Movie Guide; or,
An A to Z Encyclopedia to the
Cinema of the Fantastic* (J.
Stanley), 605

*Creature Features Movie Guide Strikes
Again* (J. Stanley), 605

*Creature Features: The Science Fiction,
Fantasy, and Horror Movie Guide*
(J. Stanley), 605

*Critical Terms for Science Fiction and
Fantasy: a Glossary and Guide to
Scholarship* (Wolfe), 20

*Cult Horror Films: From Attack of the 50-
Foot Woman to Zombies Mora Tau*
(Everman), 582

*Cult Science Fiction Films: From the
Amazing Colossal Man to Yog—
Monster from Space* (Everman), 583

Cyclopaedia of Ghost Writers (A. Gunn),
683

*Cyril M. Kornbluth, the Cynical
Scrutineer: A Working Bibliography*
(Stephensen-Payne & G. Benson),
406

Dansk Science Fiction Guide 1974
(Schiøler & Swiatek), 219

Dansk Science Fiction Indeks, 1741-1976
(Schiøler & Swiatek), 219

*The Dark Shadows Companion: 25th
Anniversary Collection* (K. Scott),
618

Dark Shadows Tribute (Gross & Van
Hise), 617

*The Darkover Concordance: A Reader's
Guide* (Breen), 540

*Daughter of the Night: A Tanith Lee
Bibliography* (Soanes & J. Pattison),
413

DAW Science-Fiction Books (Robinson),
288

*De Camp: An L. Sprague de Camp
Bibliography* (Laughlin, Levack, &
L. Hall), 364

*"Death Angel: A Bibliography of Karl
Edward Wagner"* (Marek), 501

Deep Space Crew Book (Van Hise), 644

*Deep Space Log Book: A First Season
Companion* (Altman & Gross), 629

Delap's F & SF Review (Delap), 701

The Destiny Index of Fantasy-1953 (E.
Wood & Kemp), 172

*Dictionary Catalog of the J. Lloyd Eaton
Collection of Science Fiction and
Fantasy Literature* (University of
California, Riverside), 134

The Dictionary of Imaginary Places
(Manguel & Guadalupi), 26

The Dictionary of Science Fiction Places
(Stableford), 28

*A Dictionary of the Characters and Scenes
in the Novels, Romances, and Short
Stories of H. G. Wells* (Connes), 577

Doctor Who: The Handbook (Howe,
Stammers & Walker), 621

Doctor Who: The Time-Travelers' Guide
(Haining), 619

SUBJECT INDEX

References are to item numbers.